Microeconomic Theory

Basic Principles and Extensions

Fourth Edition

Microeconomic Theory

Basic Principles and Extensions
Fourth Edition

Walter Nicholson
Amherst College

The Dryden Press

Chicago   New York   San Francisco   Philadelphia
Montreal   Toronto   London   Sydney   Tokyo

Acquisitions Editor: Elizabeth Widdicombe
Developmental Editor: Joanne Smith
Project Editor: Teresa Chartos
Design Supervisor: Rebecca Lemna
Production Manager: Barb Bahnsen
Director of Editing, Design, and Production: Jane Perkins

Text and Cover Designer: Mark Feldman
Copy Editor: Patricia Lewis
Indexer: Leoni McVey
Compositor: G & S Typesetters, Inc.
Text Type: 10/12 Sabon

Library of Congress Cataloging-in-Publication Data

Nicholson, Walter.
　Microeconomic theory.

　Includes bibliographies and index.
　1. Microeconomics.　I. Title.
HB172.N49　1989　　338.5　　88-25663
ISBN 0-03-021669-9

Address orders:
The Dryden Press
Orlando, Florida 32887

Address editorial correspondence:
The Dryden Press
908 N. Elm St.
Hinsdale, IL 60521

The Dryden Press
Holt, Rinehart and Winston
Saunders College Publishing

To Emily H. Walker and her grandchildren, Kate, David, Tory, and Paul.

The Dryden Press Series in Economics

Asch and Seneca
Government and the Marketplace,
Second Edition

Breit and Elzinga
The Antitrust Casebook: Milestones in Economic
Regulation, *Second Edition*

Breit and Ransom
The Academic Scribblers,
Second Edition

Campbell, Campbell, and Dolan
Money, Banking, and Monetary Policy

Dolan and Lindsey
Economics, *Fifth Edition*

Dolan and Lindsey
Macroeconomics, *Fifth Edition*

Dolan and Lindsey
Microeconomics, *Fifth Edition*

Eckert and Leftwich
The Price System and Resource
Allocation, *Tenth Edition*

Fort and Lowinger
Applications and Exercises in
Intermediate Microeconomics

Gardner
Comparative Economic Systems

Hyman
Public Finance: A Contemporary
Application of Theory to Policy,
Second Edition

Johnson and Roberts
Money and Banking: A Market-Oriented
Approach, *Third Edition*

Kaufman
The Economics of Labor Markets and
Labor Relations, *Second Edition*

Kidwell and Peterson
Financial Institutions, Markets,
and Money, *Third Edition*

Landsburg
Price Theory and Applications

Link, Miller, and Bergman
EconoGraph II: Interactive Software for
Principles of Economics

Nicholson
Intermediate Microeconomics and Its
Application, *Fourth Edition*

Nicholson
Microeconomic Theory: Basic Principles
and Extensions, *Fourth Edition*

Pappas and Hirschey
Fundamentals of Managerial Economics,
Third Edition

Pappas and Hirschey
Managerial Economics, *Fifth Edition*

Puth
American Economic History,
Second Edition

Rukstad
Macroeconomic Decision Making in the
World Economy: Text and Cases,
Second Edition

Welch and Welch
Economics: Theory and Practice,
Third Edition

Yarbrough and Yarbrough
The World Economy: Trade and Finance

Preface

As in prior editions, the primary goal of this fourth edition of *Microeconomic Theory: Basic Principles and Extensions* is to provide a comprehensive and intuitive approach to microeconomic theory using elementary calculus as an analytical tool. This edition, however, represents a major revision and, I hope, a substantial improvement on the previous versions. The primary change in this edition has been a reorganization in the structure of the book:

- Efficiency concepts and their relationships to competitive markets are now covered much earlier in the text. This reorganization provides a complete development of the model of general competitive equilibrium early in the text and thereby helps to sharpen and clarify the discussions of market imperfections that follow. This new structure also seems to follow current teaching practices better than the previous approach, which left general equilibrium ideas until the book's final chapters.

Four other major changes in this edition serve to update the book and make it more suitable for students' needs:

- A greater emphasis on topics from the theory of information and uncertainty including new chapters on Information and Competitive Equilibrium (Chapter 17) and Strategy and Game Theory (Chapter 20);
- Inclusion of a number of numerical and algebraic examples that illustrate in a concrete way the theoretical concepts being introduced;
- Major revisions to the problems in the book together with the inclusion of new "Extension" problems that ask the student to pursue a particular theoretical point in somewhat greater detail than is possible within the body of the text; and
- Availability of an innovative student workbook (written by David Stapleton of Dartmouth College) that offers additional insights into the material being covered. Workbook problems are of varying levels of difficulty and include many that lead the student through the solutions in a step-by-step manner.

This edition also incorporates many minor improvements in presentation throughout. The most important of these are the inclusion of more results from duality theory—a topic first approached seriously in the third edition, and a greater attention to general equilibrium results so that students can visualize what is happening "elsewhere" in the economy. Despite this somewhat sharper theoretical focus, the goal in this revision has been to continue to provide a generally intuitive approach to most topics. By proceeding in this way, I hope that the book will continue to be accessible to any student with a mathematical bent who has had some introductory economics.

Although the 25 chapters in this book represent an increase of four over the number in the prior edition, only two of these are truly new. The remaining expansion represents an attempt to divide some of the more difficult material in the text into more nearly bite-sized chapters and to follow an organizational scheme that reflects most course outlines. Still, covering all of the chapters in the book in a single term of 12–14 weeks may be too rushed for many users. For those wishing to stress only core concepts, I would recommend a focus on Chapters 3–7 (Demand), Chapters 10–12 (Costs and Supply), Chapters 14–16 (Perfect Competition), and Chapters 18–19 (Imperfect Competition). Other topics can then be added to these basic ones to meet the needs of individual instructors.

As with previous editions, a *Solutions Manual* is provided to instructors with complete, worked-out answers to the text problems. Brief descriptions overview the nature of the problems in each chapter, and each individual problem has its own statement noting its significance and level of difficulty.

ACKNOWL-EDGMENTS

Detailed reviews by the following people were a great help to me in preparing this fourth edition: Douglas K. Agbetsiafa, *Indiana University at South Bend*; Keith Brown, *Purdue University*; Tran Dung, *Wright State University*; Belton Fleisher, *Ohio State University*; Carroll B. Foster, *University of California, LaJolla*; Christopher Grandy, *Barnard College, Columbia University*; Kala Krishna, *Harvard University*; Anthony Marino, *University of Southern California*; Pat McCarthy, *Purdue University*; Jack Meyer, *Michigan State University*; Charles Plourde, *York University*; Charles F. Revier, *Colorado State University*; Joaquim Silvestre, *University of California, Davis*; Susan Vroman, *Georgetown University*; and Meng-Hua Ye, *George Washington University*. I have tried to incorporate most of the suggestions since they invariably served to make some of my muddled thoughts clearer. I have also benefited greatly from conversations about the book with Bernie Saffran (Swarthmore), David Stapleton (Dartmouth), and Frank Westhoff and Beth Yarbrough (Amherst). Many other friends and colleagues (and even competing authors) have made helpful suggestions about the book, and for these I am also grateful. The book remains my own production, however, and none of these individuals are responsible for the errors I have been too bullheaded to change.

Happi Cramer of Word-for-Word, Inc., created most of this edition out of my illegible scrawl, and she deserves great credit for keeping things organized. At The Dryden Press, Liz Widdicombe provided her usual careful oversight for this edition and offered the occasional prod to keep things on track. Joanne Smith greatly helped with many facets of the text's development. Holly Crawford and Teresa Chartos organized the production of the book with remarkable good humor given the complexities involved. Pat Lewis caught several errors at the copyediting stage. I appreciate all of this help—producing the book would have been impossible without it. Once again my wife (Susan) and children (Kate, David, Tory, and Paul) suffered through the final stages of getting the book out. Although they are old hands at this sort of thing, they must surely be starting to wonder when it will all end!

Walter Nicholson
Amherst, Massachusetts
December 1988

About the Author

Walter Nicholson is professor of economics at Amherst College. He received a B. A. degree in mathematics from Williams College and a Ph.D. in economics from the Massachusetts Institute of Technology. Professor Nicholson's primary research interests focus on the econometric analysis of labor market policies. He has published many articles on unemployment, social insurance and welfare policy, and the domestic impact of international trade. He is currently chair of the Economics Committee for the Graduate Record Examination in Economics and is also the author of *Intermediate Microeconomics and Its Application*, fourth edition (The Dryden Press, 1987). Professor Nicholson lives in Amherst, Massachusetts. He and his wife, Susan, are beginning the process of paying college tuition bills for their four children.

Contents

PART
I

Introduction

This introductory part consists of two chapters that provide some background for the study of microeconomic theory. Chapter 1 describes the general approach used in microeconomics, with particular attention to showing how economists devise and verify simple models of the economy. The chapter points out that all scientific theorizing involves the specification of simplified theoretical models within which very complex processes (such as the interactions of atoms in radioactive material or, in our case, the operation of a modern economy) can be isolated and examined. Some of the philosophical issues involved in the construction of such models, together with an analysis of how "good" models might be differentiated from "bad" ones, are also discussed. In addition, Chapter 1 provides a general outline for the book.

Chapter 2, which has a mathematical orientation, describes several methods that can be used to solve maximization and minimization problems. Because many economic models start with the assumption that economic agents (individuals, firms, government agencies, and so forth) are seeking the maximum value of something, given their limited resources, such problems provide a major focus for this book. The mathematical techniques introduced in Chapter 2 are used repeatedly in later chapters to derive implications about the behavior of economic agents who attempt to reach such goals. An appendix to Chapter 2 pursues this mathematical analysis a bit further by investigating "second-order" conditions that are required to assure that the choices made by economic agents will truly be the best of those available.

CHAPTER 1

Economic Models

As most of you know by now, economics is usually defined as the study of *the allocation of scarce resources among competing end uses*. This definition stresses two important features of economics that will concern us throughout this book. First, productive resources are scarce—they do not exist in sufficient amounts to satisfy all human wants. This scarcity imposes a variety of constraints on both the choices available to a society and the opportunities open to its members: No individual can spend more than his or her income; no one can use more than 24 hours in one day. Rather, choices must be made about how resources will be used. The necessity to make choices leads to the second feature of the definition of economics: the concern with discovering how those choices are made among competing ends. By examining the activities of consumers, producers, suppliers of resources, governments, and voters, economists seek to understand how resources are allocated. Illustrating some of the tools economists use to do this is the purpose of this book.

In this chapter we provide an introduction to these subjects. First, we discuss the role of theoretical models in scientific inquiry, with particular attention to the ways in which such models are used in economics. This discussion is followed by an examination of how economic models might be verified with information from the real world. Then, as an extended theoretical example of an economic model, we trace the historical development of the familiar supply-demand model of price determination. This discussion should provide a review, in cursory form, of some of the material you covered in your introductory economics course. Some simple mathematics is used here, however, as a brief warm-up for the material that follows. Finally, this introductory chapter concludes with a brief discussion of the contents of the remainder of the book.

THEORETICAL MODELS

The most striking feature of any developed economy is its overall complexity. Thousands of firms are engaged in producing millions of different goods. Millions of individuals work in all sorts of occupations and purchase a wide variety of products, ranging from peanuts to house trailers. And in some way, all of those actions must be coordinated. Take peanuts, for example. They must be harvested at the right time; they must be shipped to processors who turn them into peanut butter, peanut oil, peanut brittle, and numerous other delicacies. These processors, in turn, must make certain that their products arrive at thousands of retail outlets in the proper quantities to meet individual demand. Since it would be impossible to describe such features of an economy in complete detail, economists have chosen to abstract from the vast complexities of real-world economies and to develop rather simple models that capture the "essentials" of the economic process. Just as a road map proves to be helpful, even though it does not record every house or every blade of grass, economic models of, say, the market for peanuts are also very useful even though they do not record every minute feature of the peanut economy. In this book we shall be studying the most widely used economic models; we shall see that even though they are heroic abstractions from the true complexities of the real world, they nonetheless capture certain essentials that are common to all economic activities.

The use of models is widespread in both the physical and social sciences. In physics, the notion of a "perfect" vacuum or an "ideal" gas is an abstraction that permits scientists to study real-world phenomena in simplified settings. In chemistry, the idea of an atom or a molecule is in actuality a very simplified model of the structure of matter. Architects use mock-up models to plan buildings. Television repairers refer to wiring diagrams to locate problems. So too, economists have developed their models as aids to understanding economic issues, models that portray the way individuals make decisions, the way firms behave, and the way in which these two groups interact in "the market."

VERIFICATION OF ECONOMIC MODELS

Of course, not all models prove to be "good." For example, the earth-centered model of planetary motion devised by Ptolemy was eventually disregarded because it proved incapable of explaining accurately how the planets move around the sun. An important purpose of scientific investigation is to sort out the "bad" models from the "good." Two general methods have been used for verifying economic models in this way: (1) the *direct approach*, which seeks to establish the validity of the basic assumptions on which a model is based; and (2) the *indirect approach*, which attempts to confirm validity by showing that a simplified model correctly predicts real-world events. To illustrate the basic differences in the two approaches, we briefly examine a model that we will use extensively in later chapters of this book—the model of a firm that has as its single goal of operation the maximization of profits.

The Profit-Maximization Model

The model of a firm seeking to maximize profits is obviously a simplification of reality. It ignores the personal motivations of a firm's managers and does not treat personal conflicts among them. It assumes that profits are the only relevant goal of a firm; other possible goals, such as obtaining power or prestige, are treated as unimportant. The simple model also assumes that a firm has sufficient information about its costs and the nature of the market to which it sells to be able to discover what its profit-maximizing decisions actually are. Most real-world firms, of course, do not have this information readily available. Yet, such shortcomings in the model are not necessarily serious. As we have been suggesting, no model can describe reality exactly. The real question is whether this simple model has any claim to being a good one.

Direct Test of Assumptions

Now let us test the model of a profit-maximizing firm by taking the direct approach and investigating its basic assumption: Do firms really seek maximum profits? Economists have made numerous frontal assaults on that question, most commonly by sending a questionnaire to executives asking them to specify what goals they pursue. The results of such studies have been varied. Business people often mention goals other than profits or claim they only do "the best they can" given their limited information. On the other hand, most respondents also mention a strong "interest" in profits and express the view that profit maximization is an appropriate goal. The direct approach to testing the profit-maximizing model by testing its assumptions therefore has proved to be inconclusive.

Indirect Empirical Tests

Some economists, most notably Milton Friedman, object to the notion that a model can be tested by inquiring into the "reality" of its assumptions.[1] They argue that all theoretical models are based on "unrealistic" assumptions; the very nature of theorizing demands that we make certain abstractions. These economists conclude that the only way to determine the validity of a model is to see whether it is capable of explaining and predicting real-world events. The ultimate test of an economic model comes when it is confronted with data from the economy itself.

Friedman provides an important illustration of that principle. He asks what kind of a theory one should use to explain the shots expert pool players will make. He argues that the laws of velocity, momentum, and angles from classical physics would be a suitable theoretical model. Pool players shoot shots *as if* they followed these laws. But if we ask players whether they understand the physical principles behind the game of pool, most will undoubtedly answer that they do not. Nonetheless, Friedman argues, the physical laws provide very accurate predictions and therefore should be accepted as appropriate theoretical models of how pool is played by experts. That approach provides the second way in which models can be tested.

A test of the profit-maximization model, then, would be provided by trying to predict the behavior of real-world firms by assuming that these firms behave *as if* they were maximizing profits. If these predictions are reasonably in accord with reality, we may accept the profit-maximization hypothesis, even though direct methods of verification yield ambiguous information regarding the "reality" of the basic assumption. The fact that firms respond to questionnaires by disclaiming any precise attempt at profit maximization is no more damaging to the validity of the basic hypothesis than are pool players' disclaimers of

---

[1]See M. Friedman, *Essays in Positive Economics* (Chicago: University of Chicago Press, 1953), chap. 1. For an alternative view stressing the importance of using "realistic" assumptions, see H. A. Simon, "Rational Decision Making in Business Organizations," *American Economic Review* 69, no. 4 (September 1979): 493–513.

knowledge of the laws of physics. Rather, the ultimate test of either theory is its ability to predict *real-world events*. In later chapters we will study the profit-maximization hypothesis in considerable detail and will show that in many ways the hypothesis does make predictions that accord well with real-world experience.

Uses of Empirical Examples

This book is about theoretical economic models, but since our objective is to learn something about the real world, we must be concerned with the validity of our models. Sometimes we will seek to establish the validity of a model by pointing to the fact that it is based on "reasonable" assumptions. More often, however, we will examine examples from the real world that are in accord with the predictions that would be made from a simple model. Although the space devoted to such examples in this book must necessarily be limited,[2] each chapter concludes with an extended *application* that illustrates how empirical verification can be provided for the models being discussed. It is also hoped these examples will succeed in sparking readers' interest in pursuing studies of the application of economic models to real-world problems on their own.

GENERAL FEATURES OF ECONOMIC MODELS

The variety of economic models in current use is, of course, very large. Specific assumptions used and the degree of detail provided vary greatly depending on the problem being addressed. The types of models employed to explain the overall level of economic activity in the United States, for example, must be considerably more aggregated and complex than those that seek to interpret the pricing of Arizona strawberries. Despite this variety, however, practically all economic models incorporate three common elements: (1) the *ceteris paribus* (other things the same) assumption; (2) the supposition that economic decision-makers seek to optimize something; and (3) a careful distinction between "positive" and "normative" questions. Because we will use these elements throughout this book, it may be helpful at the outset to describe briefly the philosophy behind each of them.

The Ceteris Paribus *Assumption*

As is the case in most sciences, models used in economics attempt to portray relatively simple relationships. A model of the market for wheat, for example, might seek to explain wheat prices with a small number of quantifiable variables, such as wages of farm workers, rainfall, and consumer incomes. This parsimony in model specification permits the study of wheat pricing in a simplified setting in which it is possible to understand how the specific forces operate. Although any researcher will recognize that many "outside" forces (presence of wheat diseases, changes in the prices of fertilizers or of tractors, or shifts in consumer attitudes about eating bread) affect the price of wheat, these other forces are held constant in the construction of the model. This is what is meant by employing the *ceteris paribus* assumption. It is important to recognize that economists are *not* assuming that other factors do not affect wheat prices, but, rather, such other variables are assumed to be unchanged

[2] For a more extensive set of empirical examples, see W. Nicholson, *Intermediate Microeconomics and Its Application*, 4th ed. (Hinsdale, Ill.: The Dryden Press, 1987).

during the period of study. In this way the effect of only a few forces can be studied in a simplified setting. Such *ceteris paribus* assumptions are used in all economic modeling.

Use of the *ceteris paribus* assumption does pose some difficulties for the empirical verification of economic models from real-world data. In other sciences such problems may not be so severe because of the ability to conduct controlled experiments. For example, a physicist who wishes to test a model of the force of gravity would probably not do so by dropping objects from the Empire State Building. Experiments conducted in that way would be subject to too many extraneous forces (wind currents, particles in the air, variations in temperature, and so forth) to permit a precise test of the theory. Rather, the physicist would probably conduct experiments in a laboratory, using a partial vacuum in which most other forces could be controlled or eliminated. In this way the theory could be verified in a simple setting, without needing to consider all the other forces that affect falling bodies in the real world. Indeed the model verified in the vacuum-tube experiments may provide fairly good predictions of real-world behavior, even though these other forces are not explicitly taken into account.

With a few notable exceptions, economists have not been able to conduct controlled experiments to test their models. The cost, complexity, and, in some cases, ethics of devising such experiments have generally made them prohibitive. Instead, economists have been forced to rely on various statistical methods to control for other forces when testing their theories. Although these statistical methods are in principle as valid as the controlled experiment methods used by other scientists, as a few of the empirical examples in the text will illustrate, in practice they raise a number of thorny issues. For that reason, the limitations and precise meaning of the *ceteris paribus* assumption in economics are subject to somewhat greater controversy than in the laboratory sciences.

Optimization Assumptions

Many economic models start from the assumption that the economic actors being studied are rationally pursuing some goal. We briefly discussed such an assumption previously when investigating the notion of firms maximizing profits. Other examples that we will encounter in this book include consumers maximizing their own well-being (utility), firms minimizing costs, and government regulators attempting to maximize public welfare. Although, as we will show, all of these assumptions (and many others related to optimization) are somewhat controversial, all have won widespread acceptance as good starting places for developing economic models. There seem to be two reasons for this acceptance. First, the optimization assumptions are very productive in terms of generating precise, solvable models. That primarily results from the ability of such models to draw on a variety of mathematical techniques suitable for optimization problems that would not otherwise be available. Many of these techniques, together with the logic behind them, are reviewed in Chapter 2. A second reason for the popularity of optimization models concerns their apparent empirical validity. Such models seem to be fairly good at explaining reality. In all then, optimization models have come to occupy a prominent position in modern economic theory.

Positive-Normative Distinction

A final feature central to most economic models is the attempt to differentiate carefully between "positive" and "normative" questions. So far we have been talking primarily about the role of *positive* economic theories. Such "scientific" theories take the real world as an object to be studied, attempting to explain those economic phenomena that are observed. Positive economics seeks to determine how resources are *in fact* allocated in an economy. A somewhat different analysis of economic theory is *normative,* taking a definite moral position on what *should be* done. Under the heading of normative analysis, economists have a great deal to say about how resources *should be* allocated. For example, an economist engaged in positive analysis might investigate why and how the American health care industry uses the quantities of capital, labor, and land that are currently devoted to providing medical services. The economist might also choose to measure the costs and benefits of devoting even more resources to health care. But when economists advocate that more resources *should* be allocated to health, they have implicitly moved into normative analysis. If economists adopt the profit-maximization hypothesis because it seems to explain reality, they are engaging in positive analysis. But economists who argue that firms should maximize profits (and not pursue other "social" goods, say) are taking a normative position.

Some economists believe that the only proper economic analysis is positive analysis. Drawing an analogy with the physical sciences, they argue that "scientific" economics should concern itself only with the description (and possibly prediction) of real-world events. To take moral positions and to plead for special interests is considered to be outside the competence of an economist acting as an economist.

"Positive" economists believe that one reason for the success of economics as a discipline is that it has been able to emulate successfully the positive approach taken by the physical sciences rather than becoming involved in the value-laden normative approach taken by some of the other social sciences. To other observers, however, strict application of the positive-normative distinction to economic matters is inappropriate, since such issues must necessarily involve the researchers' own views about ethics, morality, and fairness. To search for scientific "objectivity" in such circumstances is hopeless.

Although this book generally will avoid philosophical investigations of such difficult issues, it does take a rather definite position by adopting a primarily positive orientation. That is, economic models that are presented purport to explain how the world works and some empirical evidence about the validity of those models is discussed. For the most part no judgment is made about the ethical, normative significance of the models. The principal exception to this approach occurs in Part V, where explicit attention is paid to analyzing the normative significance of a perfectly competitive price system with respect to economic efficiency and equity. In this part of the book also, however, some care is taken to differentiate between positive and normative issues so that the reader can judge the type of argument being made.

The specific roles of these three features of economic models will become clear only as the models themselves are studied in detail. As a starting point in that process, we review the general historical development of the economic model of price determination. The reader should notice that the three features described previously occur repeatedly throughout that development.

DEVELOP-MENT OF THE ECONOMIC THEORY OF VALUE

Although economic activity has been a central feature of all societies, it is surprising that these activities were not studied in any detail until fairly recently. For the most part, economic phenomena were treated as a basic aspect of human behavior that was not sufficiently interesting to deserve specific attention. It is, of course, true that individuals have always studied economic activities with a view toward making some kind of personal gain. Roman traders were certainly not above making profits on their transactions. But investigations into the basic nature of these activities did not begin in any depth until the eighteenth century.[3] Since this book is about economic theory as it stands today, not about the history of economic thought, our discussion of the evolution of economic theory will be brief. Only one area of economic study will be examined in its historical setting: the *theory of value*, which has been of interest to economists—or their philosopher predecessors—from the earliest times to the present.

The theory of value, not surprisingly, concerns the determinants of the "value" of a commodity. The study of this subject is at the center of modern microeconomic theory and is closely intertwined with the subject of the allocation of scarce resources for alternative ends. One of our primary intentions is to develop this interconnection. Only recently have the theoretical interrelationships between the determinants of value and the optimal allocation of resources been made clear. Earlier economists were concerned primarily with explaining the determinants of "value," and these efforts are outlined in this chapter.

The logical place to start is with a definition of the word *value*. Unfortunately, the meaning of this term has not been consistent throughout the development of the subject. Today we regard "value" as being synonymous with the "price" of a commodity.[4] Earlier philosopher-economists, however, made a distinction between the market price of a commodity and its value. The term "value" was then thought of as being in some sense synonymous with "importance," "essentiality," or (at times) "godliness." Since "price" and "value" were separate concepts, they could differ, and most early economic discussions centered on these divergences.

Just Price

St. Thomas Aquinas believed value to be divinely determined. Since prices were set by humans, it was possible for the price of a commodity to differ from its value. A person accused of charging a price in excess of a good's value was guilty of charging an "unjust" price. For example, St. Thomas believed the "just" rate of interest to be 0. Any lender who demanded a payment for the use

[3] See the discussion that follows for a brief mention of earlier work. For a far more detailed treatment, see J. A. Schumpeter, *History of Economic Analysis* (New York: Oxford University Press, 1954), pt. II, chaps. 1, 2, and 3.

[4] This, in a sense, is not completely true (see Part VIII of this text, especially Chapter 24).

of money was charging an unjust price and could be—and often was—prosecuted by church officials.

Controversies over the *just price* for a commodity dominated the economic discussions of the Middle Ages. Such discussions laid some analytical foundations for the economic advances of the eighteenth and nineteenth centuries. However, the idea of a just price gradually came to have less importance in economic discussions as the general methods of analysis moved away from the concept of natural law toward the scientific method. Rather than attempting to ascertain a divine pattern in economic affairs, emphasis shifted toward understanding economic phenomena in their own right. The scientific method of proposing and testing hypotheses became the predominant means of investigation in the Age of Reason.

Value in Exchange: the Labor Theory of Value

The early scientific economists, such as Adam Smith (1723–1790) and David Ricardo (1772–1823), continued to distinguish between value and price. To Smith, for example, the value of a commodity meant its "value in use," whereas the price represented its "value in exchange." The distinction between these two concepts was illustrated by the famous water-diamond paradox. Water, which obviously has great value in use, has little value in exchange (it has a low price); diamonds are of little practical use but have a great value in exchange. The paradox with which early economists struggled derives from the observation that some very "useful" items have low prices whereas certain "nonessential" items have high prices.

Neither Smith nor Ricardo ever satisfactorily resolved this paradox. The concept of value in use was left for philosophers to argue over, while economists turned their attention to explaining the determinants of value in exchange (that is, to explaining relative prices). One obvious possible explanation is that exchange values of goods are determined by what it costs to produce them. Costs of production are primarily influenced by labor costs—at least this was so in the time of Smith and Ricardo—and therefore it was a short step to embrace a labor theory of value. For example, to paraphrase an example from Smith, if killing a deer takes twice the number of labor-hours as killing a beaver, then one deer should exchange for two beavers. In other words, the price of a deer should be twice that of a beaver. Similarly, diamonds are relatively costly because their production requires substantial labor input.

But how does that explanation of exchange value apply to other productive resources? How do payments for rent and for capital equipment enter into the determination of price? Ricardo answered this problem with an ingenious analysis. He argued that the cost of using capital could also be regarded as labor costs, with the labor being invested some years ago at the time the machines were produced. In this way, any capital cost could ultimately be traced back to some primary labor input. Ricardo disposed of rent by theorizing that rent is not a determinant of price (see Ricardo's analysis of rent in Chapter 21). Therefore, we are left with a pure labor theory of value: The relative price of two commodities is determined by the direct and indirect labor inputs used in each good.

To students with even a passing knowledge of what we now call the *law of supply and demand,* Ricardo's explanation must seem strange. Didn't he recognize the effects of demand on price? The answer to this question is both "yes" and "no." He did observe periods of both rapidly rising and rapidly falling prices and attributed such changes to demand shifts. However, he regarded such changes as abnormalities that produced only a temporary divergence of market price from labor value. Because he had not really solved the paradox of value in use, he was unwilling, or unable, to assign demand any more than a transient role in determining exchange value. Rather, Ricardo believed long-run exchange values were determined solely by the labor costs of production.

Karl Marx (1818–1883) used Ricardo's analysis of the determinants of value as the cornerstone for his theory of political economy. Since labor is the source of all value, Marx reasoned, labor deserved to receive the total proceeds of the productive process. Capitalists and landowners syphon off value that only labor can create, which makes capitalists and landowners exploiters. This notion of exploitation is most notable for the central role it plays in Marxian political theories. However, by placing a labor theory of value at the heart of his system, Marx was also laying down a challenge to future economists to propose some alternative explanation of exchange value that would serve as the cornerstone for a different theory of the allocation of economic goods.

Marginalist Revolution: Value in Use Reconsidered

Between 1850 and 1880, economists became increasingly aware that to construct an adequate alternative to Ricardo's theory of value, they had to come to grips with the paradox of value in use. During the 1870s several economists proposed that it is not the total usefulness of a commodity that helps to determine its exchange value but, rather, the usefulness of the *last unit consumed.* For example, water is certainly very useful—it is necessary for all life. But, because water is relatively plentiful, consuming one more pint (*ceteris paribus*) has a relatively low value to people. These "marginalists" redefined the concept of value in use from an idea of overall usefulness to one of marginal, or incremental, usefulness—the usefulness of an *additional unit of a commodity.* The concept of the demand for an incremental unit of output was now contrasted to Ricardo's analysis of production costs in order to derive a comprehensive picture of price determination.[5]

Marshallian Supply-Demand Synthesis

The clearest statement of these marginal principles was presented by the English economist Alfred Marshall (1842–1924) in his *Principles of Economics,* published in 1890. Marshall showed that demand and supply *simultaneously* operate to determine price. As Marshall noted, just as you cannot tell which

[5] Ricardo had earlier provided an important first step in marginal analysis in his discussion of rent. Ricardo theorized that as the production of corn increased, land of inferior quality would be used and this would cause the price of corn to rise. In his argument Ricardo implicitly recognized that it is the marginal cost—the cost of producing an additional unit—that is relevant to pricing. Notice that Ricardo implicitly held other inputs constant when discussing diminishing land productivity; that is, he employed one version of the *ceteris paribus* assumption.

Figure 1.1   *The Marshallian Supply-Demand Cross*

Marshall theorized that demand and supply interact to determine the equilibrium price
(*P**) and the quantity (*Q**) that will be traded in the market. He concluded that it is not
possible to say that either demand or supply alone determines price or therefore that
either costs or usefulness to buyers alone determines exchange value.

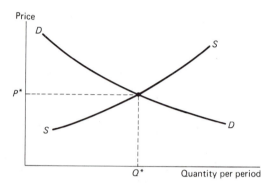

blade of a scissors does the cutting, so too you cannot say that either demand
or supply alone determines price. That analysis is illustrated by the famous
Marshallian cross shown in Figure 1.1. In the diagram the quantity of a good
purchased per period is shown on the horizontal axis, and its price appears on
the vertical axis. The curve *DD* represents the quantity of the good demanded
per period at each possible price. The curve is negatively sloped to reflect the
marginalist principle that as quantity increases, people are willing to pay less
and less for the last unit purchased. It is the value of this last unit that sets the
price for all units purchased. The curve *SS* shows how (marginal) production
costs rise as more output is produced. This reflects the increasing cost of producing one more unit as total output expands. In other words, the upward
slope of the *SS* curve reflects increasing marginal costs, just as the downward
slope of the *DD* curve reflects decreasing marginal value. The two curves intersect at *P**, *Q**. This is an *equilibrium* point—both buyers and sellers are
content with the quantity being traded and the price at which it is traded. If
one of the curves should shift, the equilibrium point would shift to a new
location. Thus price and quantity are simultaneously determined by the joint
operation of supply and demand.

   Marshall's model resolves the water-diamond paradox. Prices reflect both
the marginal evaluation that demanders place on goods and the marginal costs
of producing the goods. Viewed in this way, there is no paradox. Water is low
in price because it has both a low marginal value and a low marginal cost of
production. On the other hand, diamonds are high in price because they have
both a high marginal value (because they are relatively scarce) and a high marginal cost of production. This basic model of supply and demand lies behind
much of the analysis presented in this book.

*An Algebraic
Representation*

The supply-demand model shown in Figure 1.1 can also be developed using simple algebra. Although graphical presentations are adequate for some purposes, often economists present their model algebraically both to clarify their arguments and to make them more precise. For example, suppose we wished to study the market for peanuts and, on the basis of historical data, concluded that the quantity of peanuts demanded each week (Q—measured in bushels) depended on the price of peanuts (P—measured in dollars per bushel) according to the equation

$$\text{quantity demanded} = Q_D = 1000 - 100P. \tag{1.1}$$

Since this equation for Q_D contains only the single independent variable P, we are implicitly holding constant all other factors that might affect the demand for peanuts. Equation 1.1 indicates that, if other things do not change, at a price of $5 per bushel people will demand 500 bushels of peanuts, whereas at a price of $4 per bushel they will demand 600 bushels. The negative coefficient for P in Equation 1.1 reflects the marginalist principle that a lower price will cause more people to buy more peanuts. To complete this simple model of pricing, suppose that the quantity supplied of peanuts also depends on price:

$$\text{quantity supplied} = Q_S = -125 + 125P. \tag{1.2}$$

Here the positive coefficient of price also reflects the marginal principle that a higher price will call forth increased supply—primarily because the higher price encourages firms to incur higher marginal costs of production.

Equations 1.1 and 1.2 therefore reflect our model of price determination in the market for peanuts. An equilibrium price can be found by setting quantity supplied equal to quantity demanded:

$$\begin{aligned}\text{quantity supplied} = -125 + 125P = \\ \text{quantity demanded} = 1000 - 100P\end{aligned} \tag{1.3}$$

or

$$225P = 1125 \tag{1.4}$$

so,

$$P^* = 5. \tag{1.5}$$

At a price of $5 per bushel, this market is in equilibrium—at this price people want to purchase 500 bushels and that is exactly what peanut producers are willing to supply.

In Figure 1.2 this supply-demand model is given a graphical representation. As in Figure 1.1, the demand curve has a negative slope whereas the supply curve is positively sloped. In this case, however, we can assign the actual numerical values to quantity and price, and the equilibrium price (where the two curves intersect) can be determined using simple algebra. Stating Marshall's model algebraically has therefore added a bit to our ability to explain economic events (that is, the pricing of peanuts). Later in this book we will encounter many similar cases in which a graphic analysis may help us to get

Figure 1.2   *Hypothetical Supply-Demand Equilibrium in the Market for Peanuts*

With a demand curve given by $Q_D = 1000 - 100P$ and a supply curve given by $Q_S = -125 + 125P$, the market for peanuts is in equilibrium at a price of $P^* = \$5$. At this price, demanders wish to buy 500 bushels of peanuts, and that is precisely what suppliers are willing to produce.

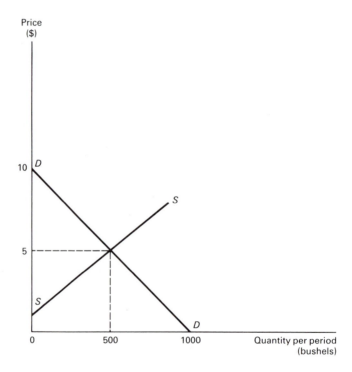

started on a problem, but in which a formal algebraic approach adds substantially to our understanding.

Shift in the Supply-Demand Equilibrium

In your introductory economics course, you probably studied the various factors that shift the demand or supply curve for a product and thereby lead to a new price-quantity equilibrium. In later chapters in this book, we will examine this type of analysis in detail. Here we will use the algebraic model from the previous section to illustrate its application to such a *comparative statics* problem. That is, we will compare our initial equilibrium to a new one that results from changing conditions.

Assuming the model portrayed by Equations 1.1 and 1.2 accurately reflects the peanut market, the only way to explain a new price-quantity equilibrium is by hypothesizing that either the supply or the demand curve has shifted.

Figure 1.3 *Effect of a Shift in Demand Depends on the Shape of Both the Supply and Demand Curves*

When demand shifts outward to $Q_D = 1450 - 100P$, both equilibrium price and quantity increase. To determine the extent of these increases, one must know the forms of both the demand and supply curves. In this particular case, price increases to $P = \$7$ and quantity increases to $Q = 750$ bushels.

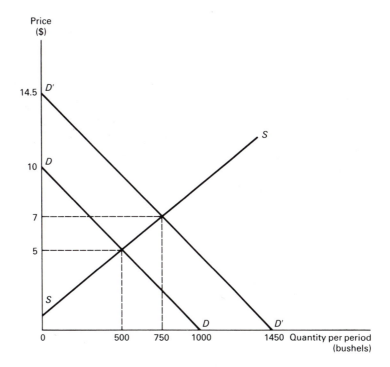

Without such a shift, the model would continue to "predict" a price of $P = \$5$ and a quantity of $Q = 500$.

One way to incorporate a shift into our simple model is to assume that the demand for peanuts increases to

$$\text{quantity demanded} = Q_D = 1450 - 100P. \tag{1.6}$$

As Figure 1.3 shows, this new demand curve (labeled $D'D'$) represents a parallel shift outward of the old demand—at every price 450 more bushels of peanuts are demanded than was the case for the old demand. As we will see in Chapters 5 and 6, such a shift might result from an increase in consumers' incomes, from an increase in the price of a product that substitutes for peanuts (pretzels, for example), or simply from an increased desire by consumers to eat peanuts. Whatever the cause of the shift in demand, Marshall's model predicts that both the equilibrium price and the quantity for peanuts will rise, as

Figure 1.3 illustrates. We can find an explicit algebraic solution, as before, by setting quantity demanded equal to quantity supplied:

$$\text{quantity demanded} = Q_D = 1450 - 100P = \\ \text{quantity supplied} = Q_S = -125 + 125P \tag{1.7}$$

or

$$225P = 1575, \tag{1.8}$$

$$P^* = 7, \tag{1.9}$$

and

$$Q_D = Q_S = 750.$$

This new solution illustrates Marshall's scissors analogy—the new price-quantity equilibrium is determined by the forces of both demand and supply. Although demand has increased by 450 bushels at every price, the rise in price brought about by this shift causes a movement upward along the new demand curve and therefore reduces quantity demanded below what would have been chosen at a price of $5 (950 bushels). Only by using information from the supply curve is it possible to compute the new equilibrium price and the final effect on the quantity of peanuts produced (which only increases to 750 bushels).

This simple algebraic analysis therefore illustrates two important features of Marshall's model. First, the model clearly shows the meaning of market equilibrium. The supply and demand equations have only one price-quantity point in common. This simultaneous solution to the two equations shows precisely what economists mean by a market equilibrium. Here, as in many other places in this book, simple mathematical ideas provide a precise way of developing this economic model of market equilibrium. Similarly, developing the supply-demand model in this way permitted a rather precise answer to the comparative statics question of how the market would respond to a shift outward in the demand curve. Again, the mathematical representation of Marshall's ideas helped to clarify the analysis and make it more precise. As we will see throughout this book, that is indeed the general purpose of building mathematical models of economic activities.

General Equilibrium Models

Although the Marshallian model is an extremely useful and versatile tool, it is a *partial equilibrium model,* looking at only one market at a time. For some questions this narrowing of perspective gives valuable insights and analytical simplicity. For other, broader questions such a narrow viewpoint may prevent the discovery of important interrelations. To answer more general questions we must have a model of the whole economy that suitably mirrors the interrelationships among various markets and various economic agents. The French economist Leon Walras (1831–1910), building on a long Continental tradition in such analysis, created the basis for modern investigations into those broad questions. His method of representing the economy by a large number of simultaneous equations forms the basis for an understanding of the interrelationships implicit in *general equilibrium* analysis. Walras recognized that one cannot talk about a single market in isolation; what is needed is a model that permits the effects of a change in one market to be followed through other markets.

For example, suppose that the price of wheat were to increase. Marshallian analysis would seek to understand the reason for this increase by looking at conditions of supply and demand in the wheat market. General equilibrium analysis would look not only at the wheat market but also at repercussions in other markets. A rise in the price of wheat would cause increased costs for bakers, which would, in turn, affect the supply curve for bread. Similarly, the rising price of wheat might mean higher land prices for landowners, which would affect the demand curves for all products that landowners buy. The demand curves for landowners' automobiles, furniture, and trips to Europe would all shift out, and that might create additional incomes for the providers of those products. Consequently, the effects of the initial increase in demand for wheat eventually would spread throughout the economy. General equilibrium analysis attempts to develop models that permit us to examine such effects in a simplified setting. Several models of this type are described in Part V of this text.

Here we briefly introduce these models by using another graph you should remember from introductory economics—the *production possibility frontier*. This graph shows the various amounts of two goods that an economy can produce during some period (say, one week). Because the production possibility frontier shows two goods, rather than the single good in Marshall's model, it is used as a basic building block for general equilibrium models.

Figure 1.4 shows the production possibility frontier for two goods, food and clothing. The graph illustrates the supply of these goods by showing the combinations that can be produced with this economy's resources. For example, 10 pounds of food and 3 units of clothing could be produced, or 4 pounds of food and 12 units of clothing. Many other combinations of food and clothing could also be produced. The production possibility frontier shows all of them. Combinations of food and clothing outside the frontier cannot be produced because not enough resources are available. The production possibility frontier reminds us of the basic economic fact that resources are scarce—there are not enough resources available to produce all we might want of every good.

This scarcity means that we must choose how much of each good to produce. Figure 1.4 makes clear that each choice has its costs. For example, if this economy produces 10 pounds of food and 3 units of clothing at point *A*, producing 1 more unit of clothing would "cost" 1/2 pound of food—increasing the output of clothing by 1 unit means the production of food would have to decrease by 1/2 pound. Economists would say that the *opportunity cost* of 1 unit of clothing at point *A* is 1/2 pound of food. On the other hand, if the economy initially produces 4 pounds of food and 12 units of clothing at point *B*, it would cost 2 pounds of food to produce 1 more unit of clothing. The opportunity cost of 1 more unit of clothing at point *B* has increased to 2 pounds of food. Because more units of clothing are produced at point *B* than

Figure 1.4   *Production Possibility Frontier*

The production possibility frontier shows the different combinations of two goods that can be produced from a certain amount of scarce resources. It also shows the opportunity cost of producing more of one good as the amount of the other good that cannot then be produced. The opportunity cost at two different levels of clothing production can be seen by comparing points *A* and *B*.

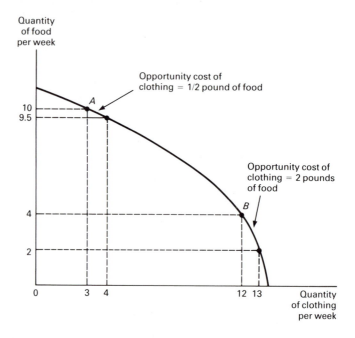

at point *A*, both Ricardo's and Marshall's ideas of increasing incremental costs suggest that the opportunity cost of an additional unit of clothing will be higher at point *B* than at point *A*. This effect is just what Figure 1.4 shows.

The production possibility frontier in Figure 1.4 gives us two general equilibrium results that are not clear in Marshall's supply and demand model of a single market. The first result is that producing more of one good means producing less of another good because resources are scarce. Economists often (perhaps too often!) use the expression "there is no such thing as a free lunch" to explain that every economic action has opportunity costs. The second result shown by the production possibility frontier is that these opportunity costs depend on how much of each good is produced. The frontier is like a supply curve for two goods—it shows the opportunity cost of producing more of one good as the decrease in the amount of the second good. The production possibility frontier is therefore a particularly useful tool for studying several markets at the same time. In later chapters we will use this concept a great deal.

Welfare Economics

In addition to their use in examining positive questions about how the economy operates, the tools used in general equilibrium analysis have also been applied to the study of normative questions about the social desirability of various economic arrangements. Although such questions were a major focus of the great eighteenth- and nineteenth-century economists (Smith, Ricardo, Marx, Marshall, and so forth), perhaps the most significant advances in their study were made by the British economist Francis Y. Edgeworth (1848–1926) and the Italian economist Vilfredo Pareto (1848–1923) in the early years of the twentieth century. These economists helped to provide a precise definition for the concept of "economic efficiency" and to demonstrate the conditions under which markets will be able to achieve that goal. By clarifying the relationship between the allocation of resources and the pricing of resources, they provided further insights into the determinants of value. Parts V and VIII of this book focus on some of these welfare issues.

Recent Advances

In the years following World War II, research activity in economics expanded rapidly, aided by increasing use of economic analysis by governments and firms and by the advent of electronic computers. Three areas of research on the general subject of price determination might be specifically highlighted. First, the mathematical foundations of economic models were further clarified and expanded. The 1947 publication of Paul A. Samuelson's *Foundations of Economic Analysis* was a major landmark in this regard.[6] This book, together with several others published between 1945 and 1955, made it inescapably clear that to understand the modern theory of price determination, some mathematical background is required.

A second major area of recent advances in economic research is in the analysis of general equilibrium and welfare economics. Following on the earlier work of Edgeworth and Pareto, this research has added greatly to an understanding of the structure of multimarket models by developing compact ways of describing very complicated interrelationships. Economists, such as Kenneth J. Arrow,[7] who have developed this area of research have been interested not only in devising positive models that explain and predict effects that occur in many markets simultaneously but also in using these models to study the welfare consequences of various kinds of market organizations and imperfections.

Finally, and perhaps of greatest significance, has been the increasing use of computers in economic research. The ability of such machines to make extremely rapid calculations and to store vast amounts of data has revolutionized the approach taken toward many topics. For example, general equilibrium systems involving literally thousands of markets and traders can now be modeled explicitly rather than having to rely solely on abstract mathematical represen-

---

[6] Paul A. Samuelson, *Foundations of Economic Analysis* (Cambridge, Mass.: Harvard University Press, 1947).

[7] Two books might be mentioned: Kenneth J. Arrow and F. H. Hahn, *General Competitive Analysis* (San Francisco: Holden-Day, 1971) and Kenneth J. Arrow, *Social Choice and Individual Values* (New Haven, Conn.: Yale University Press, 1951).

tations. And sophisticated tests of economic models using actual data can now be easily undertaken, whereas previously it was possible only to make simple, and perhaps not very relevant, calculations.[8] Hence, computers have greatly aided the process of relating economic theory to the real world. Many of the examples presented in this book are based on such computer-related research. Of course, not all computer research is of high quality—the need for a firmly based economic theory behind the calculations remains as significant today as for economists in the precomputer age. The example at the end of this chapter illustrates how overreliance on computer-generated output that is not well grounded in theory can lead to models with little empirical validity.

OUTLINE OF THE BOOK

These various themes from the historical development of the theory of value are also reflected in the organization of this book. In all, the book is divided into 25 chapters that are, in turn, grouped into eight major parts. Part I (Chapters 1 and 2) provides some basic methodological and mathematical background for the study of economics. The material in Chapter 2 is especially important because the mathematical tools introduced there will be used in many other places in the book.

The formal economic analysis of this text begins in Part II (Chapters 3–7), which develops the economic theory of choice. A primary purpose of this part is to develop Marshall's demand curve in a formal way. Doing so provides a good background for understanding how individuals respond to price changes and why demand curves might shift their positions.

Although economists' principal use for the theory of individual choice is to derive demand curves, that is not the sole application of the theory. In Part III (Chapters 8 and 9), we survey some additional applications. Especially important is our discussion of uncertainty in economics (Chapter 9) and why individuals will find it in their interest to acquire information. The observation that not all economic decisions (say, buying a car) have perfectly predictable outcomes (you might get a "lemon") has important implications for many market transactions. We will encounter these implications at many other places in this book.

In Part IV (Chapters 10–13), we begin our study of the behavior of firms (organizations that produce economic goods). Our principal goal is to examine firms' supply decisions and to show how those decisions are affected by input costs that firms incur. Some attention is also devoted to issues surrounding decisions that are internal to the firm; that is, how the production process is organized and how managers behave.

The elements of demand and supply developed in Parts II and IV, respectively, are then combined in Part V (Chapters 14–17) to discuss price determination in perfectly competitive markets. This part provides a full explanation of Marshall's model in its modern form and describes how that model can be

---

[8]Most significantly, computers, together with the sophisticated statistical techniques they make possible, have provided ways of incorporating the *ceteris paribus* assumption that were not previously available.

adapted to general equilibrium analysis as well. Part V concludes with an analysis of the welfare properties of the perfectly competitive model. This discussion provides several benchmarks against which other types of market organization (for example, monopoly) and several related market imperfections (such as imperfect information) might be judged.

Models of imperfect competition are considered explicitly in Part VI (Chapters 18–20). This part examines not only the model of monopoly price determination (which may already be familiar to you), but also explores more recent innovations in the study of imperfect competition such as the effects of potential competition for markets and the modeling of firms' strategies when they face uncertain situations. Thus Part VI illustrates the issues that arise when the rigid assumptions of Marshall's perfectly competitive model are relaxed.

Parts VII and VIII show how the Marshallian model can be applied in contexts other than the pricing of goods. In Part VII (Chapters 21–23), we examine how the model can explain the pricing of factors of production (that is, labor, capital, or specific components of these large aggregates). In this application, the actors in Marshall's model play roles opposite to those assumed in the traditional model of the pricing of goods: Individuals now supply services whereas firms demand these services. Despite this reversal of roles, however, much of the traditional analysis has direct analogies in the study of the pricing of factors of production.

Finally, in Part VIII (Chapters 24 and 25), we explore some limitations of the market mechanism. We develop models to explain why some goods (such as those that generate pollution) may be overproduced by reliance on standard market incentives whereas other goods (such as those that provide public benefits to all) may be underproduced. This part therefore offers some warnings about the ability of private markets, even perfectly competitive ones, to solve all problems in the allocation of resources. But these conclusions are not universal, and some of the analysis of Part VIII suggests that private market mechanisms may be quite robust in dealing with certain types of problems. Indeed, some of the models in Part VIII suggest that in certain cases market intervention intended to improve matters may actually make things worse.

SUMMARY

This chapter has provided some background on how economists approach the study of the allocation of resources. Much of the material discussed here should be familiar to you—and that's the way it should be. In many respects, the study of economics represents acquiring increasingly sophisticated tools for addressing the same basic problems. The purpose of this book (and, indeed, for most upper-level books on economics) is to provide you with more of these tools. As a starting place, this chapter reminded you of the following points:

- Economics is the study of how scarce resources are allocated among alternative uses. Economists seek to develop simple models to help understand that process. Many of these models have a mathematical basis because the use of mathematics offers a precise shorthand for stating the models and exploring their consequences.

- The most commonly used economic model is the supply-demand model first thoroughly developed by Alfred Marshall in the latter part of the nineteenth century. This model shows how observed prices can be taken to represent an equilibrium balancing of the production costs incurred by firms and the willingness of demanders to pay for those costs.
- Marshall's model of equilibrium is only "partial"—that is, it looks only at one market at a time. To look at many markets together requires that we develop an expanded set of tools.
- Testing the validity of an economic model is perhaps the most difficult task economists face. Occasionally, a model's validity can be appraised by asking whether it is based on "reasonable" assumptions. More often, however, models are judged by how well they can explain economic events in the real world.

Application

ECONOMIC MODELS AND THE LIMITS-TO-GROWTH DEBATE

In the early 1970s a number of books and reports predicting dire consequences for the future of humanity were published. The most influential of these were *World Dynamics*[9] by Jay W. Forrester and *The Limits to Growth*[10] (which was based largely on the Forrester book) by Donnella H. Meadows et al. Through the use of complex computer models, these books purported to show that by the mid-1980s and on into the twenty-first century, the world would be experiencing major economic disruptions, with per capita consumption of food and other necessities falling at a disturbingly rapid rate. Thus the authors foresaw world population growth outstripping sustainable increases in production, a specter first suggested in the writings of T. R. Malthus (1766–1834) in the late eighteenth century. We will briefly examine whether the evidence supports such a model

and whether its predictions should therefore be trusted. Of course, the twenty-first century has not yet arrived, so definitive evidence with which to test the model's predictions is not yet available. But since the models were published, the assumptions behind them have been subjected to intensive scrutiny, and major questions regarding their validity have been raised. Here we will discuss three of these: how the models described the production relationship, how they treated population growth, and how much importance they gave to prices. We will conclude that the evidence suggests that the models probably were not very good ones, primarily because they paid little attention to economic theory.

Mathematical Assumptions

Any computer model consists of mathematical equations that must be programmed by the model's author. To examine the properties of the *Limits* models, therefore, we must investigate the equations their authors chose to use. Perhaps the most crucial of these was the production relationship in which the total annual volume of economic output (Q) depends on the

[9] J. W. Forrester, *World Dynamics* (Cambridge, Mass.: Wright Allen Press, 1971).

[10] Donnella H. Meadows et al., *The Limits to Growth* (New York: Universe Books, 1972).

amount of resources available (R) and the quantity of capital in existence (K) according to the equation

$$Q = A \cdot R \cdot K \qquad (1.10)$$

where A is a numerical constant. Most of the extreme and disastrous estimates that the *Limits* authors obtained resulted from this assumed model. But the model of production is questionable on at least three grounds. First, as we describe more fully in Chapter 10, this model assumes strongly increasing returns to scale—for example, if the inputs R and K were to double, output would expand fourfold. In literally thousands of studies, however, economists have failed to find such increasing returns to scale. Instead, they have tended to conclude that constant returns to scale seem more in accord with the facts.[11] Because the *Limits* authors ran their model "in reverse" (that is, they studied the effects of declining resources), the effect of assuming increasing returns to scale was to build in the assumption that output would crash downward if resources became more scarce.

A second feature of the production relationship assumed in Equation 1.10 is that it does not model labor input or possible improvements in the quality of this input (through education, for example). Instead, the authors focused only on workers as consumers of economic output. Moreover, the *Limits* authors adopted what another author termed a "fruit-fly" theory;[12] that is, they assumed that increasing affluence in the world would bring increasing population growth. This assumption also provided the basis for many of the authors' dire predictions because, from the start, they as-

sumed increases in output would lead to vast increases in the number of mouths to feed. But experience from the 1960s and 1970s shows that almost universally, increasing affluence has been associated with declining, not increasing, rates of population growth. In Chapter 22 we discuss some of the economic factors behind that trend. Because the *Limits* authors did not take such factors into account, their models, and probably the predictions they made, tended to confuse completely the role of population change in the growth process.

Role of Prices

For economists, probably the major weakness of the *Limits* models was their failure to model prices. The authors assumed that available natural resources would be used no matter what their prices. But this approach takes no account of the fact (clearly recognized by Ricardo and Marshall in the nineteenth century) that resource prices provide producers with signals of the need to economize on their use. One of the most dramatic examples is the case of energy, particularly oil. During the 1970s the real price of oil increased more than sixfold, primarily in response to the forming of the OPEC cartel early in the decade. This increase led to large increases in the prices for all types of energy. As might have been expected, a principal way in which the world economy responded to this increasing price was to cut back on the use of energy. That was particularly true later in the decade as individuals and firms had increasing opportunities to change their behavior (for example, individuals could buy smaller cars, and firms could purchase more energy-efficient machinery). In the U.S. economy, for example, real overall energy prices rose about 60 percent between 1973 and 1980, and energy use per dollar of real gross national product declined by nearly 20 percent. The authors of the *Limits* books, however, did not allow for such possibilities in their models.

In conclusion, then, although the *Limits* books received a great deal of publicity (and their authors made frequent appearances on

---

[11] In Chapter 10 we show that a production function based on R and K would have such constant returns to scale if the authors had used the following form instead:

$$Q = A \sqrt{R \cdot K}.$$

[12] W. D. Nordhaus, "World Dynamics: Measurement without Data," *Economic Journal* 83 (December 1973): 1156–1183.

talk shows), it appears that the models that underlaid their analysis were seriously flawed. The models' predictions for the 1980s have proved to be quite wrong, and there is reason to believe that will continue to be true into the future. Since the *Limits* models were developed, a number of similar computer models have been published that purport to predict accurately the effects of economic disasters ranging from ballooning Latin American debt to nuclear war. In some cases, these models are solidly grounded in economic theory, but in many others they incorporate some of the same bizarre properties that the *Limits* models did. The constantly increasing power of modern computers makes the problem of GIGO ("garbage in, garbage out") even more significant today than in the early 1970s. As we will see throughout this book, computer technology cannot substitute for careful attention to economic principles and to the use of real-world data to test these principles. Only by subjecting economic models to such theoretical and empirical testing can good ones be differentiated from bad ones.

SUGGESTED READINGS

On Methodology

Boland, Lawrence E. "A Critique of Friedman's Critics." *Journal of Economic Literature* (June 1979): 503–522.

Good summary of criticisms of positive approaches to economics and of the role of empirical verification of assumptions.

Friedman, Milton. "The Methodology of Positive Economics." In *Essays in Positive Economics,* pp. 3–43. Chicago: University of Chicago Press, 1953.

Basic statement of Friedman's positivist views.

Harrod, Roy F. "Scope and Method in Economics." *Economic Journal* 48 (1938): 383–412.

Classic statement of appropriate role for economic modeling.

Koopmans, Tjalling. *Three Essays on the State of Economic Science.* New York: McGraw-Hill Book Company, 1957.

Literate discussion of both methodology and relatively advanced theory. Part II, "The Construction of Economic Knowledge," is especially recommended.

Nagel, Ernest. "Assumptions in Economic Theory." *American Economic Review* (May 1963): 211–219.

Thoughts on economic methods by a philosopher.

Robbins, Lionel. *An Essay on the Nature and Significance of Economic Science.* 2d ed. London: The Macmillan Co., 1935.

Excellent, literate statement of economic methodology, as applied to policy questions.

Primary Sources on the History of Economics

Edgeworth, F. Y. *Mathematical Psychics.* London: Kegan Paul, 1881.

Initial investigations of welfare economics, including rudimentary notions of economic efficiency and the contract curve.

Marshall, A. *Principles of Economics.* 8th ed. London: Macmillan & Co., 1920.

Complete summary of neoclassical view. A long-running, popular text. Detailed mathematical appendix.

Marx, K. *Capital.* New York: Modern Library, 1906.

Full development of labor theory of value. Discussion of "transformation problem" provides a (perhaps faulty) start for general equilibrium analysis. Presents fundamental criticisms of institution of private property.

Ricardo, D. *Principles of Political Economy and Taxation.* London: J. M. Dent & Sons, 1911.

Very analytical, tightly written work. Pioneer in developing careful analysis of policy questions, especially trade-related issues. Discusses first basic notions of marginalism.

Smith, A. *The Wealth of Nations.* New York: Modern Library, 1937.

First great economics classic. Very long and detailed, but Smith had the first word on practically every economic matter. This edition has helpful marginal notes.

Walras, L. *Elements of Pure Economics.* Translated by W. Jaffé. Homewood, Ill.: Richard D. Irwin, 1954.

Beginnings of general equilibrium theory. Rather difficult reading.

Secondary Sources on the History of Economics
Blaug, Marc. *Economic Theory in Retrospect.* Rev. ed. Cambridge: Cambridge University Press, 1978.

Very complete summary stressing analytical issues. Excellent "Readers' Guides" to the classics in each chapter.

Heilbroner, Robert L. *The Worldly Philosophers.* 5th ed. New York: Simon and Schuster, 1980.

Fascinating, easy-to-read biographies of leading economists. Chapters on Utopian Socialists and Thorstein Veblen highly recommended.

Keynes, John M. *Essays in Biography.* New York: W. W. Norton, 1963.

Essays on many famous persons (Lloyd George, Winston Churchill, Leon Trotsky) and on several economists (Malthus, Marshall, Edgeworth, F. P. Ramsey, and Jevons). Shows the true gift of Keynes as a writer.

Lekachman, Robert. *A History of Economic Ideas.* 2d ed. New York: McGraw-Hill Book Company, 1976.

Brief but complete summary. Has an interesting part on economics prior to Adam Smith.

Schumpeter, J. A. *History of Economic Analysis.* New York: Oxford University Press, 1954.

Encyclopedic treatment. Covers all the famous and many not-so-famous economists. Also briefly summarizes concurrent developments in other branches of the social sciences.

CHAPTER 2

The Mathematics of Optimization

An important starting place for many economic models is the hypothesis that an economic agent is seeking to achieve some kind of best, or "optimal," result given his or her circumstances. Managers of a firm are assumed to be striving for maximum profits; consumers seek to maximize their well-being (or, more formally, their *utility*); and governments may pursue programs to maximize total economic output. All such assumptions are obviously abstractions from reality. They take no account of "irrational" behavior by firms, consumers, or governments, nor do they consider that those agents may not possess sufficient information to decide whether they have achieved a maximum. But, as we discussed in the previous chapter, all theories must abstract from reality: Their ultimate test depends on their ability to explain real-world phenomena. As we shall see, judged by that criterion, the optimization hypothesis has been very useful indeed.

Two factors probably account for the widespread application of the optimization hypothesis to economic problems. First, the concept is precise. One may argue about what in fact is optimized (this is the case in the theory of the firm, for example, as will be discussed in Chapter 13), but the alternative behavioral assumptions to optimization have proved to be imprecise and unquantifiable. For example, if consumers or firms are assumed to strive toward "satisfactory" performance in certain endeavors, one is forced to specify exactly what "satisfactory" means, and the theory may lose much of its simplicity.[1]

A second factor accounting for the widespread application of the optimization hypothesis is the extent to which mathematical techniques have been developed to investigate such problems. Since maximization (and minimization)

---

[1] The distinction between optimization and "satisfaction" is not as clear as we imply here. In many respects satisfaction can be regarded as merely an example of maximization subject to constraints. For example, a firm that seems to achieve only satisfactory profits might be assumed to be maximizing something else (perhaps the prestige of its manager) subject to the constraint of earning a required level of profits.

problems occur quite often in the natural sciences, mathematicians have long been interested in general solutions to these problems. Fortunately, economists have been able to make use of those mathematical developments and have found that such analyses give many insights into economic behavior.

MAXIMIZA-TION OF A FUNCTION OF ONE VARIABLE

Suppose that a manager of a firm desires to maximize the profits received from selling a particular good.[2] Suppose also that the profits (π) received depend only on the quantity (Q) of the good sold. Mathematically,

$$\pi = f(Q). \tag{2.1}$$

Figure 2.1 shows a possible relationship between π and Q. Clearly, to achieve maximum profits, the manager should produce output Q^*, which yields profits π^*. If more or less than this amount were produced, profits would not be maximized. How will the manager find this point of maximum profits? If a graph such as that of Figure 2.1 were available, this would seem to be a simple matter to be accomplished with a ruler.

Suppose, however, as is more likely, the manager does not have such an accurate picture of the market. He or she may then try varying Q to see where a maximum profit is obtained. For example, by starting at Q_1, profits from sales would be π_1. Next, the manager may try output Q_2, observing that profits have increased to π_2. The commonsense idea that profits have increased in response to an increase in Q can be stated formally as

$$\frac{\pi_2 - \pi_1}{Q_2 - Q_1} > 0 \quad \text{or} \quad \frac{\Delta \pi}{\Delta Q} > 0, \tag{2.2}$$

where the Δ notation is used to mean "the change in" π or Q. So long as $\Delta\pi/\Delta Q$ is positive, profits are increasing and the manager will continue to increase output. For increases in output to the right of Q^*, however, $\Delta\pi/\Delta Q$ will be < 0 and the manager will realize that a mistake has been made if he or she continues to expand Q.

Derivatives

In calculus, mathematicians study the limit of ratios such as $\Delta\pi/\Delta Q$ for very small changes in Q. This limit is called the *derivative* of the function, $\pi = f(Q)$, and is denoted by $d\pi/dQ$ or df/dQ or $f'(Q)$. More formally, the derivative of a function $\pi = f(Q)$ at the point Q_1 is defined as

$$\frac{d\pi}{dQ} = \frac{df}{dQ} = \lim_{h \to 0} \frac{f(Q_1 + h) - f(Q_1)}{h}, \tag{2.3}$$

where the symbol $\lim_{h \to 0}$ means that we are interested in the ratio

$$\frac{f(Q_1 + h) - f(Q_1)}{h}$$

---

[2] In this chapter we will generally explore maximization problems. A virtually identical approach would be taken to study minimization problems.

Figure 2.1 *Hypothetical Relationship between Quantity Produced and Profits*

If a manager wishes to produce the level of output that maximizes profits, Q^* should be produced. Notice that at Q^*, $d\pi/dQ = 0$.

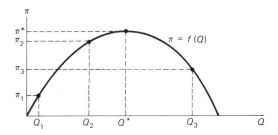

as h becomes small. Notice that the value of this ratio obviously depends on the point Q_1 that is chosen and that there is a close similarity between this definition and the Δ notation developed earlier.

A notational convention should be mentioned: Sometimes one wishes to note explicitly the point at which the derivative is to be evaluated. For example, the evaluation of the derivative at the point $Q = Q_1$ could be denoted by

$$\left.\frac{d\pi}{dQ}\right|_{Q\,=\,Q_1} \tag{2.4}$$

At other times one is interested in the value of $d\pi/dQ$ for all possible values of Q, and no explicit mention of a particular point of evaluation is made.

In the example of Figure 2.1,

$$\left.\frac{d\pi}{dQ}\right|_{Q\,=\,Q_1} > 0,$$

whereas

$$\left.\frac{d\pi}{dQ}\right|_{Q\,=\,Q_3} < 0.$$

What is the value of $d\pi/dQ$ at Q^*? It would seem to be 0, since the value is positive for values of Q less than Q^* and negative for values greater than Q^*. The derivative is the slope of the curve in question; this slope is positive to the left of Q^* and negative to the right of Q^*. At the point Q^* the slope of $f(Q)$ is 0.

First-Order Condition for a Maximum

This result is quite general. For a function of one variable to attain its maximum value at some point, the derivative at that point (if it exists) must be 0. Hence, if a manager could estimate the function $f(Q)$ from some sort of real-

Figure 2.2   *Graph of* df/dQ *from Figure 2.1*

The value of df/dQ depends on the value of Q. For values of Q to the left of Q*, df/dQ is positive: An increase in output would cause profits to increase. For Q to the right of Q*, df/dQ is negative: Increases in Q would decrease profits (a decrease in Q, on the other hand, would increase profits). At Q*, df/dQ is equal to 0 and profits are at a maximum.

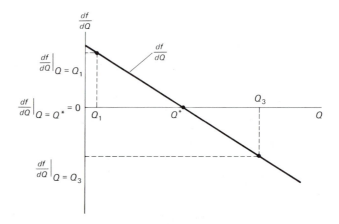

world data, it would be theoretically possible (using the techniques described below) to find the point where $df/dQ = 0$. By graphing all the values of df/dQ (see Figure 2.2), for example, output Q^* would be chosen, since

$$\frac{df}{dQ}\bigg|_{Q\ =\ Q^*} = 0. \tag{2.5}$$

Second-Order Conditions

An unsuspecting manager could be tricked, however, by a naïve application of this rule alone. For example, suppose that the profit function looks like that shown in either Figure 2.3a or 2.3b. If the profit function is that shown in Figure 2.3a, the manager, by producing where $d\pi/dQ = 0$, will choose point Q_a^*. This point in fact yields minimum, not maximum, profits for the manager. Similarly, if the profit function is that shown in Figure 2.3b, the manager will choose point Q_b^*, which, although it yields a profit greater than that for any output lower than Q_b^*, is certainly inferior to any output greater than Q_b^*. These situations point up the mathematical fact that $d\pi/dQ = 0$ is a *necessary* condition for a maximum, but not a *sufficient* condition. To ensure that the chosen point is indeed a maximum point, an additional condition must be imposed.

   Intuitively, this additional condition is clear: The profit available by producing either a bit more or a bit less than Q^* must be smaller than that available from Q^*. If this is not true, the manager can do better than Q^*. Mathematically, this means that $d\pi/dQ$ must be greater than 0 for $Q < Q^*$ and must be

---

Figure 2.3   *Two-Profit Functions That Give Misleading Results if the First Derivative Rule Is Applied Uncritically*

In (a) the application of the first derivative rule would result in point Q_a^* being chosen. This point is in fact a point of minimum profits. Similarly, in (b) output level Q_b^* would be recommended by the first derivative rule, but this point is inferior to all outputs greater than Q_b^*. This demonstrates graphically that finding a point at which the derivative is equal to 0 is a necessary, but not a sufficient, condition for a function to attain its maximum value.

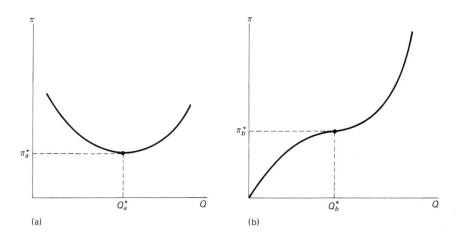

less than 0 for $Q > Q^*$. Therefore, at Q^*, $d\pi/dQ$ must be decreasing. Another way of saying this is that the derivative of $d\pi/dQ$ must be negative at Q^*.

Second Derivatives

The derivative of what is already a derivative is called a *second derivative* and is denoted by

$$\frac{d^2\pi}{dQ^2} \quad \text{or} \quad \frac{d^2 f}{dQ^2} \quad \text{or} \quad f''(Q).$$

The additional condition for Q^* to represent a true maximum is therefore

$$\left.\frac{d^2\pi}{dQ^2}\right|_{Q\,=\,Q^*} = \left. f''(Q) \right|_{Q\,=\,Q^*} < 0, \tag{2.6}$$

where the notation is again a reminder that this second derivative is to be evaluated at Q^*. The reader should check the slopes of the curves in Figure 2.3 to see that the "second-order" condition of Equation 2.6 does not hold at those points[3] where $d\pi/dQ = 0$.

---

[3] It might also be instructive to draw graphs of $d\pi/dQ$ for the functions in Figure 2.3. Notice that at Q^* the slope of $\left.\dfrac{d\pi}{dQ}\right|_{Q\,=\,Q^*}$ is positive for Figure 2.3a and is 0 for Figure 2.3b. A more detailed treatment of second-order conditions is provided in the appendix to this chapter.

Hence, although Equation 2.5 ($d\pi/dQ = 0$) is a necessary condition for a maximum, that equation must be combined with Equation 2.6 ($d^2\pi/dQ^2 < 0$) to ensure that the function is truly maximized. Equations 2.5 and 2.6 together are therefore sufficient conditions for a maximum. Of course, it is possible that by a series of trials the manager may be able to decide on Q^* by relying on market information rather than on mathematical reasoning (remember Friedman's pool player analogy). In this book we shall be less interested in how the point is discovered than in its properties and how the point changes when conditions change. The present mathematical development will be very helpful in answering these questions.

Numerical Example

As an example, suppose that the specific relationship between profits and quantity produced is given by

$$\pi = 4Q - Q^2. \tag{2.7}$$

Here Q represents a variable that is under the firm's explicit control whereas the coefficients 4 and -1 represent *parameters* of the problem that are determined by forces (such as product demand or input costs) that are beyond the firm's control. One could try to graph this expression (it would look much like Figure 2.1) or try several guesses in order to find the Q that gives maximum profits. However, the most straightforward method is to apply Equations 2.5 and 2.6 after calculating the derivatives of this profit function:

$$\frac{d\pi}{dQ} = \lim_{h \to 0} \frac{4(Q + h) - (Q + h)^2 - 4Q + Q^2}{h}$$

$$= \lim_{h \to 0} \frac{4Q + 4h - Q^2 - 2Qh - h^2 - 4Q + Q^2}{h} \tag{2.8}$$

$$= \lim_{h \to 0} \frac{4h - 2Qh - h^2}{h} = \lim_{h \to 0} 4 - 2Q - h$$

$$= 4 - 2Q,$$

and therefore $d\pi/dQ = 0$ when $Q = 2$. At this point, $\pi = 4$. By trying a few other values for Q, you may convince yourself that $\pi = 4$ is the highest value for profits obtainable in this situation.

As a more formal check of whether this is a true maximum, we must computer $d^2\pi/dQ^2$. Applying the definition of a derivative of $d\pi/dQ$ (which was shown to be $4 - 2Q$) gives

$$\frac{d^2\pi}{dQ^2} = \lim_{h \to 0} \frac{4 - 2(Q + h) - 4 + 2Q}{h} \tag{2.9}$$

$$= \lim_{h \to 0} \frac{-2h}{h} = -2 < 0.$$

Therefore Equation 2.6 is satisfied and $Q = 2$ is a true maximum. Notice that in this case $d^2\pi/dQ^2$ is negative at every point, not just at $Q = 2$. This means that $Q = 2$ is a "global" maximum for this function—for every other value of

Q profits are smaller. If the second-order condition were satisfied only near $Q = 2$, we could only be sure that this point was a "local" maximum. In that case we might have to examine other values of Q where the first-order conditions are satisfied to find the global maximum.

Rules for Finding Derivatives   The repeated application of the definition of a derivative can be tedious. For this reason several elementary derivatives are presented below. The proof of these results is left to the reader or can be found in any book on elementary calculus (see the references at the end of this chapter).

1.   If b is a constant, then

$$\frac{db}{dx} = 0.$$

This result says that changing the value of a variable in a problem does not change the values of the parameters in a problem.

2.   If a and b are constants and $b \neq 0$, then

$$\frac{dax^b}{dx} = bax^{b-1}.$$

3. $\dfrac{d \log_e x}{dx} = \dfrac{1}{x}$,

where $\log_e$ signifies the logarithm to the base e ($= 2.71828$). Such logarithms are generally used in calculus because of property 3. These are called *natural* logarithms and denoted by "*ln*" in this book.

4. $\dfrac{da^x}{dx} = a^x \, ln \, a$ for any constant a.

A particular case of this rule is $de^x/dx = e^x$. The function e^x is the only function that is its own derivative.

Now suppose that $f(x)$ and $g(x)$ are two functions of x and that $f'(x)$ and $g'(x)$ exist. Then

5. $\dfrac{d[f(x) + g(x)]}{dx} = f'(x) + g'(x).$

6. $d[f(x) \cdot g(x)] = f(x)g'(x) + f'(x)g(x).$

7. $d\left(\dfrac{f(x)}{g(x)}\right) = \dfrac{f'(x)g(x) - f(x)g'(x)}{[g(x)]^2},$

provided that $g(x) \neq 0$.

Finally, if $y = f(x)$ and $x = g(z)$ and if both $f'(x)$ and $g'(z)$ exist, then

8. $\dfrac{dy}{dz} = \dfrac{dy}{dx} \cdot \dfrac{dx}{dz} = \dfrac{df}{dx} \cdot \dfrac{dg}{dz}.$

This result is sometimes called the *chain rule,* which provides a convenient way for studying how one variable (z) affects another variable (y) solely through its influence on some intermediate variable (x). Most of you will have encountered these rules for differentiation before. For some practice with them, see Problem 2.1.

FUNCTIONS OF SEVERAL VARIABLES

Economic problems seldom involve functions of a single variable only. Most goals of interest to economic agents depend on several variables and the values for each of these must be chosen. For example, the *utility* an individual receives from activities as a consumer depends on the amount of each good consumed. For a firm's *production function,* the amount produced depends on the quantity of labor, capital, and land devoted to the production process. In these circumstances this dependence of one variable (y) on a series of other variables ($x_1, x_2, \ldots, x_n$) is denoted by

$$y = f(x_1, x_2, \ldots, x_n). \tag{2.10}$$

Partial Derivatives

We are interested in the point at which y reaches a maximum and how an economic agent might find that point. It is again convenient to picture this agent as changing the variables at his or her disposal (the x's) in order to locate a maximum. Unfortunately, for a function of several variables, the idea of *the* derivative is not well defined. Just as in climbing a mountain the steepness of ascent depends on which direction you go, so does the slope (or derivative) of the function depend on the direction in which it is taken. Usually, the only directional slopes of interest are those that are obtained by increasing one of the x's while holding all the other variables constant (the analogy of mountain climbing might be to measure slopes only in a north-south or east-west direction). These directional slopes are called *partial derivatives.* The partial derivative of y with respect to (that is, in the direction of) x_1 is denoted by

$$\frac{\partial y}{\partial x_1} \quad \text{or} \quad \frac{\partial f}{\partial x_1} \quad \text{or} \quad f_{x_1} \quad \text{or} \quad f_1.$$

It is understood that in calculating this derivative all of the other x's are held constant. Again it should be emphasized that the numerical value of this slope depends on the value of x_1 and on the (preassigned) values of $x_2, \ldots, x_n$.

A somewhat more formal definition of the partial derivative is

$$\frac{\partial f}{\partial x_1}\bigg|_{\bar{x}_2, \ldots, \bar{x}_n} = \lim_{h \to 0} \frac{f(x_1 + h, \bar{x}_2, \ldots, \bar{x}_n) - f(x_1, \bar{x}_2, \ldots, \bar{x}_n)}{h}, \tag{2.11}$$

where the notation is intended to indicate that $x_2, \ldots, x_n$ are all held constant at the preassigned values $\bar{x}_2, \ldots, \bar{x}_n$ so that the effect of changing x_1 can be studied. Partial derivatives with respect to the other variables ($x_2, \ldots, x_n$) would be calculated in a similar way.

Partial Derivatives and the Ceteris Paribus *Assumption*

In Chapter 1 we described the way in which economists use the *ceteris paribus* assumption in their models to hold constant a variety of outside influences so that the particular relationship being studied can be explored in a simplified setting. Partial derivatives are a precise mathematical way of representing this approach; that is, they show how changes in one variable affect some outcome when other influences are held constant—exactly what economists need for their models. For example, Marshall's demand curve shows the relationship between price (P) and quantity (Q) demanded when other factors are held constant. Using partial derivatives, we could represent the slope of this curve by $\partial Q/\partial P$ to indicate the *ceteris paribus* assumptions that are in effect. The fundamental law of demand—that price and quantity move in opposite directions when other factors do not change—is therefore reflected by the mathematical statement "$\partial Q/\partial P < 0$." Again, the use of a partial derivative serves as a reminder of the *ceteris paribus* assumptions that surround the law of demand. As we showed in the previous chapter, a change in some external factor would shift the supply-demand equilibrium, and then it would no longer be valid to speak of the "law of demand" since the *ceteris paribus* assumption would be violated. Considerably more complex mathematical formulations would have to be used to study such an effect, and the simple partial derivative notation would no longer be appropriate.

Later in this book we will make considerable use of this relationship between partial derivatives and the *ceteris paribus* assumption. Many of the results of economic models can be stated in the form: "Other things being constant, a change in x will affect y in the following way." A compact way of writing this statement is by describing the direction and magnitude of the partial derivative, $\partial y/\partial x$.

Calculating Partial Derivatives

Using the rules developed for finding derivatives, it is easy to calculate some simple partial derivatives. The calculation proceeds as for the usual derivative by *treating the* $x_2, \ldots, x_n$ *as constants* (which indeed they are in the definition of a partial derivative). Consider the following examples:

1.   If $y = f(x_1, x_2) = ax_1^2 + bx_1x_2 + cx_2^2$,

then

$$\frac{\partial f}{\partial x_1} = f_1 = 2ax_1 + bx_2$$

and

$$\frac{\partial f}{\partial x_2} = f_2 = bx_1 + 2cx_2.$$

Notice that $\partial f/\partial x_1$ is in general a function of both x_1 and x_2 and therefore will depend on the particular values assigned to these variables. It also depends on the parameters a, b, and c, which do not change as x_1 and x_2 change.

2.   If $y = f(x_1, x_2) = e^{ax_1 + bx_2}$,

then

$$\frac{\partial f}{\partial x_1} = f_1 = ae^{ax_1 + bx_2}$$

and

$$\frac{\partial f}{\partial x_2} = f_2 = be^{ax_1 + bx_2}.$$

3.   If $y = f(x_1, x_2) = a \log x_1 + b \log x_2$,

then

$$\frac{\partial f}{\partial x_1} = f_1 = \frac{a}{x_1}$$

and

$$\frac{\partial f}{\partial x_2} = f_2 = \frac{b}{x_2}.$$

Notice that the treatment of x_2 as a constant in the derivation of $\partial f / \partial x_1$ causes the term $b \log x_2$ to disappear upon differentiation because it does not change when x_1 changes. In this case changes in x_1, say, affect y, but the size of that effect is independent of the value for x_2 because there are no terms in the original function that contain the product of x_1 times x_2.

Second-Order Partial Derivatives   The partial derivative of a partial derivative is directly analogous to the second derivative of a function of one variable and is called a *second-order partial derivative*. This may be written as

$$\frac{\partial(\partial f / \partial x_i)}{\partial x_j}$$

or more simply as

$$\frac{\partial^2 f}{\partial x_i \partial x_j} = f_{ij}. \tag{2.12}$$

For the examples above:

1. $\dfrac{\partial^2 f}{\partial x_1 \partial x_1} = f_{11} = 2a$

$$f_{12} = b$$
$$f_{21} = b$$
$$f_{22} = 2c.$$

2. $f_{11} = a^2 e^{ax_1 + bx_2}$

$$f_{12} = abe^{ax_1 + bx_2}$$

$$f_{21} = abe^{ax_1 + bx_2}$$

$$f_{22} = b^2 e^{ax_1 + bx_2}.$$

3. $f_{11} = \dfrac{-a}{x_1^2}$

$$f_{12} = 0$$

$$f_{21} = 0$$

$$f_{22} = \dfrac{-b}{x_2^2}$$

Young's Theorem   These examples illustrate the mathematical result that, under quite general conditions, the order in which differentiation is conducted to evaluate second-order partial derivatives does not matter. That is,

$$f_{ij} = f_{ji} \tag{2.13}$$

for any pair of variables x_i, x_j. This result is sometimes called "Young's theorem." For an intuitive explanation of the theorem, we can return to our mountain-climbing analogy. In this example the theorem states that the gain in elevation a hiker experiences depends on the directions and distances traveled, but not on the order in which these occur. That is, the gain in altitude is independent of the actual path taken as long as the hiker proceeds from one set of map coordinates to another. He or she may, for example, go one mile north, then one mile east or proceed in the opposite order by going one mile east first, then a mile north. In either case, the gain in elevation is the same since in both cases the hiker is moving from one specific place to another. In later chapters we will make quite a bit of use of this result because it provides a very convenient way of showing some of the predictions that economic models make about behavior.

**MAXIMIZA-
TION OF
FUNCTIONS
OF SEVERAL
VARIABLES**   Using partial derivatives, it is possible to discuss the maximization of functions of several variables. To understand the mathematics used in solving this problem, an analogy to the one-variable case is helpful. In this one-variable case, we can picture an agent varying x by a small amount, dx, and observing the change in y (call this dy). This change is given by

$$dy = f'(x)\, dx. \tag{2.14}$$

The identity in Equation 2.14 then records the fact that the change in y is equal to the change in x times the slope of the function. This formula is equivalent to the *point-slope* formula used for linear equations in high school algebra. As before, the necessary condition for a maximum is that $dy = 0$ for small changes in x around the optimal point. Otherwise, y could be increased by suitable changes in x. But since dx does not necessarily equal 0 in Equation 2.14, $dy = 0$ must imply that at the desired point, $f'(x) = 0$. This is another way of obtaining the result we already derived.

Using this analogy it is possible to envision the decisions made by an economic agent who must choose the levels of several variables. Suppose that this agent wishes to find a set of x's that will maximize the value of $y = f(x_1, x_2, \ldots, x_n)$. The agent might consider changing only one of the x's, say x_1, while holding all the others constant. The change in y (that is, dy) that would result from this change in x_1 is given by

$$dy = \frac{\partial f}{\partial x_1} \, dx_1 = f_1 \, dx_1.$$

This says that the change in y is equal to the change in x_1 times the slope measured in the x_1 direction. Using the mountain analogy again, this would say that the gain in altitude a climber heading north would achieve is given by the distance northward traveled times the slope of the mountain measured in a northward direction.

Total Differential   If all the x's are varied by a small amount, the total effect on y will be the sum of effects such as that shown above. Therefore the total change in y is defined to be

$$dy = \frac{\partial f}{\partial x_1} \, dx_1 + \frac{\partial f}{\partial x_2} \, dx_2 + \cdots + \frac{\partial f}{\partial x_n} \, dx_n \qquad (2.15)$$
$$= f_1 dx_1 + f_2 dx_2 + \cdots + f_n dx_n.$$

This expression is called the *total differential* of y (or of f) and is directly analogous to the expression for the single-variable case given in Equation 2.14. The equation is intuitively sensible: The total change in y is the sum of changes brought about by varying each of the x's.[4]

First-Order Condition for a Maximum   A necessary condition for a maximum (or a minimum) of the function $f(x_1, x_2, \ldots, x_n)$ is that $dy = 0$ for any combination of small changes in the x's. The only way this can happen is if at the point being considered

$$f_1 = f_2 = \cdots = f_n = 0. \qquad (2.16)$$

---

[4]The total differential in Equation 2.15 also can be used to demonstrate the chain rule as it applies to functions of several variables. Suppose $y = f(x_1, x_2)$ and that $x_1 = g(z)$ and $x_2 = h(z)$. If all these functions are differentiable, it is possible to calculate the effects of a change in z on y. The total differential of y is

$$dy = f_1 \, dx_1 + f_2 \, dx_2.$$

Dividing this equation by dz gives

$$\frac{dy}{dz} = f_1 \frac{dx_1}{dz} + f_2 \frac{dx_2}{dz} = f_1 \frac{dg}{dz} + f_2 \frac{dh}{dz}.$$

Hence, calculating the effect of z on y requires calculating how z affects both of the determinants of y (that is, x_1 and x_2). If y depends on more than two variables, an analogous result holds. This result acts as a reminder to be rather careful to include all possible effects when calculating derivatives of functions of several variables.

A point where Equations 2.16 hold is called a *critical point*. Equations 2.16 are the necessary conditions for a maximum. To see this intuitively, note that if one of the partials (say f_i) were greater (or less) than 0, then y could be increased by increasing (or decreasing) x_i. An economic agent then could find this maximal point by finding the spot where y does not respond to very small movements in any of the x's. This is an extremely important result for economic analysis. It says that any activity (that is, the x's) should be pushed to the point where its "marginal" contribution to the objective (that is, y) is 0. To stop short of that point would fail to maximize y.

Second-Order Conditions

Again, however, the conditions of Equations 2.16 are not sufficient to ensure a maximum. This can be illustrated by returning to an already overworked analogy: All hilltops are (more or less) flat, but not every flat place is a hilltop. A second-order condition similar to Equation 2.6 is needed to ensure that the point found by applying Equations 2.16 is a true maximum. Intuitively, for a true maximum, y should be decreasing for any small changes in the x's away from the critical point. As in the single-variable case, this necessarily involves looking at the second-order partial derivatives of the function f. These second-order partials must obey certain restrictions (analogous to the restriction that was derived in the single-variable case) if the critical point found by applying Equations 2.16 is to be a true maximum. These restrictions are discussed briefly in the appendix to this chapter.

Since only functions of certain shapes satisfy these restrictions everywhere, it is only for these functions that the necessary conditions of Equations 2.16 are also automatically sufficient. Conveniently (or perhaps by design), most functions we shall encounter in this book do obey these restrictions, and we shall usually be interested only in applying the first-order conditions. This, however, should not be taken to imply that second-order conditions are somehow unimportant. As will be seen in several portions of the book, second-order conditions have a great deal of economic significance. But usually such examples will be discussed in exposition rather than in a formal, mathematical way.

Numerical Example

Suppose that y is a function of x_1 and x_2 given by

$$y = -(x_1 - 1)^2 - (x_2 - 2)^2 + 10 \qquad (2.17)$$

or

$$y = -x_1^2 + 2x_1 - x_2^2 + 4x_2 + 5.$$

We wish to find values for x_1 and x_2 that make y as large as possible. Taking the partial derivatives of y with respect to x_1 and x_2 and applying the necessary conditions given by Equations 2.16 yields

$$\frac{\partial y}{\partial x_1} = -2x_1 + 2 = 0$$

$$\frac{\partial y}{\partial x_2} = -2x_2 + 4 = 0 \qquad (2.18)$$

or

$$x_1 = 1$$

$$x_2 = 2.$$

The function is therefore at a critical point when $x_1 = 1$, $x_2 = 2$. At that point $y = 10$ (as the reader may easily verify), and a bit of experimentation should provide convincing evidence that this is the greatest value y can have. For example, if $x_1 = x_2 = 0$, then $y = 5$, or if $x_1 = x_2 = 1$, then $y = 9$. Values of x_1 and x_2 larger than 1 and 2, respectively, reduce y because the negative quadratic terms in Equation 2.17 become large. Consequently, the point found by applying the necessary conditions is in fact a true maximum.[5]

IMPLICIT FUNCTIONS

Although mathematical equations are often written with a "dependent" variable (y) as a function of one or more independent variable(s) (x), this is not the only way to write such a relationship. As a trivial example, the equation

$$y = mx + b \tag{2.19}$$

can also be written as

$$y - mx - b = 0 \tag{2.20}$$

or, even more generally, as

$$f(x, y, m, b) = 0 \tag{2.21}$$

where this functional notation indicates a relationship between x and y that also depends on the slope (m) and intercept (b) parameters of the function, which do not change. Functions written in the form given by Equations 2.20 and 2.21 are sometimes called implicit functions because the relationships between the variables and parameters are implicitly present in the equation rather than being explicitly calculated as, say, y as a function of x and the parameters m and b.

Often it is a simple matter to translate from implicit functions to explicit ones. For example, the implicit function

$$x + 2y - 4 = 0 \tag{2.22}$$

can easily be "solved" for x as

$$x = -2y + 4 \tag{2.23}$$

or for y as

$$y = \frac{-x}{2} + 2. \tag{2.24}$$

[5]More formally, the point $x_1 = 1$, $x_2 = 2$ is a true maximum because, at that point (as is true everywhere in this particular case), the own second-order partial derivatives, $\partial^2 y/\partial x_1^2$ and $\partial^2 y/\partial x_2^2$, are negative, and the cross second-order partial derivatives, $\partial^2 y/\partial x_1\partial x_2$, are 0 (see the appendix for a discussion of why these conditions imply a maximum).

Often, for purposes of economic analysis, equations such as 2.23 or 2.24 are more convenient to work with because the effect of x on y (or vice versa) is readily apparent; it is much easier to calculate dy/dx from Equation 2.24 than from Equation 2.22, for example.[6]

Implicit Function Theorem

It may not always be possible to solve implicit functions for unique explicit functions, however. The implicit function

$$x^2 + y^2 = 25, \qquad (2.25)$$

for example, can be represented by a circle with radius 5 centered at the origin. But, there is no well-defined explicit functional relationship between y and x since any particular value of x (say, 3) is consistent with two values of y (in this example, $+4$ and -4). To assure the existence of an explicit functional relationship between x and y, it would be necessary to look only at some restricted portion of this function (say, those points where $y \geq 0$) or to impose some other type of restriction.

Mathematicians have analyzed the conditions under which a given implicit function can be solved explicitly with one variable (or set of variables) being a function (or functions) of other variables and various parameters. Although we will not investigate these conditions here, they involve requirements on the various partial derivatives of the function that are sufficient to ensure that problems such as those posed by our circle example cannot arise.[7] In many economic applications, these derivative conditions are precisely those required to assure that the second-order conditions for a maximum (or a minimum) hold. Hence, in these cases, we will assert that the *implicit function theorem* holds and that it is therefore possible to solve explicitly for various optimal values for the variables being examined as functions of the parameters of the problem. We will, for example, show that the quantity of a good that is demanded by a person is a function of the prices that person faces and his or her income. Even though the demand relationship between price and quantity is implicitly worked out in each consumer's head, the implicit function theorem permits an explicit solution that illustrates the choices being made and the way they are affected by outside forces.

---

[6] In many circumstances, however, it is still possible to compute derivatives directly from implicit functions. For example, the implicit function $f(x, y) = 0$ has a total differential of $0 = f_x\,dx + f_y\,dy$ so

$$\frac{dy}{dx} = -\frac{f x}{f y}.$$

Hence, the derivative dy/dx can be found as the negative of the ratio of the partial derivatives of the implicit function, providing $f_y \neq 0$. In Chapter 3 we will make considerable use of this method for directly finding derivatives of implicit functions.

[7] For a detailed discussion, see Alpha C. Chiang, *Fundamental Methods of Mathematical Economics*, 2d ed. (New York: McGraw-Hill Book Company, 1974), pp. 216–227.

Table 2.1 *Optimal Values of* y *and* x *for Alternative Values of* a *in* y $= -x^2 + $ ax

Value of *a*	Value of *x**	Value of *y**
0	0	0
1	½	¼
2	1	1
3	³⁄₂	⁹⁄₄
4	2	4
5	⁵⁄₂	²⁵⁄₄
6	3	9

THE ENVELOPE THEOREM

One major application of the implicit function theorem, which will be used at many places in this book, is called the *envelope theorem;* it concerns how the optimal value for a particular function changes when a parameter of the function changes. Because many of the economic problems we will be studying concern the effects of changing a parameter (for example, the effects that changing the market price of a commodity will have on an individual's purchases), this is a type of calculation we will frequently make.

Perhaps the easiest way to understand the envelope theorem is through an example. Suppose y is a function of a single variable (x) and a parameter (a) given by

$$y = -x^2 + ax. \qquad (2.26)$$

For different values of the parameter a, this function represents a family of inverted parabolas. If a is assigned a specific value, Equation 2.26 is a function of x only, and the value of x that maximizes y can be calculated. For example, if $a = 1$, $x^* = $ ½ and, for these values of x and a, $y = $ ¼ (its maximal value). Similarly, if $a = 2$, $x^* = 1$ and $y = 1$. Hence an increase of 1 in the value of the parameter a has increased the maximum value of y by 3/4. In Table 2.1 integral values of a between 0 and 6 have been used to calculate the optimal values for x and the associated values of the objective function y. Notice that as a increases, the maximal value for y also increases. This is also illustrated in Figure 2.4, which shows that the relationship between a and y^* is quadratic. Now we wish to calculate how y^* changes as the parameter a changes.

The envelope theorem states that there are two equivalent ways we can make this calculation. First, we can calculate the slope of the function in Figure 2.4 directly. To do so we must first solve Equation 2.26 for the optimal value of x for any value of a:

$$\frac{dy}{dx} = -2x + a = 0;$$

Figure 2.4   *Illustration of the Envelope Theorem*

The envelope theorem states that the slope of the relationship between y^* (the maximum value of y) and the parameter a can be found by calculating the slope of the auxiliary relationship found by substituting the respective optimal values for x into the objective function and calculating $\partial y / \partial a$.

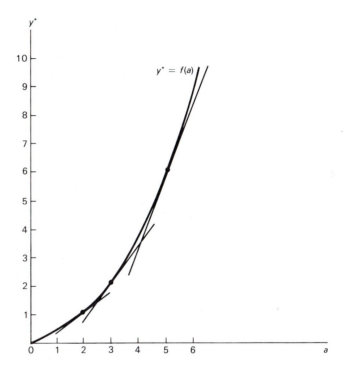

hence

$$x^* = \frac{a}{2}. \tag{2.27}$$

Substituting this value of x^* in Equation 2.26 gives

$$y^* = -(x^*)^2 + a(x^*)$$

$$= -\left(\frac{a}{2}\right)^2 + a\left(\frac{a}{2}\right) \tag{2.28}$$

$$= -\frac{a^2}{4} + \frac{a^2}{2} = \frac{a^2}{4},$$

and this is precisely the relationship shown in Figure 2.4. From Equation 2.28 it is easy to see that

$$\frac{dy^*}{da} = \frac{2a}{4} \tag{2.29}$$

and, for example, at $a = 2$, $dy^*/da = 1$. That is, at $a = 2$ an increase of a by 1 increases y^* also by 1. Table 2.1 verifies that fact (remembering that in the case of derivatives, we are dealing with only small changes rather than the discrete changes reflected in the table).

Arriving at this result was a bit complicated. We had to find the optimal value of x for each value of a and then substitute this value for x^* into the equation for y. In more general cases this may be quite burdensome since it requires repeatedly maximizing the objective function. The envelope theorem, providing an alternative approach, states that for small changes in a, dy^*/da can be computed by holding x constant *at its optimal value* and simply calculating $\partial y/\partial a$ from the objective function directly. At $a = 2$, for example, $x^* = 1$. Substituting this value in Equation 2.26 gives

$$y = -(1)^2 + a(1)$$
$$= -1 + a \tag{2.30}$$

and

$$\frac{\partial y}{\partial a} = 1. \tag{2.31}$$

This is precisely the result obtained earlier. The reason that the two approaches yield similar results is illustrated in Figure 2.4. For $a = 2$ the linear relationship given by Equation 2.30 is tangent to the y^* curve. Hence at that point the equations have the same slope. This result is quite general, and we will use it at several places in this book to simplify our results. To summarize, the envelope theorem states that the change in the optimal value of a function with respect to a parameter of that function can be found by partially differentiating the objective function while holding x (or several x's) constant at its optimal value. That is,

$$\frac{dy^*}{da} = \frac{\partial y}{\partial a} \{x = x^*(a)\}, \tag{2.32}$$

where the notation provides a reminder that $\partial y/\partial a$ must be computed at that value of x which is optimal for the particular value of the parameter a being examined.

The reason this result is called the "envelope theorem" is also illustrated in Figure 2.4. There, additional tangent relationships have been computed for $a = 3$ ($x^* = 3/2$) and $a = 5$ ($x^* = 5/2$). Notice how these auxiliary relationships seem to trace out the true y^* curve. In this situation y^* is said to be an "envelope" for the auxiliary curves. In Chapter 11 we will describe this relationship in its most important economic context: the relationship between long-run and short-run total cost curves.

Many-Variable Case

An analogous envelope theorem holds for the case where y is a function of several variables. Suppose that y depends on a set of x's $(x_1, \ldots, x_n)$ and on a particular parameter of interest, say a,

$$y = f(x_1, \ldots, x_n, a). \tag{2.33}$$

Finding an optimal value for y would consist of solving n first-order equations of the form

$$\partial y / \partial x_i = 0 \quad (i = 1, n), \tag{2.34}$$

and a solution to this process would yield optimal values for these x's (x_1^*, $x_2^*, \ldots, x_n^*$) that would implicitly depend on the parameter a. Assuming the second-order conditions are met, the implicit function theorem would apply in this case and assure that we could solve each x_i^* explicitly as a function of the parameter a:

$$x_1^* = x_1^*(a)$$

$$x_2^* = x_2^*(a) \tag{2.35}$$

$$x_n^* = x_n^*(a).$$

Substituting these functions into our original objective (Equation 2.33) yields an expression in which the optimal value of y (say, y^*) depends on the parameter a both directly and indirectly through the effect of a on the x^*'s.

$$y^* = f[x_1^*(a), x_2^*(a), \ldots, x_n^*(a), a] \tag{2.36}$$

Differentiating this expression with respect to a yields

$$\frac{dy^*}{da} = \frac{\partial f}{\partial x_1} \cdot \frac{dx_1}{da} + \frac{\partial f}{\partial x_2} \cdot \frac{dx_2}{da} \cdots + \frac{\partial f}{\partial x_n} \cdot \frac{dx_n}{da} + \frac{\partial f}{\partial a}. \tag{2.37}$$

But, because of the first-order conditions in Equation 2.34, all of these terms except the last are equal to 0 if the x's are at their optimal values. Hence again we have the envelope result:

$$\frac{dy^*}{da} = \frac{\partial f}{\partial a}. \tag{2.38}$$

Changes in the optimal value of y brought about by changing the parameter can be calculated directly from the original function through partial differentiation since all the x's are assumed to be adjusted to their optimal values.

Numerical Example

Earlier in Equation 2.17, we examined the maximum values for the function

$$y = -(x_1 - 1)^2 - (x_2 - 2)^2 + 10 \tag{2.39}$$

and found that

$$x_1^* = 1,$$

$$x_2^* = 2, \tag{2.40}$$

and

$$y^* = 10.$$

Suppose now we use the arbitrary parameter a instead of the constant 10 in Equation 2.39. Hence

$$y = -(x_1 - 1)^2 - (x_2 - 2)^2 + a. \tag{2.41}$$

In this case the optimal values for x_1 and x_2 do not depend on a (they are always $x_1^* = 1$, $x_2^* = 2$) so at those optimal values we have

$$y^* = a \tag{2.42}$$

and

$$\frac{dy^*}{da} = 1. \tag{2.43}$$

But this is precisely what the envelope theorem indicates because

$$\frac{dy^*}{da} = \frac{\partial f}{\partial a} = 1 \tag{2.44}$$

from Equation 2.41. Increasing the parameter a simply increases the optimal value for y^* by an identical amount.

CON- STRAINED MAXIMIZA- TION

So far we have focused our attention on finding the maximum value of the function f without restricting the choices of the x's available. In most economic problems not all values for the x's are permissible, however. In many situations it is required, for example, that all the x's be positive. This would be true for the problem faced by the manager choosing output to maximize profits; a negative output would have no meaning. In other instances the x's may be constrained by different economic considerations. For example, in choosing the items to consume, an individual is not able to choose any quantities desired. Rather, choices are constrained by the amount of purchasing power available, that is, by the budget constraint. Such constraints necessarily lower the maximum value for the function we are seeking to maximize. Because we are not able to choose freely among all the x's, y will not be as large as it can be. If this were not true, the constraints would be said to be "ineffective," since we could obtain the same level of y with or without imposing the constraint.

Lagrangian Multiplier Method

One method for solving constrained maximization problems is the *Lagrangian multiplier method*, which involves a clever mathematical trick that also turns out to have a useful economic interpretation. The rationale of this method is quite simple, although no rigorous presentation will be attempted here.[8] In a prior section the necessary conditions for a maximum were discussed. It was shown that at the optimal point all the partial derivatives of f must be 0. There are therefore n equations ($f_i = 0$ for $i = 1, \ldots, n$) in n unknowns (the x's). Generally, these equations can be solved for the optimal x's. When the x's are

[8] For a formal presentation see Knut Sydsaeter, *Topics in Mathematical Analysis for Economists* (New York: Academic Press, 1981), pp. 272–279.

constrained, however, there is at least one additional equation (the constraint) but no additional variables. The set of equations therefore is overdetermined. The Lagrangian technique introduces an additional variable (the Lagrangian multiplier), which not only helps to solve the problem at hand (since there are now $n + 1$ equations in $n + 1$ unknowns) but also has an interpretation that is useful in a variety of economic circumstances.

More specifically, suppose that we wish to find the values of $x_1, x_2, \ldots, x_n$ that maximize:

$$y = f(x_1, x_2, \ldots, x_n),\tag{2.45}$$

subject to a constraint that permits only certain values of the x's to be used. A general way of writing that constraint is

$$g(x_1, x_2, \ldots, x_n) = 0,\tag{2.46}$$

where the function[9] g represents the relationship that must hold among all the x's.

The Lagrangian multiplier method starts with setting up the expression

$$\mathcal{L} = f(x_1, x_2, \ldots, x_n) + \lambda g(x_1, x_2, \ldots, x_n),\tag{2.47}$$

where λ is an additional variable that is called the Lagrangian multiplier. Later we shall interpret this new variable. First, however, notice that when the constraint holds, $\mathcal{L}$ and f have the same value [since $g(x_1, x_2, \ldots, x_n) = 0$]. Consequently, if we restrict our attention only to values of the x's that satisfy the constraint, finding the maximum value of f is equivalent to finding a stationary value of $\mathcal{L}$. Let us proceed then to do so, treating λ also as a variable (in addition to the x's). From Equation 2.47 the first-order conditions are

$$\frac{\partial \mathcal{L}}{\partial x_1} = f_1 + \lambda g_1 = 0$$

$$\frac{\partial \mathcal{L}}{\partial x_2} = f_2 + \lambda g_2 = 0$$

$$\cdot$$
$$\cdot \tag{2.48}$$
$$\cdot$$

$$\frac{\partial \mathcal{L}}{\partial x_n} = f_n + \lambda g_n = 0$$

$$\frac{\partial \mathcal{L}}{\partial \lambda} = g(x_1, x_2, \ldots, x_n) = 0.$$

---

[9] As we pointed out earlier, any function of $x_1, x_2, \ldots, x_n$ can be written in this implicit way. For example, the constraint $x_1 + x_2 = 10$ could be written $10 - x_1 - x_2 = 0$. In later chapters we shall usually follow this procedure in dealing with constraints.

Equations 2.48 are then the conditions for a critical point for the function $\mathcal{L}$. Notice that there are $n + 1$ equations (one for each x and a final one for λ) in $n + 1$ unknowns. The equations can generally be solved for $x_1, x_2, \ldots, x_n$, and λ. Such a solution will have two properties: (1) the x's will obey the constraint since the last equation in 2.48 imposes that condition; and (2) among all those values of x's that satisfy the constraint, those that also solve Equations 2.48 will make $\mathcal{L}$ (and hence f) as large as possible. The Lagrangian multiplier method therefore provides a way to find a solution to the constrained maximization problem we posed at the outset.[10]

The solution to Equations 2.48 will differ in general from that in the unconstrained case (see Equations 2.16). Rather than proceeding to the point where the marginal contribution of each x is 0, Equations 2.48 require us to "stop short" because of the constraint. Only if the constraint were ineffective (in which case, as we show below, λ would be 0) would the constrained and unconstrained equations (and their respective solutions) agree.

Of course, Equations 2.48 are only necessary conditions for a maximum. There are also second-order conditions that must be checked to ensure that the solution calculated is indeed a maximum. These conditions are examined briefly in the appendix to this chapter, and some simple examples for which the necessary conditions do not yield a true maximum are illustrated in later chapters.

Interpretation of the Lagrangian Multiplier

So far we have used the Lagrangian multiplier (λ) only as a mathematical "trick" to arrive at the solution we wanted. In fact, that variable also has an important economic interpretation, which will be central to our analysis at many points in this book. To develop this interpretation, rewrite the first n equations in 2.48 as

$$\frac{f_1}{-g_1} = \frac{f_2}{-g_2} = \cdots = \frac{f_n}{-g_n} = \lambda. \tag{2.49}$$

In other words, at the maximum point, the ratio of f_i to g_i is the same for every x_i. But the numerators in Equation 2.49 are simply the marginal contributions of each x to the function f. They show the *marginal benefit* that one more unit of x_i will have for the function we are trying to maximize (that is, for f).

To interpret the denominators in Equation 2.49 requires an additional step. The total differential of the constraint is

$$g_1 \, dx_1 + g_2 \, dx_2 + \cdots + g_n \, dx_n = 0. \tag{2.50}$$

---

[10] Strictly speaking, these are the necessary conditions for an interior maximum. In some economic problems, it is necessary to amend these conditions (in fairly obvious ways) to take account of the possibility that some of the x's may be on the boundary of the region of permissible x's. For example, if all the x's are required to be non-negative, it may be that the conditions of Equations 2.48 will not hold exactly, since these may require negative x's. We shall not detail the ways in which these conditions must be modified to take account of such problems, although some of these modifications will be hinted at throughout the book.

Suppose now that x_1 is increased by one unit (that is, $dx_1 = 1$). Then using Equation 2.50, it must be that

$$g_1 + g_2\, dx_2 + \cdots + g_n\, dx_n = 0$$

or   (2.51)

$$-g_1 = g_2\, dx_2 + \cdots + g_n\, dx_n.$$

Equation 2.51 shows how the x's other than x_1 must change when x_1 is increased by one unit if the constraint is to continue to hold. The expression $-g_1$ reflects all these changes in the other variables $x_j (j = 2 \ldots n)$, where each required change is weighted by g_j, a measure of the variable's importance in the constraint. Hence $-g_i$ is an approximation to the *marginal cost* incurred by reducing $x_2 \ldots x_n$ when we wish to increase x_1 by 1 (in later chapters we will be able to present a more intuitive economic analysis of the nature of this cost). A similar argument can be made for any of the x variables we might have chosen.

Equations 2.49 now can be given an intuitive interpretation. They indicate that, at the optimal choices for the x's, the ratio of the marginal benefit of increasing x_i to the marginal cost of increasing x_i should be the same for every x. To see that this is an obvious condition for a maximum, suppose that it were not true: Suppose that the "benefit-cost ratio" were higher for x_1 than for x_2. In this case slightly more x_1 should be used in order to achieve a maximum. This can be shown by considering employing additional x_1 but giving up enough x_2 to keep g (the constraint) constant. Hence the marginal cost of the additional x_1 used would equal the cost released by using less x_2. But since the benefit-cost ratio (the amount of benefit per unit of cost) is greater for x_1 than for x_2, the additional benefits from using more x_1 would exceed the loss in benefits from using less x_2. The use of more x_1 and appropriately less x_2 will then increase y since x_1 provides more "bang for your buck." Only if the marginal benefit–marginal cost ratios are equal for all the x's will there be a true maximum, one in which no changes in the x's can increase the objective. Concrete applications of this basic principle are developed in many places in this book. The result is a fundamental one for the microeconomic theory of optimizing behavior.

The Lagrangian multiplier (λ) now may be interpreted in the light of this discussion. λ is the common benefit-cost ratio for all the x's. That is,

$$\lambda = \frac{\text{marginal benefit of } x_i}{\text{marginal cost of } x_i}$$ (2.52)

for every x_i. If the constraint were relaxed slightly, it would not matter exactly which x is changed (indeed all the x's could be altered), since, at the margin, each promises the same ratio of benefits to costs. The Lagrangian multiplier then provides a measure of how such an overall relaxation of the constraint would affect the value of y. λ in essence assigns a "value" to the constraint. A high λ indicates that y could be increased substantially by relaxing the constraint, since each x has a high benefit-cost ratio. A low value of λ, on the other hand, indicates that there is not much to be gained by relaxing the constraint. If the constraint is not effective at all, λ will have a value of 0, thereby indicating that the constraint is not restricting the value of y. In such a case finding the maximum value of y subject to the constraint would be identical to finding an unconstrained maximum. This interpretation of λ can also be shown using the envelope theorem as we describe later in this chapter.

Duality

The previous discussion indicates that there is a clear relationship between the problem of maximizing a function subject to constraints[11] and the problem of assigning values to constraints. This reflects what is called the mathematical principle of "duality": Any constrained maximization problem has associated with it a dual problem in constrained *minimization* that focuses attention on the constraints in the original ("primal") problem. For example, to jump a bit ahead of our story, economists assume that individuals maximize their utility, subject to a budget constraint. This is the consumer's primal problem. The dual problem for the consumer is to minimize the expenditure needed to achieve a given level of utility. Or, a firm's primal problem may be to minimize the total cost of inputs used to produce a given level of output, whereas the dual problem is to maximize output for a given cost of inputs purchased. Many similar examples will be developed in later chapters. Each illustrates that there are always two ways to look at any constrained optimization problem. Sometimes taking a frontal attack by analyzing the primal problem can lead to greater insights. In other instances the "back door" approach of examining the dual problem may be more instructive. Whichever route is taken, the results will generally, though not always, be identical, so that the choice made will mainly be a matter of convenience.

Numerical Examples

Although the concepts outlined in the previous chapter will become familiar only as they are applied in analyzing economic problems in later chapters, we shall present here two mathematical examples of their use. First, consider again the example of Equation 2.17.

Example A

$$\text{Maximize } y = -x_1^2 + 2x_1 - x_2^2 + 4x_2 + 5,$$

but now assume that choices of x_1 and x_2 are constrained by

$$x_1 + x_2 = 1 \tag{2.53}$$

or

$$1 - x_1 - x_2 = 0.$$

[11] The discussion in the text concerns problems involving a single constraint. In general, one can handle m constraints ($m < n$) by simply introducing m new variables (Lagrangian multipliers) and proceeding in an analogous way to that discussed above.

Notice that the original optimal point ($x_1 = 1$, $x_2 = 2$) is no longer attainable because of the constraint: Other values must be found. To do so we first set up the Lagrangian expression:

$$\mathcal{L} = -x_1^2 + 2x_1 - x_2^2 + 4x_2 + 5 + \lambda(1 - x_1 - x_2). \qquad (2.54)$$

Differentiation of $\mathcal{L}$ with respect to x_1, x_2, and λ and application of the necessary condition for a constrained maximum yield

$$\frac{\partial \mathcal{L}}{\partial x_1} = -2x_1 + 2 - \lambda = 0$$

$$\frac{\partial \mathcal{L}}{\partial x_2} = -2x_2 + 4 - \lambda = 0 \qquad (2.55)$$

$$\frac{\partial \mathcal{L}}{\partial \lambda} = 1 - x_1 - x_2 = 0.$$

Equations 2.55 must now be solved for the optimal values of x_1, y_2, and λ. Using the first and second equations gives

$$-2x_1 + 2 = \lambda = -2x_2 + 4 \qquad (2.56)$$

or

$$x_1 = x_2 - 1.$$

Substitution of this value for x_1 into the constraint 2.53 yields the solution:

$$x_2 = 1$$
$$x_1 = 0 \qquad (2.57)$$

and, by using either of the first two equations, it is easy to show that

$$\lambda = 2. \qquad (2.58)$$

This, then, is the solution to the constrained-maximum problem. If $x_1 = 0$, $x_2 = 1$, then y takes on the value 8. Constraining the values of x_1 and x_2 to sum to 1 has reduced the maximum value of y from 10 to 8.[12]

Example B

As a second example, consider the following geometric problem:

Prove that a rectangle with a fixed perimeter encloses the maximum possible area when it is a square.

---

[12] To see that this is indeed the maximum value when x_1 and x_2 are subject to the constraint, the reader may wish to try other combinations of x_1 and x_2 that also satisfy the constraint. For example, if $x_1 = 1$, $x_2 = 0$, then $y = 6$; and if $x_1 = -2$, $x_2 = 3$, then $y = 0$. The reader may also wish to examine the consequences of relaxing the constraint to be $x_1 + x_2 = 2$, in which case the maximum value of y increases to 9.5. For $x_1 + x_2 = 3$, the original optimal solution is attainable and $\lambda = 0$ since the constraint is not effective.

To demonstrate that this is a simple constrained maximization problem, let X be the length of one side of the rectangle and Y be the length of the other side. The problem then is to choose X and Y so as to maximize the area of the rectangle (given by $A = X \cdot Y$), subject to the constraint that the perimeter is fixed at $P = 2X + 2Y$.

Setting up the Lagrangian expression as in Equation 2.47 gives

$$\mathscr{L} = X \cdot Y + \lambda(P - 2X - 2Y), \tag{2.59}$$

where λ is an unknown Lagrangian multiplier. The first-order conditions for a maximum are

$$\frac{\partial \mathscr{L}}{\partial X} = Y - 2\lambda = 0$$

$$\frac{\partial \mathscr{L}}{\partial Y} = X - 2\lambda = 0 \tag{2.60}$$

$$\frac{\partial \mathscr{L}}{\partial \lambda} = P - 2X - 2Y = 0.$$

The three equations in 2.60 now must be solved simultaneously for X, Y, and λ. The first two equations say that $Y/2 = X/2 = \lambda$, showing that X must be equal to Y and that X and Y should be chosen so that the ratio of marginal benefits to marginal cost is the same for both variables. The benefit (in terms of area) of one more unit of X is given by Y (area is increased by $1 \cdot Y$), and the marginal cost (in terms of perimeter) is 2 (the available perimeter is reduced by 2 for each unit that the length of side X is increased). The maximum conditions then state that this ratio should be equal for each of the variables.

Since we have shown that $X = Y$, we can use the constraint to prove that

$$X = Y = \frac{P}{4}, \tag{2.61}$$

and because $Y = 2\lambda$, it must be the case that

$$\lambda = \frac{P}{8}. \tag{2.62}$$

Interpretation of the Lagrangian Multiplier   It is possible to use this solution for λ to show how much more area would be obtained if the perimeter of the rectangle were increased by one unit. For example, suppose that a farmer were interested in knowing how much more field could be fenced by adding an extra yard of fence. This problem could be solved by simply calculating the present perimeter and dividing by 8. Some specific numbers might make this clear. Suppose that the field currently has a perimeter of 400 yards. If the farmer has planned "optimally," the field will be a square with 100 yards ($= P/4$) on a side. The enclosed area will be 10,000 square yards. Suppose now that the perimeter were enlarged by 1 yard. Equation 2.62 would then "predict" that the total area would be increased by approximately 50 ($= P/8$)

square yards.[13] That this is indeed the case can be shown as follows: Since the perimeter is now 401 yards, each side of the square will be 401/4 yards. The total area of the field is therefore $(401/4)^2$, which, according to the author's calculator, works out to be 10,050.06 square yards. Hence the "prediction" of a 50-square-yard increase provided by the Lagrangian multiplier proves to be remarkably close.

  Duality   The dual of this constrained maximization problem is that for a given area of a rectangular field, minimize the fence required to surround it. Mathematically, the problem is to minimize

$$P = 2X + 2Y, \tag{2.63}$$

subject to the constraint

$$A = X \cdot Y. \tag{2.64}$$

Setting up the Lagrangian expression

$$\mathscr{L}^D = 2X + 2Y + \lambda^D(A - X \cdot Y) \tag{2.65}$$

(where the D denotes the dual concept) yields the following first-order conditions for a minimum:

$$\frac{\partial \mathscr{L}^D}{\partial X} = 2 - \lambda^D \cdot Y = 0$$

$$\frac{\partial \mathscr{L}^D}{\partial Y} = 2 - \lambda^D \cdot X = 0 \tag{2.66}$$

$$\frac{\partial \mathscr{L}^D}{\partial \lambda^D} = X \cdot Y - A = 0.$$

  Solving these equations as before yields the result:

$$X = Y = \sqrt{A}. \tag{2.67}$$

  Again, the field should be square if the length of fence is to be minimized. The value of the Lagrangian multiplier in this problem is

$$\lambda^D = \frac{2}{Y} = \frac{2}{X} = \frac{2}{\sqrt{A}}. \tag{2.68}$$

  As before, this Lagrangian multiplier indicates the relationship between the objective (minimizing fence) and the constraint (surrounding the field). If the field were 10,000 square yards, a fence 400 yards long would be needed, as we saw before. Increasing the field by 1 square yard would require about .02 more yards of fence ($= 2/\sqrt{A} = 2/100$). The reader may wish to fire up his or her calculator to show this is indeed the case—a fence 100.005 yards on each side will exactly enclose 10,001 square yards. Here, as in most duality problems,

---

[13] The word *approximately* is used here because the result, as is true for all calculus types of analysis, holds only for "small" changes.

the value of the Lagrangian multiplier in the dual is simply the reciprocal of the value for the Lagrangian multiplier in the primal problem. Both provide the same information, although in somewhat different form.

ENVELOPE THEOREM IN CONSTRAINED-MAXIMUM PROBLEMS

The envelope theorem, which we discussed previously in connection with unconstrained maximization problems, also has important applications in constrained-maximum problems. Here we will provide only a brief presentation of the theorem. Later in the text a number of applications will be illustrated.

Suppose we seek the maximum value of

$$y = f(x_1 \ldots x_n; a), \tag{2.69}$$

subject to the constraint

$$g(x_1 \ldots x_n; a) = 0, \tag{2.70}$$

where we have made explicit the dependence of the functions f and g on some parameter, a. As we have shown, one way to solve this problem is to set up the Lagrangian expression

$$\mathcal{L} = f(x_1 \ldots x_n; a) + \lambda g(x_1 \ldots x_n; a) \tag{2.71}$$

and solve the first-order conditions (see Equations 2.48) for the optimal values $x_1^* \ldots x_n^*$. Alternatively, it can be shown that

$$\frac{dy^*}{da} = \frac{\partial \mathcal{L}}{\partial a} (x_1^* \ldots x_n^*; a). \tag{2.72}$$

That is, the change in the maximal value of y that results when the parameter a changes (and all the x's are recalculated to new optimal values) can be found by partially differentiating the Lagrangian expression (Equation 2.71) and evaluating the resultant partial derivative at the optimal point.[14] Hence the Lagrangian expression plays the same role in applying the envelope theorem to constrained problems as does the objective function itself in unconstrained problems (see Equation 2.44). As a simple exercise the reader may wish to show that this result holds for the problem of fencing a rectangular field described in the previous section.[15]

MAXIMIZATION WITHOUT CALCULUS

Not all economic maximization problems can be solved using the calculus methods outlined above. For example, the manager of a firm may not know its profit function exactly but may only be able to approximate parts of it by straight lines. This situation is illustrated in Figure 2.5a. Here Q^* is clearly the quantity that produces maximum profits, but this point cannot be found by

---

[14] For a more complete discussion, see Eugene Silberberg, *The Structure of Economics* (New York: McGraw-Hill Book Company, 1978), pp. 170–171.

[15] For the primal problem the perimeter P is the parameter of principal interest here. By solving for the optimal values of X and Y and substituting into the expression for the area (A) of the field, it is easy to show that $dA/dP = P/8$. Differentiation of the Lagrangian expression (Equation 2.59) yields $\frac{\partial \mathcal{L}}{\partial P} = \lambda$ and, at the optimal values of X and Y, $\frac{\partial A}{\partial P} = \frac{\partial \mathcal{L}}{\partial P} = \lambda = \frac{P}{8}$

Figure 2.5   *Possible Profit Functions for Which the Calculus Maximization Techniques Would Be Inappropriate*

In (a), calculus methods would not succeed in finding that level of output that yields maximum profits (Q^*) since the derivative is not defined as such a point. Similarly, in (b) the manager may choose only integral values for Q. In this case the small changes required to apply calculus reasoning cannot be made. In order to find either of these maximum points, various kinds of "programming" techniques must be utilized.

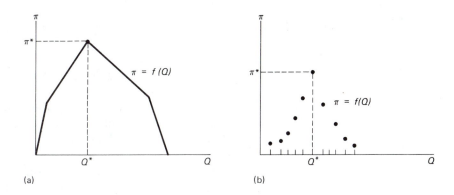

(a)   (b)

calculus methods since $d\pi/dQ$ does not exist[16] at Q^*. Some other method must be found in order to locate a point such as Q^* systematically.

A second example of the failure of traditional calculus methods is illustrated in Figure 2.5b. Here the manager can produce only integral units of Q—it makes no sense to produce 4⅓ cars. In this case again $d\pi/dQ$ is not defined at Q^*—calculus will not provide a systematic method for finding Q^*.

Specific mathematical "programming" techniques have been developed for dealing with problems such as those illustrated in Figure 2.5. The example illustrated in 2.5a is an extremely simple case of a problem that can be solved by "linear programming" methods; that illustrated in 2.5b can be solved by "integer programming" methods.[17] These techniques provide powerful tools for solving constrained maximization problems and have proved extremely useful in analyzing difficult real-world situations. In this book, however, we shall be concerned primarily with calculus methods of solving constrained maximization problems. This choice is made both for simplicity and because calculus methods and programming techniques have numerous similarities. Most economically interesting aspects of programming techniques are illustrated by the calculus methods.

One similarity between most maximization procedures should be mentioned—the concept of duality. Many constrained maximization problems

---

[16] To see this, note that the slope of $f(Q)$ changes very abruptly at Q^*.

[17] For a simple discussion of these methods, see R. Dorfman, P. A. Samuelson, and R. M. Solow, *Linear Programming and Economic Analysis* (New York: McGraw-Hill Book Company, 1958).

yield, as a concomitant of their solution, dual variables that assign values to the constraints. These are directly analogous to the Lagrangian multipliers discussed above. They indicate how much is added to the objective by relaxing a constraint slightly. If the constraint is ineffective, the value of its corresponding dual variable is 0. Otherwise, the dual variable can give an indication of how "binding" the constraint is. Using these methods for assigning values to constraints provides a variety of important economic insights, as will be seen throughout the text.

SUMMARY

Despite the formidable appearance of some parts of this chapter, this is not a book on mathematics. Rather, the intention here was to gather together a variety of tools that will be used to develop economic models throughout the remainder of the text. You should not expect to understand these tools fully at this stage. The mathematics will become far more accessible as it is used in connection with the economics to be developed later. Material in this chapter will then be useful as a handy reference.

One way to summarize the mathematical tools introduced in this chapter is by stressing again the economic lessons that these tools illustrate:

- Using mathematics provides a convenient, shorthand way for economists to develop their models. Implications of various economic assumptions can be studied in a simplified setting through the use of such mathematical tools.

- The mathematical concept of the derivatives of a function is widely used in economic models because economists are often interested in how changes in one variable affect another variable. Partial derivatives are especially useful for this purpose because they are defined to represent such changes when all other factors are held constant. In this way, partial derivatives incorporate the *ceteris paribus* assumption found in most economic models.

- The mathematics of optimization is an important tool for the development of models that assume that economic agents rationally pursue some goal. In the unconstrained case, the first-order conditions state that any activity that contributes to the agent's goal should be expanded up to the point at which the marginal contribution of further expansion is 0. In mathematical terms, the first-order condition for an optimum requires that all partial derivatives be 0.

- Most economic optimization problems involve constraints on the choices agents can make. In this case the first-order conditions for a maximum suggest that each activity be operated at a level at which the ratio of the marginal benefit of the activity to its marginal cost is the same for all activities actually used. This common marginal benefit–marginal cost ratio is also equal to the Lagrangian multiplier, which is often introduced to help solve constrained optimization problems.

- The implicit function theorem is a useful mathematical device for illustrating the dependence of the choices that result from an optimization problem on the parameters of that problem (for example, market prices). The envelope theorem is useful for examining how these optimal choices change when the problem's parameters (prices) change.

Application

OPTIMIZATION IN THE SCIENCES: SNELL'S LAW

Optimization problems quite similar to those described in this chapter occur in many other sciences. The hypothesis that something is being maximized or minimized has as great a predictive value in physics, chemistry, or biology as it does in economics. In biology, for example, a useful hypothesis is that trees locate their leaves so as to maximize the amount of sunlight received or, more generally, that genes make "choices" that maximize the probability of long-term survival. In chemistry, there are a number of hypotheses about the ways in which molecules may be arranged so as to minimize surface area for a given volume. And, in physics, effects of forces such as gravity or magnetism can be explained as the results of particular minimization problems. Of course, just as Friedman's pool player does not understand the laws of physics, trees, genes, molecules, and atoms do not set out consciously to maximize or minimize anything. Nonetheless, models based on such optimization hypotheses have proved to be extremely accurate in predicting real-world events.

One application that illustrates the use of such optimization principles concerns the way in which light waves behave as they travel through space. Specifically, physicists have developed models based on the assumption that light travels in such a way as to minimize the travel time between any two points. Obviously, light waves do not consciously choose such a time-minimizing path, but the hypothesis that

the waves behave *as if* they made such choices provides excellent predictions.

The most important of these predictions concerns the way in which light is bent as it travels through different substances. Everyone has had the experience of having distances and directions distorted when looking into a pool or lake. Formally, this phenomenon can be explained through an examination of what has come to be known as Snell's law of refraction.

The problem is illustrated in Figure 2.6 where the line LL represents the boundary between two substances, say air (white) and water (shaded). Light is to pass from point A to point B, and we wish to describe the path it will take. The important fact in this problem is that light travels at different speeds through the two media, so there is reason to believe it may not take a straight-line path. Intuitively, it seems clear that the total time that it takes for light to travel between A and B will be minimized if the path chosen takes some advantage of the higher-speed medium. If, for example, light travels much faster through air (to the left of LL) than water (to the right of LL), then a path like ADB would be the fastest since the distance in air would be maximized. If (contrary to fact) light travels faster in water, a path such as AEB would be fastest since the light would get to the (faster) water by the quickest route possible. In general then, the problem is to choose the point C so that the path ACB requires the least time.

To explore the mathematics of this problem, let

v_1 = velocity of light in medium 1 (air)

Figure 2.6   *Illustration of Snell's Law*

Snell's law refers to the fact that light is refracted as it passes through two media (divided by *LL*). The actual, most rapid path (*ACB*) can be found by approaching the question as a constrained minimization problem.

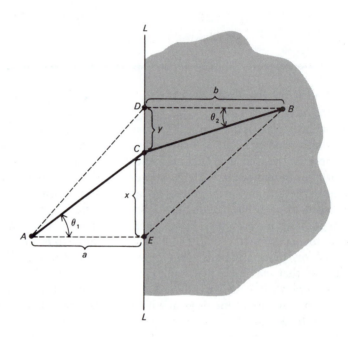

v_2 = velocity of light in medium 2 (water)

x = distance *CE*

y = distance *DC*

k = distance *DE*

a = distance *AE*

b = distance *BD*

θ_1 = angle *CAE*

θ_2 = angle *CBD*.

Now total time spent in medium 1 (T_1) is given by

$$T_1 = \frac{\text{distance } AC}{v_1}$$

$$= \frac{\sqrt{a^2 + x^2}}{v_1},$$

(2.73)

and the time spent in medium 2 (T_2) is given by

$$T_2 = \frac{\text{distance } CB}{v_2}$$

$$= \frac{\sqrt{b^2 + y^2}}{v_2}.$$

(2.74)

Hence total time of travel (T) is given by

$$T = T_1 + T_2$$

$$= \frac{\sqrt{a^2 + x^2}}{v_1} + \frac{\sqrt{b^2 + y^2}}{v_2},$$

(2.75)

and the mathematical problem is to choose x and y (that is, the location of point *C*) to minimize *T*, subject to the constraint

$$k = x + y.$$

(2.76)

Setting up the Lagrangian expression for this problem yields

$$\mathcal{L} = \frac{\sqrt{a^2 + x^2}}{v_1} + \frac{\sqrt{b^2 + y^2}}{v_2}$$

$$+ \lambda(k - x - y). \tag{2.77}$$

The first-order conditions for a maximum are

$$\frac{\partial \mathcal{L}}{\partial x} = \frac{x}{\dfrac{\sqrt{a^2 + x^2}}{v_1}} - \lambda = 0,$$

$$\frac{\partial \mathcal{L}}{\partial y} = \frac{y}{\dfrac{\sqrt{b^2 + y^2}}{v_2}} - \lambda = 0, \tag{2.78}$$

and

$$\frac{\partial \mathcal{L}}{\partial \lambda} = k - x - y = 0.$$

The first two equations in 2.78 imply that

$$\frac{x}{\dfrac{\sqrt{a^2 + x^2}}{v_1}} = \frac{y}{\dfrac{\sqrt{b^2 + y^2}}{v_2}}. \tag{2.79}$$

Now, introducing the mathematical notion of the sine of an angle, we have[18]

[18] The sine of an angle in a right triangle is the ratio of the length of the side opposite the angle to the length of the hypotenuse of the triangle. For Θ_1, $\sin \Theta_1 = x/AC$.

$$\frac{\sin \theta_1}{v_1} = \frac{\sin \theta_2}{v_2} \tag{2.80}$$

or

$$\frac{v_1}{v_2} = \frac{\sin \theta_1}{\sin \theta_2}. \tag{2.81}$$

This is Snell's law: The total time for light to pass from A to B is minimized if C is chosen so that the ratio of the velocity of light in the two media is equal to the ratio of the sines of the two angles.[19] This law gives a very accurate way of predicting how light (or other waves) is refracted. The law is used in applications ranging from astronomy (where light moves faster in space than in the earth's atmosphere) to searching for submarines by plane (since radar waves travel faster through air than through water). Although light doesn't consciously seek to minimize its travel time, a theory based on the assumption that it does is very useful indeed.

[19] Notice, for example, if v_1 is much larger than v_2, $\sin \Theta_2$ approaches 0, which means the path ADB would be appropriate, as intuition suggests.

SUGGESTED READINGS

Allen, R. G. D. *Mathematical Analysis for Economists.* New York: St. Martin's Press, 1938.

A complete summary. Some notation is cumbersome and outdated, however.

Chaing, A. C. *Fundamental Methods of Mathematical Economics.* 2d ed. New York: McGraw-Hill Book Company, 1974.

A compact, complete treatment. Fairly low level and easy to follow.

Henderson, James M., and Quandt, Richard F. *Microeconomic Theory: A Mathematical Approach.* 3d ed. New York: McGraw-Hill Book Company, 1980. Pp. 358–393.

A good mathematical appendix but requires use of linear algebra.

Intriligator, Michael D. *Mathematical Optimization and Economic Theory.* Englewood Cliffs, N.J.: Prentice-Hall, 1971.

Comprehensive treatment of maximization techniques, including several "programming" methods applicable when calculus methods are not appropriate.

Samuelson, Paul A. *Foundations of Economic Analysis.* Cambridge, Mass.: Harvard University Press, 1947. Mathematical Appendix A.

A basic reference. Mathematical appendix A pro-

vides an advanced treatment of necessary and sufficient conditions for a maximum.

Silberberg, Eugene. *The Structure of Economics: A Mathematical Analysis.* New York: McGraw-Hill Book Company, 1978.

A mathematical microeconomics text that stresses the observable predictions of economic theory. The text makes extensive use of the envelope theorem.

Sydsaeter, Knut. *Topics in Mathematical Analysis for Economists.* New York: Academic Press, 1981.

An advanced mathematical text that provides detailed discussions of the mathematical intricacies of maximization techniques.

Taylor, Angus E., and Mann, W. Robert. *Advanced Calculus.* 3d ed. New York: John Wiley, 1983. Pp. 183–195.

A comprehensive calculus text with a good discussion of the Lagrangian technique.

Thomas, George B., and Finney, Ross L. *Calculus and Analytic Geometry.* 5th ed. Reading, Mass.: Addison-Wesley Publishing Co., 1979. Pp. 620–627.

Basic calculus text with excellent coverage of differentiation techniques.

PROBLEMS

Note: These problems are all mathematical and do not introduce economic concepts. Students who feel comfortable with the mathematics in this chapter may wish to proceed to Chapter 3 where the economic problems in the text begin.

2.1

For each function, calculate the derivative with respect to x:

- a. $f(x) = 17$
- b. $f(x) = 5x^3$
- c. $f(x) = 3x^{1/3}$
- d. $f(x) = 1/x^2$
- e. $f(x) = \ln(x^3)$
- f. $f(x) = e^x$
- g. $f(x) = 5e^{3x}$
- h. $f(x) = x^3 - 5x^2 + 6x + 2$
- i. $f(x) = x^3 \cdot x^5$
- j. $f(x) = e^x(x^2 - 2x + 2)$

2.2

Compute f_x and f_y for the following functions:

- a. $f(x, y) = x^3 y^4$
- b. $f(x, y) = x/y$
- c. $f(x, y) = e^{x/y}$
- d. $f(x, y) = x^2 y^3 + e^{x^2 y}$
- e. $f(x, y) = 2x + 4y + x^2 + \ln(x^2 + y^2)$
- f. $f(x, y) = x/(x^2 + y^2)$

2.3

For each of the following functions of one variable, determine all local maxima and minima and indicate points of inflexion.

- a. $f(x) = 4x^3 - 12x$
- b. $f(x) = 4x - x^2$
- c. $f(x) = x^3$

2.4

If we cut four congruent squares out of the corners of a square piece of cardboard 12 inches on a side, we can fold up the four remaining flaps to obtain a tray without a top. What size squares should be cut in order to maximize the volume of the tray? (See figure.)

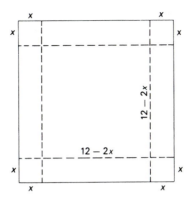

2.5
The height of a ball t seconds after it is thrown straight up is $-\frac{1}{2}gt^2 + 40t$ (where g is the acceleration due to gravity).

    a.   If $g = 32$ (as on the earth), when does the ball reach a maximum height? What is that height?

    b.   If $g = 5.5$ (as on the moon), when does the ball reach a maximum in height and what is that height? Can you explain the reasons for the difference between this answer and the answer for part a.

    c.   In general, develop an expression for the change in maximum height for a unit change in g. Explain why this value depends implicitly on the value of g itself.

2.6
$U = f(x, y) = 4x^2 + 3y^2$

    a.   Calculate $\partial U/\partial x$, $\partial U/\partial y$.

    b.   Evaluate these partial derivatives at $x = 1$, $y = 2$.

    c.   Write the total differential for U.

    d.   Calculate dy/dx for $dU = 0$.

    e.   Show $U = 16$ when $x = 1$, $y = 2$.

    f.   In what ratio must x and y change to hold U constant at 16?

2.7
Find the critical points for the function $f(x, y, z) = x^2 + y^2 + z^2$. Is that value a maximum or minimum?

2.8
Show that a solid rectangular block with a given volume has minimum surface area when it is a cube. How do you interpret the Lagrangian multiplier in this problem? Develop a numerical example of the connection between volume and surface area of a cube to illustrate your interpretation.

2.9
For $f(x, y, z) = x + 2z + yz - x^2 - y^2 - z^2$, find any critical points and whether or not they imply a maximum or minimum.

2.10
Suppose that $f(x, y) = xy$. Find the maximum value for f if x and y are constrained to sum to 1. Solve this problem in two ways: by substitution and by using the Lagrangian multiplier method.

2.11
Find the point on the plane $x + 2y + 3z - 6 = 0$ closest to the origin. (*Hint:* if

x_1, y_1, z_1 is any point in the plane, the distance from the point to the origin is given by $D = \sqrt{x_1^2 + y_1^2 + z_1^2}$. For this problem it may be easier to minimize D^2.)

2.12

A rectangular box is to be constructed of materials such that the base of the box costs twice the dollars per square foot as do the sides and top. If there are D dollars to spend on the box, how should these be allocated so that the box contains the maximum possible volume?

2.13

Use the Lagrangian method to find the minimum distance between the circle $x^2 + y^2 = 1$ and the rectangular hyperbola $x \cdot y = 9$.

2.14

Find the square of greatest area that will fit into the circle given by $x^2 + y^2 = r^2$. How does the area of this square change as r changes?

Appendix to Chapter 2

Second-Order Conditions

In Chapter 2 we showed that for a function to attain its maximum value at some point, specific "marginal" conditions must necessarily hold.[1] We also showed that points at which those conditions hold should be regarded only as potential candidates for a true maximum and that, in fact, naïve application of the necessary conditions may at times result in choosing the wrong point. To ensure that the critical point selected by the necessary conditions is a true maximum, additional properties must be examined. The basic purpose of those properties is to ensure that the value of the objective function actually decreases for movements away from the critical point. If so, the critical point is a true maximum (at least locally); if not, the necessary conditions are misleading and points other than the critical point yield higher values for the objective function. The purpose of this appendix is to examine briefly a few mathematical aspects of the *second-order conditions* that are required to assure a true maximum. Rather than presenting an exhaustive study of that subject, however, we consider only three examples of second-order conditions for maximizing a function of (1) a single independent variable; (2) two independent variables; and (3) two independent variables subject to a linear constraint on those variables. Such examples are representative of the types of maximizing problems we shall be investigating throughout this book. They provide sufficient coverage so as to permit us to illustrate most of the economic significance of second-order conditions.

FUNCTIONS OF A SINGLE INDEPENDENT VARIABLE

First we consider the case in which our objective, y, is a function of only a single variable, x. That is,

$$y = f(x). \tag{2A.1}$$

In Chapter 2 we saw that a necessary condition for this function to attain its maximum value at some point is that

$$\frac{dy}{dx} = f'(x) = 0 \tag{2A.2}$$

at that point. But as we saw, an uncritical application of the necessary condition given in Equation 2A.2 may lead to choosing a point that is not a true maximum. To ensure that the point is indeed a maximum, we must have y decreasing for movements away from it. We already know (by Equation 2A.2) that for small changes in x, the value of y does not change; what we need to check is whether or not y is increasing before that "plateau" is reached and declining thereafter. In other words, we must check whether or not, at the

---

[1] Throughout this appendix we discuss second-order conditions required for a local maximum. In most cases the conditions required for a local minimum will be identical but opposite in sign to those described here.

critical point, the change in y is decreasing (that is, going from positive to negative). We have already derived an expression for the change in y (dy), which is given by the total differential:

$$dy = f'(x) \, dx. \tag{2A.3}$$

What we now require is that dy be decreasing for small increases in the value of x. The differential of Equation 2A.3 is given by:

$$d(dy) = d^2y = \frac{d[f'(x) \, dx]}{dx} \cdot dx = f''(x) \, dx \cdot dx = f''(x) \, dx^2, \tag{2A.4}$$

where, as in Chapter 2, $f''(x)$ denotes the second derivative of the function f. But

$$d^2y < 0$$

implies that

$$f''(x) \, dx^2 < 0 \tag{2A.5}$$

and since dx^2 must be positive, we have

$$f''(x) < 0 \tag{2A.6}$$

as the required second-order condition.[2] Equations 2A.2 and 2A.6 therefore provide sufficient conditions for a maximum. They state that for a particular point to be a true maximum of a function, the slope of the function at that point must be 0, and the slope at the point must also be diminishing.

Numerical Example

In Chapter 2 we considered the problem of finding the maximum of the function

$$\pi = 4Q - Q^2. \tag{2A.7}$$

The first-order condition for a maximum requires

$$\frac{d\pi}{dQ} = 4 - 2Q = 0 \tag{2A.8}$$

or

$$Q^* = 2. \tag{2A.9}$$

The second derivative of the function is given by

$$\frac{d^2\pi}{dQ^2} = -2 < 0 \tag{2A.10}$$

and hence Equation 2A.6 is satisfied. The point $Q = 2$ obeys the sufficient conditions for a true maximum.

---

[2] By an argument analogous to that presented here, it is easy to show that for a critical point to represent a true *minimum*, d^2y must be positive and that implies that $f''(x)$ must also be positive.

FUNCTIONS OF TWO INDEPENDENT VARIABLES

As a second case we consider y as a function of two independent variables:

$$y = f(x_1, x_2). \tag{2A.11}$$

In Chapter 2 we showed that a necessary condition for such a function to attain its maximum value is that its partial derivatives in both the x_1 and the x_2 directions be 0. That is,

$$\frac{\partial y}{\partial x_1} = f_1 = 0$$

$$\frac{\partial y}{\partial x_2} = f_2 = 0. \tag{2A.12}$$

A point that satisfies the conditions of Equations 2A.12 will be a "flat" spot on the function (a point where $dy = 0$) and therefore will be a candidate for a maximum. To ensure that the point is a true (local) maximum, y must diminish for movements in any direction away from the critical point: In pictorial terms there is only one way to leave a true mountain top and that is to go down.

Before describing the mathematical properties required of such a point, an intuitive approach may be helpful. If we consider only movements in the x_1 direction, the required condition is clear: The slope in the x_1 direction (that is, the partial derivative f_1) must be diminishing at the critical point. This is simply an application of our discussion of the single-variable case and it shows that for a maximum, the second partial derivative in the x_1 direction must be negative. An identical argument holds for movements only in the x_2 direction. Hence we have shown that both own second partial derivatives (f_{11} and f_{22}) must be negative for a true maximum. In our mountain analogy, if attention is confined only to north-south or east-west movements, the slope of the mountain must be diminishing as we cross its summit—the slope must change from positive to negative.

The particular complexity that arises in the two-variable case involves movements through the initial point that are not solely in the x_1 or in the x_2 directions (say, movements from northeast to southwest). In such cases the own second-order partial derivatives do not provide complete information about how the slope is changing near the critical point. Conditions must also be placed on the cross-partial derivative ($f_{12} = f_{21}$) to ensure that dy is decreasing for movements through the critical point in any direction. As we shall see, those conditions amount to requiring that the own second-order partial derivatives be sufficiently large so as to counterbalance any possible "perverse" cross-partial derivatives that may exist. Intuitively, if the mountain falls away steeply enough in the north-south and east-west directions, relatively minor failures to do so in other directions can be compensated for.

We now proceed to make these points more formally. What we wish to discover are the conditions that must be placed on the second partial derivatives of the function f to ensure that d^2y is negative for movements in any direction through the critical point. Recall first that the total differential of the function is given by

$$dy = f_1 \, dx_1 + f_2 \, dx_2. \tag{2A.13}$$

The differential of that function is given by

$$d^2y = (f_{11} \, dx_1 + f_{12} \, dx_2) \, dx_1 + (f_{21} \, dx_1 + f_{22} \, dx_2) \, dx_2 \tag{2A.14}$$

or

$$d^2y = f_{11} \, dx_1^2 + f_{12} \, dx_2 \, dx_1 + f_{21} \, dx_1 \, dx_2 + f_{22} \, dx_2^2. \tag{2A.15}$$

Since, by Young's theorem, $f_{12} = f_{21}$, we can arrange terms to get

$$d^2y = f_{11} \, dx_1^2 + 2f_{12} \, dx_1 \, dx_2 + f_{22} \, dx_2^2. \tag{2A.16}$$

For Equation 2A.16 to be unambiguously negative for any change in the x's (that is, for any choices of dx_1 and dx_2), it is obviously necessary that f_{11} and f_{22} be negative. If, for example, $dx_2 = 0$, then

$$d^2y = f_{11} \, dx_1^2 \tag{2A.17}$$

and $d^2y < 0$ implies

$$f_{11} < 0. \tag{2A.18}$$

An identical argument can be made for f_{22} by setting $dx_1 = 0$. If neither dx_1 nor dx_2 is 0, we then must consider the cross partial, f_{12}, in deciding whether or not d^2y is unambiguously negative. Relatively simple algebra can be used to show that the required condition is [3]

$$f_{11}f_{22} - f_{12}^2 > 0. \tag{2A.19}$$

Hence Equations 2A.12, 2A.18, and 2A.19 are sufficient conditions for a true maximum. [4] A function that obeys Equations 2A.18 and 2A.19 everywhere is called a *concave function*. Such functions graphically resemble inverted tea-cups. It is obvious that for such functions, the flat places are indeed true maximum points. The necessary conditions for a maximum are, in those cases, also sufficient.

Numerical Example

In Chapter 2 we considered the function

$$y = f(x_1, x_2) = -x_1^2 + 2x_1 - x_2^2 + 4x_2 + 5. \tag{2A.20}$$

The first-order conditions for a maximum were shown to be

$$f_1 = -2x_1 + 2 = 0 \tag{2A.21}$$
$$f_2 = -2x_2 + 4 = 0$$

[3] The proof proceeds by the method of "completing the square." See, for example, A. C. Chiang, *Fundamental Methods of Mathematical Economics*, 2d edition (New York: McGraw Hill, 1974), p. 194. Equation 2A.16 is one example of a "quadratic form" in the variables dx_1 and dx_2. There exist many tools in matrix algebra for dealing with such forms and for deciding on their negativity.

[4] Equations 2A.18 and 2A.19 together imply that $f_{22} < 0$. For a minimum it is required that $f_{11} > 0$ and $f_{11}f_{22} - f_{12}^2 > 0$.

or

$$x_1 = 1 \tag{2A.22}$$
$$x_2 = 2.$$

The second-order partial derivatives for Equation 2A.20 are

$$f_{11} = -2$$
$$f_{22} = -2 \tag{2A.23}$$
$$f_{12} = 0.$$

These derivatives therefore obey Equations 2A.18 and 2A.19, and hence both necessary and sufficient conditions for a maximum are satisfied.[5]

FUNCTIONS OF TWO IN-DEPENDENT VARIABLES SUBJECT TO A LINEAR CONSTRAINT

As a final case, consider the problem of choosing x_1 and x_2 to maximize

$$y = f(x_1, x_2), \tag{2A.24}$$

subject to the linear constraint

$$c - b_1 x_1 - b_2 x_2 = 0 \tag{2A.25}$$

(where c, b_1, b_2 are constant parameters in the problem). This problem is of a type that will be frequently encountered in this book and is a special case of the constrained-maximum problems that were examined in Chapter 2. There we showed that the first-order conditions for a maximum may be derived by setting up the Lagrangian expression

$$\mathscr{L} = f(x_1, x_2) + \lambda(c - b_1 x_1 - b_2 x_2). \tag{2A.26}$$

Partial differentiation with respect to x_1, x_2, and λ yields

$$f_1 - \lambda b_1 = 0$$
$$f_2 - \lambda b_2 = 0 \tag{2A.27}$$
$$c - b_1 x_1 - b_2 x_2 = 0.$$

These equations can in general be solved for the optimal values of x_1, x_2, and λ. To assure that the point derived in that way is a true maximum, we must again examine movements away from the critical points by using the "second" total differential already presented in Equation 2A.16:

$$d^2 y = f_{11}\, dx_1^2 + 2f_{12}\, dx_1\, dx_2 + f_{22}\, dx_2^2. \tag{2A.28}$$

Now, however, not all possible small changes in the x's are permissible. Only those values of x_1 and x_2 that continue to satisfy the constraint can be consid-

---

[5] Notice that Equations 2A.23 obey the sufficient conditions not only at the critical point but for all possible choices of x_1 and x_2. That is, the function is concave. In more complex examples this need not be the case: The second-order conditions need only be satisfied at the critical point for a local maximum.

ered as valid alternatives to the critical point. To examine such changes, we must calculate the total differential of the constraint (Equation 2A.25):

$$-b_1\, dx_1 - b_2\, dx_2 = 0 \tag{2A.29}$$

or

$$dx_2 = -\frac{b_1}{b_2}\, dx_1. \tag{2A.30}$$

Equation 2A.30 therefore shows the relative changes in x_1 and x_2 that are allowable in considering movements from the critical point. To proceed further on this problem, it is necessary to use the first-order conditions (Equation 2A.27). The first two of these imply

$$\frac{f_1}{f_2} = \frac{b_1}{b_2}, \tag{2A.31}$$

and combining this result with Equation 2A.30 yields

$$dx_2 = -\frac{f_1}{f_2}\, dx_1. \tag{2A.32}$$

We now substitute this expression for dx_2 in Equation 2A.28 to demonstrate the conditions that must hold for d^2y to be negative:

$$d^2y = f_{11}\, dx_1^2 + 2f_{12}\, dx_1\left(-\frac{f_1}{f_2}\, dx_1\right) + f_{22}\left(-\frac{f_1}{f_2}\, dx_1\right)^2 \tag{2A.33}$$

$$= f_{11}\, dx_1^2 - 2f_{12}\, \frac{f_1}{f_2}\, dx_1^2 + f_{22}\, \frac{f_1^2}{f_2^2}\, dx_1^2.$$

Combining terms and putting each over a common denominator gives

$$d^2y = (f_{11}f_2^2 - 2f_{12}f_1f_2 + f_{22}f_1^2)\, \frac{dx_1^2}{f_2^2}. \tag{2A.34}$$

Consequently, for $d^2y < 0$ it must be the case that

$$f_{11}f_2^2 - 2f_{12}f_1f_2 + f_{22}f_1^2 < 0. \tag{2A.35}$$

Although this expression appears to be little more than an inordinately complex mass of symbols, in reality it has considerable significance. Functions that obey the inequality 2A.35 everywhere are sometimes termed *quasi-concave functions*.[6] Such functions are used widely in microeconomics and are the principal ones that will be encountered in this book. Usually our assumptions of quasi-concavity will be more intuitive than mathematical, but we shall occa-

---

[6] As the name implies, such functions represent generalizations of the concept of concave functions. It is easy to show that all concave functions are quasi-concave (the proof proceeds by recognizing that the quadratic form in f_1 and f_2 represented by Equation 2A.35 is quite similar to that analyzed in Equation 2A.16). The converse is not true, however. Most of the quasi-concave functions we shall examine in this book are not, in general, concave.

sionally point out (in footnotes) their formal aspects. The importance of our present analysis is to show that in maximizing such functions subject to linear constraints, the necessary conditions for a maximum are also sufficient. We shall have occasion to refer to that result at several places in the text.

Numerical Example

To demonstrate the second-order conditions in the constrained case, we will examine the geometric problem analyzed in Chapter 2.[7] In formal terms that problem required that we maximize

$$A = f(X, Y) = XY, \tag{2A.36}$$

subject to the constraint

$$P - 2X - 2Y = 0. \tag{2A.37}$$

Setting up the Lagrangian expression,

$$\mathscr{L} = XY + \lambda(P - 2X - 2Y), \tag{2A.38}$$

yields the following necessary conditions for a maximum:

$$\frac{\partial \mathscr{L}}{\partial X} = Y - 2\lambda = 0$$

$$\frac{\partial \mathscr{L}}{\partial Y} = X - 2\lambda = 0 \tag{2A.39}$$

$$\frac{\partial \mathscr{L}}{\partial \lambda} = P - 2X - 2Y = 0.$$

Solving these for the optimal values of X, Y, and λ yields

$$X = Y = \frac{P}{4}$$

$$\lambda = \frac{P}{8}. \tag{2A.40}$$

To examine the second-order conditions given by Equation 2A.35, we compute

$$f_1 = f_X = Y$$

$$f_2 = f_Y = X$$

$$f_{11} = f_{XX} = 0 \tag{2A.41}$$

$$f_{12} = f_{XY} = 1$$

$$f_{22} = f_{YY} = 0.$$

[7]Proof of the second-order condition for the algebraic problems analyzed in Chapter 2 is trivial since we have already shown that function to be strictly concave. The function analyzed here ($A = XY$) is, for positive values of X and Y, a simple example of a quasi-concave function that is not concave. We shall use the function repeatedly in examples and problems later in the text.

Making the appropriate substitutions in Equation 2A.35, we have

$$0 \cdot X^2 - 2 \cdot 1 \cdot X \cdot Y + 0 \cdot Y^2 = -2XY. \qquad \text{(2A.42)}$$

Since X and Y are both positive in this problem, the second-order conditions for a constrained maximum are satisfied.

SUGGESTED READINGS

Chiang, A. C. *Fundamental Methods of Mathematical Economics.* 2d ed. New York: McGraw-Hill Book Company, 1974. Pp. 383–390.

A basic, lower-level reference. Good, intuitive presentation of second-order conditions.

Courant, R. *Differential and Integral Calculus.* Vol. II. New York: Interscience Publishers, 1936. Pp. 183–209.

Classic calculus reference. Sophisticated proofs of sufficient conditions for a maximum.

Henderson, James M., and Quandt, Richard E. *Microeconomic Theory: A Mathematical Approach.* 3d ed. New York: McGraw-Hill Book Company, 1980. Pp. 379–386.

Compact discussion of sufficient conditions but requires linear algebra.

Hitch, C. J., and McKean, R. N. *The Economics of Defense in the Nuclear Age.* Cambridge, Mass.: Harvard University Press, 1960. Appendix, prepared by A. C. Enthoven, pp. 361–379.

Appendix has nice treatment of quasi-concave functions and of Kuhn-Tucker programming methods.

Sydsaeter, Knut. *Topics in Mathematical Analysis for Economists.* New York: Academic Press, 1981. Pp. 229–294.

Sophisticated treatment of second-order conditions in an economics context.

PART

II

Choice and Demand

In Part II we will investigate the economic theory of choice. The final goal of this examination is to develop the notion of market demand in a formal way so that this concept can be used in later sections of the text. A more general goal of the part is to illustrate the theory that economists use to explain how individuals make choices in a wide variety of contexts.

Part II begins with a description of the way economists model individual preferences, which are usually referred to by the formal term "utility." Chapter 3 shows how economists are able to conceptualize utility in a mathematical way.

Particularly important is the development of "indifference curves," which show the various exchanges that individuals are willing to make voluntarily.

The utility concept is next used in Chapter 4 to illustrate the theory of choice. The fundamental hypothesis of the chapter—the first economic example of an optimization hypothesis that we have encountered—is that individuals who are faced with limited incomes will make economic choices in such a way as to achieve as much utility as possible. Chapter 4 uses both mathematical and intuitive analyses to indicate the insights that this hypothesis provides about economic behavior.

Chapters 5 and 6 then use the model of utility maximization to investigate how individuals will respond to changes in their circumstances. Chapter 5 is primarily concerned with responses to changes in the price of a commodity, an analysis that leads directly to the demand curve notion. Chapter 6 continues this type of analysis and applies it to other types of reactions that individuals might have to changes in their economic environment.

Finally, Chapter 7 makes use of the material from Chapters 3–6 to derive the familiar market demand curve for a commodity. By developing this curve from the basic economic theory of choice, this chapter offers a fairly complete understanding of the factors that determine the location of the curve and the factors that might cause it to shift to a new position. The chapter also introduces the notion of elasticity as a way to measure the responsiveness of market demand to changes in various economic parameters such as income and prices. Such elasticities are widely used in empirical studies of market responses in the real world.

CHAPTER 3

Preferences and Utility

Because any economic system is in essence a collection of individuals, it is natural to start our analysis with an examination of individual behavior. Every individual operates in at least three roles that are of interest to economists:

1. *The individual is a consumer.* Individuals demand a variety of consumption goods and services. Presumably, they derive some welfare from those items that they demand. There may be a "higher order" of demands for the necessities of life than for the luxuries, but this dividing line is a difficult one to draw in practice (especially in rich, developed economies). Rather, economists treat all goods as providing some satisfaction to consumers and study how choices are made among them.

2. *The individual provides productive services.* The most obvious resource provided by the individual is labor. He or she must decide how much labor to expend in the market in exchange for goods or services. Individuals, by their saving (that is, abstaining from current consumption), also provide capital as a productive resource to the economic system. Savings may be invested by the individual directly in tangible capital, or they may be used to buy financial assets, which in turn permit the borrower of these funds to invest in tangible capital goods. An individual may also decide to invest in his or her own education or health. In this respect he or she invests in "human" capital.

3. *The individual participates in the political process.* By voting and other political activities, the individual expresses his or her preferences regarding the government's provision of goods and services (national defense, police protection, and trash collection, for example). He or she also expresses willingness to pay for these services by paying taxes. Individuals express their tastes in regard to other major political issues, and the social consensus that emerges sets the legal framework in which the economic system operates.

It is important to recognize that these roles cannot be separated from one another. Any decision an individual makes as a consumer, say, to buy a new car, will undoubtedly have an effect on his or her decisions as a provider of resources (the individual may save less or work harder) and as a voter (he or she may favor spending for new highways on which to drive the new car). Modern microeconomics explicitly recognizes this mixture of roles and has developed tools to aid in understanding these interrelationships. The analysis of the individual in these various roles is discussed in several parts of this book.[1] Before beginning this analysis, however, we must talk in general about individual preferences and the concept of utility. This discussion will provide a framework for all of our later analyses.

AXIOMS OF RATIONAL CHOICE

One way to begin an analysis of individuals' choices is to specify a basic set of postulates, or axioms, that characterize "rational" behavior. Although a number of sets of such axioms have been proposed, all have similarities in that they begin with the concept of "preference": When an individual reports that "A is preferred to B," it is taken to mean that all things considered, he or she feels better off under situation A than under situation B. This preference relation is usually assumed to have three basic properties:

I.   *Completeness:* If A and B are *any* two situations, the individual can always specify exactly one of the following three possibilities:
   1.   "A is preferred to B,"
   2.   "B is preferred to A," or
   3.   "A and B are equally attractive."
Individuals are consequently assumed not to be paralyzed by indecision: They completely understand and can always make up their minds about the desirability of any two alternatives. The assumption also rules out the possibility that the individual can report both that A is preferred to B and that B is preferred to A.

II.   *Transitivity:* If an individual reports that "A is preferred to B" and that "B is preferred to C," then he or she must also report that "A is preferred to C."

This assumption states that the individual's choices are internally consistent. Such an assumption can be subjected to empirical study, and in our application for this chapter, we report on some of these studies. Generally, they conclude that a person's choices are indeed transitive, but that conclusion must be modified in cases where the individual may not fully understand the consequences of the choices he or she is making. Since, for the most part, we will assume choices are fully informed (but see the discussion on uncertainty in Chapter 9 and elsewhere), the transitivity property seems an appropriate assumption to make about preferences.

III.   *Continuity:* If an individual reports "A is preferred to B," then situations suitably "close to" A must also be preferred to B.

---

[1] Parts II and III are concerned primarily with individuals as consumers; Part VII addresses individuals' supply of productive resources; and Part VIII examines individuals' participation in the political process.

This rather technical assumption is required if we wish to analyze individuals' responses to relatively small changes in income and prices. The purpose of the assumption is to rule out certain kinds of unusual preferences that pose problems for the theory of choice. Some of these odd preferences are described in the problems in this chapter. Assuming continuity does not seem to run the risk of missing types of economic behavior that are important in the real world.

UTILITY

Given the assumptions of completeness, transitivity, and continuity, it is possible to show formally that people are able to rank in order all possible situations from the least desirable to the most.[2] Following the terminology introduced by the nineteenth-century political theorist Jeremy Bentham, economists call this ranking *utility*.[3]

We also will follow Bentham by saying that more desirable situations offer more utility than do less desirable ones. That is, if a person prefers situation A to situation B, we would say that the utility assigned to option A, denoted by $U(A)$, exceeds the utility assigned to B, $U(B)$.

Non-Uniqueness of Utility Measures

We might even attach numbers to these utilities. But these numbers will not be unique. Any set of numbers we arbitrarily assign that accurately reflects the original preference ordering will imply the same set of choices. It makes no difference whether we say $U(A) = 5$ and $U(B) = 4$ or that $U(A) = 1,000,000$ and $U(B) = 0.5$. In either case the numbers clearly report that A is preferred to B. In technical terms, our notion of utility is defined only up to an order-preserving ("monotonic") transformation.[4] Any set of numbers that accurately reflects a person's preference ordering will do. Consequently, it makes no sense to ask "how much more is A preferred than B?" since that question has no unique answer. Surveys that ask people to rank their "happiness" on a scale of 1 to 10 could just as well use a scale of 7 to 1,000,000. About all that can be hoped for is that a person who reports he or she is a "6" on the scale one day and a "7" on the next day is indeed happier on the second day.

This lack of uniqueness in the assignment of utility numbers also reflects the assumption that it is not possible to compare utilities between people. If one person reports that a steak dinner provides a utility of "5" and another reports

---

[2] These properties and their connection to representation of preferences by a utility function are discussed in Donald W. Katzner, *Static Demand Theory* (New York: The Macmillan Company, 1970), chap. 1.

[3] J. Bentham, *Introduction to the Principles of Morals and Legislation* (London: Hafner, 1848).

[4] We can denote this idea mathematically by saying that any numerical utility ranking (U) can be transformed into another set of numbers by the function F providing that $F(U)$ is order preserving. This can be assured if $F'(U) > 0$. For example, the transformation $F(U) = U^2$ is order preserving as is the transformation $F(U) = \ln U$. At some places in the text and problems, we may find it convenient to make such transformations in order to make a particular utility ranking easier to analyze. As long as the transformation is order preserving, no inaccuracies will be introduced since either utility measure represents the same underlying ranking of preferences.

that the same dinner offers a utility of "100," we cannot say which individual values the dinner more since they could be using very different scales. Similarly, we have no way of measuring whether a move from situation *A* to situation *B* provides more utility to one person or to another. Nonetheless, as we will see, economists can say quite a bit about such situations by examining what people voluntarily choose to do.

The Ceteris Paribus *Assumption*

Because *utility* refers to overall satisfaction, such a measure clearly is affected by a variety of factors. A person's utility is affected not only by his or her consumption of physical commodities but also by psychological attitudes, peer group pressures, personal experiences, and the general cultural environment. Although economists do have a general interest in examining such influences, usually a narrowing of focus is necessary. Consequently, a common practice is to devote attention exclusively to choices among quantifiable options (for example, the relative quantities of food and shelter bought, the number of hours worked per week, or votes among specific taxing formulas) while holding constant the other things that affect behavior. This *ceteris paribus* (other things being equal) assumption is invoked in all economic analysis of utility-maximizing choices so as to make the analysis of choices manageable within a simplified setting. Of course, what is held constant and what is allowed to vary will depend on the particular question being examined.

As an important example of the *ceteris paribus* assumption, consider the individual's problem of choosing, at a single point in time, among n consumption goods $X_1, X_2, \ldots, X_n$. We shall assume that the individual's ranking of these goods can be represented by a utility function of the form:

$$\text{utility} = U(X_1, X_2, \ldots, X_n; \text{other things}), \quad (3.1)$$

where the X's refer to the quantities of the goods chosen and the "other things" notation is used to remind the reader that many aspects of individual welfare are being held constant in the analysis. Not only must we hold "tastes" constant, but we must also hold constant such quantifiable items as the individual's consumption in some future time periods, the number of hours worked (this amounts to holding income constant), and the amount of income saved. All these quantifiable aspects of individual behavior can be (and will be) investigated in their own right. But in the most common problems in the theory of choice, they are held constant.

Quite often it is easier to write Equation 3.1 as

$$\text{utility} = U(X_1, X_2, \ldots, X_n) \quad (3.2)$$

or, if only two goods are being considered,

$$\text{utility} = U(X, Y), \quad (3.2')$$

where it is clear that everything is being held constant (that is, outside the frame of analysis) except the goods actually referred to in the utility function. It would be tedious to remind the reader at each step what is being held constant in the analysis, but it should be remembered that some form of the *ceteris paribus* assumption will always be in operation.

<table>
<tr><td>*Indirect Utility
Functions*</td><td>The utility function notation therefore will be used to indicate how an individual ranks the particular arguments of the function being considered. In the most usual case the utility function (Equation 3.2) will be used to represent how an individual ranks certain bundles of goods that are available at one point in time. On occasion it will be useful to use other arguments in the utility function, and it is best to clear up certain conventions at the outset. For example, it may be useful to talk about the utility an individual receives from real income (I). Therefore we shall use the notation:</td></tr>
</table>

$$\text{utility} = U(I). \tag{3.3}$$

Unless the individual is a rather peculiar Scrooge-type of person, income in its own right gives no direct utility. Rather, it is only when this income is spent on consumption goods that any utility results. For this reason Equation 3.3 will be taken to mean that the utility from income is in fact derived by spending that income in such a way as to yield as much utility as possible. Equation 3.3 is therefore an "indirect" utility function, because those things that really provide utility (the consumption items that real income buys) are obscured from view. In Chapter 4 we will have a bit more to say about this concept and its usefulness to economic analysis.

Two other utility functions of this indirect type will be used in later chapters. In Chapter 22 we shall be concerned with the individual's labor-leisure choice and will therefore have to consider the presence of leisure in the utility function. A function of the form

$$\text{utility} = U(C, H) \tag{3.4}$$

will be used. Here C represents consumption and H represents hours of leisure. This function is also an indirect representation of utility because the uses to which leisure time is put are what directly provide utility.

In Chapter 23 we shall be interested in the individual's consumption decisions in different time periods. In that chapter we shall use a utility function of the form

$$\text{utility} = U(C_1, C_2), \tag{3.5}$$

where C_1 is consumption in this period and C_2 is consumption in the next period. This extremely simple case will prove to be useful in analyzing important aspects of an individual's behavior over time. It should be recognized that the use of an aggregate such as "consumption next period" is also indirect because it is based on the assumption that such a magnitude is allocated optimally (so as to maximize utility) over a collection of specific individual goods in each period.

Economic Goods
and Utility

In summary then, we start our examination of individual behavior with the following definition:

Definition:

Utility

Individuals' preferences are assumed to be represented by a utility function of the form

$$U(X_1, X_2, \ldots, X_n),\qquad\qquad (3.6)$$

where $X_1, X_2, \ldots, X_n$ are the quantities of each of n goods consumed in a period. This function is unique only up to an order-preserving transformation.

In this representation the X's are taken to be "goods"—that is, whatever they represent, we assume that more of any particular X_i during some period is preferred to less. That is what we mean by a "good," be it a simple consumption item such as a hot dog or a complex aggregate such as income or leisure. We have pictured this convention for a two-good utility function in Figure 3.1. There, all consumption bundles in the shaded area are preferred to the bundle X^*, Y^* because any bundle in the shaded area provides more of at least one of the goods.[5] By our definition of "goods," then, bundles of goods in the shaded area are ranked more highly than X^*, Y^*. Similarly, bundles in the area marked "worse" are clearly inferior to X^*, Y^* since they contain less of at least one of the goods and no more of the other. Bundles in the other two areas are difficult to compare to X^*, Y^* because they contain more of one of the goods and less of the other.

In actuality, of course, some economic commodities are regarded as "bads," rather than "goods." Most people certainly prefer fewer termites, mosquitoes, or suspended particles in the air or water. Our assumption that the X's in the utility function represent goods is made for convenience only. Later in this chapter, we briefly describe how preferences for "bads" can be handled in the utility framework.

TRADES AND SUBSTITU-TION

Most economic activity involves voluntary trading among people. When someone buys, say, a loaf of bread, he or she is voluntarily giving up one thing (money) for something else (bread) that is of greater value. To examine this kind of voluntary transaction, we need to develop a formal apparatus for illustrating trades in the utility function context. To start the discussion, consider a hypothetical situation in which we focus attention on a person's consumption of two specific goods—say, hamburgers (which we will call good Y) and soft drinks (which we will call good X). This person intends to consume a certain amount of each of these goods during a particular period of time. Suppose we

---

[5] For all bundles in the shaded area to be strictly preferred to X^*, Y^*, we also require that the person not be satiated by either of the goods; that is, additional amounts of each good will increase the person's utility.

Figure 3.1   *More of a Good Is Preferred to Less*

The shaded area represents those combinations of *X* and *Y* that are unambiguously preferred to the combination *X**, *Y**. In a sense this is why goods are called "goods": Because, *ceteris paribus,* individuals prefer more of any good rather than less.

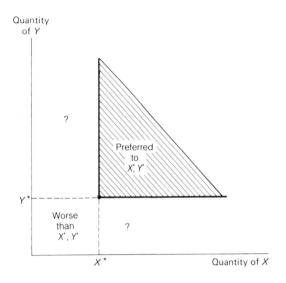

now ask how many hamburgers he or she will willingly give up to get one more soft drink. The answer to this question might very well depend on what kind of a consumption bundle this particular person is starting out with. If, for example, he or she has quite a few hamburgers and no soft drinks, this individual might willingly trade quite a few burgers for a drink. Alternatively, if the same person starts with many soft drinks and only one hamburger, he or she might be very reluctant to part with that burger. This supposition is termed by economists the assumption of a diminishing marginal rate of substitution (of one good for another). It is based on the notion that people prefer some balance in the consumption bundles they choose. Because this simple-minded idea lies at the heart of the economic theory of choice, we will spend considerable space on developing it precisely using a number of mathematical tools.

Indifference Curves and the Marginal Rate of Substitution

To discuss rigorously the principle of a diminishing marginal rate of substitution, it is easiest first to develop the idea of an *indifference curve*. In Figure 3.2 the curve U_1 represents all the alternative combinations of *X* and *Y* for which an individual is equally well off (remember again that all other arguments of the utility function are being held constant). The individual is equally happy consuming, for example, either the combination of goods X_1, Y_1 or the combination X_2, Y_2. This curve representing all the consumption bundles that the individual ranks equally is called an *indifference curve:*

Indifference Curve
An *indifference curve* (or, in many dimensions, indifference surface) shows a set of consumption bundles among which the individual is indifferent. That is, the bundles all provide the same level of utility.

The slope of the indifference curve in Figure 3.2 is negative, showing that if the individual is forced to give up some Y, he or she must be compensated by an additional amount of X to remain indifferent between the two bundles of goods. The curve is also drawn so that the slope increases as X increases (that is, the slope starts at negative infinity and increases toward 0). This is a graphical representation of the assumption of a diminishing marginal rate of substitution.

Marginal Rate of Substitution
The negative of the slope of an indifference curve (U_1) at some point is termed the *marginal rate of substitution* (MRS) at that point. That is,

$$MRS = -\frac{dY}{dX}\bigg|_{U = U_1,}$$

(3.7)

where the notation indicates that the slope is to be calculated along the U_1 indifference curve.

The slope of U_1 and the MRS therefore tell us something about the trades this person will voluntarily make. At a point such as X_1, Y_1, the person has quite a lot of Y and is willing to trade away a significant amount to get one more X. The indifference curve at X_1, Y_1 is therefore rather steep. This is the situation where the person has many hamburgers (Y) and little to drink with them (X). This person would gladly give up a few burgers (say, 5) to quench his or her thirst with one more drink.

At X_2, Y_2, on the other hand, the indifference curve is flatter. Here this person has quite a few drinks and is willing to give up relatively few burgers (say, 1) to get another soft drink. Consequently, the MRS diminishes between X_1, Y_1 and X_2, Y_2. The changing slope of U_1 shows how the particular consumption bundle available influences the trades this person will freely make.

Indifference Curve Map

In Figure 3.2 only one indifference curve was drawn. The X, Y quadrant, however, is full of such curves, each corresponding to a different level of utility. Since every bundle of goods can be ranked and yields some level of utility, each point in Figure 3.2 must have an indifference curve passing through it. Indifference curves are similar to contour lines on a map in that they represent lines of equal "altitude" of utility. In Figure 3.3 several indifference curves are shown to indicate that there are infinitely many in the plane. The level of utility represented by these curves increases as we move in a northeast direction—the

Figure 3.2   A Single Indifference Curve

The curve U_1 represents those combinations of X and Y from which the individual derives the same utility. The slope of this curve represents the rate at which the individual is willing to trade X for Y while remaining equally well off. This slope (or, more properly, the negative of the slope) is termed the *marginal rate of substitution*. In the figure the indifference curve is drawn on the assumption of a diminishing marginal rate of substitution.

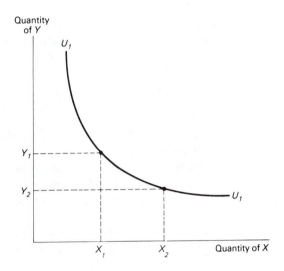

Figure 3.3   *There Are Infinitely Many Indifference Curves in the* X-Y *Plane*

There is an indifference curve passing through each point in the X-Y plane. Each of these curves records combinations of X and Y from which the individual receives a certain level of satisfaction. Movements in a northeast direction represent movements to higher levels of satisfaction.

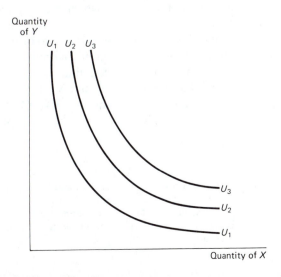

utility of curve U_1 is less than that of U_2, which is less than that of U_3. This is because of the assumption made in Figure 3.1: More goods are preferred to less. As was discussed earlier, there is no unique way to assign numbers to these utility levels. All the curves show is that the combinations of goods on U_3 are preferred to those on U_2, which are preferred to those on U_1.

Indifference Curves and Transitivity

As an exercise in examining the consistency of preferences, consider the following question: Can any two of an individual's indifference curves intersect? Two such intersecting curves are shown in Figure 3.4. We wish to know if they violate our basic axioms of rationality. Using our map analogy, there would seem to be something wrong at point E—there "altitude" is equal to two different numbers, U_1 and U_2. But no point can be both 100 and 200 feet above sea level.

To proceed formally, let us analyze the bundles of goods represented by points A, B, C, and D. By the definition of "goods," "A is preferred to B" and "C is preferred to D." But the individual is equally satisfied with either B or C (they lie on the same indifference curve), so the axiom of transitivity implies that A must be preferred to D. But that cannot be true, since A and D are on the same indifference curve and must be regarded as equally desirable. Hence the axiom of transitivity shows that indifference curves cannot intersect. We therefore should always draw indifference curve maps as they appear in Figure 3.3.

Convexity of Indifference Curves

It is possible to develop these representations of individual preferences in many ways. For example, an interesting alternative way of stating the principle of a diminishing marginal rate of substitution uses the mathematical notion of a convex set. A set of points is said to be *convex* if any two points within the set can be joined by a straight line that is contained completely within the set. The assumption of a diminishing MRS is equivalent to the assumption that all combinations of X and Y, which are preferred to or indifferent to a particular combination X^*, Y^*, form a convex set.[6] This is illustrated in Figure 3.5a, where all combinations preferred to or indifferent to X^*, Y^* are in the shaded area. Any two of these combinations—say, X_1, Y_1 and X_2, Y_2—can be joined by a straight line also contained in the shaded area. In Figure 3.5b this is not true. A line joining X_1, Y_1 and X_2, Y_2 passes outside the shaded area. Therefore the indifference curve through X^*, Y^* in 3.5b does not obey the assumption of a diminishing MRS, since the set of points preferred or indifferent to X^*, Y^* is not convex.

[6] This definition is equivalent to the assumption that the utility function is assumed to be quasi-concave. Such functions were discussed in the appendix to Chapter 2, and we shall return to examine them in the next section. Sometimes the term *strict quasi-concavity* is used to rule out the possibility of indifference curves having flat portions. We generally will assume strict quasi-concavity but in a few places will indicate the complications posed by linear portions of indifference curves.

Figure 3.4   *Intersecting Indifference Curves Imply Inconsistent Preferences*

Combinations *A* and *D* lie on the same indifference curve and therefore are equally
desirable. But the axiom of transitivity can be used to show that *A* is preferred to *D*.
Hence intersecting indifference curves are not consistent with rational preferences.

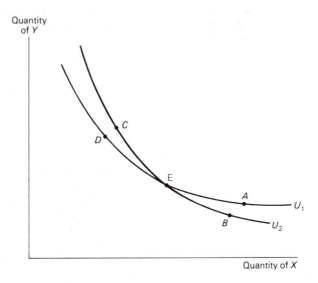

Figure 3.5   *The Notion of Convexity as an Alternative*
Definition of a Diminishing MRS

In (a) the indifference curve is *convex* (any line joining two points above U_1 is also
above U_1). In (b) this is not the case, and the curve shown here does not everywhere
have a diminishing *MRS*.

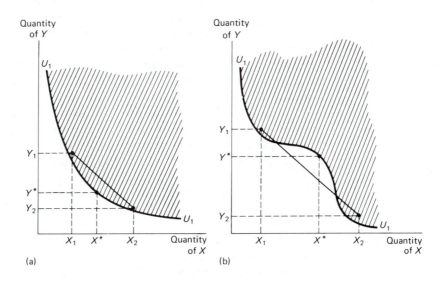

Figure 3.6 *Balanced Bundles of Goods Are Preferred to Extreme Bundles*

If indifference curves are convex (if they obey the assumption of a diminishing *MRS*), then the line joining any two points that are indifferent will contain points preferred to either of the initial combinations. Intuitively, balanced bundles are preferred to unbalanced ones.

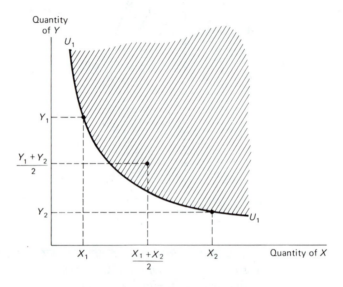

Convexity and Balance in Consumption

By using the notion of convexity, we can show an interesting implication of the assumption that the *MRS* diminishes as the ratio of X to Y increases. Suppose that an individual is indifferent between the combination X_1, Y_1 and X_2, Y_2. What the assumption of a diminishing *MRS* means, then, is that the combination $(X_1 + X_2)/2$, $(Y_1 + Y_2)/2$ will be preferred to either of the initial combinations.[7] Intuitively, "well-balanced" bundles of commodities are preferred to bundles that are heavily weighted toward one commodity. This fact is illustrated in Figure 3.6. Since the indifference curve is assumed to be convex, all points on the straight line joining (X_1, Y_1) and (X_2, Y_2) are preferred to or indifferent to these initial points. This therefore will be true of the point $(X_1 + X_2)/2$, $(Y_1 + Y_2)/2$, which lies at the midpoint of such a line. Indeed, if the indifference curve is strictly convex (not a straight line), any proportional combination of the two indifferent bundles of goods will be preferred to the initial bundles, since it will represent a more balanced combination. Thus strict convexity is equivalent to the assumption of a diminishing *MRS*, and either assumption rules out the possibility of an indifference curve being straight over any portion of its length.

[7] In the degenerate case in which the indifference curve is a straight line, the individual will be indifferent among all three combinations.

Figure 3.7   *Indifference Curve for Utility* $= \sqrt{X \cdot Y}$

This indifference curve illustrates the function $10 = U = \sqrt{X \cdot Y}$. At point *A* (5, 20), the *MRS* is 4 implying that this person is willing to trade 4*Y* for an additional *X*. At point *B* (20, 5), however, the *MRS* is 0.25 implying a greatly reduced willingness to trade.

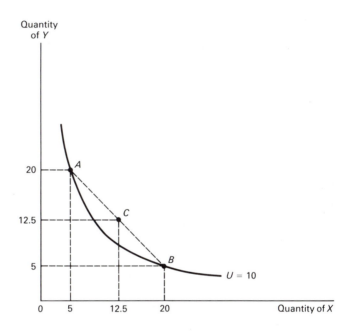

Numerical Example

Suppose a person's ranking of hamburgers (Y) and soft drinks (X) could be represented by the utility function

$$\text{utility} = \sqrt{X \cdot Y}. \tag{3.8}$$

An indifference curve for this function is found by identifying that set of combinations of X and Y for which utility has the same value. Suppose we arbitrarily set utility equal to 10. Then the equation for this indifference curve is

$$\text{utility} = 10 = \sqrt{X \cdot Y}. \tag{3.9}$$

Since squaring this function is order preserving, the indifference curve is also represented by

$$100 = X \cdot Y, \tag{3.10}$$

which is easier to graph. In Figure 3.7 we show this indifference curve—it is a rectangular hyperbola. To calculate the *MRS*, we solve Equation 3.10 for Y,

$$Y = 100/X, \tag{3.11}$$

and then we use Equation 3.7:

$$MRS = -dY/dX \text{ (along } U_1) = 100/X^2. \tag{3.12}$$

This derivation shows that for a point such as A on the indifference curve with a lot of hamburgers (say, $X = 5$, $Y = 20$), the slope is steep so the MRS is high:

$$MRS \text{ at } (5, 20) = 100/X^2 = 100/25 = 4. \tag{3.13}$$

Here the person is willing to give up 4 hamburgers to get one more soft drink. On the other hand, at B, where there are relatively few hamburgers (here $X = 20$, $Y = 5$), the slope is flat and the MRS is low:

$$MRS \text{ at } (20, 5) = 100/X^2 = 100/400 = 0.25. \tag{3.14}$$

Now he or she will only give up 1/4 of a hamburger for another soft drink.

   Notice also how convexity of the indifference curve U_1 is illustrated by this numerical example. Point C is midway between points A and B—at C this person has 12.5 hamburgers and 12.5 soft drinks. Now, however, utility is given by

$$\text{utility} = \sqrt{X \cdot Y} = \sqrt{(12.5)^2} = 12.5, \tag{3.15}$$

which clearly exceeds the utility along U_1 (which was assumed to be 10).

AN ALTER-NATIVE DERIVATION: MARGINAL UTILITY

The development of the MRS given here is the preferred one in modern economic discussions because the concepts involved are, at least in principle, observable. It is possible to conceive of asking individuals about their psychic rates of trade-off over various combinations of commodities. The assumption of a diminishing MRS can be discussed without the necessity of actually referring to the utility function. Originally, however, the concept of the MRS was developed using the ideas of utility and marginal utility. Since this derivation provides both insights and some practice in mathematical manipulation, it is presented here.

   Suppose that an individual ranks goods by a utility function of the form

$$\text{utility} = U(X_1, X_2, \ldots, X_n), \tag{3.16}$$

where $X_1, X_2, \ldots, X_n$ are the amounts of each of n goods X consumed. By the marginal utility of good X_1, we mean the function

$$\text{marginal utility of } X_1 = MU_{X_1} = \frac{\partial U}{\partial X_1}. \tag{3.17}$$

The marginal utility of X_1 is the extra utility obtained from slightly more X_1 while holding the amount of all other commodities constant. Obviously, the value of the marginal utility depends on the point at which the partial derivative is to be evaluated—it depends on how much $X_1, X_2, \ldots, X_n$ the individual is currently consuming. It also depends on the particular scale used to measure utility.

   We can write the total differential of U as

$$dU = \frac{\partial U}{\partial X_1} dX_1 + \frac{\partial U}{\partial X_2} dX_2 + \cdots + \frac{\partial U}{\partial X_n} dX_n$$

$$= MU_{X_1} dX_1 + MU_{X_1} dX_2 + \cdots + MU_{X_n} dX_n. \tag{3.18}$$

Equation 3.18 says that the extra utility obtainable from slightly more X_1, X_2, ..., X_n is simply the sum of the additional utility provided by each of these increments. Again, this value depends on how utility is measured.

To develop the concept of *MRS*, consider changing only the level of two goods, X and Y, so as to keep the individual indifferent (that is, $dU = 0$). By Equation 3.18

$$dU = 0 = \frac{\partial U}{\partial X} dX + \frac{\partial U}{\partial Y} dY = MU_X\, dX + MU_Y\, dY. \tag{3.19}$$

Notice that all other goods are held constant, hence dU is only affected by changing the quantities of the two goods in question. This is the same approach used in the development of indifference curves in the previous section.

Rearranging terms a bit gives

$$\left. \frac{-dY}{dX} \right|_{U\,=\,\text{constant}} = \frac{MU_X}{MU_Y} = \frac{\partial U/\partial X}{\partial U/\partial Y}, \tag{3.20}$$

where the notation is a reminder that Y and X are constrained to change so as to hold the level of utility constant.[8] But Equation 3.20 is simply the definition of the *MRS* given in Equation 3.7. Hence the result of this section is that the marginal rate of substitution (of X for Y) is equal to the ratio of the marginal utility of X to the marginal utility of Y. That conclusion makes intuitive sense. Suppose that the marginal utility of an extra soft drink were 4 utils and that of an extra hamburger were 2 utils. Then the *MRS* (of soft drinks for hamburgers) should be 4 utils/2 utils = 2. The individual can trade two hamburgers for one extra soft drink and remain equally well off: The loss of hamburgers reduces utility by 4 utils, whereas the gain of a soft drink raises utility by 4 utils. Notice also that the units of utility measure (what we have, for lack of a better name, termed a util) drop out when constructing the *MRS*. This result is quite general—the *MRS* is independent of how utility is measured even though marginal utility itself is not.[9]

---

[8] Holding utility constant creates an implicit relationship between X and Y. Equation 3.20 shows how this implicit relationship can be differentiated. More formally, if $U(X, Y) - U_1 = 0$ is the implicit function for the indifference curve U_1, then $dY/dX = -U_x/U_y$. This method of differentiation is sometimes called the *implicit function rule*.

[9] More formally, let $F(U)$ be any arbitrary order-preserving transformation of U (that is, $F'(U) > 0$). Then for this revised function

$$MRS = \frac{\partial F/\partial X}{\partial F/\partial Y} = \frac{F'(U)\, \partial U/\partial X}{F'(U)\, \partial U/\partial Y}$$

$$= \frac{\partial U/\partial X}{\partial U/\partial Y},$$

which is the *MRS* for the original function U—the fact that the $F'(U)$ terms cancel out shows that the *MRS* is independent of how utility is measured.

Diminishing
Marginal Utility
and the MRS

In Chapter 1 it was shown how the assumption of diminishing marginal utility was used by Marshall to solve the paradox of value. Marshall theorized that it is the marginal valuation that an individual places on a good that determines its value: It is the amount that an individual is willing to pay for one more pint of water that determines the price of water. Since it might be thought that this marginal value declines as the quantity of water that is consumed increases, Marshall showed why water has a low exchange value. Intuitively, it seems clear that the assumption of the decreasing marginal utility of a good is related to the assumption of a decreasing *MRS*; both concepts seem to refer to the same commonsense idea of an individual becoming relatively satiated with a good as more of it is consumed. Unfortunately the two concepts are quite different. (See Problem 3.7.) Exhibiting the interrelationship between the two concepts involves some degree of mathematical complication, which will be pursued only in a footnote.[10] In modern usage the concept of a decreasing *MRS* has replaced Marshall's idea because a discussion of the *MRS* does not depend so heavily on the utility concept and appears to be a more empirically verifiable statement of the relative satiation idea.

[10] We have shown that if utility is given by $U = f(X, Y)$, then

$$MRS = \frac{f_X}{f_Y} = \frac{f_1}{f_2} = -\frac{dY}{dX}.$$

The assumption of a diminishing *MRS* means that $dMRS/dX < 0$, but

$$\frac{dMRS}{dX} = \frac{f_2(f_{11} + f_{12} \cdot dY/dX) - f_1(f_{21} + f_{22} \cdot dY/dX)}{f_2^2}.$$

Using the fact that $f_1/f_2 = -dY/dX$, we have

$$\frac{dMRS}{dX} = \frac{f_2[f_{11} - f_{12}(f_1/f_2)] - f_1[f_{21} - f_{22}(f_1/f_2)]}{f_2^2}.$$

Combining terms and recognizing that $f_{12} = f_{21}$ yields

$$\frac{dMRS}{dX} = \frac{f_2 f_{11} - 2f_1 f_{12} + (f_{22}f_1^2)/f_2}{f_2^2},$$

or, multiplying numerator and denominator by f_2,

$$\frac{dMRS}{dX} = \frac{f_2^2 f_{11} - 2f_1 f_2 f_{12} + f_1^2 f_{22}}{f_2^3}.$$

If we assume that $f_2 > 0$ (that marginal utility is positive), then the *MRS* will diminish provided that

$$f_2^2 f_{11} - 2f_1 f_2 f_{12} + f_1^2 f_{22} < 0.$$

Notice that diminishing marginal utility ($f_{11} < 0$ and $f_{22} < 0$) will not ensure this inequality. One must also be concerned with the f_{12} term. That is, one must know how increases in X affect the marginal utility of Y. In general it is not possible to predict the sign of that term.

The condition required for a diminishing *MRS* is precisely that discussed in the appendix to Chapter 2 (see Equation 2A.35) to ensure that the function f is strictly quasi-concave. The condition shows that the necessary conditions for a maximum of f subject to a linear constraint are also sufficient.

Numerical Example

In our previous numerical example, we assumed that the utility provided by hamburgers (Y) and soft drinks (X) was given by

$$\text{utility} = U(X, Y) = \sqrt{X \cdot Y} = X^{.5}Y^{.5}. \tag{3.21}$$

Hence the marginal utility from additional soft drinks is

$$\text{marginal utility} = MU_X = \partial U/\partial X = .5X^{-.5}Y^{.5}. \tag{3.22}$$

Notice that marginal utility declines as X increases and that, as is generally the case, the marginal utility for good X also depends on the amount of Y consumed. In this particular case, the marginal utility from extra soft drinks (X) increases as the number of hamburgers (Y) increases, but that need not always be so.

The marginal utility for hamburgers is calculated in a similar way:

$$MU_Y = \partial U/\partial Y = .5X^{.5}Y^{-.5}. \tag{3.23}$$

Now we can use Equation 3.20 to calculate the *MRS*:

$$MRS = \left. \frac{-dY}{dX} \right|_{U \,=\, \text{constant}} = \frac{MU_X}{MU_Y} = \frac{.5X^{-.5}Y^{.5}}{.5X^{.5}Y^{-.5}} = \frac{Y}{X}. \tag{3.24}$$

This result is somewhat more general than the one we derived previously (Equation 3.12) because it applies to any bundle, not just bundles on one indifference curve. As before, however, at the point $X = 5$, $Y = 20$, Equation 3.24 shows that the *MRS* is 4.0 whereas at the point $X = 20$, $Y = 5$, it is 0.25.

EXAMPLES OF UTILITY FUNCTIONS

Individuals' rankings of commodity bundles and the utility functions implied by these rankings are unobservable. All we can learn about people's preferences must come from the behavior we observe when they respond to changes in income, prices, and other factors.

It is nevertheless useful to examine a few of the forms particular utility functions might take, both because such an examination may offer some insights into observed behavior and (more to the point) because understanding the properties of such functions can be of some help in solving problems. Here we will examine four specific examples of utility functions for two goods. Indifference curve maps for these functions are illustrated in the four panels of Figure 3.8. As should be visually apparent, these cover quite a few possible shapes. Even greater variety is possible once we move to functions for three or more goods, however, and some of these possibilities are mentioned in later chapters.

Cobb-Douglas Utility

Figure 3.8a shows the familiar shape of an indifference curve. One commonly used utility function that generates such curves has the form

$$\text{utility} = U(X, Y) = X^{\alpha}Y^{\beta}, \tag{3.25}$$

where α and β are positive constants.

In the previous numerical examples in this chapter, we studied a particular case of this function for which $\alpha = \beta = 0.5$. The more general case presented

Figure 3.8   *Examples of Utility Functions*

This figure illustrates four possible shapes for the indifference curve map. In (a), the Cobb-Douglas case, $U = X^\alpha Y^\beta$, is represented; (b) illustrates the case of perfect substitutes whereas (c) illustrates perfect complements. Case (d) shows a situation where good Y is an economic "bad." This person requires more X if he or she is to be willing to consume more Y and remain equally well-off.

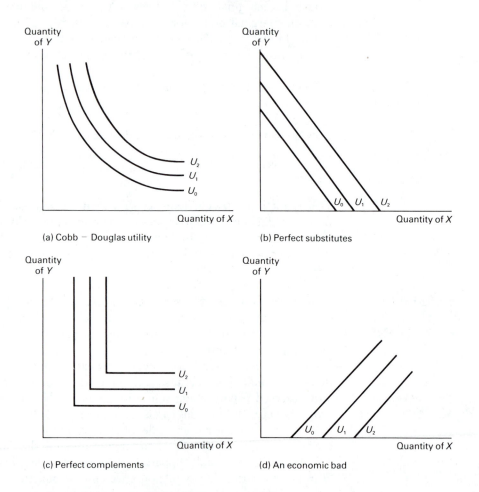

(a) Cobb − Douglas utility

(b) Perfect substitutes

(c) Perfect complements

(d) An economic bad

in Equation 3.25 is usually termed a *Cobb-Douglas utility function* after two researchers who used such a function for their detailed study of production relationships in the U.S. economy (see Chapter 10). Not only does the Cobb-Douglas function possess a familiar indifference curve map, but it is also easy to show that this map is *homothetic*—that is, each indifference curve has essentially the same shape as every other one. The curves are "radial extensions" of each other in that their slopes at any point depend only on the ratio of Y to

X, but not on the absolute amounts of Y and X.[11] In the next chapter we will see how this property of the curves leads to a particularly simple (and perhaps unrealistic) proportional relationship between a person's income and how much of a particular good he or she will buy.

Perfect Substitutes   The straight line indifference curves in Figure 3.8b are generated by a utility function of the form

$$\text{utility} = U(X, Y) = \alpha X + \beta Y, \tag{3.26}$$

where, again, α and β are positive constants. That the indifference curves for this function are straight lines should be readily apparent: Any particular curve can be calculated by setting $U(X, Y)$ equal to a constant that, given the linear form of the function, clearly specifies a straight line. The linear nature of these indifference curves gave rise to the term *perfect substitutes* to describe the implied relationship between X and Y. Because the *MRS* is constant (and equal to α/β) along the entire indifference curve, our previous notions of a diminishing *MRS* do not apply in this case. A person with these preferences would be willing to give up the same amount of Y to get one more X no matter how much X was being consumed. Such a situation might describe the relationship between different brands of what is essentially the same product. For example, many people (including the author) don't care where they buy gasoline. A gallon of gas is a gallon of gas in spite of the best efforts of the Exxon and Mobil advertising departments to convince us otherwise. Given this fact, I am always willing to give up 10 gallons of Exxon in exchange for 10 gallons of Mobil because it doesn't matter to me which I use or where I got my last tankful. Indeed, as we will see in the next chapter, one implication of such a relationship is that I will buy all my gas from the least expensive seller. Since I don't experience a diminishing *MRS* of Exxon for Mobil, I have no reason to seek a balance among the gasoline types I use.

Perfect Complements   A situation directly opposite to the case of perfect substitutes is illustrated by the L-shaped indifference curves in Figure 3.8c. These preferences would apply to goods that "go together"—coffee and cream, peanut butter and jelly, or cream cheese and lox would be familiar examples. The indifference curves shown in Figure 3.8c imply that these pairs of goods will be used in the fixed proportional relationship represented by the vertices of the curves. A person who prefers 1 ounce of cream with 8 ounces of coffee will want 2 ounces of cream with 16 ounces of coffee. Extra coffee without cream is of no value to this person just as extra cream would be of no value without coffee. Only by choosing the goods together can utility be increased.

---

[11] Proof: If $U(X, Y) = X^\alpha Y^\beta$, $\partial U/\partial X = \alpha X^{\alpha-1} Y^\beta$, and $\partial U/\partial Y = \beta X^\alpha Y^{\beta-1}$, then, by Equation 3.20

$$MRS = \frac{\partial U/\partial X}{\partial U/\partial Y} = \frac{\alpha X^{\alpha-1} Y^\beta}{\beta X^\alpha Y^{\beta-1}} = \frac{\alpha}{\beta} \cdot \frac{Y}{X}.$$

These concepts can be formalized by examining the mathematical form of the utility function that generates these L-shaped indifference curves:

$$utility = U(X, Y) = \min(\alpha X, \beta Y). \tag{3.27}$$

Here α and β are positive parameters, and the operator "min" means that utility is given by the smaller of the two terms in the parentheses. In the coffee-cream example, if we let ounces of coffee be represented by X and ounces of cream by Y, utility would be given by

$$utility = U(X, Y) = \min(X, 8Y). \tag{3.28}$$

Now 8 ounces of coffee and 1 ounce of cream provide 8 units of utility. But 16 ounces of coffee and 1 ounce of cream also provide only 8 units of utility because $\min(16, 8) = 8$. The extra coffee without cream is of no value as shown by the horizontal section of the indifference curves for movement away from a vertex—utility does not increase when only X increases (with Y constant). Only if coffee and cream are both doubled (to 16 and 2, respectively) will utility increase to 16.

More generally, neither of the two goods in Equation 3.27 will be in excess only if

$$\alpha X = \beta Y. \tag{3.29}$$

Hence

$$Y/X = \alpha/\beta, \tag{3.30}$$

which shows the fixed proportional relationship between the two goods that must occur if choices are to be at the vertices of the indifference curves.

Economic Bads   Finally, the positively sloped indifference curves in Figure 3.8d illustrate a case in which one of the goods (say, Y) is really a "bad"—this person will choose more Y only if compensated with additional X also. Commodity Y might represent mosquito contacts whereas X could represent beach quality. The positive slope of the curve therefore implies that this person will choose to swim at a mosquito-infested beach only if the sand and surf are of exceptional quality.

The mathematical function that generates the indifference curve map in Figure 3.8d is

$$utility = U(X, Y) = \alpha X + \beta Y, \tag{3.31}$$

where α is a positive parameter and β is a negative parameter. Increases in X therefore increase utility whereas increases in Y decrease utility. Utility can be kept constant when Y increases only by increasing X also.

A simple comparison of Equation 3.31 and Equation 3.26 (perfect substitute) shows that the only difference between these cases is the sign of the parameter β.[12] The other functions in this section can also sometimes be used to

---

[12] A middle ground might be $\beta = 0$. In this case utility would depend only on the amount of X consumed, and the individual would be indifferent to how much Y is available.

illustrate economic bads by simply changing the sign of the parameter or by making other alterations in the functional form. Since the study of economic bads will not play a major role in the analysis of this book (bads generally will not have a positive price, for example, so there is no incentive to "produce" them), we will not pursue such matters here.[13]

Generalizations to More Than Two Goods

These specific utility functions can easily be generalized to many goods. For example, a many-good Cobb-Douglas function might be written as

$$\text{utility} = U(X_1, X_2, \ldots, X_n) = X_1^{\beta_1}, X_2^{\beta_2}, \ldots, X_n^{\beta_n}, \tag{3.32}$$

or a many-good case of perfect substitutes might be written as

$$\text{utility} = U(X_1, X_2, \ldots, X_n) = \beta_1 X_1 + \beta_2 X_2 + \cdots + \beta_n X_n, \tag{3.33}$$

where for both cases the β's are all positive constants. Notions of indifference surfaces and marginal rates of substitution can also be discussed for these functions using the definitions developed previously. Some of the problems in this and later chapters ask students to make use of such many-good functions.

Unfortunately, the extremely simple nature of these functions is even more constraining in describing real-world choices among many goods than it is for illustrating choices among just two goods. Use of such a function generally makes it impossible to portray the rich variety of relationships that exist among all the kinds of goods that people consume. Adoption of more complex functional forms may, to some extent, reduce these problems, but, since individuals' "true" utility functions will always be unobservable, economists have little direct evidence on which to choose among the vast number of mathematical functions that might be used. Instead, the usual approach is to use fairly simple functions to illustrate concepts and then to rely on direct market evidence to learn more about the complex relationships among goods. We also will follow that approach here.

SUMMARY

In this chapter we have described the way in which economists formalize individuals' preferences about the goods they choose. We derived several conclusions about such preferences that will play a central role in our analysis of the theory of choice in the following chapters:

- If individuals obey certain basic behavioral postulates in their preferences among goods, they will be able to rank all commodity bundles, and that ranking can be represented by a utility function. In making choices, individuals will behave as if they were maximizing this function.

---

[13] Alternatively, we might define disposal of economic bads as an economic good and study choices made about that good. For example, rather than focusing on mosquitoes or garbage, it might be more useful to study people's preferences for mosquito control or garbage disposal.

- Utility functions for two goods can be illustrated by an indifference curve map. Each indifference curve contour on this map shows all the commodity bundles that yield a given level of utility.

- The negative of the slope of an indifference curve is defined to be the marginal rate of substitution (*MRS*). This shows the rate at which an individual would willingly give up an amount of one good (*Y*) if he or she were compensated by receiving one more unit of another good (*X*).

- The assumption that the *MRS* decreases as *X* is substituted for *Y* in consumption is consistent with the notion that individuals prefer some balance in their consumption choices. If the *MRS* is always decreasing, individuals will have convex indifference curves.

- The *MRS* can also be represented as the ratio of the marginal utility of one good to that of another good. Although the marginal utility concept itself is not especially useful (because it can be affected by how utility is measured), it is quite helpful in deriving the *MRS* in some cases. Because the *MRS* itself is the ratio of marginal utilities, it is not affected by the way in which utility is measured.

Application

TRANSITIVITY

Whether or not people obey the assumption of transitivity and thereby make consistent decisions has been a subject of some controversy among economists and psychologists. Many examples have been proposed that purport to show the assumption is widely violated in the real world. One popular counter-example is scoring at sporting events. By invoking (incorrectly) the assumption of transitivity, it is often possible to draw absurd conclusions about how games might turn out. Consider the following question: Can Amherst College (a major football power of the Connecticut Valley) beat the University of Oklahoma? Using the assumption of transitivity the answer is a definite yes. In the 1975 season, for example, Amherst beat Bowdoin, Bowdoin beat Bates, Bates beat C. W. Post, and (to make a very long story short) C. W. Post beat a team that beat a team that beat a team that beat Pitt. Since Pitt beat Kansas and (in that year) Kansas beat Oklahoma,

the result is proved.[14] An Amherst-Oklahoma match-up would be no contest since the law of transitivity assures that Amherst would win in a walk-away.

The absurdity of the above conclusion stems from the fact that football games do not necessarily obey the assumption of transitivity. Rather, the outcomes of games depend mostly on relatively random happenings between the players; drawing conclusions from comparative scores is a very inexact business.

Experimental Data
Of greater interest to economists is whether individuals' choices obey or violate the transitivity assumption. A number of experiments have been undertaken to try to answer that question. Here we describe two of them. In a

---

[14] This example was developed by Frank Westhoff, an economist and die-hard football fan.

1958 study, J. M. Davis asked a group of undergraduate male students to express their marital preferences from among a set of written descriptions of nine women.[15] These descriptions included (relatively sexist) adjectives such as: woman 1—plain, average charm, wealthy; woman 2—pretty, average charm, wealthy; woman 3—pretty, very charming, average income; and so forth. The students were then asked to make choices between pairs of women. Such choices were judged intransitive if a subject reported, for example, that he preferred woman 1 to woman 3, that he preferred woman 3 to woman 7, and that he preferred woman 7 to woman 1. In all, Davis examined nearly 4,000 such triples, looking for intransitivities and finding relatively few. Only about 1 out of 8 of the triples examined showed intransitivity, and most of those failed to be repeated in a second test on the same subjects. Fewer than 1 percent of all the triples examined were intransitive on both replications of the test. Davis concluded that the vast majority of preferences were transitive, and those intransitivities that were observed could probably be explained as random choices among women judged to be equally desirable by the subjects.

A similar approach to the study of consistency of preferences was taken by A. A. Weinstein in a 1968 experiment that examined how individuals ranked consumption items.[16] Overall, 10 items were used (ranging from $3 in cash to three Beatles records or a 15-inch pizza) and, following the Davis study, the author looked at

individuals' ranking of three items to see how many intransitivities occurred. For example, an inconsistency would occur if someone reported preferring the cash to the Beatles records and the records to the pizza, but that he or she preferred pizza to cash. Among adults, Weinstein found few (less than 7 percent) such intransitivities. Again, those that did occur might be attributed to relatively random rankings among goods viewed as equally attractive to the subjects being examined. The author did find, however, that younger people (notably children ages 9 through 12) exhibited considerably more intransitivities (about 20 percent of the choices made). This led him to conclude that consistency may to some extent be an acquired skill.

Data from Actual Consumption Patterns
Actual consumption data are also broadly consistent with the notion of transitivity. In a detailed study of families' food purchases over a four-year period in Michigan, for example, relatively few intransitive choices were found.[17] As in the experimental studies, the occurrence of intransitivities seemed to be related to some extent to family circumstances. Families where both spouses were employed tended to have relatively larger numbers of intransitivities whereas families with many children (and large food demands) tended to have fewer. Such observations suggest that the rationality required to exhibit consistent, transitive preferences may to some extent be costly to families. So a varying degree of "optimal irrationality" may sometimes be observed.

[15] J. M. Davis, "Transitivity of Preferences," *Behavioral Science* (Fall 1958), 26–33.

[16] A. A. Weinstein, "Transitivity of Preferences," *Journal of Political Economy* (March/April 1968), 307–311.

[17] A. Y. C. Koo and Georg Haverkamp, "Structure of Revealed Preference: Some Preliminary Evidence," *Journal of Political Economy*, July/August, 1972, pp. 724–744.

SUGGESTED READINGS

Katzner, Donald W. *Static Demand Theory.* New York: The Macmillan Company, 1970. Chaps. 2 and 3.

Theoretical treatment of preferences and of the

conditions under which preferences can be represented by a utility function.

Leibenstein, H. "Bandwagon, Snob, and Veblen Effects in the Theory of Consumers' Demand."

Quarterly Journal of Economics 64 (May 1970): 183–207.

Discusses some ways of formalizing common-sense ideas of how preferences are formed and whether they change over short periods.

Marshall, A. *Principles of Economics.* 8th ed. London: Macmillan & Co., Ltd., 1920. Chaps. I–IV. Book III.

Early basic text. Still a very readable and interesting treatment of consumer theory.

Russell, R. Robert, and Wilkinson, Maurice. *Microeconomics: A Synthesis of Modern and Neoclassical Theory.* New York: John Wiley & Sons, 1979. Chaps. 2 and 3.

Advanced but readable treatment of the relationship between preference orderings and utility theory.

Samuelson, P. A. *Foundations of Economic Analysis.* Cambridge, Mass.: Harvard University Press, 1947. Chap. 5.

Detailed, calculus-based treatment of consumer theory. One of the first to introduce the revealed preference concept and the integrability problem.

Silberberg, Eugene. *The Structure of Economics: A Mathematical Approach.* New York: McGraw-Hill Book Company, 1978. Chap. 8.

Good discussion of preference theory and the integrability problem. Makes significant use of duality relations and the envelope theorem.

Stigler, G. "The Development of Utility Theory," *Journal of Political Economy* 59, pts. 1–2 (August–October 1950), pp. 307–327, 373–396.

A lucid and complete survey of the history of utility theory. Has many interesting insights and asides.

Theil, Henri. *Theory and Measurement of Consumer Demand.* Vol. I. Amsterdam: North-Holland Publishing Co., 1975. Chap. 1.

Shows how utility-based demand functions can be estimated and the restrictions imposed by theory.

Weymark, John A. "Duality Results in Demand Theory." *European Economic Review,* November 1980, pp. 377–385.

Nice summary of primal and dual relationships in demand theory. Some graphical treatment of the issues being presented.

PROBLEMS

3.1

Laidback Al derives utility from 3 goods: music (M), wine (W), and cheese (C). His utility function is of the simple linear form

$$\text{Utility} = U(M, W, C) = M + 2W + 3C.$$

a.   Assuming Al's consumption of music is fixed at 10, sketch the indifference curves for W and C for $U = 40$ and $U = 70$.

b.   Show that Al's *MRS* of wine for cheese is constant for all values of W and C on the indifference curves calculated in part a.

c.   Suppose Al's consumption of music increases to 20. How would this change your answers to parts a and b? Explain your results intuitively.

3.2

Suppose the utility function for two goods, X and Y, has the simple form

$$\text{Utility} = U(X, Y) = \sqrt{X \cdot Y}.$$

a.   Graph the $U = 10$ indifference curve associated with this utility function.

b.   If $X = 5$, what must Y equal to be on the $U = 10$ indifference curve? What is the *MRS* at this point?

c.   In general, develop an expression for the *MRS* for this utility function. Show how this can be interpreted as the ratio of the marginal utilities for X and Y.

d.   Consider a logarithmic transformation of this utility function:

$$U' = \log U$$

where log is the logarithmic function to base 10. Show that for this transformation the $U' = 1$ indifference curve has the same properties as the $U = 10$ curve calculated in parts a and b. What is the general expression for the *MRS* of this transformed utility function?

3.3

Georgia always eats hot dogs in a bun together with 1 oz. of mustard. Each hot dog eaten in this way provides 15 units of utility, but any other combination of hot dogs, buns, and mustard is worthless to Georgia.

    a.   Explain the nature of Georgia's utility function and indicate the form of her indifference curve map.

    b.   Suppose hot dogs cost $1, buns cost $.40, and mustard costs $.10 per ounce. Show how Georgia's utility can be represented by the total amount of money she spends on these three items.

    c.   How would your answer to part b change if the price of hot dogs rose to $1.50?

3.4

For each of the following expressions, state the formal assumption that is being made about the individual's utility function:

    a.   It (margarine) is just as good as the high-priced spread (butter);

    b.   Peanut butter and jelly go together like a horse and carriage;

    c.   Things go better with Coke;

    d.   Popcorn is addictive—the more you eat, the more you want;

    e.   Mosquitoes ruin a nice day at the beach;

    f.   A day without wine is like a day without sunshine;

    g.   It takes two to tango.

3.5

Graph a typical indifference curve for the following utility functions and determine whether or not they have convex indifference curves (that is, whether they obey the assumption of a diminishing *MRS*):

    a. $U = 3X + Y$.

    b. $U = \sqrt{X \cdot Y}$.

    c. $U = \sqrt{X^2 + Y^2}$.

    d. $U = \sqrt{X^2 - Y^2}$.

    e. $U = X^{2/3} Y^{1/3}$.

    f. $U = \log X + \log Y$.

3.6

In footnote 10 of Chapter 3, we showed that in order for a utility function for two goods to have a strictly diminishing *MRS* (that is, to be strictly quasi-concave), the following condition must hold:

$$f_2^2 f_{11} - 2 f_1 f_2 f_{12} + f_1^2 f_{22} < 0.$$

Use this condition to check the convexity of the indifference curves for each of the utility functions in Problem 3.5. Describe any shortcuts you discover in this process.

3.7

Consider the following utility functions

    (i) $U(X, Y) = XY$

    (ii) $U(X, Y) = X^2 Y^2$

    (iii) $U(X, Y) = \log X + \log Y$

Show that each of these has a diminishing *MRS*, but that they exhibit constant, increasing, and decreasing marginal utility, respectively. What do you conclude?

3.8

As pointed out in Chapter 3, indifference curves are said to be "homothetic" (a term we will examine also in the theory of production) if the *MRS* depends only on the ratio of the two goods *X* and *Y*. That is, a doubling of both *X* and *Y* would not change the *MRS*.

a. Show that the indifference curves for perfect substitutes, perfect complements, and for the Cobb-Douglas utility function are homothetic;

b. Show that the indifference curves for

$$U(X, Y) = X + \log Y$$

are not homothetic. Develop an intuitive explanation of why a doubling of *X* and *Y* in this function causes the *MRS* to change.

3.9

Two goods have independent marginal utilities if

$$\frac{\partial^2 U}{\partial Y \, \partial X} = \frac{\partial^2 U}{\partial X \, \partial Y} = 0.$$

Show that if we assume diminishing marginal utility for each good, then any utility function with independent marginal utilities will have a diminishing *MRS*. Provide an example to show that the converse of this statement is not true.

EXTENSIONS

ODD PREFERENCES

In Chapter 3 we devoted relatively little attention to the formal theory of individual preferences. Instead, we moved quickly to the assumption that such preferences could be accurately represented by a utility function with a well-behaved indifference curve map. This approach, although it did permit us to begin our study of individual behavior without an unnecessarily long and formal introduction, may obscure difficult issues in preference theory. Here we develop some exercises that permit the student to examine these issues.

In formal terms, any preference relation (call this relation "P") defines how an individual feels about bundles of commodities (which we will denote by A, B, C, and so forth). We write APB to record that the individual prefers A to B and BPA to denote the converse of this statement. We use AIB to indicate that the individual is indifferent between A and B. Throughout, we assume that there are only two goods (X and Y) although the results are easily generalized.

The following four preference relations violate at least one of the principles developed in Chapter 3 (completeness, transitivity, or continuity). For each, identify the principle(s) that is (are) violated and illustrate why the relationship cannot be represented by a utility function with a well-defined indifference curve map.

E3.1 Threshold Effects.

Suppose individuals must consume a significant amount of extra *X* (with *Y* constant) before they feel better-off. For example, adding an extra 3 or 4 square feet to existing living space may make no difference whereas an addition of 200 square feet does improve well-being. Such a possibility is termed a "threshold effect." Formally, if AIB, then $A'IB$ where $Y_A = Y_{A'}$, and $X_{A'} \leq X_A + d$ where d is the "threshold."

E3.2 Lexicographic Preferences.
With lexicographic preferences, the individual orders goods so that additional units of the first are always preferred to additional units of the second, additional units of the second are preferred to additional units of the third, and so forth. The goods are therefore ordered as in a dictionary (or lexicon). Formally, APB if and only if $X_A > X_B$ regardless of the values of Y_A and Y_B.

E3.3 Bliss.
The term "bliss" refers to the possibility of total satiation in one or both of the goods. For two goods, a bundle A (consisting of X_A and Y_A) would be a bliss point if APB for any other bundle B, even if $X_B > X_A$ and $Y_B > Y_A$.

E3.4 Ignorance.
If the individual has no experience with one or both of the goods, he or she may not be able to express a preference or may articulate preferences randomly. A person with no musical experiences, asked to rank bundles of commodities containing Mozart and Wagner operas, may sometimes report APB and other times report BPA.

REFERENCES

Deaton, A., and Muellbauer, J. *Economics and Consumer Behavior.* Cambridge: Cambridge University Press, 1980. Chapter 2.

Katzner, D. W. *Static Demand Theory.* New York: Macmillan, 1970. Chapters 1–3.

CHAPTER 4

Utility Maximization and Choice

In this chapter we will examine the basic model of choice that economists use to explain individuals' behavior. That model assumes that individuals who are constrained by limited incomes will behave as if they were using their purchasing power in such a way as to achieve the highest utility possible. That is, individuals are assumed to behave as if they maximized utility subject to a budget constraint. Although the specific applications of this model are quite varied, as we will show, all of them are based on the same fundamental mathematical model, and all arrive at the same general conclusion: In order to maximize utility, individuals will choose bundles of commodities for which the rate of trade-off among those commodities (the *MRS*) reflects the commodities' market prices. Market prices convey information about opportunity costs to individuals, and this information plays an important role in affecting the choices actually made. All of the applications we study reach this same fundamental conclusion.

Before starting our formal study of the theory of choice, it may be appropriate to dispose of two complaints non-economists often make about the approach we will take. First is the charge that probably no person can make the kinds of "lightning calculations" required for utility maximization. According to this complaint, when moving down a supermarket aisle, people just grab what is available with no real pattern or purpose to their actions. Economists are not persuaded by this complaint. They doubt that people behave randomly (everyone, after all, is bound by some sort of budget constraint), and they view the lightning calculation charge as misplaced. Recall, again, Friedman's pool player. He or she also cannot make the lightning calculations required to plan a shot according to the laws of physics, but those laws still predict the player's behavior. So too, as we shall see, the utility-maximization model predicts behavior even though no one carries around a computer with his or her utility function programmed into it. To be precise, economists assume that people behave *as if* they made such calculations so the complaint that the calculations are not actually made is irrelevant.

A second complaint against our model of choice is that it appears to be extremely selfish—no one, according to this complaint, has such solely self-centered goals. Although economists are probably more ready to accept self-interest as a motivating force than are some other, more Utopian thinkers (Adam Smith observed, "We are not ready to suspect any person of being deficient in selfishness"[1]), this charge is also misplaced. Nothing in the utility-maximization model prevents individuals from deriving satisfaction from philanthropy or generally "doing good." These activities also can be assumed to provide utility. Indeed, economists have used the utility-maximization model extensively to study such issues as donating time and money to charity, leaving bequests to children, or even giving blood. One need not take a position on whether such activities are "selfish" or "selfless" since economists doubt people would undertake them if they were against their own best interests, broadly conceived.

AN INITIAL SURVEY

Before starting our formal study of the utility-maximization model, it may be useful to indicate where we are going. The general results of our examination can be stated succinctly:

Optimization Principle:

Utility Maximization

In order to maximize utility, given a fixed amount of money to spend, an individual will buy those quantities of goods which exhaust his or her total income and for which the psychic rate of trade-off between any two goods (the *MRS*) is equal to the rate at which the goods can be traded one for the other in the marketplace.

That spending all one's income is required for utility maximization is obvious. Since extra goods provide extra utility (there is no satiation) and since there is no other use for income (there is no saving in this model), to leave any unspent would be to fail to maximize utility. Throwing money away is not a utility-maximizing activity in this model.

The condition specifying equality of trade-off rates requires a bit more explanation. Since the rate at which one good can be traded for another in the market is given by the ratio of their prices, this result can be restated to say that the individual will equate the *MRS* (of X for Y) to the ratio of the price of X to the price of Y (P_X/P_Y). This equating of a psychic trade-off rate to a market trade-off rate is a result common to all individual utility-maximization problems (and to many other types of maximization problems). It will occur again and again throughout this text.

To see the intuitive reasoning behind this result, assume that it were not true that the individual had equated the *MRS* to the ratio of the prices of goods.

---

[1] Adam Smith, *The Theory of Moral Sentiments* (1759; reprint, New Rochelle, N.Y.: Arlington House, 1969), p. 446.

Specifically, assume that the individual's *MRS* is equal to 1, that he or she is willing to trade 1 unit of *X* for 1 unit of *Y* and remain equally well off. Assume also that the price of *X* is $2 per unit and of *Y* $1 per unit. It is easy to show in this case that the individual can be made better off. Give up 1 unit of *X* and trade it in the market for 2 units of *Y*. But only 1 extra unit of *Y* was needed to keep the individual as happy as before the trade—the second unit of *Y* is a net addition to welfare. Therefore the individual's money could not have been allocated rationally in the first place. A similar method of reasoning can be used whenever the *MRS* and the price ratio P_X/P_Y differ. The condition for maximum utility must be the equality of these two magnitudes.

This discussion seems eminently reasonable, but it can hardly be called a proof. Rather, we must now show the result in a rigorous manner and, at the same time, illustrate several other important attributes of the maximization process.

THE TWO-GOOD CASE: A GRAPHIC ANALYSIS

Budget Constraint

First, using a graphic approach, we illustrate utility maximization for the two-good case. We begin with an analysis of the budget constraint.

Assume that the individual has *I* dollars to allocate between good *X* and good *Y*. If P_X is the price of good *X* and P_Y is the price of good *Y*, then the individual is constrained by

$$P_X X + P_Y Y \le I. \tag{4.1}$$

That is, no more than *I* can be spent on the two goods in question. This budget constraint is shown graphically in Figure 4.1. The individual can only afford to choose combinations of *X* and *Y* in the shaded triangle of the figure. If all of *I* is spent on good *X*, it will buy I/P_X units of *X*. Similarly, if all is spent on *Y*, it will buy I/P_Y units of *Y*. The slope of the constraint is easily seen to be $-P_X/P_Y$. For example, suppose that hamburgers (*Y*) cost $1, soft drinks (*X*) cost 25 cents, and that the individual has $2 (*I*), which must be spent on these two goods. In this situation he or she can buy two hamburgers (I/P_Y) or eight soft drinks (I/P_X) or a variety of combinations of the goods (such as one hamburger and four soft drinks). The rate at which the individual can trade soft drinks for hamburgers is four for one because this is the ratio of the prices of the goods. Economists would say that the *opportunity cost* of one hamburger is four soft drinks.

First-Order Conditions for a Maximum

This budget constraint can be imposed on the individual's indifference curve map to show the utility-maximization process. Figure 4.2 illustrates this procedure. The individual would be irrational to choose a point such as *A*—he or she can get to a higher utility level just by spending some of the unspent portion of *I*. Similarly, by reallocating expenditures, the individual can do better than point *B*. Point *D* is out of the question because *I* is not large enough to purchase *D*. It is clear that the position of maximum utility is at point *C*, where

Figure 4.1   *The Individual's Budget Constraint for Two Goods*

Those combinations of X and Y that the individual can afford are shown in the shaded triangle. If, as we usually assume, the individual prefers more rather than less of every good, the outer boundary of this triangle is the relevant constraint where all of the available funds are spent on either X or on Y. The slope of this straight-line boundary is given by $-P_X/P_Y$.

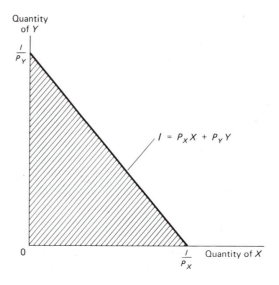

the combination X^*, Y^* is chosen. This is the only point on indifference curve U_2 that can be bought with I dollars; no higher utility level can be bought. C is a point of tangency between the budget constraint and the indifference curve. Therefore at C,

$$\text{slope of budget constraint} = \frac{-P_X}{P_Y} = \text{slope of indifference curve}$$

$$= \left. \frac{dY}{dX} \right|_{U \,=\, \text{constant}} \tag{4.2}$$

or

$$\frac{P_X}{P_Y} = \left. -\frac{dY}{dX} \right|_{U \,=\, \text{constant}} = MRS \text{ (of } X \text{ for } Y\text{).} \tag{4.3}$$

The result is proved—for a utility maximum, all income should be spent and the *MRS* should equal the ratio of the prices of the goods. It is obvious from the diagram that if this condition is not fulfilled, the individual could be made better off by reallocating expenditures.

Figure 4.2 *A Graphic Demonstration of Utility Maximization*

Point *C* represents the highest utility level that can be reached by the individual, given the budget constraint. The combination *X**, *Y** is therefore the rational way for the individual to allocate purchasing power. Only for this combination of goods will two conditions hold: All available funds will be spent; and the individual's psychic rate of trade-off (*MRS*) will be equal to the rate at which the goods can be traded in the market (P_x/P_y).

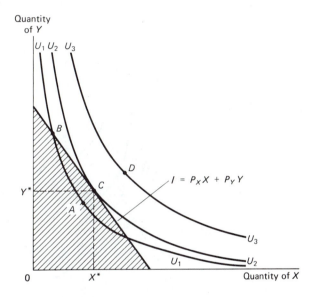

Second-Order Conditions for a Maximum

The tangency rule is only a necessary condition for a maximum. To see that it is not a sufficient condition, consider the indifference curve map shown in Figure 4.3. Here a point of tangency (*C*) is inferior to a point of nontangency (*B*). Indeed the true maximum is at another point of tangency (*A*). The failure of the tangency condition to produce an unambiguous maximum can be attributed to the peculiar shape of the indifference curves in Figure 4.3. If the indifference curves are shaped like those in Figure 4.2, no such problem can arise. But we have already shown that "normally" shaped indifference curves result from the assumption of a diminishing *MRS*. Therefore, if the *MRS* is assumed to be diminishing, the condition of tangency is both a necessary and sufficient condition for a maximum.[2] Without this assumption one would have to be very careful in applying the tangency rule.

[2] In mathematical terms, because the assumption of a diminishing *MRS* is equivalent to assuming quasi-concavity, the necessary conditions for a maximum subject to a linear constraint are also sufficient. See the appendix to Chapter 2 and footnote 10 in Chapter 3.

Figure 4.3   *Example of an Indifference Curve Map for Which the Tangency Condition Does Not Ensure a Maximum*

If indifference curves do not obey the assumption of a diminishing *MRS,* not all points of tangency (points for which *MRS* = P_x/P_y) may truly be points of maximum utility. In this example tangency point *C* is inferior to many other points, which can also be purchased with the available funds. In order that the necessary conditions for a maximum (that is, the tangency conditions) also be sufficient, one usually assumes that the *MRS* is diminishing; that is, the utility function is quasi-concave.

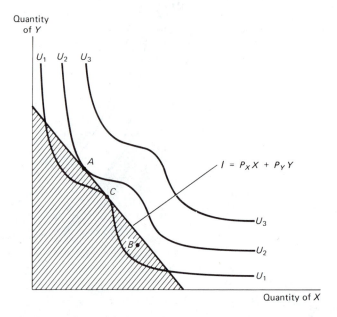

Corner Solutions   The utility-maximization problem illustrated in Figure 4.2 resulted in an "interior" maximum, in which positive amounts of both goods were consumed. In some situations individuals' preferences may be such that they can obtain maximum utility by choosing to consume no amount of one of the goods. If someone does not like hamburgers very much, there is no reason to allocate any income to their purchase. This possibility is reflected in Figure 4.4. There utility is maximized at *E,* where $X = X^*$ and $Y = 0$—any point on the budget constraint where positive amounts of *Y* are consumed yields a lower utility than does point *E*. Notice that at *E* the budget constraint is not precisely tangent to the indifference curve U_2. Instead at the optimal point the budget constraint is flatter than U_2, indicating that the rate at which *X* can be traded for *Y* in the market is lower than the individual's psychic trade-off rate (the *MRS*). At prevailing market prices the individual is more than willing to trade away *Y* to get extra *X*. Because it is impossible in this problem to consume negative amounts of *Y*, however, the physical limit for this process is the *X*-axis, along which purchases of *Y* are 0. Hence, as this discussion makes clear, it is necessary to amend the first-order conditions for a utility maximum a bit to allow

Figure 4.4 *Corner Solution for Utility Maximization*

With the preferences represented by this set of indifference curves, utility maximization occurs at *E,* where 0 amounts of good *Y* are consumed. The first-order conditions
for a maximum must be modified somewhat to accommodate this possibility.

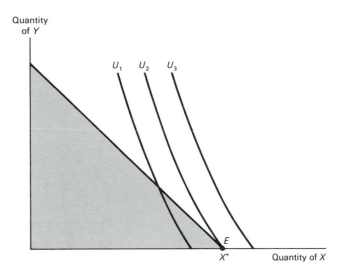

for corner solutions of the type shown in Figure 4.4. Following our discussion
of the general *n*-good case, we will show how this can be accomplished.

THE *n*-GOOD CASE

The results derived in the case of two goods carry over directly for the case of
n goods. Again it can be shown that for an interior maximum, the *MRS* between any two goods must equal the ratio of the prices of these goods for a
utility maximum. However, because the case of *n* goods cannot be presented
graphically, we shall adopt a mathematical proof, which provides additional
insights into the maximization assumption.

First-Order Conditions

When there are *n* goods to choose from, the individual's objective is to maximize utility from these *n* goods:

$$\text{utility} = U(X_1, X_2, \ldots, X_n), \tag{4.4}$$

subject to the budget constraint: [3]

$$I = P_1 X_1 + P_2 X_2 + \cdots + P_n X_n \tag{4.5}$$

or

$$I - P_1 X_1 - P_2 X_2 - \cdots - P_n X_n = 0. \tag{4.6}$$

---

[3] The budget constraint has been written as an equality here because, given the assumption of
nonsatiation, it is clear that the individual will spend all available income.

Following the techniques developed in Chapter 2 for maximizing a function subject to a constraint, we set up the Lagrangian expression:

$$\mathcal{L} = U(X_1, X_2, \ldots, X_n) + \lambda(I - P_1X_1 - P_2X_2 - \cdots - P_nX_n). \quad (4.7)$$

Setting the partial derivatives of $\mathcal{L}$ (with respect to X_1, X_2, ..., X_n and λ) equals to 0 yields $n + 1$ equations representing the necessary conditions for an interior maximum:

$$\frac{\partial \mathcal{L}}{\partial X_1} = \frac{\partial U}{\partial X_1} - \lambda P_1 = 0$$

$$\frac{\partial \mathcal{L}}{\partial X_2} = \frac{\partial U}{\partial X_2} - \lambda P_2 = 0$$

$$\cdot$$

$$\cdot \quad (4.8)$$

$$\cdot$$

$$\frac{\partial \mathcal{L}}{\partial X_n} = \frac{\partial U}{\partial X_n} - \lambda P_n = 0$$

$$\frac{\partial \mathcal{L}}{\partial \lambda} = I - P_1X_1 - P_2X_2 - \cdots - P_nX_n = 0.$$

These $n + 1$ equations can usually be solved for the optimal X_1, X_2, ..., X_n and for λ (see the example in the next section to be convinced that such a solution is possible).

Equations 4.8 are necessary but not sufficient for a maximum. The second-order conditions that ensure a maximum are relatively complex. However, the assumption of quasi-concavity (a diminishing *MRS* in the two-good case) is sufficient to ensure that any point obeying Equations 4.8 is in fact a true maximum. Hereafter, therefore, only first-order conditions will usually be discussed with the implication that the assumption of a diminishing *MRS* assures that these conditions are sufficient for a true maximum.[4]

Implications of First-Order Conditions

The first-order conditions represented by Equation 4.8 can be rewritten in a variety of interesting ways. For example, for any two goods X_i and X_j, we have

$$\frac{\partial U/\partial X_i}{\partial U/\partial X_j} = \frac{P_i}{P_j}. \quad (4.9)$$

But previously it was shown that the ratio of the marginal utilities of two goods is in fact identical to the marginal rate of substitution between the two goods. Therefore, the conditions for an optimal allocation of income become

---

[4]For a full statement of the sufficient conditions for a maximum, see Knut Sydsaeter, *Topics in Mathematical Analysis for Economists* (New York: Academic Press, 1981), pp. 282–288.

$$MRS\ (X_i\ \text{for}\ X_j)\ =\ \frac{P_i}{P_j}. \tag{4.10}$$

This is exactly the result derived earlier in this chapter; in order to maximize utility, the individual should equate the psychic rate of trade-off to the market trade-off rate.

Another result can be derived by solving Equation 4.8 for λ:

$$\lambda\ =\ \frac{\partial U/\partial X_1}{P_1}\ =\ \frac{\partial U/\partial X_2}{P_2}\ =\ \cdots\ =\ \frac{\partial U/\partial X_n}{P_n} \tag{4.11}$$

or

$$\lambda\ =\ \frac{MU_{X_1}}{P_1}\ =\ \frac{MU_{X_2}}{P_2}\ =\ \cdots\ =\ \frac{MU_{X_n}}{P_n}.$$

This equation says that at the utility-maximizing point, each good purchased should yield the same marginal utility per dollar spent on that good. Each good therefore should have an identical (marginal) benefit to (marginal) cost ratio. If this were not true, one good would promise more "marginal enjoyment per dollar" than some other good, and funds would not be optimally allocated.

Although the reader is again warned against talking very confidently about marginal utility, what Equation 4.11 says is that an extra dollar should yield the same "additional utility" no matter which good it is spent on. The common value for this extra utility is given by the Lagrangian multiplier of I (that is, by λ). Therefore, λ can be regarded as the marginal utility of an extra dollar of consumption expenditure (the marginal utility of "income").

One final way to rewrite the necessary conditions for a maximum is

$$P_i\ =\ \frac{MU_i}{\lambda} \tag{4.12}$$

for every good i that is bought. This equation says that for every good that an individual buys, the price of that good represents his or her evaluation of the utility of the last unit consumed. The price obviously represents how much the individual is willing to pay for that last unit. In Chapter 5 (and elsewhere) we will make considerable use of this result when discussing the value of a good to a consumer and the "consumer surplus" received by some purchasers when they are able to buy a good for less than the maximum they would be willing to pay.

Corner Solutions   The first-order conditions of Equation 4.8 hold exactly only for interior maxima for which some positive amount of each good is purchased. When corner solutions (such as those illustrated in Figure 4.4) arise, the conditions have to be modified slightly.[5] In this case Equation 4.8 becomes

---

[5] Formally, these conditions are called the "Kuhn-Tucker" conditions for nonlinear programming. For a more complete explanation, see Michael D. Intriligator, *Mathematical Optimization and Economic Theory* (Englewood Cliffs, N.J.: Prentice-Hall, 1971), chap. 4.

$$\frac{\partial \mathscr{L}}{\partial X_i} = \frac{\partial U}{\partial X_i} - \lambda P_i \leq 0 \quad (i = 1 \ldots n), \tag{4.13}$$

and, if

$$\frac{\partial \mathscr{L}}{\partial X_i} = \frac{\partial U}{\partial X_i} - \lambda P_i < 0, \tag{4.14}$$

then

$$X_i = 0. \tag{4.15}$$

To interpret these conditions, we can rewrite Equation 4.14 as

$$P_i > \frac{\frac{\partial U}{\partial X_i}}{\lambda} = \frac{MU_{X_i}}{\lambda}. \tag{4.16}$$

Hence the optimal conditions are as before, except that any good whose price (P_i) exceeds its marginal value to the consumer (MU_X/λ) will not be purchased $(X_i = 0)$. Thus, the mathematical results conform to the commonsense idea that individuals will not purchase goods that they believe are not worth the money. Although such corner solutions will not provide a major focus for our analysis in this book, the reader should keep in mind the possibilities for such solutions arising and the economic interpretation that can be attached to the optimal conditions in such cases.

Numerical Example

To illustrate these various ideas we return to the Cobb-Douglas function for hamburgers (Y) and soft drinks (X) proposed in the previous chapter:

$$\text{utility} = U(X, Y) = \sqrt{X \cdot Y} = X^{.5}Y^{.5}. \tag{4.17}$$

Assume now that hamburgers cost \$1 each $(P_Y = 1.00)$ and soft drinks cost \$.25 $(P_X = .25)$ and that this person has \$2.00 to spend $(I = 2.00)$. Now the budget constraint is

$$1.00Y + .25X = 2.00. \tag{4.18}$$

Setting up the Lagrangian expression

$$\mathscr{L} = X^{.5}Y^{.5} + \lambda(2.00 - Y - .25X) \tag{4.19}$$

yields the following first-order conditions for a constrained maximum:

$$\frac{\partial \mathscr{L}}{\partial X} = .5X^{-.5}Y^{.5} - .25\lambda = 0$$

$$\frac{\partial \mathscr{L}}{\partial Y} = .5X^{.5}Y^{-.5} - \lambda = 0 \tag{4.20}$$

$$\frac{\partial \mathscr{L}}{\partial \lambda} = 2.00 - Y - .25X = 0.$$

Notice that the final equation simply repeats the budget constraint here. Moving the terms to the right side of the first and second equations yields

$$.5X^{-.5}Y^{.5} = .25\lambda \tag{4.21}$$
$$.5X^{.5}Y^{-.5} = \lambda.$$

Dividing the second of these by the first, we have

$$\frac{.5X^{.5}Y^{-.5}}{.5X^{-.5}Y^{.5}} = \frac{\lambda}{.25\lambda} \tag{4.22}$$

or

$$\frac{X}{Y} = 4 \tag{4.23}$$

so, for a constrained maximum

$$X = 4Y. \tag{4.24}$$

Now, using the budget constraint, we have

$$.25X + Y = .25(4Y) + Y = 2.00 \tag{4.25}$$

or

$$2Y = 2.00 \tag{4.26}$$
$$Y^* = 1$$
$$X^* = 4 \tag{4.27}$$

as the utility-maximizing values for X and Y. At this choice

$$\text{utility} = \sqrt{X \cdot Y} = \sqrt{4} = 2. \tag{4.28}$$

A General Solution
More generally, we could solve this example for any prices (P_X, P_Y) and income level (I) by setting up the Lagrangian expression

$$\mathcal{L} = X^{.5}Y^{.5} + \lambda(I - P_XX - P_YY) \tag{4.29}$$

and deriving the first-order conditions

$$\frac{\partial \mathcal{L}}{\partial X} = .5X^{-.5}Y^{.5} - \lambda P_X = 0$$

$$\frac{\partial \mathcal{L}}{\partial Y} = .5X^{.5}Y^{-.5} - \lambda P_Y = 0 \tag{4.30}$$

$$\frac{\partial \mathcal{L}}{\partial \lambda} = I - P_XX - P_YY = 0.$$

As before, this problem can be solved most easily by moving the terms in λ to the right and then dividing the second equation by the first:

$$\frac{.5\,X^{.5}\,Y^{-.5}}{.5\,X^{-.5}\,Y^{.5}} = \frac{P_Y}{P_X} \tag{4.31}$$

or

$$\frac{X}{Y} = \frac{P_Y}{P_X} \tag{4.32}$$

and

$$P_X X = P_Y Y. \tag{4.33}$$

In words, with this particular utility function, expenditures on good X should always equal expenditures on Y (this is one reason the function may be unrealistic). Substituting Equation 4.33 into the budget constraint

$$I = P_X X + P_Y Y \tag{4.34}$$

yields

$$I = P_X X + P_X X = 2P_X X$$

so

$$X^* = \frac{I}{2P_X} \tag{4.35}$$

and

$$Y^* = \frac{I}{2P_Y}. \tag{4.36}$$

Equations 4.35 and 4.36 show that utility-maximization problems can often be solved for the optimal values of X and Y as the functions of the problems' parameters, P_X, P_Y, and I. For the case where $P_X = .25$, $P_Y = 1$, and $I = 2.00$, these equations yield the optimal results derived previously ($X^* = 4$, $Y^* = 1$). Now we could also compute such optimal values for any other pre-assigned values of the parameters P_X, P_Y, and I. As we shall see, Equations 4.35 and 4.36 are called the *demand functions* for X and Y, respectively.

Interpretation of λ

Returning to our specific numerical example, the first-order conditions (Equation 4.20 or 4.21) can also be solved for λ at the optimal point. Since

$$.5\,X^{-.5}\,Y^{.5} = .25\lambda \tag{4.37}$$

and $X^* = 4$ and $Y^* = 1$, we have

$$.5(4)^{-.5}(1)^{.5} = .25\lambda \tag{4.38}$$

or

$$.25 = .25\lambda \tag{4.39}$$

and so

$$\lambda = 1. \tag{4.40}$$

Somewhat loosely speaking, this equation says that an extra dollar of income, if spent optimally, would yield an extra unit of utility. Suppose, for example, income were to be $2.10. Assuming $P_X = .25$ and $P_Y = 1$, Equations 4.35 and 4.36 can be used to show that with this new income

$$X^* = \frac{2.10}{.50} = 4.2$$

$$(4.41)$$

$$Y^* = \frac{2.10}{2} = 1.05,$$

and now utility is given by

$$\text{utility} = \sqrt{X \cdot Y} = \sqrt{4.2 \cdot 1.05} = \sqrt{4.41} = 2.10. \quad (4.42)$$

An increase in income of $.10 has raised utility by .10, as λ predicted.

Corner Solutions

This simple example can also be used to illustrate corner solutions. Consider a third good, say ice cream sundaes (Z), which cost $2.00 each. Suppose utility for the three goods (soft drinks, hamburgers, and sundaes) is given by

$$\text{utility} = U(X, Y, Z) = X^{.5}Y^{.5}(1 + Z)^{.5}. \quad (4.43)$$

We could slog through the first-order conditions for a maximum here,[6] but an alternative route may offer greater insight. Let us compute the marginal utilities for X, Y, and Z:

$$MU_X = \frac{\partial U}{\partial X} = .5 X^{-.5} Y^{.5}(1 + Z)^{.5}$$

$$MU_Y = \frac{\partial U}{\partial Y} = .5 X^{.5} Y^{-.5}(1 + Z)^{.5} \quad (4.44)$$

$$MU_Z = \frac{\partial U}{\partial Z} = .5 X^{.5} Y^{.5}(1 + Z)^{-.5}.$$

Notice that for all of these functions marginal utility is a declining function of the good in question. Consider now the point $X = 4$, $Y = 1$, and $Z = 0$. This point is clearly affordable with an income of $2.00. For this consumption bundle,

$$MU_X = .25$$

$$MU_Y = 1 \quad (4.45)$$

$$MU_Z = 1$$

[6] The reader may wish to show that the optimal Z here is $Z^* = -1/3$. But, although short selling can occur in some contexts, such a negative consumption level has no meaning in the current problem, so $Z^* = 0$ is the optimal choice.

and

$$\frac{MU_X}{P_X} = \frac{.25}{.25} = 1$$

$$\frac{MU_Y}{P_Y} = \frac{1}{1} = 1 \tag{4.46}$$

$$\frac{MU_Z}{P_Z} = \frac{1}{2} = 0.5.$$

Hence, with this hypothetical consumption bundle, goods X and Y yield the same marginal utility per dollar spent, but good Z falls short of this common marginal benefit–marginal cost ratio. Even when no sundaes are bought, the marginal gain from buying a small amount would fall short of the opportunity cost incurred. Choosing $Z = 0$ is the best this person can do in these circumstances. Of course, if he or she had more income and chose to buy more X and Y, the marginal utilities of these goods would fall. Eventually, with more money to spend, it might make sense to buy a sundae to complement the hamburgers and soft drinks being consumed.[7]

INDIRECT UTILITY FUNCTION

The example in the previous section illustrated the principle that it is often possible to manipulate the first-order conditions for a constrained utility-maximization problem to solve for the optimal values of $X_1, X_2, \ldots, X_n$. These optimal values in general will depend on the prices of all the goods and on the individuals' income. That is,

$$X_1^* = X_1(P_1, P_2, \ldots, P_n, I)$$

$$X_2^* = X_2(P_1, P_2, \ldots, P_n, I)$$

$$\cdot \tag{4.47}$$

$$\cdot$$

$$\cdot$$

$$X_n^* = X_n(P_1, P_2, \ldots, P_n, I).$$

In later chapters we will analyze in more detail this set of *demand functions*, which show the dependence of the quantity of each X_i demanded on $P_1, P_2, \ldots, P_n$ and I. Here we wish to point out that the optimal values of the X's from Equations 4.47 can be substituted in the original utility function (Equation 4.4) to yield

---

[7] Again, the reader may wish to show that with an income of $10 (and prices unchanged), the optimal choices are $X^* = 16$, $Y^* = 4$, $Z^* = 1$.

$$\text{maximum utility} = U(X_1^*, X_2^*, \ldots, X_n^*)$$

$$= U[X_1(P_1, P_2, \ldots, P_n, I),$$

$$X_2(P_1, P_2, \ldots, P_n, I), \tag{4.48}$$

$$\ldots X_n(P_1, P_2, \ldots, P_n, I)]$$

$$= V(P_1, P_2, \ldots, P_n, I).$$

In other words, because of the individual's desire to maximize utility, given a budget constraint, the optimal level of utility obtainable will depend *indirectly* on the prices of the goods being bought and on the individual's income. This dependence is reflected by the indirect utility function V. If either prices or income were to change, the level of utility that can be attained would also be affected. Sometimes, in both consumer theory and in many other contexts, it is possible to use this indirect approach to study how changes in economic circumstances affect various kinds of outcomes, such as utility or (later in this book) firms' costs.

Numerical Example

In our two-good example, we found (Equations 4.35 and 4.36)

$$X^* = \frac{I}{2P_X}$$

$$Y^* = \frac{I}{2P_Y}. \tag{4.49}$$

Substituting these into the utility function gives

$$\text{maximum utility} = U(X^*, Y^*) = (X^*)^{.5}(Y^*)^{.5} \tag{4.50}$$

$$= \left(\frac{I}{2P_X}\right)^{.5}\left(\frac{I}{2P_Y}\right)^{.5} \tag{4.51}$$

$$= \frac{I}{2P_X^{.5}P_Y^{.5}}. \tag{4.52}$$

With $I = 2$, $P_X = .25$, and $P_Y = 1$, Equation 4.52 shows that maximum utility can be indirectly computed as

$$\text{maximum utility} = \frac{2}{2(.25)^{.5}(1)^{.5}} = 2, \tag{4.53}$$

which is the same value we derived from the direct utility function (Equation 4.28). More generally, notice that increases in income raise (indirect) utility whereas increases in prices cause utility to fall.

DUAL TO THE UTILITY-MAXIMUM PROBLEM

In Chapter 2 we pointed out that many constrained-maximum problems have associated "dual" constrained-minimum problems. For the case of utility maximization, the associated dual minimization problem concerns allocating income in such a way as to achieve a given utility level with the minimal expen-

Figure 4.5   *The Individual's Dual Expenditure Minimization Problem*

The dual of the individual's utility-maximization problem is to attain a given utility level (U_2) with minimal expenditures. An expenditure level of E_1 does not permit U_2 to be reached, whereas E_1 provides more spending power than is strictly necessary. With expenditures E_2 the individual can just reach U_2 by consuming X^* and Y^*.

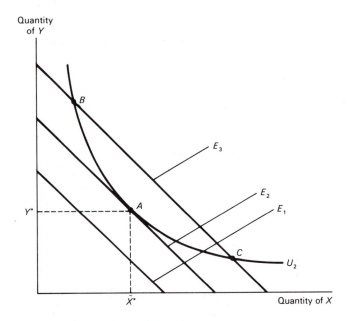

diture. This problem is clearly analogous to the primary utility-maximization problem, but the goals and constraints of the problems have been reversed. Figure 4.5 illustrates this dual expenditure minimization problem. There the individual must attain utility level U_2—this is now the constraint in the problem. Three possible expenditure amounts (E_1, E_2, and E_3) are shown as three "budget constraint" lines in the figure. Expenditure level E_1 is clearly too small to achieve U_2. Hence it cannot solve the dual problem. With expenditures given by E_3, the individual can reach U_2 (at either of the two points B or C), but this is not the minimal expenditure level required. Rather, E_2 clearly provides just enough total expenditures to reach U_2 (at point A), and this is in fact the solution to the dual problem. By comparing Figures 4.2 and 4.5, it is obvious that both the primary utility-maximization approach and the dual expenditure minimization approach yield the same solution (X^*, Y^*)—they are simply alternative ways of viewing the same process. Often the expenditure minimization approach is more useful, however, because expenditures are directly observable whereas utility is not.

More formally, the individual's dual expenditure minimization problem is to choose $X_1, X_2, \ldots, X_n$ so as to minimize

$$\text{total expenditures} = E = P_1X_1 + P_2X_2 + \cdots + P_nX_n, \quad (4.54)$$

subject to the constraint

$$\text{utility} = U_2 = U(X_1, X_2, \ldots, X_n). \tag{4.55}$$

The optimal amounts of $X_1, X_2, \ldots, X_n$ chosen in this problem will depend on the prices of the various goods $(P_1, P_2, \ldots, P_n)$ and on the required utility level U_2. If any of the prices were to change or if the individual had a different utility "target," another commodity bundle would be optimal. This dependence can be summarized by an *expenditure function*.

Definition:

Expenditure Function
The individual's expenditure function shows the minimal expenditures necessary to achieve a given utility level for a particular set of prices. That is,

$$\text{minimal expenditures} = E(P_1, P_2, \ldots, P_n, U). \tag{4.56}$$

This statement shows that the expenditure function and the indirect utility function are inverse functions of one another (compare Equations 4.48 and 4.56). In the next chapter we will see how this relationship is quite useful in allowing us to examine the theory of how individuals respond to price changes. The application in that chapter also indicates how the expenditure function approach can be useful for addressing practical problems involved in constructing price indices.

Numerical Example

Returning again to our simple Cobb-Douglas case, the individual's dual problem is to minimize

$$E = P_X X + P_Y Y \tag{4.57}$$

subject to

$$\text{utility} = \overline{U} = X^{.5} Y^{.5}, \tag{4.58}$$

where $\overline{U}$ is the utility target.

The Lagrangian expression for this problem is

$$\mathcal{L} = P_X X + P_Y Y + (\overline{U} - X^{.5} Y^{.5}), \tag{4.59}$$

and the first-order conditions for a minimum are

$$\frac{\partial \mathcal{L}}{\partial X} = P_X - .5\lambda X^{-.5} Y^{.5} = 0$$

$$\frac{\partial \mathcal{L}}{\partial Y} = P_Y - .5\lambda X^{.5} Y^{-.5} = 0 \tag{4.60}$$

$$\frac{\partial \mathcal{L}}{\partial \lambda} = \overline{U} - X^{.5} Y^{.5} = 0.$$

These can again be solved by moving the terms in λ to the right and dividing:

$$\frac{P_Y}{P_X} = \frac{.5\lambda X^{.5}Y^{-.5}}{.5\lambda^{-.5}Y^{.5}} = \frac{X}{Y} \tag{4.61}$$

or

$$P_X X = P_Y Y, \tag{4.62}$$

which is precisely the same first-order condition we had before (see Equation 4.33). Now, however, we wish to solve for expenditures as a function of P_X, P_Y, and U—that is, we wish to eliminate X and Y from Equation 4.57. Although the algebra here is not difficult, it is important to keep this end goal in mind because you can easily become confused as to whether you have found a solution or not. Substituting Equation 4.61 into the expenditure function yields

$$E = P_X X^* + P_Y Y^* = 2P_X X^* \tag{4.63}$$

so

$$X^* = \frac{E}{2P_X} \tag{4.64}$$

and similarly,

$$Y^* = \frac{E}{2P_Y}. \tag{4.65}$$

But, the utility target requires

$$\overline{U} = (X^*)^{.5}(Y^*)^{.5} \tag{4.66}$$

so

$$\overline{U} = \left(\frac{E}{2P_X}\right)^{.5}\left(\frac{E}{2P_Y}\right)^{.5} = \frac{E}{2P_X^{.5}P_Y^{.5}}. \tag{4.67}$$

Making use of the inverse relationship between indirect utility and expenditures, we have the function

$$E = 2\overline{U}P_X^{.5}P_Y^{.5} \tag{4.68}$$

as the minimum expenditure necessary to reach $\overline{U}$. If, as before, $\overline{U} = 2$, $P_X = .25$, and $P_Y = 1$, we have a required expenditure of

$$E = 2(2)(.25)^{.5}(1)^{.5} = 2. \tag{4.69}$$

Notice this was the original value for income with which we started this problem. We know that this income level is indeed sufficient to attain a utility level of 2. Of course, as the expenditure function in Equation 4.68 shows, a higher utility target would require greater expenditures. Similarly, an increase in P_X or P_Y would also require greater expenditures to attain a given utility target. Without such added expenditures, the utility target would have to be reduced—the individual would be worse off.

Our example from the theory of choice has therefore come full circle. We have now demonstrated two dual ways to solve the utility-maximization problem. In later chapters we will use this specific example (especially the expenditure function in Equation 4.68) to illustrate many of our theoretical analyses.

SUMMARY

In this chapter we examined the basic economic model of utility maximization subject to a budget constraint. Although we approached this problem in a variety of ways, all of these approaches lead to the same basic result:

- To reach a constrained maximum, an individual should spend all available income and should choose a commodity bundle such that the *MRS* between any two goods is equal to the ratio of those goods' market prices. This basic tangency will result in the individual equating the ratios of the marginal utility to market price for every good that is actually consumed. Such a result is common to most constrained optimization problems.

- The tangency conditions are only the first-order conditions for a constrained maximum, however. To ensure that these conditions are also sufficient, the individual's indifference curve map must exhibit a diminishing *MRS*. In formal terms, the utility function must be quasi-concave.

- The tangency conditions must also be modified to allow for corner solutions in which the optimal level of consumption of some goods is 0. In this case, the ratio of marginal utility to price for such a good will be below the common marginal benefit–marginal cost ratio for goods actually bought.

- A consequence of the assumption of constrained utility maximization is that the individual's optimal choices will depend implicitly on the parameters of his or her budget constraint. That is, the choices observed will be implicit functions of all prices and income. Utility will therefore also be an indirect function of these parameters.

- The dual to the constrained utility-maximization problem is to minimize the expenditure required to reach a given utility target. Although this dual approach yields the same optimal solution as the primal constrained-maximum problem, it also yields additional insight into the theory of choice. Specifically, this approach leads to expenditure functions in which the spending required to reach a given utility target depends on the goods' market prices.

Application

THE LUMP-SUM PRINCIPLE

The constrained utility-maximization model introduced in this chapter can be used to derive many insights about economic behavior. Here we will examine one of the most important of these—the "lump-sum" principle. In very general terms this principle states that government taxation or subsidy policies can achieve their goals at minimal costs if they focus on the overall purchasing power of individuals rather than on taxing or subsidizing specific commodities. Here we will examine the principle directly

Figure 4.6   *The Efficiency of Lump-Sum Taxes*

A per-unit tax on good X causes the utility-maximizing point to shift to X_1, Y_1, and utility to fall from U_2 to U_1. A lump-sum tax that collects the same revenue would shift the budget constraint to I'' and would reduce utility only to U_2. The lump-sum tax therefore may be preferred on efficiency grounds.

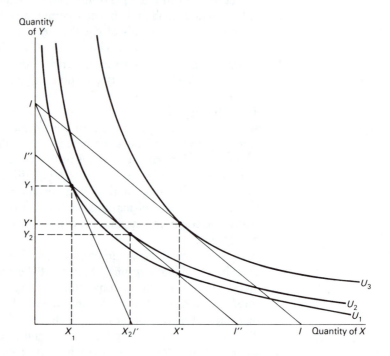

as it applies to taxes, but will offer a few observations on subsidies at the conclusion of the example.

What we specifically wish to show is that if two taxes—one a lump-sum tax on general purchasing power and the other a tax on a specific commodity—collect equal tax revenue, then the lump-sum tax will do so at lower cost since it will reduce the individual's utility the least. The proof is illustrated for the two-good case in Figure 4.6.

Initially, the individual has I to spend and chooses to consume X^* and Y^*, since that point obeys the budget constraint

$$I = P_X X^* + P_Y Y^* \qquad (4.70)$$

and the tangency condition for a maximum. A tax on good X of t dollars per unit would raise its price to $P_X + t$, and the budget constraint would become

$$I = (P_X + t)X + P_Y Y. \qquad (4.71)$$

With that budget constraint (shown as line I' in Figure 4.6), the individual would be forced to accept a lower utility level and would choose to consume the combination X_1, Y_1. Total tax revenues (T) would be given by

$$T = tX_1. \qquad (4.72)$$

A general purchasing power tax that also collected T dollars in revenue would leave the individual with $I - T$ dollars to spend, and the budget constraint would be given by

$$I'' = I - T = P_X X + P_Y Y. \quad (4.73)$$

With that budget constraint,[8] the individual will choose to consume X_2, Y_2, as shown in Figure 4.6. Notice that even though the individual pays the same tax bill in both instances, the combination chosen under the purchasing-power tax yields a higher utility than does the single commodity tax. An intuitive explanation of this result is based on the recognition that a single commodity tax affects an individual's well-being in two ways. It reduces general purchasing power, and it directs consumption away from the taxed commodity. A purchasing-power tax incorporates only the first effect, and hence individuals are better off under it. Now we examine some practical illustrations of this principle.

Applications to Tax Policy
Although the previous theoretical development shows that lump-sum taxes are more efficient than taxes on a single commodity (because they minimize the utility lost for a given amount of tax revenue), some care must be taken in extrapolating this result to the real world. For example, it is not accurate to use the result to argue that income taxes are preferably to excise taxes on certain commodities in the belief that income taxes approximate the lump-sum principle. Since, as we show later (in Chapter 22), income taxes affect an individual's net, after-tax wage rate, they may also affect his or her work behavior, and hence they are not truly lump-sum in nature. Indeed, in an important 1981 study, J. Hausman found that the average taxpayer loses about 22 percent more utility (or real income) under the existing U.S. progressive

income tax than would be lost from paying lump-sum taxes of an equal magnitude.[9] Hausman also finds that the losses from income taxation could be roughly halved if a proportional rather than progressive income tax were used, since the proportional tax avoids the distorting effects of high, progressive tax rates. Of course, all taxes violate the lump-sum principle to some extent, since all affect relative prices in some way. Other considerations (such as ease of collection) may also affect some taxes' desirability. But Hausman's (and other researchers') results suggest that it may be possible to design "optimal" tax policies that collect desired amounts of governmental revenues with the minimal utility losses to individuals.

Applications to Transfer Policy
One of the fastest growing portions of government budgets throughout the world is transfer payment programs. Such programs can be categorized into two broad types: income maintenance programs and in-kind transfer programs. Transfer payments of the former type are provided to families in cash. In the United States the largest such programs are social security, aid to families with dependent children, and unemployment insurance. In-kind programs, on the other hand, provide specific goods to individuals at below-market prices. These programs include medicare, food stamps, and subsidized housing. Such in-kind programs have grown somewhat more rapidly than the cash transfer programs, largely because they seem quite popular with legislators and voters.

A direct application of the lump-sum principle, however, suggests some caution in following the in-kind transfer route. By reversing the logic of Figure 4.6, it is easy to show that a given dollar amount of transfers will raise

---

[8] The budget constraint given by Equation 4.73 must pass through the point X_1, Y_1 (as drawn in Figure 4.6). Since $I = (P_X + t)X_1 + P_Y Y_1$, it must be true that $I'' = I - tX_1 = P_X X_1 + P_Y Y_1$.

[9] Jerry A. Hausman, "Labor Supply," in Henry J. Aaron and Joseph A. Pechman, *How Taxes Affect Economic Behavior* (Washington, D.C.: Brookings Institution, 1981), p. 54.

utility more if it is provided in a lump-sum way than if it is provided by subsidizing the purchase of specific commodities. Again the intuitive reasoning behind this result is that the ability of subsidies to raise individuals' utility levels is mitigated to a degree because of the distortion of choices brought about by such subsidies whereas lump-sum subsidies contain no such distortions. Hence a dollar in in-kind transfers is worth less to the individual than is a dollar in cash.

Empirical evidence tends to support this proposition. In a 1977 report on the antipoverty effects of various transfer programs, T. Smeeding used an analysis of individuals' expenditure functions to show that $1 of existing subsidies for food, housing, and medical care was worth

considerably less than $1 in cash to the individuals who received the subsidies:[10] Specifically, the author found that food subsidies were worth about 88 percent, housing subsidies about 56 percent, and medical care subsidies about 68 percent of their actual cash values. The author therefore concluded that the ability of such programs to increase the overall well-being of poor people was considerably lessened by providing subsidies for specific goods rather than cash.

[10] Timothy M. Smeeding, "The Antipoverty Effectiveness of In-Kind Transfers," *Journal of Human Resources* 12, no. 3 (Summer 1977): 365.

SUGGESTED READINGS

Hicks, J. R. *Value and Capital.* Oxford: Clarendon Press, 1939.

A classic work. Detailed development of notions of substitutes and complements and of the "composite commodity" theorem (see Chapter 6). Results discussed both intuitively and (in an appendix) mathematically.

Katzner, Donald W. *Static Demand Theory.* New York: The Macmillan Company, 1970. Chaps. 2 and 3.

Theoretical treatment of preferences and of the conditions under which preferences can be represented by a utility function.

Leibenstein, H. "Bandwagon, Snob, and Veblen Effects in the Theory of Consumers' Demand." *Quarterly Journal of Economics* 64 (May 1970): 183–207.

Discusses some ways of formalizing commonsense ideas of how preferences are formed and whether they change over short periods.

Marshall, A. *Principles of Economics.* 8th ed. London: Macmillan & Co., Ltd., 1920. Chaps. I–IV. Book III.

Early basic text. Still a very readable and interesting treatment of consumer theory.

Russell, R. Robert, and Wilkinson, Maurice. *Microeconomics: A Synthesis of Modern and Neoclassical Theory.* New York: John Wiley & Sons, 1979. Chaps. 2 and 3.

Advanced but readable treatment of the relationship between preference orderings and utility theory.

Samuelson, P. A. *Foundations of Economic Analysis.* Cambridge, Mass.: Harvard University Press, 1947. Chap. 5.

Detailed, calculus-based treatment of consumer theory. One of the first to introduce the revealed preference concept and the integrability problem (see Chapter 6).

PROBLEMS

4.1

Each day Paul, who is in third grade, eats lunch at school. He only likes Twinkies (T) and Orange Slice (S), and these provide him a utility of

$$\text{utility} = U(T, S) = \sqrt{TS}.$$

    a.   If Twinkies cost $.10 each and Slice costs $.25 per cup, how should Paul spend the $1 his mother gives him in order to maximize his utility?

    b.   If the school tries to discourage Twinkie consumption by raising the price to $.40, by how much will Paul's mother have to increase his lunch allowance to provide him with the same level of utility he received in part (a)? How many Twinkies and cups of Slice will he buy now (assuming that it is possible to purchase fractional amounts of both of these goods)?

4.2

    a.   One young connoisseur has $300 to spend to build a small wine cellar. She enjoys two vintages in particular: an expensive 1981 French Bordeaux (W_F) at $20 per bottle and a less expensive 1983 California varietal wine (W_C) priced at $4. How much of each wine should she purchase if her utility is characterized by the following function?

$$U(W_F, W_C) = W_F^{2/3} W_C^{1/3}.$$

    b.   When she arrived at the wine store, our young oenologist discovered that the price of the 1981 French Bordeaux had fallen to $10 a bottle because of a decline in the value of the franc. If the price of the California wine remains stable at $4 per bottle, how much of each wine should our friend purchase to maximize utility under these altered conditions?

4.3

    a.   On a given evening J. P. enjoys the consumption of cigars (C) and brandy (B) according to the function

$$U(C, B) = 20C - C^2 + 18B - 3B^2.$$

How many cigars and glasses of brandy does he consume during an evening? (Cost is no object to J. P.)

    b.   Lately, however, J. P. has been advised by his doctors that he should limit the sum of brandy and cigars consumed to 5. How many glasses of brandy and cigars will he consume under these circumstances?

4.4

    a.   Mr. Odde Ball enjoys commodities X and Y according to the utility function

$$U(X, Y) = \sqrt{X^2 + Y^2}.$$

Maximize Mr. Ball's utility, if $P_X = \$3$, $P_Y = \$4$, and he has $50 to spend.

Hint: It may be easier here to maximize U^2 rather than U. Why won't this alter your results?

    b.   Graph Mr. Ball's indifference curve and its point of tangency with his budget constraint. What does the graph say about Mr. Ball's behavior? Have you found a true maximum?

4.5

Suppose that an individual consumes three goods—food, clothing, and automobiles. Denote the quantities of these goods consumed by X_1, X_2, and X_3, respectively. Suppose that the individual's utility function is given by

$$U = 5 \log X_1 + 4 \log X_2 + \log (1 + X_3),$$

that the prices of the goods are given by

$$P_1 = 1$$

$$P_2 = 2$$

$$P_3 = 2000,$$

and that the individual's total income is $9,000. Automobiles, however, have the property that they must be bought in discrete units (that is, X_3 must equal 0, 1, 2, and so on). It is impossible, in this simple model, to buy one-half of a car.

Given these constraints, how will an individual allocate income so as to maximize utility? Discuss the corner solution inherent in the problem. A graph may help your explanation.

4.6

Ms. Caffeine enjoys coffee (C) and tea (T) according to the function

$$U(C, T) = 3C + 4T.$$

What does her utility function say about her *MRS* of coffee for tea? If coffee and tea cost $3 each and Ms. Caffeine has $12 to spend on these products, how much coffee and tea should she buy to maximize her utility? Draw the graph of her indifference curve and budget constraint, and show that the utility-maximizing point is a boundary solution at which the usual utility-maximizing condition does not hold. Under what condition would the usual condition hold? Would there be a unique maximizing point in that case?

4.7

Mr. A derives utility from martinis (M) in proportion to the number he drinks:

$$U(M) = M.$$

Mr. A is very particular about his martinis, however: He only enjoys them made in the exact proportion of two parts gin (G) to one part vermouth (V). Hence we can rewrite Mr. A's utility function as

$$U(M) = U(G, V) = \min\left(\frac{G}{2}, V\right).$$

a.   Graph Mr. A's indifference curve in terms of G and V for various levels of utility. Show that regardless of the prices of the two ingredients, Mr. A will never alter the way he mixes martinis.

b.   Calculate the demand functions for G and V.

c.   Using the results from part (b), what is Mr. A's indirect utility function?

d.   Calculate Mr. A's expenditure function; for each level of utility, show spending as a function of P_G and P_V.

4.8

Assume that consumers are choosing between housing services measured in square feet and consumption of other goods aggregated and measured in dollars.

a.   Show the equilibrium position in a diagram.

b.   Now suppose that the government agrees to subsidize consumers by paying 50 percent of their housing cost. How will their budget line change? Show the new equilibrium.

c.   Show in a diagram the minimum amount of income supplement the government would have to give individuals instead of housing subsidy to make them as well-off as they were in situation (b).

4.9

Suppose that an individual has three uses for his time: sleeping, working, and consuming goods. Let

$$S = \text{hours of sleep}$$

$$L = \text{hours of work}$$

$$C = \text{hours of consumption.}$$

Consumption, of course, is costly, so assume that consumption costs a flat rate of 10 cents per minute. Consequently,

$$\text{cost of consumption} = \$6 \times C.$$

Suppose that the individual receives utility from sleeping and consumption given by

$$U(S, C) = S^{1/4} C^{3/4}.$$

Finally, assume that the individual's entire income comes from working and that for his work he receives \$4 per hour.

    a.   If this person is to maximize utility, how many hours should he spend sleeping, working, and consuming?

    b.   More generally, explain why this is really a problem in choosing two "goods," S and C. What is the budget constraint for these two goods? That is, what are the opportunity costs of S and C, and how much "income" does this person have to devote to them?

    c.   What kind of utility function does this person have? Using the results for this type of function described in the chapter, can you calculate his demand functions for S and C as functions of the prices and income described in part (b)?

    d.   What is this person's expenditure function—that is, what are his minimum necessary expenditures as a function of utility and the "prices" of S and C? What is unusual about this function?

4.10

    a.   Ms. J, a sports buff, enjoys playing golf (G) and tennis (T) each week and derives enjoyment according to the utility function

$$U(G, T) = G^{1/2} T^{1/2}.$$

    If she has \$24 a week to spend on these two activities, and the price of a round of golf equals that of a game of tennis, \$4, how will Ms. J pursue her athletic activities in order to maximize utility?

    b.   Being a businesswoman with a heavy schedule, however, Ms. J has only a limited amount of time—16 hours—to devote to athletic activities each week. If a round of golf takes 4 hours and a game of tennis 2 hours, how many hours would Ms. J pursue athletic activities under the circumstances of part (a)? How should she reallocate her activities in order to maximize her utility under the time constraint now imposed? Graph this new (lower) level of utility maximization and show graphically that it also satisfies the constraint of part (a).

4.11

Develop a graphical argument analogous to Figure 4.6 to show that a given government expenditure on lump-sum transfers provides greater utility than does the same expenditure on subsidies for the purchase of a particular good.

EXTENSIONS

USEFUL
FORMS OF
UTILITY
FUNCTIONS

In Chapter 4 we showed that the hypothesis of utility maximization together with a particular form for the utility function allow us to solve for demand functions for the various goods consumed. Here we examine a few specific utility functions and ask the student to verify that these lead to particular kinds of demand functions. These demand functions are often used in empirical work. All of the examples presented are based on only two goods (X_1 and X_2 with prices P_1 and P_2), but these are easily generalized to many goods.

E4.1 Cobb-Douglas.

Suppose utility $= U(X_1, X_2) = X_1^{\beta_1} \cdot X_2^{\beta_2}$, where $\beta_1, \beta_2 > 0$ and, for convenience, assume $\beta_1 + \beta_2 = 1$.

a. Show that the utility-maximization hypothesis implies that the quantities of X_1 and X_2 chosen will obey

$$\frac{P_1 X_1}{I} = \beta_1 \quad \text{and} \quad \frac{P_2 X_2}{I} = \beta_2.$$

b. How do you interpret these demand functions? What do they say about the fraction of income spent on good X_1 or good X_2? Does this form seem quite restrictive?

c. How do changes in P_2 affect the quantity of X_1 chosen (and vice versa)? Does this seem realistic?

E4.2 Linear Expenditure System.

Suppose utility $= U(X_1, X_2) = \beta_1 \log(X_1 - \gamma_1) + \beta_2 \log(X_2 - \gamma_2)$, where β_1, $\beta_2 > 0$ and $\beta_1 + \beta_2 = 1$ and $X_1 > \gamma_1 > 0$, $X_2 > \gamma_2 > 0$.

a. Show that the Cobb-Douglas function represents a special case of this utility function where $\gamma_1 = \gamma_2 = 0$.

b. Show that the utility-maximizing choices for X_1 and X_2 with this utility function are given by

$$P_1 X_1 = P_1 \gamma_1 + \beta_1 [I - (P_1 \gamma_1 + P_2 \gamma_2)]$$

and

$$P_2 X_2 = P_2 \gamma_2 + \beta_2 [I - (P_1 \gamma_1 + P_2 \gamma_2)].$$

How would you interpret these "linear expenditure" functions? Show that the γ's represent minimum necessary expenditures on X_1 and X_2 and that the β's represent marginal budget shares for each X for expenditures above the minimal amounts.

c. Explain how changes in P_2 affect the quantity of X_1 chosen in this system of demand equations. In what way does this generalize the assumption implicit in the Cobb-Douglas case?

This particular system of demand functions was first utilized by Richard Stone in "Linear Expenditure Systems and Demand Analysis: An Application to the Pattern of British Demand," *The Economic Journal* (September 1954): 511–527. It has been widely used in empirical work ever since.

E4.3 CES.

Suppose utility $= U(X_1, X_2) = X_1^\beta + X_2^\beta$, where $\beta \le 1$.

a. What is the form for this utility function if $\beta = 1$? How would the indifference curves look in this case? How would they look for $\beta < 1$?

b. Show that for the case $\beta < 1$, maximizing this function subject to the usual budget constant yields

$$\frac{P_1 X_1}{I} = \frac{P_1^\kappa}{P_1^\kappa + P_2^\kappa} \quad \text{and} \quad \frac{P_2 X_2}{I} = \frac{P_2^\kappa}{P_1^\kappa + P_2^\kappa}, \text{ where } \kappa = -\beta/(1 - \beta).$$

c. How do you interpret these budget share equations? Does the share devoted to, say, good X_1 depend on both P_1 and P_2? In what special case would the budget shares be independent of both prices? What would these shares be? What Cobb-Douglas function would give the same result?

d. Show that if $\beta < 0$, changes in P_1 move the budget share in the same direction (that is, show that $ds_1/dP_1 > 0$, where $s_1 = P_1 X_1/I$). Alternatively, show that if $\beta > 0$ then $ds_1/dP_1 < 0$. How do you interpret these results?

e. In what ways might this utility function be generalized? Describe the results of some of these generalizations.

Note: The acronym CES stands for "Constant Elasticity of Substitution," a function that is commonly used in production theory. In Chapter 10 we will describe the elasticity of substitution concept and investigate the CES function in more detail.

CHAPTER 5

Effects of Changes in Income or in a Good's Price

In this chapter we will use the utility-maximization model to study how the quantity of a good that an individual chooses is affected by a change in that good's price. This examination will result in our being able to construct the individual's demand curve for the good. In the process we will provide a number of insights into the nature of this price response and into the kinds of *ceteris paribus* assumptions that lie behind most analyses of demand. Before starting, however, we will find it helpful to explore in a general way how changes in purchasing power affect individuals' choices. The study of such responses is perhaps the most elementary application of the utility-maximization model and will also prove useful when we come to discussing price changes.

HOMOGE-NEITY OF DEMAND FUNCTIONS

As we pointed out in Chapter 4, in principle it will always be possible to solve the necessary conditions of a utility maximum for the optimal levels of X_1, X_2, ..., X_n (and λ) as functions of all prices and income. Mathematically, this can be expressed as n demand functions of the form

$$X_1^* = D_1(P_1, P_2, \ldots, P_n, I)$$

$$X_2^* = D_2, (P_1, P_2, \ldots, P_n, I)$$

$$\cdot$$

$$\cdot \qquad\qquad\qquad\qquad\qquad\qquad (5.1)$$

$$\cdot$$

$$X_n^* = D_n(P_1, P_2, \ldots, P_n, I),$$

where we now use the functional notation D for "demand." Once we know the functions $D_1, D_2, \ldots, D_n$ and the values of $P_1, P_2, \ldots, P_n$ and I, we can "predict" how much of each good the individual will buy. In later sections we shall be interested in what happens to the optimal amount of, say, X_1 when P_1 changes. We shall also investigate what happens to X_1 when income changes or (in Chapter 6) when the price of another good changes. Such questions involve the study of the derivatives of the demand functions; we are interested in comparing utility-maximization choices under alternative circumstances, and the demand functions provide a shorthand way for recording the results of this *comparative statics analysis*.

One comparative statics "theorem" can easily be demonstrated here. If we were to double all prices and income (indeed if we were to multiply them all by any positive constant), the optimal quantities demanded would remain unchanged. Doubling all prices and income changes only the units by which we count, not the "real" quantity of goods demanded. This result can be seen in a number of ways, although perhaps the easiest is through a graphic approach. Referring back to Figures 4.1 and 4.2, it is clear that if we double P_X, P_Y, and I, we shall not affect the graph of the budget constraint. Hence X^*, Y^* will still be the combination that is chosen. $P_X X + P_Y Y = I$ is the same constraint as $2P_X X + 2P_Y Y = 2I$. Somewhat more technically, we can write this result as saying that for any good X_i,

$$X_i^* = D_i(P_1, P_2, \ldots, P_n, I) = D_i(tP_1, tP_2, \ldots, tP_n, tI) \tag{5.2}$$

for any $t > 0$. Functions that obey the property illustrated in Equation 5.2 are said to be homogeneous of degree 0.[1] Hence we have shown that individual *demand functions are homogeneous of degree 0 in all prices and income*. Changing all prices and income in the same proportions will not affect the physical quantities of goods demanded. This result shows that individuals' demands will not be affected by a "pure" inflation during which all prices and incomes rise proportionally. They will continue to demand the same bundle of goods. Of course, if an inflation were not pure (that is, if some prices rose more rapidly than others), this would not be the case.

CHANGES IN INCOME

As an individual's purchasing power rises, it is natural to expect that the quantity of each good purchased will also increase. This situation is illustrated in Figure 5.1. As expenditures increase from I_1 to I_2, to I_3, the quantity of X demanded increases from X_1 to X_2, to X_3. Also, the quantity of Y increases from Y_1 to Y_2, to Y_3. Notice that the budget lines I_1, I_2, and I_3 are all parallel, reflecting the fact that only income is changing, not the relative prices of X and Y. Since the ratio P_X/P_Y stays constant, the utility-maximizing conditions also require that the *MRS* stay constant as the individual moves to higher levels of satisfaction. The *MRS* is therefore the same at point (X_3, Y_3) as at (X_1, Y_1).

The information from Figure 5.1 can be used to construct *Engel curves*, which record the relationship between the quantity of X purchased and total

---

[1]More generally, a function $f(X_1, X_2, \ldots, X_n)$ is said to be homogeneous of degree k if $f(tX_1, tX_2, \ldots, tX_n) = t^k f(X_1, X_2, \ldots, X_n)$ for any $t > 0$. The most common cases of homogeneous functions are $k = 0$ and $k = 1$. If f is homogeneous of degree 0, doubling all of its arguments leaves f unchanged in value. If f is homogeneous of degree 1, doubling all its arguments will double the value of f. We shall encounter functions homogeneous of degree 1 in Part IV. Notice that the demand functions calculated in Chapter 4 are indeed homogeneous of degree 0.

Figure 5.1   *Effect of an Increase in Income on the Quantities of* X *and* Y *Chosen*

As income increases from I_1 to I_2 to I_3, the optimal (utility-maximizing) choices of *X* and *Y* are shown by the successively higher points of tangency. Notice that the budget constraint shifts in a parallel way because its slope (given by $-P_X/P_Y$) does not change.

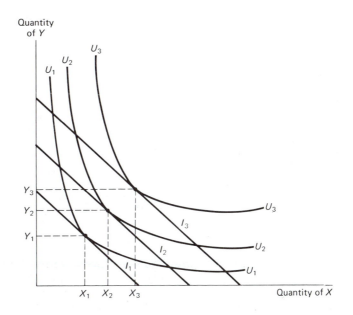

expenditures.[2] Examples of Engel curves appear in Figure 5.2. Notice that these curves are not necessarily straight lines. The demand for some "luxury" goods may increase proportionately more rapidly than income, whereas the demand for "necessities" may grow proportionately less rapidly than income.

Normal and Inferior Goods

In Figures 5.1 and 5.2, both *X* and *Y* increase as income increases—$\partial X/\partial I$ and $\partial Y/\partial I$ are both positive. This might be considered the usual situation, and goods that exhibit this property are called *normal goods* over the range of income change being observed.

For some goods, however, the quantity chosen may decrease as income increases in some ranges. Some examples of these goods might be rotgut whiskey, potatoes, and secondhand clothing. A good *Z* for which $\partial Z/\partial I$ is negative is called an *inferior good*. This phenomenon is illustrated in Figure 5.3. In this diagram the good *Z* is inferior because, for increases in income in the range

---

[2] The curves are named for the Prussian economist Ernst Engel (1821–1896), who was one of the first persons to study systematically the relation between the quantity of a good demanded and income. (See the discussion of Engel's results later in this chapter.)

Figure 5.2   *Engel Curves Derived from the Individual's Indifference Curves*

Engel curves depict the relationship between total expenditures and the quantity of a particular good purchased. In both (a) and (b), the goods are normal because the quantity purchased increases as income increases. The good pictured in (a), however, is a "necessity" in the sense that the *fraction* of expenditures devoted to X declines as income increases. On the other hand, in (b), good Y is a "luxury."

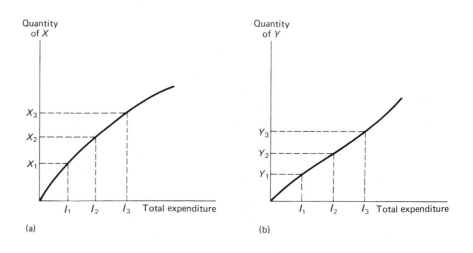

(a)   (b)

Figure 5.3   *An Indifference Curve Map Exhibiting Inferiority*

In this diagram, good Z is inferior because the quantity purchased actually declines as income increases. Y is a normal good (as it must be if there are only two goods available), and purchases of Y increase as total expenditures increase.

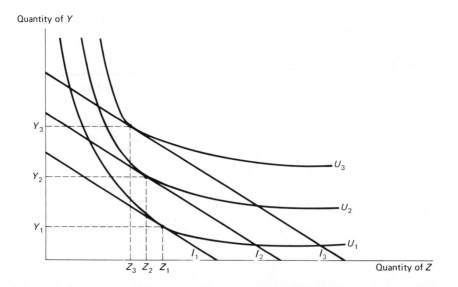

shown, less of Z is actually chosen. Notice that indifference cuves do not have to be "oddly" shaped to exhibit inferiority; although the curves shown in Figure 5.3 continue to obey the assumption of a diminishing MRS, they exhibit inferiority. Good Z is inferior because of the way it relates to the other goods available (good Y here), not because of a peculiarity unique to it. It is clear that for an inferior good, the Engel curve will be negatively sloped. Hence we have developed the following definitions:

Definitions:

Inferior and Normal Goods

A good X_i for which $\partial X_i/\partial I < 0$ over some range of income changes is an *inferior good* in that range. If $\partial X_i/\partial I \geq 0$ over some range of income variation, the good is a *normal,* or "noninferior," *good* in that range.

Engel's Law

Since the eighteenth century, the relationship between income and the consumption of specific items has been studied extensively by economists. Most commonly, expenditure data are collected from a sample of families and are then classified by income levels (or by "social class") to see if any important regularities are visible. Probably the most widely referenced sample data are those used by Engel in his original studies. An abbreviated set of these data, showing the average budgetary allocations made by a sample of 153 Belgian families in 1857, appears in Table 5.1.

From these data Engel drew what was perhaps the first empirical generalization about consumer behavior: The proportion of total expenditure devoted to food declines as income rises. In other words, food is a necessity whose consumption rises less rapidly than does income. That hypothesis has come to

Table 5.1   *Percentage of Total Expenditures on Various Items by Belgian Families in 1857*

	Annual Income		
Expenditure Item	$225–$300	$450–$600	$750–$1000
Food	62.0%	55.0%	50.0%
Clothing	16.0	18.0	18.0
Lodging, light, and fuel	17.0	17.0	17.0
Services (education, legal, health)	4.0	7.5	11.5
Comfort and recreation	1.0	2.5	3.5
Total	100.0	100.0	100.0

Source: Adapted from A. Marshall, *Principles of Economics,* 8th ed. (London: Macmillan & Co., 1920), p. 97.

be known as "Engel's law," and it has been verified in hundreds of studies. It holds true not only within a particular geographic area but also across countries and continents: Cross-country comparisons show that, on the average, individuals in less-developed countries spend a larger percentage of their incomes on food than do individuals in the industrial economies. The percentage of income spent on food also tends to decline over time as incomes rise. For example, in nineteenth-century America, individuals spent nearly 50 percent of their incomes on food. Today that figure has fallen to below 20 percent. Indeed Engel's law appears to be such a consistent empirical finding that some economists have suggested that the proportion of income spent on food might be a useful indicator of poverty. Families that spend more than, say, 35 percent of their income on food might be regarded as "poor," whereas those who spend less than that percentage would not be so regarded.

CHANGES IN A GOOD'S PRICE

The effect of a price change on the quantity of a good demanded is somewhat more complex to analyze than is the effect of a change in income. Geometrically, this is because changing a price involves changing not only the position of the budget constraint but also its slope. Consequently, moving to the new utility-maximizing choice entails not only moving to another indifference curve but also changing the *MRS*. When a price changes, therefore, two analytically different effects come into play. One of these is a *substitution effect*—even if the individual were to stay on the *same* indifference curve, consumption patterns would be allocated so as to equate the *MRS* to the new price ratio. A second effect, the *income effect,* arises because a price change necessarily changes an individual's "real" income—the individual cannot stay on the initial indifference curve but must move to a new one. We begin by analyzing these effects graphically. Then we will provide a mathematical development.

Graphic Analysis of a Fall in Price

Income and substitution effects are illustrated in Figure 5.4. The individual is initially maximizing utility (subject to total expenditures, I) by consuming the combination X^*, Y^*. The initial budget constraint is $I = P_X^1 X + P_Y Y$. Now suppose that the price of X falls to P_X^2. The new budget constraint is given by the equation $I = P_X^2 X + P_Y Y$ in Figure 5.4. It is clear that the new position of maximum utility is at X^{**}, Y^{**}, where the new budget line is tangent to the indifference curve U_2. The movement to this new point can be viewed as being composed of two effects. First, the change in the slope of the budget constraint would have motivated the individual to move to point B, even if choices had been confined to those on the original indifference curve U_1. The dashed line in Figure 5.4 has the same slope as the new budget constraint ($I = P_X^2 X + P_Y Y$), but is drawn to be tangent to U_1 because we are conceptually holding "real" income (that is, utility) constant. A relatively lower price for X causes a move from X^*, Y^* to B if we do not allow the individual to be made better off as a result of the lower price. This movement is a graphic demonstration of the *substitution effect*. The further move from B to the optimal point X^{**}, Y^{**} is analytically identical to the kind of change exhibited earlier for changes in income. Because the price of X has fallen, the individual has a greater "real"

Figure 5.4   *Demonstration of the Income and Substitution Effects of a Fall in the Price of* X

When the price of X falls from P_x^1 to P_x^2, the utility-maximizing choice shifts from X^*, Y^* to X^{**}, Y^{**}. This movement can be broken down into two analytically different effects: first, the substitution effect, involving a movement along the initial indifference curve to point B, where the *MRS* is equal to the new price ratio; and secondly, the income effect, entailing a movement to a higher level of utility, since real income has increased. In the diagram, both the substitution and income effects cause more X to be bought when its price declines. Notice that point I/P_Y is the same as before the price change. This is because P_Y has not changed. Point I/P_Y therefore appears on both the old and new budget constraints.

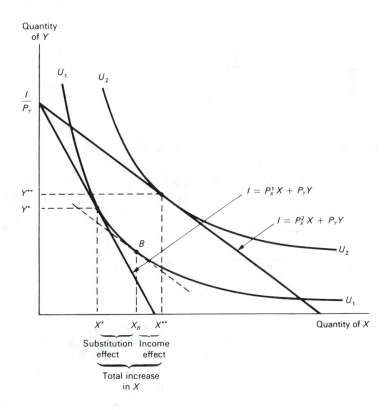

income and can afford a utility level (U_2) that is greater than that which could previously be attained. If X is a normal good, the individual will demand more of it in response to this increase in purchasing power. This observation explains the origin of the term *income effect* for the movement. Overall then, the result of the price decline is to cause more X to be demanded.

It is important to realize that the individual does not actually move from X^*, Y^* to B and then to X^{**}, Y^{**}. We never observe point B; only the two optimal positions are reflected in the individual's behavior. However, the notion of income and substitution effects is analytically valuable because it shows that a price change affects the quantity of X that is demanded in two conceptually different ways. For example, suppose that the price of soft drinks fell from 25 cents to 20 cents while the price of hamburgers stayed at $1. This price change has the effect of increasing the individual's purchasing power. For example, whereas earlier $2 could buy 8 soft drinks, now $2 can buy 10. Therefore the price decline represents an increase in welfare. The individual will choose a different combination of hamburgers and soft drinks than before, if only because the previous optimal selection (say, 1 hamburger and 4 soft drinks) now leaves some extra purchasing power (40 cents in this example). In moving to this new preferred consumption choice, two different effects come into play. First, even if we conceptually hold constant the individual's "real income" (that is, if we *compensate* for the positive effect of the price decline on purchasing power), expenditures still will be adjusted so that the *MRS* is brought into line with the new price ratio (now 5 to 1). We call this compensating response the *substitution effect*. Even at a constant real income, there is an incentive to substitute soft drinks for hamburgers. In actuality, real income has also increased, and in order to assess the total effect of the price change on the demand for soft drinks, we must also investigate the income effect.

Graphic Analysis of an Increase in Price

If the price of good X were to increase, a similar analysis would be used. In Figure 5.5 the budget line has been shifted inward because of an increase in the price of X from P_X^1 to P_X^2. The movement from the initial point of utility maximization (X^*, Y^*) to the new point (X^{**}, Y^{**}) can be decomposed into two effects. First, even if the individual could stay on the initial indifference curve (U_2), there would still be an incentive to substitute Y for X and move along U_2 to point B. However, because purchasing power has been reduced by the rise in the price of X, the individual must move to a lower level of utility. This movement is again called the income effect. Notice in Figure 5.5 that both the income and substitution effects work in the same direction and cause the quantity of X demanded to be reduced in response to an increase in its price.

Effects of Price Changes for Inferior Goods

So far we have shown that substitution and income effects tend to reinforce one another. For a price decline, both cause more of the good to be demanded, whereas for a price increase, both cause less to be demanded. Although this analysis is accurate for the case of normal (noninferior) goods, the possibility of inferior goods complicates the story somewhat. In this case, income and substitution effects work in opposite directions, and the total result of a price change is indeterminate. A fall in price, for example, will always cause an individual to consume more of a good because of the substitution effect. But if the good is inferior, the increase in purchasing power caused by the price decline may cause less of the good to be bought. The result is therefore indeterminate—the substitution effect tends to increase the quantity of the inferior good bought whereas the (perverse) income effect tends to reduce this quantity. Unlike the situation for normal goods, it is not possible here to predict exactly how the price change will affect the quantity chosen.

Figure 5.5   *Demonstration of the Income and Substitution Effects of an Increase in the Price of Good* X

When the price of *X* increases, the budget constraint shifts inward. The movement from the initial utility-maximizing point (*X**, *Y**) to the new point (*X***, *Y***) can be analyzed as two separate effects. The substitution effect would be depicted as a movement to point *B* on the initial indifference curve (U_2). The price increase, however, would create a loss of purchasing power and a consequent movement to a lower indifference curve. This is the income effect. In the diagram, both the income and substitution effects cause the quantity of *X* to fall as a result of the increase in its price. Again, the point I/P_Y is not affected by the change in the price of *X*.

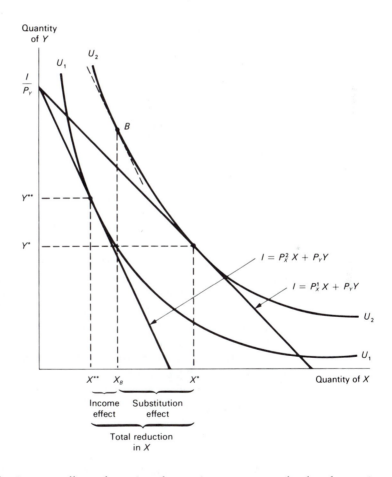

Giffen's Paradox   If the income effect of a price change is strong enough, the change in price and the resulting change in the quantity demanded could actually move in the same direction. Legend has it that the English economist Robert Giffen observed this paradox in nineteenth-century Ireland—when the price of potatoes rose, people reportedly consumed more of them. This peculiar result can be explained by looking at the size of the income effect of a change in the price of

Figure 5.6   *Giffen's Paradox*

The total effect of an increase in the price of *X* is to *increase* the quantity of *X* demanded. This happens because the negative substitution effect (the movement from *X**, *Y** to point *B*) is outweighed by a strong positive income effect resulting from the inferiority of good *X* (compare Figure 5.3). Not every inferior good exhibits Giffen's paradox.

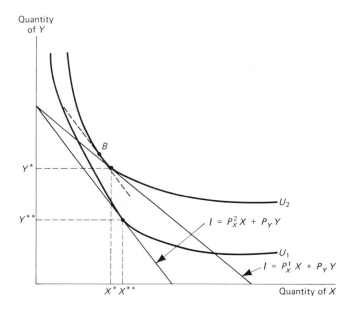

potatoes. Potatoes were not only inferior goods but also used up a large portion of the Irish people's income. An increase in the price of potatoes therefore reduced real income substantially. The Irish were forced to cut back on other luxury food consumption in order to buy more potatoes. Even though this rendering of events is historically implausible, the possibility of an increase in the quantity demanded in response to the price increase of a good has come to be known as *Giffen's paradox*.[3]

The paradox is illustrated graphically in Figure 5.6, which shows potato consumption on the *X*-axis and all other goods on the *Y*-axis. The graph shows that in response to the increase in the price of potatoes, more are de-

[3]A major problem with this explanation is that it disregards Marshall's observation that both supply and demand factors must be taken into account when analyzing price changes. If potato prices increased because of the potato blight in Ireland, then supply should have become smaller, so how could *more* potatoes possibly have been consumed? Also, since many Irish people were potato farmers, the potato price increase should have increased real income for them. For a detailed discussion of these and other fascinating bits of potato lore, see G. P. Dwyer and C. M. Lindsey, "Robert Giffen and the Irish Potato," *American Economic Review* (March 1984): 188–192.

manded. Even though the substitution effect reduces consumption, the "perverse" income effect is strong enough to make the total effect of the price increase positive. Real income falls and, since potatoes are inferior goods, the demand for them increases.

This paradox is probably quite rare in the real world—not only must the good be inferior, but the positive income effect must be strong enough to outweigh the negative substitution effect. A strong income effect will not usually exist unless the good makes up a large part of the individual's expenditures (as with potatoes in nineteenth-century Ireland). We can therefore conclude that price and quantity demanded of a good will usually move in opposite directions, even when the good is inferior. That is, Giffen's paradox will not occur except in unusual circumstances.

A Summary   Hence our graphical analysis leads to the following conclusions:

Optimization Principle:

Substitution and Income Effects
The utility-maximization hypothesis suggests that for normal goods, a fall in the price of a good leads to an increase in quantity purchased because (1) the *substitution effect* causes more to be purchased as the individual moves *along* an indifference curve; and (2) the *income effect* causes more to be purchased because the price decline has increased the individual's purchasing power, thereby permitting movement to a *higher* indifference curve. When the price of a normal good rises, similar reasoning predicts a decline in the quantity purchased. For inferior goods, substitution and income effects work in opposite directions, and no definite predictions can be made.

Later in this chapter we will present a mathematical derivation of substitution and income effects that will permit more precise statements to be made about the size and direction of such effects. First, however, we will develop two different ways of showing an individual's demand for a good graphically.

THE INDIVID-UAL'S DE-MAND CURVE   So far we have shown that an individual's demand for a good (say, X_1) depends on the shape of the utility function and on all prices and income:

$$X_1^* = D_1(P_1, P_2, \ldots, P_n, I). \tag{5.3}$$

Frequently, it is convenient to graph X_1 as simply a function of its own price (P_1), with the understanding that all other prices and income are being held constant. To show the construction of such a graph, we assume that there are only two goods (X and Y) and that the demand function for good X is given by

$$X^* = D_X(P_X, P_Y, I). \tag{5.4}$$

Figure 5.7a shows utility-maximizing choices of X and Y as the individual is presented with successively lower prices of good X (while holding P_Y and I constant). It is assumed that the quantities of X chosen increase from X' to X'' to X''' as that good's price falls from P_X' to P_X'' to P_X'''. Such an assumption

Figure 5.7   *Construction of an Individual's Demand Curve*

In (a) the individual's utility-maximizing choices of X and Y are shown for three different prices of X (P'_x, P''_x, and P'''_x). In (b) this relationship between P_x and X is used to
construct the demand curve for X. The demand curve is drawn on the assumption
that P_Y, I, and preferences remain constant as P_x varies.

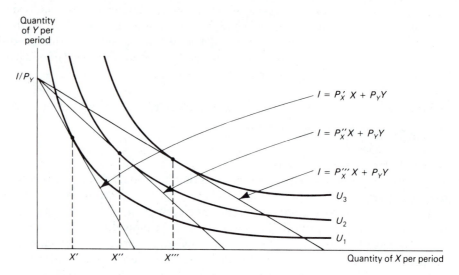

(a) Individual's Indifference Curve Map

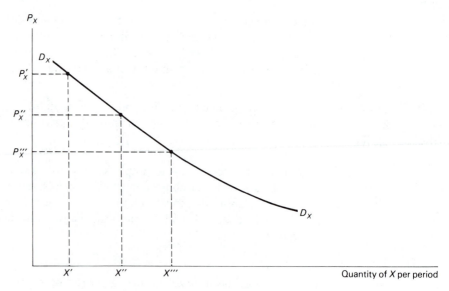

(b) Demand Curve

is in accord with our general conclusion that, except in the unusual case of Giffen's paradox, $\partial X/\partial P_X$ is negative.

In Figure 5.7b information about the utility-maximizing choices of good X is transferred to a *demand curve*, having P_X on the vertical axis and sharing the same horizontal axis as that in Figure 5.7a. The negative slope of the curve again reflects the assumption that $\partial X/\partial P_X$ is negative. Hence we have:

Definition:

Individual Demand Curve

An *individual demand curve* shows the relationship between the price of a good and the quantity of that good purchased, assuming that all other determinants of demand are held constant.

The demand curve illustrated in Figure 5.7 stays in a fixed position only so long as all other determinants of demand remain unchanged. If one of these other factors does change, the curve will shift to a new position, as we now describe.

Shifts in the Demand Curve

Three basic factors were held constant in deriving the demand curve in Figure 5.7b: (1) income; (2) prices of other goods (say, P_Y); and (3) the individual's preferences. If any of these were to change, the entire demand curve would shift to a new position. For example if I were to increase, the curve would shift outward (provided that $\partial X/\partial I > 0$; that is, that the good is a "normal" good over this income range). More X would be demanded at *each* price. If another price, say, P_Y, were to change, the curve would shift inward or outward, depending precisely on how X and Y are related. In the next chapter we will examine that relationship in detail. Finally, the curve would shift if the individual's preferences for good X were to change. A sudden advertising blitz by the McDonald's Corporation might shift the demand for hamburgers outward, for example.

As this discussion makes clear, one must remember that the demand curve drawn in Figure 5.7b is only a two-dimensional representation of the true demand function (Equation 5.3 or 5.4) and that it is stable only if other things in fact stay constant. It is important to keep clearly in mind the difference between a movement along a given demand curve caused by a change in P_X and a shift in the entire curve caused by a change in income, in one of the other prices, or in preferences. Traditionally, the term "an increase in demand" is reserved for an outward shift in the demand curve, whereas the term "an increase in the quantity demanded" refers to a movement along a given curve.

Compensated Demand Curves

In Figure 5.7 the individual's utility varies along the demand curve. As P_X falls, the individual is made increasingly better off as shown by the increase in utility from U_1 to U_2 to U_3. The reason this happens is that the demand curve is drawn on the assumption that nominal income and other prices are held constant; hence a decline in P_X makes the individual better off by increasing his or her real purchasing power. Although this is the most common way to impose

Figure 5.8   *Construction of a Compensated Demand Curve*

The curve h_x shows how the quantity of X demanded changes when P_x changes, holding P_Y and *utility* constant. That is, the individual's income is "compensated" so as to keep utility constant. Hence h_x reflects only substitution effects of changing prices.

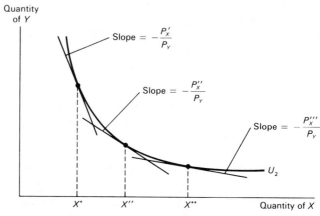

(a) Individual's Indifference Curve Map

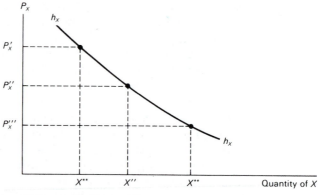

(b) Compensated Demand Curve

the *ceteris paribus* assumption in developing a demand curve, it is not the only way. An alternative approach holds the individual's *real* income (or utility) constant while examining reactions to changes in P_X. The derivation is illustrated in Figure 5.8. There we hold utility constant (at U_2) while successively reducing P_X. As P_X falls, the individual's nominal income is effectively reduced to prevent any increase in utility from occurring. In other words, the effects of the price change on purchasing power are "compensated" so as to constrain the individual to remain on U_2. If we were instead to examine increases in P_X, such compensation would be positive: The individual's income would have to be increased to permit him or her to stay on the U_2 indifference curve in response to the price rises. We can summarize these results by

---

Definition:

Compensated Demand Curve

A *compensated demand curve* shows the relationship between the price of a good and the quantity purchased on the assumption that other prices *and utility* are held constant. Mathematically, the curve is a two-dimensional representation of the *compensated demand function*

$$X^* = h_X(P_X, P_Y, U). \tag{5.5}$$

Relationship between Compensated and Uncompensated Demand Curves

This relationship between the two demand curve concepts we have developed is illustrated in Figure 5.9. At P_X'' the curves intersect, since at that price the individual's income is just sufficient to attain utility level U_2 (compare Figures 5.7 and 5.8). Hence X'' is demanded under either demand concept. For prices below P_X'', however, the individual suffers a negative income compensation on the curve h_X to prevent an increase in utility from the lower price. Hence, assuming X is a normal good, less X is demanded at P_X''' along h_X than along the uncompensated curve D_X. Alternatively, for a price above P_X'' (such as P_X'), income compensation is positive, since the individual needs some help to remain on U_2. Hence, again assuming X is a normal good, at P_X' more X is demanded along h_X than along D_X. In general then, for a normal good, the compensated demand curve is somewhat less responsive to price changes than is the uncompensated curve because the latter reflects both substitution and income effects of price changes whereas the compensated curve reflects only substitution effects.

The choice between using compensated or uncompensated demand curves in economic analysis is largely a matter of convenience. In most empirical work uncompensated curves are used since the data on prices and nominal incomes needed to estimate them are readily available. In Chapter 7 we will describe some of these estimates and show how they might be employed for practical policy purposes. For some theoretical purposes, however, compensated demand curves are a more appropriate concept, since the ability to hold utility constant offers a considerable number of advantages. Our discussion of "consumer surplus" in the final section of this chapter offers one illustration of these advantages.

A MATHEMATICAL DEVELOPMENT OF RESPONSE TO PRICE CHANGES

Up to this point we have largely relied on graphical devices to describe how individuals respond to price changes. Since additional insights are provided by a more mathematical approach, we will now pursue such an analysis. Our basic goal is to examine the partial derivative $\partial X/\partial P_X$; that is, how a *ceteris paribus* change in the price of a good affects its purchase. Later we take up the question of how changes in the price of one commodity affect purchases of another commodity.

Figure 5.9   *Comparison of Compensated and Uncompensated Demand Curves*

The compensated (h_x) and uncompensated (D_x) demand curves intersect at P''_x since X'' is demanded under each concept. For prices above P''_x, the individual's income is increased with the compensated demand curve, so more X is demanded than with the uncompensated curve. For prices below P''_x, income is reduced for the compensated curve, so less X is demanded than with the uncompensated curve. The curve D_x is flatter because it incorporates both substitution and income effects whereas the curve h_x reflects only substitution effects.

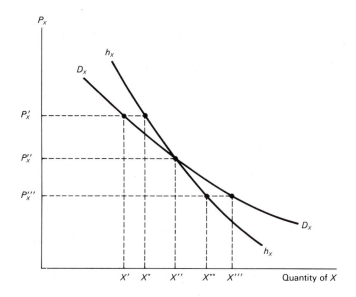

Direct Approach   Our goal is to use the utility-maximization model to learn something about how the demand for good X changes when P_X changes; that is, we wish to calculate $\partial D_X / \partial P_X$. The direct approach to this problem makes use of the first-order conditions for a utility maximization (Equations 4.8). Differentiation of these $n + 1$ equations yields a new system of $n + 1$ equations, which eventually can be solved for the derivative we seek.[4] Unfortunately, obtaining this solution is quite cumbersome and the steps required yield little in the way of economic insights. Hence, we will instead adopt an indirect approach that relies on the concept of duality. In the end, both results yield the same conclusion, but the indirect approach is much richer in terms of the economics it contains.

[4]See, for example, James M. Henderson and Richard F. Quandt, *Microeconomic Theory: A Mathematical Approach*, 3d ed. (New York: McGraw-Hill Book Company, 1980), pp. 25–27.

Indirect Approach   In order to begin our indirect approach,[5] we will assume there are only two goods (X and Y) and focus on the compensated demand function, $h_X(P_X, P_Y, U)$, introduced in Equation 5.5. We now wish to illustrate the connection between this demand function and the ordinary demand function, $D_X(P_X, P_Y, I)$. In Chapter 4 we introduced the notion of the expenditure function, which records the minimal expenditure necessary to attain a given utility level. If we denote this function by

$$\text{minimum expenditure} = E(P_X, P_Y, U), \tag{5.6}$$

then by definition,

$$h_X(P_X, P_Y, U) = D_X[P_X, P_Y, E(P_X, P_Y, U)]. \tag{5.7}$$

This conclusion was already introduced in connection with Figure 5.9, which showed that the quantity demanded is identical for the compensated and uncompensated demand functions when the individual's income is exactly what is needed to attain the required utility level. Equation 5.7 is obtained by inserting that expenditure level into the demand function, D_X. Now we can proceed by partially differentiating Equation 5.7 with respect to P_X and recognizing that P_X enters into the ordinary demand function in two places. Hence

$$\frac{\partial h_X}{\partial P_X} = \frac{\partial D_X}{\partial P_X} + \frac{\partial D_X}{\partial E} \cdot \frac{\partial E}{\partial P_X}, \tag{5.8}$$

and rearranging terms,

$$\frac{\partial D_X}{\partial P_X} = \frac{\partial h_X}{\partial P_X} - \frac{\partial D_X}{\partial E} \cdot \frac{\partial E}{\partial P_X}. \tag{5.9}$$

Consequently, the derivative we seek has two terms. We now examine each of these. Interpretation of the first term is straightforward: It is the slope of the compensated demand curve. More precisely, it is the substitution effect that comes about from a change in P_X.

The second term in Equation 5.9 reflects the way in which changes in P_X affect the demand for X through changes in necessary expenditure levels (that is, changes in purchasing power). This term therefore reflects the income effect. The negative sign in Equation 5.9 shows the precise direction of the effect. For example, an increase in P_X increases the expenditure level necessary to attain a given utility level (mathematically, $\partial E/\partial P_X > 0$). But because nominal income is in fact held constant, these extra expenditures are not available, so X must be reduced to meet this shortfall. The extent of the reduction is given by $\partial D_X/\partial E$. On the other hand, if P_X falls, the minimum expenditure level required to attain a given utility level falls too. The decline in X that would normally accompany such a fall in expenditures is precisely the amount that must be added back through the income effect (by subtracting a negative change in X)

[5] The following proof is adapted from Phillip J. Cook, "A 'One Line' Proof of the Slutsky Equation," *American Economic Review* 62 (March 1972): 139.

to account for the increase in X brought about by this increase in real purchasing power.

The Slutsky Equation

The relationships embodied in Equation 5.9 were first discovered by the Russian economist Eugen Slutsky in the late nineteenth century. A slight change in notation is required to illustrate Slutsky's precise result. First, we write the substitution effect as

$$\text{substitution effect} = \frac{\partial h_X}{\partial P_X} = \frac{\partial X}{\partial P_X}\bigg|_{U = \text{constant}} \tag{5.10}$$

to indicate movement along an indifference curve. For the income effect we have

$$\text{income effect} = -\frac{\partial D_X}{\partial E} \cdot \frac{\partial E}{\partial P_X} = -\frac{\partial X}{\partial I} \cdot \frac{\partial E}{\partial P_X}, \tag{5.11}$$

since changes in income or expenditures amount to the same thing in the function D_X.

It is a relatively easy matter to show that

$$\frac{\partial E}{\partial P_X} = X. \tag{5.12}$$

Intuitively, a \$1 increase in P_X raises necessary expenditures by X dollars since \$1 extra must be paid for each unit of X purchased. A formal proof of this assertion, which relies on the envelope theorem (see Chapter 2), will be relegated to a footnote.[6]

By combining Equations 5.10–5.12 we can arrive at the following:

Optimization Principle:

Slutsky Equation

The utility-maximization hypothesis shows that the substitution and income effects arising from a price change can be represented by

[6] Remember that the individual's dual problem is to minimize $E = P_X X + P_Y Y$, subject to $\overline{U} = U(X, Y)$. The Lagrangian expression for this problem is

$$\mathcal{L} = P_X X + P_Y Y + \lambda[\overline{U} - U(X, Y)],$$

and the envelope theorem applied to constrained minimization problems (see Equation 2.72) states that at the optimal point,

$$\frac{\partial E}{\partial P_X} = \frac{\partial \mathcal{L}}{\partial P_X} = X.$$

This is the result that was to be shown. The result, and similar ones that we will encounter in the theory of firms' costs, is sometimes called Shephard's lemma. Its importance in empirical work is that the *demand function* for good X can be found directly from the expenditure function by simple partial differentiation. The demand functions generated in this way will depend on $\overline{U}$, so they should be interpreted as compensated demand functions.

$$\frac{\partial D_X}{\partial P_X} = \text{substitution effect} + \text{income effect} \tag{5.13}$$

$$= \left.\frac{\partial X}{\partial P_X}\right|_{U \,=\, \text{constant}} - X\frac{\partial X}{\partial I}. \tag{5.14}$$

The Slutsky equation allows us to give a more definitive treatment of the direction and size of substitution and income effects than was possible with only a graphic analysis. First, the substitution effect $(\partial X/\partial P_X | U = \text{constant})$ is always negative as long as the MRS is diminishing. A fall (rise) in P_X reduces (increases) P_X/P_Y, and utility maximization requires that the MRS fall (rise) too. But this can only occur along an indifference curve if X increases (or, in the case of a fall in P_X, decreases). Hence, insofar as the substitution effect is concerned, price and quantity must move in opposite directions. Equivalently, the slope of the compensated demand curve must be negative.[7] We will show this result in a somewhat different way in the next section.

The sign of the income effect $(-X\,\partial X/\partial I)$ depends on the sign of $\partial X/\partial I$. If X is a normal good, $\partial X/\partial I$ is positive and the entire income effect is negative. As for the substitution effect, price and quantity move in opposite directions. For example, a fall in P_X raises real income, and because X is a normal good, purchases of X rise. Similarly, a rise in P_X reduces real income and purchases of X fall. Overall then, as we described previously using a graphic analysis, substitution and income effects work in the same direction to yield a negatively sloped demand curve.

REVEALED PREFERENCE AND THE SUBSTITUTION EFFECT

As we have seen, the principal prediction that can be derived from the utility-maximization model is that the slope of the compensated demand curve (that is, the substitution effect of a price change) is negative. Our proof of this assertion relies on the assumption of a diminishing MRS and the related observation that with a diminishing MRS the necessary conditions for a utility maximum are also sufficient. To some economists, such reliance on a hypothesis about an unobservable utility function represented a weak foundation indeed on which to base a theory of demand. An alternative approach, which leads to the same result, was first proposed by Paul Samuelson in the late 1940s.[8] This approach, which Samuelson termed the *theory of revealed preference*, defines a principle of rationality that is based on observed behavior and then uses this principle to approximate an individual's utility function. In this sense, a person who follows Samuelson's principle of rationality behaves *as if* he or she were maximizing a proper utility function and exhibits a negative substitution ef-

---

[7] It is possible that substitution effects would be 0 if indifference curves have an L-shape (implying that X and Y are used in fixed proportions). Some examples are provided in the Chapter 5 problems.

[8] Paul A. Samuelson, *Foundations of Economic Analysis* (Cambridge, Mass.: Harvard University Press, 1947).

Figure 5.10   *Demonstration of the Principle of Rationality*
in the Theory of Revealed Preference

With income I_1 the individual can afford both points *A* and *B*. If *A* is selected, *A* is revealed preferred to *B*. It would be irrational for *B* to be revealed preferred to *A* in some other price-income configuration.

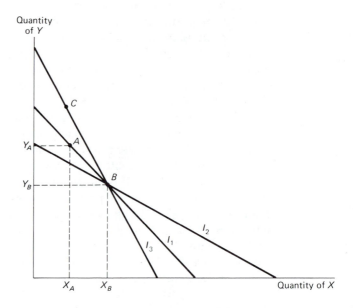

fect. Because Samuelson's approach provides considerable additional insights into our model of consumer choice, we will briefly examine it here.

Graphic Approach

The principle of rationality in the theory of revealed preference is as follows: Consider two bundles of goods, *A* and *B*. If at some prices and income level, the individual can afford both *A* and *B* but chooses *A*, we say that *A* has been "revealed preferred" to *B*. The principle of rationality states that under any different price-income arrangement, *B* can never be revealed preferred to *A*. If *B* is in fact chosen at some price-income configuration, it must be because the individual cannot afford *A*. The principle is illustrated in Figure 5.10. Suppose that when the budget constraint is given by I_1, point *A* is chosen, even though *B* also could have been purchased. *A* then has been revealed preferred to *B*. If for some other budget constraint, *B* is in fact chosen, it must be a case such as that represented by I_2—where *A* could not have been bought. If *B* were chosen when the budget constraint is I_3, this would be a violation of the principle of rationality, since with I_3 both *A* and *B* can be bought. With budget constraint I_3 it is likely that some point other than either *A* or *B*, say, *C*, will be bought. Notice how this principle uses observable reactions to alternative budget constraints to rank commodities rather than assuming the existence of a utility function itself.

Negativity of the Substitution Effect

Using the principle of rationality, we can now show why the substitution effect must be negative (or 0). Suppose that an individual is *indifferent* between two bundles, C (composed of X_C and Y_C) and D (composed of X_D and Y_D). Let P_X^C, P_Y^C be the prices at which bundle C is chosen and P_X^D, P_Y^D be the prices at which bundle D is chosen.

Since the individual is indifferent between C and D, it must be the case that when C was chosen, D cost at least as much as C:

$$P_X^C X_C + P_Y^C Y_C \leq P_X^C X_D + P_Y^C Y_D. \tag{5.15}$$

A similar statement holds when D is chosen:

$$P_X^D X_D + P_Y^D Y_D \leq P_X^D X_C + P_Y^D Y_C. \tag{5.16}$$

Rewriting Equations (5.15) and (5.16) gives

$$P_X^C(X_C - X_D) + P_Y^C(Y_C - Y_D) \leq 0 \tag{5.17}$$

$$P_X^D(X_D - X_C) + P_Y^D(Y_D - Y_C) \leq 0. \tag{5.18}$$

Adding these together we get

$$(P_X^C - P_X^D)(X_C - X_D) + (P_Y^C - P_Y^D)(Y_C - Y_D) \leq 0. \tag{5.19}$$

Now suppose that only the price of X changes; assume that $P_Y^C = P_Y^D$. Then[9]

$$(P_X^C - P_X^D)(X_C - X_D) \leq 0. \tag{5.20}$$

But Equation 5.20 simply says that price and quantity move in the opposite direction when utility is held constant (remember, bundles C and D are equally attractive). This is precisely a statement about the non-positive nature of the substitution effect:

$$\left. \frac{\partial X}{\partial P_X} \right|_{U \,=\, \text{constant}} \leq 0. \tag{5.21}$$

We have arrived at the result by an approach that requires neither the existence of a utility function nor the assumption of a diminishing *MRS*.

Mathematical Generalization

Generalizing the revealed preference idea to n goods is relatively trivial. If at prices P_i^0, bundle X_i^0 is chosen and bundle X_i^1 is also affordable, then

$$\sum_{i=1}^{n} P_i^0 X_i^0 \geq \sum_{i=1}^{n} P_i^0 X_i^1; \tag{5.22}$$

that is, bundle 0 has been "revealed preferred" to bundle 1. Consequently, at the prices that prevail when bundle 1 is bought (say, P_i^1), it must be the case that X_i^0 is more expensive:

[9]This proof follows that developed by Samuelson, *Foundations of Economic Analysis*, p. 109. It should be pointed out that the proof is not strictly correct and is presented for pedagogic purposes only. The principal problem in the development of a complete proof is that the concept of "indifference" is not defined in revealed preference theory.

$$\sum_{i=1}^{n} P_i^1 X_i^0 > \sum_{i=1}^{n} P_i^1 X_i^1. \qquad (5.23)$$

Although this initial definition of revealed preference focuses on the relationship between two bundles of goods, the most often used version of the basic principle requires a degree of transitivity for preferences among an arbitrarily large number of bundles. This is summarized by the following "strong" axiom:

Definition:

Strong Axiom of Revealed Preference

The *strong axiom of revealed preference* states that if commodity bundle 0 is revealed preferred to bundle 1, and if bundle 1 is revealed preferred to bundle 2, and if bundle 2 is revealed preferred to bundle 3, . . . , and if bundle $K - 1$ is revealed preferred to bundle K, *then* bundle K cannot be revealed preferred to bundle 0 (where K is any arbitrary number of commodity bundles).

Most other properties that have been developed using the concept of utility can be proved using this revealed preference axiom instead. For example, it is an easy matter to show that demand functions are homogeneous of degree 0 in all prices and income. It therefore is apparent that the revealed preference axiom and the existence of "well-behaved" utility functions are somehow equivalent conditions. That this is in fact the case was first shown by H. Houthakker in 1950. Houthakker showed that a set of indifference curves can always be derived for an individual who obeys the strong axiom of revealed preference.[10] Hence this axiom provides a quite general and believable foundation for utility theory based on relatively simple comparisons among alternative budget constraints.

CONSUMER SURPLUS

An important problem in applied economics is to develop a monetary measure of the gains or losses that individuals experience as a result of price changes. For example, as we will show in Part VI, if sellers of a commodity are relatively few in number, they may be able to raise the market price of the commodity in order to obtain greater profits. In order to put a monetary cost on this distortion, we need some way of evaluating the welfare loss that consumers experience from the price rise. Similarly, some inventions cause the price of products to fall dramatically (consider the invention of the electronic calculator, for example), and in this case we might wish to evaluate how much consumers gain. In order to make such calculations, economists have developed the concept of *consumer surplus,* which permits welfare gains or losses to be estimated from knowledge of the market demand curve for a product. In this section we will show how these calculations are made; we will then use the consumer surplus notion at several places later in the text.

---

[10]H. Houthakker, "Revealed Preference and the Utility Function," *Economica* 17 (May 1950): 159–174.

Consumer Surplus and Expenditure Functions

In Chapter 4 we developed the concept of the expenditure function as a way of recording the minimum expenditure necessary to achieve a desired level of utility given the prices of various goods. We denoted this function as

$$\text{expenditure} = E(P_X, P_Y, U_0), \tag{5.24}$$

where U_0 is the "target" level of utility that is sought. One way to evaluate the welfare cost of a price increase (say, from P_X^0 to P_X^1) would be to compare the expenditures required to achieve U_0 under these two situations:

$$\text{expenditures at } P_X^0 = E_0 = E(P_X^0, P_Y, U_0) \tag{5.25}$$

$$\text{expenditures at } P_X^1 = E_1 = E(P_X^1, P_Y, U_0), \tag{5.26}$$

so the loss in welfare would be measured as the increase in needed expenditures. Thus,

$$\text{welfare change} = E_0 - E_1. \tag{5.27}$$

Since $E_1 > E_0$, this change would be negative, indicating that the price rise makes this person worse off. On the other hand, if P_X fell, E_0 would exceed E_1 and the individual would experience a welfare gain. Knowledge of the expenditure function is therefore sufficient to make the kind of calculations we need.

A Graphic Approach

We can make further headway in this problem by using the envelope theorem result (see footnote 6 of this chapter). The derivative of the expenditure function with respect to P_X yields the compensated demand function, h_X:

$$\frac{dE(P_X, P_Y, U_0)}{dP_X} = h_X(P_X, P_Y, U_0). \tag{5.28}$$

In words, the change in necessary expenditures brought about by a change in P_X is given by the quantity of X demanded. For evaluating this change in expenditures over a "large" price change (from P_X^0 to P_X^1), we must integrate Equation 5.28:

$$\text{change in expenditures} = \int_{P_X^0}^{P_X^1} dE = \int_{P_X^0}^{P_X^1} h_X(P_X, P_Y, U_0)\, dP_X \tag{5.29}$$

The integral in Equation 5.29 has a straightforward interpretation—it is the area to the left of the compensated demand curve (h_X) between P_X^0 and P_X^1. This is our measure of welfare loss. It is illustrated as the shaded area between P_X^0 and P_X^1 in Figure 5.11. For a fall in price below P_X^0, the welfare gain would be shown by a similar area below P_X^0.

To understand the origin of the term *consumer surplus* to describe the welfare changes we have been examining, consider the following question: How much would the person whose demand curve is illustrated in Figure 5.11 be willing to pay for the right to consume X_0 at a price of P_X^0 rather than being forced to do without the good? A price of P_X^2 would be sufficiently high to prompt this person to reduce purchases of X to 0. Hence, by our previous discussion, it would require extra expenditures given by area $P_X^2 A P_X^0$ to com-

Figure 5.11   *The Welfare Loss of a Price Change*

The shaded area to the left of the compensated demand curve, h_x, shows the amount that would have to be given to this individual to keep him or her as well-off at a price of P_x as at a price of P_x^0. A consumer who buys X_0 at a price of P_x^0 receives a consumer surplus of $P_x^2 A P_x^0$ since this is the increase in expenditures that would have to be provided to make this person willing to do without X completely.

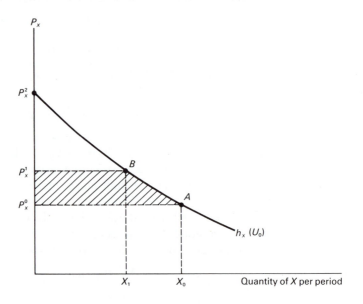

pensate this individual for doing without good X. Similarly, a person faced by the price P_X^0 chooses to consume X_0 and spends a total of $P_X^0 \cdot X_0$ on good X. In making these expenditures, he or she receives extra (or "surplus") welfare represented by the area $P_X^2 A P_X^0$ relative to a situation in which X is not available at all. In our study of monopoly and other market imperfections, we will see how these often result in a loss of this consumer surplus or, in some cases, a transfer of consumer surplus from individual consumers to other market participants.

Welfare Changes and the Marshallian Demand Curve

So far, our graphic analysis of consumer surplus has made use of the compensated demand curve h_X. Because the location of this curve depends on the target level of utility assumed, there is some ambiguity about which curve to use. For example, in connection with Figure 5.11 we described the extra expenditures required to attain U_0 when good X costs P_X^1 rather than P_X^0. But in most actual applications this price rise will result in both substitution and income effects and a loss in utility to this individual (from, say, U_0 to U_1). That is, the actual market reaction to the rise in P_X would be to move from the point X_0, P_X^0 on the Marshallian demand curve (D_X) in Figure 5.12 to the point X_1, P_X^1 on that curve. At this new point, the individual will receive utility U_1, and

Figure 5.12   *Welfare Effects of Price Changes and the Marshallian Demand Curve*

D_x is the usual Marshallian (nominal income constant) demand curve for good X. $h_x(U_0)$ and $h_x(U_1)$ denote the compensated demand curves associated with the utility levels experienced when P_x^0 and P_x^1, respectively, prevail. The area to the left of D_x between P_x^0 and P_x^1 is bounded by the similar areas to the left of $h_x(U_0)$ and $h_x(U_1)$. Hence, for small changes in price, the area to the left of D_x is a good measure of welfare loss.

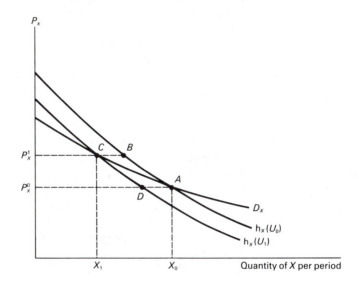

for this level of utility the compensated demand curve is represented by $h_X(U_1)$ rather than the original curve, $h_X(U_0)$. The ambiguity then is whether the welfare loss is best described by the area $P_X^1 BAP_X^0$ (as in Figure 5.11) or by the area $P_X^1 CDP_X^0$ associated with the new curve, $h_X(U_1)$. Since the new area represents the reduction in expenditures that can be made in order to retain utility U_1 when the price of X falls from P_X^1 to P_X^0, it is unclear whether our original measure or this alternative measure more appropriately captures the change in welfare we seek to describe. It all depends on whether we assume that U_0 or U_1 is the appropriate utility target.

Fortunately we have a compromise measure available. The size of the area to the left of the Marshallian demand curve between P_X^0 and P_X^1 (given by $P_X^1 CAP_X^0$ clearly falls between the size of the welfare losses defined by $h_X(U_0)$ and $h_X(U_1)$. Since information in the Marshallian curve is also more likely to be available from real-world data, this seems a very good compromise indeed.[11]

---

[11] For a further discussion, see R. C. Willig, "Consumer's Surplus without Apology," *American Economic Review* (September 1976): 589–597.

Of course, if the price changes we were examining were quite small, there would be little distinction among these three measures, and it is common in many economic discussions of welfare gains or losses to be rather imprecise about exactly what type of demand curve is being used for the analysis.

SUMMARY

In this chapter we have used the utility-maximization model to study how the quantity of a good that an individual chooses responds to changes in income or to changes in that good's price. The final result of this examination is the derivation of the familiar downward-sloping demand curve. In arriving at that result, however, we have drawn a wide variety of insights from the general economic theory of choice:

- Proportional changes in all prices and income do not shift the individual's budget constraint and therefore do not change the quantities of goods chosen. In formal terms, demand functions are homogeneous of degree 0 in all prices and income.

- When purchasing power changes (that is, when income increases with prices remaining unchanged), budget constraints shift and individuals will choose new commodity bundles. For normal goods an increase in purchasing power causes more to be chosen. In the case of inferior goods, however, an increase in purchasing power causes less to be purchased. Hence the sign of $\partial X_i/\partial I$ could be either positive or negative, although $\partial X_i/\partial I \geq 0$ is the most common case.

- A fall in the price of a good causes substitution and income effects that, for a normal good, cause more of the good to be purchased. For inferior goods, however, substitution and income effects work in opposite directions and no unambiguous prediction is possible.

- Similarly, a rise in price induces both substitution and income effects that, in the normal case, cause less to be demanded. For inferior goods the net result is again ambiguous.

- The Marshallian demand curve summarizes the total quantity of a good demanded at each possible price. Changes in price induce both substitution and income effects that prompt movements along the curve. For a normal good, $\partial X_i/\partial P_i \leq 0$ along this curve. If income, prices of other goods, or preferences change, the curve will shift to a new location.

- Compensated demand curves illustrate movements along a given indifference curve for alternative prices. They are constructed by holding utility constant and exhibit only the substitution effects from a price change. Hence their slope is unambiguously negative (or 0).

- Income and substitution effects can be analyzed precisely by using the Slutsky equation. These effects can also be examined by using the revealed preference approach to theory of choice, thereby mitigating the need to assume the existence of utility functions.

- The welfare changes that accompany price changes can sometimes be measured by the changing area under demand curves. These changes in consumer surplus are quite useful for evaluating the net effects on the allocation of resources of economic phenomena such as monopoly or taxation.

Application

SUBSTITUTION EFFECTS AND THE CONSUMER PRICE INDEX

One practical problem for which the study of substitution and income effects offers considerable insights is the construction of price indexes by which to measure inflation. The most common procedure in developing such measures is to choose a "market basket" of commodities in a base year and then to examine how the cost of this basket changes over time. For example, suppose that the market basket of commodities is denoted by X_i^0 and that prices P_i^0 prevail in the base year. Then

$$\text{cost of basket in year } 0 = \sum_{i=1}^{n} P_i^0 X_i^0. \quad (5.30)$$

If, in some future year, prices change to P_i^1, the cost of the original market basket would be

$$\text{cost of basket in year } 1 = \sum_{i=1}^{n} P_i^1 X_i^0, \quad (5.31)$$

and the consumer price index (CPI) would be

$$\text{CPI} = 100 \times \frac{\sum_i P_i^1 X_i^0}{\sum_i P_i^0 X_i^0} \quad (5.32)$$

(where multiplication by 100 is used to put the index into a convenient form). For example, if bundle X_i^0 costs 25 percent more in year 1 than in year 0, the CPI in year 1 would be 125 and this might be regarded as a considerable loss in purchasing power between the two years.

A simple analysis of expenditure functions shows that the CPI computed in this way may overstate the welfare loss from inflation, since use of a fixed market basket does not permit commodity substitution in response to changing relative prices. Suppose that in year 0 the typical individual obtained utility U_0 from consuming X_i^0:

$$\text{minimum expenditures in year } 0$$
$$= E(P_i^0, U_0). \quad (5.33)$$

Then it is relatively easy to show that

$$\text{minimum expenditures in year } 1$$
$$= E(P_i^1, U_0) \leq \sum P_i^1 X_i^0, \quad (5.34)$$

since the typical individual can always choose to obtain U_0 by purchasing X_i^0 again but may be able to attain U_0 more cheaply by consuming some other bundle. Because construction of the CPI does not permit such substitution, it may overstate the effect of inflation on individual welfare.

Some Empirical Evidence

Several economists have used this type of expenditure analysis to estimate the extent to which a fixed market basket-type price index overstates the true rate of price increase. Table 5.2 reports the results of one such study by S. D. Braithwait. In this study the author compared the actual performance of the U.S. consumer price index between the years 1958 and 1973 with the performance of an estimated "true" cost of living index that takes account of substitution in consumption. As the table shows, the actual CPI rose 47.5 percent during the 15-year interval being examined (from 100 to 147.5), whereas the true index rose only 46.0 percent. Hence over the entire period the CPI tended to overstate inflation by about 1.5 percent, due to failure to consider substitution among items in the market basket. The resulting bias worked out to about 0.1 percent per year.

Table 5.2   *Estimated Substitution Bias in the U.S. Consumer Price Index, 1958–1973*

Consumption Category	Actual CPI (1958 = 100)	True Cost of Living Index (1958 = 100)	Bias (column 1 − column 2)
Food	156.1	155.4	0.7
Clothing	149.3	148.5	0.8
Shelter	136.8	135.8	1.0
Transportation	134.0	132.5	1.5
Personal services	172.6	168.1	4.5
Recreation and entertainment	146.9	139.9	7.0
Total Consumption	147.5	146.0	1.5

Source: S. D. Braithwait, "The Substitution Bias of the Laspeyres Price Index: An Analysis Using Estimated Cost of Living Indices," *American Economic Review* (March 1980): 70.

For major consumption categories within the CPI, resulting biases were variable. In the case of food and clothing, little substitution tended to occur among specific items within each category in response to changing relative prices (and indeed relative prices within the categories changed only slightly), so that these biases were quite small (less than 1 percent over the entire period). In the recreation and entertainment category, on the other hand, relative prices changed more significantly and substitution was more prevalent, hence the bias was larger, amounting to nearly 0.5 percent per year. By failing to account for individuals' shifting demands among such items as TVs, spectator events, and use of hotels and motels, the CPI tended to exaggerate the general inflation rate for the goods in this category.

One question that the data in Table 5.2 shed some light on is how often CPI weights should be revised. Since gathering new data with which to develop weights is quite costly (the 1972 revisions cost about $100 million),

there is a natural desire to delay in doing so. From the table it appears that the 15-year period between revisions, at least between the years 1958 and 1972, did not seriously bias the index. There is some evidence that delays of longer periods, however, would result in major biases. Of course, the judgment that 15 years is about the right length of time for a CPI revision depends on whether the 1958 to 1972 period was a normal period or whether more recent experience suggests more frequent revisions. Changes in energy prices during the 1970s, for example, may have changed relative prices to a much greater extent than experienced previously, and therefore a more frequent revision may be required to account for the substitution that may take place. Individuals purchase a much larger number of small automobiles than was previously the case, for example. Similarly, during a period when many new goods are coming on the market (as during the 1980s with the microelectronic revolution), more frequent revisions may also be called for.

SUGGESTED READINGS

Cook, P. J. "A 'One Line' Proof of the Slutsky Equation." *American Economic Review* 62 (March 1972): 139.

Clever use of duality to derive the Slutsky equation; uses the same method as in Chapter 5 but with rather complex notation.

Fisher, F. M., and Shell, K. *The Economic Theory of Price Indices*. New York: Academic Press, 1972.

Complete, technical discussion of the economic properties of various price indexes; describes "ideal" indexes in detail.

Henderson, James M., and Quandt, Richard E. *Microeconomic Theory: A Mathematical Approach*. 3d ed. New York: McGraw-Hill Book Company, 1980. Pp. 18–33.

Concise calculus-based approach. Derives the Slutsky equation directly from first-order conditions.

Russell, R. R., and Wilkinson, M. *Microeconomics: A Synthesis of Modern and Neoclassical Theory*. New York: John Wiley and Sons, 1979. Chaps. 4 and 5.

Good proof of Roy's theorem (Chapter 5), which shows how demand functions can be found from the indirect utility function.

Silberberg, E. *The Structure of Economics: A Mathematical Analysis*. New York: McGraw-Hill Book Company, 1978. Chap. 8.

Good discussion of expenditure functions and the use of indirect utility functions.

Slutsky, E. E. "On the Theory of the Budget of the Consumer," reprinted in American Economic Review, *Readings in Price Theory*. Homewood, Ill.: Richard D. Irwin, 1952. Pp. 27–56.

Original derivation of formal statement of income and substitution effects.

Varian, H. *Microeconomic Analysis*, 2d ed. New York: W. W. Norton and Co., 1984, pp. 111–153.

Formal development of preference notions. Extensive use of expenditure functions and their relationship to the Slutsky equation.

PROBLEMS

5.1

Ms. Boring maximizes her utility by spending her entire income on goods A, B, and C (whose prices stay constant in this problem). Ms. Boring makes $300 per week and purchases 10 units of good A, 10 units of good B, and 10 units of good C. When Ms. Boring's income rises to $400 per week, she buys 9 units of good A, 17 units of good B, and 14 units of good C. Finally, Ms. Boring gets another pay increase to $500 per week and purchases 8 units of good A, 26 units of good B, and 16 units of good C.

a. Using the above information, construct the Engel curve for goods A, B, and C.

b. Explain the nature of each good: is it normal or inferior? A "luxury" or "necessity?"

5.2

David N. gets $3 per month as an allowance to spend any way he pleases. Since he only likes peanut butter and jelly sandwiches, he spends the entire amount on peanut butter (at $.05 per ounce) and jelly (at $.10 per ounce). Bread is provided free of charge by a concerned neighbor. David is a particular eater and makes his sandwiches with exactly 1 oz. of jelly and 2 oz. of peanut butter. He is set in his ways and will never change these proportions.

a. How much peanut butter and jelly will David buy with his $3 allowance in a week?

b. Suppose the price of jelly were to rise to $.15 an ounce. How much of each commodity would be bought?

c. By how much should David's allowance be increased to compensate for the rise in the price of jelly in part (b)?

d. Graph your results of parts (a) to (c).

e. In what sense does this problem only involve a single commodity, peanut butter and jelly sandwiches? Graph the demand curve for this single commodity.

f.   Discuss the results of this problem in terms of the income and substitution effects involved in the demand for jelly.

5.3

Show that if Mr. Green is forced to spend a fixed amount of his income on a particular good, his utility level will be lower than if he could freely allocate his income.

5.4

Show that if there are only two goods (X and Y) to choose from, both cannot be inferior goods.

5.5

Suppose that an individual receives utility from consuming X and Y and that the form of the utility function is

$$U(X, Y) = (X \cdot Y)^{1/2}.$$

a.   If $P_X = 20$, $P_Y = 10$, and the individual's income = 200, how much X and Y should be bought to maximize utility?

b.   In general, using the above function, calculate the individual's demand functions for X and Y as a function of P_X, P_Y.

c.   Calculate $\partial X/\partial I$, $\partial X/\partial P_X$, $\partial X/\partial P_Y$. What do you conclude? Is the utility function used here rather special?

5.6

Consider a consumer who purchases 100 units of good X and 80 units of good Y, along with quantities of many other goods. Suppose that the price of good X rises by 40 cents per unit and the price of good Y drops by 50 cents per unit; other prices and the consumer's income remain unchanged. Will the consumer buy more, less, or the same amount of good X? Does your answer depend on the income elasticity of demand? Explain.

5.7

An indifference map is "vertically parallel" if the marginal rate of substitution is constant for every fixed level of X. Graphically, this says that a vertical line cuts all indifference curves at points of equal slope.

a.   What implications does this assumption have for individuals' behavior? Show that price and quantity must move in opposite directions. (Hint: Use the Slutsky Equation.)

b.   Show that the indifference curve map for the function $U(X, Y) = ln(X) + Y$ is vertically parallel. What are the Engel curves for this function?

c.   Show that an indifference map is both "vertically parallel" and "horizontally parallel" (analogously defined) if and only if X and Y are perfect substitutes (that is, the MRS is constant for all X and Y).

5.8

As defined in problem 3.7, an indifference map is homothetic if any straight line through the origin cuts all indifference curves at points of equal slope: The MRS depends on the ratio Y/X.

a.   Prove that the Engel curves for a homothetic indifference map are straight lines.

b.   Prove that if an individual's tastes can be represented by a homothetic indifference map, price and quantity must move in opposite directions.

c.   Show that the indifference curves for the utility function

$$U(X, Y) = X^{1/2}Y^{1/2}$$

are homothetic. What are the Engel curves for this function?

5.9

Suppose the individual's utility function for three goods, X_1, X_2, and X_3, is "separable"; that is, assume that

$$U(X_1, X_2, X_3) = U_1(X_1) + U_2(X_2) + U_3(X_3)$$

$$\text{and } U_i' > 0 \qquad U_i'' < 0 \qquad \text{for } i = 1, 2, \text{ or } 3.$$

Show that

a.   None of the goods can be inferior;

b. $\partial X_i / \partial P_i$ must be < 0

In the Chapter 6 problems we will return to examine this separable utility case in more detail.

EXTENSIONS

SHEPHARD'S LEMMA AND ROY'S IDENTITY

In Chapters 4 and 5 we showed that there are a number of ways of viewing the individual's choice problem and, similarly, a variety of ways of deriving demand relationships. In this extension, we illustrate all of these relationships for a simple utility function of the form

$$U(X, Y) = X^a Y^{1-a}$$

where $0 < a < 1$. Readers with a sense of adventure may wish to attempt a similar exercise for some of the other utility functions in the Extension Exercises from Chapter 4.

E5.1

Show that the Marshallian demand functions associated with this utility function are

$$X = a\frac{I}{P_X}$$

$$Y = (1 - a)\frac{I}{P_Y}$$

E5.2

Use the results from E5.1 to show that the indirect utility function in this case is

$$V(P_X, P_Y, I) = a(1 - a)IP_X^{-a}P_Y^{a-1}$$

$$= KIP_X^{-a}P_Y^{a-1}$$

where $K = a(1 - a)$

E5.3

Use the results of E5.2 to derive the expenditure function (the inverse of the indirect utility function) as:

$$E(P_X, P_Y, U) = \frac{1}{K}P_X^a P_Y^{1-a}$$

E5.4
Shephard's Lemma states that the compensated demand function for, say, X is given by

$$\frac{\partial E}{\partial P_X} = h(P_X, P_Y, U).$$

Show that in this case

$$h(P_X, P_Y, U) = aU \frac{1}{K} P_X^{a-1} P_Y^{1-a}$$

E5.5
Use the results of E5.1 and E5.4 to prove the Slutsky Equation for good X. That is, show

$$\frac{\partial X}{\partial P_X} = \frac{\partial h}{\partial P_X} - X \frac{\partial X}{\partial I}$$

E5.6
Rather than computing the Marshallian demand curve directly from the utility function (as in E5.1), it is sometimes easier to use the indirect utility function together with "Roy's Identity."

This identity states that the demand function for X can be found by

$$X(P_X, P_Y, I) = -\frac{\dfrac{\partial V(P_X, P_Y, I)}{\partial P_X}}{\dfrac{\partial V(P_X, P_Y, I)}{\partial I}}$$

Use this result together with the results from E5.2 to provide an alternative derivation of the Marshallian demand function for X in E5.1.

For a derivation of Roy's Identity together with a useful summary of the concepts described in this Extension, see A. Deaton and J. Muellbauer. *Economics and Consumer Behavior.* Cambridge: Cambridge University Press, 1980, Chapter 2; or E. Silberberg. *The Structure of Economics: A Mathematical Analysis.* New York: McGraw-Hill, 1978, Chapter 8.

CHAPTER 6

Demand Relationships between Goods

In Chapter 5 we examined how changes in the price of a particular good (say, good X) affected the quantity of that good purchased. Throughout the discussion we held the prices of all other goods constant. It should be clear, however, that a change in one of these other prices could also affect the quantity of X chosen. For example, if X were taken to represent the quantity of automobile miles that an individual drives, then this quantity might be expected to decline when the price of gasoline rises or to increase when air and bus fares rise. In this chapter we will use the utility-maximization model to study such reactions.

THE TWO-GOOD CASE

Figure 6.1 presents two examples of how the quantity of X chosen might be affected by a change in the price of good Y. In both panels of the figure, P_Y has fallen, thereby shifting the budget constraint outward from I_0 to I_1. In both cases also, the quantity of good Y chosen has increased from Y_0 to Y_1 as a result of the decline in P_Y, as would be expected if Y is a normal good. For good X, however, the results shown in the two panels differ. In (a) the indifference curves are nearly L-shaped, implying a fairly small substitution effect. A decline in P_Y does not induce a very large move along U_0 as Y is substituted for X. That is, X drops relatively little as a result of the substitution effect. The income effect, however, reflects the greater purchasing power now available, and this causes the total quantity of X chosen to increase. Hence $\partial X / \partial P_Y$ is negative (X and P_Y move in opposite directions).

In Figure 6.1b this situation is reversed—there $\partial X / \partial P_Y$ is positive. The relatively flat indifference curves in Figure 6.1b result in a large substitution effect from the fall in P_Y. The quantity of X declines sharply as Y is substituted for X along U_0. As in Figure 6.1a, the increased purchasing power from the decline in P_Y causes more X to be bought, but now the substitution effect dominates and the quantity of X declines to X_1. In this case, then, X and P_Y move in the same direction.

A Mathematical Treatment

The ambiguity in the effect of changes in P_Y can be further illustrated by a Slutsky-type equation. By using procedures similar to those in Chapter 5, it is fairly simple to show that

---

Figure 6.1   *Differing Directions of Cross-Price Effects*

In both panels the price of Y has fallen. In (a) substitution effects are small so that the quantity of X consumed increases along with Y. Since $\partial X/\partial P_Y < 0$, X and Y are gross complements. In (b) substitution effects are large so the quantity of X chosen falls. Since $\partial X/\partial P_Y > 0$, X and Y would be termed gross substitutes.

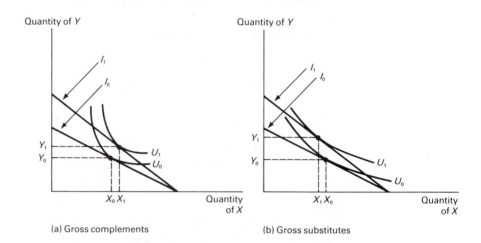

(a) Gross complements   (b) Gross substitutes

$$\frac{\partial X}{\partial P_Y} = \frac{\partial X}{\partial P_Y}\bigg|_{U\ =\ \text{constant}} - Y\frac{\partial X}{\partial I}, \tag{6.1}$$

where the first term on the right, as before, represents the substitution effect and the second term is the income effect. Notice that in the income effect, the derivative $\partial X/\partial I$ is now multiplied by the amount of Y purchased since that quantity reflects the extent to which changes in P_Y affect purchasing power.

For the two-good case, the terms on the right side of Equation 6.1 have different signs. Assuming that indifference curves are convex, the substitution effect $\partial X/\partial P_Y|U = \text{constant}$ is positive. If we confine ourselves to moves along one indifference curve, increases in P_Y increase X and vice versa. But, assuming X is a normal good, the income effect $(-Y\ \partial X/\partial I)$ is clearly negative. Hence the combined effect in Equation 6.1 is ambiguous; $\partial X/\partial P_Y$ could be either positive or negative. Even in the two-good case, the demand relationship between X and P_Y is rather complex.

RELATIONS AMONG MANY GOODS

For the case of many goods, it is a simple matter to generalize the Slutsky analysis (as represented by Equations 5.14 and 6.1) as

$$\frac{\partial X_i}{\partial P_j} = \frac{\partial X_i}{\partial P_j}\bigg|_{U\ =\ \text{constant}} - X_j\frac{\partial X_i}{\partial I} \tag{6.2}$$

for any i and j (including i = j). This simply says that the change in the price of any good (here good j) induces income and substitution effects that may change the quantity of every good demanded. Equation 6.2 can be used to discuss the idea of substitutes and complements. Intuitively, these ideas are rather simple. Two goods are *substitutes* if one good may, as a result of changed conditions, replace the other in use. Some examples are tea and coffee, hamburgers and hot dogs, and butter and margarine. *Complements,* on the other hand, are goods that "go together," such as coffee and cream, fish and chips, or brandy and cigars. In some sense "substitutes" substitute for one another in the utility function, whereas "complements" complement each other.

There are two different ways to make these intuitive ideas precise. One of these focuses on the "gross" effects of price changes by including both income and substitution effects, while the other looks at substitution effects alone. Since both definitions are used, we will examine each in detail.

Gross Substitutes and Complements   A direct way to define substitute and complementary relationships is

---

Definitions:

Gross Substitutes and Complements
Two goods, X_i and X_j, are said to be gross substitutes if

$$\frac{\partial X_i}{\partial P_j} > 0 \qquad\qquad (6.3)$$

and gross complements if

$$\frac{\partial X_i}{\partial P_j} < 0. \qquad\qquad (6.4)$$

That is, two goods are gross substitutes if a rise in the price of one good causes *more* of the other good to be bought. They are gross complements if a rise in the price of one good causes *less* of the other good to be purchased. For example, if the price of coffee rises, the demand for tea might be expected to increase (they are substitutes), whereas the demand for cream might decrease (coffee and cream are complements). Equation 6.2 makes it clear that this definition is a "gross" definition in that it includes both income and substitution effects that arise from price changes. Since these effects are in fact combined in any real-world observation we can make, it might be reasonable always to speak only of "gross" substitutes and "gross" complements.

There are, however, several things that are undesirable about the gross definitions of substitutes and complements. Most important of these failures is that the definitions are not symmetric. It is possible, by the definitions, for X_1 to be a substitute for X_2 and at the same time for X_2 to be a complement of X_1. The presence of income effects can produce paradoxical results. For example, consider two consumption items: food (X_1) and yo-yos (X_2). If the price of food (P_1) rises, it may be that $\partial X_2/\partial P_1 < 0$. Because food is an important item in consumption, a rise in its price will substantially reduce real income and may reduce the demand for X_2 even though there may be a substitution effect favoring an increase in yo-yo consumption as a replacement for food. On the other hand, if the price of yo-yos (P_2) rises, it is quite likely that $\partial X_1/\partial P_2$ will be positive. A rise in the price of yo-yos will not induce important income effects, and the principal effect may be a substitution of food for yo-yos. Consequently, X_2 would be termed a "complement" for X_1, whereas X_1 would be classed as a "substitute" for X_2. Clearly this asymmetry can lead to possible confusion.

A Numerical Example

As an explicit example, suppose the utility function for two goods (X and Y) is given by

$$U(X, Y) = \ln X + Y. \tag{6.5}$$

Setting up the Lagrangian expression

$$\mathcal{L} = \ln X + Y + (I - P_X X - P_Y Y) \tag{6.6}$$

yields the following first-order conditions:

$$\frac{\partial \mathcal{L}}{\partial X} = \frac{1}{X} - \lambda P_X = 0$$

$$\frac{\partial \mathcal{L}}{\partial Y} = 1 - \lambda P_Y = 0 \tag{6.7}$$

$$\frac{\partial \mathcal{L}}{\partial \lambda} = I - P_X X - P_Y Y = 0.$$

Moving the terms in λ to the right and dividing the first equation by the second yields

$$\frac{1}{X} = \frac{P_X}{P_Y} \tag{6.8}$$

$$P_X X = P_Y. \tag{6.9}$$

Substitution into the budget constraint now permits us to solve for the Marshallian demand function for Y:

$$I = P_X X + P_Y Y = P_Y + P_Y Y. \tag{6.10}$$

Hence

$$P_Y Y = I - P_Y. \tag{6.11}$$

This equation shows that an increase in P_Y must decrease spending on good Y (that is, $P_Y Y$). Therefore, since P_X and I are unchanged, spending on X and purchases of X must rise. So

$$\frac{\partial X}{\partial P_Y} > 0 \tag{6.12}$$

and we would term X and Y gross substitutes. On the other hand, Equation 6.11 shows that spending on Y is independent of P_X. Consequently,

$$\frac{\partial Y}{\partial P_X} = 0 \tag{6.13}$$

and, looked at in this way, X and Y would be said to be independent of each other—they are neither gross substitutes nor gross complements. Relying on market-based responses to define the relationship between X and Y would run into some ambiguity.

NET SUBSTI-TUTES AND COMPLE-MENTS

Because of the ambiguities involved in the definition of gross substitutes and complements, an alternative definition that focuses only on substitution effects is sometimes used:

Definitions:

Net Substitutes and Complements[1]
X_i and X_j are said to be net substitutes if

$$\left. \frac{\partial X_i}{\partial P_j} \right|_{U \,=\, \text{constant}} > 0 \tag{6.14}$$

and net complements if

$$\left. \frac{\partial X_i}{\partial P_j} \right|_{U \,=\, \text{constant}} < 0. \tag{6.15}$$

These definitions, then, look only at the substitution terms to determine whether two goods are substitutes or complements. This definition is both intuitively appealing (because it looks only at the shape of an indifference curve) and theoretically desirable (because it is unambiguous). Once X_i and X_j have been discovered to be substitutes, they stay substitutes, no matter in which direction the definition is applied. As a matter of fact, it can be shown that the definitions are symmetric in that

$$\left. \frac{\partial X_i}{\partial P_j} \right|_{U \,=\, \text{constant}} = \left. \frac{\partial X_j}{\partial P_i} \right|_{U \,=\, \text{constant}} \tag{6.16}$$

The substitution effect of a change in P_i on good X_j is identical to the substitution effect of a change in P_j on the quantity of X_i chosen. This symmetry is important in both theoretical and empirical work.[2]

---

[1] Sometimes these are called "Hicksian" substitutes and complements, named after the British economist John Hicks, who originally developed the definitions.

[2] This symmetry is easily shown by using Shephard's lemma (see footnote 6, Chapter 5). Since $X_i = \partial E / \partial P_i$,

$$\left. \frac{\partial X_i}{\partial P_j} \right|_{U \,=\, \text{constant}} = \frac{\partial E^2}{\partial P_i \partial P_j},$$

but

$$\frac{\partial E^2}{\partial P_i \partial P_j} = \frac{\partial E^2}{\partial P_j \partial P_i} = \left. \frac{\partial X_j}{\partial P_i} \right|_{U \,=\, \text{constant}}$$

since, by Young's theorem (see Chapter 2), the order of partial differentiation is irrelevant.

The differences between the two definitions of substitutes and complements are easily demonstrated in Figure 6.1a. In this figure X and Y are gross complements, but they are net substitutes. The derivative $\partial X/\partial P_Y$ turns out to be negative (X and Y are gross complements) because the (positive) substitution effect is outweighed by the (negative) income effect (a fall in the price of Y causes real income to increase greatly and, consequently, actual purchases of X increase). However, as the figure makes clear, if there are only two goods from which to choose, they must be net substitutes. This fact is obvious by a simple geometric argument identical to that used to prove that the own-price substitution effect is negative. Because we have assumed a diminishing MRS, the own-price substitution effect must be negative and, consequently, the cross-price substitution effect must be positive. In a world of only two goods, they must be net substitutes although they may be either gross substitutes or gross complements. Indeed, it can be shown that there can be only a "few" complementary relationships in the net sense.[3] Net substitution is the prevalent relationship among goods.

The symmetry of net cross-substitution effects (Equation 6.16) and the negativity of the own-substitution effect (discussed in Chapter 5) are the major results of the theory of individual choice. These results can, in principle, be tested using real-world data. However, because most actual market data involve the behavior of many demanders and because adding demand across individuals involves some difficult methodological problems (see Chapter 7), there are few convincing tests of the propositions. Instead, the results are used mainly in theoretical work and in the specification of useful demand functions that obey these properties.

COMPOSITE COMMODITIES

Our discussion in the previous section showed that the demand relationships among goods are quite complicated. In the most general case, an individual who consumes n goods will have demand functions that reflect $n(n + 1)/2$ different substitution effects.[4] When n is very large (as it surely is for all the specific goods that individuals actually consume), this general case can be unmanageable. It is often far more convenient to group goods into larger aggregates such as food, clothing, shelter, and so forth. At the most extreme level of aggregates, we might wish to examine one specific good (say, gasoline, which we might call X) and its relationship to "all other goods," which we might call Y. This is the procedure we have been using in many of our two-dimensional graphs, and we will continue to do so at many other places in this book. In this section we show the conditions under which this procedure can be defended. In the extension problems to this chapter, we explore more general issues involved in aggregating goods into larger groupings.

---

[3] See J. R. Hicks, *Value and Capital* (Oxford: Oxford University Press, 1939), p. 312 and problem 6.8.

[4] This can be shown by recognizing that all substitution effects, s_{ij}, could be recorded in an $n \times n$ matrix. However, symmetry of the effects ($s_{ij} = s_{ji}$) implies that only those terms on and below the principal diagonal of this matrix may be distinctly different from each other.

Composite
Commodity
Theorem

Suppose consumers choose among n goods, but that we are only interested specifically in one of them, say X_1. In general, the demand for X_1 will depend on the individual prices of the other $n - 1$ commodities. But if all these prices move together, it may make sense to lump them into a single "composite commodity," Y. Formally, if we let $P_2 \ldots P_n$ represent the initial prices of these goods, then we assume that these prices can only vary together. They might all double, or all decline by 50 percent, but the relative prices of $X_2 \ldots X_n$ would not change. Now we define the composite commodity Y to be total expenditures on $X_2 \ldots X_n$, using the initial prices $P_2 \ldots P_n$:

$$Y = P_2 X_2 + P_3 X_3 + \cdots + P_n X_n. \tag{6.17}$$

This person's initial budget constraint is given by

$$I = P_1 X_1 + P_2 X_2 + \cdots + P_n X_n = P_1 X_1 + Y. \tag{6.18}$$

By assumption, all of the prices $P_2 \ldots P_n$ change in unison. Assume all of these prices change by a factor of $t (t > 0)$. Now the budget constraint is

$$I = P_1 X_1 + t P_2 Y_2 + \cdots + t P_n X_n = P_1 X_1 + tY. \tag{6.19}$$

Consequently, the factor of proportionality, t, plays the same role in this person's budget constraint as did the price of Y (P_Y) in our earlier two-good analysis. Changes in P_1 or in t induce the same kinds of substitution effects we have been analyzing. So long as $P_2 \ldots P_n$ move together, we can therefore confine our examination of demand to choices between buying X_1 or buying "everything else."[5] Simplified graphs that show these two goods on their axes can therefore be defended rigorously so long as the conditions of this "composite commodity theorem" (that all other prices move together) are satisfied. Notice, however, that the theorem makes no predictions about how choices of $X_2 \ldots X_n$ behave—they need not move in unison. The theorem focuses only on total spending on $X_2 \ldots X_n$, not on how that spending is allocated among specific items (although this allocation is assumed to be done in a utility-maximizing way).

Generalizations
and Limitations

The composite commodity theorem can be shown to apply to any group of commodities whose relative prices all move together. It is possible to have more than one such commodity if there are several groupings that obey the theorem (i.e., expenditures on "food," "clothing," and so forth). Hence we have developed the following:

---

[5] For a complete proof, see E. Silberberg, *The Structure of Economics: A Mathematical Approach* (New York: McGraw-Hill Book Company, 1978), pp. 343–345. The idea of a "composite commodity" was introduced by J. R. Hicks in *Value and Capital*, 2d ed. (Oxford: Oxford University Press, 1946), pp. 312–313. Proof of the theorem relies on the notion that to achieve maximum utility, the ratio of the marginal utilities for $X_2 \ldots X_n$ must remain unchanged when $P_2 \ldots P_n$ all move together. Hence, the n-good problem can be reduced to the two-dimensional problem of equating the ratio of the marginal utility from X to that for Y to the "price ratio" P_1/t.

Definition:

Composite Commodity

A composite commodity is a group of goods for which all prices move together. These goods can be treated as a single "commodity" in that the individual behaves as if he or she were choosing between other goods and total spending on the entire composite group.

This definition and the related theorem are very powerful results. They help to simplify many problems that would otherwise be intractable. Still, one must be rather careful in applying the theorem to the real world because its conditions are quite stringent. Finding a set of commodities whose prices move together may be quite rare. Slight departures from strict proportionality may negate the composite commodity theorem if cross-substitution effects are large. In these cases, assuming the theorem to be true may seriously distort one's analysis. Still, in some cases, the conditions of the theorem may be approximately true (prices of energy-related commodities did tend to rise more or less together during the 1970s), and in these cases the theorem can be quite helpful in simplifying the analysis.

ATTRIBUTES OF GOODS AND IMPLICIT PRICES

Thus far our discussion in this chapter has focused on what one can learn about the relationship between goods by observing individuals' reactions to changes in market prices. This analysis thus skirts the crucial question of *why* coffee and cream go together or *why* people tend to view fish and chicken as partial substitutes. To understand what characteristics of goods lead to these relationships, economists have begun to develop a new approach to the traditional theory of choice.[6] This new approach argues that individuals do not desire goods directly but rather desire the "attributes" that goods provide. That is, a person who buys, say, a blanket is doing so not because he or she wishes to own a blanket, but because of the desire to obtain the warmth, beauty, protection, and so forth that the blanket provides. Similarly, individuals do not simply wish to buy "cars," but they desire combinations of horsepower, style, miles per gallon, and convenience. The reason one individual purchases one make of automobile whereas another purchases another make of about the same price is that the attributes of the two models appeal differently to the two individuals. Hence, the novelty of this approach is the notion that the attributes of goods provide utility to individuals and that goods themselves provide utility only to the extent that they contain desirable attributes. Here we will briefly examine this alternative approach and show how it complements the standard theory.

Graphic Analysis

The importance of the attribute approach can be illustrated graphically with a simple example. Suppose that individuals care only about two attributes of the food they buy: the amount of calories provided and the amount of vitamins

---

[6]For an initial statement of this theory of individual choices, see K. J. Lancaster, "A New Approach to Consumer Theory," *Journal of Political Economy* 74 (April 1966): 132–157.

Figure 6.2 *Attributes Provided by Rice Consumption*

The ray *OR* shows the combinations of calories and vitamins provided by various levels of rice consumption. Dashes on *OR* show dollars of spending on rice. Hence an individual who spent \$5 on rice would obtain C^* in calories, V^* in vitamins, and a utility level of U_2.

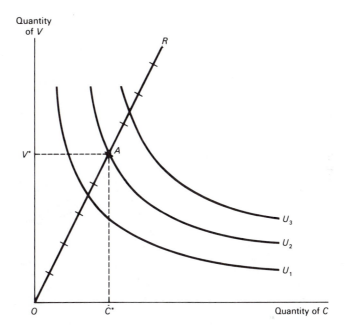

provided. Quantities of these two attributes are shown on the axes of the indifference curve map in Figure 6.2. The indifference curves in the diagram have been drawn in the same way they were in Chapters 3 and 4, except now each curve shows combinations of the two attributes (that is, calories and vitamins) that offer the same utility. Movements to the northeast in Figure 6.2, as in previous diagrams, provide more utility because such movements provide greater amounts of desirable attributes.

Of course, individuals cannot buy calories and vitamins directly. Rather they must purchase various food items that possess those attributes. Consider a particular food item—rice, for example. One pound of rice contains a particular combination of calories and vitamins, and two pounds contain twice as much of each attribute. Hence all possible levels of the attributes offered to an individual who purchases rice are shown by the ray *OR*. The small dashes on *OR* show various amounts of rice purchased (say, in pounds). The calories and vitamins provided by these amounts can be read directly off the diagram, together with the levels of utility provided by them.

For our future analysis we will find it more convenient to consider dollar expenditures on rice (and on other goods) than to record the physical quanti-

Figure 6.3   *Introduction of Another Good Whose Attributes Provide More Utility Per Dollar*

Five dollars spent on wheat (along ray *OW*) yields *C*** calories and *V*** vitamins. This combination (point *B*) yields a higher utility than does a similar expenditure on rice (point *A*).

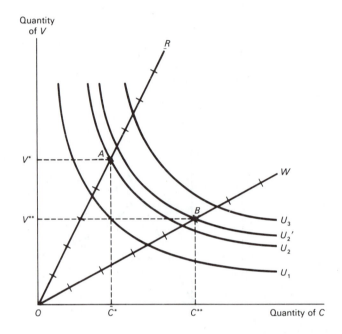

ties of the good purchased. If we assume that rice costs $1 per pound, the dashes on *OR* will serve equally well to represent dollars of expenditure on the product. Hence if an individual chose to spend $5 on rice, he or she would consume at point *A*, obtain *C** in calories and *V** in vitamins from rice purchases, and enjoy a utility level of U_2. In this case utility can be raised or lowered by spending more or less on rice and thereby moving along *OR*.

New Goods and Utility Improvements

Using the notion of goods' attributes and the diagrammatic treatment just presented, we can illustrate the relationship between goods by asking under what conditions this individual will turn to a different source of vitamins and calories. Suppose that another food source, say, wheat, is introduced and that the combinations of calories and vitamins offered by wheat are shown along the ray *OW* in Figure 6.3. As before, the dashes along *OW* represent dollars of expenditure on wheat, with more calories and vitamins being provided when more is spent on wheat. The figure clearly shows why, for this consumer, wheat is a better buy than rice. For equal amounts of expenditures on wheat and rice, the calories and vitamins yielded by wheat purchases provide more utility than do those yielded by rice purchases. With an expenditure of $5, for example,

Figure 6.4 *Mixed Bundles and Implicit Prices*

By combining wheat and rice, expenditures of $5 will permit purchase of any point along *AB*. Point *C* maximizes utility with *C'* calories and *V'* vitamins.

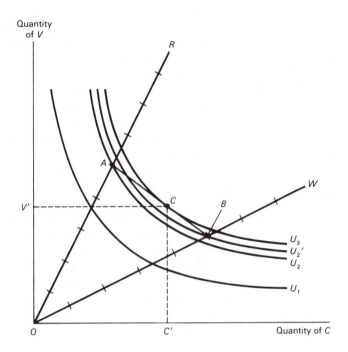

buying wheat provides C^{**} and V^{**}, which results in a utility level of U_2' (point *B*). Clearly, an individual with the preferences shown and $5 to spend on only one of the two grains will choose to buy only wheat. Availability of the wheat has resulted in a higher utility because of the attributes the good provides. A fall in the price of rice could reverse the situation, however.

Mixed Bundles and Implicit Prices

There is no reason why an individual must buy only wheat or only rice with his or her funds. In geometric terms, nothing requires that consumption take place only along the ray *OR* or *OW*. By purchasing some of each grain, it may be possible to obtain a combination of calories and vitamins that yields an even higher level of utility. That possibility is illustrated in Figure 6.4. Suppose again that the person we have been studying has $5 to spend on the two grains and hence could afford either point *A* or point *B* if only one or the other were chosen exclusively. Possible combinations of calories and vitamins obtainable by purchasing a mixed market basket of wheat and rice that costs $5 are shown along the line *AB*. Points near *A* would represent bundles with a large amount of rice and relatively little wheat, whereas those near *B* would reverse those proportions. In a sense then, the line *AB* represents the individual's budget constraint between calories and vitamins when he or she has $5 to spend on those attributes. Given this budget constraint, the individual will choose the mixed bundle C (consisting of C' calories and V' vitamins) and obtain utility level U_3. This result then illustrates in another way why individuals choose mixed bundles of commodities (as we first described in Chapter 3), because mixed bundles make available combinations of attributes not available when only one good or a limited number of goods are bought.

Figure 6.4 provides one other important piece of information: It shows the rate at which vitamins can be traded for calories in the marketplace by substituting wheat for rice. That is, the slope of the "budget constraint" AB shows the ratio of the relative "price" of calories to that of vitamins. To make this notion explicit, consider some (obviously hypothetical) numbers. Suppose point A represents 100 vitamins and 50 calories whereas B represents 75 vitamins and 100 calories. Then in moving from A to B, the individual gives up 25 vitamins to get 50 calories and hence the relative "price" of each extra calorie is half a vitamin. This trade-off rate is the same all along AB. Hence the relative price of extra calories is implicit in the relationship between the attributes provided by rice and wheat.

We can go even further than this, assigning actual monetary values to the implicit prices of calories and vitamins. A little algebra (which is mercifully relegated to a footnote) yields the result that the implicit price of each calorie is 2 cents whereas each vitamin "sells for" 4 cents.[7] These prices make clear again that the cost of an extra calorie is half a vitamin. But they also show much more, since they now show how calories and vitamins may be traded off against other items (or attributes) the individual might choose to buy. Hence we have developed the following definition:

Definition:

Implicit Price
The *implicit prices* of the attributes of goods show how particular attributes may be traded for one another by making substitutions in consumption. These prices can often be computed from information on the physical characteristics of various goods and those goods' market prices.[8]

[7]Let P_C be the implicit price of calories and P_V be the implicit price of vitamins. For rice then, we know that

$$50P_C + 100P_V = 500 \text{ (that is, \$5),}$$

since $5 worth of rice yields 50 calories and 100 vitamins. Similarly, for wheat

$$100P_C + 75P_V = 500.$$

Multiplying the first equation by 2 and subtracting the second yields

$$125P_V = 500,$$

or $P_V = 4$. Substituting this value into the first equation gives $P_C = 2$.

[8]Implicit prices are sometimes called "hedonic" (derived from the same root as the word *hedonism*) prices to indicate that they apply to utility-producing attributes.

An Assessment of the New Approach to Consumer Theory

Focusing on the attributes of goods offers some clear benefits for studying consumer behavior. On a theoretical level, the foundations of utility theory are made clearer by such a focus because it provides a more precise view of why people derive utility from various goods. Similarly, several aspects of behavior that are difficult to conceptualize within the framework of traditional utility analysis (such as why individuals choose a good newly introduced to the market or why goods are substitutes rather than complements) are easily explained using the notion of the good's attributes. On a more practical level, the notion that the attributes of goods have implicit prices and that those prices might be measured offers the possibility of addressing questions as seemingly diverse as how much is clean air "worth" to individuals or how should houses be appraised fairly for tax purposes. The increasing availability of economic data and sophisticated statistical procedures has greatly expanded the types of estimates of implicit prices that can be made. Some of these are discussed in the application to this chapter.

Despite these obvious advantages, the new attribute approach to consumer theory has several disadvantages as well. Most important of these is the fact that transactions take place among buyers and sellers of goods, not attributes. Hence the prices of attributes are not readily observable but instead must be inferred from the prices of goods. Indeed the attributes of goods themselves may not be clearly defined. Imagine trying to list all the factors that are of value to a buyer of a complicated good such as an automobile or a house. Undoubtedly, there would be disagreement among various buyers about what constitutes an attribute and how it might be measured (how automobile "styling" is to be measured, for example). For this reason studies of consumption based on attributes have a tendency to engender more significant disputes about issues in measurement than do studies based on readily observable goods with unchanging characteristics.[9]

SUMMARY

In this chapter we used the utility-maximizing model of choice to examine relationships among consumer goods. Although these relationships may be quite complex, the analysis presented here provided a number of ways of categorizing and simplifying them:

- When there are only two goods, the income and substitution effects from the change in the price of one good (say, P_Y) on the demand for another good (X) usually work in opposite directions. The sign of $\partial X/\partial P_Y$ is therefore ambiguous—its substitution effect is positive whereas its income effect is negative.

---

[9] For a further discussion of some difficulties with the implicit price notion, see S. Rosen, "Hedonic Prices and Implicit Markets," *Journal of Political Economy* 82 (January/February 1974): 34–55.

- In cases of more than two goods, demand relationships can be specified in two ways: Two goods (X_i and X_j) are "gross substitutes" if $\partial X_i/\partial P_j > 0$ and "gross complements" if $\partial X_i/\partial P_j < 0$. Unfortunately, since these price effects include income effects, they need not be symmetric. That is, $\partial X_i/\partial P_j$ does not necessarily equal $\partial X_j/\partial P_i$.

- Focusing only on the substitution effects of price changes does provide a symmetric definition. Two goods are "net substitutes" if $\partial X_i/\partial P_j|\overline{U} > 0$ and "net complements" if $\partial X_i/\partial P_j|\overline{U} < 0$. Since $\partial X_i/\partial P_j|\overline{U} = \partial X_j/\partial P_i|\overline{U}$, there is no ambiguity about these definitions.

- If a group of goods have prices that always move in unison, expenditures on these goods can be treated as a "composite commodity" whose "price" is given by the size of the proportional change in the individual goods' prices.

- An alternative way to develop the theory of choice among goods is to focus on the attributes of those goods. In some cases implicit prices of goods' attributes can be identified from market data.

Application

HOUSES AND THEIR CHARACTERISTICS

Owner-occupied homes represent most individuals' principal asset and spending on housing constitutes more than 40 percent of total consumption. Because houses are very complicated goods, incorporating probably thousands of specific characteristics such as living space or built-in trash compactors, studying the demand for housing has created many difficulties for economists. As part of the Application for Chapter 7 we explore some of the important policy issues that surround the demand for housing. Here we will look at some of the conceptual issues associated with this demand.

Housing Characteristics and Implicit Prices
Each house represents a unique bundle of characteristics. It has a location, age, size, exterior and interior design, and a set of accompanying fixtures that differentiate it from any other house. For this reason it is somewhat misleading to speak of the demand for "housing" since housing is not a homogeneous good. Instead, some economists have tried to estimate the

demand for various attributes of housing and these studies have helped to clarify the basic nature of the product. For example, a 1984 study by Raymond Palmquist examined data on more than 30 different characteristics of recently bought homes in seven urban areas (Atlanta, Denver, Houston, Louisville, Miami, Oklahoma City, and Seattle).[10] Using data from more than 20,000 homes he was able to calculate an implicit price for such attributes as living space ($15 per square foot in 1977), extra bathrooms ($1,800), and central air conditioning ($2,000). Palmquist also found that proximity to places of employment tended to increase the value of a house whereas presence of particulate air pollution tended to decrease that value. Other authors have made use of such observations about housing values to estimate how much individuals appear to be willing to pay to avoid air pollution, airport noise, or city crime. For example, one important study of the

---

[10] Raymond B. Palmquist, "Estimating the Demand for the Characteristics of Housing," *Review of Economics and Statistics* August, 1984, pp. 394–404.

Boston metropolitan area concluded that individuals appeared to be willing to pay about $2,000 (in 1970) for a 25 percent reduction in nitrogen oxide levels in the air.[11] Clearly, then, environmental amenities may be as important in determining the overall price of a house as are the house's basic physical characteristics.

Complementarity in Housing Characteristics
The Palmquist study of housing characteristics estimated a different implicit price for each characteristic in each of the seven areas studied. Hence the author was also able to examine how demanders responded to differences in these prices. As expected, he found that most housing characteristics had negative own-price effects. That is, in cities where housing cost more per square foot, for example, other things being the same, people tended to demand smaller houses. Perhaps more interesting, Palmquist found that most housing characteristics were complementary with living space. People tend to consume housing characteristics in "bundles" of progressively higher quality rather than making substitutions among characteristics and purchasing

[11] David Harrison and Daniel L. Rubinfeld, "The Air Pollution and Property Value Debate: Some Empirical Evidence," *Review of Economics and Statistics,* November, 1978, pp. 635–638.

bundles that are quite heterogeneous in terms of quality.

Housing Characteristics and
Property Tax Assessments
Data on the implicit prices of housing attributes are widely used for assigning values to houses for purposes of property taxation. Most localities base their property taxes on the current market value of houses. But only a small portion of the houses in an area change hands in any one year, so tax assessors are faced with the problem of assigning prices to the majority of houses for which current market information is not available. One method for doing this is to use information for those houses that do sell to put current prices on those houses' attributes. Then, since the assessor knows the characteristics of all houses (they have historical data on living space, bathrooms, garages, swimming pools, and so forth), a current price can be assigned to each by viewing it as simply a bundle of attributes. In this way property tax assessments can be defined in ways that treat both houses that have sold and those that have not symmetrically. Of course, none of this stops irate taxpayers from arguing about their assessments and many lively debates over implicit pricing can be seen throughout the country at tax time.

SUGGESTED READINGS

Borcherding, T. E., and Silberberg, E. "Shipping the Good Apples Out—The Alchian-Allen Theorem Reconsidered." *Journal of Political Economy* (February 1978): 131–138.

Good discussion of the relationships among three goods in demand theory. See also Problems 6.5 and 6.6.

Eppel, Dennis. "Hedonic Prices and Implicit Markets: Estimating Demand and Supply Functions for Differentiated Products." *Journal of Political Economy* (February 1987): 59–80.

Good survey of the problems in defining implicit markets for the attributes of goods.

Hicks, J. R. *Value and Capital,* 2d ed. Oxford: Oxford University Press, 1946. Chaps. I–III and related appendices.

Proof of the composite commodity theorem. Also has one of the first treatments of net substitutes and complements.

Lancaster, K. J. "A New Approach to Consumer Theory." *Journal of Political Economy* 74 (April 1966): 132–157.

Develops the attribute concept and discusses some of the problems associated with defining the "market" for attributes.

Rosen, S. "Hedonic Prices and Implicit Markets." *Journal of Political Economy* (January/February 1974): 34–55.

Nice graphical and mathematical treatment of the attribute approach to consumer theory and of the concept of "markets" for attributes.

Samuelson, P. A. "Complementarity—An Essay on the 40th Anniversary of the Hicks-Allen Revolution in Demand Theory." *Journal of Economic Literature* (December 1977): 1255–1289.

Reviews a number of definitions of complementarity and shows the connections among them. Contains an intuitive, graphical discussion and a detailed mathematical appendix.

Silberberg, E. *The Structure of Economics: A Mathematical Analysis.* New York: McGraw-Hill Book Company, 1978. Chap. 8.

Good discussion of expenditure functions and the use of indirect utility functions to illustrate the composite commodity theorem and other results.

PROBLEMS

6.1

Heidi receives utility from two goods, goat's milk (M) and strudel (S), according to the utility function

$$U(M, S) = M \cdot S$$

a.   Show that increases in the price of goat's milk will not affect the quantity of strudel Heidi buys—that is, show that $\partial S/\partial P_M = 0$.

b.   Develop an intuitive argument that explains why the substitution and income effects of a change in P_M are exactly offsetting in their effect on S in this problem.

6.2

HardTimes-Burt buys only rotgut whiskey and jelly donuts to sustain him. For Burt, rotgut whiskey is an inferior good that exhibits Giffen's paradox, although rotgut whiskey and jelly donuts are Hicksian substitutes in the customary sense. Develop an intuitive explanation to suggest why a rise in the price of rotgut must cause fewer jelly donuts to be bought. That is, the goods must also be gross substitutes.

6.3

Donald, a frugal graduate student, consumes only coffee (C) and buttered toast (BT). He buys these items at the university cafeteria and always uses two pats of butter for each piece of toast. Donald spends exactly half of his meager stipend on coffee and the other half on buttered toast.

a.   In this problem, buttered toast can be treated as a composite commodity. What is its price in terms of the prices of butter (P_B) and toast (P_T)?

b.   Explain why $\partial C/\partial P_{BT} = 0$.

c.   Is it also true here that $\partial C/\partial P_B$ and $\partial C/\partial P_T$ are equal to zero?

6.4

Ms. Sarah Traveler does not own a car and travels only by bus, train, or plane. Her utility function is given by

$$\text{Utility} = B \cdot T \cdot P$$

where each letter stands for miles traveled by a specific mode. Suppose that the ratio of the price of train travel to that of bus travel (P_T/P_B) never changes.

a.   How might one define a composite commodity for ground transportation?

b.   Phrase Sarah's optimization problem as one of choosing between ground (G) and air (P) transportation.

c.   What are Sarah's demand functions for G and P?

     d.   Once Sarah decides on how much to spend on G, how will she allocate those expenditures between B and T?

6.5

Suppose that an individual consumes three goods, X_1, X_2, and X_3, and that X_2 and X_3 are similar commodities (i.e., cheap and expensive restaurant meals) with $P_2 = KP_3$ where $K < 1$—that is, the goods' prices have a constant relationship to one another.

     a.   Show that X_2 and X_3 can be treated as a composite commodity.

     b.   Suppose both X_2 and X_3 are subject to a transaction cost of t per unit (for some examples, see Problem 6.6). How will this transaction cost affect the price of X_2 relative to that of X_3? How will this effect vary with the value of t?

     c.   Can you predict how an income-compensated increase in t will affect expenditures on the composite commodity X_2 and X_3? Does the composite commodity theorem strictly apply to this case?

     d.   How will an income-compensated increase in t affect how total spending on the composite commodity is allocated between X_2 and X_3?

(For a further discussion of the complications involved in this problem, see T. E. Borcherding and E. Silberberg, "Shipping the Good Apples Out: The Alchian and Allen Theorem Reconsidered," *Journal of Political Economy* (February 1978): 131–138.)

6.6

Apply the results of Problem 6.5 to explain the following observations:

     a.   It is difficult to find high quality apples to buy in Washington state or good fresh oranges in Florida.

     b.   People with significant baby-sitting expenses are more likely to have those meals they eat out at expensive restaurants than are those without such expenses.

     c.   Those individuals with a high value of time are more likely to fly the Concorde than those with a lower value of time.

     d.   Individuals are more likely to search for bargains for expensive items than for cheap ones.

(Note: Observations b and d form the bases for perhaps the only two murder mysteries in which an economist solves the crime. See Marshall Jevons, *Murder at the Margin* and *The Fatal Equilibrium*.)

6.7

In general, uncompensated cross price effects are not equal. That is,

$$\frac{\partial X_i}{\partial P_j} \neq \frac{\partial X_j}{\partial P_i}$$

Use the generalized Slutsky equation to show that these effects are equal if the individual spends a constant fraction of income on each good regardless of relative prices.

6.8

Hicks' "second law" of demand states that the predominant relationship among goods is net substitutability (see footnote 3 of Chapter 6). To prove this result:

     a.   Show why compensated demand functions

$$X_i = f(P_1, \ldots, P_n, U)$$

are homogeneous of degree zero in $P_1 \ldots P_n$ for a given level of U.

b. Use Euler's Theorem for homogeneous functions (for a statement of this theorem, see footnote 5 of Chapter 7) to show that

$$\sum_{j=1}^{n} P_j \left. \frac{\partial X_i}{\partial P_j} \right|_{U = \text{Constant}} = 0 \qquad \text{(for all } i = 1, n)$$

c. Use the "first law of demand"

$$\left(\text{that } \left. \frac{\partial X_i}{\partial P_i} \right|_{U = \text{constant}} \leq 0 \right)$$

to conclude that

$$\sum_{j \neq i} P_j \left. \frac{\partial X_i}{\partial P_j} \right|_{U = \text{Constant}} \geq 0$$

that is, net substitution $(\partial X_i / \partial P_j | U = \text{Constant} \geq 0$ for $i \neq j)$ must prevail.

EXTENSIONS

SEPARABLE UTILITY

In Chapter 6 we saw that general utility theory implies rather little about demand relationships among goods. Other than the fact that net cross substitution effects are symmetric, practically any type of relationship is possible. In this extension we examine a particular type of utility function for which it is possible to make somewhat more definitive statements. These utility functions are called "separable" in the sense (to be made more precise later) that consumption decisions about one good or group of goods do not affect the utility received from some other good or group of goods. If this assumption is tenable, a number of useful results can be observed.

E6.1
Suppose an individual consumes only three goods X_1, X_2, and X_3 and that his or her utility function is of the separable form

$$U(X_1, X_2, X_3) = U_1(X_1) + U_2(X_2) + U_3(X_3)$$

where

$$U_i' > 0 \qquad U_i'' < 0 \quad \text{for } i = 1, 2, 3.$$

Show that $\partial X_2 / \partial P_1$ and $\partial X_3 / \partial P_1$ must both have the same sign—X_2 and X_3 must both be either gross substitutes for X_1 or gross complements for X_1.
(Hint: use the fact that MU_i / P_i must be equal for all goods.)

E6.2
Does the result described in E6.1 hold generally if utility is a separable function of n goods?

E6.3
A more general statement of separability is

$$U(X_1, X_2, \ldots, X_n) =$$
$$U[U_1(X_{g1}), U_2(X_{g2}), \ldots, U_k(X_{gk})]$$

where the set of goods $X_1, X_2, \ldots, X_n$ is partitioned into k mutually exclusive groups, $X_{g1} \ldots X_{gk}$ (i.e., food, clothing, shelter, and so forth). What does this functional representation assume about the effect of changes in the consumption of a good from one group (food) on the subutility obtained from goods in another group (clothing)?

E6.4

Explain why an individual whose utility function is characterized by the type of separability defined in E6.3 will engage in "two stage budgeting." That is, he or she will allocate total income among the groups of goods and then seek to maximize U_i ($i = 1, k$) given the expenditure to be devoted to each commodity group.

E6.5

Use E6.4 to show that changes in the price of a good in one group affect the optimal choices of goods in another group only by affecting total expenditures on that other group.

E6.6

Show how the results of E6.3 and E6.4 might be applied to:

- **a.** Utility maximization for a family of k members.
- **b.** Intertemporal income allocation over k time periods into the future.

REFERENCES

A. Deaton and J. Muellbauer, *Economics and Consumer Behavior* (Cambridge: Cambridge University Press, 1980), pp. 127–141.

W. M. Gorman, "Separable Utility and Aggregation," *Econometrica* (September/October), 1959, pp. 469–481.

CHAPTER 7

Market Demand and Elasticity

In Chapter 5 we showed how to construct the individual's demand curve for a good by examining changes in the utility-maximizing choices for the good in response to changing prices. In this chapter we will be concerned with "adding up" these individual demand curves to create a market demand curve, a concept that plays a crucial role in all of microeconomic theory. Considerable attention is devoted to examining how the position of the market demand curve might change in response to changing conditions. We also will be concerned with defining various "elasticity" measures of the market demand curve since those measures are widely used in empirical work.

MARKET DEMAND CURVES

For ease of exposition, assume that there are only two goods (X and Y) and only two individuals (numbered 1 and 2) in an economy. The first person's demand function for good X is given by

$$X_1 = D_X^1(P_X, P_Y, I_1) \tag{7.1}$$

and the second person's demand for X by

$$X_2 = D_X^2(P_X, P_Y, I_2). \tag{7.2}$$

Two features of these demand functions should be explicitly emphasized. First, both individuals are assumed to face the same prices (P_X and P_Y). Each person is assumed to be a *price taker,* who must accept the prices prevailing in the market. Second, each person's demand depends on his or her own income since each is bound by a budget constraint that determines how much he or she can buy with income I_1 or I_2, respectively.

The total demand for X is simply the sum of the amounts demanded by the two individuals. Obviously, this market demand will depend on the parameters P_X, P_Y, I_1, and I_2. Mathematically,

$$\text{total } X = X_1 + X_2 = D_X^1(P_X, P_Y, I_1) + D_X^2(P_X, P_Y, I_2) \tag{7.3}$$

or

$$\text{total } X = MD_X(P_X, P_Y, I_1, I_2),$$

Figure 7.1   *Construction of a Market Demand Curve*
from Individual Demand Curves

A market demand curve is the "horizontal sum" of each individual's demand curve. At each price the quantity demanded in the market is the sum of the amounts each individual demands. For example, at P_x^* the demand in the market is $X_1^* + X_2^* = X^*$.

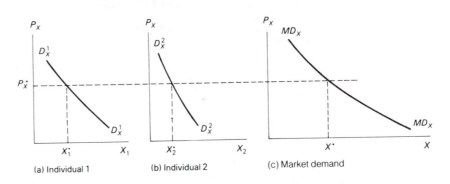

(a) Individual 1   (b) Individual 2   (c) Market demand

where the function MD_X represents the market demand function for good X. Notice that in this case, market demand depends on the prices of both good X and good Y and on the incomes of each individual. To construct the market demand curve (as we do graphically in the next section), P_X is allowed to vary while P_Y, I_1, and I_2 are held constant. If we assume that each individual's demand for good X is downward sloping, the market demand curve will also be. That is, a decrease in P_X will cause the quantity of X demanded in the market to increase because each individual will demand more.

A Graphic
Construction

Figure 7.1 shows the construction of the market demand curve for X. For each price, the point on the market demand curve is found by summing the quantities demanded by each individual. For example, at a price of P_X^* individual 1 demands X_1^* and individual 2 demands X_2^*. The total quantity demanded in the market at P_X^* is therefore the sum of these two amounts: $X^* = X_1^* + X_2^*$. Consequently, the point X^*, P_X^* is one point on the market demand curve MD_X. The other points on the curve are derived in a similar way. The market curve is simply the "horizontal sum" of each individual's demand curve.[1]

Shifts in the
Market Demand
Curve

The market demand curve, then, summarizes the *ceteris paribus* relationship between X and P_X. If the factors underlying the construction of this curve do not change, the position of the curve will remain fixed. If we are to analyze the reasons why a market demand curve might shift, we must first examine how individual demand curves shift and then see how a horizontal summation of

---

[1]Although the construction here applies to uncompensated demand curves (that is, nominal income is being held constant), an identical procedure could be used to construct compensated market demand curves from compensated individual demand curves.

Figure 7.2 *Increases in Each Individual's Income Cause the Market Demand Curve to Shift Outward*

An increase in income for each individual causes each demand curve for X to shift out (assuming X is a normal good). For example, at P_X^* individual 1 now demands X_1^{**} instead of X_1^*. Consequently, the market demand curve shifts out to MD_X'. At P_X^* previously X^* was demanded; now X^{**} $(= X_1^{**} + X_2^{**})$ is demanded.

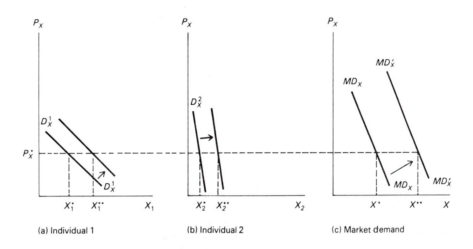

(a) Individual 1   (b) Individual 2   (c) Market demand

these new demand curves compares to the old market demand. In some cases the direction in which the market demand curve will shift is reasonably unambiguous. For example, if both individuals' incomes increase and if both regard X as a normal good, then each person's demand curve would shift outward, and the market demand curve would also shift outward. At each price, more would be demanded in the market because each person's income has increased. This situation is illustrated in Figure 7.2.

Other cases, however, may be more complex. If some individuals' demand curves shift outward while others' shift inward, the resultant effect on market demand will be ambiguous. For example, suppose that I_1 increases and I_2 decreases. The total effect on the location of the market demand curve will then depend on the relative shifts that these income changes induce in individuals' demand functions. It is possible that the total demand curve could shift inward, even though the increase in I_1 exceeded the decrease in I_2, if the reaction of the second person's demand response to income was great and the first person's was small. The effect of changes in total income on market demand therefore will depend greatly on how the income changes are distributed among individuals. For example, an income tax cut that favored low-income individuals might have a substantial effect on the demand for food and general retail purchases but relatively little effect on the demand for luxuries. A tax cut of a similar magnitude that favored those with high incomes might have the opposite effect.

Similar comments apply when discussing the effect that a change in the price of some other good (Y) will have on the market demand for X. For example, if P_Y rises and X and Y are regarded by "most" people as being gross substitutes (see Chapter 6), the market demand for X will shift outward. It would be expected, for example, that a rise in the price of chicken would shift the market demand curve for beef outward. On the other hand, if most people regard the two goods as gross complements, an increase in P_Y will cause the market demand curve for X to shift inward. An increase in the price of sugar may shift the coffee demand curve inward.

Generalizations   Although the construction illustrated previously concerned only two goods and two individuals, it is easily generalized. Suppose there are n goods (denoted by X_i, $i = 1$, n) with prices P_i, $i = 1$, n. Assume also there are m individuals in society. Then the jth individual's demand for the ith good will depend on all prices and on I_j, the income of this person. This can be denoted by

$$X_{ij} = X_{ij}(P_1, \ldots, P_n, I_j). \tag{7.4}$$

where $i = 1$, n and $j = 1$, m.

Using these individual demand functions, market demand concepts are provided by the following definitions.

Definition:

Market Demand

The *market demand function* for a particular good (X_i) is the sum of each individual's demand for that good:

$$X_i = \sum_{j=1}^{m} X_{ij} = X_i(P_1, \ldots, P_n, I_1, \ldots, I_m). \tag{7.5}$$

The *market demand curve* for X_i is constructed from the demand function by varying P_i while holding all other determinants of X_i constant. Assuming each individual's demand curve is downward sloping, this market demand curve also will be downward sloping.

Of course, this definition is just a generalization of our prior discussion, but three features warrant repetition. First, the functional representation of Equation 7.5 makes clear that the demand for X_i depends not only on P_i but also on the prices of all other goods. A change in one of those other prices would therefore be expected to shift the demand curve to a new position. Second, the functional notation indicates that the demand for X_i depends on the entire distribution of individuals' incomes. Although in some economic discussions it is customary to refer to the effect of changes in aggregate total purchasing power on the demand for a good, this approach may be a misleading simplification, since the actual effect of such a change on total demand will depend on precisely how the income changes are distributed among individuals. For example, a general rise in income throughout the economy might not affect purchases in a particular area, if no one there shared in the boom. Finally, although they are obscured somewhat by the notation we have been using, the role of changes in preferences should be mentioned. We have constructed individuals' demand functions with the assumption that preferences (as represented by indifference curve maps) remain fixed. If preferences were to change, so would individual and market demand functions. Hence market demand curves can clearly be shifted by changes in preferences. In many economic analyses, however, it is assumed that these changes occur so slowly that they may be implicitly held constant without misrepresenting the situation.

A Word on Notation

Often in this book we shall be looking at only one market. In order to simplify the notation, in these cases we shall use the letter Q to refer to the quantity of the particular good demanded in this market and P to denote its price. As always, when we draw a demand curve in the Q–P plane, the *ceteris paribus* assumption is in effect. If any of the factors mentioned in the previous section (other prices, individuals' incomes, or preferences) should change, the Q–P demand curve will shift, and we should keep that possibility in mind. When we turn to consider relationships among two or more goods, however, we will return to the notation we have been using up until now (that is, denoting goods by X and Y).

ELASTICITY

Economists frequently wish to summarize the way in which changes in one variable, say, A, affect some other variable, say, B. For example, an economist might be interested in measuring how the change in the price of a good affects the quantity demanded or how a change in income affects total expenditures. One problem that arises in attempting to develop such summary measures is that quite often A and B are not measured in the same units. The quantity of steak purchased is measured in pounds and ounces per week, and the price of steak is measured in dollars. We might then speak of an increase of 10 cents in the price of steak, leading to a fall of 2 pounds per week of steak purchases. Similarly, we could speak of a fall in the price of oranges by 10 cents per dozen, leading to an increase of orange purchases of one-half dozen per week. However, there now would be no easy way to answer the question of whether steak is more or less responsive to price changes than are oranges. The problem exists because the commodities are measured in different units. As a solution economists have developed the concept of *elasticity*, which will be introduced in this section.

Suppose that a particular variable B depends on another variable A and that this dependence is denoted by

$$B = f(A \ldots),\qquad (7.6)$$

where the dots in the equation indicate that B may depend on other variables as well. We define the elasticity of B with respect to A (denoted by $e_{B,A}$) as

$$e_{B,A} = \frac{\text{percentage change in } B}{\text{percentage change in } A} = \frac{\Delta B/B}{\Delta A/A} = \frac{\partial B}{\partial A} \cdot \frac{A}{B}. \qquad (7.7)$$

This expression shows how the variable B responds, *ceteris paribus*, to a 1 percent change in variable A. Although the partial derivative $\partial B/\partial A$ also shows how B changes when A changes, it is not as useful as the elasticity measures because it is measured in units of B per unit change in A. In the elasticity measure, multiplication of that partial derivative by A/B causes the unit to "drop out," and the remaining expression is purely in terms of percentages. In our orange-steak example, we might know that a 1 percent change in the price of steak leads to a 2 percent change in the quantity bought, whereas a 1 percent change in the price of oranges leads to a 1 percent change in the quantity bought. Consequently, we could conclude that steak purchases were more responsive to price. The fact that steak and oranges are measured in different units no longer presents a problem because we are dealing only in relative percentage changes.

Price Elasticity of Demand

Although we shall come across many different applications of the concept of elasticity in this book, probably the most important is that of the price elasticity of demand. Changes in the price of a good (P) will lead to changes in the quantity purchased (Q), and the price elasticity of demand is intended to measure this response. Applying Equation 7.7 the price elasticity of demand would be defined as

Definition:

Price Elasticity of Demand ($e_{Q,P}$)

$$e_{Q,P} = \frac{\text{percentage change in } Q}{\text{percentage change in } P} = \frac{\partial Q}{\partial P} \cdot \frac{P}{Q}. \tag{7.8}$$

This elasticity, then, records how Q changes (in percentage terms) in response to a percentage change in P. Since $\partial Q/\partial P$ is usually negative (that is, P and Q move in opposite directions, except in the case of Giffen's paradox), $e_{Q,P}$ usually will be negative.[2] For example, a value of $e_{Q,P}$ of -1 would mean that a 1 percent rise in price leads to a 1 percent decline in quantity, whereas a value of $e_{Q,P}$ of -2 would record the fact that a 1 percent rise in price causes quantity to decline by 2 percent.

A distinction is often made among values of $e_{Q,P}$ that are less than, equal to, or greater than -1. Specifically, the terminology used is as shown in Table 7.1. For an elastic curve, a price increase is met by a more than proportionate quantity decrease. For a unit elastic curve, the price increase and the quantity decrease are of identical proportional magnitudes. For an inelastic curve, price increases proportionally more than quantity decreases. If a curve is elastic,

[2] Sometimes the elasticity of demand is defined as the absolute value of the definition in Equation 7.8. Consequently, under this alternative definition, elasticity is never negative; curves are classified as elastic, unit elastic, or inelastic, depending on whether $|e_{Q,P}|$ is greater than, equal to, or less than 1. The reader should recognize this distinction in examining empirical work, since there is no consistent usage in economic literature.

Table 7.1   *Terminology for a Demand Curve to Distinguish Values of $e_{Q,P}$*

Value of $e_{Q,P}$ at a Point	Terminology of Curve at This Point
$e_{Q,P} < -1$	Elastic
$e_{Q,P} = -1$	Unit elastic
$e_{Q,P} > -1$	Inelastic

price affects quantity "a lot"; if a curve is inelastic, price does not have as much of an effect on quantity demanded. We might classify goods by their elasticities of demand. For example, the quantity of medical services demanded is undoubtedly very inelastic. The market demand curve may be almost vertical in this case, indicating that the quantity demanded is not responsive to price. On the other hand, it is likely that price changes will have a great effect on the quantity of candy bought (the demand is elastic). Here the market demand curve would be relatively flat. If market price were to change even slightly, the quantity demanded would change significantly.

Price Elasticity and Total Expenditure

The total expenditure on any good is the product of the price of the good (P) times the quantity chosen (Q). By using the concept of price elasticity of demand, it is possible to examine how total expenditure changes when the price of a good changes. Differentiating PQ with respect to P yields

$$\frac{\partial PQ}{\partial P} = Q + P \cdot \frac{\partial Q}{\partial P}. \tag{7.9}$$

Dividing both sides by Q, we have

$$\frac{\partial PQ/\partial P}{Q} = 1 + \frac{\partial Q}{\partial P} \cdot \frac{P}{Q} = 1 + e_{Q,P}. \tag{7.10}$$

Since Q is positive, the sign of $\partial PQ/\partial P$ will depend on whether $e_{Q,P}$ is greater than or less than -1. If $e_{Q,P} > -1$, demand is inelastic and the derivative is positive: Price and total expenditures move in the same direction. For example, an increase in price would raise total expenditures, since P would rise proportionally more than Q would fall. That situation has been observed in the demand for agricultural products. Since the demand for food (as we show later in this chapter) is price inelastic, an increase in its price, perhaps due to bad weather, actually increases total expenditures on food.

On the other hand, if $e_{Q,P} < -1$, price and total expenditures will move in opposite directions. For example, an increase in price will reduce total expenditures, since quantity purchased will fall proportionately more than price rises. Table 7.2 (which is constructed from Equation 7.10) summarizes these responses of total expenditure to a change in price. These results will be useful for our examination of the behavior of firms in Parts IV–VI.

Table 7.2   *Responses of Total Expenditure to Price Changes*

	Responses of PQ	
Demand	Price Increase	Price Decrease
Elastic	Falls	Rises
Unit elastic	No change	No change
Inelastic	Rises	Falls

Income Elasticity of Demand

Another type of elasticity frequently encountered in economics is the income elasticity of demand ($e_{Q,I}$). This concept records the relationship between income changes and quantity changes and is another application of the general definition given in Equation 7.7.

Definition:

Income Elasticity of Demand ($e_{Q,I}$)

$$e_{Q,I} = \frac{\text{percentage change in quantity}}{\text{percentage change in income}} = \frac{\partial Q}{\partial I} \cdot \frac{I}{Q} \qquad (7.11)$$

For a normal good, $e_{Q,I}$ is positive since $\partial Q/\partial I$ is positive. For an inferior good, on the other hand, $e_{Q,I}$ is negative.

   Among normal goods there is considerable interest about whether $e_{Q,I}$ is greater than or less than 1. Goods for which $e_{Q,I} > 1$ might be called luxury goods in the sense that purchases of these goods increase more rapidly than income. For example, if the income elasticity of demand for automobiles is 2.0, then the implication is that a 10 percent rise in income will lead to a 20 percent increase in automobile purchases. On the other hand, a good such as food probably has an income elasticity of less than 1. If the income elasticity of demand for food were 0.5, then the implication is that a 10 percent rise in income would result in only a 5 percent increase in food purchases.[3]

Cross-Price Elasticity

The final concept of elasticity we introduce in this chapter measures the reaction of quantity purchased (Q) to changes in the price of some other good (P'). We define this cross-price elasticity of demand as

---

[3] In light of our previous discussion, these definitions of income elasticity might be generalized to include possible changes in the distribution of income as well. In practice, however, the distinction is often disregarded.

Definition:

Cross-Price Elasticity of Demand ($e_{Q,P'}$)

$$e_{Q,P'} = \frac{\partial Q}{\partial P'} \cdot \frac{P'}{Q}. \qquad (7.12)$$

If Q and the other goods are gross substitutes, $\partial Q/\partial P'$ will be positive, as will be $e_{Q,\,P'}$. When the goods are gross complements, $\partial Q/\partial P'$ and $e_{Q,P'}$ will be negative.

RELATION-SHIPS AMONG ELASTICITIES

We have developed elasticity concepts as they apply to the market demand for a product because these provide convenient, measurable summaries of the responsiveness of quantity demanded to changes in various factors. By treating market demand as being composed of the demands of many "typical" individuals, it is possible to derive some important relationships among these elasticities. For this purpose, suppose that there are only two goods (X and Y) for the typical individual to choose from in maximizing utility and that, as before, the budget constraint is given by[4]

$$P_X X + P_Y Y = I. \qquad (7.13)$$

The typical individual's demand functions for X and Y are given by

$$X = D_X(P_X, P_Y, I)$$
$$Y = D_Y(P_X, P_Y, I), \qquad (7.14)$$

and these demand functions are homogeneous of degree 0 in all prices and income. We shall now derive some relationships among the demand elasticities for this typical individual that can then be taken to hold for the market demand function as a whole.

Sum of Income Elasticities for All Goods

Differentiation of the budget constraint (Equation 7.13) with respect to I yields

$$P_X \frac{\partial X}{\partial I} + P_Y \frac{\partial Y}{\partial I} = 1 \qquad (7.15)$$

or, multiplying each term by (a complex form of) 1,

$$\frac{P_X \cdot X}{I} \cdot \frac{\partial X}{\partial I} \cdot \frac{I}{X} + \frac{P_Y \cdot Y}{I} \cdot \frac{\partial Y}{\partial I} \cdot \frac{I}{Y} = 1. \qquad (7.16)$$

Now $P_X \cdot X/I$ is simply the proportion of income spent on good X, and $P_Y \cdot Y/I$ is a similar expression for good Y. Using s_X to denote the proportion

---

[4] For most of the results presented here, the generalization to n goods is straightforward. However, the treatment of market demand reflecting the behavior of a typical individual raises many complications, some of which are examined in the Extension problems to this chapter.

of income spent on X, s_Y for the proportion income spent on Y, and the definition of income elasticity of demand (Equation 7.11), we have

$$s_X e_{X,I} + s_Y e_{Y,I} = 1. \tag{7.17}$$

The weighted sum of the income elasticities of demand for *all* goods must be unity; that is, when income increases by 10 percent, the budget constraint requires that purchases as a whole increase by 10 percent. Equation 7.17 is sometimes referred to as a "generalized" Engel's law. It shows that for "every" good (or group of goods) that has an income elasticity of demand less than 1, there must exist goods that have income elasticities greater than 1. In fact, if there are only two goods, Equation 7.17 implies that knowledge of one good's income elasticity and of the share of income devoted to that good permits calculation of the income elasticity for the other good.

Slutsky Equation in Elasticities

In Chapter 5 we derived the Slutsky equation to show how an individual's demand for a good (say, X) responds to a change in its price. That equation was written as

$$\frac{\partial X}{\partial P_X} = \left. \frac{\partial X}{\partial P_X} \right|_{U \,=\, \text{constant}} - X \frac{\partial X}{\partial I}. \tag{7.18}$$

Multiplication of Equation 7.18 by P_X/X yields

$$\frac{\partial X}{\partial P_X} \cdot \frac{P_X}{X} = \left. \frac{\partial X}{\partial P_X} \cdot \frac{P_X}{X} \right|_{U \,=\, \text{constant}} - P_X \cdot X \cdot \frac{\partial X}{\partial I} \cdot \frac{1}{X}. \tag{7.19}$$

Multiplying numerator and denominator of the final term in this expression by I, we have

$$\frac{\partial X}{\partial P_X} \cdot \frac{P_X}{X} = \left. \frac{\partial X}{\partial P_X} \cdot \frac{P_X}{X} \right|_{U \,=\, \text{constant}} - \frac{P_X \cdot X}{I} \cdot \frac{\partial X}{\partial I} \cdot \frac{I}{X}. \tag{7.20}$$

Now we introduce a definition of the "substitution elasticity":

$$e_{X,P_X}^S = \left. \frac{\partial X}{\partial P_X} \cdot \frac{P_X}{X} \right|_{U \,=\, \text{constant}}, \tag{7.21}$$

which shows how the compensated demand for X responds to proportional compensated price changes. Combining that definition with the others developed in this chapter, Equation 7.20 becomes

$$e_{X,P_X} = e_{X,P_X}^S - s_X e_{X,I}. \tag{7.22}$$

This equation therefore incorporates the Slutsky relationship in elasticity form. It shows how the price elasticity of demand can be disaggregated into substitution and income components and that the relative size of the income component depends on the proportion of total expenditures devoted to the good in question (that is, on s_X). The equation also shows that if a good has no substitutes ($e_{X,P_X}^S = 0$), price elasticity of demand is proportional to income elasticity, the factor of proportionality being s_X. Similarly, the extent to which that proportionality does hold can be used to judge the extent to which individuals are willing to make substitutions in their consumption choices. Hence empirical estimates of income and uncompensated price elasticities can be used with Equation 7.22 to estimate compensated demand elasticities. Some of the problems at the end of this chapter ask the reader to do just that.

Sum of All Price and Income Elasticities for a Single Good

As a final example of deriving relationships among elasticities, we make use of the fact that demand functions are homogeneous of degree 0 in all prices and income. Focusing on the demand for good X, for example, Euler's theorem for homogeneous functions shows that[5]

$$\frac{\partial X}{\partial P_X} \cdot P_X + \frac{\partial X}{\partial P_Y} \cdot P_Y + \frac{\partial X}{\partial I} \cdot I = 0. \tag{7.23}$$

Dividing this expression by X gives

$$\frac{\partial X}{\partial P_X} \cdot \frac{P_X}{X} + \frac{\partial X}{\partial P_Y} \cdot \frac{P_Y}{X} + \frac{\partial X}{\partial I} \cdot \frac{I}{X} = 0 \tag{7.24}$$

or, using our definitions,

$$e_{X,P_X} + e_{X,P_Y} + e_{X,I} = 0. \tag{7.25}$$

The fact that the demand elasticities for X with respect to all prices and income sum to 0 is an alternative way of stating the homogeneity property of demand functions: An equal percentage change in all prices and income will leave the demand for X unaffected.

TYPES OF DEMAND CURVES

A wide variety of specific mathematical functions have been used by economists to represent demand functions and their related demand curves. In this section we will examine only two such functional forms—linear functions and constant elasticity functions. Other forms are illustrated in various problems throughout the book.

Linear Demand

Probably the simplest way of recording the relationship between quantity demanded (Q), the price of the good (P), income (I), and the price of other goods (P') is by means of a linear function of the form:[6]

$$Q = a + bP + cI + dP', \tag{7.26}$$

---

[5] Euler's theorem states that if a function $f(X_1, X_2, \ldots, X_n)$ is homogeneous of degree m [that is, if $f(tX_1, tX_2, \ldots, tX_n) = t^m f(X_1, X_2, \ldots, X_n)$ for any $t > 0$], then $f_1 \cdot X_1 + f_2 \cdot X_2 + \cdots + f_n \cdot X_n = mf(X_1, X_2, \ldots, X_n)$. Here we apply the theorem for the case in which $m = 0$. In Chapter 21 we make use of the theorem when $m = 1$ to show that competitively determined factor prices will cause total factor costs to equal the total value of output. Proof of Euler's theorem is fairly straightforward—it proceeds by differentiating the equation defining homogeneity with respect to t, and then setting $t = 1$.

[6] Notice that this equation is not homogeneous of degree zero in all prices and income. To make it so would require that $a = 0$ and that P, I, and P' be measured relative to an overall measure of prices (say, the CPI).

where a, b, c, and d are various demand parameters and

- $\partial Q / \partial P = b \le 0$ (assuming Giffen's paradox does not occur);
- $\partial Q / \partial I = c \ge 0$ (assuming the good is normal); and
- $\partial Q / \partial P' = d \gtreqless 0$ (depending on whether P' is the price of a gross substitute or a gross complement).

If I and P' are held constant at $\bar{I}$ and $\bar{P}'$, respectively, then the demand function in Equation 7.26 can be written as

$$Q = a' + bP, \tag{7.27}$$

where $a' = a + c\bar{I} + d\bar{P}'$. The linear form of Equation 7.27 makes clear that the demand curve implied by this demand function is a straight line. Changes in I or P' would shift this curve to alternative positions by altering its Q-intercept,[7] a'.

Numerical Example

Consider a linear demand function for oranges of the form

$$Q = 10 - 2P + .1I + .5P', \tag{7.28}$$

where per capita

- Q = quantity of oranges demanded per year in dozens;
- P = price of oranges in dollars per dozen;
- I = income (in thousands of dollars) for the typical consumer;
- P' = price of grapefruits (a gross substitute for oranges) in dollars per dozen.

Then, for given values for I (say, $I = 20$) and P' (say, $P' = 4$), Equation 7.28 can be "compressed" into a simple linear relationship between Q and P:

$$Q = 10 - 2P + .1(20) + .5(4) \tag{7.29}$$

or

$$Q = 14 - 2P, \tag{7.30}$$

and it would be a simple matter to graph this curve. If income (I) rose (to, say, $I = 30$), this equation would shift to

$$Q = 15 - 2P, \tag{7.31}$$

and if the price of grapefruits fell (to, say, 2) the curve would shift to

$$Q = 13 - 2P. \tag{7.32}$$

Additional influences on Q could be captured by adding more terms to Equation 7.28.

---

[7]Notice here that, following usual economic convention, the dependent variable, Q, is shown graphically on the horizontal axis. Hence, a' represents the intercept on that axis.

Figure 7.3   *The Elasticity of Demand Varies along a Straight-Line Demand Curve*

A straight-line demand curve may be inappropriate for empirical work because it implies that reaction to proportional price changes will be quite different depending on whether prices are high or low.

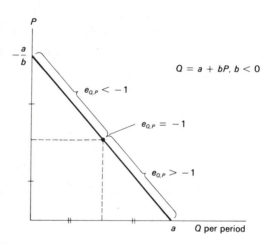

Linear Demand and Elasticity

Although the simple form for a linear demand curve is easy to graph, it may at times be inappropriate for economic applications. Along a linear demand curve, $\partial Q/\partial P$ is constant. This means that a change in price from \$1 to \$2 (a doubling of price) is assumed to have the same effect on quantity demanded as a change from \$20 to \$21 (a 5 percent increase). In many applications this assumed similarity of response to very different proportional changes in price may be untenable.

An alternative way of stating this objection is to observe that the price elasticity of demand is not constant along a linear demand curve. If demand is reflected by Equation 7.27, then applying the definition of the price elasticity of demand (Equation 7.8) yields

$$e_{Q,P} = \frac{\partial Q}{\partial P} \cdot \frac{P}{Q} = b \cdot \frac{P}{Q}. \tag{7.33}$$

But the value for this elasticity obviously varies along the demand curve $Q = a' + bP$; as P rises, Q falls and $e_{Q,P}$ becomes a larger negative number (remember, $b < 0$). In other words, demand becomes more elastic for higher prices. Figure 7.3 illustrates this fact. When price, P, is halfway between 0 and where the curve hits the vertical axis (where $P = -a'/b$), $e_{Q,P}$ has a value of -1.[8] Above this midpoint, demand is elastic ($e_{Q,P} < -1$) and for a price below this

---

[8] Proof: If $P = -a'/2b$ (i.e., halfway between 0 and $-a'/b$), then $Q = a' + b(-a'/2b) = a'/2$. Hence, $e_{Q,P} = bP/Q = b(-a'/2b) \div (a'/2) = -1$.

point, demand is inelastic ($e_{Q,P} > -1$). Hence $e_{Q,P}$ can take on any non-positive value depending on which point on the curve happens to be observed. In our prior numerical example we assumed that $Q = 14 - 2P$. If $P = 2$, then $Q = 10$ and $e_{Q,P} = (\partial Q/\partial P) \cdot (P/Q) = -2 \cdot (2/10) = -.4$. On the other hand, if $P = 4$, $Q = 6$ and $e_{Q,P} = -2 \cdot (4/6) = -1.33$. Thus orange demand can be either inelastic or elastic depending on the price.

Constant
Elasticity
Functions

If one wished to assume that elasticities were relatively constant in response to changing prices, an exponential demand function might be used:

$$Q = aP^b I^c P'^d, \tag{7.34}$$

where now $a > 0$, $b \le 0$, $c \ge 0$, $d \gtreqless 0$. For particular values of the shift variables (say, $\bar{I}$ and $\bar{P}'$) this could be written as

$$Q = a'P^b, \tag{7.35}$$

where $a' = aI^c P'^d$. An alternative way of writing Equation 7.34 is

$$\ln Q = \ln a' + b \ln P, \tag{7.36}$$

which shows that the equation is linear in the logarithms (denoted by "ln") of Q and P.

Applying the definition of price elasticity to this case yields

$$e_{Q,P} = \frac{\partial Q}{\partial P} \cdot \frac{P}{Q} = \frac{ba' P^{b-1} \cdot P}{a' P^b} = b. \tag{7.37}$$

Consequently, the price elasticity of demand is constant (and equal to b) for this demand curve. Notice that the elasticity can be read directly from the mathematical form of the curve—it is given by the exponent of P and does not have to be calculated.[9] If, for example,

$$Q = 100P^{-1.5}, \tag{7.38}$$

you would know that $e_{Q,P} = -1.5$. Demand is therefore elastic; each 1 percent rise in price is met by a fall of 1.5 percent in quantity.[10]

Figure 7.4 illustrates a constant elasticity demand curve. The curve never reaches the Q- or P-axes—Q is undefined when $P = 0$. As in the linear case, changes in I and P' would shift this curve to a new location.

We have, of course, examined only two simple mathematical forms for demand functions. In practice, a wide variety of forms have been used. Ultimately, the choice among them depends both on the underlying economic theory the function is supposed to represent and on which type of function seems to fit the data best. In the application at the end of this chapter, we examine such issues in a bit more detail and illustrate some of the results that have been obtained from actual studies of demand.

---

[9]Similarly, if the entire demand function is given by Equation 7.34, then $e_{Q,I} = c$ and $e_{Q,P'} = d$.

[10]Using Equation 7.38, if $P = 1$, $Q = 100$. If $P = 1.01$, $Q = 100(1.02)^{-1.5} = 98.5$. A 1 percent increase in price results in a 1.5 percent fall in price as might be predicted by the exponent of P.

Figure 7.4   *Constant Elasticity Demand Curve*

A curve of this mathematical form (or, equivalently, one that is linear in the logarithms of *P* and *Q*) exhibits a constant elasticity of demand along its entire length. This feature may make such curves more suitable for empirical work, since demand functions of this form seem to fit historical data rather well.

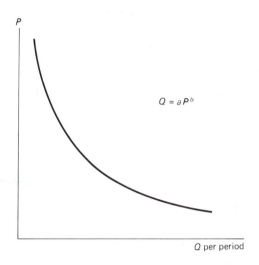

SUMMARY

In this chapter we used the theory of individual demand to construct the market demand function and related market demand curves. The demand curve shows the *ceteris paribus* relationship between the price of a good and the total quantity demanded by all potential buyers. This concept, which is a fundamental tool for practically all economic analysis, will be used repeatedly in later chapters. Hence some conclusions about the market demand curve bear repeating here:

- The market demand curve is negatively sloped on the assumption that most individuals will buy more when the price of a good falls. That is, most individuals are assumed to view most goods as normal goods, or, if the good is inferior, it is assumed that Giffen's paradox does not occur.
- For the usual Marshallian market demand curve, the utility level of the individual demander varies along the curve. Because nominal income is held constant, lower prices raise utility and higher prices lower utility.
- It is also possible to construct income-compensated market demand curves by horizontally summing each individual's compensated demand curve. Although we will use these at some places in the text, for the most part we will develop our analysis using the more familiar Marshallian curve.

- Movements along a given demand curve are measured by the price elasticity of demand, $e_{Q,P}$. This shows the percentage change in quantity from a 1 percent change in price, when all other influences on demand are held constant.
- Changes in total expenditures on a good induced by changes in price can be predicted from the price elasticity of demand. If demand is inelastic ($0 \geq e_{Q,P} > -1$), price and total expenditures move in the same direction. If demand is elastic ($e_{Q,P} < -1$), price and total expenditures move in opposite directions.
- If other factors that enter the demand function (other prices, income, and preferences) change, the market demand curve will shift to a new position. Effects of changes in these other factors on quantity demanded (at a given price) can be measured by the income elasticity of demand ($e_{Q,I}$) or the cross-price elasticity of demand ($e_{Q,P'}$).

Application

EMPIRICAL STUDIES OF MARKET DEMAND

For many years economists have been interested in studying the demand for various goods. Some of the earliest studies looked at the expenditure patterns of a small sample of families, attempting to generalize from those empirical regularities that were observed. Probably the most widely quoted result of those early studies was Engel's law (see Chapter 5), which states that the percentage of income that families spend on food declines as their incomes increase. The conclusion drawn was that the income elasticity of the demand for food, although positive, was considerably less than 1.

Estimating Demand Curves: the Ceteris Paribus Assumption

More recent studies have examined a wide variety of goods and have attempted to estimate both income and price elasticities. Although it is not possible for us to discuss here the statistical techniques used in such studies, it should be useful to suggest in an intuitive way how economists have proceeded. The first important problem faced in any empirical investigation is

how to implement the *ceteris paribus* assumption. In examining the relationship between the price of a good and the quantity demanded, for example, our theory requires that income, other prices, and all other factors be held constant. If income and other prices are not held constant, observed combinations of P and Q will lie on many different demand curves.

At a conceptual level this problem is a straightforward one to solve. If we could measure the quantity of the product bought at several points in time where different prices prevailed but "everything else" was the same, we could plot these P, Q points as in Figure 7.5. Then we could use some type of curve-fitting technique to draw a demand curve that represents them fairly accurately. Similarly, if we could measure quantities bought in different locations that were identical in every respect except the prices people face (perhaps the price varies because of transport charges), we could conduct a similar exercise. In these conceptual cases then, demand analysis is simply a matter of plotting points and fitting curves.

Unfortunately, the real world does not provide these kinds of data. No two time periods will exhibit exactly the same influences on de-

Figure 7.5   *Fitting a Demand Curve to Empirical Observations*

The points in this figure show observed combinations of *P* and *Q*. It is important that these points be observed while the other factors that affect the demand for *Q* are held constant.

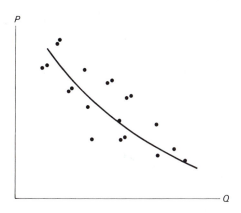

mand except the price of the commodity. Two geographic areas will always differ along many dimensions that are relevant to the market in question. A partial answer to imposing the *ceteris paribus* assumption in these circumstances is to use statistical tools to estimate the entire demand function. If, for example, the demand for some product (*Q*) were believed to depend on its price (*P*), income (*I*), the price of a close substitute (*P'*), a variable representing preferences (*X*), and a set of unexplained "random" influences (*U*), it would be possible to use multiple regression analysis to estimate the demand function:[11]

$$Q = a + bP + cI$$
$$+ dP' + eX + U, \quad (7.39)$$

where *a, b, c, d,* and *e* are the parameters to be estimated. With sufficient data for the variables *Q, P, I, P',* and *X*, it is a simple matter to estimate such an equation using modern com-

puters. Knowledge of the demand function in Equation 7.39 can then be used to calculate the market demand curve (as we did in the final section of Chapter 7) by holding *I, P',* and *X* at preassigned fixed values. In this way we can use statistical techniques to impose the *ceteris paribus* assumption.

Supply and the Identification Problem
A naïve application of these techniques may still encounter difficulties, however, because they disregard Marshall's lesson that price and quantity are set jointly by the influence of demand *and* supply. Figure 7.6 illustrates the nature of the problem. Both panels of the figure are based on the same observed "data"—that is, both panels record the same four (*P, Q*) points. In Figure 7.6a these price-quantity equilibria were generated by a shifting supply curve tracing out a stable and relatively inelastic demand curve. In this situation a statistical procedure that fit a curve such as D_1 to these data would give an accurate picture of the true demand curve and its price elasticity.

In Figure 7.6b, however, fitting a simple curve would give inaccurate information. For

[11]For a discussion, see Edwin Mansfield, *Statistics for Business and Economics,* 3d ed. (New York: W. W. Norton and Co., 1987), chap. 12.

Figure 7.6   *The Identification Problem*

The price quantity data in these two panels are identical. In (a) they arose from a stable, inelastic demand curve that intersected a shifting supply curve. In (b) the same points were generated by an elastic demand curve that shifted simultaneously with the supply curve. Discovering whether (a) or (b) represents the true situation is a difficult theoretical problem.

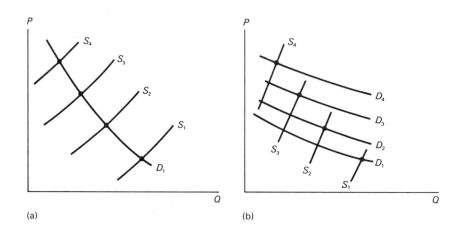

(a)   (b)

this case the four points represent four different demand curves because the demand and supply curves have been shifted by a common cause. The demand curves in (b) are actually quite elastic, but this could not be detected from the data unless the reasons for the shifts in both curves could be analyzed independently.

The possible confusion illustrated by Figure 7.6 is an example of what economists call the *identification problem*.[12] Although we will not pursue this problem here, it should be noted that it is perhaps the most difficult problem faced by researchers who wish to study a situation in which two variables (P and Q) are determined simultaneously (here by demand and

supply). The authors who developed all the price elasticity estimates we will study had to address this problem to ensure that their estimates were valid.

Some Elasticity Estimates

Table 7.3 lists a few income and price elasticities of demand that economists have estimated. Although these estimates come from a variety of sources, they do exhibit certain similarities. The income elasticities for "necessities" (food and medical services) are considerably below those for "luxuries" (automobiles). This is in accord with *a priori* expectations about the way in which the purchases of such goods respond to income changes. A second observation is that most of the price elasticities are fairly low (although, as we expected, they are all negative). Price changes do not induce substantial proportional changes in quantities.

A few of the elasticities in Table 7.3 might be discussed explicitly. For example, the findings

[12]This problem was first analyzed by E. J. Working in "What Do Statistical 'Demand Curves' Show?" *Quarterly Journal of Economics* 41(1927): 217–235. For a more recent extensive treatment, see Franklin M. Fisher, *The Identification Problem in Econometrics* (New York: McGraw-Hill Book Company, 1966).

Table 7.3 *Representative Income and Price Elasticities*

Item	Income Elasticity	Price Elasticity
Food	0.28	−0.21
Medical services	0.22	−0.20
Automobiles	3.00	−1.20
Housing		
Rental	1.00	−0.18
Owner-occupied	1.20	−1.20
Gasoline	1.06	−0.54
Electricity	0.61	−1.14
Giving to charity	0.70	−1.29
Beer	0.93	−1.13
Marijuana	0	−1.50

Sources: Food—H. Wold and L. Jureen, *Demand Analysis* (New York: John Wiley & Sons, 1953), p. 203. Medical services—income elasticity from R. Andersen and L. Benham, "Factors Affecting the Relationship Between Family Income and Medical Care Consumption"; price elasticity from G. Rosenthal, "Price Elasticity of Demand for Short-Term General Hospital Services"; both in *Empirical Studies in Health Economics*, ed. Herbert Klarman (Baltimore, Md.: Johns Hopkins Press, 1970). Automobiles—Gregory C. Chow, *Demand for Automobiles in the United States* (Amsterdam: North-Holland Publishing Co., 1957). Housing—income elasticities from F. de Leeuw, "The Demand for Housing," *Review of Economics and Statistics* (February 1971); price elasticities from H. S. Houthakker and L. D. Taylor, *Consumer Demand in the United States* (Cambridge, Mass.: Harvard University Press, 1970), pp. 166–167. Gasoline—Data Resources, "A Study of the Quarterly Demand for Gasoline" (Prepared for the Council on Environmental Quality, December 1973). Electricity—R. F. Halvorsen, "Residential Demand for Electricity" (Ph.D. diss., Harvard University, December 1972). Giving to charity—M. Feldstein and A. Taylor, "The Income Tax and Charitable Contributions," *Econometrica* 44, no. 6 (November 1976): 1201–1222. Beer—T. F. Hogarty and K. G. Elsinger, "The Demand for Beer," *Review of Economics and Statistics* 54, no. 2 (May 1972): 195–198. Marijuana—T. C. Misket and F. Vakil, "Some Estimates of Price and Expenditure Elasticities among UCLA Students," *Review of Economics and Statistics* 54, no. 4 (November 1972): 474–475.

suggest that the demand for electricity is price elastic. Hence one result of the sharply increasing energy prices of the 1970s was to curtail significantly the demand for electric power. As a consequence, a number of major power plant projects were canceled when utility companies discovered that their demand growth patterns were significantly overstated.

For housing, the finding that the income elasticity of demand equals or exceeds unity has interesting implications for the fairness of prop-

erty taxation. If housing expenditures increase more rapidly than income, a tax on housing values will tend to be relatively progressive, since higher-income people will pay proportionally more in taxes than will low-income people. Hence the "commonsense notion" that property taxes are regressive because housing is a "necessity" is simply erroneous.

Finally, the estimate for the "price elasticity" of giving to charity presented in Table 7.3 warrants some explanation. In this case the price elasticity refers to how individuals respond to the favorable tax treatment of charitable contributions under the federal income tax. Under current law such contributions may be deducted from taxable income, thereby effectively reducing the net cost of making them. For example, a taxpayer facing a marginal income tax rate of 33 percent essentially pays only 67 percent of the cost of his or her charitable contributions, with the government paying the remainder in terms of reduced tax revenues. For someone in a higher tax bracket, the net price of giving is even lower, thereby providing greater incentives to give. Because the elasticity estimate in Table 7.3 is below -1.00 (that is, demand is elastic), the special tax treatment of contributions can be shown to generate a greater total amount in such contributions than is lost in potential tax revenues. Hence the special tax treatment is somewhat more effective at promoting charitable purposes than simply having the government make contributions directly. We now show in somewhat more detail two specific examples of how estimates of particular demand elasticities can be used for policy purposes.

National Health Insurance

Most developed countries have some form of national health insurance plan, and a number of such plans have been proposed for the United States in recent years. These proposed plans vary greatly in cost, with some having annual price tags higher than $100 billion. A principal determinant of a plan's cost is the precise mix of services that it covers. Very basic plans cover only hospital stays and physicians' costs for major illnesses, whereas more extensive plans may cover a wide variety of services, ranging from family counseling to dental care. An important policy issue that must be addressed in choosing among such plans is how their adoption will affect the quantity demanded of specific medical services. Because insurance lowers the out-of-pocket cost to patients who receive services,

there is certain to be some increase in quantity demanded. The empirical question is how large that increase might be.

The estimated price elasticity of demand for medical services given in Table 7.3 (the value is -0.20) might be a starting point in making such assessments. As would be expected, this figure indicates that the demand for overall medical services is quite inelastic, though it does suggest that there will be some expansion in demand as a result of reductions in effective prices through insurance coverage. Of course, the figure in Table 7.3 applied to all medical services, and the true situation may differ significantly among specific services. For example, in a study of patients' actual responses to out-of-pocket costs for medical services, J. P. Newhouse and C. E. Phelps found very low price elasticities of demand (between 0 and -0.10) for the lengths of stays in hospitals and for office visits to physicians.[13] Hence these services might experience relatively little expansion in demand were they included in national health insurance plans. On the other hand, several authors have found much larger price elasticities for services, such as dental care, ophthalmological services and devices, and psychiatric counseling, that may have a somewhat greater discretionary element to their consumption. For these items then, a substantial increase in demand as a result of insurance coverage might be expected. Suggestions for ways of limiting this expansion have ranged from outright exclusion of such services from national health insurance coverage to imposition of some sort of cost-sharing on patients using the services. Information on price elasticities will continue to play a major role in shaping legislation in this area.

[13] J. P. Newhouse and C. E. Phelps, "Price and Income Elasticities for Medical Care Services," in *The Economics of Health and Medical Care*, ed. M. Perlman (New York: John Wiley & Sons, 1974), pp. 139–161.

Federal Tax Benefits for Homeowners

Elasticity estimates can be used to suggest how current federal tax benefits to individuals living in their own homes affect the demand for owner-occupied housing. Federal tax policy makes it more advantageous to own rather than rent housing because an owner can deduct mortgage interest payments and property taxes from his or her taxable income whereas a renter (who presumably pays these same costs to his or her landlord) cannot. There is a benefit to homeowners to the extent that interest payments and property taxes make up the total costs of owning or renting. Most authors estimate that these two costs in fact make up about 70 percent of total gross rents. Consequently, it is argued that homeowners are permitted by law to deduct 70 percent of the implicit "rental" costs from their income before they pay taxes whereas renters are not able to do so. The value of this benefit, of course, will depend on the income tax rate that particular families pay. If, for example, a home-owning family faces a marginal tax rate of 30 percent,

then essentially the government pays 21 percent of true rental costs (= 70 percent deduction times 30 percent tax rate). The deductibility of mortgage payments and property taxes causes the government to be subsidizing the price of an owner's house to the extent of 21 percent. The effective price is 21 percent lower than it would be in the absence of preferential treatment. Of course, this subsidy may or may not be in some sense desirable from the viewpoint of national policy, but the effect on the demand for housing is clear-cut: Individuals will respond to the lower price by demanding more owner-occupied housing. In fact we can use the price elasticity for housing reported in Table 7.3 (given as −1.20) to estimate that the 21 percent reduction in price will lead to approximately a 25 percent (= 21 percent times 1.20) increase in the quantity of owner-occupied housing demanded. The effect of the governmental subsidy, then, is to provide a considerable impetus to home ownership. For families facing a higher tax rate, the subsidy (and the impetus to own their homes) is even greater.

SUGGESTED READINGS

Barten, A. P. "The Systems of Demand Function Approach: A Review." *Econometrica* (January 1977): 23–51.

A good survey of the statistical questions involved in trying to estimate a complete set of demand functions for consumer expenditures. Stresses theoretical restrictions that must hold across the equations.

Bell, F. W. "The Pope and the Price of Fish." *American Economic Review* 58 (December 1968): 1346–1350.

Brief, empirical study of how the demand for fish shifted in response to the papal relaxation of the meatless Friday custom.

Deaton, A. J. "Demand Analysis" in Z. Grilicher and M. D. Intriligator, eds. *Handbook of Econometrics*. Amsterdam: North Holland Publishing Co., 1984.

Good survey of the technical econometric issues that arise in demand analysis. Limited references to the empirical literature.

Ferber, R. "Consumer Economics, A Survey." *Journal of Economic Literature* 11 (December 1973): 1303–1342.

Good summary of the empirical literature on consumer behavior. Very complete bibliography (up to only 1973, however).

Houthakker, H. J., and Taylor, I. D. *Consumer Demand in the United States*. 2d ed. Cambridge, Mass.: Harvard University Press, 1970.

Complete analysis of all the categories of expenditures in the GNP consumption series; has several empirical anomalies but generally plausible elasticity estimates for most items.

Theil, H. *Theory and Measurement of Consumer*

Demand, Vol. 1. Amsterdam: North Holland Publishing Co., 1975. Chaps. 5 and 6.

Complete development of the "linear expenditure" system of demand equations; includes substantial theoretical background material.

Wold, H., and Jureen, I. *Demand Analysis*. New York: John Wiley & Sons, 1953.

Classic work on the empirical analysis of demand. Outdated but provides insights on many important issues of empirical specification.

Working, E. "What Do Statistical 'Demand Curves' Show?" *Quarterly Journal of Economics* 41 (1927): 212–235.

Basic statement of the "identification" problem and its relevance to demand analysis.

PROBLEMS

7.1

Imagine a market for X's composed of four individuals: Mr. Pauper (P), Ms. Broke (B), Mr. Average (A), and Ms. Rich (R). All four have the same demand function for X: It is a function of income (I), P_X, and the price of an important substitute (Y) for X:

$$X = \frac{\sqrt{IP_Y}}{2P_X}.$$

a. What is the market demand function for X? If $P_X = P_Y = 1$, and $I_P = I_B = 16$, $I_A = 25$, and $I_R = 100$, what is the total market demand for X? What is e_{X,P_X}? e_{X,P_Y}? $e_{X,I}$?

b. If P_X doubled, what would be the new level of X demanded? If Mr. Pauper lost his job and his income fell 50 percent, how would that affect the market demand for X? What if Ms. Rich's income were to drop 50 percent? If the government imposed a 100 percent tax on Y, how would the demand for X be affected?

c. If $I_P = I_B = I_A = I_R = 25$, what would be the total demand for X? How does that figure compare with your answer to (a)? Answer (b) for these new income levels and $P_X = P_Y = 1$.

d. If Ms. Rich found Z's a necessary complement to X's, her demand function for X's might be described by the function

$$X = \frac{IP_Y}{2P_XP_Z}.$$

What is the new market demand function for X? If $P_X = P_Y = P_Z = 1$ and income levels are those described by (a), what is the demand for X? What is e_{X,P_X}? e_{X,P_Y}? $e_{X,I}$? e_{X,P_Z}? What is the new level of demand for X if the price of Z rises to 2? Notice that Ms. Rich is the only one whose demand for X drops.

7.2

Suppose there are n individuals, each with a linear demand curve for Q of the form

$$Q_i = a_i + b_iP + c_iI + d_iP' \qquad i = 1, n,$$

where the parameters a_i, b_i, c_i, and d_i differ among individuals. Show that at any point, the price elasticity of the market demand curve is independent of P' and the distribution of income. Would this be true if each individual's demand for Q were instead linear in logarithms? Explain.

7.3

The market demand for potatoes is given by:

$$Q = 1,000 + 0.3I - 300P + 200P'$$

where:

$$Q = \text{Annual demand in pounds}$$
$$I = \text{Average income in dollars per year}$$
$$P = \text{Price of potatoes in cents per pound}$$
$$P' = \text{Price of rice in cents per pound.}$$

a.   Suppose $I = \$10,000$ and $P' = \$.25$; what would be the market demand for potatoes? At what price would $Q = 0$? Graph this demand curve.

b.   Suppose I rose to $\$20,000$ with P' staying at $\$.25$. Now what would the demand for potatoes be? At what price would $Q = 0$? Graph this demand curve. Explain why more potatoes are demanded at every price in this case than in part a.

c.   If I returns to $\$10,000$ but P' falls to $\$.10$, what would the demand for potatoes be? At what price would $Q = 0$? Graph this demand curve. Explain why fewer potatoes are demanded at every price in this case than in part a.

7.4

Tom, Dick, and Harry constitute the entire market for scrod. Tom's demand curve is given by:

$$Q_1 = 100 - 2P$$

for $P \le 50$. For $P > 50$, $Q_1 = 0$. Dick's demand curve is given by:

$$Q_2 = 160 - 4P$$

for $P \le 40$. For $P > 40$, $Q_2 = 0$. Harry's demand curve is given by:

$$Q_3 = 150 - 5P$$

for $P \le 30$. For $P > 30$, $Q_3 = 0$. Using this information, answer the following.

a.   How much scrod is demanded by each person at $P = 50$? At $P = 35$? At $P = 25$? At $P = 10$? And at $P = 0$?

b.   What is the total market demand for scrod at each of the prices specified in part a?

c.   Graph each individual's demand curve.

d.   Use the individual demand curves and the results of part b to construct the total market demand curve for scrod.

7.5

Suppose the quantity of good X demanded by individual 1 is given by

$$X_1 = 10 - 2P_X + 0.01I_1 + 0.4P_Y$$

and the quantity of X demanded by individual 2 is

$$X_2 = 5 - P_X + 0.02I_2 + 0.2P_Y.$$

a.   What is the market demand function for total X ($= X_1 + X_2$) as a function of P_X, I_1, I_2, and P_Y?

b. Graph the two individual demand curves (with X on the horizontal axis, P_X on the vertical axis) for the case $I_1 = 1,000$, $I_2 = 1,000$, and $P_Y = 10$.

c. Using these individual demand curves, construct the market demand curve for total X. What is the algebraic equation for this curve?

d. Now suppose I_1 increases to 1,100 and I_2 decreases to 900. How would the market demand curve shift? How would the individual demand curves shift? Graph these new curves.

e. Finally, suppose P_Y rises to 15. Graph the new individual and market demand curves that would result.

7.6
A *luxury* is defined as a good for which the income elasticity of demand is greater than 1. Show that for a two-good economy, both goods cannot be luxuries. (*Hint:* What happens if both goods are luxuries and income is increased by 10 percent?)

7.7
The "expenditure elasticity" for a good is defined as the proportional change in total expenditures on the good in response to a 1 percent change in income. That is,

$$e_{P_X \cdot X, I} = \frac{\partial P_X X}{\partial I} \cdot \frac{I}{P_X X}.$$

Prove that $e_{P_X \cdot X, I} = e_{X, I}$. Show also that $e_{P_X \cdot X, P_X} = 1 + e_{X, P_X}$. Both of these results are useful for empirical work in cases where quantity measures are not available, since income and price elasticities can be derived from expenditure elasticities.

7.8
Show that for a two-good world,

$$s_X e_{X, P_X} + s_Y e_{Y, P_X} = -s_X.$$

If the own price elasticity of demand for X is known, what do we know about the cross price elasticity for Y?

(*Hint:* Begin by taking the total differential of the budget constraint and setting $dI = 0 = dP_Y$.)

7.9
Suppose that ham and cheese are pure complements—they will always be used in the ratio of one slice of ham to one slice of cheese to make a sandwich. Suppose also that ham and cheese sandwiches are the only goods that a consumer can buy and that bread is free. Show that if the price of a slice of ham equals the price of a slice of cheese,

a. The own price elasticity of demand for ham is $-\frac{1}{2}$; and

b. The cross price elasticity of a change in the price of cheese on ham consumption is also $-\frac{1}{2}$.

How would your answers to (a) and (b) change if a slice of ham cost twice as much as a slice of cheese?

(*Hint:* Use the Slutsky Equation.)

7.10
For the linear demand curve illustrated, show that the price elasticity of demand at any given point (say, point E) is given by minus the ratio of distance X to distance Y in the figure. How might you apply this result to a non-linear demand curve?

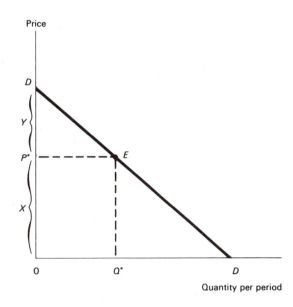

EXTENSIONS

THEORETICAL ISSUES IN MARKET DEMAND ANALYSIS

In Chapters 4–6 we showed that the assumption of utility maximization implies several properties for individual demand functions:

- *The functions are continuous;*
- *The functions are homogeneous of degree zero in all prices and income;*
- *Income compensated substitution effects are negative; and*
- *Cross-price substitution effects are symmetric.*

In this extension problem we will examine the extent to which these properties would be expected to hold for aggregated market demand functions and what, if any, restrictions should be placed on such functions. In addition, we illustrate some additional issues that arise in estimating these functions.

E7.1
Explain why the continuity of individual demand functions implies the continuity of market demand functions. Are there situations in which market demand functions might be continuous whereas individual functions are not? (*Hint:* Consider the case where goods—such as an automobile—must be bought in large, discrete units.)

E7.2
Show that market demand functions are homogeneous of degree zero in all prices and all incomes. Are they necessarily homogeneous of degree zero in all prices and total income?

E7.3

Suppose all individuals' demand functions obey the usual restrictions on own and cross-price substitution effects. Would you expect market demand functions to obey such restrictions? Explain.

E7.4

Suppose individual i's demand for X is given by

$$X_i = a_i(P) + b(P)y_i \qquad i = 1, n$$

where P is the vector of all market prices, $a_i(P)$ is a set of individual-specific price effects and $b(P)$ is a marginal propensity to spend function that is the same across all individuals (although the value of this parameter may depend on market prices). Show that in this case the market demand functions will depend on P and on total income

$$Y = \sum_{i=1}^{n} y_i.$$

Hence, show that market demand reflects the behavior of a single typical consumer. (Gorman, 1959, shows that this is the most general form of demand function that can represent such a typical consumer.)

E7.5

Suppose a typical individual buys k items and that the demand for each is given by

$$P_j X_j = \sum_{i=1}^{k} a_{ij} P_i + b_j Y \qquad j = 1, k$$

If expenditures on these k items exhaust total income, that is,

$$\sum_{j=1}^{k} P_j X_j = Y,$$

show that

$$\sum_{j=1}^{k} a_{ij} = 0$$

for all i and that

$$\sum_{j=1}^{k} b_j = 1.$$

What does this imply about the ability of researchers to estimate these j expenditure functions independently?

REFERENCES

Gorman, W. M., "Separable Utility and Aggregation," *Econometrica* (November 1959): 469–481.

Shafer, W., and Sonnenschein, H., "Market Demand and Excess Demand Functions," in K. J. Arrow and M. D. Intriligator (Eds.), *Handbook of Mathematical Economics,* Vol. II (Amsterdam: North Holland, 1982), pp. 671–693.

Theil, H., *Principles of Econometrics* (New York: John Wiley and Sons, Inc., 1971), pp. 326–346.

PART

III

Additional Applications of the Theory of Choice

In Part II we used the economic theory of choice to develop a rather complete analysis of demand concepts. These concepts are widely used later in this book and throughout the entire study of economics. The theory of choice has many other applications to economics, however, and in this brief part we will examine two of them. First, in Chapter 8 we investigate the theory of exchange—that is, voluntary trading between individuals. There we show that even in the absence of any notion of production and supply (the quantities of goods are fixed in an exchange model), people may have considerable incentive to trade with each other. We show

that some trades may make everyone better off and that there will be ample motivation to exploit such trading opportunities. Hence the material in Chapter 8 represents a rudimentary beginning to our eventual study of market interactions in a very simplified setting.

Our second application of the theory of choice is the study of individual decision making in uncertain situations. In Chapter 9 we show how consumption that involves uncertain outcomes (such as betting on games of chance, investing in risky assets, or buying a used car that may be a "lemon") can be handled in the traditional utility-maximization framework. We use this expanded model to examine two related aspects of individual behavior in uncertain situations: risk aversion and the demand for information. That is, we show that individuals will generally dislike risky situations (say, buying a used car) and will often pay something to acquire more information about such situations (for example, hiring a mechanic to look at the car). Such motives lead to flourishing markets in such risk-reducing products as insurance, mutual funds, and consumer-testing services.

Although the concepts introduced in this part will not be used as widely later in the book as the demand concepts from Part II, their applications to later material will often be mentioned. The gains from voluntary trade, for example, provide an implicit motivation for much of our discussion of the efficiency of various market organizations in later chapters. Similarly, the concepts of risk and information can in principle affect outcomes in all of the types of markets we will be examining. Hence these concepts should not be regarded as tangential to the main thrust of the analysis in this book.

CHAPTER 8

Exchange

In *The Wealth of Nations* Adam Smith observed a widespread tendency in all human societies to "truck, barter, and exchange one thing for another."[1] To Smith such activities represented a fundamental foundation for all economic activity. In this chapter we will use the model of utility maximization that we developed in Chapters 3 and 4 to show how the incentives for such trading arise and to illustrate what efficient trading outcomes might look like. We begin with a few simple, seemingly trivial examples. As the chapter proceeds, however, we address some rather difficult issues which have relevance to a wide variety of market and non-market activities.

THE GAINS FROM VOLUNTARY TRADE

One of the first observations to be made about voluntary trade is that everyone involved in it might possibly be made better off. Trade between two people does not necessarily have a "winner" and a "loser," but can be mutually beneficial. For example, everyone participates in voluntary trade by giving up some amount of money to buy something (say, a candy bar) that he or she values more highly than the cash. The seller also benefits from this transaction—the seller values the cash more highly than the candy bar. Hence voluntary market transactions are usually of mutual benefit to the participants. To study the essentials of the situation, however, we begin with a case in which no markets exist.

A Simple Exchange Situation

Assume that only two goods, hamburgers (which we will call Y) and soft drinks (which we will call X) are available. Assume also that there are fixed amounts of $X = 15$ and $Y = 15$, and that persons 1 and 2 have unequal amounts of X and Y. Person 1 starts out with $X = 5$ and $Y = 10$, and person 2 starts out with $X = 10$ and $Y = 5$. These initial quantities appear in the first columns of Table 8.1.

[1]A. Smith, *The Wealth of Nations* (New York: Random House, Modern Library Edition, 1937), p. 13.

Table 8.1   *A Trade in Which Both Parties Gain*

	Initial Quantity		Results of Trade		Final Quantity	
	X	Y	X	Y	X	Y
Person 1	5	10	+1	−1	6	9
Person 2	10	5	−1	+1	9	6

To look at voluntary trades away from this initial position, we need to know these people's preferences to determine what trades would make each of them better off. Figure 8.1 presents indifference curve maps for our two traders, including the initial allocations of X and Y. At X = 5, Y = 10, person 1 has a marginal rate of substitution (*MRS*) of 2; because she has an abundance of hamburgers, she is willing to give up two of them to get one more soft drink. For person 2, on the other hand, the *MRS* is ½; because she has quite a lot of soft drinks already, she is rather unwilling to give up hamburgers to get even more of them.

Suppose now that these two people reach an agreement under which person 1 trades 1 Y to person 2 for 1 X. Results of this trade are recorded in Table

Figure 8.1   *Both Individuals Gain from a Trade*

Person 1 starts with 10 units of Y and 5 units of X and has an *MRS* of 2. Person 2 starts with 10 units of X and 5 units of Y and has an *MRS* of ½. If person 1 trades 1 X to person 2 for 1 Y, both individuals will be on a higher indifference curve than in their initial situation. In other examples, the actual distribution of the trading gains depends on the terms of trade that are established.

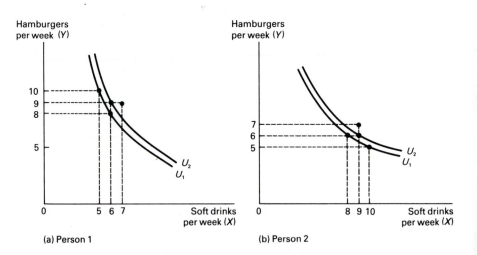

(a) Person 1   (b) Person 2

8.1 and shown graphically in Figure 8.1. The striking fact of the trade is that it makes both people better off. Person 1 now has $X = 6$ and $Y = 9$. Since she would have been as well off as in her initial situation if the trade had resulted in $X = 6$, $Y = 8$ (because her *MRS* is assumed to be 2), the posttrade allocation is clearly better—she still gets the same amount of X and more Y. Person 2 now has $X = 9$, $Y = 6$, which improves her utility. She would have been willing to accept $X = 8$, $Y = 6$ (with her assumed *MRS* of ½), but the trade leaves her with an additional X over what would have been acceptable. The voluntary trade makes both people better off.

A similar demonstration could be made any time two people have combinations of goods that result in their having different marginal rates of substitution (if their *MRS*'s were the same, the individuals would not gain from trading). If they agree to trade goods in some ratio that lies between these two *MRS*'s, both people will benefit from the trade.

Distribution of the Gains from Trade

Although both individuals may gain from a voluntary trading situation, the gains may sometimes be unevenly distributed. We would not expect people to agree to a trade that actually resulted in lower utility (people may be forced into such trades, however—a gun is an effective form of coercion for a mugger!). But, even in voluntary trades, one person may get the bulk of the gains. Two such situations are illustrated in Table 8.2. In Case 1, our two people have decided to exchange Y for X in the ratio of 2 Y for 1 X. This trade leaves person 1 (with $X = 6$, $Y = 8$) precisely as well off as before the trade. As Figure 8.1 shows, both the initial combination of goods and this new posttrade

Table 8.2   *Distribution of Gains from Trade Depends on the Terms of Trade*

Case 1: 1 X trades for 2 Y—only person 2 gains.

	Initial Quantity		Results of Trade		Final Quantity	
	X	Y	X	Y	X	Y
Person 1	5	10	+1	−2	6	8
Person 2	10	5	−1	+2	9	7

Case 2: 2 X trade for 1 Y—only person 1 gains.

	Initial Quantity		Results of Trade		Final Quantity	
	X	Y	X	Y	X	Y
Person 1	5	10	+2	−1	7	9
Person 2	10	5	−2	+1	8	6

combination lie on the same indifference curve, U_1. Although person 1 does not lose from the trade, she does not gain anything either.

In this new trade, person 2 is the big winner. She now has $X = 9$, $Y = 7$, which, as Figure 8.1 shows, not only is preferred to her initial position but also makes her better off than in our first trading example.

Case 2 of Table 8.2 shows a trade in which person 1 gets the better deal. Now the two individuals have agreed to trade at a ratio of 1 Y for 2 X. After this trade, person 2 is still on her initial indifference curve. Person 1 with $X = 7$, $Y = 9$ is now better off than in any of the previous cases. With these "terms of trade," person 1 is the primary gainer from trading.

EDGEWORTH BOX DIAGRAM

Obviously, the numbers in this example were purely arbitrary. Any allocation in which the MRS's of two individuals differ and in which the individuals consume both goods can be shown to be "inefficient" in that these goods can be reallocated in an unambiguously better way; that is, a "better" allocation can be found. There may be many such allocations, however, and we can most easily demonstrate them by using a graphic device known as the *Edgeworth box*,[2] the construction of which is shown in Figure 8.2. The Edgeworth box has dimensions given by the total (fixed) quantities of the two goods (call these goods simply X and Y). The horizontal dimension of the box represents the total quantity of X available, whereas the vertical height of the box is the total quantity of Y. The point O_S is considered to be the origin for person 1 (call her Smith). Quantities of X are measured along the horizontal axis rightward from O_S; quantities of Y, along the vertical axis upward from O_S. Any point in the box can then be regarded as some allocation of X and Y to Smith. For example, at point A, Smith gets X_S^A and Y_S^A. The unusual property of the Edgeworth box is that the quantities received by person 2 (say Jones) are also recorded by point A. Jones simply gets that part of the total quantity that is "left over." In fact, we can regard Jones's quantities as being measured from the origin O_J. Point A therefore also corresponds to the quantities X_J^A and Y_J^A for Jones. Notice that the quantities assigned to Smith and Jones in this manner exactly exhaust the total quantities of X and Y available.

Mutually Beneficial Trades

Any point in the Edgeworth box represents an allocation of the available goods between Smith and Jones, and all possible allocations are contained within the box. The reader may wish to choose any point in the box and demonstrate that this point represents a unique division of goods X and Y between these two people. To discover which of the allocations offer mutually beneficial trades, we must introduce preferences. In Figure 8.3 Smith's indifference curve map is drawn with origin O_S. Movements in a northeasterly direction represent higher levels of utility to Smith. In the same figure, Jones's indifference curve map is drawn with the corner O_J as an origin. We have taken Jones's indiffer-

[2]Named for F. Y. Edgeworth (1854–1926), who in 1881 derived the concept of a contract curve in his *Mathematical Psychics: An Essay on the Application of Mathematics to the Moral Sciences* (New York: August M. Kelley, 1953).

Figure 8.2   Edgeworth Box Diagram

The Edgeworth box diagram permits all possible allocations of two goods (X and Y) to be visualized. If we consider the corner O_S to be Smith's (person 1) "origin" and O_J to be Jones's (person 2), then the allocation represented by point A would have Smith getting X_S^A and Y_S^A, and Jones would receive what is left over (X_J^A, Y_J^A). The purpose of this diagram is to discover which of the possible locations within the box are efficient.

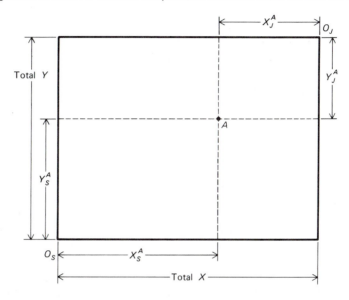

Figure 8.3   Edgeworth Box Diagram of Pareto Efficiency in Exchange

The points on the curve O_S, O_J are efficient in the sense that at these allocations Smith cannot be made better off without making Jones worse off, and vice versa. An allocation such as A, on the other hand, is inefficient because both Smith and Jones can be made better off by choosing to move into the shaded area. Notice that along O_S, O_J the *MRS* for Smith is equal to that for Jones. The line O_S, O_J is called the *contract curve*.

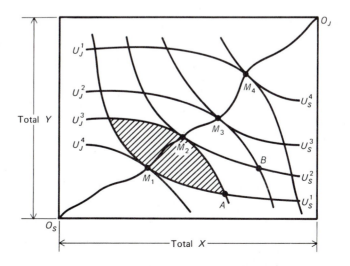

ence curve map, rotated it 180°, and fit it into the northeast corner of the Edgeworth box. Movements in a southwesterly direction represent increases in Jones's utility level.

Using these superimposed indifference curve maps, we can identify the allocations from which some mutually beneficial trades might be made. Any point for which the *MRS* for Smith is unequal to that for Jones presents such an opportunity. Consider the potential allocation A in Figure 8.3. This point lies on the point of intersection of Smith's indifference curve U_S^1 and Jones's indifference curve U_J^3. Obviously, the marginal rates of substitution (the slopes of the indifference curves) are not equal at A. Any allocation in the oval-shape shaded area in Figure 8.3 represents a mutually beneficial trade for these two people—they can both move to a higher level of utility by adopting a trade that moves them into this area.

Efficiency in Exchange

When the marginal rates of substitution of Smith and Jones are equal, however, such mutually beneficial trades are not available. The points M_1, M_2, M_3, and M_4 in Figure 8.3 indicate tangencies of these individuals' indifference curves, and movement away from such points must make at least one of the people worse off. A move from M_2 to A, for example, reduces Smith's utility from U_S^2 to U_S^1 even though Jones is made no worse off by the move. Alternatively, a move from M_2 to B makes Jones worse off, but keeps the utility level of Smith constant. In general, then, these points of tangency do not offer the promise of additional mutually beneficial trading. Such points are called *Pareto efficient* allocations of resources after the Italian scientist Vilfredo Pareto (1878–1923) who pioneered in the development of the formal theory of exchange. In precise terms we define

Definition:

Pareto Efficient Allocation

An allocation of available resources in which no mutually beneficial trading opportunities are unexploited. That is, an allocation in which no one person can be made better off without someone else being made worse off.

Notice that the Pareto definition of efficiency does not require any interpersonal comparisons of utility—we never have to compare Jones's gains to Smith's losses or vice versa. Rather, individuals decide for themselves whether particular trades improve utility. For efficient allocations there are no such additional trades to which both parties would agree.

Contract Curve

The set of all the efficient allocations in an Edgeworth box diagram is called the *contract curve*. In Figure 8.3 this set of points is represented by the line running from O_S to O_J and includes the tangencies M_1, M_2, M_3, and M_4 (and many other such tangencies). Points off the contract curve (such as A or B) are inefficient, and mutually beneficial trades are possible. But, as its name implies, the contract curve represents the exhaustion of all such trading opportunities. Even a move along the contract curve (say, from M_1 to M_2) cannot represent a mutually beneficial trade since there will always be a winner (Smith) and a loser (Jones). These observations are summarized by

---

Definition:

Contract Curve
In an exchange economy, all efficient allocations of the existing goods lie along a (multidimensional) *contract curve*. Points off that curve are necessarily inefficient, since individuals can be made unambiguously better off by moving to the curve. Along the contract curve, however, individuals' preferences are rivals in the sense that one individual's situation may be improved only if someone else is made worse off.

In the case where the contract curve is interior to the Edgeworth box (as in Figure 8.3), individuals' *MRS*'s will be equal along the contract curve. If preferences are such that for some efficient allocations some individuals choose not to consume all goods, corner solutions will arise in which rates of substitution are not necessarily equalized (for a simple case, see problem 8.2). Whatever their quantitative nature, all such efficient allocations are depicted on the contract curve.

A Numerical Illustration

To fix these ideas, consider an exchange economy in which there are exactly 1000 soft drinks (X) and 1000 hamburgers (Y). If we let Smith's utility be represented by

$$U_S(X_S, Y_S) = X_S^{2/3} Y_S^{1/3} \tag{8.1}$$

and Jones's utility by

$$U_J(X_J, Y_J) = X_J^{1/3} Y_J^{2/3}, \tag{8.2}$$

we can compute the efficient ways of allocating soft drinks and hamburgers. Notice at the start that the differing exponents in the utility functions of the two individuals indicate that Smith has a relative preference for soft drinks whereas Jones tends to prefer hamburgers. We might therefore expect that efficient allocations would give relatively more soft drinks to Smith and relatively more hamburgers to Jones.

To find the efficient points in this situation, suppose we let Smith start at any preassigned utility level, $\overline{U}_S$. Our problem now is to choose X_S, Y_S, X_J, and Y_J to make Jones's utility as large as possible given Smith's utility constraint.[3] Setting up the Lagrangian expression for this problem yields

$$\begin{aligned}\mathcal{L} &= U_J(X_J, Y_J) + \lambda[U_S(X_S, Y_S) - \overline{U}_S] \\ &= X_J^{1/3} Y_J^{2/3} + \lambda(X_S^{2/3} Y_S^{1/3} - \overline{U}_S).\end{aligned} \tag{8.3}$$

Remember now that Jones simply gets what Smith doesn't and vice versa.

---

[3] We could have obtained the same solution by assigning Jones a set utility level and maximizing Smith's utility.

Table 8.3   *Pareto Efficient Allocations of 1000 Soft Drinks and 1000 Hamburgers to Smith and Jones*

X_S	Y_S	$U_S = X_S^{2/3} Y_S^{1/3}$	$X_J =$ $1000 - X_S$	$Y_J =$ $1000 - Y_S$	$U_J = X_J^{1/3} Y_J^{2/3}$
0	0	0	1000	1000	1000
100	27	65	900	973	948
200	59	133	800	941	891
300	97	206	700	903	830
400	143	284	600	857	761
500	200	369	500	800	684
600	273	462	400	727	596
700	368	565	300	632	493
800	500	684	200	500	369
900	692	825	100	308	212
1000	1000	1000	0	0	0

Hence

$$X_J = 1000 - X_S$$

and   (8.4)

$$Y_J = 1000 - Y_S.$$

Our Lagrangian expression is therefore only a function of the two variables, X_S and Y_S:

$$\mathcal{L} = (1000 - X_S)^{1/3}(1000 - Y_S)^{2/3} + \lambda(X_S^{2/3} Y_S^{1/3} - \overline{U}_S). \quad (8.5)$$

The first-order conditions for a maximum are

$$\frac{\partial \mathcal{L}}{\partial X_S} = -\frac{1}{3}\left(\frac{1000 - Y_S}{1000 - X_S}\right)^{2/3} + \frac{2\lambda}{3}\left(\frac{Y_S}{X_S}\right)^{1/3} = 0$$

$$\frac{\partial \mathcal{L}}{\partial Y_S} = -\frac{2}{3}\left(\frac{1000 - X_S}{1000 - Y_S}\right)^{1/3} + \frac{\lambda}{3}\left(\frac{X_S}{Y_S}\right)^{2/3} = 0. \quad (8.6)$$

Moving the terms in λ to the right side of these equations and dividing the top equation by the bottom gives[4]

$$\frac{1}{2}\left(\frac{1000 - Y_S}{1000 - X_S}\right) = 2\left(\frac{Y_S}{X_S}\right) \quad (8.7)$$

---

[4] Notice that Equation 8.7 is a restatement of the condition that the individuals' marginal rates of substitution must be equal for an efficient allocation. That is, MRS (for Smith) = $(\partial U_S/\partial X)/(\partial U_S/\partial Y) = 2(Y/X)$ and MRS (for Jones) = $(\partial U_J/\partial X)/(\partial U_J/\partial Y) = 1/2(Y/X)$.

Figure 8.4 *Contract Curve in an Exchange Economy for Soft Drinks and Hamburgers*

The contract curve in this example is computed from the individuals' utility functions. The bowed shape of the curve reflects Smith's relative preference for soft drinks (X) and Jones's relative preference for hamburgers (Y). If the individuals start from an initial endowment of equal amounts of each good (A), they can both be made better off by moving to an allocation between B and C on the contract curve.

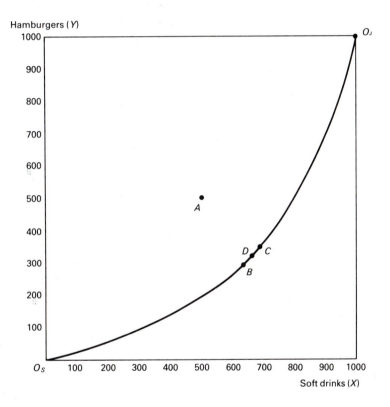

or

$$\frac{X_S}{(1000 - X_S)} = 4\left(\frac{Y_S}{1000 - Y_S}\right), \qquad (8.8)$$

which is our required condition for efficiency. We can now use Equation 8.8 to calculate any number of efficient allocations. In Table 8.3 we have done so for values of X_S ranging from 0 to 1000 (that is, for situations in which Smith gets nothing to situations where she gets everything). These efficient allocations are also graphed in Figure 8.4. In this case the contract curve O_S, O_J is bowed below the diagonal of the Edgeworth box showing that efficient allocations require Smith to get relatively more soft drinks and Jones to get relatively more hamburgers. As shown in Table 8.3, Smith's utility increases and Jones's decreases as we move along the contract curve from O_S toward O_J.

To illustrate why points off this contract curve are inefficient, consider allocation A in which Smith and Jones share X and Y equally. With 500 units of each item, both Smith and Jones receive a utility of 500 (assuming that such utility measurement is meaningful). But, by using your basic scientific calculator, it is a relatively simple matter to show that there are many allocations on the contract curve that offer more utility to both people. Table 8.3 shows that this is nearly true for the allocations where Smith gets 600 or 700 soft drinks and the precise boundaries of such mutually beneficial trades are given by points B and C in Figure 8.4. At a point such as D, for example, $X_S = 660$, $Y_S = 327$, $X_J = 340$, and $Y_J = 673$. For this allocation Smith's utility is 522 and Jones's is 536. They are clearly both better off at D than at A, and one might expect some sort of trading to take place that moves them toward the contract curve.

EXCHANGE WITH INITIAL ENDOWMENTS AND THE DISTRIBUTION OF GAINS FROM TRADE

In our previous discussion we assumed that fixed quantities of the two goods in question existed and that these could be allocated in any way conceivable. A somewhat different, more restricted analysis would hold if the individuals participating in the exchange possessed various quantities of the goods in question at the start. An example of such a situation would occur if two people were marooned on an island and each was in possession of certain basic commodities. There would be a very definite possibility that each person could benefit from voluntary trade (supposing that force is ruled out by social conventions), since it is unlikely that the initial allocations would be efficient ones. On the other hand, neither person would engage in a trade that would leave him or her worse off than would be the case without trading. Hence only a portion of the contract curve can be regarded as efficient allocations that might result from exchange.

Those ideas are illustrated in Figure 8.5. The initial endowments of Smith and Jones are represented by point A in the Edgeworth box. As before, the dimensions of the box are taken to be the total quantities of the two goods (X and Y) available. The contract curve of efficient allocations is represented by the line O_S, O_J. Let the indifference curve of Smith, which passes through point A, be called U_S^A and, similarly, let Jones's indifference curve through A be denoted by U_J^A. Notice that at point A, the individuals' indifference curves are not tangent, and therefore the initial endowments are not efficient. Neither Smith nor Jones will accept trading outcomes that give a utility level of less than U_S^A or U_J^A, respectively. It would be preferable for an individual to refrain from trading rather than accept such an inferior outcome. Thus only those efficient allocations between M_1 and M_2 on the contract curve can occur as a result of free exchange. The range of efficient outcomes from voluntary exchange has been narrowed by considering the initial endowments with which the individuals enter into trading. If the initial distribution of goods favors Jones, any final allocation will also favor Jones, since it is in Jones's interest to refuse to accept bargains that provide less utility. Nevertheless, it is clear that

---

Figure 8.5   *Exchange with Initial Endowments*

If individuals start with initial endowments (such as those represented by point A), neither would be willing to accept an allocation that promised a lower level of utility than point A does. Smith would not accept any allocation below U_S^A, and Jones would not accept any allocation below U_J^A. Therefore, not every point on the contract curve can result from free exchange. Only the efficient allocations between M_1 and M_2 are eligible if each individual is free to refrain from trading, and we require that the final allocation be efficient.

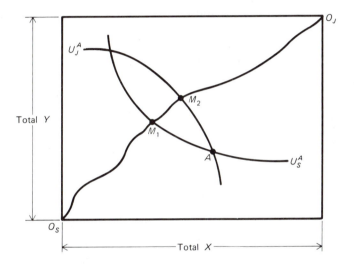

both individuals *can* benefit from trading. Moving to the line segment M_1, M_2 is an unambiguous improvement over point A for both Smith and Jones.

Exactly which allocation on the segment of the contract curve M_1, M_2 might be chosen by the participants in exchange is difficult to predict. Obviously, Smith would prefer points closer to M_2, whereas Jones would desire points close to M_1. The desires of the two individuals are in conflict, and bargaining between the two will determine the final allocation. In the desert island example, it would require particularly narrow and antisocial individuals not to recognize that some trade would be beneficial, however. A steadfast refusal to trade by either person would not be in either individual's self-interest.

Numerical Example Revisited

In our prior numerical example, we illustrated all of the efficient allocations in this exchange situation. Suppose now that each individual starts with 500 units of each good. That is, assume that the initial endowment is point A in Figure 8.4. In this case Smith's minimum acceptable level of utility is 500 since she can obtain that without trading. At point B in Figure 8.4 ($X_S = 638$, $Y_S = 306$), Smith's utility is exactly 500 so she is indifferent between A and B. At B, however, Jones is the big winner with a utility of 559—the maximum she can obtain from voluntary trading in this situation.

Allocation C ($X_S = 694$, $Y_S = 362$) in Figure 8.4 is Smith's best deal. Here Jones's utility remains at the minimum acceptable level of 500 whereas Smith's is now 559. Hence, when point A is the initial endowment, only a relatively small portion of the contract curve (segment B–C) represents allocations that may result from unrestricted trading.

VIABLE BARGAINS AND THE CORE

A somewhat different approach to Pareto efficiency can be developed from game theory concepts (see Chapter 20). In that approach, stress is placed on the kinds of trading bargains individuals in an exchange economy might reach and whether those bargains are "viable" in that the parties involved do not have an incentive to renege on them. Once a particular allocation has been decided upon, if a subgroup of individuals find they can better their positions still further by engaging in additional trading, the initial allocation does not represent a viable bargain. If, on the other hand, an allocation offers no such possibilities for further betterment, it then represents a viable bargain. The set of all such allocations is called the "core" of an exchange economy. More formally

Definition:

Core of an Exchange Economy
The *core of an exchange economy* is composed of those allocations of available goods for which no group of individuals in the economy will find it attractive to strike additional bargains.

It is obvious that allocations in the core must be Pareto efficient. For inefficient allocations there is always the possibility that one or more persons can be made unambiguously better off, so that they would have an incentive to seek out the efficient alternative. Since this model implicitly assumes that it is costless to arrive at such bargains, nothing prevents them from being achieved. Hence inefficient allocations would not be viable.

Not all efficient allocations are in the core of an exchange economy, however. In the previous section we showed that individuals who start with initial endowments will not accept allocations that provide a lower level of utility than is provided by the initial endowment. In Figure 8.5 only those allocations on the contract curve between M_1 and M_2 might result from uncoerced trade. In the context of the concept of the core, Smith would block any allocation on the contract curve southwest of M_1 whereas Jones would block allocations northeast of M_2. Hence, in the two-person exchange economy illustrated in Figure 8.5, the core consists of those allocations along the segment M_1, M_2. With more individuals the core might even be smaller, a possibility we will now briefly examine.

Increasing Numbers of Traders and the Core

Intuitively, there are good reasons to believe that with larger numbers of traders, there will be relatively fewer allocations in the core of an exchange economy. With more traders there are more potential trading coalitions, and hence the likelihood that an allocation in the core will be immune to the at-

Figure 8.6   *Coalitions and the Viability of the Core*

The exchange situation illustrated here contains two Smiths and two Joneses. The allocation M_1 is not viable against a coalition of two Smiths and Jones-1 since a trade among the members will yield a higher utility level for both Smiths (at C_1) and for Jones-1 (at C_2). Hence the allocation M_1 is not in the core of the four-person exchange economy, although it was in the core of the two-person exchange economy in Figure 8.5.

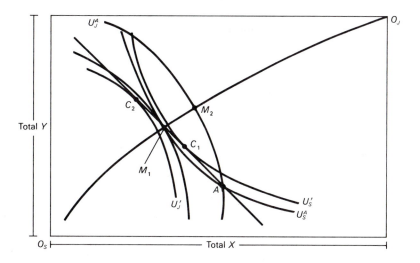

tractions of such coalitions is reduced. This possibility is illustrated for a simple case in Figure 8.6. There we initially assume only two traders, Smith and Jones, with initial endowments given by point A. As before, the core of this economy is represented by the curve M_1, M_2. Now suppose that we double the number of traders by assuming that there are two individuals exactly like Smith (call them Smith-1 and Smith-2) and two exactly like Jones (Jones-1 and Jones-2). Although it would take a four-dimensional Edgeworth box to explore fully all of the trades possible among these individuals, our two-dimensional diagram can be used to indicate the types of trading coalitions that might arise. Consider, for example, the allocation M_1 that was in the core of the two-person exchange economy. Suppose both Smiths would obtain a higher utility level than M_1 provides by giving up one unit of Y for one unit of X. That is, both Smiths trade away less X and keep more Y in going from A to their preferred point than they would in going from A to M_1. This new allocation for the Smiths is represented by point C_1 in Figure 8.6; it provides a utility level of U'_S. Of course, point C_1 is a feasible allocation only if *one* of the Joneses is willing to satisfy both Smiths' desires for more X and less Y than they had at point M_1. That is, a Jones must be willing to meet the trades of both Smiths in going from A to C_1. Suppose that is the case for, say, Jones-1. Then Jones-1 moves from A to point C_2 whereas Jones-2 stays at the initial endowment, A. The line passing through A, M_1, C_1, and C_2 represents the terms of trade among the three coalition members, all of whom are now better off. Thus the allocation M_1 is not in the core of the four-person exchange economy, since it is not viable against a trading coalition of Smith-1, Smith-2, and Jones-1.[5] We have shown that replication of our simple two-person exchange economy leads to the possibility of removing points (here M_1) from the core.

Of course, the numbers in this example were hypothetical, and Figure 8.6 had to be very carefully drawn so that the coalition specified would indeed benefit from the trade. But the result that expanding the numbers of traders has the effect of "shrinking" the core is in fact quite general. Expanding the number of traders in an exchange economy, by increasing the likelihood that mutually beneficial coalitions will be formed, reduces the proportion of allocations that are in the core.[6] This result has a number of applications both in formal game theory and (as we shall see later in the chapter) in the study of the properties of a price system.

EFFICIENT TRADING WITH EQUILIBRIUM PRICES

Our discussion of exchange thus far has been applicable to barter situations. That is, each individual trades one of the goods for the other good and betters his or her situation by doing so. Now we will show that a similar argument can be made for a situation in which individuals respond to trading options on the basis of market prices. Specifically, we show that if both Smith and Jones are price takers and respond to equilibrium prices for the goods (P_X^* and P_Y^*), then they will also be led to the contract curve. In this situation market prices can show the way toward efficient allocations of resources.

Offer Curves

A graphic proof of these assertions can readily be developed for the simple case of a two-person, two-good (X and Y) exchange economy. In order to diagram this proof, it is helpful to introduce the concept of an *offer curve*. This curve shows those quantities of X and Y for which an individual is willing to trade away from his or her initial endowment at various price ratios.

To construct the offer curve, consider the set of indifference curves shown in Figure 8.7. Suppose that this individual has an initial endowment of goods X and Y that is denoted by point A. If "the market" quotes a price ratio (P_X/P_Y) to the individual, then the trades that can be made from the initial endowment

---

[5] Notice that this allocation is feasible with the three-person coalition since Jones-1 gets what the Smiths give up and vice versa in moving from A to the C_1, C_2 combination. If both Joneses tried to participate in the coalition, they would have to settle at a feasible point such as M_1. But then there would be an incentive for the three-person coalition to re-form. Notice also, however, that the C_1, C_2 allocation is not efficient since the *MRS* for Jones-2 (who stays at point A) no longer is equal to that of the other individuals. Thus further trades that return the allocation to the contract curve may be expected.

[6] The mathematics associated with this analysis is quite advanced, and the statements made here are of necessity vastly oversimplified. For a more complete analysis see K. J. Arrow and F. Hahn, *General Competitive Analysis* (San Francisco: Holden-Day, 1971), chap. 8.

Figure 8.7   *Construction of an Individual's Offer Curve*

An individual's offer curve shows the quantities of X and Y for particular initial endowments that the individual would choose when presented with different price ratios. For example, if a price ratio of P_X/P_Y were quoted by the market, the individual would choose point B. In so doing he or she would be willing to trade $(X^A - X^B)$ of good X for $(Y^B - Y^A)$ of good Y. By varying the price ratio, all points such as B can be traced out as the offer curve.

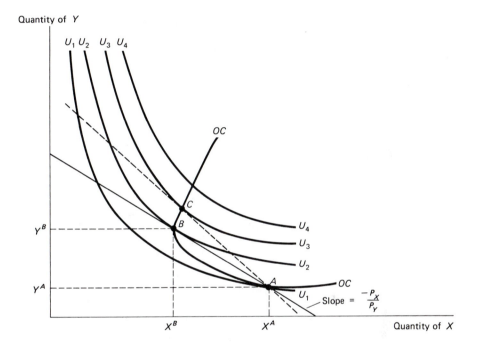

are along a straight line with slope $-P_X/P_Y$ passing through point A.[7] Given this budget constraint, the individual's preferred point is B, where the tangency conditions for a maximum are satisfied. To reach this point by trading in the market, the individual will trade some of the initial endowment of X, $(X^A - X^B)$, for an additional amount of Y, $(Y^B - Y^A)$. The ratio in which these two quantities can be traded is given by the market price ratio of goods (that is, by the slope of the budget constraint).

The individual's offer curve can now be constructed as the locus of the trade points, such as B, that result from being presented with all possible price ratios. For example, an alternative budget constraint arising from a different price ratio might be represented by the dashed line in Figure 8.7 where the

---

[7] The individual can afford any combination of X and Y such that $P_X \cdot X + P_Y \cdot Y \leq P_X \cdot X^A + P \cdot Y^A$. Hence the budget constraint passes through X^A, Y^A with slope $-P_X/P_Y$.

utility-maximizing position would be at point C. The locus of all points such as A, B, and C would be the offer curve, which is labeled OC in the figure.[8] This construction can be summarized by

---

Definition:

Offer Curve

An individual's offer curve shows those trades he or she would willingly make away from a particular initial endowment at alternative price ratios.

Graphic Demonstration of Pareto Efficiency

The offer curve concept is a useful graphic device for demonstrating the reactions of an individual being presented with fixed prices and an initial endowment of the two goods. By using offer curves for the two individuals in an Edgeworth box diagram, it is possible to demonstrate how such a price system can lead to efficiency in exchange. In Figure 8.8 the indifference curves of the two individuals (Smith and Jones) are drawn together with the offer curves (OC_S and OC_J) associated with the initial endowments represented by point A. These curves record the responses of Smith and Jones to all possible price ratios. At the points of intersection of OC_S and OC_J, exchange is in equilibrium: The demands of Smith and Jones exactly exhaust the total quantities of the two goods available. For example, point A is an exchange equilibrium since both individuals could choose to keep their initial endowments. If the offer curves intersect at a point other than A, say, E, it can be shown that this new equilibrium point is on the contract curve and hence is an efficient allocation of X and Y. Consider the straight line joining A and E. The slope of this line ($-P_X^*/P_Y^*$) represents an equilibrium price ratio, since Smith and Jones react to this ratio by demanding combinations of goods that exhaust the total quantities of X and Y. At E the line AE is tangent to Smith's indifference curve U_S^2, since this is the way the offer curve was constructed (see Figure 8.7). Similarly, the line AE is also tangent to an indifference curve of Jones (U_J^2) at E. Hence, Smith's and Jones's indifference curves must be tangent to each other at E. Providing that the indifference curves have the normal convex shape, this point of tangency will be on the contract curve and will represent an efficient allocation of X and Y between the two individuals. The generation of equilibrium prices has ensured both that what is demanded will in fact be supplied and that the resultant trade will be Pareto optimal.

Exchange Equilibrium and the Core

Because the exchange equilibrium illustrated in Figure 8.8 lies on the contract curve and represents (at least) no loss in utility for either Smith or Jones, the equilibrium must also lie in the core of this exchange economy. In the previous section, however, we showed that the relative size of the core shrinks as addi-

---

[8]Notice that the initial point A is included on the offer curve. At some price ratio, the individual's optimal choice would be to abstain from trade. Also notice that the offer curve never passes below the indifference curve passing through point A. An individual would never choose to trade if forced to accept a utility level lower than that available from the initial endowment.

Figure 8.8   *Demonstration of the Efficiency of Perfect Competition in an Exchange Economy*

In this exchange box diagram, the initial endowment is given by point *A*. The offer curves are drawn through point *A*; the intersection of these curves at point *E* represents an exchange equilibrium since Smith is willing to trade what Jones wants, and vice versa. The price ratio P_X^*/P_Y^* will be able to bring about this equilibrium point. It can also be seen that *E* lies on the contract curve since Smith's and Jones's indifference curves are tangent at *E*. Hence the price ratio of P_X^*/P_Y^* will also promote efficiency.

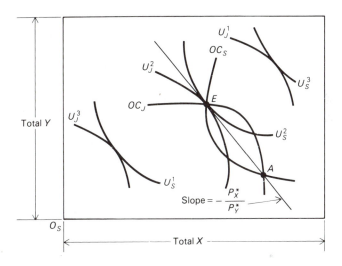

tional traders are added and the possibilities for side coalitions expand. Questions might therefore be raised about the relationship between exchange equilibria and the core concept as the number of traders expands. Although to pursue this question in detail would take us far beyond the scope of this book, it is possible here to indicate in an intuitive way why the connection between the two concepts is very close.[9] First, the proof that any competitive equilibrium must be in the core of an exchange economy is straightforward. Suppose a coalition of individuals chose to break away from an exchange equilibrium in the belief that they could do better by trading among themselves. Then, for each individual, the value (measured in terms of the equilibrium prices) of the goods received through such bargaining must exceed the value of that individual's initial endowment because, if it does not, the new allocation would have been obtainable directly and no side bargaining would have been necessary. Thus, the aggregate value of the new allocations for all members of the coalition must exceed the aggregate value of the members' endowments. But that is impossible since, in the aggregate, the coalition's aggregate final allocations

[9] For a more formal treatment, see Arrow and Hahn, *General Competitive Analysis*, chap. 8.

must be identical to their endowments; therefore they must have the same aggregate value. Hence there is a contradiction and no such coalition can exist—an exchange equilibrium must be in the core and not blocked by any side coalition.[10]

In Figure 8.8 many allocations appear to be in the core in addition to the competitive equilibrium. However, as the number of traders expands, we know some of these allocations will be blocked by potential coalitions. Still, by the argument of the previous paragraph, the competitive equilibrium will remain in the core. One of the more remarkable results of modern mathematical economics is to show that under certain circumstances, the only allocations remaining in the core of an exchange economy as the number of traders expands are those that are "close" to the price-exchange equilibrium.[11] Consequently, it appears not only that such equilibria are efficient but also that these equilibria might be expected to emerge out of uncoerced bargaining situations even in the absence of a formal market mechanism. Exchange equilibria brought about by reliance on the price mechanisms are very sturdy, and individuals who seek further gains outside this process may be doomed to failure.

Additional
Efficiency Issues
In this chapter we have only studied the issue of Pareto efficiency in a simple exchange context. Many additional questions arise in models in which production takes place. For these models the relationship between price mechanism and Pareto efficiency is far more complex than in the exchange case. Once we introduce production, we must not only worry about firms' behavior and possible coalitions among producers, but we must also recognize that there may be situations in which production activities have effects that extend be-

---

[10] Algebraically, suppose there are only two goods, X and Y, and let S represent a coalition attempting to make a side bargain. Let X', Y' be the allocation of X and Y decided upon by this bargain, and let X^A and Y^A be the initial endowments of these goods. Then, if P_X^* and P_Y^* are the equilibrium prices for X and Y, it must be the case that

$$P_X^* \cdot X' + P_Y^* \cdot Y' > P_X^* \cdot X^A + P_Y^* \cdot Y^A,$$

since otherwise X', Y' would be attainable under the competitive equilibrium. Hence, summing over all coalition members yields

$$P_X^* \sum_S X' + P_Y^* \sum_S Y' > P_X^* \sum_S X^A + P_Y^* \cdot \sum_S Y^A.$$

But we know

$$\sum_S X' = \sum_S X^A$$

and

$$\sum_S Y' = \sum_S Y^A,$$

and therefore

$$P_X^* \sum_S X' + P_Y^* \sum_S Y' = P_X^* \sum_S X^A + P_Y^* \sum_S Y^A,$$

which is a contradiction.

[11] See Arrow and Hahn, *General Competitive Analysis*, pp. 188–195.

yond the buyer-seller relationship (for example, environmental side effects). How efficiency should be defined in these contexts and whether market-type mechanisms can yield efficient solutions are subjects we will be examining at many other places in this book.

SUMMARY

The primary goal of this chapter is to show how the utility-maximization model of choice can be used to examine voluntary trades among individuals. Making the observation that such trade can be mutually beneficial may seem obvious, but a full exploration is central to understanding how markets arise and why they are usually efficiency enhancing. Our examination of exchange situations (that is, situations in which there is no production) reached the following basic conclusions:

- If individuals possess quantities of goods that result in their having unequal marginal rates of substitution, they may be able to achieve mutually beneficial trades of these goods.
- The gains that individuals are able to achieve through voluntary trade will depend on the terms on which the trades take place. In general, individuals for whom the terms of trade differ substantially from their initial *MRS* will gain significantly whereas those for whom the terms of trade are close to their initial *MRS* will gain little.
- All of the possible allocations in an exchange situation can be illustrated in an Edgeworth box diagram. Pareto efficient allocations (those for which no one can be made better off without making another person worse off) are illustrated by the contract curve in this diagram. Along the contract curve, marginal rates of substitution are equal.
- Voluntary trading can lead to the contract curve, but only to that portion of the curve in which each individual is at least as well off as with his or her initial endowment. This portion of the contract curve is termed the "core" of an exchange economy.
- Voluntary trading with equilibrium prices may allow individuals to reach Pareto efficient allocations. Such price-exchange equilibria will also be in the core of the exchange economy.

Application

BLACK MARKETS AND VOLUNTARY EXCHANGE

The illegal buying and selling of goods through black markets is often the subject of public annoyance and outrage. People who "scalp"

World Series tickets or who sell their government-provided surplus food (rather than eating it) are regarded as anti-social deviants or worse. To economists, however, such activities may be quite innocuous, reflecting instead the basic

Pareto principles of mutually beneficial trade. If for some reason an individual finds that he or she has some item that others value more highly, such transactions become likely and economists tend to favor prohibition of them only in relatively rare cases (such as the buying and selling of babies). In this application we will examine the development of black markets in three specific instances. Readers may wish to think about whether they would have favored stiff legal sanctions against these transactions.

Wartime Rationing

During World War II most of the belligerents adopted rationing for important commodities that were experiencing shortages. Germany, the United Kingdom, and the United States, for example, had rather strict rationing for gasoline and for some food items, especially meat. Typically families were provided with weekly or monthly ration coupons that permitted the purchase of rather small amounts of these rationed goods at controlled prices. In principle these coupons were not exchangeable and wartime ethics strongly discouraged such trading. Still, black markets in ration coupons were commonplace and it was well known that any rationed commodity was available if the demander was willing to pay the going price.[12] Individuals with "initial endowments" of ration coupons were willing to trade these away voluntarily if they were compensated with sufficient amounts of other goods.

A particularly interesting example of wartime exchange is provided by R. A. Radford's discussion of his experiences in a German prisoner of war camp.[13] In these camps, Radford explains, "initial endowments" were provided by periodic receipt of Red Cross packages and rates of exchange quickly developed among the various items contained therein. Tins of jam traded for one-half pound of margarine, whereas tins of diced carrots were worth practically nothing. Cigarettes became the customary medium of exchange for making most transactions—every item had a price in terms of cigarettes. Some of the camp's medical officers worried that smokers would trade away their Red Cross necessities in order to get cigarettes and therefore tried to enforce price controls on these necessities. But the desire to seek out mutually beneficial trades was a strong one and these controls usually broke down.

Food Stamps

Food Stamps are provided to low income people to be used to purchase food. The program is one of the largest income transfer programs in the United States. In its original form, the Food Stamp program required that low income families pay, say, $50 in cash to receive $100 in Food Stamps each month. Such a procedure offered participating families several incentives to engage in further (technically illegal) transactions to improve their welfare. They could, for example, with the help of a friendly merchant, use the stamps to buy non-food items, thereby essentially converting the program into a simple cash grant of $50. Or, more directly, they could sell their $100 in Food Stamps on the black market for some price (say $75) that would be beneficial both to them and to the purchaser (who can now get $100 worth of food for $75). In some locales this type of black market in Food Stamps was quite well-developed with current price quotations being widely known. In Puerto Rico, for example, Food Stamps traded on a par with cash and some analyses of the Puerto Rican economy have even included Food Stamps as part of the money supply.

These incentives for the formation of black markets provided one of the arguments for major revisions in the Food Stamp program in the late 1970s. At that time the "purchase requirement" was eliminated, thereby reducing substantially the dollar amount of Food Stamps that a family would receive. In our prior example, the family would get $50 in Food

[12] For a discussion see *Wartime Rationing and Consumption* (Geneva: League of Nations Intelligence Service, 1941).

[13] R. A. Radford, "The Economic Organization of a P.O.W. Camp," *Economica* (November 1945): 189–201.

Stamps at no cost rather than $100 of stamps for $50. The effect of this change was to reduce the possibilities for engaging in black market transactions because now most families would choose to spend their entire allotment on food. In 1982 Puerto Rico went even further than this by "cashing out" its Food Stamp program—a cash grant was substituted for the Food Stamp allotment. This had the effect of completely eliminating the prior black markets (which had already been reduced in scope) with little apparent effect on actual food consumption.[14] A similar cash-out program has been suggested for the entire United States and some demonstration programs that move in this direction have been conducted. The political coalition that supports Food Stamps has so far blocked this move toward a more efficient transfer system, however.

Ticket Scalping

The number of people who want to see popular sporting or entertainment events often exceeds the seating capacity available. In principle, promoters could simply raise ticket prices to the point at which the number of people willing to pay met this seating capacity. Usually, however, tickets are allocated on some more-or-less ran-

dom basis among those willing to pay a lower, "fair" price. For example, World Series tickets are usually offered first to season ticket-holders of the participating teams and remaining tickets are then awarded on a lottery basis (except for those given to players and management). Similarly, tickets to the Jackson Brothers tour in 1984 were vastly over-subscribed and were, in many cities, awarded using elaborate drawing procedures.

The Edgeworth model of voluntary exchange makes a straightforward prediction about such allocational procedures—the tickets will tend to be resold. Since the procedures take no account of the value of the tickets to those receiving them, there will likely be consumers who value the tickets quite highly who are unable to get them. Such individuals have an incentive to try to obtain the tickets from the lottery winners. The resulting process of ticket reallocation is sometimes called "scalping." Many cities have laws that forbid such activities (although, to economists, they seem innocuous enough) and the fines can be rather severe. Still, tickets for popular events are widely scalped, in some cases selling for more than ten times their original price. According to some sources, for example, $25 tickets for the NBA championship at Boston Garden in 1987 sold for nearly $300 on the street and $28 tickets to the Jackson Brothers' Madison Square Garden concert sold for as much as $700. Presumably such transactions were mutually beneficial.

---

[14] See B. Devaney and T. Fraker, "Cashing Out Food Stamps: Impacts on Food Expenditures and Diet Quality," *Journal of Policy Analysis and Management* (Summer, 1986): 725–741.

SUGGESTED READINGS

Anderson, R. M. "An Elementary Core Equivalence Theorem." *Econometrica* (November 1978): 1483–1487.

Very difficult mathematics, but a good introduction and set of references on the theory of the core.

Arrow, K. J., and Hahn, F. *General Competitive Analysis.* San Francisco: Holden-Day, 1971. Chaps. 1, 2, and 4.

Sophisticated mathematical treatment of general equilibrium analysis. Each chapter has a good literary introduction.

Aumann, R. J. "Markets with a Continuum of Traders." *Econometrica* (January/February 1964): 39–50.

Important early paper on the mathematical theory of the core. Difficult mathematics, but offers some intuitive explanations.

Debreu, G. *Theory of Value.* New York: John Wiley & Sons, 1959.

Basic reference, difficult mathematics. Does have a good introductory chapter on the mathematical tools used.

Debreu, G., and Scarf, H. "A Limit Theorem on the Core of an Economy." *International Economic Review* (1963): 235–246.

A fairly readable treatment of the mathematical theory of the core.

Dorfman, R.; Samuelson, P. A.; and Solow, R. M. *Linear Programming and Economic Analysis.* New York: McGraw-Hill Book Company, 1958. Chap. 13.

Good introduction to efficiency notion and its relationship to perfect competition.

Feldman, A. *Welfare Economics and Social Choice Theory.* Amsterdam: Martinus Nijhoff, 1980.

First two chapters give a good summary of efficiency notion in general equilibrium models.

Hildenbran, W. "Core of an Economy" in K. J. Arrow and M. D. Intriligator, eds. *Handbook of Mathematical Economics,* Vol. 2. Amsterdam: North Holland Publishing Co., 1982. Pp. 831–877.

Good review article with a very readable introductory section.

Koopmans, T. C. *Three Essays on the State of Economic Science.* New York: McGraw-Hill Book Company, 1957.

Uses activity analysis to develop several efficiency notions.

Sen, A. K. *Collective Choice and Social Welfare.* San Francisco: Holden-Day, 1970. Chaps. 1 and 2.

Basic reference on social choice theory. Early chapters have a good discussion of the meaning and limitations of the Pareto efficiency concept.

Shapley, L. S., and Shubik, M. "On the Core of an Economic System with Externalities." *Econometrica* (September 1969): 678–684.

A brief introduction to a generalized concept in the presence of externalities.

PROBLEMS

8.1

Backyard Jack has a yard full of trees and firewood, but cannot grow very much corn due to poor sunlight. Sunshine Steve, on the other hand, has wide open cornfields but little firewood to keep him warm. Jack starts out with 20 cords of firewood and only 5 bushels of corn and has an *MRS* (of firewood for corn) of 1/3. Steve begins with 25 bushels of corn and only 10 cords of firewood and has an *MRS* of 2. How can both men be made better off through trade? Illustrate this situation with a graph.

8.2

"Jack Sprat can eat no fat, his wife can eat no lean." Construct a box diagram for this pair (assuming fixed quantities of "fat" and "lean") and indicate the contract curve.

8.3

Illustrate a situation in which every allocation in an Edgeworth box is Pareto efficient. Can you describe a situation to which this example might apply?

8.4

Nothing in the analysis of this chapter requires that exchange equilibrium be unique. Draw an example of an Edgeworth box diagram in which there are two different, interior equilibria arising from the same initial endowments. Explain intuitively why these occur and show the offer curves for the individuals involved.

8.5

Smith and Jones are stranded on a desert island. Each has in his possession some slices of ham (H) and cheese (C). Smith is a very choosy eater and will eat ham and cheese only in the fixed proportions of 2 slices of cheese to 1 slice of ham. His utility function is given by $U_S = \min(H, C/2)$

Jones is more flexible in his dietary tastes and has a utility function given by $U_J = 4H + 3C$. Total endowments are 100 slices of ham and 200 slices of cheese.

- a. Draw the Edgeworth box diagram that represents the possibilities for exchange in this situation. What is the only exchange ratio that can prevail in any equilibrium?
- b. Suppose that Smith initially had $40H$ and $80C$. What would the equilibrium position be?
- c. Suppose that Smith initially had $60H$ and $80C$. What would the equilibrium position be?
- d. Suppose that Smith (much the stronger of the two) decides not to play by the rules of the game. Then what could the final equilibrium position be?

8.6

Suppose, as in Problem 8.5, that there are only two individuals (Smith and Jones) and two goods (ham and cheese) in an exchange economy. Smith chooses to consume ham and cheese in fixed proportions of $2C$ to $1H$. Smith's utility function is therefore

$$U_S = \min(H, C/2).$$

Jones has flexible preferences and utility is given by

$$U_J = 4H + 3C.$$

Initial endowments for Smith are $H = 60$, $C = 80$ and for Jones $H = 40$, $C = 120$.

- a. Graph the Edgeworth box diagram for this exchange economy and indicate the core of the economy given the initial endowments specified.
- b. Graph the offer curves for Smith and Jones and show that these intersect in the core.
- c. At the competitive equilibrium, what will be the equilibrium price ratio? Who will obtain the gains from competitive trading?

8.7

In an economy with two individuals (A and B), discuss the results of exchange in the following situations.

- a. Perfect competition in which A and B accept prices as given by the market.
- b. A is a monopolist and can set any price it chooses.
- c. A is a perfect price discriminator and can charge a different price for each unit traded.

Does each of these lead to a Pareto efficient solution? It would be useful to work with an Edgeworth box diagram to present your solution. (See Chapter 18 for additional discussions of monopoly and price discrimination.)

8.8

In the numerical example of exchange in Chapter 8 each individual has an initial endowment of 500 units of each good.

- a. Express the demand of Smith and Jones for goods X and Y as functions of P_X and P_Y and their initial endowments.
- b. Use the demand functions from part a together with the observation

that total demand for each good must be 1,000 to calculate the equilibrium price ratio, P_X/P_Y, in this situation. What are the equilibrium consumption levels of each good by each person?

c.   Develop an offer curve analysis for this problem. What is the equilibrium price ratio where these curves intersect? Does this ratio agree with
the ratio computed in part b above?

8.9

How would the answers to Problem 8.8 change for the following initial
endowments?

	Smith's Endowment		Jones's Endowment	
	X	Y	X	Y
a.	0	1,000	1,000	0
b.	600	600	400	400
c.	400	400	600	600
d.	1,000	1,000	0	0

Explain the reason for these varying results.

CHAPTER 9

Choice in Uncertain Situations

In previous chapters it has been implicitly assumed that individuals make decisions in an environment characterized by an absence of uncertainty. When individuals purchase goods, they know exactly what they are getting and how much utility the goods will yield. Once the allocation of the budget is determined, no uncertainty is associated with the utility derived.

In a variety of real-world situations, this assumption cannot be considered tenable. First, some goods that individuals purchase are in the nature of games or lotteries for which the outcome is uncertain. Racetrack bets, craps, insurance purchases, and stock market transactions all fit into this general category: The purchase of the good does not guarantee any particular outcome. A second way in which uncertainty affects individual behavior is in dealings with others. Many encounters between individuals are in the form of adversary proceedings in which the reward that anyone receives depends on what others do. This type of uncertainty is manifest in numerous situations ranging from poker games to the conduct of diplomacy.

Finally, the individual is confronted by uncertainty through a lack of understanding or of information concerning the problem to be solved. An individual is not able to predict the weather with any degree of certainty, or to decide specifically which refrigerator offers the best quality for the money. In such situations the individual lacks knowledge and might be willing to pay something for additional information.

Of these three types of uncertainty, the first is the most easily investigated and will occupy the major portion of this chapter. That is, we will be primarily interested in studying how individuals make choices in risky situations when the likelihood of various outcomes (for example, winning at the track) is reasonably well understood. We will also show how consideration of this question leads naturally into the examination of the ways in which individuals attempt to gather information to use in making their decisions. As anyone who has ever thought about buying a used car knows, information (say, about the car's defects) has real economic value, and individuals will often devote considerable resources (hiring a mechanic, say) to acquiring it. In the latter part of this chapter, we will look at that process in some detail. For the moment, however, we will delay our discussion of uncertainty in dealing with other people. That topic is taken up as a part of our discussion of game theory and inter-firm strategy in Chapter 20.

PROBABILITY AND EXPECTED VALUE

The study of individual behavior under uncertainty and the mathematical study of probability and statistics have a common historical origin in attempts to understand (and presumably to win) games of chance. The study of simple coin-flipping games, for example, has been unusually productive both in mathematics and in illuminating certain characteristics of human behavior that the games exhibit. Two statistical concepts that originated in such games, and will be quite useful in the remainder of this chapter, are *probability* and *expected value*.

The *probability* of an event happening is, roughly speaking, the relative frequency with which it will occur. For example, to say that the probability of obtaining a head on the flip of a fair coin is one-half means that one would expect that if a fair coin were flipped a large number of times, a head would appear in approximately one-half of the trials. Similarly, the probability of rolling a 2 on a single die is one-sixth. In approximately one out of every six rolls, a 2 will come up.

Suppose that a lottery offers n prizes (some of which may be 0), X_1, X_2, . . . , X_n, and that the probabilities of winning these prizes are $\pi_1, \pi_2, . . . , \pi_n$. If we assume that one and only one prize will be awarded to a player, it must be the case that

$$\sum_{i=1}^{n} \pi_i = 1. \tag{9.1}$$

Equation 9.1 simply says that some outcome has to occur. To provide a measure of the average payoff in this lottery, we define

---

Definition:

Expected Value

For a lottery (X) with prizes X_1, X_2, . . . , X_n and probabilities of winning $\pi_1, \pi_2, . . . , \pi_n$, the *expected value* of the lottery is [1]

$$\text{expected value} = E(X) = \pi_1 X_1 + \pi_2 X_2 + \cdots + \pi_n X_n$$

$$= \sum_{i=1}^{n} \pi_i X_i. \tag{9.2}$$

---

[1] If the situation being examined has continuous outcomes (for example, the change in the price of a stock measured very precisely), then we need to modify this definition a bit. If the probability

The expected value of the lottery is a weighted sum of the prizes, where the weights are the respective probabilities. It is simply the size of the prize that the player will win on the average. For example, suppose that Jones and Smith agree to flip a coin once. If a head comes up, Jones will pay Smith $1; if a tail, Smith will pay Jones $1. From Smith's point of view, there are two prizes in this game: For a head, $X_1 = +\$1$; for a tail, $X_2 = -\$1$, where the minus sign indicates that Smith must pay. From Jones's point of view, the game is exactly the same except the signs of the outcomes are reversed. Thus the expected value of the game is

$$\frac{1}{2} X_1 + \frac{1}{2} X_2 = \frac{1}{2} (\$1) + \frac{1}{2} (-\$1) = 0. \tag{9.3}$$

The game has an expected value of 0. If the game were to be played a large number of times, it is not likely that either player would come out very far ahead.

   Now suppose that the prizes of the game were changed slightly so that (again from Smith's point of view) $X_1 = \$10$, $X_2 = -\$1$. Smith will win $10 if a head comes up but will lose only $1 if a tail appears. The expected value of this game is

$$\frac{1}{2} X_1 + \frac{1}{2} X_2 = \frac{1}{2} (\$10) + \frac{1}{2} (-\$1) = \$5 - \$.50 = \$4.50. \tag{9.4}$$

If this game is played many times, Smith will certainly end up the big winner. In fact, Smith might be willing to pay Jones something for the privilege of playing the game. He might even be willing to pay as much as $4.50 for a chance to play. Games such as those in Equation 9.3, which have an expected value of 0, or those in Equation 9.4, which cost their expected values (here $4.50) for the right to play, are called (actuarially) *fair games*. A common observation is that, in many situations, people refuse to play actuarially fair games. This point is central to understanding developments in the theory of uncertainty and is taken up in the next section.

---

that an outcome of such a random event (X) is in a small interval (dx) is given by $f(x)\ dx$, then Equation 9.1 can be modified as

$$\int_{-\infty}^{\infty} f(x)\ dx = 1.$$

In this case the expected value of X is given by

$$E(X) = \int_{-\infty}^{\infty} x f(x)\ dx.$$

In many situations (for example, when X has a normal distribution), manipulation of such expected values can be much simpler than for the discrete case represented in Equation 9.2.

FAIR GAMES AND THE EXPECTED UTILITY HYPOTHESIS

People are generally unwilling to play fair games.[2] I may at times agree to flip a coin for small amounts of money, but if I were offered the chance to wager $1000 on one coin flip, I would undoubtedly refuse. Similarly, people may sometimes pay a small amount of money to play an actuarially unfair game such as a state lottery, but they will avoid paying a great deal to play risky, but fair games.

St. Petersburg Paradox

An even more convincing example is the "St. Petersburg paradox," which was first investigated rigorously by the mathematician Daniel Bernoulli in the eighteenth century.[3] In the St. Petersburg paradox the following game is proposed: A coin is flipped until a head appears. If a head first appears on the nth flip, the player is paid 2^n. This game has an infinite number of outcomes (a coin might be flipped from now until doomsday and never come up a head, although the likelihood of this is small), but the first few can easily be written down. If X_i represents the prize awarded when the first head appears on the ith trial, then

$$X_1 = \$2$$

$$X_2 = \$4$$

$$X_3 = \$8$$

$$\cdot$$

$$\cdot \tag{9.5}$$

$$\cdot$$

$$X_n = \$2^n$$

$$\cdot$$

$$\cdot$$

$$\cdot$$

The probability of getting a head for the first time on the ith trial is $(1/2)^i$; it is the probability of getting $(i - 1)$ tails and then a head. Hence the probabilities of the prizes given in Equation 9.5 are

---

[2] The games discussed here are assumed to yield no utility in their play other than the prizes; hence the observation that many individuals gamble at "unfair" odds (for instance, in the game of roulette, where there are 38 possible outcomes but the house pays only 36 to 1 for a winning number) is not necessarily a refutation of this statement. Rather, such individuals can reasonably be assumed to be deriving some utility from the circumstances associated with the play of the game. It is therefore conceptually possible to differentiate the consumption aspect of gambling from the pure risk aspect.

[3] The original Bernoulli article is well worth reading. It has been reprinted as D. Bernoulli, "Exposition of a New Theory on the Measurement of Risk," *Econometrica* 22 (January 1954): 23–36.

$$\pi_1 = \frac{1}{2}$$

$$\pi_2 = \frac{1}{4}$$

$$\pi_3 = \frac{1}{8}$$

.

.   (9.6)

.

$$\pi_n = \frac{1}{2^n}$$

.

.

.

The expected value of the St. Petersburg paradox game is infinite:

$$\text{expected value} = \sum_{i=1}^{\infty} \pi_i X_i = \sum_{i=1}^{\infty} 2^i \frac{1}{2^i}$$

$$= 1 + 1 + 1 + \cdots + 1 \cdots = \infty. \tag{9.7}$$

Some introspection, however, should convince anyone that no player would pay very much (much less than infinity) to play this game. If I charged $1 billion to play the game, I would surely have no takers, despite the fact that $1 billion is still considerably less than the expected value of the game. This, then, is the paradox: Bernoulli's game is in some sense not worth its (infinite) expected dollar value.

Expected Utility   Bernoulli's solution to this paradox was to argue that individuals do not care directly about the dollar prizes of a game; rather they respond to the utility these dollars provide. If it is assumed that the marginal utility of income declines as income increases, the St. Petersburg game may converge to a finite *expected utility* value that players would be willing to pay for the right to play. Bernoulli termed this expected utility value the "moral value" of the game because it represents how much the game is worth to the individual. Because utility may rise less rapidly than the dollar value of the prizes, it is possible that a game's moral value will fall short of its monetary expected value.

Numerical   Suppose, as did Bernoulli, that the utility of each prize in the St. Petersburg
Example   paradox is given by

$$U(X_i) = \ln (X_i). \tag{9.8}$$

This natural logarithmic utility function exhibits diminishing marginal utility (that is, $U' > 0$, but $U'' < 0$), and the expected utility value of this game converges to a finite number:

$$\text{expected utility} = \sum_{i=1}^{\infty} \pi_i U(X_i)$$

$$= \sum_{i=1}^{\infty} \frac{1}{2^i} \ln (2^i).$$

(9.9)

Some manipulation of this expression yields the result that the expected utility value of this game is 1.39.[4] An individual with this type of utility function might therefore be willing to invest resources that otherwise yield up to 1.39 units of utility in purchasing the right to play this game. Thus, assuming that the very large prizes promised by the St. Petersburg paradox encounter diminishing marginal utility permitted Bernoulli to offer a solution to the paradox.

Although Bernoulli's basic observation is extremely important to any discussion of individual behavior under uncertainty, he did not really solve the St. Petersburg paradox. As long as there is no upper bound on the utility function,[5] the prizes in the game can be suitably redefined so as to regenerate the paradox. However, Bernoulli clearly made an important observation about individual behavior, and the hypothesis that individuals look at expected utility rather than at expected dollar values has a great intuitive appeal.

THE VON NEUMANN–MORGENSTERN THEOREM

In their book, *The Theory of Games and Economic Behavior,* John von Neumann and Oscar Morgenstern developed mathematical models for examining the economic behavior of individuals under conditions of uncertainty.[6] To understand these interactions, it was necessary first to investigate the motives of the participants in such "games." Since the hypothesis that individuals make choices in uncertain situations based on expected utility seemed intuitively reasonable, the authors set out to show that this hypothesis could be derived from more basic axioms of "rational" behavior. The axioms represent an attempt by the authors to generalize some of the foundations of the theory of individual choice to cover uncertain situations. Although most of these axioms seem emi-

---

[4] Proof: Expected utility $= \sum_{i=1}^{\infty} \frac{1}{2^i} \cdot i \ln 2 = \ln 2 \sum_{i=1}^{\infty} \frac{i}{2^i}$. But the value of this final infinite series can be shown to be 2.0. Hence expected utility $= 2 \ln 2 = 1.39$.

[5] This problem and several others have prompted many investigators to adopt the assumption of a bounded utility function. It is assumed that there is some income level above which utility no longer increases with further increases in income. For example, suppose that the level of bliss is taken to be $\$2^{42}$ (which is about the total value of all physical assets in the United States). Then prizes greater than this are worth no more than $\$2^{42}$. Under this assumption the *expected value* of the St. Petersburg game is a "reasonable" $43. This level of "bliss" is so far above any observable level of income as to be irrelevant to real-world problems. In this case the assumption of boundedness is merely a convenient assumption without any stringent empirical content.

[6] J. von Neumann and O. Morgenstern, *The Theory of Games and Economic Behavior* (Princeton, N.J.: Princeton University Press, 1944). The axioms of rationality in uncertain situations are discussed in the appendix.

nently reasonable at first glance, many important questions about their tenability have been raised. We will not pursue these questions here, however. Instead, we will show why von Neumann and Morgenstern concluded that maximizing expected utility seemed to be a reasonable goal to pursue in uncertain situations.[7]

The von Neumann–Morgenstern Utility Index

To begin, suppose that there are n possible prizes that an individual might win by participating in a game. Let these prizes be denoted by $X_1, X_2, \ldots, X_n$ and assume (without loss of generality) that these have been arranged in order of ascending desirability. X_1 is therefore the least preferred prize for the individual, and X_n is the most preferred prize. Now assign arbitrary utility numbers to these two extreme prizes. For example, it might be convenient to assume that

$$U(X_1) = 0$$
$$U(X_n) = 1,$$

(9.10)

but any other pair of numbers would do equally well.[8] Using these two values of utility, the point of the von Neumann–Morgenstern theorem is to show that a reasonable way exists to assign specific utility numbers to the other prizes available. Suppose that we choose any other prize, say, X_i. Consider the following experiment. Ask the individual at what probability, say π_i, he or she would be indifferent between X_i with *certainty*, and a *gamble* offering prizes of X_n, with probability π_i, and X_1, with probability $(1 - \pi_i)$. It seems reasonable (although again this is a questionable axiom) that such a probability will exist: The individual will always be indifferent between a gamble and a sure thing, provided that in the gamble a high enough probability of winning the best prize is offered. It also seems likely that π_i will be higher the more desirable X_i is; the better X_i is, the better a chance of winning X_n must be offered to get the individual to gamble. In some sense the probability π_i represents how desirable the prize X_i is. In fact, the von Neumann–Morgenstern technique is to define the utility of X_i as the expected utility of the gamble that the individual considers equally desirable to X_i:

$$U(X_i) = \pi_i \cdot U(X_n) + (1 - \pi_i) \cdot U(X_1).$$

(9.11)

Because of our choice of scale in Equation 9.10 we have

$$U(X_i) = \pi_i \cdot 1 + (1 - \pi_i) \cdot 0 = \pi_i.$$

(9.12)

---

[7] For a discussion of some of the issues raised in the debate over the von Neumann–Morgenstern axioms, see Mark J. Machina, "Choice under Uncertainty: Problems Solved and Unsolved," *Journal of Economic Perspectives* (Summer 1987): 121–154.

[8] Technically, a von Neumann–Morgenstern utility index is unique only up to a choice of scale and origin—that is, only up to a "linear transformation." This is also true, for example, of temperature scales (centigrade, Fahrenheit, Kelvin).

Notice that the requirement that these utility numbers be unique up to a linear transformation is more stringent than the requirement (discussed in Chapter 3) that a utility function be unique up to a monotonic transformation.

By judiciously choosing the utility numbers to be assigned to the best and worst prizes, we have been able to show that the utility number attached to any other prize is simply the probability that was defined above. This choice of utility numbers is totally arbitrary. Any other two numbers could have been used to construct this utility scale, but our initial choice (Equation 9.10) will prove to be a particularly convenient one.

Expected Utility Maximization

In line with the choice of scale and origin represented by Equation 9.10, suppose that probability π_i has been assigned to represent the utility of every prize X_i. Notice in particular that $\pi_1 = 0$ and $\pi_n = 1$ and that the other utility values range between these extremes. Using these utility numbers, it is possible to show that a "rational" individual will choose among gambles based on their expected "utilities" (that is, based on the expected value of these von Neumann–Morgenstern utility index numbers).

As an example, consider two gambles. One gamble offers X_2, with probability q, and X_3, with probability $(1 - q)$. The other offers X_5, with probability t, and X_6, with probability $(1 - t)$. We want to show that the individual will choose gamble 1 if and only if the expected utility of gamble 1 exceeds that of gamble 2. Now for the gambles:

$$\text{expected utility (1)} = q \cdot U(X_2) + (1 - q) \cdot U(X_3)$$
$$\text{expected utility (2)} = t \cdot U(X_5) + (1 - t) \cdot U(X_6). \tag{9.13}$$

Substituting the utility index numbers (that is, π_2 is the "utility" of X_2, and so forth) gives

$$\text{expected utility (1)} = q \cdot \pi_2 + (1 - q) \cdot \pi_3$$
$$\text{expected utility (2)} = t \cdot \pi_5 + (1 - t) \cdot \pi_6. \tag{9.14}$$

We wish to show that the individual will prefer gamble 1 to gamble 2 if and only if

$$q \cdot \pi_2 + (1 - q) \cdot \pi_3 > t \cdot \pi_5 + (1 - t) \cdot \pi_6. \tag{9.15}$$

To show this, recall the definitions of the utility index. The individual is indifferent between X_2 and a gamble promising X_1, with probability $(1 - \pi_2)$, and X_n, with probability π_2. Now use this fact to substitute gambles involving only X_1 and X_n for all utilities in Equation 9.14 (even though the individual is indifferent between these, the assumption that this substitution can be made is another of the important von Neumann–Morgenstern axioms):

$$\text{expected utility (1)} = q[\pi_2 \cdot U(X_n) + (1 - \pi_2) \cdot U(X_1)]$$
$$+ (1 - q)[\pi_3 \cdot U(X_n) + (1 - \pi_3) \cdot U(X_1)]$$
$$= [q\pi_2 + (1 - q)\pi_3] \cdot U(X_n) + [q(1 - \pi_2)$$
$$+ (1 - q)(1 - \pi_3)] \cdot U(X_1). \tag{9.16}$$

expected utility $(2) = t[\pi_5 \cdot U(X_n) + (1 - \pi_5) \cdot U(X_1)]$

$$+ (1 - t)[\pi_6 \cdot U(X_n) + (1 - \pi_6) \cdot U(X_1)]$$

$$= [t\pi_5 + (1 - t)\pi_6] \cdot U(X_n) + [t(1 - \pi_5)$$

$$+ (1 - t)(1 - \pi_6)] \cdot U(X_1).$$

Consequently, gamble 1 is equivalent to a gamble promising X_n, with probability $q\pi_2 + (1 - q)\pi_3$, and gamble 2 is equivalent to a gamble promising X_n, with probability $t\pi_5 + (1 - t)\pi_6$. The individual will presumably prefer the gamble with the highest probability of winning the best prize. Consequently, he or she will choose gamble 1 if and only if

$$q\pi_2 + (1 - q)\pi_3 > t\pi_5 + (1 - t)\pi_6. \qquad (9.17)$$

But this is precisely what we wanted to show in Equation 9.15. Consequently, we have proved that an individual will choose the gamble that provides the highest level of expected (von Neumann–Morgenstern) utility.

In a sense, then, the von Neumann–Morgenstern index plays the role of a utility function, and individuals can be shown to make choices among risky options so as to maximize expected "utility." Since much debate and confusion have centered on the exact relationship, if any, between von Neumann–Morgenstern "utility" and the more traditional concept, it is best to keep the two ideas distinct. In the remainder of this chapter, the "utility" functions that are used will represent von Neumann–Morgenstern orderings. We will assume that the basic von Neumann–Morgenstern axioms hold and therefore that it is possible to talk about individuals maximizing *expected utility:*

Optimization Principle:

Expected Utility Maximization
In certain situations individuals are assumed to choose the option that maximizes the expected value of their von Neumann–Morgenstern utility index.

RISK AVERSION

Two lotteries may have the same expected monetary value but may differ in their riskiness. For example, flipping a coin for $1 and flipping a coin for $1000 are both fair games, and both have the same expected value (0). However, the latter is in some sense more "risky" than the former, and fewer people would participate in the game where the prize was winning or losing $1000. The purpose of this section is to discuss the meaning of the term "risky" and to explain the widespread aversion to risk.

The term *risk* refers to the variability of the outcomes of some uncertain activity.[9] If variability is low, the activity may be approximately a sure thing.

---

[9]Often the statistical concept of "variance" is used as a proxy for risk. Although we will not discuss this statistical notion in the body of this chapter, it is defined in the chapter's extension problems and used in a few of those problems.

Figure 9.1   *Utility of Wealth from Two Fair Bets of Differing Variability*

If the individual's utility of wealth function is concave (that is, exhibits a diminishing marginal utility of wealth), he or she will refuse fair bets. A 50–50 bet of winning or losing *h* dollars, for example, yields less utility [$C^h(W^*)$] than does refusing the bet. The reason for this is that winning *h* dollars means less to such an individual than does losing *h* dollars.

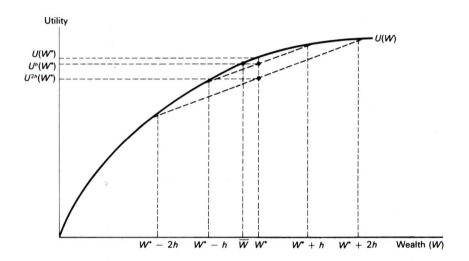

With no more precise notion of variability than this, it is possible to show why individuals, when faced with a choice between two gambles with the same expected value, usually will choose the one with a smaller variability of return. Intuitively, the reason behind this is that we usually assume that the marginal utility from extra dollars of prize money (that is, wealth) declines as the prizes get larger. A flip of a coin for $1000 promises a relatively small gain of utility if you win but a large loss of utility if you lose. A bet of only $1 is "inconsequential," and the gain in utility from a win approximately counterbalances the decline in utility from a loss.

Risk Aversion and Fair Bets

This argument is illustrated in Figure 9.1. Here W^* represents the individual's current wealth and $U(W)$ is a von Neumann–Morgenstern utility index that reflects how the individual feels about various levels of wealth. $U(W)$ is drawn as a concave function of W to reflect the assumption of a diminishing marginal utility. It is assumed that obtaining an extra dollar adds less to enjoyment as total wealth increases. Now suppose that the individual is offered two fair gambles: a 50–50 chance of winning or losing $\$h$ or a 50–50 chance of winning or losing $\$2h$. The utility of present wealth is $U(W^*)$. The expected utility if he or she participates in gamble 1 is given by $U^h(W^*)$:

$$U^h(W^*) = \frac{1}{2} U(W^* + h) + \frac{1}{2} U(W^* - h), \tag{9.18}$$

and expected utility of gamble 2 is given by $U^{2h}(W^*)$:

$$U^{2h}(W^*) = \frac{1}{2} U(W^* + 2h) + \frac{1}{2} U(W^* - 2h). \qquad (9.19)$$

It is geometrically clear from the figure that [10]

$$U(W^*) > U^h(W^*) > U^{2h}(W^*). \qquad (9.20)$$

The individual therefore will prefer current wealth to that wealth combined with a fair gamble and will prefer a small gamble to a large one. The reason for this is that winning a fair bet adds to the individual's enjoyment less than losing hurts. Although the prizes are equal in dollar terms, in utility terms the loss is more serious.

Risk Aversion and Insurance

As a matter of fact, the individual might be willing to pay some amount to avoid participating in any gamble at all. Notice that a certain wealth of $\overline{W}$ provides the same utility as does participating in gamble 1. The individual will be willing to pay anything up to $W^* - \overline{W}$ to avoid participating in the gamble. This undoubtedly explains why people buy insurance. They are giving up a small, certain amount (the premium) to avoid the risky outcome that they are insured against. The premium a person pays for automobile collision insurance, for example, provides a policy that agrees to repair his or her car should an accident occur. The widespread use of such insurance would seem to imply that aversion to risk is quite common. Hence we introduce the following definition:

Definition:

Risk Aversion

An individual who always refuses fair bets is said to be *risk averse*. If individuals exhibit a diminishing marginal utility of wealth, they will be risk averse. As a consequence, they will be willing to pay something to avoid taking fair bets.

Numerical Example

To illustrate the connection between risk aversion and insurance, consider an individual with a current wealth of $100,000 who faces the prospect of a 25 percent chance of losing his or her $20,000 automobile through theft during the next year. Suppose also that this person's von Neumann–Morgenstern utility index is logarithmic—that is, $U(W) = \ln(W)$.

If this person faces next year without insurance, expected utility will be

[10] To see why the expected utilities for bet h and bet $2h$ are those shown, notice that these expected utilities are simply the average of the utilities from a favorable and an unfavorable outcome. Since W^* is halfway between $W^* + h$ and $W^* - h$, U^h is also halfway between $U(W^* + h)$ and $U(W^* - h)$.

$$\text{expected utility} = .75\,U(100{,}000) + .25\,U(80{,}000)$$

$$= .75 \ln 100{,}000 + .25 \ln 80{,}000 \qquad (9.21)$$

$$= 11.4571.$$

In this situation a fair insurance premium would be $5,000 (25 percent of $20,000, assuming that the insurance company has only claim costs and that administrative costs are 0). Consequently, if this person completely insures the car, his or her wealth will be $95,000 regardless of whether the car is stolen. In this case, then,

$$\text{expected utility} = U(95{,}000)$$

$$= \ln (95{,}000) \qquad (9.22)$$

$$= 11.4616.$$

This person is clearly better off when he or she purchases insurance. Indeed we can determine the maximum amount that might be paid for this insurance protection (x) by setting

$$\text{expected utility} = U(100{,}000 - x)$$

$$= \ln (100{,}000 - x) \qquad (9.23)$$

$$= 11.4571.$$

Solving this equation for x yields

$$100{,}000 - x = e^{11.4571} = 94{,}570. \qquad (9.24)$$

Hence

$$x = 5430. \qquad (9.25)$$

Thus this person would be willing to pay up to $430 in administrative costs to an insurance company (in addition to the $5,000 premium to cover the expected value of the loss). Even when such costs are paid, this person is as well off as he or she would be if forced to face the world uninsured.

MEASURING RISK AVERSION

In the study of economic choices in risky situations, it is sometimes convenient to have a quantitative measure of how averse to risk a person is. The most commonly used measure of risk aversion was initially developed by J. W. Pratt in the 1960s.[11] This risk aversion measure, $r(W)$, is defined as

$$r(W) = -\frac{U''(W)}{U'(W)}. \qquad (9.26)$$

Since the distinguishing feature of risk-averse individuals is a diminishing marginal utility of wealth $[U''(W) < 0]$, Pratt's measure is positive in such cases. It

[11] J. W. Pratt, "Risk Aversion in the Small and in the Large," *Econometrica* (January/April 1964): 122–136.

is easy to show that the measure is invariant with respect to linear transformations of the utility function; hence it is not affected by which particular von Neumann–Morgenstern ordering is used.

Risk Aversion and Insurance Premiums

Perhaps the most useful feature of the Pratt measure of risk aversion is that it can be shown to be proportional to the amount an individual will pay for insurance against taking a fair bet. Suppose the winnings from such a fair bet are denoted by the random variable h (this variable may be either positive or negative). Since the bet is fair, $E(h) = 0$ (where E means "expected value"). Now let p be the size of the insurance premium that would make the individual exactly indifferent between taking the fair bet h and paying p with certainty to avoid the gamble:

$$E[U(W + h)] = U(W - p), \tag{9.27}$$

where W is the individual's current wealth. We now expand both sides of Equation 9.27 using Taylor's series.[12] The right side of the equation becomes

$$U(W - p) = U(W) - pU'(W) + \text{higher order terms}, \tag{9.28}$$

and the left side is

$$E[U(W + h)] = E[U(W) + hU'(W) + \frac{h^2}{2} U''(W) \tag{9.29}$$

$$+ \text{ higher order terms}]$$

$$= U(W) + E(h)U'(W) + \frac{E(h^2)}{2} U''(W) \tag{9.30}$$

$$+ \text{ higher order terms.}$$

Now, remembering $E(h) = 0$, dropping the higher order terms, and using the constant k to represent $E(h^2)/2$, we can equate Equations 9.28 and 9.30 as

$$U(W) - pU'(W) \simeq U(W) + kU''(W) \tag{9.31}$$

or

$$p \simeq -\frac{kU''(W)}{U'(W)} = kr(W) \tag{9.32}$$

as was to be shown. That is, the amount that a risk-averse individual is willing to pay to avoid a fair bet is approximately proportional to Pratt's risk aversion measure. Since insurance premiums paid are observable in the real world, these are often used to estimate individuals' risk aversion coefficients or to compare

---

[12] Taylor's series provides a way of approximating any differentiable function around some point. If $f(x)$ has derivatives of all orders, it can be shown that

$$f(x + h) = f(x) + hf'(x) + h^2/2 f''(x) + \text{higher order terms.}$$

The point-slope formula learned in high school algebra is a simple example of Taylor's series.

such coefficients among groups of individuals. It is therefore possible to use market information to learn quite a bit about attitudes toward risky situations.

Risk Aversion and Wealth

An important question is whether an individual's degree of risk aversion increases or decreases for higher levels of wealth. Intuitively, one might assume that the willingness to pay to avoid a given fair bet would decline as wealth increases, since diminishing marginal utility would make potential losses less serious for high-wealth individuals. Such an intuitive answer is not generally correct, however, because diminishing marginal utility also makes the gains from winning gambles less attractive. So the net result is indeterminate, depending on the precise shape of the utility function. Indeed, if utility is quadratic in wealth,

$$U(W) = a + bW + cW^2, \tag{9.33}$$

where $b > 0$, $c < 0$, Pratt's risk aversion measure is

$$r(W) = -\frac{U''(W)}{U'(W)} = \frac{-2c}{b + 2cW}, \tag{9.34}$$

which increases as wealth increases.[13]

On the other hand, if utility is logarithmic in wealth,

$$U(W) = \ln (W + a) \qquad (a > 0), \tag{9.35}$$

we have

$$r(W) = -\frac{U''(W)}{U'(W)} = \frac{1}{W + a}, \tag{9.36}$$

which does indeed decrease as wealth increases. Since there seems to be no strong theoretical reason for preferring one of these assumed utility functions for wealth over the other, the question of the relationship between wealth and risk-avoiding behavior remains theoretically ambiguous.[14]

THE STATE-PREFERENCE APPROACH TO CHOICE UNDER UNCERTAINTY

Although our analysis thus far in this chapter has offered insights on a number of issues, it has been very different from the approach we took in other chapters. The basic model of utility maximization subject to a budget constraint seems to have been lost. In order to make further progress in our examination of behavior under uncertainty, we must therefore develop some new terminology that will permit us to bring the discussion of such behavior back into our standard choice-theoretic framework.

[13] For reasons to be described in the extension problems at the end of this chapter, utility functions that are quadratic in wealth are quite popular in some empirical research. This result indicates one reason to be hesitant about the assumptions underlying the use of such a function.

[14] A function "midway" between the quadratic and logarithmic cases is the exponential utility function $U(W) = k - e^{aW}$, where k is a positive constant and a is a negative constant. For this case $r(W) = -a$, which is constant for all levels of wealth.

States of the World and Contingent Commodities

To accomplish this goal, we start by assuming that outcomes of any random event can be categorized into a certain number of *states of the world*. We cannot predict exactly what will happen, say, tomorrow, but we assume that it is possible to categorize all of the possible things that might happen into a number of well-defined *states*. For example, we might make the very crude approximation of saying that the world will be in only one of two possible states tomorrow: It will be either "good times" or "bad times." One could make a much finer gradation of states of the world (involving even millions of possible states), but most of the essentials of the theory can be developed using only two states; therefore no more complex definition will be used here.

A conceptual idea that can be developed concurrently with the notion of states of the world is that of *contingent commodities*. These are goods delivered only if a particular state of the world occurs. "$1 in good times" is an example of a contingent commodity that promises the individual $1 in good times but nothing should tomorrow turn out to be bad times. It is even possible, by stretching one's intuitive ability somewhat, to conceive of being able to purchase this commodity—I might be able to buy from someone the promise of $1 if tomorrow turns out to be good times. If someone were also willing to sell me the contingent commodity, "$1 in bad times," then I could assure myself of having $1 tomorrow by buying the two contingent commodities "$1 in good times" and "$1 in bad times." Notice that even though I buy both of these commodities today, only one will "pay off" tomorrow, since tomorrow will be either good times or bad times but not both. Similarly, it is possible to guarantee a winner in a horse race by betting on all the horses. Some horse has to come in first, and therefore some winnings are generated.

This concept of a contingent commodity can be extended to include claims on any good in the future. One can envision a hamburger to be delivered tomorrow with certainty as in reality the combination of two contingent claims: "A hamburger if tomorrow is good times" plus "a hamburger if tomorrow is bad times." There may be markets for these two distinct contingent goods, and conceivably an individual could buy one without buying the other. If an individual did buy a contingent claim on "one hamburger in good times," then, if tomorrow turned out to be bad times, nothing would be received.

Utility Analysis

A utility analysis involving the choice of contingent commodities proceeds formally in much the same way as did the analysis of individual choices in Chapter 4. The principal difference is that in choosing goods individuals usually consume both goods, whereas in choosing contingent commodities they will ultimately consume only one of the goods. This distinction makes possible a simple assumption that might be made about the form of the utility function for contingent commodities. This assumption is illuminating in what it shows about individual behavior in uncertain situations. Specifically, denote consumption in good times by C_g and in bad times by C_b. The individual will choose among these contingent commodities in such a way as to maximize an expected utility function of the form $U(C_g, C_b)$. The assumption to be made about this function is that the utility an individual receives from consumption is *independent of the state of the world*. Formally, this assumes that

$$\text{utility in state } g = V(C_g) \tag{9.37}$$

and

$$\text{utility in state } b = V(C_b),$$

where the function V is the same in both states of the world. Also we will assume that V is concave in consumption. That is, $V'(C) > 0$, $V''(C) < 0$. If π_g is the (subjective)[15] probability of good times and π_b is the probability of bad times, then the expected utility of any bundle of contingent consumption choices is given by

$$U(C_g, C_b) = \pi_g \cdot V(C_g) + \pi_b \cdot V(C_b). \tag{9.38}$$

Fair Markets for Contingent Commodities

Given the assumption of state independence of utility, it is an easy matter to show that if the market for contingent commodities is perceived as "fair," the individual will be "risk averse." To make this clear, some definitions are necessary. By a "fair market" for contingent commodities, we simply mean that the prices of the contingent commodities (call them P_g and P_b) are proportional to the subjective probabilities (π_g and π_b) of the two states of the world:

$$\frac{P_g}{P_b} = \frac{\pi_g}{\pi_b}. \tag{9.39}$$

This equation is one way of phrasing the assumption that buying contingent commodities is perceived as a fair game. This may be true if there are a large number of buyers and sellers in the market and if the probabilities are known to all. In the racetrack example, Equation 9.39 is satisfied when the odds on each horse reflect the true probability of its winning the race.

Risk Aversion

A possible definition of "risk aversion" in this model (one on which we shall cast some doubt below) is that individuals prefer to ensure the same level of consumption in all states of the world: that is, they will choose $C_g = C_b$ so that it does not matter which state actually occurs. Given our assumptions so far, it can be shown that the individual is risk averse in this sense. To maximize Equation 9.38 subject to the budget constraint $I = P_g C_g + P_b C_b$ (where I is the amount the individual has decided to devote to the purchase of contingent commodities), the first-order conditions for a maximum require that the individual equate the *MRS* (of C_g for C_b) to the ratio of the prices P_g/P_b:

$$\frac{P_g}{P_b} = \frac{\partial U/\partial C_g}{\partial U/\partial C_b} = \frac{\pi_g V'(C_g)}{\pi_b V'(C_b)}. \tag{9.40}$$

But, on the assumption that P_g and P_b represent actuarially fair prices, Equation 9.39 implies

[15] Notice that we are now assuming that individuals base their decisions on what they believe the probabilities of various outcomes are. This assumption will permit us to study why individuals might pay something to obtain better probability estimates.

Figure 9.2   *Utility Maximization for Contingent Commodities*

The indifference curve U_1 represents alternative combinations of "consumption in good times" (C_g) and "consumption in bad times" (C_b) about which the individual is indifferent. The 45° line is a certainty line since along it $C_g = C_b$; along this line the individual gets the same quantity whichever state of the world occurs. If the market for contingent commodities is fair, and if the utility an individual gets from consumption is independent of the state of the world, then the utility-maximizing point will be on the certainty line, and the individual will have the same consumption in both states.

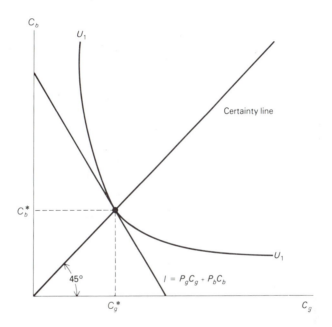

$$\frac{V'(C_g)}{V'(C_b)} = 1 \quad \text{or} \quad V'(C_g) = V'(C_b) \tag{9.41}$$

and since utility is state independent,

$$C_g = C_b. \tag{9.42}$$

That is, the individual assures himself or herself the same consumption in each state of the world. This result can also be presented graphically. In Figure 9.2 the individual's indifference map for C_g and C_b is drawn. In this figure the 45° line is labeled the "certainty line," since this is the locus of points for which $C_g = C_b$. Now the assumption we made in Equation 9.37 means that along the certainty line, the *MRS* is simply $-\pi_g/\pi_b$. But if the market is fair (that is, if Equation 9.39 holds), this will also be the slope of the individual's budget constraint, and hence maximization of expected utility will involve moving to the certainty line. The individual will act in this case so as to ensure the same consumption level at all eventualities.

Generalizations: Reasons for Incomplete Insurance

The model diagrammed in Figure 9.2 suggests that individuals will completely insure themselves against all risk: that is, they will choose $C_g = C_b$ so that consumption is independent of which state of the world occurs. But a variety of observations about behavior in risky situations suggests that such complete insurance is not the norm. Relatively few travelers buy flight insurance policies; practically no one has complete health insurance coverage; and most parents do not insure their children's lives. In each of these instances, individuals are essentially choosing to consume relatively more in "good times" and relatively less in "bad times" than under complete insurance. To understand why such choices might be made, it is helpful to reexamine the assumption of our model.

A first way in which our assumptions may be at variance with the real world is that the market for contingent commodities may not be "fair": that is, Equation 9.39 may not hold. For example, if the price of C_b exceeds what would be suggested by the perceived likelihood of "bad times" occurring, individuals might choose points to the right of the certainty line (with $C_g > C_b$). Such a high price of C_b might occur if there were significant costs in selling insurance or if the insurance market were not competitive. This may be the case for airline flight insurance. There is some evidence that such insurance is in fact not actuarially fair: It is much more costly than is warranted by the probabilities primarily because of the high costs of selling such insurance.[16]

A related reason for the failure of contingent insurance markets to offer actuarially fair prices concerns the problem of "moral hazard" (see the application at the end of this chapter). If the purchase of insurance actually changes the probability of an event occurring, it may be impossible to have fair, market-determined prices. A classic case is the problem of insuring old barns. Generally, one cannot buy insurance on such structures because, once insured, they seem prone to succumb to fires of "mysterious origin." Perhaps more relevant, because insurance lowers the out-of-pocket cost of some services to 0, individuals may respond to being insured by increasing their utilization of those services. That reaction probably explains the absence of some types of dental insurance (particularly for cosmetic types of work): Having insurance would tend to increase the probability that an individual would visit the dentist.

A final reason for the absence of complete insurance concerns the assumption we made in Equation 9.37 that utility is independent of the state of the world that actually occurs. If that assumption does not hold, there are reasons to expect movements away from the certainty line even when contingent markets are fair. The utility of a given level of income for a parent may be quite different when children are alive than when they are not, and hence utility might be maximized by not insuring against such a loss.

THE ECONOMICS OF INFORMATION

In a sense all individual behavior in uncertain situations can be regarded as being motivated by a lack of information. If individuals knew that a coin were going to come up heads or that it was not going to rain tomorrow, they would be better off. They may, in fact, be willing to pay for additional information

---

[16] See R. Eisner and R. H. Strotz, "Flight Insurance and the Theory of Choice," *Journal of Political Economy* 69 (1961): 355–368.

and will do so as long as the expected gains from this information exceed its cost. For example, an individual trying to decide whether to go on a picnic may invest in the price of a phone call to the weather bureau to help in deciding on a strategy.

More important illustrations of the willingness of persons to pay for additional information when faced with uncertainty are easy to find. Better weather forecasting undoubtedly has reduced the uncertainty associated with crop cultivation and mitigated the dangers of living on the Gulf Coast. A similar service is provided by Consumers Union, in that it supplies additional information on consumer goods, presumably permitting more rational purchasing decisions. Increasingly, government has attempted to compensate for the uncertainty faced by individuals in purchasing decisions both by providing various types of testing information and by setting minimal safety standards. Although such policies impose costs on consumers and on taxpayers, the benefits of those policies may exceed their costs if they provide information in a relatively efficient way.

Information and Subjective Probabilities

The relationship of information to behavior under uncertainty can be most readily studied using the state-preference approach that we introduced in the previous section. There we assumed that an individual formed subjective opinions about the probabilities of the two states of the world, "good times" and "bad times." In this model, information is valuable because it allows the individual to revise his or her estimates of these probabilities. For example, information that foretold that tomorrow would definitely be "good times" would cause the individual to revise his or her probabilities to be $\pi_g = 1$, $\pi_b = 0$. When the information received is less definitive, the individual may only revise the probabilities slightly, but even small revisions may be quite valuable. If you ask some friends about their experiences with a few brands of cassette players you are thinking of buying, you may not want their opinions to determine your choice. The prices of the players and other types of information (say, from reading *Consumer Reports*) will also affect your views. Ultimately, however, you must process all of these factors into a decision that reflects your assessment of the probabilities of various "states of the world" (in this case, the outcomes from buying various brands). To the extent that information alters *a priori* probabilities and allows individuals to make better decisions, it is a resource that has economic value.

A Formal Model

To illustrate how the quest for information might be integrated with our model of individual choice, suppose that information can be measured by the number of "messages" (m) received. Suppose also that the individual decision maker adjusts his or her subjective probabilities in response to these messages. Hence π_g and π_b will be functions of m. The individual's goal now is to maximize

$$\text{expected utility} = \pi_g V(C_g) + \pi_b V(C_b) \tag{9.43}$$

subject to

$$I = P_g C_g + P_b C_b + P_m m, \tag{9.44}$$

where P_m is the per unit cost of information messages (that is, the cost of a mechanic's time, of a phone call to gather price information, and so forth). Setting up the Lagrangian expression for this problem

$$\mathcal{L} = \pi_g V(C_g) + \pi_b V(C_b) + \lambda(I - P_g C_g - P_b C_b - P_m m) \qquad (9.45)$$

yields the following first-order conditions for a constrained maximum:

$$\frac{\partial \mathcal{L}}{\partial C_g} = \pi_g V'(C_g) - \lambda P_g = 0$$

$$\frac{\partial \mathcal{L}}{\partial C_b} = \pi_b V'(C_b) - \lambda P_b = 0$$

$$\frac{\partial \mathcal{L}}{\partial m} = \pi_g V'(C_g) \frac{dC_g}{dm} + \pi_b V'(C_b) \frac{dC_b}{dm} \qquad (9.46)$$

$$+ V(C_g) \frac{d\pi_g}{dm} + V(C_b) \frac{d\pi_b}{dm} - \lambda P_m = 0$$

$$\frac{\partial \mathcal{L}}{\partial \lambda} = I - P_g C_g - P_b C_b - P_m m = 0.$$

The first two of these equations simply restate the optimality result derived earlier. At a maximum the (subjective) ratio of expected marginal utilities should equal the price ratio P_g/P_b. The third equation states the basic marginal principle that this individual should purchase additional information messages up to the point at which the expected marginal gain from another message is equal to its cost. Notice that additional information increases utility in two ways: (1) It permits the individual to revise his or her choices of C_g and C_b so as to achieve a higher expected utility at given probability estimates; and (2) it may raise the expected utility associated with a particular choice of C_g and C_b by revising the probabilities attached to the two states. In general, it might be expected that the first of these reasons would be the most important motive for a risk-averse individual to acquire information.[17]

Asymmetry of Information

The principal implication of this model is that the level of information that an individual acquires will depend on the per unit price of information messages. Unlike the market price for most goods (which are assumed to be the same for everyone), there are many reasons to believe that these information costs may differ significantly among individuals. Some people may possess specific skills relevant to information acquisition (they may be trained mechanics, for example) whereas others may not possess such skills. Some individuals may have other types of experiences that yield valuable information whereas others may

---

[17] In the case of state independence and fair markets for contingent commodities, we have shown that $V(C_g) = V(C_b)$. Since $\pi_g + \pi_b = 1$, $d\pi_g/dm = -d\pi_b/dm$. Hence the second part of the expression for optimal information choice is equal to 0, and only the first motive for acquiring information is operative.

lack that experience. For example, the seller of a product will usually know more about its limitations than will a buyer since the seller will know precisely how the good was made and where possible problems might arise. Similarly, large-scale repeat buyers of a good may have greater access to information about it than do first-time buyers. Finally, some individuals may have invested in some types of information services (for example, by having a computer link to a brokerage firm or by subscribing to *Consumer Reports*) that make the marginal cost of obtaining additional information lower than for someone without such an investment.

All of these factors suggest that the level of information may differ among the participants in market transactions. Of course, in many instances, information costs may be low and such differences may be minor. Most people can appraise the quality of fresh vegetables fairly well just by looking at them, for example. But when information costs are high and variable across individuals, we would expect them to find it advantageous to acquire different amounts of information. Some of the implications of that possibility are described in later sections of this book.

Special Properties of Information

Acquiring information and using it in making market transactions are in many ways activities quite different from most other types of economic transactions. Although we cannot pursue all of these differences here, a brief discussion can indicate some of the issues that arise.[18] Most important of the special properties of information is that it may not be a purely private good for the individual who acquires it. It may have some characteristics of a *public good* (see Chapters 16 and 24) in that many individuals may benefit from it. The principal example of this is scientific inventions. Once a scientific discovery is made, the information from it is relatively available to anyone. It is very hard for an inventor to keep an important new technology a secret, especially if it is used to produce products to be sold openly in the market. In order to preserve the incentive to acquire scientific information, most countries offer some degree of patent protection to inventors to permit them to garner most of the gains of the invention. In this way, scientific information that would normally be public in nature can be privatized. Patent laws are usually designed to seek a balance between preserving the incentive to innovate and providing scientific information for everyone in a timely manner.

Many other information-acquisition activities yield side benefits to third parties. The information from government and private product testing, for example, is widely disseminated. Perhaps the most important way in which privately acquired information is spread, however, is through its effects on market prices. If people discover that one brand of television receiver is superior to other brands, the price of the better brand may rise. Similarly, when people learn that a particular product is unsafe, its price may fall. In financial markets

---

[18] For a more detailed summary, see J. Hirshleifer and J. G. Riley, "The Analytics of Uncertainty and Information: An Expository Survey," *Journal of Economic Literature* (December 1979): 1375–1421.

it is generally assumed that new information is rapidly disseminated through changes in prices of stocks or foreign exchange. A stringent form of the assumption that financial information is disseminated quickly is the *efficient markets hypothesis*, which asserts that prevailing market prices accurately reflect all presently available information. This hypothesis is widely used in economic literature on financial topics and we shall encounter it at several places in this book. One implication of the efficient markets hypothesis is that the private return to information acquisition may be rather low since in efficient markets, prices will already reflect all there is to know.

SUMMARY

In this chapter we have briefly surveyed the economic analysis of individual behavior in uncertain situations. From that survey we reached several conclusions that have relevance throughout the study of microeconomics.

- In uncertain situations individuals are concerned with the expected utility associated with various outcomes. If they obey the von Neumann–Morgenstern axioms, they will make choices so as to maximize this expected utility.
- If individuals have a diminishing marginal utility for wealth, they will be risk averse. That is, they will generally refuse actuarially fair bets.
- Risk-averse individuals will purchase insurance that allows them to avoid participating in fair bets. Even if the premium is somewhat unfair (in an actuarial sense), they will still buy insurance in order to minimize risk. Willingness to pay for insurance is related to the individual's degree of risk aversion.
- New information may prompt individuals to alter their subjective probabilities for various states of the world. Such information is valuable because it permits them to make different choices that increase expected utility.
- Individuals may face differing costs of obtaining information and may therefore acquire different amounts of it. Information may also have some characteristics of a public good (it may sometimes be available to everyone at zero cost). In particular, information may sometimes be reflected in the market prices of goods.

Application

THE VALUE OF INFORMATION

For many years economists have been interested in the relationship between individuals' behavior in uncertain situations and the value of the information they receive. Here we will examine three specific examples: (1) the value of weather forecasts; (2) the value of price information; and (3) the problem of risk assessment by insurers.

Weather Forecasts and Raisins

Obtaining accurate weather forecasts is crucial to a wide variety of situations in which individuals' and firms' decisions depend on the weather. People must make decisions about where to spend their vacations or whether to go to a baseball game; commuters must decide how they will get to work in inclement weather; builders must organize their work; and ski slope operators must decide whether to turn on their artificial snow machines. Probably the most important examples of the impact of the weather on production occur in agriculture, where anticipated rainfall affects a number of decisions, such as which crop to plant, when to harvest, and whether to take advantage of the sun or use natural gas for crop drying. Although all such decisions are subject to considerable uncertainty, economic calculations clearly affect the choices that are made.

One industry in which such calculations are particularly important is the raisin industry of the San Joaquin valley in California. Raisins are produced by sun-drying grapes in the early fall. If conditions for drying are unfavorable, the grapes can be crushed to produce wine, although this may be somewhat less profitable than raisin production. A farmer who opts for drying raisins, however, takes a considerable gamble because rain could virtually destroy the raisin crop, leaving the grapes with only a "scrap" value if sold to a distillery. Weather forecasting therefore plays a major role in affecting growers' decisions: A forecast of rain in the fall would prompt many to sell their grapes for wine, whereas a sunny forecast would encourage growers to try to make it through the required 21-day drying period unscathed.

In an important 1963 study, Lester Lave attempted to estimate the value that more accurate weather forecasts would have for raisin growers.[19] He first carefully outlined all of the relevant decisions that growers must make as the fall harvest approaches and calculated how each of these depends on the expected weather. He then compared expected profits under average but uncertain weather patterns to profits that might be expected if rain could be accurately forecast over a three-week period. Using this procedure, Lave was able to estimate that improved forecasting accuracy would increase raisin growers' profits by about $91 per acre. When applied to all acres planted in 1960, this figure yielded an estimate of over $20 million for the value of better weather information to the industry as a whole.[20] Hence, even for a relatively small segment of the economy, the value of information can be substantial.

Price Information

It should come as no surprise to anyone who has ever searched for bargains that it is important to know the prices being quoted by various sellers. Obtaining such information is undoubtedly subject to economic calculations. If one were buying a major item (say, a color television), it would probably make sense to call around to find the best price available. When buying a tube of toothpaste, on the other hand, such an effort may be unwarranted. An illustration of this sort of situation was provided in a 1976 study of gasoline prices by H. Marvel.[21] In that study the author examined the dispersion of prices for regular-grade gasoline in 20 U.S. cities. He found that the average observed price range within the cities was nearly 5 cents per gallon and that in some instances, ranges as wide as 20 cents per gallon seemed to persist for long periods.

[19] Lester B. Lave, "The Value of Better Weather Information to the Raisin Industry," *Econometrica* 31 (January/April 1963): 151–164.

[20] Lave also pointed out, however, that the increased raisin production brought about through better information might cause raisin prices to fall, thereby resulting in this kind of aggregate estimate being an overestimate for the value to the industry as a whole (of course, consumers would gain from the lower prices).

[21] H. Marvel, "The Economics of Information and Retail Gasoline Price Behavior," *Journal of Political Economy* 84 (October 1976): 1033–1059.

Perhaps more interesting, Marvel found that the degree of price dispersion in particular cities seemed to be associated with the costs and benefits of price information to consumers. For example, cities in which gasoline use was relatively greater tended to have less price dispersion, possibly because drivers in such cities had greater incentives to seek out low prices. Similarly, cities that required gas stations to post prices that were readable from the highway tended to have smaller price dispersions. Again, this probably occurred because of the efficiency with which such posting provided price information to passing motorists. Though not examined in the Marvel study, price advertising has been found to have a similar effect on reducing dispersions in the prices of eyeglasses, lawyers' fees, and prescription drug prices. Because advertising prices reduces search costs to potential buyers, a smaller spread in prices will result.

Insurance and Risk Appraisal

Our previous discussion showed why risk-averse individuals may choose to buy insurance, even though they know that on the average, the expected dollar value of benefits they receive will fall short of their premium costs. The study of insurance markets in the real world is made more complicated than our simple examples imply by the fact that the probabilities of certain risks may not be known (what, for example, is the probability of a baseball strike that affects television broadcast revenues?) or that the probabilities may be affected by the behavior of the people insured. Here we examine two types of this latter behavior: "moral hazard" and "adverse selection."

The moral hazard problem arises when being covered by insurance against some event actually increases the expected value of loss. Fires of "suspicious origin" often take place in heavily insured buildings, for example, possibly because of the desire to collect insurance proceeds. The moral hazard problem need not be quite so sinister, however. In the study of medical insurance (as we described in Chapter 7), it is well-known that coverage for certain types of medical procedures such as psychiatric or dental care increases patient usage substantially. Once a person is covered by insurance, his or her cost for such services becomes 0, so it is not surprising that demand increases. In order to control that phenomenon, many medical policies contain various cost-sharing provisions so that patients incur directly some (usually small) proportion of the expenses their treatment entails.[22]

Adverse selection occurs in situations where individuals are in a better position to assess the risks they face than an insurance provider is. In this case, individuals who know they have small risks will not buy insurance coverage (because it is too expensive given what they know), whereas high-risk individuals will purchase coverage (because, for them, it is a good buy). Hence, only high-risk individuals will buy insurance, thereby raising its cost. For example, most life insurance companies require physical examinations for individuals seeking to buy insurance. Those exams are intended to provide information to the company that the individual may already know. Similarly, medical policies sold to groups (usually through an employer) are much less expensive than individual policies, since coverage of the entire group prevents the sort of adverse selection that arises when individuals who know their own medical needs are able to accept or decline coverage.

---

[22] For a further discussion see M. Pauly, "The Economics of Moral Hazard: Comment," *American Economic Review* 58 (June 1968): 531–537.

SUGGESTED READINGS

Alchian, A. A. "The Meaning of Utility Measurement." *American Economic Review* 42 (1953): 26–50.

Concise, readable discussion of the meaning and implications of the von Neumann–Morgenstern axioms.

Arrow, K. J. "The Role of Securities in the Optimal Allocation of Risk Bearing." *Review of Economic Studies* 31 (1963): 91–96.

Introduces the state-preference concept and interprets securities as claims on contingent commodities.

————. "Uncertainty and the Welfare Economics of Medical Care." *American Economic Review* 53 (1963): 941–973.

Excellent discussion of the welfare implications of insurance. Has a clear, concise, mathematical appendix. Should be read in conjunction with Pauly's article on moral hazard (see below).

Bernoulli, D. "Exposition of a New Theory on the Measurement of Risk." *Econometrica* 22 (1954): 23–36.

Reprint of the classic analysis of the St. Petersburg paradox.

Friedman, M., and Savage, L. J. "The Utility Analysis of Choice." *Journal of Political Economy* 56 (1948): 279–304.

Analyzes why individuals may both gamble and buy insurance. Very readable.

Hirshleifer, J. "The Investment Decision under Uncertainty: Choice Theoretic Approaches." *Quarterly Journal of Economics* 79 (1965): 509–536.

Illustrates the state-preference approach as applied to investment decisions.

Hirshleifer, J., and Riley, J. G. "The Analytics of Uncertainty and Information: An Expository Survey." *Journal of Economic Literature* (December 1979): 1375–1421.

Good survey of literature on the expected utility model. Contains a complete set of references.

Machina, M. J. "Choice under Uncertainty: Problems Solved and Unsolved." *Journal of Economic Perspectives* (Summer 1987): 121–154.

Thorough and readable survey of the expected utility-maximization hypothesis. Nice discussion of the normative implications of various theories.

Pauly, M. "The Economics of Moral Hazard: Comment." *American Economic Review* (June 1968): 531–537.

Uses a simple graphic analysis to show how the behavioral effects of insurance can produce inefficient outcomes.

Pratt, J. W. "Risk Aversion in the Small and in the Large." *Econometrica* 32 (1964): 122–136.

Theoretical development of risk aversion measures. Fairly technical treatment but readable.

Spence, A. M., and Zeckhauser, R. "Insurance, Information and Individual Action." *American Economic Review* (May 1971): 380–387.

Examines some issues in optimal insurance contracts when behavior of the insured cannot be fully monitored by the insurance company.

Stigler, G. J. "The Economics of Information." *Journal of Political Economy* (June 1961): 213–225.

Classic examination of price uncertainty and of the role of search in obtaining price information.

PROBLEMS

9.1

Two fast-food restaurants are located next to each other and offer different procedures for ordering food. The first offers five lines leading to a server, whereas the second has a single line leading to five servers, with the next person in the line going to the first available server. Use the assumption that most individuals are risk-averse to discuss which restaurant will be preferred.

9.2

Show that if an individual's utility of wealth function is convex (rather than concave, as shown in Figure 9.1), he or she will prefer fair gambles to income certainty and may even be willing to accept somewhat unfair gambles. Do you believe this sort of risk-taking behavior is common? What factors might tend to limit its occurrence?

9.3

An individual purchases a dozen eggs and must take them home. Although making trips home is costless, there is a 50 percent chance that all of the eggs carried on any one trip will be broken during the trip. The individual considers two strategies:

> Strategy 1: Take all 12 eggs in one trip.
> Strategy 2: Take two trips with 6 in each trip.

a. List the possible outcomes of each strategy and the probabilities of these outcomes. Show that on the average, 6 eggs will remain unbroken after the trip home under either strategy.

b. Develop a graph to show the utility obtainable under each strategy. Which strategy will be preferable?

c. Could utility be improved further by taking more than two trips? How would this possibility be affected if additional trips were costly?

9.4

Suppose there is a 50–50 chance that a risk-averse individual with a current wealth of $20,000 will contract a debilitating disease and suffer a loss of $10,000.

a. Calculate the cost of actuarially fair insurance in this situation and use a utility of wealth graph (such as shown in Figure 9.1) to show that the individual will prefer fair insurance against this loss to accepting the gamble uninsured.

b. Suppose two types of insurance policies were available:
(1) A fair policy covering the complete loss.
(2) A fair policy covering only half of any loss incurred.
Calculate the cost of the second type of policy and show that the individual will generally regard it as inferior to the first.

c. Suppose individuals who purchase cost-sharing policies of the second type take better care of their health, thereby reducing the loss suffered when ill to only $7,000. In this situation what will be the cost of a cost-sharing policy? Show that some individuals may now prefer this type of policy. (This is an example of the "Moral Hazard" problem in insurance theory.)

9.5

Ms. Fogg is planning an around-the-world trip on which she plans to spend $10,000. The utility from the trip is a function of how much she actually spends on it (Y), given by

$$U(Y) = \ln Y.$$

a. If there is a 25 percent probability that Ms. Fogg will lose $1,000 of her cash on the trip, what is the trip's expected utility?

b. Suppose that Ms. Fogg can buy insurance against losing the $1,000 (say, by purchasing traveler's checks) at an "actuarially fair" premium of $250. Show that her expected utility is higher if she purchases this insurance than if she faces the chance of losing the $1,000 without insurance.

c. What is the maximum amount that Ms. Fogg would be willing to pay to insure her $1,000?

d. Suppose that people who buy insurance tend to become more careless with their cash than those who don't and that the probability of their losing $1,000 is 30 percent. What will be the actuarially fair insurance premium? Will Ms. Fogg buy insurance in this situation? (Another example of the moral hazard problem—what do you conclude by comparing this answer to the one from Problem 9.4c?)

9.6

In deciding to park in an illegal place, any individual knows that the probability of getting a ticket is p and that the fine for receiving the ticket is f. Suppose that all individuals are risk averse (that is, $U''(W) < 0$, where W is the individual's wealth).

Will a proportional increase in the probability of being caught or a proportional increase in the fine be a more effective deterrent to illegal parking? *Hint:* Use the Taylor series approximation $U(W - f) = U(W) - fU'(W)$.

9.7

Jimmy the Greek is seen to place an even money $100,000 bet on the Lakers to win their NBA Championship final with the Pistons. If Jimmy has a logarithmic utility of wealth function and if his current wealth is $1,000,000, what must he believe the minimum probability that the Lakers will win is?

9.8

Blue-eyed people are more likely to lose their expensive watches than are brown-eyed people. Specifically there is an 80 percent probability that blue-eyed people will lose a $1,000 watch during a year, but only a 20 percent probability that a brown-eyed person will. Blue-eyed and brown-eyed people are equally represented in the population.

    a.   If an insurance company assumes blue-eyed and brown-eyed people are equally likely to buy watch loss insurance what will the actuarially fair insurance premium be?

    b.   If blue-eyed and brown-eyed people have logarithmic utility of wealth functions and current wealths of $10,000 each, will these individuals buy watch insurance at the actuarially fair premium?

    c.   Given your results from part b, will the insurance premium be correctly computed? What should the premium be? What will the utility for each type of person be?

    d.   Suppose that an insurance company charged different premiums for blue-eyed and brown-eyed people. How would these individuals' maximum utilities compare to those computed in parts b and c? (This problem is an example of adverse selection in insurance.)

9.9

In Chapter 9 we showed that the amount that a risk-averse individual is willing to pay to avoid a fair bet is (approximately) proportional to $r(W) = -U''(W)/U'(W)$. Suppose an individual places a fair bet that involves winning or losing a fixed proposition, h, of his or her wealth. That is, in accepting the bet wealth will be $W(1 + h)$ where $E(h) = 0$.

    a.   Use the approach from Chapter 9 to show that the amount an individual will pay to avoid such a bet is given by the "relative risk aversion" measure

$$rr(W) = \frac{-WU''(W)}{U'(W)}$$

    b.   Do the quadratic and logarithmic utility functions exhibit increasing or decreasing relative risk aversion?

c.   What form of utility of wealth function exhibits constant relative risk aversion?

EXTENSIONS

MEAN-VARIANCE ANALYSIS OF CHOICES INVOLVING RISK

Much applied work in the theory of risk assumes that individuals choose among assets on the basis of the mean return promised by such assets and on the variance of that return. In this extension we explore some of the results and limitations of this approach. To start, we need to introduce some results from mathematical statistics.

Suppose that a random variable (X) has outcomes X_1, X_2 ... X_n that occur with probabilities $\pi_1, \ldots, \pi_n$. The expected value (or mean) of this variable is, as we have shown, defined as:

$$E(X) = \sum_{i=1}^{n} \pi_i X_i = \mu_X.$$

The variance of X (σ_X^2) is defined as

$$\sigma_X^2 = E[(X - \mu_X)^2] = \sum_{i=1}^{n} \pi_i (X_i - \mu_X)^2.$$

The variance is therefore the weighted average squared deviation from the mean. Using the definition it is easy to show that

(1) $\sigma_{aX}^2 = a^2 \sigma_X^2$ for any constant, a;

(2) $\sigma_X^2 = E[X^2] - \mu_X^2$, where $E[X^2] = \sum_{i=1}^{n} \pi_i X_i^2$;

and that if X and Y are two independent variables,

(3) $\sigma_{X+Y}^2 = \sigma_X^2 + \sigma_Y^2$.

In what follows we use these various results to show how choices among assets with different values for μ_X and σ_X^2 might be made.

E9.1

Suppose an individual's utility of wealth function is given by the quadratic expression

$$U(W) = a + bW + cW^2,$$

where $b > 0$, $c < 0$ and for all relevant values of W, $b + 2cW > 0$. If W is a random variable, show that expected utility $E[U(W)]$ is a quadratic function of the mean of W (μ_W) and its variance (σ_W^2).

E9.2

Show that the indifference curves between μ_W and σ_W^2 for the expected utility function calculated in E9.1 have a positive slope; that is, show that the individual will accept a higher σ_W^2 only if promised a higher μ_W $(d\sigma_W^2/d\mu_W > 0)$. Graph your results.

E9.3
Show that the indifference curves calculated in E9.2 have a "diminishing MRS" in the sense that along any indifference curve, $d^2\sigma_W^2/d\mu_W^2 > 0$. Graph your results and discuss the possible limitations of this type of utility representation.

E9.4 (Diversification)
Suppose an individual with a quadratic utility of wealth function is thinking of investing in two independent assets X and Y and that $\mu_X = \mu_Y$, $\sigma_X^2 = \sigma_Y^2$. Will he or she be indifferent about how available wealth is distributed between these assets? What is the utility maximizing division of wealth?

E9.5 (Portfolio Theory)
As a generalization to E9.4, suppose $\mu_X < \mu_Y$ and $\sigma_X^2 < \sigma_Y^2$. How might the individual's wealth be allocated between these two assets? How might you generalize this result further to allow for correlations between the returns on the two assets?

E9.6 (Portfolio Separation)
Suppose only two investments are available: (1) risk-free cash; and (2) investment in a risky asset, X. For ease of notation, assume that the risky asset is denominated in units such that if all of W is invested in it, $W = X$. If some fraction α ($0 \le \alpha \le 1$) of wealth is invested in X, the total investment is given by αX. The fraction of wealth not invested in the risky asset [which is $(1 - \alpha)W$] is invested in risk-free cash. Hence, for any given α, total net wealth (N) is given by the random variable

$$N = \alpha X + (1 - \alpha)W.$$

a. Assuming the random variable X has a mean μ_X (which must be $> W$ or none will be bought) and variance σ_X^2 and W is simply a constant with zero variance, compute the mean and variance of N (these obviously will be functions of α).

b. Using a graph with the mean of N on the horizontal axis and its variance on the vertical axis, plot the relationship between these two magnitudes for values of α ranging from 0 to 1. Is this relationship linear?

c. Assuming utility of net wealth is a quadratic, show graphically how the indifference curves from E9.2 and E9.3 can be superimposed on the graph developed in part (b) to find the optimal fraction, α, to invest in the risky asset.

d. Use the utility function to compute expected utility as a function of α and the parameters a, b, c, μ_X, σ_X^2, and W. Solve for the utility maximizing value of α as a function of those parameters.

e. If α^* is the utility maximizing value of α, show that

$$\frac{\partial \alpha^*}{\partial \sigma_X^2} < 0$$

and that if $(\mu_X - W)$ remains a constant,

$$\frac{\partial \alpha^*}{\partial W} < 0.$$

Explain your results intuitively.

f.   Show that the sign of $\partial\alpha^*/\partial(\mu_X - W)$ is indeterminate. Use the generalized notions of income and substitution effects to explain this result.

REFERENCES

Bierwag, G. V., and Grove, M. A., "Indifference Curves in Asset Analysis," *Economic Journal* (June 1966): 337–373.

Markowitz, H., *Portfolio Selection: Efficient Diversification of Investments* (New York: John Wiley and Sons, Inc.) 1959.

Tobin, J., "Liquidity Preference as Behavior Toward Risk," *Review of Economic Studies* (February 1958): 65–86.

PART
IV

Production and Supply

In this part we examine the production and supply of economic goods—goods that are produced by combining various inputs (land, labor, capital, and so forth) using the best available technology. Institutions that coordinate this transformation of inputs into outputs are called *firms*. They may be large institutions (such as General Motors, IBM, or the U.S. Department of Defense) or small ones (such as "Mom and Pop" stores or self-employed individuals). Although they may pursue different goals (IBM may seek maximum profits, whereas a Soviet collective farm may try to make members of the collective as well off as possible), all firms must make certain basic choices in the production process. The purpose of Part IV is to develop some methods of conceptualizing those choices.

In Chapter 10 we examine ways of modeling the physical relationship between inputs and outputs. We introduce the concept of a production function, a useful abstraction from the complexities of real-world production processes. Two measurable aspects of the production function are stressed: its returns to scale (that is, how output expands when all inputs are increased) and its elasticity of substitution (that is, how easily one input may be replaced by another while maintaining the same level of output). We also briefly describe how technical improvements are reflected in production functions.

The production function concept is then used in Chapter 11 to discuss costs of production. It is assumed that all firms seek to produce their output at the lowest possible cost, an assumption that permits the development of cost curves for the firm. Chapter 11 focuses on how the shapes of those curves may differ, depending on the amount of time a firm has to respond to changing circumstances. Both short-run and long-run cost curves are important components of our derivation of the supply decision.

In Chapters 12 and 13 we investigate the firm's supply decision; that is, we examine the factors that determine how much output a firm will produce. To answer that question we must first ask what goals the firm is pursuing. Perhaps the most basic assumption about a firm's motivation is that its manager will make output choices so as to achieve the maximum possible profit. In Chapter 12 we study the implications of this profit-maximization hypothesis in some detail. The chapter concludes with the fundamental model of supply behavior by profit-maximizing firms that we will use in many subsequent chapters.

The profit-maximization hypothesis is not a universal explanation of all firms' behavior, however, and in Chapter 13 we examine a few alternatives. In the first part of the chapter, we look at other possible goals that a profit-maximizing firm might pursue (e.g., maximum sales). The second part of Chapter 13 examines a few situations in which the goals of the different economic actors associated with a firm may be in conflict. In particular, we develop a model of the agent relationship between a firm's owners and their hired managers. This model both provides an interesting application of theories developed previously in this book and offers an introduction to a number of topics in the modern theory of financial markets.

Overall, Part IV is concerned with modeling firms' activities in much the same way that Parts II and III were concerned with the individual. Thus, after completing these chapters, we will have developed theoretical descriptions of the behavior of economic actions on both sides of any market transaction. We can then use these models in later parts of the book to study such transactions.

CHAPTER 10

Production Functions

The principal activity of any firm is to turn inputs into outputs. Because economists are interested in the choices that the firm makes in accomplishing this goal, but wish to avoid discussing many of the engineering intricacies involved, they have chosen to construct an abstract model of production. In this model the relationship between inputs and outputs is formalized by a *production function* of the form

$$Q = f(K, L, M, \dots), \tag{10.1}$$

where Q represents the output of a particular good during a period,[1] K represents the machine (that is, capital) usage during the period, L represents hours of labor input,[2] M represents raw materials used, and the notation indicates the possibility of other variables affecting the production process.[3] Equation 10.1 is assumed to provide, for any conceivable set of inputs, the engineer's solution to the problem of how best to combine those inputs to get output. For example, the production function might represent a farmer's output of wheat during one year as being dependent on the amount of labor used on the farm that year, the quantity of capital equipment employed during the year, the amount of land under cultivation, and so forth. The function records the fact

---

[1] The term "output of a particular good" is used here to indicate that we are considering only productive processes that produce identical goods. For example, "cheap" shoes and "good" shoes are two different goods and presumably have different production functions. We shall see in later chapters that it may be difficult in some productive processes to specify exactly what output is (for example, consider the problem of defining the output of a hospital).

[2] Capital and labor inputs are assumed to be homogeneous. This is a great simplification, since in reality there are numerous kinds of labor and many types of machines. The recognition that these inputs are in fact not homogeneous raises many technical problems in the theory of aggregation, but we will generally not discuss them here.

[3] In a purely formal way, technical progress can be accommodated within the formulation of Equation 10.1 by assuming that variable "time" enters into the production function. We take up this topic later in this chapter.

that there are many different ways in which, say, 100 bushels of wheat could be produced. The farmer could use a very labor-intensive technique with only a small amount of mechanical equipment; alternatively, the 100 bushels could be produced by using huge amounts of equipment with very little labor. Similarly, techniques could be adopted to produce the 100 bushels of wheat that were very land-intensive, or relatively little land could be used together with great amounts of labor, equipment, and fertilizer (as in Japanese or British agriculture). All of those possible techniques are represented by the general production function in Equation 10.1. For any possible choices of land, equipment, and labor input, the function records the maximum of wheat output that can be produced from those given inputs. The important question from an economic point of view is how the levels of Q, K, L, and M are chosen by the firm. We take up this question in detail in the next several chapters.

This chapter will not touch on questions of optimal choice. Rather our intention is to describe a few concepts that have been developed for the purpose of understanding the relationship between inputs and outputs. The chapter centers on purely physical relationships in contrast to later chapters, which will concentrate on costs and profit maximization. Production functions represent constraints on the activities of producers that are imposed by the existing technology. Our purpose is to examine the way in which these constraints can be formalized.

VARIATIONS IN ONE INPUT

In this section we shall study the change in output that is brought about by a change in one of the productive inputs. For the purposes of this examination (and indeed for most of the purposes of this book), it will be more convenient to use a simplified production function defined as

---

Definition:

Production Function

The *production function* for a particular good, Q,

$$Q = f(K, L) \tag{10.2}$$

shows the maximum amount of the good that can be produced using alternative combinations of capital (K) and labor (L).

Of course, most of our analysis will hold for any two inputs to the production process we might wish to examine. The terms "capital" and "labor" are used only for convenience. Similarly, it would be a simple matter to generalize our discussion to cases involving more than two inputs; and, occasionally, we will do so. For the most part, however, limiting our discussion to two inputs will be quite helpful because we can show these inputs on two-dimensional graphs.

Marginal Physical Product

The earliest economists who studied production were concerned with how increasing labor utilization on a fixed plot of land might affect output. Hence there are historical reasons to start by studying variations in a single input, although as we will see, the general theory focuses on the firm's ability to change all inputs together.

To study variation in a single input, we define

Definition:

Marginal Physical Product

The *marginal physical product* of an input is the additional output that can be produced by employing one more unit of that input while holding all other inputs constant. Mathematically,

$$\text{marginal physical product of capital} = MP_K = \frac{\partial Q}{\partial K} = f_K$$

(10.3)

$$\text{marginal physical product of labor} = MP_L = \frac{\partial Q}{\partial L} = f_L.$$

Notice that the mathematical definitions of marginal product use partial derivatives, thereby properly reflecting the fact that all other input usage is held constant while the input of interest is being varied. As a physical example of these definitions, let us consider the case of a farmer hiring one more laborer to harvest the crop but holding all other inputs constant. The extra output this laborer produces is that farmhand's marginal physical product, measured in physical quantities, such as bushels of wheat, crates of oranges, or heads of lettuce. We might observe, for example, that 50 workers on a farm are able to produce 100 bushels of wheat per year, whereas 51 workers, with the same land and equipment, can produce 102 bushels. The marginal physical product of the fifty-first worker is then 2 bushels per year.

Diminishing Marginal Productivity

We might expect that the marginal physical product of an input depends on how much of that input is used. Labor, for example, cannot be added indefinitely to a given field (while keeping the amount of equipment, fertilizer, and so forth fixed) without eventually exhibiting some deterioration in its productivity. This possibility is illustrated in Figures 10.1a and 10.1b. The relationship between the quantity of a particular input (labor) and total output is recorded in Figure 10.1a as TP_L. For small amounts of L, output increases rapidly as additional L is added. However, because other inputs are held constant, eventually the ability of additional labor to generate additional output begins to deteriorate. Finally, at L^{***} ouput reaches its maximum level. Any additional labor added beyond this point actually decreases output. Beyond L^{***} additional laborers get in each other's way to such an extent that total output begins to decline.

The TP_L curve in Figure 10.1a therefore embodies the assumption that labor's marginal physical productivity eventually declines as more labor is added to the production of a good while other inputs are held constant. Mathematically, the assumption of diminishing marginal physical productivity is an assumption about the second-order partial derivatives of the production function:

$$\frac{\partial MP_K}{\partial K} = \frac{\partial^2 Q}{\partial K^2} = f_{KK} < 0$$

$$\frac{\partial MP_L}{\partial L} = \frac{\partial^2 Q}{\partial L^2} = f_{LL} < 0. \tag{10.4}$$

This assumption is an extremely important one in economic analysis. Thomas Malthus, for example, argued that additional labor cannot be added constantly to a fixed supply of land without the productivity of labor in food production eventually beginning to diminish. This must be the case, Malthus argued, for otherwise new lands would never be opened for cultivation in response to population pressures. Since it was clear to Malthus that new (and relatively inferior) land was in fact being brought into cultivation as populations expanded, the productivity of labor on existing farm plots must have been declining as more labor was added.[4] Because in the long run the quantity of land is absolutely fixed, to Malthus the principle of a diminishing marginal productivity of labor implied serious problems for the future of humanity. In fact, Malthus's prediction that the diminishing productivity of labor eventually would lead to a situation in which population growth would outpace the growth in food supplies caused economics to be called the "dismal science." Most modern economists would agree that Malthus did not adequately recognize the possibility that increases in capital equipment and technical advances (which, although held constant in our definition, in fact change over time) would prevent the decline of labor's productivity in agriculture. Nevertheless, the basic observation that the marginal productivity of labor (or any other input) declines when *all other inputs* are held constant is still recognized by economists as an empirically valid proposition.

Marginal Physical Productivity Curve

To illustrate these ideas graphically, we begin by recognizing that the marginal physical productivity of labor is simply the slope of the curve TP_L. This should be clear from Equation 10.3: The slope of the TP_L curve shows how output expands as additional labor is added, and this is what is required by the definition of the marginal physical productivity of labor. In Figure 10.1b the marginal productivity curve (MP_L) is drawn. Notice that MP_L reaches a maximum at L^* and declines as labor input is added beyond this point. This is a reflection of the assumption of a diminishing marginal physical productivity of labor. MP_L is equal to 0 at the level L^{***} at which TP_L reaches a maximum. Beyond L^{***} further additions of labor input actually reduce output. The point L^{***} is sometimes called the *intensive margin* of production. Production will not take place beyond L^{***}, since using more labor (which is presumably costly to the firm) will result in less output being produced.

---

[4] A somewhat facetious "proof" of the diminishing marginal productivity of an input argues that if it were not true that marginal productivities diminish, the entire world food supply could be grown in a single flowerpot if a sufficient quantity of labor were applied to the pot. Since this situation is obviously absurd, the marginal product of labor, after some point, must diminish.

Figure 10.1   *Deriving Average and Marginal Productivity of Labor Curves from the Total Product Curve*

These curves show how the average and marginal productivity of labor curves can be derived from the total product curve. The curve TP_L in (a) represents the relationship between labor input and output, assuming that all other inputs are held constant. As (b) shows, the slope of the TP_L curve is the marginal product of labor (MP_L), and the slope of a chord joining the origin to a point on the TP_L curve gives the average product of labor (AP_L). The relationship between the AP_L and MP_L curves is geometrically obvious from the figures.

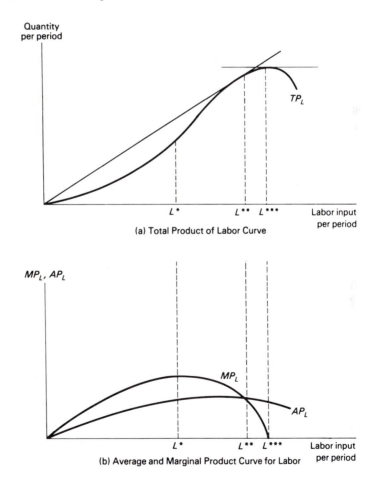

(a) Total Product of Labor Curve

(b) Average and Marginal Product Curve for Labor

Average Physical Productivity Curve

In common usage the term "labor productivity" usually means *average productivity*. When it is said that a certain industry has experienced productivity increases, this is taken to mean that output per unit of labor input has increased. Although this concept of average productivity is not nearly as important in theoretical economic discussions as marginal productivity is, it receives a great deal of attention in empirical discussions. Because average productivity is easily measured (say, as so many bushels of wheat per labor-hour input), it is often used as a measure of efficiency.

Deriving average productivity relationships from the total product curve is a simple matter, as Figure 10.1 shows. We define the average product of labor (AP_L) to be

$$AP_L = \frac{\text{output}}{\text{labor input}} = \frac{Q}{L}. \tag{10.5}$$

Geometrically, the value of AP_L for any quantity of labor input is the slope of the chord drawn from the origin to the relevant point on the TP_L curve. By drawing a series of such chords through the origin to various points on the total product curve (TP_L), the average product of labor curve (AP_L) can be constructed.

The AP_L curve is shown in Figure 10.1b. From the diagram it can be seen that the average and marginal productivities of labor are equal at L^{**}. For this level of labor input, the chord through the origin in Figure 10.1a is just tangent to the TP_L curve. Hence the average and marginal products of labor are equal. Also, at L^{**} the average product of labor is at its *maximum value*. For levels of labor input less than L^{**}, the marginal product of labor (MP_L) exceeds its average product (AP_L). Consequently, adding one more worker will raise the average productivity of all workers, since the increment to output from hiring this additional worker exceeds the output produced by the average worker previously. An analogous situation would occur if a baseball team with a team batting average of .260 acquired a .300 hitter: The team average would rise. A similar argument would show that for labor input greater than L^{**}, the average product of labor is falling. Beyond L^{**}, labor's average productivity exceeds its marginal productivity so that average product is falling. Adding a worker to the production process causes output to rise by less than the average that previously prevailed. Consequently, the average productivity of labor will fall. In our baseball analogy, adding a .200 hitter to the team will cause the team average to fall.

We have shown that to the left of L^{**}, the AP_L curve is rising; to the right of L^{**}, it is falling. Therefore the average productivity of labor reaches its maximum value[5] at L^{**}. The point L^{**} is sometimes called the *extensive*

---

[5] Mathematically, we wish to find that L for which AP_L ($= Q/L$) is a maximum. Differentiating AP_L with respect to L gives

$$\frac{L \cdot (\partial Q/\partial L) - Q}{L^2} = \frac{L \cdot MP_L - Q}{L^2} = 0$$

as the condition for a maximum. But this says that

$$L \cdot MP_L - Q = 0$$

or

$$MP_L = \frac{Q}{L} = AP_L$$

at the maximum point.

margin of production. Only for levels of labor usage greater than L^{**} will output per labor hour (AP_L) exceed what an extra worker is able to produce (and hence what the worker might be paid). Hence production is profitable only beyond L^{**}.[6]

Numerical Example

Suppose the production function for flyswatters during a particular period can be represented by

$$Q = f(K, L) = 600K^2L^2 - K^3L^3. \tag{10.6}$$

To construct the total, marginal, and average productivity relations of labor (L) for this function, we must assume a particular value for the other input, capital (K). Suppose $K = 10$. Then the total productivity relationship is given by

$$Q = TP_L \quad (\text{for } K = 10) \quad = 60{,}000L^2 - 1{,}000L^3. \tag{10.7}$$

The marginal productivity function is given by

$$MP_L = \frac{\partial Q}{\partial L} = 120{,}000L - 3{,}000L^2, \tag{10.8}$$

which, because it is an inverted parabola, resembles the inverted U-shaped MP_L curve in Figure 10.1. Setting MP_L equal to 0,

$$120{,}000L - 3{,}000L^2 = 0 \tag{10.9}$$

yields

$$40L = L^2 \tag{10.10}$$

or

$$L = 40 \tag{10.11}$$

as the point at which TP_L reaches its maximum value (labeled L^{***} in the figure). Labor input beyond 40 units per period actually reduces total output. For example, when $L = 40$, Equation 10.7 shows that $Q = 32$ million flyswatters, whereas when $L = 50$, production of flyswatters amounts to only 25 million.

To find the average productivity of labor in flyswatter production, we divide TP_L (Equation 10.7) by L:

$$AP_L = \frac{TP_L}{L} = 60{,}000L - 1{,}000L^2. \tag{10.12}$$

Again, this is an inverted parabola that resembles the curve shown in Figure 10.1. AP_L reaches its maximum value when

$$\frac{\partial AP_L}{\partial L} = 60{,}000 - 2{,}000L = 0, \tag{10.13}$$

[6]See also problem 10.8 for a further analysis of why a level of use of less than L^{**} is not profitable.

which occurs when $L = 30$. At this value for labor input, Equation 10.12 shows that $AP_L = 900,000$ and Equation 10.8 shows that MP_L is also 900,000. When AP_L is a maximum, average and marginal productivities of labor are equal.

Notice the relationship between total and average productivity that this example illustrates. Even though total production of flyswatters is greater with 40 workers (32 million) than with 30 workers (27 million), output per worker is higher in the second case. With 40 workers, each worker produces 800,000 flyswatters per period, whereas with 30 workers each worker produces 900,000. Because capital input (flyswatter presses) is held constant, after some point diminishing marginal productivity results in a declining level of output per worker.

Limitations of Single-Input Analysis

Our examination of variations in the level of employment of a single input has yielded some important conclusions, which are sometimes applied to actual economic problems. For example, macroeconomic studies of firms' hiring and layoff decisions over the business cycle often assume that all other inputs (especially capital inputs) are held fixed and that firms only have the freedom to vary their labor input. In general, however, this approach to firms' input decisions seems overly restrictive. It obscures the fact that firms may change their levels of use of several inputs at the same time, presumably in response to cost considerations. But, when several inputs change, the total marginal and average productivity curves for any particular input will shift in ways that may be difficult to predict. In our prior numerical example, increases in capital input (from the initially assumed level of $K = 10$) would result in quite different productivity relationships since, for this function, the curves would not shift in a simple linear way. For production functions with more than two inputs, the situation can become even more complex. Hence, to provide a general approach to the theory of production, we must examine the shape of the entire production function when all inputs are variable, at least to some degree.

ISOQUANT MAPS AND THE RATE OF TECHNICAL SUBSTITUTION

One way to picture the whole production function in two dimensions is by using its *isoquant map*. Again we shall use a production function of the form $Q = f(K, L)$, with the understanding that "capital" and "labor" are simply convenient examples of any two inputs that might happen to be of interest. An isoquant (from *iso*, meaning "equal") records those combinations of K and L that are able to produce a given level of output. For example, all those combinations of K and L that fall on the curve labeled "$Q = 10$" in Figure 10.2 are capable of producing ten units of output per period. This isoquant then records the fact that there are many alternative ways of producing ten units of output. One way might be represented by point A: We would use L_A and K_A to produce ten units of output. Alternatively, we might prefer to use relatively less capital and more labor and therefore would choose a point such as B. Hence we have

Figure 10.2 An Isoquant Map

Isoquants record the alternative combinations of inputs that can be used to produce a given level of output. The slope of these curves shows the rate at which L can be substituted for K while keeping output constant. The negative of this slope is called the (marginal) rate of technical substitution (*RTS*). In the figure the *RTS* is positive and diminishing for increasing inputs of labor.

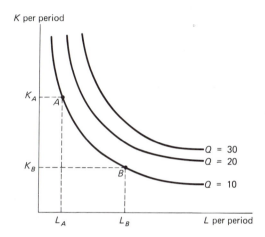

Isoquant

An *isoquant* shows those combinations of K and L that can produce a given level of output (say, Q_0). Mathematically, an isoquant records the set of K and L that satisfies

$$f(K, L) = Q_0. \tag{10.14}$$

There are many isoquants in the $K–L$ plane. Each isoquant represents a different level of output. Isoquants record successively higher levels of output as we move in a northeasterly direction. Presumably, using more of each of the inputs will permit output to increase. Several other isoquants (for $Q = 20$ and $Q = 30$) are shown in Figure 10.2. These record those combinations of inputs that can produce the required output. The reader will probably notice the similarity between an isoquant map and the individual's indifference curve map discussed in Parts II and III. These are indeed similar concepts, since both represent "contour" maps of the particular function of interest. For isoquants, however, the labeling of the curves is measurable (an output of ten units has a quantifiable meaning), and we therefore shall be somewhat more interested in studying the shape of these curves and their related production function than we were in examining the exact shape of utility functions.

The Marginal Rate of Technical Substitution (RTS)

The slope of an isoquant shows how one input can be traded for another while holding output constant. Examining the slope will give us some information about the technical possibility of substituting labor for capital. Therefore we have

Definition:

Marginal Rate of Technical Substitution

The *marginal rate of technical substitution* (RTS) shows the rate at which labor can be substituted for capital while holding output constant along an isoquant. In mathematical terms,

$$RTS \quad (L \text{ for } K) \quad = \left. \frac{-dK}{dL} \right|_{Q\ =\ Q_0}. \tag{10.15}$$

In this definition the notation is intended as a reminder that output is to be held constant as L is substituted for K. The particular value of this trade-off rate will depend not only on the level of output but also on the quantities of capital and labor being used. Its value depends on the point on the isoquant map at which the slope is to be measured.

RTS and Marginal Productivities

In order to examine the shape of production function isoquants, it is useful to prove the following result: the *RTS* (of L for K) is equal to the ratio of the marginal physical productivity of labor (MP_L) to the marginal physical productivity of capital (MP_K). The proof of this assertion proceeds by setting up the total differential of the production function:

$$dQ = \frac{\partial f}{\partial L} \cdot dL + \frac{\partial f}{\partial K} \cdot dK = MP_L \cdot dL + MP_K \cdot dK, \tag{10.16}$$

which records how small changes in L and K affect output. Along an isoquant, $dQ = 0$ (output is constant) so

$$MP_L \cdot dL = -MP_K \cdot dK. \tag{10.17}$$

This says that along an isoquant, the gain in output from increasing L slightly is exactly balanced by the loss in output from suitably decreasing K. Rearranging terms a bit gives

$$-\left. \frac{dK}{dL} \right|_{Q\ =\ Q_0} = RTS \quad (L \text{ for } K) \quad = \frac{MP_L}{MP_K} \tag{10.18}$$

as was to be shown.

   We can use the result of Equation 10.18 to see that those isoquants that we observe must be negatively sloped. Since both MP_L and MP_K will be positive (no firm would choose to produce where a marginal productivity is negative), the *RTS* also will be positive. Because the slope of an isoquant is the negative of the *RTS*, any firm we observe must be operating in the negatively sloped portion of an isoquant. Although it is mathematically possible to have isoquants with positive slopes at some points, it would not make economic sense for a firm to operate at these points. If both L and K had to be increased to keep output constant, one of these inputs would, of necessity, have a negative marginal productivity.

Law of a Diminishing RTS   The isoquants in Figure 10.2 are drawn not only with a negative slope (as they should be) but also as convex curves. Along any one of the curves, the RTS is *diminishing*. For high ratios of K to L, the RTS is a large positive number, indicating that a great deal of capital can be given up if one more unit of labor becomes available. On the other hand, when a lot of labor is already being used, the RTS is low, signifying that only a small amount of capital can be traded for an additional unit of labor if output is to be held constant. This shape seems intuitively reasonable: The more labor (relative to capital) that is used, the harder it is to substitute labor for capital. In some sense labor becomes less potent as a substitute as more of it is used. This assumption is closely related to the assumption of diminishing marginal productivities, as Equation 10.18 implies. But the assumptions are not identical: It is not possible to derive a diminishing RTS from the assumption of diminishing marginal productivities alone.

To see why this is so, assume that $Q = f(K, L)$ and that f_K and f_L are positive (that is, the marginal productivities are positive). Assume also that $f_{KK} < 0$ and $f_{LL} < 0$ (that the marginal productivities are diminishing). In order to show that isoquants are convex, we would like to show that $d(RTS)/dL < 0$. Since by Equation 10.18 $RTS = f_L/f_K$, we have

$$\frac{dRTS}{dL} = \frac{d(f_L/f_K)}{dL}. \tag{10.19}$$

Because f_L and f_K are functions of both K and L, we must take the total derivative of this expression:

$$\frac{dRTS}{dL} = \frac{[f_K(f_{LL} + f_{LK} \cdot dK/dL) - f_L(f_{KL} + f_{KK} \cdot dK/dL)]}{(f_K)^2} \tag{10.20}$$

Using the fact that $dK/dL = -f_L/f_K$ along an isoquant and that Young's theorem implies $f_{KL} = f_{LK}$, we have

$$\frac{dRTS}{dL} = \frac{(f_K^2 f_{LL} - 2f_K f_L f_{KL} + f_L^2 f_{KK})}{(f_K)^3}. \tag{10.21}$$

Since we have assumed $f_K > 0$, the denominator of this function is positive. Hence the whole fraction will be negative if the numerator is negative. Because f_{LL} and f_{KK} are both assumed to be negative, the numerator definitely will be negative if f_{KL} is positive. If we can assume this, we have shown that $dRTS/dL < 0$ (that the isoquants are convex).

Intuitively, it seems reasonable that the cross–partial derivative $f_{KL} = f_{LK}$ should be positive. Since $f_{LK} = \partial MP_L/\partial K$, we are interested in how an increase in capital affects the marginal physical productivity of labor (or vice versa), and it seems plausible that if workers had more capital, they would have higher marginal productivities. But, although this is probably the most prevalent case, it does not necessarily have to be so. Many plausible production functions have $f_{KL} < 0$, at least for some input values.[7] When we assume a diminishing *RTS* (as we have used throughout most of our discussion), we are therefore making a somewhat stronger assumption than simply diminishing productivities for each input.

RETURNS TO SCALE

Using the production function and its isoquant map, we can now proceed to develop some ways of characterizing these functions. Providing such a characterization is not only useful for developing mathematical examples, but, more importantly, the terminology used for this purpose is encountered in a wide variety of economic applications. In order to understand those applications, one must know precisely how the various terms are defined.

The first important question that might be asked about production functions is how output responds to increases in all inputs together. For example, suppose that all inputs were doubled: Would output double or would the relationship not be quite so simple? This is a question of the *returns to scale* exhibited by the production function that has been of interest to economists ever since Adam Smith intensively studied the production of pins. Smith identified two forces that came into operation when the conceptual experiment of doubling all inputs was performed. First, a doubling of scale permits a greater division of labor and specialization of function. Hence there is some presumption that efficiency might increase—production might more than double. Second, doubling of the inputs also entails some loss in efficiency because managerial overseeing may become more difficult given the larger scale of the firm. Which of these two tendencies will have a greater effect is an important empirical question.

Presenting a technical definition of these concepts is misleadingly simple:

Definition:

Returns to Scale
If the production function is given by $Q = f(K, L)$ and all inputs are multiplied by the same positive constant, m (where $m > 1$), we classify the *returns to scale* of the production function by

Effect on Output	Returns to Scale
I. $f(mK, mL) = mf(K, L) = mQ$	Constant
II. $f(mK, mL) < mf(K, L) = mQ$	Decreasing
III. $f(mK, mL) > mf(K, L) = mQ$	Increasing

In intuitive terms, if a proportionate increase in inputs increases output by the same proportion, the production function exhibits constant returns to scale.[8]

[7]In our previous numerical example $f_{KL} = 2,400KL - 9K^2L^2$, which is positive only for $KL \le$ 266. When $K = 10$, $L = 30$, for example, $f_{KL} < 0$. Additional implications of the sign of f_{KL} are explored in the problems to this chapter.

[8]Mathematically, such constant returns-to-scale functions are said to be "homogeneous of degree 1" or, sometimes, "linear homogeneous." The general notion of homogeneous functions was discussed briefly in Chapter 5 (see especially footnote 1).

If output increases less than proportionately, the function exhibits diminishing returns to scale. And if output increases more than proportionately, there are increasing returns to scale. It is theoretically possible for a function to exhibit constant returns to scale for some levels of input usage and increasing or decreasing returns for other levels. Often, however, economists refer to *the* degree of returns to scale of a production function with the implicit notion that only a fairly narrow range of variation in input usage and the related level of output are being considered.

Constant Returns to Scale and the RTS

Constant returns-to-scale production functions occupy an important place in economic theory. This is not only because such functions occupy a mathematical middle ground between increasing and decreasing returns but also because there are economic reasons for expecting an industry's production function to exhibit constant returns. If all production in an industry is carried on in plants of an "efficient" size, then doubling all inputs could most reasonably be accomplished by doubling the number of these plants. But presumably this would double output since there are now exactly twice as many plants. Hence the *industry* would have a constant returns-to-scale production function. As long as doubling of inputs is brought about by doubling the number of optimally sized plants, this will be the case.

Constant returns-to-scale production functions also have the interesting theoretical property that the *RTS* between two factors, say, K and L, depends only on the *ratio* of K to L, not on the scale of production. This can be shown with a simple argument. Suppose that we have a constant returns-to-scale production function such that when $K = 10$ and $L = 10$, $Q = 20$. Suppose also that at this point the *RTS* of L for K is equal to 2. Therefore 8 units of K and 11 units of L also will yield $Q = 20$. Now consider doubling all inputs. What we want to show is that the *RTS* at the new input configuration ($K = 20$, $L = 20$) is also equal to 2. We know, because of the assumption of constant returns to scale, that the input combination ($K = 20$, $L = 20$) will produce 40 units of output and so will the input combination ($K = 16$, $L = 22$). Therefore the *RTS* at ($K = 20$, $L = 20$) is given by $-(-4)/2 = 2$. That was the result to be shown: The *RTS* does not depend on the scale of production, but only on the ratio of K to L.

Geometrically, all the isoquants of a constant returns-to-scale production function are "radial blowups" of the unit isoquant. Along any ray through the origin (a line along which K/L is constant), the slope of the isoquants is the same. This is illustrated in Figure 10.3, which also shows that the isoquants are equally spaced as output expands; thus they exhibit the constant proportional relationship between increases in all inputs and increases in output.[9]

---

[9] More generally, production functions for which each isoquant is a radial expansion of the unit isoquant but which do not necessarily exhibit constant returns to scale are called *homothetic*. All of the production functions illustrated at the end of this chapter are homothetic even in cases of non-constant returns to scale.

Figure 10.3   *Isoquant Map for a Constant Returns-to-Scale Production Function*

For a constant returns-to-scale production function, the *RTS* depends only on the ratio of *K* to *L*, not on the scale of production. Consequently, each isoquant will simply be a radial blowup of the unit isoquant. Along any ray through the origin (a ray of constant *K/L*), the *RTS* will be the same on all isoquants.

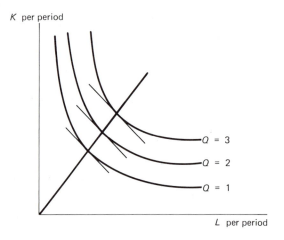

Mathematical Proof

We can use a straightforward mathematical proof to show that for a constant returns-to-scale production function, the *RTS* depends only on the ratio of K to L (and therefore not on the scale of production). By the definition of constant returns to scale,

$$mQ = mf(K, L) = f(mK, mL) \tag{10.22}$$

for any $m > 0$. Partial differentiation of this equation with respect to either input (say, K) gives

$$m \frac{\partial f(K, L)}{\partial K} = \frac{\partial f(mK, mL)}{\partial mK} \cdot \frac{\partial mK}{\partial K} = m \frac{\partial f(mK, mL)}{\partial mK}. \tag{10.23}$$

Hence

$$\frac{\partial f(K, L)}{\partial K} = \frac{\partial f(mK, mL)}{\partial mK} \tag{10.24}$$

or, if we let $m = 1/L$,

$$MP_K = \frac{\partial f(K, L)}{\partial K} = \frac{\partial f\left(\frac{K}{L}, 1\right)}{\partial \left(\frac{K}{L}\right)}. \tag{10.25}$$

Therefore the marginal product of capital depends only on the ratio K/L. Since an identical proof holds for labor input and since the RTS is simply the ratio of the input's marginal productivities, the RTS also must depend only on the ratio K/L.[10]

The n-Input Case

The definition of returns to scale can be easily generalized to a production function with n inputs. If that production function is given by

$$Q = f(X_1, X_2, \ldots, X_n), \tag{10.26}$$

and all inputs are multiplied by a positive constant m, we have

$$f(mX_1, mX_2, \ldots, mX_n) = m^k f(X_1, X_2, \ldots, X_n) = m^k Q \tag{10.27}$$

for some constant k. If $k = 1$, the production function exhibits constant returns to scale. Diminishing and increasing returns to scale correspond to the cases $k < 1$ and $k > 1$, respectively.

The crucial part of this mathematical definition is the requirement that all inputs be increased by the same proportion, m. In many real-world production processes, this provision may make little economic sense. For example, a firm may have only one "boss" and that number would not necessarily be doubled even if all other inputs were. Or the output of a farm may depend on the fertility of the soil. It may not be literally possible to double the acres planted while maintaining fertility, since the new land may not be as good as that already under cultivation. Hence some inputs may have to be fixed (or at least imperfectly variable) for most practical purposes. In such cases some degree of diminishing productivity (a result of increasing employment of variable inputs) seems likely, although this cannot properly be called "diminishing returns to scale" because of the presence of quasi-fixed inputs.

THE ELAS-TICITY OF SUBSTITU-TION

Another important characteristic of the production function is how "easy" it is to substitute one input for another. Is it, for example, relatively simple to substitute capital for labor while keeping output constant? This is essentially a question of the shape of a single isoquant rather than a question about the whole isoquant map. Along one isoquant it has been assumed that the rate of technical substitution will decrease as the capital-labor ratio decreases (that is, as K/L decreases); now we wish to define some parameter that measures this degree of responsiveness. If the RTS does not change at all for changes in K/L, we might say that substitution is easy, since the ratio of the marginal productivities of the two inputs does not change as the input mix changes. Alternatively, if the RTS changes rapidly for small changes in K/L, we would say that substitution is difficult, since minor variations in the input mix will have a

---

[10] This proof is one example of a general mathematical theorem that states that if a function is homogeneous of degree k, its partial derivatives are homogeneous of degree $k - 1$. Since the production function is homogeneous of degree 1, its marginal productivity functions will be homogeneous of degree 0. A doubling of all inputs will not change marginal productivities in the constant returns-to-scale case.

substantial effect on the inputs' relative productivities. A scale-free measure of this responsiveness is provided by the *elasticity of substitution:*

Definition:

Elasticity of Substitution

For the production function $Q = f(K, L)$, the *elasticity of substitution* (σ) measures the proportionate change in K/L relative to the proportionate change in the RTS along an isoquant. That is,

$$\sigma = \frac{\text{percent } \Delta(K/L)}{\text{percent } \Delta RTS} = \frac{dK/L}{dRTS} \cdot \frac{RTS}{K/L}. \tag{10.28}$$

Since, along an isoquant, K/L and RTS are assumed to move in the same direction, the value of σ is always positive. Graphically, this concept is illustrated in Figure 10.4 as a movement from point A to point B on an isoquant. In this movement both the RTS and the ratio K/L will change, and we are interested in the relative magnitude of these changes. If σ is high, the RTS will not change much relative to K/L, and the isoquant will be relatively flat. On the other

---

Figure 10.4   *Graphic Description of the Elasticity of Substitution*

In moving from point A to point B on the $Q = Q_0$ isoquant, both the capital-labor ratio (K/L) and the RTS will change. The elasticity of substitution (σ) is defined to be the ratio of these proportional changes. It is a measure of how curved the isoquant is.

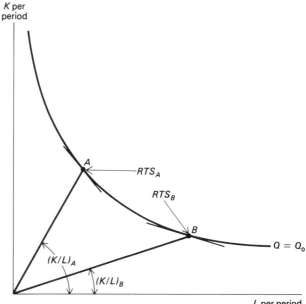

hand, a low value of σ implies a rather sharply curved isoquant: The *RTS* will change by a substantial amount as K/L changes. In general, it is possible that the elasticity of substitution will vary as one moves along an isoquant and as the scale of production changes. Frequently, however, it is convenient to assume that σ is constant along an isoquant. If constant returns to scale are also assumed, then, since all the isoquants are merely radial blowups of each other, σ will be the same along all isoquants. Many investigations of real-world production functions have centered on this *constant returns-to-scale, constant elasticity of substitution* type.[11] Some of the most important of these functions are discussed in detail later in this chapter.

The n-Input Case

Generalizing the elasticity of substitution to the many-input case raises several complications. One possible approach is to adopt a definition analogous to Equation 10.28; that is, to define the elasticity of substitution between two inputs to be the proportionate change in the ratio of the two inputs to the proportionate change in the *RTS* between them while holding output constant. To make this definition complete, it would also be necessary to require that all inputs other than the two being examined be held constant. This latter requirement (which is not needed when there are only two inputs), however, restricts the value of this potential definition. In real-world production processes, it is likely that any change in the ratio of two inputs will also be accompanied by changes in the levels of other inputs. Some of these other inputs may be complementary with the ones being changed whereas others may be substitutes, and to hold them constant creates a rather artificial restriction. For this reason an alternative definition of the elasticity of substitution that permits such complementarity and substitutability is generally used in the *n*-good case. We will briefly describe this alternative concept in the next chapter and make more extensive use of it when we examine input demands in Chapter 21. The application at the end of this chapter also describes some empirical findings about input complementarity in the real world.

SOME COMMON PRODUCTION FUNCTIONS

In this section we illustrate four simple production functions, each characterized by a different elasticity of substitution. These are illustrated only for the case of two inputs, but generalization to many inputs is easily accomplished as shown by the extension problems for this chapter.

Case 1: Linear Function ($\sigma = \infty$)

Suppose that the production function is given by

$$Q = f(K, L) = aK + bL. \tag{10.29}$$

---

[11] The elasticity of substitution can be phrased directly in terms of the production function and its derivatives in the constant returns-to-scale case as

$$\sigma = \frac{(\partial Q/\partial L) \cdot (\partial Q/\partial K)}{Q \cdot (\partial^2 Q/\partial L \partial K)}.$$

For a proof, see R. G. D. Allen, *Mathematical Analysis for Economists* (New York: St. Martin's, 1938), p. 343.

Figure 10.5   *Isoquant Maps for Production Functions with Various Values for σ*

Three possible values for the elasticity of substitution are illustrated in these figures. In (a) capital and labor are perfect substitutes. In this case the *RTS* will not change as the capital-labor ratio changes. In (b), the fixed-proportions case, no substitution is possible. The capital-labor ratio is fixed at *b/a*. A case of limited substitutability is illustrated in (c).

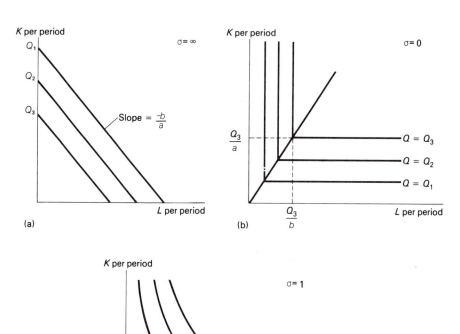

It is easy to show that this production function exhibits constant returns to scale: For any $m > 0$,

$$f(mK, mL) = amK + bmL = m(aK + bL) = mf(K, L). \quad (10.30)$$

All isoquants for this production function are parallel straight lines with slope $-b/a$. Such an isoquant map is pictured in Figure 10.5a. Since along any straight-line isoquant, the *RTS* is constant, the denominator in the definition of σ (Equation 10.28) is equal to 0, and hence σ is equal to infinity. Although this linear production function is a useful example, it is rarely encountered in practice because few production processes are characterized by such ease of substitution. Indeed, in this case capital and labor can be thought of as perfect substitutes for each other. An industry characterized by such a production function could use *only* capital or *only* labor. It is hard to envision such a production process: Every machine needs someone to press its buttons, and every laborer requires some capital equipment, however modest.

Case 2: Fixed Proportions ($\sigma = 0$)

The production function characterized by $\sigma = 0$ is the important case of a *fixed-proportions production function*. Capital and labor must always be used in a fixed ratio. The isoquants for this production function are L-shaped and are pictured in Figure 10.5b. A firm characterized by this production function will always operate along the ray where the ratio K/L is fixed at b/a. To operate at some point other than at the vertex of the isoquants would be inefficient, since the same output could be produced with fewer inputs by moving along the isoquant toward the vertex. Because K/L is a constant, it is easy to see from the definition of the elasticity of substitution that σ must equal 0.

The mathematical form of the fixed-proportions production function is given by

$$Q = \min (aK, bL) \qquad a, b > 0, \tag{10.31}$$

where the operator "min" means that Q is given by the smaller of the two values in parentheses. For example, suppose that $aK < bL$; then $Q = aK$ and we would say that capital is the binding constraint in this production process. The employment of more labor would not raise Q, and hence the marginal product of labor is 0; additional labor is superfluous in this case. Similarly, if $aK > bL$, labor is the binding constraint on output and additional capital is superfluous. When $aK = bL$, both inputs are fully utilized. When this happens, $K/L = b/a$ and production takes place at a vertex on the isoquant map. If both inputs are costly, this is the only reasonable place to operate. Thelocus of all such vertices is a straight line through the origin with a slope given by b/a.

The fixed-proportions production function has a wide range of applications.[12] Many machines, for example, require a certain number of people to run them, but any excess labor is superfluous. Consider combining capital (a

---

[12] With the form reflected by Equation 10.31, the fixed-proportions production function exhibits constant returns to scale since

$$f(mK, mL) = \min (amK, bmL) = m \cdot \min (aK, bL) = mf(K, L)$$

for any $m > 0$. Increasing or decreasing returns can be easily incorporated into the function by using a non-linear transformation of this functional form.

lawn mower) and labor to mow a lawn. It will always take one person to run the mower, and either input without the other is not able to produce any output at all. It may be that many machines are of this type and require a fixed complement of workers per machine.[13]

Case 3:
Cobb-Douglas
($\sigma = 1$)

The production function for which $\sigma = 1$ is called a *Cobb-Douglas production function*[14] and provides an interesting middle ground between the two polar cases previously discussed. Isoquants for the Cobb-Douglas case have the "normal" convex shape and are shown in Figure 10.5c. The mathematical form of the Cobb-Douglas production function is given by

$$Q = f(K, L) = AK^aL^b, \tag{10.32}$$

where A, a, and b are all positive constants.

The Cobb-Douglas function can exhibit any degree of returns scale depending on the values of a and b. Suppose all inputs were increased by a factor of m. Then

$$f(mK, mL) = A(mK)^a(mL)^b = Am^{a+b}K^aL^b \tag{10.33}$$
$$= m^{a+b}f(K, L).$$

Hence, if $a + b = 1$, the Cobb-Douglas function exhibits constant returns to scale since output also increases by a factor of m. If $a + b > 1$, the function exhibits increasing returns to scale whereas $a + b < 1$ corresponds to the decreasing returns-to-scale case. For the constant returns-to-scale case, it is a simple matter to show that the elasticity of substitution is 1 for the Cobb-Douglas function.[15] This fact has led many researchers to use the function for a general description of aggregate production relationships in many countries. In Chapter 21 we review some of the reasons why the function is sometimes considered appropriate for this purpose.

[13] The lawn mower example points up another possibility, however. Presumably there is some leeway in choosing what size of lawn mower to buy. Hence, prior to the actual purchase, the capital-labor ratio in lawn mowing can be considered variable: Any device, from a pair of clippers to a gang mower, might be chosen. Once the mower is purchased, however, the capital-labor ratio becomes fixed. Several authors have adopted this general "putty-clay" view of productive processes. In the planning stage there may be substantial possibilities for substituting capital for labor. Once investment decisions have been made (the "putty" has hardened into "clay"), the machines have to be used with a specified amount of labor.

[14] Named after C. W. Cobb and P. H. Douglas. See P. H. Douglas, *The Theory of Wages* (New York: Macmillan Co., 1934), pp. 132–135.

[15] Using Allen's definition from footnote 11 of this chapter, when $Q = AK^aL^{1-a}$,

$$\sigma = \frac{(1 - a)(Q/L) \cdot a(Q/K)}{Q^2(1 - a)(a)/KL} = 1.$$

The Cobb-Douglas function has also proved to be quite useful in many applications because it is linear in logarithms:

$$\ln Q = \ln A + a \ln K + b \ln L. \tag{10.34}$$

The constant a is then the elasticity of output with respect to capital input, and b is the elasticity of output with respect to labor input.[16] These constants can sometimes be estimated from actual data, and such estimates may be used to measure returns to scale (by examining the sum $a + b$) and for other purposes.

Case 4: CES Production Function

Although 0, 1, and ∞ are important constants, there is little reason to believe that production processes would be characterized by any of these elasticities of substitution. Rather, it is desirable to have a general production function that permits σ to take on any positive value. Such a function is provided by the *constant elasticity of substitution (CES) production function* first developed by Arrow, Chenery, Minhas, and Solow.[17] The complex mathematical form of this production function is given by

$$Q = \gamma[\delta K^\rho + (1 - \delta)L^\rho]^{\epsilon/\rho}, \tag{10.35}$$

where

$$\gamma > 0$$

$$0 \le \delta \le 1$$

$$\rho \le 1$$

$$\epsilon \ge 0.$$

These parameters can be given specific interpretations: γ is an efficiency parameter in that it merely shifts the whole production function; δ is a distribution parameter that permits the relative importance of K and L to vary in much the same way as in the Cobb-Douglas case.

Here ρ is the substitution parameter—the closer ρ is to 1 (its maximum value), the higher the elasticity of substitution. Specifically, it can be shown that for the constant returns-to-scale case (see our later discussion)

$$\sigma = \frac{1}{1 - \rho} \tag{10.36}$$

[16] The proof follows those used in Chapter 7. Define the output elasticity for capital, say, as

$$e_{Q,K} = \frac{\partial Q}{\partial K} \cdot \frac{K}{Q} = \frac{\partial \ln Q}{\partial \ln K}.$$

Hence, by Equation 10.34 $e_{Q,K} = a$. Similarly, $e_{Q,L} = b$.

[17] K. J. Arrow, H. B. Chenery, B. S. Minhas, and R. M. Solow, "Capital Labor Substitution and Economic Efficiency," *Review of Economics and Statistics* (August 1961): 225–250.

so that the CES function incorporates the linear, fixed-proportions, and Cobb-Douglas functions as special cases (for $\rho = 1$, $-\infty$, and 0 respectively).[18]

The isoquant map of the general CES production function is much like that of the Cobb-Douglas function. It is easy to show that the CES function can exhibit any degree of returns to scale depending on the parameter ε:

$$f(mK, mL) = \gamma[\delta(mK)^\rho + (1 - \delta)(mL)^\rho]$$

$$= \gamma[m^\rho]^{\varepsilon/\rho}[\delta K^\rho + (1 - \delta)L^\rho]^{\varepsilon/\rho} \qquad (10.37)$$

$$= m^\varepsilon f(K, L)$$

for any $m > 0$. Hence the function exhibits increasing, constant, or decreasing returns to scale depending on whether $\varepsilon > 1$, $\varepsilon = 1$, or $\varepsilon < 1$.

Numerical Example

Many of these production function concepts can be illustrated by a numerical example. For this purpose we shall assume that there are only two factors of production (again represented by K and L) and that the hourly production function for hamburgers is given explicitly by

$$Q = 10\sqrt{K \cdot L}, \qquad (10.38)$$

where Q represents hamburger output per hour and K and L represent grill and worker employment per period. We can write this function as

$$Q = 10K^{1/2}L^{1/2}, \qquad (10.39)$$

which makes clear that it is a Cobb-Douglas production function with constant returns to scale (since the exponents sum to 1). Hence it is a type widely used in economic studies. Table 10.1 shows that the production function does indeed exhibit constant returns to scale: As the inputs are increased proportionately, hourly hamburger output increases in the same proportion.

The isoquant map for this production function can be constructed by setting Q equal to various constant output levels and graphing the implicit relationship between K and L. For example, if $Q = 50$ hamburgers per hour,

$$50 = 10\sqrt{K \cdot L} \qquad (10.40)$$

or

$$K \cdot L = 25.$$

Similarly, if $Q = 100$ hamburgers per hour,

$$100 = 10\sqrt{K \cdot L}$$
$$K \cdot L = 100. \qquad (10.41)$$

[18] In particular, for $\rho = 0$ the CES production function approaches a Cobb-Douglas function of the form

$$Q = \gamma K^\delta L^{1-\delta}.$$

As will be pointed out in Chapter 21, this further explains the use of the term *distribution parameter* for the parameter δ.

Table 10.1   *Values of* $Q = f(K, L) = 10\sqrt{K \cdot L}$
for Proportionate Increases in K and L

Capital per Hour (K)	Labor per Hour (L)	Hamburger Output per Hour (Q)
1	1	10
2	2	20
3	3	30
4	4	40
5	5	50
6	6	60
7	7	70
8	8	80
9	9	90
10	10	100

The isoquants of the function are therefore rectangular hyperbolas. They are illustrated in Figure 10.6. The *RTS* along the isoquants can be computed by

$$RTS \quad (L \text{ for } K) \quad = \frac{\partial Q/\partial L}{\partial Q/\partial K} = \frac{5\sqrt{K/L}}{\sqrt{L/K}} = \frac{K}{L}. \tag{10.42}$$

It is obvious, therefore, that the *RTS* diminishes as K/L does and that the *RTS* does not depend on the scale of production (doubling K and L would not change the ratio of K to L). Figure 10.6 illustrates this second fact for the case where $K/L = 1$ since the slope of the isoquants at both A and B is -1.

TECHNICAL PROGRESS

Methods of production improve over time and it is important to be able to capture these improvements in the production function concept. A simplified view of such progress is provided by Figure 10.7. Initially, isoquant Q_0 records those combinations of capital and labor that can be used to produce an output level of Q_0. Following the development of superior production techniques, this isoquant shifts to Q_0'. Now the same level of output can be produced with fewer inputs. One way to measure this improvement is by noting that with a level of capital input of K, say, K_1, it previously took L_2 units of labor to produce Q_0 whereas now it takes only L_1. Output per worker has risen from Q_0/L_2 to Q_0/L_1. But one must be careful in this type of calculation. An increase in capital input to K_2 would also have permitted a reduction in labor input to L_1 along the original Q_0 isoquant. In this case output for workers would also rise, although there would have been no true technical progress. Use of the production function concept can help to differentiate between these two concepts and therefore allow economists to obtain an accurate estimate of the rate of technical advancement.

Figure 10.6   *Graph of the* Q = *50 and* Q = *100 Isoquants for the Production Function* Q = $10\sqrt{K \cdot L}$

These isoquants are taken directly from Equations 10.40 and 10.41. They show the combinations of *K* and *L* that can produce 50 and 100 hamburgers per hour, respectively. The isoquants clearly display a diminishing *RTS*.

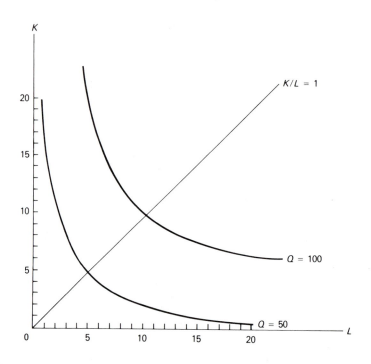

Measuring Technical Progress

The first observation to be made about technical progress is that historically the rate of growth of output over time has exceeded the growth rate that can be attributed to the growth in conventionally defined inputs. Suppose that we let

$$Q = A(t)f(K, L) \tag{10.43}$$

be the production function for some good (or perhaps for society's output as a whole). The term *A(t)* in the function represents all the influences that go into determining *Q* besides *K* (machine-hours) and *L* (labor-hours). Changes in *A* over time could represent technical progress. For this reason *A* is shown as a function of time. Presumably *dA/dt* > 0: Particular levels of input of labor and capital become more productive over time.

Differentiating Equation 10.43 with respect to time gives

$$\frac{dQ}{dt} = \frac{dA}{dt} \cdot f(K, L) + A \cdot \frac{df(K, L)}{dt}$$

$$= \frac{dA}{dt} \cdot \frac{Q}{A} + \frac{Q}{f(K, L)} \left[\frac{\partial f}{\partial K} \cdot \frac{dK}{dt} + \frac{\partial f}{\partial L} \cdot \frac{dL}{dt} \right]. \tag{10.44}$$

Figure 10.7 *Technical Progress*

Technical progress shifts the Q_0 isoquant toward the origin. The new Q_0 isoquant, Q_0', shows that a given level of output can now be produced with less input. For example, with K_1 units of capital, it now only takes L_1 units of labor to produce Q_0, whereas before the technical advance, it took L_2 units of labor.

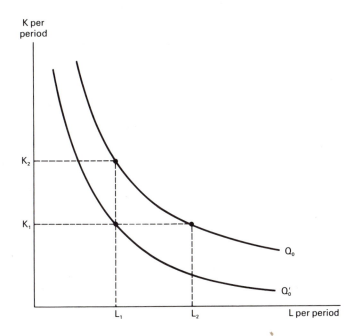

Dividing by Q gives

$$\frac{dQ/dt}{Q} = \frac{dA/dt}{A} + \frac{\partial f/\partial K}{f(K, L)} \cdot \frac{dK}{dt} + \frac{\partial f/\partial L}{f(K, L)} \cdot \frac{dL}{dt} \qquad (10.45)$$

or

$$\frac{dQ/dt}{Q} = \frac{dA/dT}{A} + \frac{\partial f}{\partial K} \cdot \frac{K}{f(K, L)} \cdot \frac{dK/dt}{K} + \frac{\partial f}{\partial L} \cdot \frac{L}{f(K, L)} \cdot \frac{dL/dt}{L}.$$

Now, for any variable x, $(dx/dt)/x$ is simply the geometric rate of growth of x per unit of time. We shall denote this by G_x. Hence Equation 10.45 can be written in terms of growth rates as

$$G_Q = G_A + \frac{\partial f}{\partial K} \cdot \frac{K}{f(K, L)} \cdot G_K + \frac{\partial f}{\partial L} \cdot \frac{L}{f(K, L)} \cdot G_L, \qquad (10.46)$$

but

$$\frac{\partial f}{\partial K} \cdot \frac{K}{f(K, L)} = \frac{\partial Q}{\partial K} \cdot \frac{K}{Q} = \text{elasticity of output with respect to capital input}$$

$$= e_{Q,K}$$

and

$$\frac{\partial f}{\partial L} \cdot \frac{L}{f(K, L)} = \frac{\partial Q}{\partial L} \cdot \frac{L}{Q} = \text{elasticity of output with respect to labor input}$$

$$= e_{Q,L}.$$

Therefore, our growth equation finally becomes

$$G_Q = G_A + e_{Q,K}G_K + e_{Q,L}G_L. \tag{10.47}$$

Hence the rate of growth in output can be broken down into the sum of two components: growth attributed to changes in inputs (K and L) and other growth (that is, changes in A).

Equation 10.47 provides a way of estimating the relative importance of technical progress (G_A) in determining the growth of output. For example, in a pioneering study of the U.S. economy between the years 1909 and 1949, R. M. Solow recorded the following values for the terms in the equation:[19]

$$G_Q = 2.75 \text{ percent per year}$$

$$G_L = 1.00 \text{ percent per year}$$

$$G_K = 1.75 \text{ percent per year}$$

$$e_{Q,L} = 0.65$$

$$e_{Q,K} = 0.35.$$

Consequently,

$$\begin{aligned} G_A &= G_Q - e_{Q,L}G_L - e_{Q,K}G_K \\ &= 2.75 - 0.65(1.00) - 0.35(1.75) \\ &= 2.75 - 0.65 - 0.60 \\ &= 1.50. \end{aligned} \tag{10.48}$$

The conclusion reached, then, is that technology advanced at a rate of 1.5 percent per year from 1909 to 1949. More than one-half of the growth in real output can be attributed to technical change rather than to growth in the physical quantities of the factors of production.

Classifying Technical Progress

The empirical question, then, is in what precise way does the technical change factor $[A(t)]$ enter into the production function? Three possible ways that this might happen are as follows:

[19] R. M. Solow, "Technical Progress and the Aggregate Production Function," *Review of Economics and Statistics* 39 (August 1957): 312–320. The data, abstracted from Solow's Table I, have been rounded off for convenience. The figures for $e_{Q,L}$ and $e_{Q,K}$ are taken from Solow's data on the shares of income accruing to labor and capital. In Chapter 21 we shall show why such data are relevant to determining the elasticity of output with respect to an input.

1.   *Neutral technical progress:*

$$Q = A(t)f(K, L). \tag{10.49}$$

Here technical progress affects all the inputs equally.

2.   *Capital augmenting technical progress:*

$$Q = f[A(t)K, L]. \tag{10.50}$$

In this case technical progress affects only capital. Machine-hours (K) become more productive over time.

3.   *Labor augmenting technical progress:*

$$Q = f[K, A(t)L]. \tag{10.51}$$

This is the case in which technical progress affects only the quality of labor-hours that enter into the production function. The productive power of labor is "augmented" over time, perhaps because workers learn to do their jobs better.

Each of these three types of technical progress has the effect of shifting the production function. Over time, more output can be obtained from any given combination of inputs. As we showed in Figure 10.7, the isoquant map shifts toward the origin as productive technology improves. Equations 10.49, 10.50, and 10.51 provide a way of classifying those shifts that do take place. It is quite likely that all three types of technical progress occur simultaneously. One important role of empirical investigations is to identify the relative importance of each of these types so that policy makers can appraise the possible effects of input changes on the increase in productivity.

Empirical Evidence

E. F. Denison's study of the U.S. economy was the first major work to attempt to determine whether the unexplained residual in the growth of gross national product was neutral or could more properly be attributed to improvements in the stocks of capital or labor.[20] Although it is impossible for us to survey all of Denison's conclusions or any of the further analysis his work has engendered, we shall mention two central findings. First, Denison found that a substantial part (about 40 percent) of the technical advance could be explained by improvements in the quality of the labor force. This result indicated the strong role that education can have in the growth process. Since Denison's work, numerous empirical studies have attempted to better explain the relationship between education and economic growth.

Second, Denison was relatively unsuccessful in demonstrating the importance of improvements in capital to the growth process. Since many economists believe that improvements in capital equipment are a major means by which

---

[20] E. F. Denison, *The Sources of Economic Growth in the United States and the Alternatives before Us* (New York: Committee for Economic Development, 1962).

new techniques are adopted, this finding provided a serious challenge for future analysis. The most interesting models to emerge from his study involve the "embodied" nature of technical progress. This view holds that new investment provides the major method by which technical change is introduced into the capital stock. Only such new equipment is able to embody the latest technology. Consequently, capital accumulation becomes far more important than is implied by studies that do not take the embodied nature of technical change into account. For example, an interesting study by Solow found that new capital equipment improves at the surprisingly fast rate of 5 percent per year.[21] In terms of productive ability, machines introduced during the current year are 5 percent more effective than machines produced the previous year. Using this estimate of the improvement experienced by the capital stock, Solow concluded that most of the unexplained growth in output found in his earlier studies can be attributed to the embodiment of improved technology in the latest additions to the capital stock.

These studies of technical progress suggest that a simple production function with only two inputs may not be adequate for examining many issues. Skilled and unskilled workers may be quite different inputs; old and new machines may have quite different characteristics. Perhaps most important, the recognition that labor and capital inputs are not homogeneous can have a major impact on longer term results when technical improvements are more likely to occur. Consequently, at many places in this book we will suggest ways in which our analysis of production might be generalized to incorporate these possibilities. For the development of basic principles, however, we will primarily rely on the two-input production function.

SUMMARY

In this chapter we illustrated the ways in which economists conceptualize the production process of turning inputs into outputs. The fundamental tool is the production function, which, in its simplest form, assumes that output per period (Q) is a simple function of capital and labor inputs during that period, $Q = f(K, L)$. Using this starting point, we developed several basic results for the theory of production:

- If all but one of the inputs are held constant, a relationship between the single variable input and output can be derived. From this relationship one can derive the marginal physical productivity (MP) of the input as the change in output resulting from a one-unit increase in the use of the input. The marginal physical productivity of an input is assumed to decline as use of the input increases.

[21] R. M. Solow, *Capital Theory and the Rate of Return* (Amsterdam: North Holland Publishing Co., 1964), chap. 3.

- The entire production function can be illustrated by its isoquant map. The (negative of the) slope of an isoquant is termed the marginal rate of technical substitution (*RTS*) since it shows how one input can be substituted for another while holding output constant. The *RTS* is the ratio of the marginal physical productivities of the two inputs.
- Isoquants are usually assumed to be convex—they obey the assumption of a diminishing *RTS*. This assumption cannot be derived exclusively from the assumption of diminishing marginal physical productivities.
- The returns to scale exhibited by a production function record how output responds to proportionate increases in all inputs. If output increases proportionately with input use, there are constant returns to scale. If there are greater than proportionate increases in output, there are increasing returns to scale, whereas if there are less than proportionate increases in output, there are decreasing returns to scale.
- The elasticity of substitution (σ) provides a scale-free measure of how easy it is to substitute one input for another in production. A high σ implies nearly straight isoquants whereas a low σ implies that isoquants are nearly L-shaped.
- Technical progress shifts the entire production function and its related isoquant map. Many technical improvements arise from the use of improved, more productive inputs.

Application

PRODUCTION FUNCTIONS

Economists have conducted literally thousands of empirical studies of real-world production relationships. Here we examine only two of them. The first shows the importance of the returns-to-scale concept in the design of cargo ships, and the second illustrates how the elasticity of substitution notion can be generalized a bit to study basic questions about energy use.

Returns to Scale and Cargo Ships

Oceangoing cargo ships provide an illustration of the importance of the returns-to-scale concept for practical decision making and of the complications that can arise in examining that concept closely. Simple geometric intuition suggests why cargo ships might exhibit increasing returns to scale. Picture a ship as just a topless cube. If the lengths of the four sides and the bottom of the cube are doubled, its overall surface area will increase fourfold. Hence the metal needed for the hull also will increase fourfold. The volume of the cube, however, will increase eightfold. Thus a doubling of inputs (here the size of the ship's hull) would more than double its carrying capacity. Because other features of the ship such as power plants, staffing needs, and control devices also probably exhibit increasing returns to scale, the cube analogy may not be very far from the truth. This undoubtedly explains why much larger oil tankers (up to 500,000 tons) have been produced in recent years, for example, and why economies of scale occur in other forms of transportation, such as oil and natural gas pipelines, for which similar geometric considerations apply.

A closer examination of cargo ships, however, reveals substantial problems with increases in size. Loading and unloading cargoes from very large ships can be a difficult and costly process: Larger cranes are needed; interior handling equipment for use in the large holds is required; goods sometimes must be moved substantial distances just to get them off the ship; and larger ships may have to anchor far offshore. Hence the geometric allure of large ships must be tempered somewhat by logistical problems involved in cargo handling.

A 1978 study by J. O. Jansson and D. Shneerson illustrated these considerations quite clearly.[22] They showed that, on the average, a 50 percent increase in the carrying capacity of a cargo ship increases the ship's capital cost by only about 25 percent. Ships' operating costs are increased even less (after all, a ship, no matter how large, needs only one captain). On the other hand, the authors found that a 50 percent increase in carrying capacity tends to increase capital costs associated with cargo handling by nearly 90 percent, with similar cost increases for operating the handling equipment. Hence shipping firms must make very careful calculations in deciding how to trade off the advantages and disadvantages of large-scale vessels.

Substitution between Energy and Capital

Although the discussion of substitutability between inputs presented thus far has focused on the relationship between capital and labor, substitution among other inputs is also an important question. One issue that has been of considerable recent interest to economists is the nature of the relationship between energy and capital in production. That interest was particularly sparked by the rapid increases in energy prices during the 1970s, which aroused concern about the flexibility with which firms could respond to those increases. If energy and capital exhibit a high degree of substitutability, firms

may be able to adapt rather quickly to rising energy prices by using more and better capital equipment that economizes on energy use. On the other hand, if such substitutions are difficult, firms may be faced with major adjustment problems.

Actual studies of the relationship between capital and energy inputs during the 1970s suggest a third possibility: that capital and energy may be *complements* in production. That is, some authors suggest that use of more sophisticated capital equipment necessarily involves using more energy to power that equipment and that the only way firms can cope with increases in energy prices is to cut back on both capital and energy usage. A 1975 study by E. R. Berndt and D. O. Wood indicated this was indeed the situation for many industries,[23] and several later investigations have reached similar conclusions. Hence the commonsense idea that energy and capital equipment tend to be used jointly in production seems to be supported by the facts.

As an example of capital-energy complementarity, consider the case of jet aircraft. Rapid increases in the price of jet fuel during the 1970s had a substantial effect on airlines' costs and made it necessary for them to think carefully about which planes to fly. Daily hours of use for fuel-inefficient versions of such planes as the 707, the DC8, and the DC9 declined as such planes were put on shortened schedules or retired altogether. Hence the airlines' use of capital services was, at least over the short term, reduced significantly.

The finding that capital and energy may be complements has been suggested as a major explanation for the decline in labor productivity in the United States during the 1970s. Prior to 1973 average output per worker in the United States grew at about 2 percent to 2.5 percent per year. Since 1973 (the year of the Arab oil

[22] J. O. Jansson and D. Shneerson, "Economics of Scale of General Cargo Ships," *Review of Economics and Statistics* 60 (May 1978): 291–296.

[23] E. R. Berndt and D. O. Wood, "Technology, Prices, and the Derived Demand for Energy," *Review of Economics and Statistics* 57 (August 1975): 259–268.

embargo and consequent rise in energy prices), productivity growth has been less than 1 percent per year. A possible reason is that, due to the complementary relationship between capital and energy, higher energy prices made use of some existing capital equipment uneconomical and reduced the demand for new machinery. Both of these influences sharply reduced the amount of equipment with which the typical employee had to work and thereby reduced his or her productivity.

SUGGESTED READINGS

Clark, J. M. "Diminishing Returns." *Encyclopaedia of the Social Sciences,* Vol. 5. New York: Crowell-Collier and Macmillan, 1931. Pp. 144–146.

Lucid discussion of the historical development of the diminishing returns concept.

Douglas, P. H. "Are There Laws of Production?" *American Economic Review* 38 (March 1948): 1–41.

Basic methodological analysis of the uses and misuses of production functions.

———. "The Cobb-Douglas Production Function Once Again: Its History, Its Testing, and Some Empirical Values." *Journal of Political Economy* 84 (October 1976): 903–916.

Comprehensive review of the literature on Cobb-Douglas production functions.

Ferguson, C. E. *The Neoclassical Theory of Production and Distribution.* New York: Cambridge University Press, 1969.

Fairly complete discussion of production function theory. Good use of three-dimensional graphs.

Fuss, M., and McFadden, D. *Production Economics: A Dual Approach to Theory and Application.* Amsterdam: North Holland Publishing Co., 1980.

Modern approach with heavy emphasis on the use of duality.

Henderson, J. M., and Quandt, R. F. *Microeconomic Theory: A Mathematical Approach.* 3d ed. New York: McGraw-Hill Book Company, 1980. Chap. 3.

Standard calculus approach, working through several useful examples.

Machlup, F. "On the Meaning of Marginal Product." Reprinted in American Economic Association, *Readings in the Theory of Income Distribution.* Philadelphia: Blakiston Co., 1951. Pp. 158–174.

Nice methodological development of the proper use of the marginal product notion.

Nadiri, M. I. "Producer's Theory." In K. J. Arrow and M. D. Intriligator, eds., *Handbook of Mathematical Economics,* Vol. 2. Amsterdam: North Holland Publishing Co., 1981.

Fairly advanced mathematical treatment but surprisingly readable.

Shephard, R. W. *Theory of Cost and Production Functions.* Princeton, N.J.: Princeton University Press, 1978.

Extended analysis of the dual relationship between production and cost functions.

Stigler, G. J. "The Division of Labor Is Limited by the Extent of the Market." *Journal of Political Economy* 59 (June 1951): 185–193.

Careful tracing of the evolution of Smith's ideas about economies of scale.

Uzawa, H. "Production Functions with Constant Elasticities of Substitution." *The Review of Economic Studies* (October 1962): 291–299.

Analyzes several potential ways of measuring substitution elasticities and demonstrates the relationships among them.

Walters, A. A. "Production and Cost Functions." *Econometrica* 31 (January/April 1963): 1–66.

Excellent though dated survey of the empirical literature.

PROBLEMS

10.1

Digging clams by hand in Sunset Bay requires only labor input. The total number of clams obtained per hour (Q) is given by

$$Q = 100\sqrt{L}$$

where L is labor input per hour.

    a.   Graph the relationship between Q and L.

    b.   What is the average productivity of labor in Sunset Bay? Graph this relationship and show that AP_1 diminishes for increases in labor input.

    c.   Show that the marginal productivity of labor in Sunset Bay is given by

$$MP_L = 50/\sqrt{L}.$$

    Graph this relationship and show that $MP_L < AP_L$ for all values of L. Explain why this is so.

10.2

Suppose the production function for widgets is given by

$$Q = KL - .8K^2 - .2L^2$$

where Q represents the annual quantity of widgets produced, K represents annual capital input, and L represents annual labor input.

    a.   Suppose $K = 10$; graph the total and average productivity of labor curves. At what level of labor input does this average productivity reach a maximum? How many widgets are produced at that point?

    b.   Again assuming that $K = 10$ graph the MP_L curve. At what level of labor input does $MP_L = 0$?

    c.   Suppose capital inputs were increased to $K = 20$. How would your answers to parts a and b change?

    d.   Does the widget production function exhibit constant, increasing, or decreasing returns to scale?

10.3

Power Goat Lawn Company uses two sizes of mowers to cut lawns. The smaller mowers have a 24-inch blade and are used on lawns with many trees and obstacles. The larger mowers are exactly twice as big as the smaller mowers and are used on open lawns where manueverability is not so difficult. The two production functions available to Power Goat are:

	Output per Hour (Square Feet)	Capital Input (# of 24" Mowers)	Labor Input
Large Mowers	8,000	2	1
Small Mowers	5,000	1	1

    a.   Graph the $Q = 40,000$ square feet isoquant for the first production function. How much K and L would be used if these factors were combined without waste?

    b.   Answer part a for the second function.

    c.   How much K and L would be used without waste if half of the 40,000 square foot lawn were cut by the method of the first production function and half by the method of the second? How much K and L would be used if three-fourths of the lawn were cut by the first method and one-fourth by the second? What does it mean to speak of fractions of K and L?

d.   On the basis of your observations in part c, draw a $Q = 40,000$ isoquant for the combined production functions.

10.4
The production of barstools (Q) is characterized by a production function of the form

$$Q = K^{1/2} \cdot L^{1/2} = \sqrt{K \cdot L}.$$

a.   What is the average productivity of labor and capital for barstool production $(AP_L$ will depend on K, and AP_K will depend on L)?

b.   Graph the AP_L curve for $K = 100$.

c.   For this particular function show that $MP_L = 1/2\ AP_L$, and $MP_K = 1/2\ AP_K$. Using that information, add a graph of the MP_L function to the graph calculated in part b (again for $K = 100$). What is unusual about this curve?

d.   Sketch the $Q = 10$ isoquant for this production function.

e.   Using the results from part c, what is the RTS on the $Q = 10$ isoquant at the points: $K = L = 10$; $K = 25$, $L = 4$; and $K = 4$, $L = 25$? Does this function exhibit a diminishing RTS?

10.5
Contrast the concepts of diminishing returns to scale and diminishing returns to a factor. Can a production function exhibit diminishing returns to scale but not have diminishing returns to a factor?

10.6
Suppose that

$$Q = L^{\alpha}K^{\beta} \qquad 0 < \alpha < 1, \quad 0 < \beta < 1, \quad \alpha + \beta = 1.$$

a.   Show that $e_{Q,L} = \alpha$, $e_{Q,K} = \beta$.

b.   Show that $MP_L > 0$, $MP_K > 0$; $\partial^2 Q/\partial L^2 < 0$, $\partial^2 Q/\partial K^2 < 0$.

c.   Show that the RTS depends only on K/L, but not on the scale of production, and that the RTS ($<$ for K) diminishes as L/K increases.

10.7
Consider a production function of the firm

$$Q = \beta_0 + \beta_1\sqrt{KL} + \beta_2K + \beta_3L$$

$$\text{where } 0 \le \beta_i \le 1 \qquad i = 0 \ldots 3$$

a.   If this function is to exhibit constant returns to scale what restrictions should be placed on the parameters $\beta_0 \ldots \beta_3$?

b.   Show that in the constant returns to scale case this function exhibits diminishing marginal productivities and that the marginal productivity functions are homogeneous of degree zero.

c.   Use Allen's formula for the elasticity of substitution (footnote 11 of this chapter) to calculate σ in this case. Is σ constant?

10.8
Show that Euler's theorem (see footnote 5 of Chapter 7) implies that for a constant returns-to-scale production function $[Q = f(K, L)]$,

$$Q = f_K \cdot K + f_L \cdot L.$$

Use this result to show that for such a production function, if $MP_L > AP_L$, MP_K must be negative. What does this imply about where production must take place in Figure 10.1 (assuming both MP_L and MP_K are positive)?

10.9

As in problem 10.8, again use Euler's theorem to prove that for a constant returns-to-scale production function with only two inputs (K and L), f_{KL} must be positive. Interpret this result.

10.10

Show that for the CES production function.

$$Q = \gamma[\delta K^\rho + (1 - \delta)L^\rho]^{1/\rho}$$

a. $MP_K = \beta_1 \left(\dfrac{Q}{K}\right)^{1-\rho}$ and $MP_L = \beta_2 \left(\dfrac{Q}{L}\right)^{1-\rho}$ where $\beta_1 + \beta_2 = 1$

b. $RTS = \dfrac{\beta_1}{\beta_2}\left(\dfrac{L}{K}\right)^{1-\rho}$

c.   Determine the output elasticities for K and L. Show that their sum equals 1.

d.   Prove that

$$\frac{Q}{L} = C\left(\frac{\partial Q}{\partial L}\right)^\sigma, \text{ where } C \text{ is a constant.}$$

Hence show

$$\ln\left(\frac{Q}{L}\right) = \ln C + \sigma \ln\left(\frac{\partial Q}{\partial L}\right).$$

Note: The latter equality is useful in empirical work, since in some cases we may approximate $\partial Q/\partial L$ by the competitively determined wage rate. Hence σ can be estimated from a regression of $\ln(Q/L)$ on $\ln W$.

EXTENSIONS

MANY INPUT PRODUCTION FUNCTIONS

Most of the production functions illustrated in Chapter 10 can be easily generalized to the many input cases. Here we show this for the Cobb-Douglas and CES cases and then examine two quite flexible forms that such production functions might take. In all of these examples the β's are non-negative parameters and the n inputs are represented by $X_1 \ldots X_n$.

E10.1 (Cobb-Douglas)
The many input Cobb-Douglas production function is given by

$$Q = \prod_{i=1}^{n} X_i^{\beta_i}$$

a.   Show that this function exhibits constant returns to scale if

$$\sum_{i=1}^{n} \beta_i = 1$$

b.   Show that this production function exhibits diminishing marginal
     productivities for each input.

E10.2 (CES)

The many input constant elasticity of substitution (CES) production function is
given by

$$Q = [\Sigma \, \beta_i X_i^\rho]^{\varepsilon/\rho} \qquad \rho \leq 1$$

a.   Show that this function exhibits constant returns to scale for $\varepsilon = 1$.
b.   Show that this production function exhibits diminishing marginal
     productivities for all inputs.

*The next two examples illustrate flexible form production functions that may
approximate any general function of n inputs. In the Chapter 11 Extensions we
examine the cost function analogues to some of these functions, which are more
widely used than the production functions themselves.*

E10.3 (Generalized Leontief)

$$Q = \sum_{i=1}^{n}\sum_{j=1}^{n} \beta_{ij}\sqrt{X_i X_j} \qquad \beta_{ij} = \beta_{ji}$$

a.   Illustrate this function for the case $n = 3$. Show that it is a generaliza-
     tion of the function in Problem 10.7.
b.   Show that this function exhibits constant returns to scale.
c.   Show that this function exhibits diminishing marginal productivity to
     each input.
d.   Why is the condition $\beta_{ij} = \beta_{ji}$ imposed for this function?

E10.4 (Translog)

$$\ln Q = \beta_0 + \sum_{i=1}^{n} \beta_i \ln X_i + 0.5 \sum_{i=1}^{n}\sum_{j=1}^{n} \beta_{ij} \ln X_i \ln X_j \qquad \beta_{ij} = \beta_{ji}$$

a.   Show that the Cobb-Douglas is a special case of this function where
     $\beta_0 = \beta_{ij} = 0$ for all i, j.
b.   Show that this function exhibits constant returns to scale. What role
     does the coefficient of 0.5 play in assuring this?
c.   Why is the condition $\beta_{ij} = \beta_{ji}$ imposed for this function?

E10.5

For each of the four production functions described here illustrate how differing
degrees of return to scale might be incorporated into the functions.

REFERENCES

Christensen, L. R., Jorgenson, D. W., and Lav, L. J., "Transcendental Logarithmic Production Frontiers," *Review of Economics and Statistics,* February 1973, pp. 28–45.

Diewert, W. E., "Functional Forms for Profit and Transformation Functions," *Journal of Economic Theory,* June 1973, pp. 284–315.

Fuss, M., and McFadden, D. (eds.), *Production Economics: A Dual Approach to Theory and Applications* (Amsterdam: North Holland, 1978 [see especially Ch. I.1, "Cost Revenue and Profit Functions," and Ch. II.1, "A Survey of Functional Forms in the Economic Analysis of Production"]).

CHAPTER 11

Costs of Production

In Chapter 10 we discussed ways of conceptualizing the relationship between inputs and outputs in the production process. Now we wish to show how this production function can be used to illustrate, in a formal way, the costs that a firm incurs in its productive activities. Ultimately, we will be able to use such information together with information about the firm's revenues to show how much it will choose to produce. But we will delay that topic until Chapters 12 and 13. Here we will only be concerned with questions about the costs associated with the inputs that the firm chooses to employ.

DEFINITIONS OF COSTS

Before we can discuss the theory of costs, some conceptual difficulties about the proper definition of "costs" must be cleared up. At least three different concepts of costs can be distinguished: opportunity cost, accounting cost, and "economic" cost. For economists the most important of these is *social,* or *opportunity, cost.* Because resources are limited, any decision in an economy to produce some good necessitates doing without some other good. When an automobile is produced, for example, an implicit decision has been made to do without, say, 15 bicycles that could have been produced using the labor, metal, chrome, and glass that went into making the automobile. The opportunity cost of one automobile is then 15 bicycles.[1] Since expressing opportunity costs in terms of physical goods is often inconvenient, monetary units are sometimes chosen instead. Indeed the price of a car may adequately reflect the goods that were given up by its being produced. If this were true, we would say that the opportunity cost of an automobile is $10,000 worth of other goods. This may not always be the case, however. If, for example, the car were produced with resources that could not be usefully employed elsewhere, the opportunity cost of its production might have been close to 0.

The opportunity cost doctrine is extremely important in economic analysis. Many problems of social choice are made conceptually clearer by recognizing

---

[1] The notion of opportunity cost in a general sense pervades all applications of the theory of choice. For example, an individual who chooses to purchase a hamburger forgoes at the same time, say, two soft drinks.

the alternatives inherent in the economic process. Because the concept, in its most general statement, is directly relevant to social decisions, a full discussion will be postponed until Part VIII. In this chapter we shall be interested primarily in defining costs in a way that is relevant to the firm's decision-making process.

The two other concepts of cost are both directly related to the firm's theory of choice. These are the accountant's concept of cost and the economist's concept of the firm's costs. The accountant's view of cost stresses out-of-pocket expenses, historical costs, depreciation, and other bookkeeping entries. The economist's definition of cost (which in obvious ways draws on the idea of opportunity cost) is that the true cost of any input is given by the size of the payment necessary to keep a resource in its present employment. The best way to distinguish between these two views is to consider how the costs of various resources (labor, capital, and entrepreneurial services) are defined under each system.

Labor Costs

Economists and accountants regard labor costs in much the same way. To accountants expenditures on labor are current expenses and hence are costs of production. For economists labor is an *explicit* cost. Labor services (labor-hours) are contracted at some hourly wage rate (w), and it is assumed that this is the amount the labor services would earn in their best alternative employment. Thus both definitions of costs look at wages, although there is a slight distinction in that accountants tend to stress the total wage bill whereas economists look at the cost of the marginal labor-hour.

Capital Costs

In the case of capital services (machine-hours), the two concepts of cost differ greatly. In calculating capital costs, accountants use the historical price of the particular machine under investigation and apply some more-or-less arbitrary depreciation rule to determine how much of that machine's original price to charge to current costs. Economists regard the historical price of a machine as a "sunk cost," which is basically irrelevant to the productive process. They instead regard the *implicit* cost of the machine to be what someone else would be willing to pay for its use. Thus the cost of one machine-hour is the *rental rate* for that machine in its best alternative use. By continuing to use the machine itself, the firm is implicitly forgoing the rental rate someone else would be willing to pay to use it. This rental rate for one machine-hour will be denoted by v.[2]

Costs of Entrepreneurial Services

The owner of a business is a residual claimant who is entitled to whatever extra revenues or losses are left after paying all input costs. To an accountant these would be called "profits" (which might be either positive or negative). Econo-

---

[2]In most other texts, the symbol r is chosen to represent the rental rate on capital. Since this variable is often confused with the related though distinct concept of the interest rate, an alternative symbol was chosen here. The exact relationship between v and the interest rate is examined in Chapter 23.

mists, however, ask whether owners (or "entrepreneurs") also encounter opportunity costs by being engaged in a particular business. If so, their entrepreneurial services should be considered an input to the firm, and some cost should be imputed to that input. For example, suppose a highly skilled computer programmer starts a software firm with the idea of keeping any (accounting) profits that might be generated. Then the programmer's time is clearly an input to the firm, and a cost should be imputed for it. Perhaps the wage that the programmer might command if he or she worked for someone else could be used for that purpose. Hence, some part of the accounting profits generated by the firm would be categorized as entrepreneurial costs by economists. Residual economic profits would be smaller than accounting profits and might be negative if the programmer's opportunity costs exceeded the accounting profits being earned by the business.

Economic Costs   In this book, not surprisingly, we shall use economists' definition of cost:

Definition:

Economic Cost

The *economic cost* of any input is the payment required to keep that input in its present employment. Equivalently, the economic cost of an input is the remuneration the input would receive in its best alternative employment.

Use of this definition is not meant to imply that accountants' concepts are irrelevant to economic behavior. Indeed, bookkeeping methods are integrally important to any manager's decision-making process because they can greatly affect the rate of taxation to be applied against profits. They also have the desirable property of being readily available sources of data. Since the "economic costs" of General Motors are never calculated (perhaps not even unambiguously defined), it is usually necessary to use some accounting concepts for empirical work. Economists' definitions, however, do have the desirable features of being broadly applicable to all firms and of forming a conceptually consistent system.[3] They therefore are best suited for a general theoretical analysis.

Two Simplifying Assumptions   Two simplifications initially will be made in this chapter about the inputs a firm uses. First, it generally will be assumed, as before, that there are only two inputs: homogeneous labor (L, measured in labor-hours) and homogeneous capital (K, measured in machine-hours). Entrepreneurial costs will be assumed to be included in capital costs. That is, it will be assumed that the primary opportunity costs faced by a firm's owner are those associated with the capital that the owner provides.

---

[3] In fact, in recent years accountants have moved toward economists' definitions. For example, the conceptual model of economic costs has been applied to several topics in depreciation accounting and to the calculation of the profits of life insurance companies.

A second simplification will be that the inputs to the firm are hired in perfectly competitive markets. Firms can buy (or sell) all the labor or capital services they want at the prevailing rental rates (w and v). In graphic terms the supply curve for these resources that the firm faces is horizontal at the prevailing factor prices. Both w and v are treated as "parameters" in the firm's decisions; there is nothing the firm can do to affect them. These conditions will be relaxed in later chapters (notably Chapter 21), but for the moment the perfectly competitive assumption is a convenient and useful one to make.

Economic Profits and Cost Minimization

Given these simplifying assumptions, total costs for the firm during a period can be represented by

$$\text{total costs} = TC = wL + vK, \tag{11.1}$$

where, as before, L and K represent input usage during the period. Assuming the firm produces only one output, its total revenues are given by the price of its product (P) times its total output [$Q = f(K, L)$ where $f(K, L)$ is the firm's production function]. Economic profits (π) are then the difference between total revenues and total economic costs:

Definition:

Economic Profits

Economic profits (π) are the difference between a firm's total revenues and its total costs.

$$\pi = \text{total revenue} - \text{total cost} = PQ - wL - vK$$
$$= Pf(K, L) - wL - vK \tag{11.2}$$

In general, then, Equation 11.2 shows that the economic profits obtained by a firm are simply a function of the amount of capital and labor employed. If, as we will assume in many places in this book, the firm seeks maximum profits, we might study its behavior by examining how K and L are chosen so as to maximize Equation 11.2. This would, in turn, lead to a theory of the "derived demand" for capital and labor inputs—a topic we take up explicitly in Chapter 21.

Here, however, we wish to develop a theory of costs that is somewhat more general and might apply to firms that are not necessarily profit maximizers. Hence we begin our study of costs by finessing a discussion of output choice for the moment. That is, we assume that for some reason the firm has decided to produce a particular output level (say, Q_0). The firm's revenues are therefore fixed at PQ_0. Now we wish to examine how the firm might choose to produce Q_0 at minimal costs. The precise connection between such a cost-minimizing choice and the assumption of profit maximization will be illustrated in Chapter 12.

COST-MINIMIZING INPUT CHOICES

Given the previous discussion, the firm's goal is to choose K and L so as to minimize the total costs (Equation 11.1) associated with producing Q_0. Mathematically, this is a constrained minimization problem. But, before proceeding with a rigorous solution, it might be useful to state the result to be derived with an intuitive argument. In order to minimize the cost of producing a given level of output, a firm should choose that point on the isoquant for that level of output at which the rate of technical substitution of L for K is equal to the ratio w/v: It should equate the rate at which K can be traded for L in the productive process to the rate at which they can be traded in the marketplace. Suppose that this were not true. In particular, suppose that the firm were producing output level Q_0 using $K = 10$, $L = 10$, and assume that the RTS was 2 at this point. Assume also that $w = \$1$, $v = \$1$, and hence that $w/v = 1$ (which is unequal to 2). At this input combination, the cost of producing Q_0 is \$20. It is easy to show this is not the minimal input cost. Q_0 can also be produced using $K = 8$ and $L = 11$; we can give up two units of K and keep output constant at Q_0 by adding one unit of L. But at this input combination the cost of producing Q_0 is \$19, and hence the initial input combination was not optimal. A proof similar to this one can be demonstrated whenever the RTS and the ratio of the input costs differ.

Mathematical Analysis

Mathematically, we seek to minimize total costs, given $Q = f(K, L) = Q_0$. Setting up the Lagrangian expression

$$\mathcal{L} = wL + vK + \lambda[Q_0 - f(K, L)], \tag{11.3}$$

the first-order conditions for a constrained minimum are

$$\frac{\partial \mathcal{L}}{\partial L} = w - \lambda \frac{\partial f}{\partial L} = 0$$

$$\frac{\partial \mathcal{L}}{\partial K} = v - \lambda \frac{\partial f}{\partial K} = 0 \tag{11.4}$$

$$\frac{\partial \mathcal{L}}{\partial \lambda} = Q_0 - f(K, L) = 0$$

or, using the first two equations,

$$\frac{w}{v} = \frac{\partial f/\partial L}{\partial f/\partial K} = RTS \quad (L \text{ for } K). \tag{11.5}$$

This says that the cost-minimizing firm should equate the RTS for the two inputs to the ratio of their prices.[4]

Graphic Analysis

The result is shown graphically in Figure 11.1. Given the output isoquant Q_0, we wish to find the least costly point on the isoquant. From Equation 11.1 all lines of equal cost are parallel straight lines with slopes $-w/v$. Three lines of

[4] Equation 11.4 also shows that

$$\frac{1}{\lambda} = \frac{\partial f/\partial L}{w} = \frac{\partial f/\partial K}{v}.$$

This means that the marginal productivity per dollar spent should be the same for all inputs used. In other words, the ratio of marginal benefit (that is, increased output) to marginal cost should be the same for all inputs actually employed. If an input did not meet this benefit-cost test, it would not be used.

Figure 11.1   *Minimization of Costs Given* Q = Q₀

A firm is assumed to choose *K* and *L* to minimize total costs. The condition for this minimization is that the rate at which *K* and *L* can be traded technically (while keeping Q = Q₀) should be equal to the rate at which these inputs can be traded in the market. In other words, the *RTS* (of *L* for *K*) should be set equal to the price ratio *w/v*. This tangency is shown in the figure; costs are minimized at *TC₁* by choosing inputs *K** and *L**.

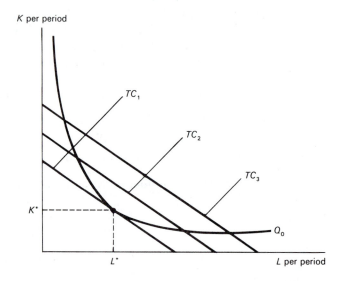

equal total cost are shown in Figure 11.1: $TC_1 < TC_2 < TC_3$. It is clear from the figure that the minimum total cost for producing Q_0 is given by TC_1, where the total cost curve is just tangent to the isoquant. The cost-minimizing input combination is L^*, K^*. This combination will be a true minimum if the isoquant is convex (if the *RTS* diminishes for decreases in K/L). Our mathematical and graphic analyses arrive at the same conclusion:

Optimization Principle:

Cost Minimization
In order to minimize the cost of any given level of input (Q_0), the firm should produce at that point on the Q_0 isoquant for which the *RTS* (of *L* for *K*) is equal to the ratio of the inputs' rental prices (*w/v*).

Dual Problem: Output Maximization

A result identical to that just derived can be obtained by considering the dual formulation of the firm's primal cost-minimization problem: For a given total cost of inputs (say, TC_1), maximize the level of output. Mathematically, the Lagrangian expression for this problem is

$$\mathcal{L}^D = f(K, L) + \lambda^D(TC_1 - wL - vK),$$

(11.6)

Figure 11.2   *Dual Output-Maximization Problem*

The dual approach to cost minimization is for the firm to maximize output for a given expenditure of total cost (TC_1). Under this approach too, the firm chooses the input combination L^*, K^* for which the *RTS* is equal to the ratio of the input's rental rates, *w/v*.

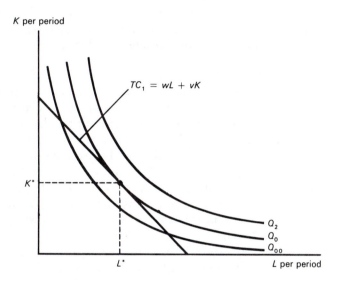

K per period

$TC_1 = wL + vK$

K^*

Q_2
Q_0
Q_{00}

L^* *L* per period

and it is a simple matter to show that the first-order conditions for this problem are identical to those already derived in Equation 11.5. A graphic demonstration is provided in Figure 11.2. There the maximum output attainable with total cost TC_1 is Q_0, which results when the input combination L^*, K^* is utilized. All other combinations of inputs that lie along TC_1 are below the Q_0 isoquant and hence yield less output than does this optimal combination. Therefore the solution derived in Figure 11.2 is identical to that in Figure 11.1. For most of our subsequent analysis we will make use of the primal cost-minimization approach, but at times we will rely on the dual formulation of the problem to provide insights into the economic consequences of cost minimization.

Derived Demand for Inputs

Figure 11.2 exhibits the formal similarity between the firm's cost-minimization problem and the individual's utility-maximization problem. In both cases we took prices as fixed parameters and derived the tangency conditions. In Chapter 5 we then asked the comparative statics question of how the utility-maximizing choice of goods would change if a price were to change. The analysis of this change permitted the construction of the familiar downward-sloping demand curve. An interesting question is whether the firm's demand for an input could be developed analogously here. Could we change some input price (change the slope of the *TC* curves) and then trace out the effects of this price change on the quantity of the factor demanded? The analogy to the individual's utility-maximization process can be misleading at this point. In order to analyze what happens to K^*, say, as v changes, we also have to know what happens to Q_0. The demand for K is a *derived demand*, based on the demand for the firm's output. We cannot answer questions about K^* without looking at the interaction of supply and demand in the goods market. Although the analogy to the theory of individual behavior is useful in pointing out basic similarities, it is not an exact analogy—the derivation of a firm's demand for an input involves additional issues about the firm's desired output level that do not arise in the consumer's problem.

The Firm's Expansion Path

A firm can perform an analysis such as that presented above for each level of output: For each Q it finds the input choice that minimizes the cost of producing Q. If input costs (w and v) remain constant for all amounts the firm may demand, we can easily trace out this locus of cost-minimizing choices. This procedure is shown in Figure 11.3. The line $0E$ records the cost-minimizing tangencies for successively higher levels of Q. For example, the minimum cost for producing output level Q_1 is given by TC_1 and inputs K_1 and L_1 are used. Other tangencies in the figure can be interpreted in a similar way. The locus of these tangencies is called the firm's *expansion path*, because it records how input usage expands as output expands while holding the prices of the inputs constant.

As Figure 11.3 shows, the expansion path need not be a straight line. The use of some inputs may increase faster than others as output expands. Which

Figure 11.3 *The Firm's Expansion Path*

The firm's expansion path is the locus of cost-minimizing tangencies. Assuming fixed input prices, the curve shows how inputs increase as output increases.

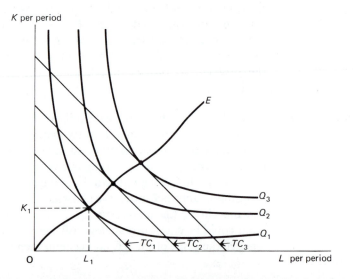

Figure 11.4   *Factor Inferiority*

With this particular set of isoquants, labor is an inferior input, since less *L* is chosen as output expands beyond Q_2.

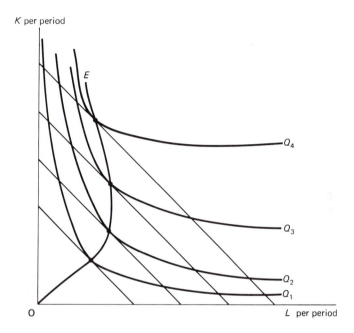

inputs expand more rapidly will depend on the shape of the production iso-quants. Since cost minimization requires that the *RTS* always be set equal to the ratio *w/v*, and since the *w/v* ratio is assumed to be constant, the shape of the expansion path will be determined by where a particular *RTS* occurs on successively higher isoquants. If the production function exhibits constant re-turns to scale (or, more generally, if it is homothetic), the expansion path will be a straight line since, as we showed in Chapter 10, the *RTS* depends only on the ratio of *K* to *L*.

It would seem reasonable to assume that the expansion path will be posi-tively sloped; that is, successively higher output levels will require more of both inputs. This need not be the case, however, as Figure 11.4 illustrates. Increases of output beyond Q_2 actually cause the quantity of labor used to decrease. In this range, labor would be said to be an *inferior input*. The occurrence of inferior inputs is then a theoretical possibility that may happen, even when isoquants have their usual convex shape.

Much theoretical discussion has centered on the analysis of factor inferi-ority. Whether inferiority is likely to occur in real-world production functions is a difficult empirical question to answer. It seems unlikely that such com-prehensive magnitudes as "capital" and "labor" could be inferior, but a finer classification of inputs may bring inferiority to light. For example, the use of shovels may decline as production of building foundations (and the use of backhoes) increases. In this book we shall not be particularly concerned with the analytical complications raised by this possibility, although results for such inputs will be mentioned in a few places.

Numerical
Example

Suppose again that the hourly production of hamburgers (Q) depends on the number of grills (K) and workers (L) hired each hour according to the Cobb-Douglas production function

$$Q = 10K^{1/2}L^{1/2} = 10\sqrt{KL}. \tag{11.7}$$

If grills can be rented for v per hour and workers can be hired at w per hour, total costs of hamburger production are given by

$$TC = vK + wL. \tag{11.8}$$

Suppose this burger emporium wished to produce, say, 40 hamburgers per hour. Then the relevant Lagrangian expression for the firm's cost-minimization problem would be

$$\mathcal{L} = vK + wL + \lambda(40 - 10K^{1/2}L^{1/2}). \tag{11.9}$$

First-order conditions for a minimum are

$$\frac{\partial \mathcal{L}}{\partial K} = v - \lambda 5(L/K)^{1/2} = 0$$

$$\frac{\partial \mathcal{L}}{\partial L} = w - \lambda 5(K/L)^{1/2} = 0 \tag{11.10}$$

$$\frac{\partial \mathcal{L}}{\partial \lambda} = 40 - 10K^{1/2}L^{1/2} = 0.$$

Dividing the first of these equations by the second yields

$$\frac{v}{w} = \frac{L}{K}. \tag{11.11}$$

If, for example, w and v were each $4 per hour, Equation 11.11 indicates that the firm should use equal amounts of K and L. In this case $K = 4$, $L = 4$ would be sufficient to produce 40 hamburgers. Total costs of the 40 hamburgers would be $32. Any other input combination that can also produce 40 hamburgers has a greater total cost. For example, $K = 8$, $L = 2$ will also yield an output of 40, but in this case total cost is $40.

Notice that in this problem the production function exhibits constant returns to scale so that the expansion path is a straight line. Equation 11.11 shows the equation for this straight line. If $w = v$, the firm will always choose $K = L$ for cost minimization. Of course, if $w \neq v$, this would not be so although the expansion path would still be linear. If, for example, grills rented for $12 per hour and wages were $4, Equation 11.11 indicates that the expansion path would be those combinations of grills and workers for which $L/K =$

3. The firm would produce hamburgers using relatively more of the less expensive input.

COST FUNCTIONS

With the construction of the cost-minimizing expansion path, we are in a position to examine the firm's overall cost structure. To do so it will be convenient to use the expansion path solutions to derive the total cost function:

Definition:

Total Cost Function

The *total cost function* shows that for any set of input costs and for any output level, the minimum total cost incurred by the firm is

$$TC = TC(v, w, Q).\qquad (11.12)$$

Figure 11.3 makes clear that total costs increase as output, Q, increases. We will begin by analyzing this relationship between total cost and output while holding input prices fixed. Then we will consider how a change in an input price shifts the expansion path and its related cost functions.

Average and Marginal Cost Functions

Although the total cost function provides complete information about the output-cost relationship, it is often convenient to analyze costs on a per unit of output basis, since that approach corresponds more closely to our analysis of demand, which focused on the price per unit of a commodity. Two different unit cost measures are widely used in economics: (1) average cost, which is the cost per unit of output; and (2) marginal cost, which is the cost of one more unit of output. The relationship of these concepts to the total cost function is described in the following definitions:

Definitions:

Average and Marginal Cost Functions

The *average cost function* (AC) is found by computing total costs per unit of output:

$$\text{average cost} = AC(v, w, Q) = \frac{TC(v, w, Q)}{Q}.\qquad (11.13)$$

The *marginal cost function* (MC) is found by computing the change in total costs for a change in output produced:

$$\text{marginal cost} = MC(v, w, Q) = \frac{\partial TC(v, w, Q)}{\partial Q}.\qquad (11.14)$$

Notice that in these definitions, average and marginal costs depend both on the level of output being produced and on the prices of inputs. In many places throughout this book we will graph simple two-dimensional relationships between costs and output. As Equations 11.12, 11.13, and 11.14 make clear, all such graphs are drawn on the assumption that the prices of inputs remain

Figure 11.5   *Total, Average, and Marginal Cost Curves for the Constant Returns-to-Scale Case*

In (a) total costs are proportional to output level. Average and marginal costs, as shown in (b), are equal and constant for all output levels.

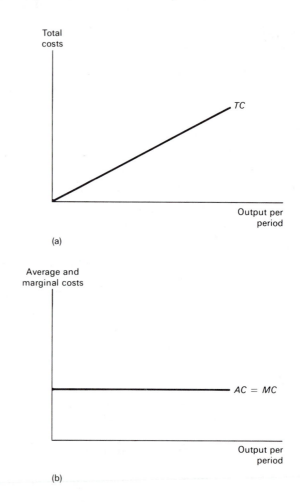

(a)

(b)

constant. If input prices change, cost curves generally will shift to new positions. Later in this chapter we will explore the likely direction and size of such shifts. For now, however, we hold input prices constant.

Graphic Analysis of Total Costs

Figures 11.5a and 11.6a illustrate two possible shapes for the relationship between total cost and the level of the firm's output. In Figure 11.5a total cost is simply proportional to output. Such a situation would arise if the underlying production function for Q exhibits constant returns to scale. In that case, suppose K_1 units of capital input and L_1 units of labor input are required to produce one unit of output. Then

Figure 11.6   *Total, Average, and Marginal Cost Curves for the Cubic Total Cost Curve Case*

If the total cost curve has the cubic shape shown in (a), average and marginal cost curves will be U-shaped. In (b) the marginal cost curve passes through the low point of the average cost curve at output level Q^*.

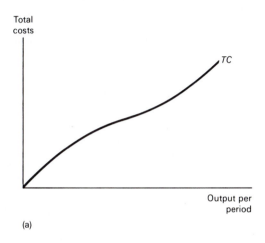

(a)

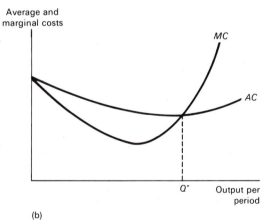

(b)

$$TC(Q = 1) = vK_1 + wL_1. \tag{11.15}$$

To produce m units of output then requires mK_1 units of capital and mL_1 units of labor because of the constant returns-to-scale assumption.[5] Hence

---

[5] The input combination mL_1, mK_1 minimizes the cost of producing m units of output, since the ratio of the inputs is still K_1/L_1 and the *RTS* for a constant returns-to-scale production function depends only on that ratio. Hence the *RTS* for the new input combination will equal the ratio w/v (as required for cost minimization), since the original input combination was assumed to minimize cost also.

$$TC \ (Q = m) \ = vmK_1 + wmL_1 = m(vK_1 + wL_1)$$

$$= m \cdot TC \ (Q = 1),$$

(11.16)

and the proportionality between output and cost is established.

The situation in Figure 11.6a is somewhat more complicated. There it is assumed that initially the TC curve is concave; although initially costs rise rapidly for increases in Q, that rate of increase slows as Q expands into the midrange of output. Beyond this middle range, however, the TC curve becomes convex, and costs begin to rise progressively more rapidly. One possible reason for such a shape for the total cost curve is that there is some third factor of production (say, the services of an entrepreneur) that is fixed as capital and labor usage expands. In this case, the initial concave section of the TC curve might be explained by the increasingly optimal usage of the entrepreneur's services—he or she needs a moderate level of production to utilize his or her skills fully. Beyond the point of inflexion, however, the entrepreneur becomes overworked in attempting to coordinate production, and diminishing returns set in. Hence total costs rise rapidly.

A variety of other explanations have been offered for the cubic-type total cost curve in Figure 11.6, but we will not examine them here. Ultimately, the shape of the TC curve is an empirical question that can only be determined by examining real-world data. Instead our purpose here is to investigate the theoretical consequences of such a shape, and we now turn to that topic.

Graphic Analysis of Average and Marginal Costs

Information from the total cost curves can be used to construct the average and marginal cost curves shown in Figures 11.5b and 11.6b. For the constant returns-to-scale case (Figure 11.5), this is quite simple. Since total costs are proportional to output, average and marginal costs are constant and equal for all levels of output.[6] These costs are shown by the horizontal line $AC = MC$ in Figure 11.5b.

For the cubic total cost curve case (Figure 11.6), computation of the average and marginal cost curves requires some geometric intuition. As the definition in Equation 11.14 makes clear, marginal cost is simply the slope of the TC curve. Hence, because of the assumed shape of the curve, the MC curve is U-shaped, with MC falling over the concave portion of the TC curve and rising beyond the point of inflexion. Since the slope is always positive, however, MC is always greater than zero. Average costs (AC) start out being equal to marginal cost for the "first" unit of output.[7] As Q expands, AC exceeds MC, how-

---

[6] Mathematically, since $TC = aQ$ (where a is the cost of 1 unit of output),

$$AC = \frac{TC}{Q} = a = \frac{\partial TC}{\partial Q} = MC.$$

[7] Technically, $AC = MC$ at $Q = 0$. This can be shown by L'Hopital's rule, which states that if $f(a) = g(a) = 0$,

$$\lim_{x \to a} \frac{f(x)}{g(x)} = \lim_{x \to a} \frac{f'(x)}{g'(x)}.$$

ever, since *AC* reflects both the marginal cost of the last unit produced and the somewhat higher marginal costs of the previously produced units. So long as *AC* > *MC*, average costs must be falling. Because the lower costs of the newly produced units are below average cost, they continue to pull average costs downward. Eventually, however, marginal costs start to rise and eventually (at Q^*), they equal average cost. Beyond this point *MC* > *AC*, and hence average costs must be rising because they are being pulled upward by increasingly higher marginal costs. Consequently, we have shown that the *AC* curve also has a U-shape and that it reaches a low point at Q^*, where *AC* and *MC* intersect.[8] In empirical studies of cost functions, there is considerable interest in this point of minimum average cost, since it reflects the optimal scale of operations for the particular production process being examined. The point also is theoretically important because of the role it plays in perfectly competitive price determination in the long run (see Chapter 14).

CHANGES IN INPUT PRICES

Thus far in our analysis of costs, we have held input prices constant so that we could study the two-dimensional relationship between costs and quantity produced. When input prices change, the firm's cost-minimizing expansion path will change, and hence the cost curves that are based on that path will shift. In this section we will examine such shifts. For simplicity we will primarily study only increases in input prices, although analogous results would hold for declines in such prices.

Homogeneity

A first obvious result we can demonstrate is that the total cost function is homogeneous of degree 1 in input prices. That is, if all input prices were to increase in the same proportion, *t*, the total costs for producing any given output level would also be multiplied by *t*. The reason for this result is that such a simultaneous increase in input prices does not change the ratio of the inputs' prices. Hence the cost-minimizing input choice is not affected by such

---

In this case $TC = 0$ at $Q = 0$, so that

$$\lim_{Q \to 0} AC = \lim_{Q \to 0} \frac{TC}{Q} = \lim_{Q \to 0} \frac{\partial TC/\partial Q}{1} = \lim_{Q \to 0} MC$$

or

$$AC = MC \text{ at } Q = 0,$$

which was to be shown.

[8] Mathematically, we can find the minimum *AC* by setting its derivative equal to 0:

$$\frac{\partial AC}{\partial Q} = \frac{\partial \frac{TC}{Q}}{\partial Q} = \frac{Q \cdot \frac{\partial TC}{\partial Q} - TC \cdot 1}{Q^2} = \frac{Q \cdot MC - TC}{Q^2} = 0$$

or

$$Q \cdot MC - TC = 0 \quad \text{or} \quad MC = TC/Q = AC.$$

an increase, and the firm's expansion path remains unaffected. If, prior to the increase in input prices, the firm employed the combination L_1, K_1 to produce Q_1, total costs would have been

$$TC_1 = vK_1 + wL_1. \tag{11.17}$$

If both v and w rise by the same fraction, t, the firm will continue to use L_1, K_1 to produce Q_1, but now total costs (TC_1') will be

$$TC_1' = tvK_1 + twL_1 = t(vK_1 + wL_1) = tTC_1, \tag{11.18}$$

which is what we wished to show.

Because the total cost function is homogeneous of degree 1 in all input prices, the average and marginal cost functions based on that total cost function also will be homogeneous of degree 1 for such price changes. If, as in Equation 11.18, we let costs following the input price change be represented by primes and assume all input prices increase by t, we have

$$TC' = tTC, \tag{11.19}$$

$$AC' = \frac{TC'}{Q} = t\frac{TC}{Q} = tAC,$$

and

$$MC' = \frac{\partial TC'}{\partial Q} = t\frac{\partial TC}{\partial Q} = tMC. \tag{11.20}$$

One consequence of these results is that in a "pure" inflationary situation (one in which all prices rise at the same rate), firms' input costs will all rise at the same rate, and there will be no incentives for the firms to alter their input choices (or, as we will see, to alter their output choice).

Change in the Price of One Input

If only one input price changes, the story is more complicated. Because such a price change alters the ratios of the inputs' prices, the firm's cost-minimizing choice of inputs will be affected and a new expansion path must be derived. Here we will examine three questions about this kind of change: (1) the qualitative direction of the effect on total, average, and marginal costs; (2) the degree of substitution among inputs introduced by such a change; and (3) the quantitative effect on total, average, and marginal costs.

Direction of Effect

An increase in the price of an input must increase the total cost for any output level (or, at least, leave TC unaffected). If the input substitutions induced by the rise in the cost of one input actually caused total costs to fall, then the firm would not have been minimizing costs in the first place, since the new input combination chosen would have been even less expensive prior to the price rise. Hence, one implication of the cost-minimization assumption is that a rise in an input cost increases total cost.[9] A similar argument holds for average costs. Since the total cost of any output level has risen, average costs for any output level (which are simply given by TC/Q) must also have risen. Again, the assumption of cost minimization provides an unambiguous result.

The situation for marginal costs is made somewhat complicated by the possibility that the input being examined may be inferior. In this (admittedly rare) case, an increase in the inferior input's price will cause firms to use relatively less of that input and, surprisingly, that will reduce marginal costs. The precise reason for this perverse result need not detain us here, although the persistent reader may wish to pursue the matter independently. When the input being examined is not inferior, it is a simple matter to show that an increase in its price will raise marginal cost as well.[10]

Input Substitution

As we remarked previously, a change in the price of an input will cause a cost-minimizing firm to alter its input choices. One way to measure this change is

---

[9] This can be shown formally by the envelope theorem. Remember that the firm's problem is to minimize $TC = vK + wL$, subject to $f(K, L) = Q_0$. The Lagrangian expression for this problem is

$$\mathcal{L} = vK + wL + \lambda[Q_0 - f(K, L)].$$

Now the envelope theorem states that at the minimum expenditure level,

$$\frac{\partial TC}{\partial v} = \frac{\partial \mathcal{L}}{\partial v} = K > 0,$$

and

$$\frac{\partial TC}{\partial w} = \frac{\partial \mathcal{L}}{\partial w} = L > 0.$$

These results not only show that an increase in input prices will increase total cost but also introduce again Shephard's lemma (see footnote 6 of Chapter 5), which in this case states that the input demand function can be found from the total cost function by partial differentiation. Since Q is held constant in this derivation, these input demand functions also are constant output demand functions. We will examine these in detail in Chapter 21. The Extension problems to this chapter also make use of this result to study input substitution.

[10] Again, the envelope theorem can be employed. Making use of the Lagrangian expression in footnote 9 (or Equation 11.2), we have the important result that

$$MC = \frac{\partial TC}{\partial Q} = \frac{\partial \mathcal{L}}{\partial Q} = \lambda.$$

As in all constrained optimization problems, the Lagrangian multiplier shows the change in the objective function (here TC) with respect to the constraint (Q). For any input (say, capital),

$$\frac{\partial MC}{\partial v} = \frac{\partial^2 \mathcal{L}}{\partial Q \partial v} = \frac{\partial^2 \mathcal{L}}{\partial v \partial Q} = \frac{\partial K}{\partial Q},$$

which is positive or negative, depending on whether K is a normal or an inferior input (see Figures 11.3 and 11.4). For a more detailed discussion, see C. E. Ferguson, *The Neoclassical Theory of Production and Distribution* (Cambridge: Cambridge University Press, 1969), pp. 136–153.

to examine how the ratio of input usage (K/L) changes in response to a change in w/v, while holding Q constant. That is, we wish to examine the derivative

$$\frac{d\left(\dfrac{K}{L}\right)}{d\left(\dfrac{w}{v}\right)} \tag{11.21}$$

along an isoquant.

Putting this in proportional terms as

$$s = \frac{d\ K/L}{d\ w/v} \cdot \frac{w/v}{K/L} \tag{11.22}$$

gives an alternative and more intuitive definition of the elasticity of substitution.[11] In the two-input case, s must be nonnegative: An increase in w/v will be met by an increase in K/L (or, in the limiting fixed-proportions case, K/L will stay constant). Large values of s indicate that firms change their input proportions significantly in response to changes in input prices, whereas low values indicate that changes in input prices have relatively little effect.

When there are only two inputs, the substitution elasticity defined in Equation 11.22 is identical to that defined in Chapter 10 (see Equation 10.28). This can be easily demonstrated by remembering that a cost-minimizing firm will equate its RTS (of L for K) to the input price ratio w/v. The great advantage of the definition given in Equation 11.22 is that it can be more easily generalized to the many-input case than can the definition of the previous chapter. Specifically,

---

Definition:

Partial Elasticity of Substitution (s_{ij})
The *partial elasticity of substitution* between two inputs (X_i and X_j) with prices w_i and w_j is given by

$$s_{ij} = \frac{\partial\ X_i/X_j}{\partial\ w_j/w_i} \cdot \frac{w_j/w_i}{X_i/X_j}, \tag{11.23}$$

where output and all other input prices are held constant.

The word *partial* is used in this definition to differentiate the concept from the production function–based definition developed in Chapter 10. In fact, s_{ij} is a very flexible concept because it permits the firm to alter the usage of inputs other than X_i or X_j when input prices change, whereas other input usage was held constant in our prior definition. Suppose, as in the application in Chapter

---

[11] This definition is usually attributed to R. G. D. Allen, who developed it in an alternative form in his *Mathematical Analysis for Economists* (New York: St. Martin's Press, 1938), pp. 504–509.

10, that energy prices rise and we wish to know how this affects the ratio of energy to capital input while holding output constant. Although we would expect energy input to fall, it is possible that the firm will substitute a third input, say labor, for *both* energy and capital so that both inputs may fall. Hence, depending on the specific sizes of these changes, it is possible that the energy-capital ratio may in fact rise. In such a case we might call energy and capital "complements," because of the way their joint usage relates to labor input. Although we will not examine the implications of these possibilities for production and cost theory here, the Extension problems in this chapter show how s_{ij} can be calculated if the cost function is known. The concept is also quite useful for studying the derived demand for inputs, as we will show in Chapter 21.

Quantitative Size of Shifts in Cost Curves

We have already shown that increases in an input price will raise total, average, and (except in the inferior input case) marginal costs. We are now in a position to judge the extent of such increases. First, and most obviously, the increase in costs will be influenced importantly by the relative significance of the input in the production process. If an input constitutes a large fraction of total costs, an increase in its price will raise costs significantly. A rise in the wage rate would sharply increase home-builders' costs because labor is a major input in construction. On the other hand, a price rise for a relatively minor input will have a small cost impact. An increase in nail prices will not raise home costs significantly.

A less obvious determinant of the extent of cost increases is input substitutability. If firms can easily substitute another input for the one that has risen in price, there may be little increase in costs. Increases in copper prices in the late 1960s, for example, had little impact on electric utilities' costs of distributing electricity because they found they could easily substitute aluminum for copper cables. Alternatively, if the firm finds it difficult or impossible to substitute for the input that has become more costly, costs may rise rapidly. The cost of gold jewelry, along with the price of gold, rose rapidly during the early 1970s because there was simply no substitute for the raw input.

Although it is possible to give a precise mathematical statement of the quantitative sizes of all of these effects, to do so would risk further cluttering the book with symbols.[12] For our purposes it is sufficient to rely on the previous intuitive discussion. This should serve as a reminder that changes in the price of an input will have the definite effect of shifting firms' cost curves, with the size of the shift depending on the relative importance of the input and the substitution possibilities that are available.

Numerical Example

Returning to our hamburger-grilling example, remember that cost minimization requires

---

[12] For a relatively complete statement, see Ferguson, *Neoclassical Theory of Production and Distribution*, pp. 154–160.

$$\frac{v}{w} = \frac{L}{K}. \tag{11.24}$$

To compute the total cost function implied by this condition requires that we use Equation 11.24 together with the production function to express total costs as a function of Q, v, and w. Sometimes that can involve quite a lot of tedious algebra, but in this case it is a relatively simple manipulation. Given the hamburger production function,

$$Q = 10K^{1/2}L^{1/2}, \tag{11.25}$$

division by K yields

$$\frac{Q}{K} = 10\left(\frac{L}{K}\right)^{1/2} \tag{11.26}$$

and, in view of Equation 11.24,

$$\frac{Q}{K} = 10\left(\frac{v}{w}\right)^{1/2} \tag{11.27}$$

Hence

$$K = \frac{Q}{10}w^{1/2}v^{-1/2} \tag{11.28}$$

and

$$vK = \frac{Q}{10}w^{1/2}v^{1/2}. \tag{11.29}$$

A similar chain of substitutions yields

$$wL = \frac{Q}{10}w^{1/2}v^{1/2} \tag{11.30}$$

and, since

$$TC = vK + wL, \tag{11.31}$$

we have

$$TC = \frac{Q}{5}w^{1/2}v^{1/2}. \tag{11.32}$$

This is the total cost function for hamburger production. For specific input prices the function implies a simple relationship between TC and Q. If $w = v = \$4$, for example,

$$TC = \frac{4Q}{5} = .8Q. \tag{11.33}$$

As before, it costs \$32 to produce 40 hamburgers if costs are minimized. Total costs of any other level of production can also be calculated quickly from Equation 11.33.

Because of the constant returns-to-scale nature of the hamburger production function, average and marginal costs are constant (and equal) for all possible output levels:

$$AC = \frac{TC}{Q} = .8 \tag{11.34}$$

$$MC = \frac{\partial TC}{\partial Q} = .8. \tag{11.35}$$

The average and marginal costs of producing a hamburger are always $.80.

If an input price should change, the firm would use K and L in different proportions, and this changed expansion path would be reflected by a shifting cost function. When $v = \$9$ and $w = \$4$, for example,

$$TC = \frac{Q}{5} w^{1/2}v^{1/2} = \frac{Q6}{5} = 1.2Q. \tag{11.36}$$

Hence the average and marginal costs of each hamburger have increased to $1.20. Knowing the total cost function makes it unnecessary to recalculate cost-minimizing input choices—this is done "automatically" once the total cost function is computed. The total cost function (and its related average and marginal cost functions) already incorporates the cost-minimization assumption.

SHORT-RUN, LONG-RUN DISTINCTION

It is customary in economics to make a distinction between the "short run" and the "long run." Although no very precise chronological definition can be provided for these terms, the general purpose of the distinction is to differentiate between a short period during which economic actors have only limited flexibility in their actions and a longer period that provides greater freedom. One area of study in which this distinction is quite important is in the theory of the firm and its costs, since economists are interested in examining supply reactions during different potential time intervals. In the remainder of the analysis in this chapter, we will examine the implications of such differential response periods.

There are several possible ways of introducing the short-run, long-run distinction into the analysis of the firm we have presented thus far. Probably the easiest method (and the one we shall use here) is to assume that one of the productive inputs is held constant in the short run. Specifically, we shall assume that capital input is held constant at a level of K_1 and that (in the short run) the firm is only free to vary its labor input. Implicitly, we are assuming that alterations in the level of capital input are infinitely costly in the short run. As a result of this assumption, we may write the short-run production function as

$$Q = f(K_1, L), \tag{11.37}$$

where this notation explicitly shows that capital inputs may not vary. Of course, the level of Q still may be changed by the firm altering its use of labor. We have already studied this possibility in Chapter 10, when we examined the marginal productivity of labor. Here we are interested in analyzing the way in which changes in a firm's output level in the short run are related to changes in total costs.

Before turning to this question, we should comment on the method of analysis we have chosen. It is obvious that any firm uses far more than two inputs in its production process. The level of usage of some of these inputs may be changed on rather short notice. Firms may ask workers to work overtime hours, hire part-time replacements from an employment agency, or rent equipment (such as power tools or automobiles) from some other firm. It may take a somewhat longer time for the level of usage of other inputs to be adjusted; for example, to hire new, full-time workers is a relatively time-consuming (and costly) process. Similarly, ordering new machines designed according to unique specifications may involve a considerable time lag. At the most lengthy extreme, new factories can be built, new managers can be recruited and trained, and raw material supplies can be discovered and extracted. To cover all such variations of input types in any detail is an impossibility. Consequently, we will proceed by using only the two-input model we have been analyzing and will hold the level of capital input fixed. Such a treatment should not be taken to imply that in some way labor is a more flexible input than capital. As we have just pointed out, this need not be the case. Rather, all we wish to do is to make a distinction between fixed and variable inputs, and this approach will enable us to do so. We could substitute any other appropriate input names for "capital" and "labor" in the discussion that follows.

Short-Run Total Costs

Total cost for the firm continues to be defined as

$$TC = vK + wL \tag{11.38}$$

for our short-run analysis, but now capital input is fixed at K_1. To denote this fact, we will write

$$STC(K_1) = vK_1 + wL, \tag{11.39}$$

where the "S" indicates that we are analyzing short-run costs with the level of capital input fixed (at K_1). Throughout our analysis we will use this method to indicate short-run costs, while the long-run costs derived previously will be denoted by TC, AC, and MC.

The two types of input costs in Equation 11.39 are given special names. The term vK_1 is referred to as (short-run) *fixed costs;* since K_1 is constant, these costs will not change in the short run. The term wL is referred to as (short-run) *variable costs,* since labor input can indeed be varied in the short run. Using the symbols $SFC(K_1)$ for short-run fixed costs and $SVC(K_1)$ for short-run variable costs, we have

$$SFC(K_1) = vK_1$$

$$SVC(K_1) = wL$$

and therefore

$$STC(K_1) = SFC(K_1) + SVC(K_1). \tag{11.40}$$

More generally, we have

Figure 11.7   *Fixed and Variable Costs in the Short Run*

The curve $SFC(K_1)$ in (a) shows that fixed costs do not vary in the short run. They are determined by the amount of fixed input of capital (here K_1) being used. Variable costs do change as the output increases. The shape of the curve in (b) assumes that initially labor exhibits an increasing marginal productivity but that, after some point, the marginal productivity of labor diminishes, thus causing short-run costs to rise rapidly.

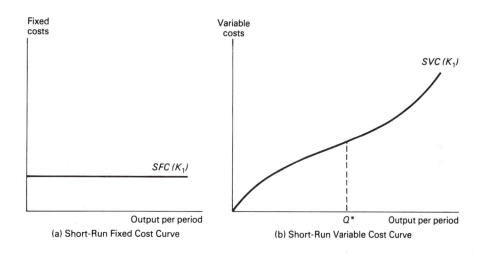

(a) Short-Run Fixed Cost Curve   (b) Short-Run Variable Cost Curve

Definitions:

Short-Run Fixed and Variable Costs
Short-run fixed costs (SFC) are costs associated with inputs that cannot be varied in the short run. *Short-run variable costs* (SVC) are costs of those inputs that can be varied in order to change the firm's output level.

The importance of this distinction is to differentiate between those variable costs that the firm can avoid by producing nothing in the short run and those costs that are fixed and must be paid regardless of the output level chosen (even zero). A graphic approach can make this distinction most efficiently.

Short-Run Fixed and Variable Cost Curves

In the short run, fixed costs are obviously "fixed." They do not change as the level of output changes. This relationship is shown in Figure 11.7a. The $SFC(K_1)$ curve is simply a horizontal line representing the cost of the fixed amount of capital being employed. Figure 11.7b records one possible relationship between short-run variable costs and output. The assumption made here is that initially the marginal productivity of labor is rising as labor is added to the production process. Since there is a fixed input of capital initially, this capital is "underutilized," and labor's marginal productivity rises as the amount of labor available to work with this fixed amount of capital increases. Because the marginal product of labor is increasing, short-run variable costs

Figure 11.8   *Short-Run Total Cost Curve*

This curve simply represents the summation of the two curves shown in Figure 11.7. Short-run fixed costs determine the 0-output intercept for the curve, whereas the short-run variable cost curve determines the total cost curve's shape.

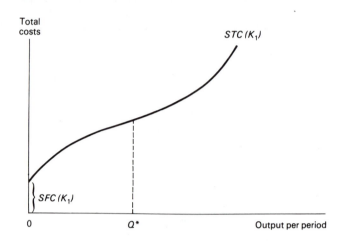

rise less rapidly as output expands—in its initial section, the $SVC(K_1)$ curve is concave downward. Beyond some output level, say Q^*, however, the marginal product of labor will begin to decline (as shown in Figure 10.1). Because capital input is constant at K_1, the ability of labor to generate extra output will diminish; since the per-unit cost of labor is assumed to be constant, costs of production will begin to rise rapidly. Beyond Q^* the $SVC(K_1)$ curve becomes concave upward to reflect this diminishing marginal productivity of labor. What we have shown, therefore, is that the shape of the $SVC(K_1)$ curve in Figure 11.7b is in general agreement with the hypotheses we made about the marginal productivity of labor.

Short-Run Total Cost Curve

We can now construct the short-run total cost curve by summing the $SFC(K_1)$ and $SVC(K_1)$ curves, as required by the definition in Equation 11.40. This total cost curve is shown in Figure 11.8. Two features of the figure should be pointed out explicitly. First, notice that when output is 0, total costs are given by fixed costs, $SFC(K_1)$. Since capital input is fixed, its rental rate must be paid even if no production takes place. The firm cannot avoid these fixed costs in the short run. It can, of course, avoid all variable costs simply by hiring no labor. A second important feature of the graph is that the shape of the curve is determined solely by the shape of the short-run variable cost curve. The way in which changes in output affect costs determines the shape of the curve; since fixed costs are constant, they play no role in determining the shape of the $STC(K_1)$ curve other than determining its 0-output intercept.

It is important to understand that the costs shown in Figure 11.8 are not the minimal costs for producing the various output levels shown. Because we are

Figure 11.9 *"Nonoptimal" Input Choices Must Be Made in the Short Run*

Because capital input is fixed at K_1 in the short run, the firm cannot bring its *RTS* into equality with the ratio of input prices. Given the input prices, Q_0 should be produced with more labor and less capital than it will be in the short run, whereas Q_2 should be produced with more capital and less labor than it will be.

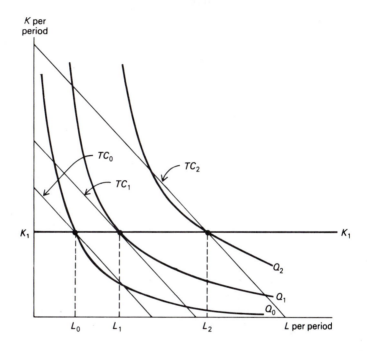

holding capital fixed in the short run, the firm does not have the flexibility of input choice that we assumed when we discussed cost minimization earlier in this chapter. Rather, to vary its output level in the short run, the firm will be forced to use "nonoptimal" input combinations: The *RTS* will not be equal to the ratio of the input prices. This is shown in Figure 11.9. In the short run, the firm is constrained to use K_1 units of capital. To produce output level Q_0, it therefore will use L_0 units of labor. Similarly, it will use L_1 units of labor to produce Q_1, and L_2 units to produce Q_2. The total costs of these input combinations are given by TC_0, TC_1, and TC_2, respectively. Only for the input combination K_1, L_1 is output being produced at minimal cost. Only at that point is the *RTS* equal to the ratio of the input prices. From Figure 11.9 it is clear that Q_0 is being produced with "too much" capital in this short-run situation. Cost minimization should suggest a southeasterly movement along the Q_0 isoquant, indicating a substitution of labor for capital in production. Similarly, Q_2 is being produced with "too little" capital, and costs could be reduced by substituting capital for labor. Neither of these substitutions is possible in the short run. Over a longer period, however, the firm will be able to change its level of capital input and will adjust its input usage to the cost-minimizing combinations. We have already discussed this flexible case earlier in this chapter and shall return to it to illustrate the connection between long-run and short-run cost curves.

Short-Run Marginal and Average Total Cost Curves

The short-run total cost curve summarizes the relationship between output levels and total costs in the short run. Since this is precisely the information relevant to firms' short-run output decisions, it would be feasible to proceed directly to analyze those decisions. Frequently, however, we shall find it more useful to analyze costs on a per-unit of output basis rather than on a total basis. The two most important per-unit curves that can be derived from the short-run total cost curve are the *short-run average total cost curve* (*SATC*) and the *short-run marginal cost curve* (*SMC*). These concepts are defined as

$$SATC(K_1) = \frac{\text{total costs}}{\text{total output}} = \frac{STC(K_1)}{Q}$$

$$SMC(K_1) = \frac{\text{change in total costs}}{\text{change in output}} = \frac{\partial STC(K_1)}{\partial Q},$$

(11.41)

where we have continued to record the level of capital input usage (K_1) that is fixed in the short run. These definitions for average and marginal costs are identical to those developed previously for the long-run, fully flexible case, and the derivation of the curves from the total cost curve proceeds in exactly the same way. Because the short-run total cost curve in Figure 11.8 has the same general type of cubic shape as did the total cost curve in Figure 11.6a, these short-run average and marginal cost curves will also be U-shaped. They are illustrated as the *SATC* and *SMC* curves in Figure 11.10. Notice that, again, the *SMC* curve intersects the *SATC* curve at its lowest point.

Short-Run Average Fixed and Variable Costs

Occasionally, it is helpful to use Equation 11.40 to divide short-run average total costs into two components: *short-run average fixed costs* (*SAFC*) and *short-run average variable costs* (*SAVC*). These are defined as

$$SAFC(K_1) = \frac{\text{total fixed costs}}{\text{output}} = \frac{SFC(K_1)}{Q}$$

$$SAVC(K_1) = \frac{\text{total variable costs}}{\text{output}} = \frac{SVC(K_1)}{Q},$$

(11.42)

where it is obvious that

$$SAFC(K_1) + SAVC(K_1) = \frac{SFC(K_1)}{Q} + \frac{SVC(K_1)}{Q}$$

$$= \frac{STC(K_1)}{Q} = SATC(K_1).$$

(11.43)

Although we shall not show the derivation of these curves in detail, the curves are shown in Figure 11.10, together with the marginal and average total

---

Figure 11.10   *Short-Run Per-Unit Cost Curves*

These cost curves are all drawn on the assumption that capital input is held constant in the short run. The *SATC* and *SMC* curves are derived from the *STC* curve in Figure 11.8 and show average and marginal costs in the short run. The *SAFC* curve shows average fixed costs and is a rectangular hyperbola. The short-run average variable cost curve (*SAVC*) approaches the *SATC* curve as output expands.

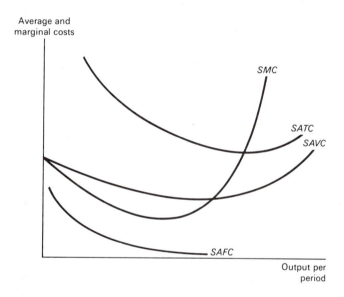

cost curves. The *SAFC* curve is simply a hyperbola reflecting that as Q increases, fixed costs are being divided by a larger and larger number. The *SAVC* curve is generally similar in shape to the *SATC* curve but always falls below it to the extent of average fixed costs. At high levels of output, the *SATC* and *SAVC* curves get very close together because average fixed costs become small. By an argument similar to the one we presented for the average total cost curve, we can show that the short-run marginal cost curve also passes through the low point of the average variable cost curve. This is also shown in Figure 11.10. In later chapters we shall make considerable use of the *SATC* and *SMC* curves. The *SAFC* and *SAVC* curves will be of less use, although they will enter the analysis on one or two occasions.

Relationship between Short-Run and Long-Run Cost Curves   By considering all possible variations in capital input, we can establish the relationship between the short-run cost curves we have just derived and the fully flexible long-run cost curves that were derived previously in this chapter. Figure 11.11 shows this relationship for both the constant returns-to-scale and cubic total cost curve cases. Short-run total costs for three different levels of capital input are shown, although of course it would be possible to show many more such short-run curves. The figures show that long-run total costs (*TC*)

Figure 11.11   *Two Possible Shapes for Long-Run Total Cost Curves*

By considering all possible levels of capital input, the long-run total cost curve (*TC*) can be traced out. In (a) the underlying production function exhibits constant returns to scale—in the long run, though not in the short run, total costs are proportional to output. In (b) the long-run total cost curve has a cubic shape, as do the short-run curves. Diminishing returns set in more sharply for the short-run curves, however, because of the assumed fixed level of capital input.

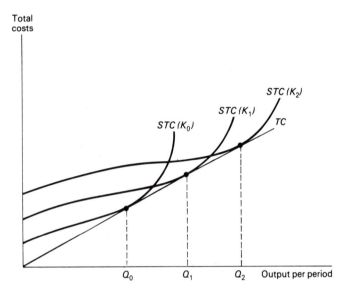

(a) Constant Returns to Scale

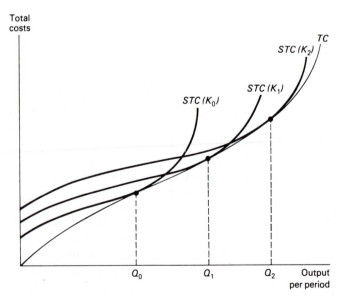

(b) Cubic Cost Curve Case

are always less than short-run total costs, except at that output level for which the assumed fixed capital input is appropriate to long-run cost minimization. For example, as we showed previously in Figure 11.9, with capital input of K_1, the firm can obtain full cost minimization when Q_1 is produced. Hence, short-run and long-run total costs are equal at this point. For output levels other than Q_1, however, $STC(K_1) > TC$, as was the case in Figure 11.9.

Technically, the long-run total cost curves in Figure 11.11 are said to be an "envelope" of their respective short-run curves. These short-run total cost curves can be represented by

$$F(Q, K) = \text{total cost}, \tag{11.44}$$

where the family of curves is generated by allowing capital input to vary. The long-run envelope curve (TC) must obey both Equation 11.44 and the further stipulation that for any Q, capital input should be chosen to minimize total cost; that is, capital input should be chosen so that for any Q,

$$\frac{\partial F(Q, K)}{\partial K} = 0. \tag{11.45}$$

By solving Equations 11.44 and 11.45 together to eliminate K, it is possible to derive the long-run total cost curve. This solution will in fact be identical to the one found by minimizing total cost directly as we did earlier in this chapter. A comparison of Figures 11.1 and 11.9 clearly shows why both procedures result in the same input combination solution. They are simply different approaches to the same cost-minimization problem. In the next section we will show this result with a numerical example.

The envelope total cost curve relationships exhibited in Figure 11.11 can be used to show geometric connections between short-run and long-run average and marginal cost curves. These are presented in Figure 11.12 for the constant returns-to-scale case and in Figure 11.13 for the cubic total cost curve case. In both cases, short-run and long-run average costs are equal at that output for which the (fixed) capital input is appropriate. At Q_1, for example, $SATC(K_1)$ = AC since K_1 is used in producing Q_1 at minimal costs. For movements away from Q_1, short-run average costs exceed long-run average costs, thus reflecting the cost-minimizing nature of the long-run total cost curve. In the constant returns-to-scale case in Figure 11.12, for example, an increase in output from Q_1 to Q_1^* raises average cost slightly from AC to C_1 whereas long-run average cost continues to be AC for such a movement. This reflects the diminishing returns that occur in the short run (because of a fixed capital input), but not in the long run.

For marginal costs, similar conclusions occur. Short-run and long-run marginal costs are equal for output levels where the short-run fixed capital stock is appropriate. But for increases in Q beyond these levels, short-run marginal costs rise rapidly. At Q_1^* in Figure 11.12, for example, short-run marginal costs of C_2 greatly exceed the constant long-run marginal cost, MC.

Because the minimum point of the long-run average cost curve (AC) plays a major role in the theory of long-run price determination, it is important

Figure 11.12 *Long-Run Average and Marginal Cost Curves for the Constant Returns-to-Scale Case*

This figure is derived from the cost curves shown in Figure 11.11a. Because the underlying production function exhibits constant returns to scale, long-run average and marginal costs will be constant (and equal) over all output ranges. In this figure, three sets of short-run curves are also shown for three different levels of capital input.

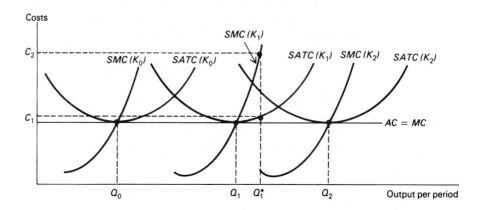

Figure 11.13 *Average and Marginal Cost Curves for the Cubic Cost Curve Case*

This set of curves is derived from the total cost curves shown in Figure 11.11b. The *AC* and *MC* curves have the usual U-shapes, as do the short-run curves. At Q_1, long-run average costs are minimized. The configuration of curves at this minimum point is quite important.

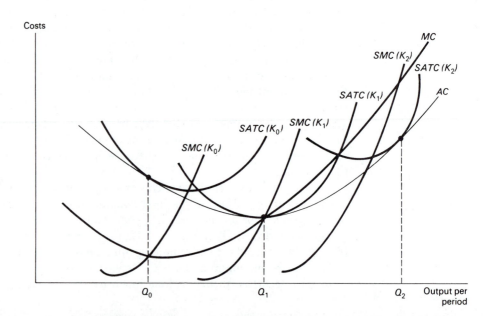

to note the various curves that pass through this point in Figure 11.13. First, as is always true for average and marginal cost curves, the MC curve passes through the low point of the AC curve. At Q_1 long-run average and marginal costs are equal. Associated with Q_1 is a certain level of capital input (say, K_1), and the short-run average cost curve for this level of capital input [$SATC(K_1)$] is tangent to the AC curve at its minimum point. The $SATC(K_1)$ curve also reaches its minimum at output level Q_1. For movements away from Q_1, the AC curve is much flatter than the $SATC(K_1)$ curve, and this reflects the greater flexibility open to firms in the long run. Short-run costs rise rapidly because capital inputs are fixed. In the long run, such inputs are not fixed, and diminishing marginal productivities do not occur so abruptly. Finally, because the $SATC(K_1)$ curve reaches its minimum at Q_1, the short-run marginal cost curve [$SMC(K_1)$] also passes through this point. The minimum point of the AC curve therefore brings together the four most important per-unit costs we have been analyzing. At this point

$$AC = MC = SATC(K_1) = SMC(K_1). \qquad (11.46)$$

For this reason, as we shall show in Chapter 14, the output level Q_1 is an important equilibrium point for the firm in the long run.

Numerical Example

Previously, we calculated total costs of hamburger production on the assumption that both inputs could be varied. Suppose now that the number of grills is fixed at K_1 in the short run. Now the short-run production function is

$$Q = 10K_1^{1/2}L^{1/2} \qquad (11.47)$$

and

$$STC = vK_1 + wL = vK_1 + \frac{wQ^2}{100K_1}. \qquad (11.48)$$

If, for example, the firm has four grills to operate, $K_1 = 4$ and

$$STC = 4v + \frac{wQ^2}{400}. \qquad (11.49)$$

Again, in order to calculate total costs we need to know w and v. Table 11.1 shows the relationship between STC and Q for the case where $w = v = \$4$ for three fixed levels of capital input: 1, 4, and 9 grills. Notice that short-run total costs are positive even when $Q = 0$ (since fixed capital costs must be paid).

In the final column of Table 11.1 we have used Equation 11.33 to calculate long-run total costs. As in Figure 11.11, for each output level except one, short-run total costs exceed long-run total costs. This is also illustrated in Figure 11.14.

An alternative way of deriving this firm's long-run total cost curve is to use the envelope procedure described earlier in this chapter. If we continue to assume $w = v = \$4$, we can use Equation 11.48 to write

$$STC = 4K + \frac{4Q^2}{100K} \qquad (11.50)$$

Table 11.1   *Short-Run and Long-Run Total Costs for* $Q = 10\sqrt{K \cdot L}$ *when* $w = v = \$4$

(1) Q	(2) $STC(K = 1)$	(3) $STC(K = 4)$	(4) $STC(K = 9)$	(5) TC
0	$ 4.00	$ 16.00	$36.00	$ 0.00
10	8.00	17.00	36.44	8.00
20	20.00	20.00	37.76	16.00
30	40.00	25.00	40.00	24.00
40	68.00	32.00	43.12	32.00
50	104.00	41.00	45.12	40.00
60	148.00	52.00	52.00	48.00
70	200.00	65.00	57.76	56.00
80	260.00	80.00	64.44	64.00
90	328.00	97.00	72.00	72.00
100	404.00	116.00	80.44	80.00

Figure 11.14   *Short-Run and Long-Run Total Cost Curves for* $Q = 10\sqrt{K \cdot L}$

Since this production function possesses constant returns to scale, the *TC* curve is a straight line. The short-run curves for $K = 1$, $K = 4$, and $K = 9$ lie above this line, except at output levels $Q = 10$, $Q = 40$, and $Q = 90$, respectively. At these output levels, the constant short-run level of K is also appropriate for long-run cost minimization. Hence at these output levels, the short-run and long-run total cost curves are tangent.

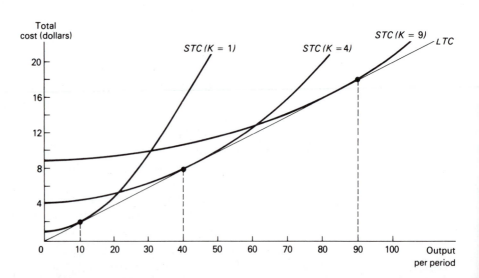

Figure 11.15   *Short-Run and Long-Run Average and Marginal Cost Curves for* $Q = 10\sqrt{K \cdot L}$

For this production function, *AC* and *MC* are constant over all ranges of output. Since $w = v = \$4$, this constant average cost is \$.80 per unit. The shcrt-run average cost curves, however, do have a general U-shape, since *K* is held constant in the short run. The *SATC* curves are tangent to the *AC* curve at output levels $Q = 10$, $Q = 40$, and $Q = 90$.

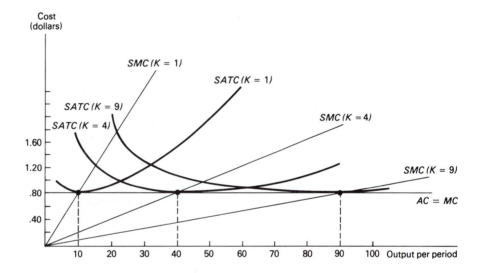

and then differentiate this expression with respect to (the now variable) *K:*

$$\frac{\partial STC}{\partial K} = 4 - \frac{4Q}{100K^2}. \qquad (11.51)$$

Setting this derivative equal to 0 (since we wish to minimize *STC* with respect to *K*, for each level of *Q*) we have

$$4 = \frac{4Q^2}{100K} \qquad (11.52)$$

or

$$K = \frac{Q}{10}. \qquad (11.53)$$

Substitution back into the short-run total cost function (Equation 11.50) yields

$$TC = .4Q + .4Q = .8Q, \qquad (11.54)$$

which is a rather long-winded way to show what we already know.

Average and marginal cost relationships can be derived from Equations 11.50 and 11.54. These are illustrated in Figure 11.15. As before, long-run average and marginal costs are constant at $.80 and the short-run average cost curves have a general U-shape. Other relationships between long-run and short-run cost curves discussed in the previous section are also apparent in the figure.

SUMMARY

In this chapter we have examined the relationship between the level of output that a firm produces and the input costs that that level of production requires. The resulting cost curves should generally be familiar to you since they are widely used in most courses in introductory economics. Here we have shown how such curves reflect the firm's underlying production function together with the firm's desire to minimize costs. By developing cost curves from these basic foundations, we were able to illustrate a number of important findings:

- A firm that wishes to minimize the economic costs of producing a particular level of output should choose that input combination for which the rate of technical substitution (RTS) is equal to the ratio of the inputs' rental prices.

- Repeated application of this minimization procedure yields the firm's expansion path. Since the expansion path shows how input usage expands with the level of output, it also shows the relationship between output level and total cost. That relationship is summarized by the total cost function—$TC(Q, v, w)$—which shows production costs as a function of output levels and input prices.

- The firm's average cost ($AC = TC/Q$) and marginal cost ($MC = \partial TC/\partial Q$) functions can be derived directly from the total cost function. If the total cost curve has a general cubic shape, the AC and MC curves will be U-shaped.

- All cost curves are drawn on the assumption that the input prices are held constant. When input prices change, cost curves will shift to new positions. The extent of the shifts will be determined by the overall importance of the input whose price has changed and by the ease with which the firm may substitute one input for another.

- In the short run, the firm may not be able to vary some inputs. It can then alter its level of production only by changing its employment of variable inputs. In so doing, it may have to use nonoptimal, higher cost input combinations than it would choose to use if it were possible to vary all inputs.

Application

THE MEASUREMENT OF LONG-RUN COSTS

Economists study long-run cost curves in order to discover something about the appropriate scale of operation for various industries. They are particularly interested in estimating the output level (or range of levels) for which long-run average cost reaches its minimum value. The location of this point of minimum long-run average cost is indicative of whether the industry in question is appropriate for the development of large-scale firms. If the point of minimum long-run average cost occurs at an output level that is small relative to the total industry output, economists would argue that it is efficient for such an industry to contain many small firms. For the U.S. economy this observation has been made most often for the agricultural industry, where it appears that long-run average costs reach a minimum for farms of a relatively small size (400 to 800 acres). On the other hand, there are industries for which long-run average cost curves seem to be downward sloping over a broad range of output levels; that is, the point of minimum average cost occurs at an output level that represents a substantial portion of total industry production. Economists sometimes refer to such industries as exhibiting "increasing returns to scale," as indicated by their negatively sloped *AC* curves. Usually that term is not meant in the strict production function sense of "returns to scale," which we discussed in Chapter 10, although there are situations in which the two definitions coincide. Whatever term is attached to the phenomenon of declining long-run average costs, this possibility does present serious problems for resource allocation in an economy because industries dominated by a few large firms may not operate efficiently. In Chapters 18 and 19 we will examine such industries and will outline the problems in resource allocation that they pose.

Some General Findings on Long-Run Average Costs

Most studies of long-run cost curves have found that average costs decrease up to some particular output level and then remain relatively constant. Average cost curves therefore have a modified L-shape, such as that shown in Figure 11.16. The industries studied therefore might be said to exhibit "increasing returns to scale" up to some point, but there is no strong evidence that long-run average costs begin to rise after some point. Adam Smith's hypotheses about the difficulties of managing large-size firms do not appear to be supported by the data.

Table 11.2 reports some representative results of studies of long-run average cost curves for six industries: banking, electric power, hospitals, life insurance, railroads, and trucking. Entries in the table represent the long-run average cost in the industry for a firm of a particular size (small, medium, or large) as a percentage of the minimum-cost firm in the industry. For example, the data for hospitals indicate that small hospitals have average costs that are about 29.6 percent greater than average costs for large ones. Hospitals therefore are one industry for which there do appear to be some cost advantages to larger-scale operations. For most other industries a picture similar to that illustrated in Figure 11.16 emerges. Average costs are lower for medium and large firms than for smaller ones. That is, there appears to be a "minimum efficient scale" (termed, appropriately, MES in the field of industrial organization). In most cases, however, these cost advantages are not great, and for at least one case (trucking), smaller firms seem to operate with lower costs. Clearly there is no overwhelming evidence of substantial benefits to large-scale operation. Of course, far more information has been gathered about cost curves than is reflected in Table 11.2.

Figure 11.16   *Long-Run Average Cost Curve*
Found in Many Empirical Studies

In most empirical studies the *AC* curve has been found to have this modified L-shape. Average costs decline up to a point and then remain constant. There is no strong evidence that after some output level is reached, average costs start to rise.

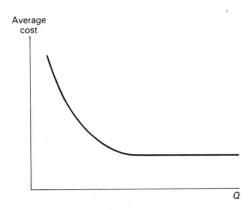

Table 11.2   *Long-Run Average Cost Estimates for Six Industries*
(Average Cost as a Percentage of Minimum Average Cost)

	Firm Size		
Industry	**Small**	**Medium**	**Large**
Commercial banking			
Demand deposits	116.1	104.7	100.0
Installment loans	102.4	101.5	100.0
Electric power generation	113.2	101.0	101.5
Hospitals	129.6	111.1	100.0
Life insurance (Canada)	113.6	104.5	100.0
Railroads			
East	100.0	127.9	119.9
South	100.0	100.0	100.0
West	106.9	108.4	100.0
Trucking	100.0	102.1	105.6

Sources: Banking—F. W. Bell and N. B. Murphy, *Costs in Commercial Banking* (Boston: Federal Reserve Bank of Boston, Research Report No. 41, 1968). Electric Power—L. H. Christensen and W. H. Greene, "Economies of Scale in U.S. Electric Power Generation," *Journal of Political Economy* 84 (August 1976): 655–676. Hospitals—H. A. Cohen, "Hospital Cost Curves" in *Empirical Studies in Health Economics,* ed. H. F. Klarman (Baltimore: Johns Hopkins Press, 1970), pp. 279–293. Life Insurance—R. Geehan, "Returns to Scale in the Life Insurance Industry," *The Bell Journal of Economics* 8, no. 2 (Autumn 1977): 497–516. Railroads—G. Borts, "The Estimation of Rail Cost Functions," *Econometrica* 28 (January 1960): 108–131. Trucking—R. Koenka, "Optimal Scale and the Size Distribution of American Trucking Firms," *Journal of Transport Economics and Policy* (January 1977): 54–67.

Here we will examine three more detailed examples.

Electric Power Generation

In an important study of electricity generation, M. Nerlove examined a cross section of 145 privately owned utilities.[13] He found strong indications of decreasing long-run average costs, although the benefits from increasing size seemed somewhat greater for small firms than for large ones. This may occur because of difficulties in managing multiplant electric firms, since large firms typically have several generating stations. Indeed, Nerlove's results do show considerably smaller returns to scale on the firm level than do reports by other authors on individual generating plants. One particularly interesting problem that Nerlove had to face in his study was that input costs were not identical for the firms in his cross section. Wage rates and fuel costs varied greatly among firms, being generally higher in the northeastern states than in the southern and western states. But Nerlove developed several ingenious analytical tools for dealing with the price differences. His work provided important guidelines for future developments in the use of cross-section data for examining long-run cost curves.

Although Nerlove's study focused on the question of declining average costs at the firm level, it might be argued that it is more appropriate to focus on individual generating units. Some economists have proposed separating the generating and distributing functions of electric utilities and have favored greater competition among generating units. One major study suggests that the efficiency gains from operation of multiple generating units are small; that is, average costs for firms that operate several generating units are not much different from those that operate only one.[14] Hence it seems possible to promote competition among generating facilities by limiting multiple plant ownership without significantly sacrificing scale economies. Several utility regulatory reform proposals therefore have suggested separating the power generation function of electric utility firms from the power distribution function (which clearly does exhibit economies of scale).

Railroads

A 1960 study by G. Borts looked at long-run cost curves for U.S. railroads.[15] Borts examined 61 class I railway firms. He defined the "output" of a railway to be either the number of car loadings or the mean length of haul. Using such a definition, he found that railways in the South and in the West exhibit decreasing long-run average costs but that those in the East seem to exhibit increasing average costs. Borts attributes that to the higher traffic density experienced by the eastern railroads. The author's technique of examining railways in different parts of the country separately indicates the necessity of trying to hold some factors constant when analyzing a cross section of rather different firms.

More recently, the question of "excess capacity" of railroads has been examined. Because various regulatory agencies require railroads to retain little-used lines, it is possible that they are not minimizing long-run average costs: They may be overcapitalized given prevailing output levels. For example, T. E. Keeler estimated a series of short-run cost curves for U.S. railroads and used those cost curves (much as we did earlier in this chapter) to calculate a long-run cost curve envelope.[16] He concluded that railroads currently possess an enormous amount of excess capacity (over 200,000 miles of track) and that adoption of a more appropriately sized rail

[13] M. Nerlove, "Returns to Scale in Electricity Supply" in *Measurement in Economics,* ed. C. F. Christ et al. (Stanford, Calif.: Stanford University Press, 1963), pp. 167–198.

[14] L. R. Christensen and W. H. Greene, "Economies of Scale in U.S. Electric Power Generation," *Journal of Political Economy* 84 (August 1976): 655–676.

[15] G. Borts, "The Estimation of Rail Cost Functions," *Econometrica* (January 1960): 108–131.

[16] T. E. Keeler, "Railroad Costs, Returns to Scale, and Excess Capacity," *Review of Economics and Statistics* 56 (May 1974): 201–208.

network might save over $2.5 billion in annual operating costs.

If railroads were deregulated to permit abandonment of excess track and mergers of smaller lines, it is possible that average costs would fall not only because of reduced capital costs but also because the remaining, larger railroads would exhibit some economies of scale. Caves, Christensen, and Swanson in a 1981 paper found that the substantial increase in haul lengths made possible by rail mergers in the 1960s and early 1970s provided substantial cost savings.[17] In years to come, the U.S. rail network is likely to exhibit many similar consolidations.

Refuse Collection

Refuse collection is a major municipal service that is carried out by both private and public enterprises. The question of scale economies plays an important role in deciding exactly how this service should be organized to achieve minimal costs. Two types of such economies might be distinguished. First, operating a number of refuse trucks may provide some reductions in average costs because of economies in maintenance facilities and in the purchasing of specialized equipment. A number of studies have found that these scale economies are relatively insignificant, however. Hence there seems to be little cost advantage to operating a large number of trucks.

A second, more important source of economies in refuse collection stems from customer density. As density increases, multiple pickups from a single stop become possible and collection times (and costs) fall dramatically. One study finds that each 10 percent increase in density of collection tonnage results in a 5 percent reduction in average costs.[18]

These research findings on refuse collection costs have two implications for how the service might be organized. First, the absence of scale economies provides little support for the notion that collection must be done on a citywide basis. Contracting with several different firms would not result in increased costs. However, existence of density economies argues strongly for offering exclusive contracts to service entire areas rather than permitting a totally free market with overlapping collection routes. With such a contracting system, overall average costs of refuse collection might be minimized.

A Note on Short-Run Costs

Economists have found it much more difficult to examine the short-run cost relationship than they have the long-run relationship. Definitional and statistical problems in using real-world data to study such curves have proved particularly vexing. For the most part economists have relied on studies of the overall (long-run) cost function and on various engineering examples to document the rapidly increasing average and marginal costs that are believed to occur in the short run. We will not examine such examples here, but we will continue to assume that diminishing marginal productivities are a quite important determinant of costs in the short run—mainly because this assumption seems to be a quite reasonable one.

[17] D. W. Caves, L. R. Christensen, and J. A. Swanson, "Productivity Growth, Scale Economies and Capacity Utilization in U.S. Railroads, 1955–74," *American Economic Review* 71 (December 1981): 994–1002.

[18] P. Kemper and J. M. Quigley, *The Economics of Refuse Collection* (Cambridge, Mass.: Ballinger Publishing Co., 1976), p. 53.

SUGGESTED READINGS

Allen, R. G. D. *Mathematical Analysis for Economists*. New York: St. Martin's Press, 1938. Various pages—see index.

Complete mathematical analysis of substitution possibilities and cost functions. Notation somewhat difficult.

Ferguson, C. E. *The Neoclassical Theory of Production and Distribution*. Cambridge: Cambridge University Press, 1969. Chap. 6.

Nice development of cost curves, especially strong on graphic analysis.

Fuss, M., and McFadden, D. *Production Economics: A Dual Approach to Theory and Applications*. Amsterdam: North Holland Publishing Co., 1978.

Difficult and quite complete treatment of the dual relationship between production and cost functions. Some discussion of empirical issues.

Knight, F. H. "Cost of Production and Price over Long and Short Periods." *Journal of Political Economy* 29 (April 1921): 304–335.

Classic treatment of the short-run, long-run distinction.

Marshall, A. *Principles of Economics*, 8th ed. New York: Crowell-Collier and Macmillan, 1970. Book 5. Chaps. 8–11.

Good literary analysis of early cost theory. See also Marshall's mathematical appendix.

Nadiri, M. I. "Producers Theory." In K. J. Arrow and M. D. Intriligater, eds., *Handbook of Mathematical Economics*. Vol. 2. Amsterdam: North

Holland Publishing Company, 1982. Pp. 431–490.

Complete description of mathematical production theory. A nice survey of the properties of production and cost functions and relationships among these properties. Also a brief discussion of multiproduct firms.

Silberberg, E. *The Structure of Economics: A Mathematical Analysis*. New York: McGraw Hill Book Company, 1978. Chaps. 7 and 8.

Extensive use of the envelope theorem to develop cost curve concepts.

Viner, J. "Cost Curves and Supply Curves." Reprinted in American Economic Association, *Readings in Price Theory*. Homewood, Ill.: Richard D. Irwin, 1952.

Classic article on the envelope relationship between short-run and long-run cost curves. Famous for Viner's criticism of his draftsman (see problem 11.1 at the end of this chapter).

Walters, A. A. "Production and Cost Functions: An Econometric Survey." *Econometrica* 31 (January/April 1963): 1–66.

Excellent but dated survey of the empirical literature on production and cost functions. Particularly interesting discussion of short-run costs.

PROBLEMS

11.1

In a famous article [J. Viner, "Cost Curves and Supply Curves," *Zeitschrift fur Nationalokonomie* 3 (September 1931): 23–46], Viner criticized his draftsman who could not draw a family of *SATC* curves whose points of tangency with the *AC* curve were also the minimum points on each *SATC* curve. The draftsman protested that such a drawing was impossible to construct. Whom would you support in this debate? Are there cases in which either might be correct?

11.2

Show that for a production function with $\sigma = \infty$, the cost-minimizing input ratio, if it is unique, will generally require the use of only capital or only labor. In such a situation, what will be the firm's expansion path? On what will the shape of its marginal and average cost curves depend? How will these cost curves shift as the price of the input that is utilized rises?

11.3

Professor Smith and Professor Jones are going to produce a new introductory textbook. As true scientists they have laid out the production function for the book as

$$Q = S^{1/2}J^{1/2},$$

where Q = the number of pages in the finished book, S = the number of working hours spent by Smith, and J = the number of hours spent working by Jones.

Smith values his labor as $3 per working hour. He has spent 900 hours preparing the first draft. Jones, whose labor is valued at $12 per working hour, will revise Smith's draft to complete the book.

   a.   How many hours will Jones have to spend to produce a finished book of 150 pages? Of 300 pages? Of 450 pages?
   b.   What is the marginal cost of the 150th page of the finished book? Of the 300th page? Of the 450th page?

11.4
Suppose that a firm's production function is given by

$$Q = \min(5K, 10L),$$

and that the rental rates for capital and labor are given by $v = 1$, $w = 3$.

   a.   Calculate the firm's long-run total, average, and marginal cost curves.
   b.   Suppose that K is fixed at 10 in the short run. Calculate the firm's short-run total, average, and marginal cost curves. What is the marginal cost of the 10th unit? The 50th unit? The 100th unit?

11.5
Suppose that a firm's production function is given by the Cobb-Douglas function

$$Q = K^\alpha L^\beta$$

(where α, $\beta > 0$) and that the firm can purchase all the K and L it wants in competitive input markets at rental rates of v and w, respectively.

   a.   Show that cost minimization requires

$$\frac{vK}{\alpha} = \frac{wL}{\beta}.$$

What is the shape of the expansion path for this firm?

   b.   Assuming cost minimization, show that total costs can be expressed as a function of Q, v, and w of the form

$$TC = BQ^{1/\alpha+\beta}w^{\beta/\alpha+\beta}v^{\alpha/\alpha+\beta},$$

where B is a constant depending on α and β.
Hint: This part may be most easily worked by using the results from part (a) to solve successively for TC as a function of L and TC as a function of K and then substituting into the production function.

   c.   Show that if $\alpha + \beta = 1$, TC is proportional to Q.
   d.   Calculate the firm's marginal cost curve. Show that

$$e_{MC,w} = \frac{\beta}{\alpha + \beta}$$

$$e_{MC,v} = \frac{\alpha}{\alpha + \beta}$$

   e.   If the growth rate of capital accumulation is denoted by G_K $[=(dK/dt)/K]$ and the rate of increase in hiring of labor is denoted by G_L $[= dL/dt)/L]$, show that the growth rate of output, G_Q $[= (dQ/dt)/Q]$, is given by

$$G_Q = \alpha G_K + \beta G_L.$$

11.6

For the total cost curve calculated in Problem 11.5, use Shephard's lemma (see Footnote 9) to compute the (constant output) demand function for L as a function of w, v, and Q_0.

11.7

A firm producing hockey sticks has a production function given by

$$Q = 2\sqrt{K \cdot L}$$

In the short run, the firm's amount of capital equipment is fixed at $K = 100$. The rental rate for K is $v = \$1$, and the wage rate for L is $w = \$4$.

  a.   Calculate the firm's short-run total cost curve. Calculate the short-run average cost curve.

  b.   What is the firm's short-run marginal cost function? What are the STC, $SATC$, and SMC for the firm if it produces twenty-five hockey sticks? Fifty hockey sticks? One hundred hockey sticks? Two hundred hockey sticks?

  c.   Graph the $SATC$ and the SMC curves for the firm. Indicate the points found in part b.

  d.   Where does the SMC curve intersect the $SATC$ curve? Explain why the SMC curve will always intersect the $SATC$ curve at its lowest point.

11.8

Suppose, as in problem 11.7, a firm produces hockey sticks with a production function of $Q = 2\sqrt{KL}$. Capital stock is fixed at $\overline{K}$ in the short run.

  a.   Calculate the firm's total costs as a function of Q, w, v, and $\overline{K}$.

  b.   Given Q, w, and v, how should the capital stock be chosen to minimize total cost?

  c.   Use your results from part b to calculate the long run total cost of hockey stick production.

  d.   For $w = \$4$, $v = \$1$ graph the long run total cost curve for hockey stick production. Show that this is an envelope for the short-run curves computed in part a by examining values of $\overline{K}$ of 100, 200, and 400.

11.9

An enterprising entrepreneur purchases two firms to produce widgets. Each firm produces identical products and each has a production function given by

$$Q = \sqrt{K_i L_i} \qquad i = 1, 2.$$

The firms differ, however, in the amount of capital equipment each has. In particular, firm 1 has $K_1 = 25$, whereas firm 2 has $K_2 = 100$. Rental rates for K and L are given by $w = v = \$1$.

  a.   If the entrepreneur wishes to minimize short-run total costs of widget production, how should output be allocated between the two firms?

  b.   Given that output is optimally allocated between the two firms, calculate the short-run total, average, and marginal cost curves. What is the marginal cost of the 100th widget? The 125th widget? The 200th widget?

  c.   How should the entrepreneur allocate widget production between the two firms in the long run? Calculate the long-run total, average, and marginal cost curves for widget production.

  d.   How would your answer to part (c) change if both firms exhibited diminishing returns to scale?

11.10

Suppose the total cost function for a firm is given by

$$TC = Qw^{2/3}v^{1/3}.$$

a.   Use Shephard's lemma (footnote 9) to compute the constant output demand functions for inputs L and K.

b.   Use your results from part (a) to calculate the underlying production function for Q.

11.11

Suppose the total cost function for a firm is given by

$$TC = (v + 2\sqrt{vw} + w)Q.$$

a.   Use Shephard's lemma to compute the constant output demand function for each input, K and L.

b.   Use the results from part (a) to compute the underlying production function for Q.

c.   You can check the result by using results from the Extension problems to show that the *CES* cost function with $\sigma = \delta = .5$ generates this total cost curve.

EXTENSIONS

INPUT SUBSTITUT-ABILITY

Throughout Chapter 11 we stressed that a change in input prices may affect all the inputs that a firm uses by changing the cost-minimizing mix. Here we examine the nature of these substitutions implied by various types of cost (and production) functions. We show that some common forms for cost functions offer very limited possibilities for input substitution and a more general form (the translog) should be considered. Throughout we use only constant returns to scale cost functions (the exponent of output, Q, is always 1), but these are readily generalizable to cases of non-constant (but homothetic) returns to scale cost functions.

E11.1

The Cobb-Douglas cost function for two inputs (K and L) is given by (see Problem 11.5)

$$TC = Q(v^{\alpha}w^{\beta}) \quad \text{where } \alpha + \beta = 1$$

a.   Use Shephard's lemma to show that the constant output demand functions for K and L are

$$K = \alpha\left(\frac{w}{v}\right)^{\beta}Q$$

$$L = \beta\left(\frac{v}{w}\right)^{\alpha}Q$$

b.   By the definition given in this chapter, the elasticity of substitution between K and L can be measured by

$$S = \frac{\partial(K/L)}{\partial(w/v)} \cdot \frac{(w/v)}{(K/L)} = \frac{\partial \ln(K/L)}{\partial \ln(w/v)}.$$

Use this definition and the results from part a to show that $s = 1$ for this case.

E11.2
The *CES* cost function for two inputs is given by

$$TC = Q[\delta^\sigma v^{1-\sigma} + (1 - \delta)^\sigma w^{1-\sigma}]^{1/1-\sigma}$$

a. For this function use Shephard's lemma to calculate the constant output demand functions for K and L as

$$K = \alpha_1 v^{-\sigma} Q$$

$$L = \alpha_2 w^{-\sigma} Q$$

where α_1 and α_2 are constants.

b. Use the results from part a together with the definition of s in Problem E11.1 to show that here

$$s = \sigma$$

That is, the elasticity of substitution is the same and constant for all values of K and L whether calculated from the production or the cost function.

c. Use the results of this problem to prove Problem 11.11, part c.

E11.3
One commonly used approximation to any cost function is the *Translog* function:

$$\ln TC = \ln Q + \beta_0 + \beta_1 \ln w + (1 - \beta_1) \ln v$$
$$+ \beta_2(\ln w)^2 + \beta_3(\ln v)^2 + \beta_4 \ln w \ln v$$

a. What restrictions must be placed on the β's here if this function is to be homogeneous of degree 1 in w and v?

b. Show that this function reduces to the Cobb-Douglas cost function if $\beta_2 = \beta_3 = \beta_4 = 0$.

c. Use Shephard's lemma to derive the constant output demand functions for K and L. Show that, contrary to the Cobb-Douglas and CES cases, the demand for each input depends on *both* input prices.

d. Show that the shares of total costs accounted for by K and L are given by

$$s_K = \frac{vK}{TC} = (1 - \beta_1) + 2\beta_3 \ln v + \beta_4 \ln w$$

$$s_L = \frac{wL}{TC} = \beta_1 + 2\beta_2 \ln w + \beta_4 \ln v$$

e. Use the definition of s given in Problem E11.1 to show that the elasticity of substitution in this problem is not constant; it depends on w and v and on the βs.

E11.4
The three cost functions given in Problems E11.1–E11.3 can be readily generalized to many inputs $(X_1 \ldots X_n)$ with prices $w_1 \ldots w_n$ as:

Cobb-Douglas

$$TC = Q \prod_{i=1}^{n} w_i^{\beta i} \quad \text{where} \sum_{i=1}^{n} \beta_i = 1$$

CES

$$TC = Q \left[\sum_{i=1}^{n} \beta_i^{\sigma} w_i^{1-\sigma} \right]^{1/1-\sigma}$$

Translog

$$\ln TC = \ln Q + \beta_0 + \sum_{i=1}^{n} \beta_i \ln w_i + 0.5 \sum_i \sum_j \beta_{ij} \ln w_i \ln w_j$$

$$\text{where} \sum \beta_i = 1 \qquad \beta_{ij} = \beta_{ji}$$

It can be shown that the partial elasticity of substitution (s_{ij}) can be computed from these cost functions as

$$s_{ij} = \frac{TC \cdot TC_{ij}}{TC_i \cdot TC_j}$$

a.   If you do not wish to take this result on faith, prove it for the two input case or see Sato and Koizumi (1973).

b.   Use this definition of s_{ij} to show that $s_{ij} = 1$ for the Cobb-Douglas case and s_{ij} is a constant for the *CES* case.

c.   Generalize the results of Problem E11.3 to show that cost shares for the Translog cost function are given by

$$s_i = \frac{w_i X_i}{TC} = \beta_i + \sum_{j=1}^{n} \beta_{ij} \ln w_j$$

d.   Show that for the Translog case

$$s_{ij} = (\beta_{ij} + s_i s_j)/s_i s_j.$$

This latter result is useful in empirical work because it shows how the partial elasticities of substitution can be computed directly from information obtained from the cost share equations in part c.

REFERENCES

Ferguson, C. E., *The Neoclassical Theory of Production and Distribution* (Cambridge: Cambridge University Press, 1969).

Fuss, M., and McFadden, D. (eds.), *Production Economics: A Dual Approach to Theory and Applications* (Amsterdam: North Holland, 1978).

Sato, R., and Koizumi, T., "On Elasticities of Substitution and Complementarity," *Oxford Economic Papers*, March 1973, pp. 44–50.

CHAPTER 12

Profit Maximization and Supply

In Chapter 11 we examined the way in which firms minimize costs for any level of output they may choose. In this chapter we will focus on how the level of output is chosen by profit maximizing firms. Before investigating that decision, however, it is appropriate to discuss briefly the nature of firms and the ways in which firms' choices may be analyzed. That discussion will lay the foundation for our discussion of profit maximization in this chapter and for the alternatives we take up in Chapter 13.

THE NATURE AND BEHAVIOR OF FIRMS

Contractual Relationships within Firms

As we pointed out at the beginning of our analysis of production, a firm is fundamentally a collection of individuals who have organized themselves for the purpose of turning inputs into outputs. Different individuals will provide different types of inputs, such as workers' skills and varieties of capital equipment, with the expectation of receiving some sort of reward for doing so.

The nature of the contractual relationship between the providers of inputs to a firm may be quite complicated. Each provider agrees to devote his or her input to production activities under a set of understandings about how it is to be used and what benefit is to be expected from that use. In some cases these contracts are explicit. Workers often negotiate contracts that specify in considerable detail what hours are to be worked, what rules of work are to be followed, and what rate of pay is to be expected. Similarly, capital owners invest in a firm under a set of explicit legal principles about the ways in which that capital may be used, the compensation the owner can expect to receive, and whether the owner retains any profits or losses after all economic costs have been paid. Despite these formal arrangements, it is clear that many of the understandings between the providers of inputs to a firm are implicit: Relationships between managers and workers follow certain procedures about who has the authority to do what in making production decisions. Among workers numerous implicit understandings exist about how work tasks are to be shared; and capital owners may delegate much of their authority to managers and workers to make decisions on their behalf (General Motors' shareholders, for example, are never involved in how assembly-line equipment will be used, though technically they own it). All of these explicit and implicit relationships change in response to experiences and events external to the firm. Much as a basketball team will try out new plays and defensive strategies, so too firms will alter the nature of their internal organizations in order to achieve better long-run results.[1]

Modeling Firms' Behavior

These complicated relationships among the providers of inputs to a firm pose some problems for economists who wish to develop theoretical generalizations about how firms behave. In our study of demand theory, it made some sense to talk about choices by a rational consumer because we were examining decisions by only a single person. But for firms, many individuals may be involved in decisions and any detailed study of such decisions may quickly become deeply mired in the subjects of psychology, sociology, and group dynamics.

Although some economists have adopted such a "behavioral" approach to studying firms' decisions, most have found that approach too cumbersome for general purposes. Rather, they have adopted a "holistic" approach that treats the firm as a single decision-making unit and sweeps away all the complicated behavioral issues about relationships among input providers. Under this approach it is often convenient to assume that a firm's decisions are made by a single dictatorial manager who rationally pursues some goal. At times issues raised by the complexities of actual decision-making procedures within the firm can be introduced to show how they influence the dictatorial manager's ability to achieve the desired goals, but for the most part, it is assumed that the manager can exercise a relatively free hand.

PROFIT MAXIMIZA- TION

In this chapter we will assume that the firm and its manager pursue the goal of achieving the largest economic profits possible. That is, we will define

---

Definition:

Profit-Maximizing Firm

A *profit-maximizing firm* chooses both its inputs and its outputs with the sole goal of achieving maximum economic profits. That is, the firm seeks to make the difference between its total revenues and its total economic costs as large as possible.

This assumption, that firms seek maximum economic profits, has a long history in economic literature. It has much to recommend it both in terms of its ability to yield interesting theoretical results and to explain actual firms' decisions. In this chapter we will illustrate some of these results. Some alternative approaches are surveyed in Chapter 13.

---

[1] For an elaboration of these points, see K. J. Arrow, *The Limits of Organization* (New York: Norton, 1974). The initial development of the theory of the firm from the notion of the contractual relationships involved can be found in R. H. Coase, "The Nature of the Firm," *Economica* (November 1937): 386–405.

*Profit
Maximization and
Marginalism*

If firms are strict profit maximizers, they will make decisions in a "marginal" way. The entrepreneur will perform the conceptual experiment of adjusting those variables that can be controlled until it is impossible to increase profits further. This involves, say, looking at the incremental, or "marginal," profit obtainable from producing one more unit of output or at the additional profit available from hiring one more laborer. As long as this incremental profit is positive, the extra output will be produced or the extra laborer will be hired. When the incremental profit of an activity becomes 0, the entrepreneur has pushed that activity far enough, and it would not be profitable to go farther.

Output Choice

This relationship between profit maximization and marginalism can be most clearly demonstrated if we examine the output level that a firm will choose to produce in attempting to obtain maximum profits. First, we must define "profits." In its activities a firm sells some level of output,[2] q, at a market price of P per unit. Total revenues (TR) are therefore given by

$$TR(q) = P(q) \cdot q, \tag{12.1}$$

where we have allowed for the possibility that the selling price the firm receives might by affected by how much it sells. In the production of q, certain *economic* costs are incurred and, as in Chapter 11, we will denote these by $TC(q)$.

The difference between revenues and costs is called economic profits (π). Because both revenues and costs depend on the quantity produced, economic profits will also. That is,

$$\pi(q) = P(q) \cdot q - TC(q) = TR(q) - TC(q). \tag{12.2}$$

The necessary condition for choosing the value of q that maximizes profits is found by setting the derivative of Equation 12.2 with respect to q equal to 0.[3]

$$\frac{d\pi}{dq} = \pi'(q) = \frac{dTR}{dq} - \frac{dTC}{dq} = 0 \tag{12.3}$$

so the first-order condition for a maximum is that

$$\frac{dTR}{dq} = \frac{dTC}{dq}. \tag{12.4}$$

This is simply a mathematical statement of the marginal revenue equals marginal cost rule usually studied in introductory economics courses. Hence we have the following:

---

[2] In this chapter and for the remainder of this book we will use a lower-case q to record the output level of a single firm. We will use an upper-case Q to refer to total output by all firms.

[3] Notice that this is an unconstrained maximization problem: The constraints in the problem are implicit in the revenue and cost functions. Specifically, the demand curve facing the firm determines the revenue function, and the firm's production function (together with input prices) determines its costs. We will explore these "built-in" constraints further later in this chapter.

Optimization Principle:	

Profit Maximization

In order to maximize economic profits, the firm should choose that output for which marginal revenue is equal to marginal cost. That is,

$$MR = \frac{dTR}{dq} = \frac{dTC}{dq} = MC. \tag{12.5}$$

We have already discussed the concept of marginal cost in Chapter 11. "Marginal revenue" refers to the revenue provided by the last unit sold. Although we shall investigate this concept in detail in the next section, it may be worthwhile here to indicate the intuitive logic behind the first-order conditions in Equation 12.5. If a firm decided to produce at an output level for which marginal revenue exceeded marginal cost, it could not be maximizing profits, since the production of one more unit of output would yield more in additional revenue than it would cost to produce. Similarly, if marginal revenue were less than marginal costs, reducing output by one unit would lower costs by a greater amount than it would lower revenue, and this action would increase profits. Assuming that it is in fact possible for the firm to make "small" adjustments, marginalism and profit maximization are synonymous.

Second-Order Conditions

Equation 12.4 or 12.5 is only the necessary condition for a profit maximum. For sufficiency it is also required that

$$\left. \frac{d^2\pi}{dq^2} \right|_{q\,=\,q^*} = \left. \frac{d\pi'(q)}{dq} \right|_{q\,=\,q^*} < 0 \tag{12.6}$$

or that "marginal" profit must be decreasing at the optimal level of q. For q less than q^* (the optimal level of output), profit must be increasing [$\pi'(q) > 0$]; and for q greater than q^*, profit must be decreasing [$\pi'(q) < 0$]. Only if this condition holds has a true maximum of profits been achieved.

Graphic Analysis

These relationships are illustrated in Figure 12.1, where the top panel depicts typical cost and revenue functions. For low levels of output, costs exceed revenues and therefore economic profits are negative. In the middle ranges of output, revenues exceed costs; this means that profits are positive. Finally, at high levels of output, costs rise sharply and again exceed revenues. This relationship between the revenue and cost curves is shown in Figure 12.1b, where profits reach a maximum at q^*. At this level of output it is also true that the slope of the revenue curve (marginal revenue) is equal to the slope of the cost curve (marginal cost). It is clear from the figure that the sufficient conditions for a maximum are also satisfied at this point, since profits are increasing to the left of q^* and decreasing to the right of q^*. Output level q^* is therefore a true profit maximum. This is not so for output level q^{**}. Even though marginal revenue is equal to marginal cost at this output, profits are in fact a minimum at that point.

Figure 12.1   *Marginal Revenue Must Equal Marginal Cost for Profit Maximization*

Since profits are defined to be revenues (*TR*) minus costs (*TC*), it is clear that profits reach a maximum when the slope of the revenue function (marginal revenue) is equal to the slope of the cost function (marginal cost). This equality is only a necessary condition for a maximum, as may be seen by comparing points q^* (a true *maximum*) and q^{**} (a true *minimum*) for both of which marginal revenue equals marginal cost.

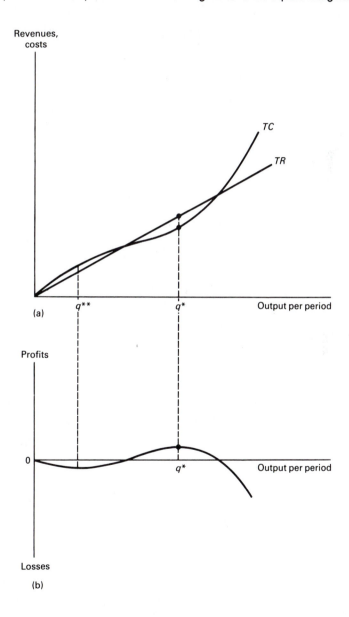

MARGINAL REVENUE

It is the revenue obtained from selling one more unit of output that is relevant to the profit-maximizing firm's output decision. If the firm can sell all it wishes without having any effect on market price, the market price will indeed be the extra revenue obtained from selling one more unit. Phrased in another way, if a firm's output decisions will not affect market price, marginal revenue is equal to the price at which a unit sells.

A firm may not always be able to sell all it wants at the prevailing market price, however. If it faces a downward-sloping demand curve for its good, more output can be sold only by reducing the good's price. In this case the revenue obtained from selling one more unit will be less than the price of that unit because, in order to get consumers to take the extra unit, the price of all other units must be lowered. This result can be easily demonstrated. As before, total revenue (TR) is simply the product of the quantity sold (q) times the price at which it is sold (P), which may depend on q also. Marginal revenue (MR) is then defined to be the change in TR resulting from a change in q:

Definition:

Marginal Revenue

$$\text{marginal revenue} = MR(q) = \frac{dTR}{dq} = \frac{d[P(q) \cdot q]}{dq} = P + q \cdot \frac{dP}{dq} \qquad (12.7)$$

Notice that the marginal revenue is a function of output. In general, MR will be different for different levels of q. From Equation 12.7 it is easy to see that if price does not change as quantity increases ($dP/dq = 0$), then marginal revenue will be equal to price. In this case we say that the firm is a *price taker* since its decisions do not influence the price it receives. On the other hand, if price falls as quantity increases ($dP/dq < 0$), then marginal revenue will be less than price. A profit-maximizing entrepreneur must know how increases in output will affect the price received before making an optimal output decision. If increases in q cause market price to fall, this must be taken into account.

Numerical Example

Suppose a firm faces a simple linear demand curve for its output over some period (q) of the form

$$q = 100 - 10P. \qquad (12.8)$$

Solving for P, we have

$$P = \frac{-q}{10} + 10, \qquad (12.9)$$

and total revenues (as a function of q) are given by

$$TR = Pq = \frac{-q^2}{10} + 10q. \qquad (12.10)$$

Hence, the firm's marginal revenue function is

$$MR = \frac{dTR}{dq} = \frac{-q}{5} + 10, \tag{12.11}$$

and, in this case, $MR < P$ for all values of q. If, for example, the firm produces 40 units of output per period, Equation 12.9 shows that it will receive a price of \$6 per unit. But at this level of output Equation 12.11 shows that MR is only \$2. If the firm produces 40 units of output, total revenue will be \$240 ($= \$6 \times 40$) whereas, if it produced 39 units, total revenue would be \$238 ($= \$6.1 \times 39$) since price will rise slightly when less is produced. Hence the marginal revenue from the fortieth unit sold is considerably less than its price. Indeed, for $q = 50$, marginal revenue is 0 (total revenues are a maximum at \$250 $= \$5 \times 50$), and any further expansion in output will actually result in a reduction in total revenue to the firm.

Marginal Revenue and Elasticity The concept of marginal revenue is directly related to the concept of demand elasticity developed in Chapter 7. Remember that the elasticity of demand ($e_{Q,P}$) was defined as the percentage change in quantity that results from a 1 percent change in price:

$$e_{Q,P} = \frac{dQ/Q}{dP/P} = \frac{dQ}{dP} \cdot \frac{P}{Q}. \tag{12.12}$$

If we use $e_{q,P}$ to denote the price elasticity of the demand curve facing the firm, this definition can be combined with Equation 12.7 to give

$$MR = P + \frac{qdP}{dq} = P\left(1 + \frac{q}{P} \cdot \frac{dP}{dq}\right) = P\left(1 + \frac{1}{e_{q,P}}\right). \tag{12.13}$$

If the demand curve facing the firm is negatively sloped, $e_{q,P} < 0$ and marginal revenue will be less than price as we have already shown. If demand is elastic ($e_{q,P} < -1$), marginal revenue will be positive. If demand is elastic, the sale of one more unit will not affect price "very much," and hence more revenue will be yielded by the sale. In fact, if demand facing the firm is infinitely elastic ($e_{q,P} = -\infty$), marginal revenue will equal price. The firm is, in this case, a price taker. However, if demand is inelastic ($e_{q,P} > -1$), marginal revenue will be negative. Increases in q can be obtained only through "large" declines in market price and these declines will actually cause total revenue to decrease.[4]

The relationship between marginal revenue and elasticity is summarized by Table 12.1

Marginal Revenue Curve Any demand curve has a marginal revenue curve associated with it. If we assume the firm must sell all its output at one price, it is sometimes convenient to think of the demand curve facing the firm as an *average revenue curve*. That

---

[4]In this light it might be pointed out that as long as marginal costs are positive, a profit-maximizing firm will not produce at a point on the demand curve for which demand is inelastic. In such a case, marginal revenue (negative) could not be equated to marginal cost (positive). This fact can be quite useful for studying market organization, as we will show in Chapter 19.

Table 12.1   *Relationship between Elasticity and Marginal Revenue*

$$e_{q,P} < -1 \qquad MR > 0$$
$$e_{q,P} = -1 \qquad MR = 0$$
$$e_{q,P} > -1 \qquad MR < 0$$

Figure 12.2   *Market Demand Curve and Associated Marginal Revenue Curve*

Since the demand curve is negatively sloped, the marginal revenue curve will fall below the demand ("average revenue") curve. For output levels beyond q_1, *MR* is negative. At q_1, total revenues ($P_1 \times q_1$) are a maximum; beyond this point additional increases in q actually cause total revenues to fall because of the concomitant declines in price.

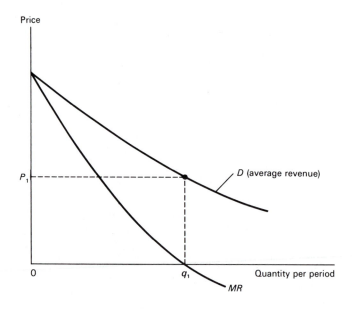

is, the demand curve shows the revenue per unit (in other words, the price) yielded by alternative output choices. The marginal revenue curve, on the other hand, shows the extra revenue provided by the last unit sold. In the usual case of a downward-sloping demand curve, the marginal revenue curve will lie below the demand curve for the reasons we analyzed earlier.[5] In Figure 12.2 we

---

[5]Notice that if demand is infinitely elastic (that is, if the demand curve is a horizontal line at some price), the average and marginal revenue curves coincide. Selling one more unit has no effect on price; therefore marginal and average revenue are equal.

have drawn such a curve, together with the demand curve from which it was derived. Notice that for output levels greater than q_1, marginal revenue is negative. As output increases from 0 to q_1, total revenues ($P \cdot q$) increase. However, at q_1 total revenues ($P_1 \cdot q_1$) are as large as possible; beyond this output level, price falls proportionately faster than output rises.

In Chapter 7 we talked in detail about the possibility of a demand curve's shifting because of changes in income, prices of other goods, or preferences. Whenever a demand curve does shift, its associated marginal revenue curve also shifts. This should be obvious, since a marginal revenue curve cannot be calculated without referring to a specific demand curve. In later analysis we shall have to keep in mind the kinds of shifts that marginal revenue curves might make when the demand for a product changes.

SHORT-RUN SUPPLY BY A PRICE-TAKING FIRM

We are now ready to study the supply decision of a profit-maximizing firm. In this chapter we will only examine the case in which the firm is a price taker since we will be looking at other cases in considerably more detail later on. Also, we will only focus on supply decisions in the short run here since long-run questions are the primary focus of Chapter 14. The firm's set of short-run cost curves are therefore the appropriate model for our analysis.

Profit-Maximizing Decision

Figure 12.3 shows the firm's short-run decision. The market price is given by P^*. The demand curve facing the firm is therefore a horizontal line through P^*. This line is labeled $P^* = MR$ as a reminder that an extra unit always can

Figure 12.3   *Short-Run Supply Curve for a Price-Taking Firm*

In the short run a price-taking firm will produce the level of output for which $SMC = P$. At P^*, for example, the firm will produce q^*. The SMC curve also shows what will be produced at other prices. For prices below $SAVC$, however, the firm will choose to produce no output. The heavy lines in the figure represent the firm's short-run supply curve.

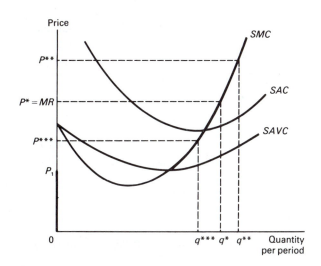

be sold by this price-taking firm without affecting the price. Output level q^* provides maximum profits, since at q^* price is equal to short-run marginal cost. The fact that profits are positive can be seen by noting that at q^* price exceeds average costs. The firm earns a profit on each unit sold. If price were below average cost (as is the case for P^{***}), the firm would have a loss on each unit sold. If price and average cost were equal, profits would be zero.

A geometric proof that profits are a maximum at q^* would proceed as follows. For output levels slightly less than q^*, price (P^*) exceeds short-run marginal cost. Reducing output below q^* would cut back on revenues more than on costs, and profits would fall. For output levels greater than q^*, marginal costs exceed P^*. Producing more than q^* would now cause costs to rise more rapidly than revenues, and again profits would fall. This means that if a firm produces either more or less than q^*, its profits will be lowered. Only at q^* are profits at a maximum. Notice that at q^* the marginal cost curve has a positive slope. This is required if profits are to be a true maximum. If $P = MC$ on a negatively sloped section of the marginal cost curve, this would not be a point of maximum profits, since increasing output would yield more in revenues (price times the amount produced) than this production would cost (marginal cost would decline if the MC curve has a negative slope). Consequently, profit maximization requires both that $P = MC$ and that marginal cost be increasing at this point.[6]

The Firm's Short-Run Supply Curve

The positively sloped portion of the short-run marginal cost curve is the short-run supply curve for this price-taking firm, since the curve shows how much the firm will produce for every possible market price. For example, as Figure 12.3 shows, at a higher price of P^{**}, the firm will produce q^{**} since it will find it in its interest to incur the higher marginal costs q^{**} entails. With a price of P^{***}, on the other hand, the firm opts to produce less (q^{***}) since only a lower output level will result in lower marginal costs to meet this lower price. By considering all possible prices that the firm might face, we can see by the marginal cost curve how much output the firm should supply at each price.

For very low prices we have to be careful about this conclusion. Should market price fall below P_1, the profit-maximizing decision would be to produce nothing. As Figure 12.3 shows, prices less than P_1 do not cover variable costs. There will be a loss on each unit produced in addition to the loss of all fixed costs. By shutting down production, the firm still must pay fixed costs, but it

[6]Mathematically, since

$$\pi(q) = Pq - TC(q),$$

profit maximization requires

$$\pi'(q) = P - MC = 0$$

and

$$\pi''(q) = -MC'(q) < 0.$$

Hence it is required that $MC'(q) > 0$; marginal cost must be increasing.

avoids the losses incurred on each unit produced. Since, in the short run, the firm cannot close down and avoid all costs, its best decision is to produce no output. On the other hand, a price only slightly above P_1 means the firm should produce some output. Even though profits may be negative (which they will be if price falls below short-run average total costs, the case at P^{***}), as long as variable costs are covered, the profit-maximizing decision is to continue production. Fixed costs must be paid in any case, and any price that covers variable costs will provide revenue as an offset to the fixed costs.[7] Hence we have a complete description of this firm's supply decisions in response to alternative prices for its output. These are summarized in the following definition:

Definition:

Short-Run Supply Curve
The firm's short-run supply curve shows how much it will produce at various possible output prices. For a profit-maximizing firm that takes the price of its output as given, this curve consists of the positively sloped segment of the firm's short-run marginal cost above the point of minimum average variable cost. For prices below this level, the firm's profit-maximizing decision is to shut down and produce no output.

Of course, any factor that shifts the firm's short-run marginal cost curve (such as changes in input prices or changes in the level of fixed inputs employed) will also shift the short-run supply curve. In Chapter 14 we will make extensive use of this type of analysis to study the operations of perfectly competitive markets.

Numerical Example   In our hamburger joint example in Chapter 11, we found that the firm's short-run total cost curve when it uses four grills was

$$STC = 4v + \frac{wq^2}{400},$$ (12.14)

where v and w are the per unit costs of capital and labor, respectively. If $v = w = \$4$, this can be written as

---

[7]Some algebra may clarify matters. Since we know total costs equal the sum of fixed and variable costs

$$STC = SFC + SVC,$$

profits are given by

$$\pi = TR - STC = P \cdot q - SFC - SVC.$$

If $q = 0$, variable costs and revenues are 0, so

$$\pi = -SFC.$$

Hence the firm will only produce something if $\pi > -SFC$. But, that means that

$$P \cdot q > SVC \quad \text{or} \quad P > SVC/q = SAVC.$$

$$STC = 16 + \frac{q^2}{100}. \qquad (12.15)$$

Hence, short-run marginal cost is given by

$$SMC = \frac{\partial STC}{\partial q} = \frac{2q}{100} = \frac{q}{50}. \qquad (12.16)$$

Profit maximization requires setting price equal to marginal cost:

$$P = SMC = \frac{q}{50}, \qquad (12.17)$$

and the short-run supply curve (with q as a function of P) is given by

$$q = 50P. \qquad (12.18)$$

To find this firm's shut-down price, we can use Equation 12.15 to calculate

$$SVC = \frac{q^2}{100} \qquad (12.19)$$

and

$$SAVC = \frac{SVC}{q} = \frac{q}{100}. \qquad (12.20)$$

Therefore, the minimum value for $SAVC$ occurs when q and $SMC = 0$. Consequently, Equation 12.18 reflects the firm's supply curve for any positive price. Notice, however, that

$$SAC = \frac{STC}{q} = \frac{16}{q} + \frac{q}{100} \qquad (12.21)$$

and minimum short-run average cost occurs when

$$\frac{dSAC}{dq} = \frac{-16}{q^2} + \frac{1}{100} = 0 \qquad (12.22)$$

and this occurs when $q = 40$ (and $SAC = .80$). For any price less than $.80 the firm will therefore incur a loss. If, for example, $P = \$.60$, Equation 12.18 shows that the firm should produce $q = 30$ hamburgers per hour. Total revenues are therefore \$18 ($= \$.60 \times 30$), but total costs are given by

$$STC = 16 + \frac{q^2}{100} = 16 + 9 = 25, \qquad (12.23)$$

and the firm will lose \$7 per hour. Of course, this is far better than producing nothing since then the firm would lose \$16 per hour.

If price exceeds \$.80, the firm will make positive economic profits. At a price of \$1 per hamburger, for example, the firm produces 50 hamburgers per hour and earns positive profits of \$5 per hour ($TR = \$50$, $STC = \$45$). When price is \$.80, profits are exactly 0 ($TR = \$32$, $TC = \$32$).

**PROFIT MAXI-
MIZATION
AND INPUT
DEMAND**

Thus far, we have treated the firm's decision problem as one of choosing a profit-maximizing level of output. But our discussion in Chapter 10 made clear that the firm's output is, in fact, determined by the inputs it chooses to employ, a relationship that is summarized by the production function $q = f(K, L)$. Consequently, the firm's economic profits can also be expressed as a function of the inputs it employs:

$$\pi(K, L) = Pq - TC(q) = Pf(K, L) - (vK + wL). \qquad (12.24)$$

Viewed in this way, the profit-maximizing firm's decision problem becomes one of choosing the appropriate levels of capital and labor input.[8] The first-order conditions for a maximum are

$$\frac{\partial \pi}{\partial K} = P \frac{\partial f}{\partial K} - v = 0$$

$$\frac{\partial \pi}{\partial L} = P \frac{\partial f}{\partial L} - w = 0. \qquad (12.25)$$

These conditions make the intuitively appealing point that a profit-maximizing firm should hire any input up to the point at which its marginal contribution to revenues is equal to the marginal cost of hiring the input. That is, the firm should implicitly perform a benefit-cost calculation for each unit of an input hired and cease hiring when the input's marginal contribution to profits reaches zero. In Chapter 21 we will examine the consequences of this observation in considerable detail since they provide the foundation of the theory of input demand. For the moment, however, we wish only to observe that the first-order conditions given in Equation 12.25 also imply cost minimization (since they imply that the $RTS = w/v$) and that these can generally be solved for the profit-maximizing levels of capital and labor input that the firm should hire.

*Second-Order
Conditions*

Because the profit function in Equation 12.24 depends on two variables, K and L, the second-order conditions for a profit maximum are somewhat more complex than in the single-variable case we examined earlier. In the Appendix to Chapter 2, we showed that in order to ensure a true maximum it is required that

$$\pi_{KK} < 0 \qquad \pi_{LL} < 0$$

and   (12.26)

$$\pi_{KK}\pi_{LL} - \pi_{KL}^2 > 0.$$

These conditions amount to requiring that the inputs capital and labor exhibit sufficiently diminishing marginal productivities so that marginal costs increase

---

[8] Throughout our discussion in this section, we will assume that the firm is a price taker so the price of its output can be treated as a fixed parameter. Results can be generalized fairly easily in the case where price depends on quantity sold.

as output expands. They therefore reflect the type of second-order conditions we have examined earlier in this chapter. To see why, notice from Equation 12.25 that $\pi_{KK} = Pf_{KK}$ and $\pi_{LL} = Pf_{LL}$. Hence diminishing marginal productivities ($f_{KK}, f_{LL} < 0$) will ensure that π_{KK} and π_{LL} will be negative. But, diminishing marginal productivity for each input is not sufficient to ensure increasing marginal costs. Since expanding output usually requires the firm to use both more capital *and* more labor, we must also ensure that increases in capital input do not raise the marginal productivity of labor (and thereby reduce marginal cost) by a large enough amount to reverse the effect of diminishing marginal productivity of labor itself. The second part of Equation 12.26 therefore requires that such cross-productivity effects be relatively small—that they be dominated by diminishing marginal productivities of the inputs. If these conditions can be satisfied, marginal costs will be increasing at the profit-maximizing choices for K and L, and the first-order conditions in Equation 12.25 will represent a true maximum.

The Supply Function

To develop the connection between supply behavior in this input-oriented view of the firm's choices and our prior discussion of output decisions, we can recognize that the first-order conditions for profit maximization (Equation 12.25) can generally be solved for the optimal input combination of capital (K^*) and labor (L^*) as functions of the parameters P, v, and w:

$$K^* = K^*(P, v, w)$$
$$L^* = L^*(P, v, w). \tag{12.27}$$

These input choices can then be substituted into the production function to yield the profit-maximizing output choice (q^*):

$$q^* = f(K^*, L^*) = f[K^*(P, v, w), L^*(P, v, w)]$$
$$= q^*(P, v, w). \tag{12.28}$$

Because this function shows how much the firm will produce at various prices for its product and various input costs, it is called a supply function:

Definition:

Supply Function
The supply function for a profit-maximizing firm that takes both output price (P) and input prices (v, w) as fixed is written as

$$\text{quantity supplied} = q^*(P, v, w) \tag{12.29}$$

to indicate the dependence of output choices on both product price and input cost considerations.

We will not make extensive use of this supply function here. It will be much easier for our purposes to rely on a graphical treatment of supply based on the firm's marginal cost curve. Usually no information will be lost by utilizing this simplification. But the supply function does provide a convenient reminder of two points that are not apparent from the marginal cost curve approach to supply: (1) The firm's output decision is fundamentally a decision about hiring inputs; and (2) changes in input costs will alter the hiring of inputs and hence affect output choices as well. Consequently, when it seems especially important to highlight this connection between input and output choices, we will want to return to this approach to supply.

Numerical Example

Our previous burger emporium example is not quite appropriate for the development of a supply function because our assumed production function is characterized by constant returns to scale. In situations where both K (grills) and L (workers) are variable, marginal costs will be constant and unaffected by how much the firm chooses to produce. If market price equals this marginal cost, the quantity supplied is indeterminate. To introduce increasing marginal costs, we must assume that a third input (say, seating capacity [F] measured in square meters) enters the burger production function, which is now given by

$$q = 10K^{.25}L^{.25}F^{.5}. \tag{12.30}$$

We assume that, in the short run, eating space is limited to an area four meters square. Hence, $F = 16$ and the short-run production function is given by

$$q = 40K^{.25}L^{.25}. \tag{12.31}$$

The firm's profit function is now given by

$$= Pq - TC$$
$$= P40K^{.25}L^{.25} - vK - wL - R, \tag{12.32}$$

where R is the (fixed) rent the firm must pay for eating space.
First-order conditions for a profit maximum are

$$\frac{\partial \pi}{\partial K} = 10PK^{-.75}L^{.25} - v = 0$$

$$\frac{\partial \pi}{\partial L} = 10PK^{.25}L^{-.75} - w = 0. \tag{12.33}$$

Hence

$$10PK^{-.75}L^{.25} = v \tag{12.34}$$

$$10PK^{.25}L^{-.75} = w. \tag{12.35}$$

As before, in these examples, division of 12.35 by 12.34 yields the cost-minimization result that

$$\frac{K}{L} = \frac{w}{v}. \tag{12.36}$$

Solving this equation for L and substitution into Equation 12.34 yields (after some manipulation) the capital demand equation

$$K = \frac{(10P)^2}{v^{1.5}w^{.5}}, \tag{12.37}$$

and a similar substitution for K in Equation 12.35 yields the labor demand equation

$$L = \frac{(10P)^2}{v^{.5}w^{1.5}}. \tag{12.38}$$

Finally, substitution of these back into the short-run production function (Equation 12.31) yields

$$q = \frac{40(10P)}{(vw)^{.5}}, \tag{12.39}$$

which is the short-run supply function we seek. Notice that this function is homogeneous of degree 0 in P, v, and w. That is, if P, w, and v were all to double, quantity supplied would not change. If $w = v = \$4$, the function becomes

$$q = 100P. \tag{12.40}$$

Hence, if $P = \$1$, the firm will supply 100 hamburgers per hour. Equations 12.37 and 12.31 show that these will be produced using 6.25 ($= {}^{100}\!/_{16}$) grills and 6.25 workers per hour. Substitution of these input values into the short-run production function (Equation 12.31) shows that they are indeed sufficient to produce 100 hamburgers per hour. With these inputs, short-run variable costs will be \$50 (6.25 × \$4 + 6.25 × \$4) and revenues will be \$100. Since revenues cover variable costs, the firm will choose to produce in the short run even if its fixed rent results in a loss in overall terms.

If the price of hamburgers were to rise, this profit-maximizing firm would produce more. If $P = \$1.50$, for example, the firm would produce 150 burgers per hour using $K = L = {}^{225}\!/_{16} = 14.1$. Hence the higher price has also led to a substantial increase in the hiring of inputs.

The supply function in Equation 12.39 also permits an examination of how the firm's supply decisions would be affected by a change in input prices. Suppose, for example, a benevolent government dictated a minimum wage for workers of \$9 per hour. Then the supply function would become

$$q = \frac{400P}{(36)^{.5}} = \frac{400P}{6}. \tag{12.41}$$

At a price of \$1 the firm would now only produce ${}^{400}\!/_{6}$ ($= 66.6$) hamburgers per hour. To do so it would utilize ${}^{100}\!/_{24} = 4.2$ grills and ${}^{100}\!/_{54} = 1.9$ workers. Notice that the higher wage has reduced the hiring of workers both because the firm chooses to produce fewer hamburgers per hour and because it substitutes capital for labor in production. In Chapter 21 we will examine this relationship between input costs and hiring in considerably more detail.

THE CONTRO- VERSY OVER THE PROFIT- MAXIMIZA- TION HYPOTHESIS

The so-called marginalist controversy about whether firms really do maximize profits, although usually dormant in the economics profession, occasionally has a revival that spurs a wide variety of theoretical and empirical research.[9] Over the years a vast amount of evidence has been brought forth that purports to refute the hypothesis that profit-making firms seek maximum profits, but on the whole, the hypothesis has withstood these assaults. The attacks on the marginalist approach can be classed into three general types: (1) that the profit-maximization approach is too simple; (2) that there exist alternative, equally simple hypotheses that can better explain reality; and (3) that real-world firms do not have suitable information to be able to maximize profits, nor would they particularly want to maximize profits if they had such information. In Chapter 13 we will examine the first two of these objections. Here we look briefly at the firm's information problem and how we might test the profit-maximization hypothesis.

Certainly, most economists would agree that real-world firms do not have adequate information to maximize profits in any exact sense. For most firms the demand and marginal revenue curves they face are only vaguely understood. It is also likely that firms do not have adequate information on their cost structure so as to be able to make delicate and precise marginal calculations. In defense of the profit-maximization hypothesis, it might be argued that only those firms that are reasonably able to approximate marginal decisions will survive in a competitive atmosphere. This *survivorship principle* implies that any firms we observe are likely to be profit maximizers (simply because they are still in business), even though their technical knowledge of precise revenue and cost factors may be minimal.

In answering questionnaires, firms often deny having adequate information to make careful marginal decisions. On the other hand, economists have found the profit-maximization hypothesis to be extremely accurate in predicting certain aspects of firms' behavior. For example, many firms seem eager to enter into the most profitable industries, and some of the larger, stagnant firms seek to diversify to increase profitability. Attempts to reconcile these two seemingly contradictory findings about profit maximization have centered on the methodological question of the role of assumptions in economic theory. As we saw in Chapter 1, Friedman and other economists argue that one cannot judge the assumption of profit maximization either by *a priori* logic or by asking firms what they do.[10] Rather, the ultimate test is the predictive ability of the hypothesis. Friedman uses the analogy of the expert pool player who has no knowledge of the rules of physics that determine the movements of the balls on the table. This ignorance on the part of the player, however, does not prevent an observer from accurately predicting the player's behavior by applying physical principles. Just as Molière's Monsieur Jourdain spoke prose all his life without

---

[9] Perhaps the most interesting of these debates over the goals of the firm was conducted by Richard A. Lester and Fritz Machlup in the *American Economic Review* during the years 1946 and 1947.

[10] See Milton Friedman, "The Methodology of Positive Economics" in *Essays in Positive Economics* (Chicago: University of Chicago Press, 1953).

knowing it, firms may in fact maximize profits despite their protests that they have no such intentions. In a sense the argument again rests on the survivorship principle: Firms are led by the rigors of the market toward profit maximization.

The alternative to Friedman's positivist position is to argue that much more can be learned about a firm's behavior by studying the behavior of its managers. Profit maximization is claimed to be too simple a hypothesis to be useful in understanding the complex workings of a modern corporation. A resolution of these conflicting methodological views may never be achieved. Clearly, both views have elements of truth and each can be valuable for certain applications. The position taken in this book will be that the profit-maximization hypothesis is the single most acceptable starting point for a theory of firm behavior. It will also be shown in later chapters that firms that operate in a profit-maximizing way (or firms that are forced to do so by the state) may perform the task of production in an efficient manner. Hence, for a theoretical overview of microeconomic behavior, profit maximization seems a reasonable and useful assumption to make, and we shall do so throughout most of this book.

SUMMARY

In this chapter we studied the supply decision of a profit-maximizing firm. Our general goal was to show how such a firm responds to price signals from the marketplace, and in addressing that question, we developed a number of analytical results:

- In order to maximize profits, the firm should choose to produce that output level for which marginal revenue (the revenue from selling one more unit) is equal to marginal cost (the cost of producing one more unit).

- If a firm is a price taker, its output decisions do not affect the price of its output so marginal revenue is given by this price. If the firm faces a downward-sloping demand for its output, however, it can sell more only by lowering its price. In this case marginal revenue will be less than price and may even be negative.

- Marginal revenue and the price elasticity of demand are related by the formula

$$MR = P\left(1 + \frac{1}{e_{q,P}}\right),$$

where P is the market price of the firm's output and $e_{q,P}$ is the price elasticity of demand for its product.

- The supply curve for a price-taking, profit-maximizing firm is given by the positively sloped portion of its marginal cost curve above the point of minimum average variable cost (AVC). If price falls below minimum

AVC, the firm's profit-maximizing choice is to shut down and produce nothing.

- The firm's profit-maximization problem can also be approached as a problem in optimal input choice. Although this alternative approach yields the same results as does an approach based on output choices, it does help to clarify the relationship between input costs and supply decisions.

Application

MARKUP PRICING

Major corporations (and minor ones also) use neither the terminology nor the analytical techniques that we have introduced in Chapter 12. Here we will examine the most common management technique, *markup pricing*, and we shall see how this technique compares to the simplified model we have developed.[11]

The markup pricing technique works as follows. Management first computes the average total cost of producing some "normal" level of output. To this cost is added a profit markup to arrive at the good's selling price. The most interesting question about the markup pricing policy is whether it is consistent with profit maximization. Taken at face value, it seems that the policy cannot possibly lead to maximum profits, since it pays no attention to demand. To see that this is so, let us consider the markup that would be required in order to maximize profits. In general the markup (m) is given by

$$m = \frac{P - AC}{AC}. \qquad (12.42)$$

Now let us assume that the firm is planning on an output level that corresponds to the low point on its long-run *AC* curve. At this "optimal" output level, *AC* is equal to marginal cost.

[11] The use of this method of pricing in particular corporations is discussed in A. D. H. Kaplan, J. B. Dirlam, and R. F. Lanzillotti, *Pricing in Big Business: A Case Approach* (Washington, D.C.: The Brookings Institution, 1958).

Therefore

$$m = \frac{P - MC}{MC}. \qquad (12.43)$$

But for profit maximization, marginal cost should equal marginal revenue. Consequently,

$$m = \frac{P - MR}{MR}. \qquad (12.44)$$

By using Equation 12.13 and performing some algebraic manipulations, we get

$$m = -\frac{1}{1 + e_{q,P}}. \qquad (12.45)$$

Equation 12.45 shows that the markup of a profit-maximizing firm should vary inversely with the elasticity of demand for its product. If this demand elasticity is -3.0, for example, $m = .50$ and a markup of 50 percent would maximize profits. If $e_{q,P} = -11.0$, on the other hand, $m = .10$ and a markup of only 10 percent would maximize profits.

Empirical Evidence for Large Corporations

Most available evidence indicates that major corporations take demand into account in their pricing policies. For example, in their study of the pricing policies of U.S. Steel Corporation, Kaplan, Dirlam, and Lanzillotti found that the markup on steel products varied inversely with the elasticity of demand for these products. Margins were high on steel rails, for example, since this was a product line in which U.S. Steel faced little competition. On the other hand, margins were low on stainless steel and tin plate, since these products faced strong competition from aluminum and lumber producers. The authors found similar results for many major corporations, including E. I. du Pont de Nemours, Standard Oil Company of New Jersey, and Aluminum Company of America.[12] In all of them, target profit margins seemed to be related to the elasticity of demand, just as profit maximization requires. In a study of Danish firms, B. Fog also found that target profit margins vary with demand conditions. He reported that many companies respond to questions about how profit margins are set by noting that they "charge what the traffic will bear" or that "market conditions determine the price."[13] In other words, markups are determined in a profit-maximizing way.

Evidence from Retailing

In their study of retailing, R. M. Cyert and J. G. March spent considerable effort analyzing the feedback from the market for the pricing of a product. Even though the firm may set prices and profit margins without considering demand, the subsequent reaction of the market (which provides information on the true demand situation) causes the firm to adjust its prices accordingly. Cyert and March applied their model to a department store's markdown policy and concluded that the prices of items are adjusted over time to meet demand conditions.[14] Any experienced bargain hunter knows that retailers adjust the prices of unpopular items downward much more rapidly than they reduce the prices of "hot" items. Price changing such as this is consistent with the notion that markups are set with profit-maximization goals in mind.

[12] Kaplan, Dirlam, and Lanzillotti, *Pricing in Big Business* pp. 172–174.

[13] B. Fog, *Industrial Pricing Policies* (Amsterdam: North Holland Publishing Co., 1969), p. 104. See especially Chapter 6.

[14] R. M. Cyert and J. G. March, *A Behavioral Theory of the Firm* (Englewood Cliffs, N.J.: Prentice-Hall, 1963), chap. 7.

SUGGESTED READINGS

Arrow, K. J. *The Limits of Organization.* New York: Norton, 1974.

A general inquiry into the internal operations of firms (and other organizations). Stresses how economic incentives affect these operations.

Baumol, W. J. *Business Behavior, Value, and Growth.* Rev. ed. New York: Harcourt Brace Jovanovich, 1967. Chap. 6.

An extended analysis of the revenue-maximization hypothesis.

Coase, R. H. "The Nature of the Firm." *Economica* (November 1937): 386–405.

Cyert, R. M., and Hedrick, C. L. "Theory of the Firm: Past, Present, and Future: An Interpretation." *Journal of Economic Literature* 10 (1972): 389–412.

A brief, succinct survey of alternative models of firms' objectives.

Cyert, R. M., and March, J. G. *A Behavioral Theory of the Firm.* Englewood Cliffs, N.J.: Prentice-Hall, 1963. Chap. 7.

Detailed development of a behavioral approach to firm decision making together with some empirical evidence.

Ferguson, C. E. "Static Models of Average-Cost Pricing." *Southern Economic Journal* 23 (1957): 272–284.

An exploration of the consequences of markup pricing behavior.

Friedman, M. "The Methodology of Positive Economics." In *Essays in Positive Economics.* Chicago: University of Chicago Press, 1953. Pp. 3–43.

Basic statement of Friedman's positivist views about the role of assumptions in economics.

Griliches, Z. "Are Farmers Rational?" *Journal of Political Economy* 68 (1960): 68–71.

A fascinating methodological discussion of the best way to treat farmers' decision making in the economics of agriculture.

Kaplan, A. D. H.; Dirlam, J. B.; and Lanzillotti, R. F. *Pricing in Big Business: A Case Approach.* Washington, D.C.: The Brookings Institution, 1958.

Classic study of pricing decisions in a sample of large corporations.

Machlup, F. "Theories of the Firm: Marginal, Behavioral, Managerial." *American Economic Review* 47 (1957): 1–33.

Influential article on the "marginalist debate" over the proper approach to theories of the firm.

Silberberg, E. *The Structure of Economics: A Mathematical Analysis.* New York: McGraw-Hill Book Company, 1978. Pp. 107–114.

Gives a detailed development of the supply function for a profit-maximizing firm.

Williamson, O. F. "The Modern Corporation: Origins, Evolution, Attributes." *Journal of Economic Literature* 19 (December 1981): 1537–1568.

A good literate survey of the nature of modern corporations.

PROBLEMS

12.1

John's Lawn Mowing Service is a small business that acts as a price taker (i.e., $MR = P$). The prevailing market price of lawn mowing is $20 per acre. John's costs are given by

$$\text{Total cost} = .1q^2 + 10q + 50$$

where q = the number of acres John chooses to cut a day.

- a. How many acres should John choose to cut in order to maximize profit?
- b. Calculate John's maximum daily profit.
- c. Graph these results and label John's supply curve.

12.2

Would a lump sum profits tax affect the profit maximizing quantity of output? How about a proportional tax on profits? How about a tax assessed on each unit of output?

12.3

Suppose that a firm faces a constant elasticity demand curve of the form

$$q = 256P^{-2}$$

and has a *marginal cost* curve of the form

$$MC = 0.001q.$$

- a. Graph these demand and marginal cost curves.
- b. Calculate the marginal revenue curve associated with the demand curve. Graph this curve.
- c. At what output level does marginal revenue equal marginal cost?

12.4

A firm faces a demand curve given by:

$$q = 100 - 2P.$$

Marginal and average costs for the firm are constant at $10 per unit.

a. What output level should the firm produce to maximize profits? What are profits at that output level?

b. What output level should the firm produce to maximize revenues? What are profits at that output level?

c. Suppose the firm wishes to maximize revenues subject to the constraint that it earn $12 in profits for each of the 64 machines it employs. What level of output should it produce?

d. Graph your results.

12.5

This problem concerns the relationship between demand and marginal revenue curves for a few functional forms. Show that:

a. for a linear demand curve, the marginal revenue curve bisects the distance between the vertical axis and the demand curve for any price.

b. for any linear demand curve, the vertical distance between the demand and marginal revenue curves is $-1/b \cdot q$, where b (<0) is the slope of the demand curve.

c. for a constant elasticity demand curve, the vertical distance between the demand and marginal revenue curves is a constant ratio of the height of the demand curve, with this constant depending on the price elasticity of demand.

d. for any downward-sloping demand curve, the vertical distance between the demand and marginal revenue curves at any point can be found by using a linear approximation to the demand curve at that point and applying the procedure described in part (b).

e. Graph the results of parts (a) through (d) of this problem.

12.6

Universal Widget produces high-quality widgets at its plant in Gulch, Nevada, for sale throughout the world. The cost function for total widget production (q) is given by

$$\text{total cost} = .25q^2.$$

Widgets are demanded only in Australia (where the demand curve is given by $q = 100 - 2P$) and Lapland (where the demand curve is given by $q = 100 - 4P$). If Universal Widget can control the quantities supplied to each market, how many should it sell in each location in order to maximize total profits? What price will be charged in each location?

12.7

The production function for a firm in the business of calculator assembly is given by

$$q = 2\sqrt{L}$$

where q is finished calculator output and L represents hours of labor input. The firm is a price taker for both calculators (which sell for P) and workers (which can be hired at a wage rate of w per hour).

a. What is the supply function for assembled calculators $[q = f(P, w)]$?

b. Explain both algebraically and graphically why this supply function is homogeneous of degree zero in P and w and why profits are homogeneous of degree one in these variables.

c. Show explicitly how changes in w shift the supply curve for this firm.

12.8

The market for high quality caviar is dependent on the weather. If the weather is good there are many fancy parties and caviar sells for $30 per pound. In bad weather it sells for only $20 per pound. A small caviar producer has a cost function given by

$$TC = \tfrac{1}{2}q^2 + 5q + 100$$

where q is weekly caviar production. Production decisions must be made before the weather (and the price of caviar) is known, but it is known that good weather and bad weather each occur with a probability of 0.5.

   a.   How much caviar should this firm produce if it wishes to maximize the expected value of its profits?

   b.   Suppose the owner of this firm has a utility function of the form

$$\text{utility} = \sqrt{\pi}$$

   where π is weekly profits. What is the expected utility associated with the output strategy defined in part a?

   c.   Can this firm owner obtain a higher utility of profits by producing some output other than that specified in parts a and b? Explain.

   d.   Suppose this firm could predict next week's price, but could not influence that price. What strategy would maximize expected profits in this case? What would expected profits be?

EXTENSIONS

PROFIT FUNCTIONS

For some applications the analysis of profit maximization provided in Chapter 12 may be too indirect and it is more expedient to focus explicitly on the firm's profits and their dependence on output and input prices. Specifically, since by definition,

$$\text{Profits} = \pi = P \cdot q - vK - wL$$

and the variables q, K, and L are endogenous (they are determined through various profit-maximizing decisions), we can write

$$\text{maximum profits} = \pi^* = \pi^*(P, v, w).$$

This representation, which is analogous to the indirect utility function that we introduced in Chapter 4, is called a profit function—*it shows how the firm's profits ultimately depend on the market parameters the firm faces (and, implicitly, on the firm's technology and on the demand for its product). Here we will examine some properties of this function and illustrate a few applications of the concept.*

E12.1
Show that the profit function is homogeneous of degree 1 in P, v, and w. That is, show that a doubling of output and input prices will double profits. Explain this result intuitively.

E12.2
Use simple partial differentiation of the profit function to show

$$\frac{\partial \pi^*}{\partial P} \geq 0, \qquad \frac{\partial \pi^*}{\partial v}, \frac{\partial \pi^*}{\partial w} \leq 0.$$

Explain these results intuitively.

E12.3

Since the function $\pi^*(P, v, w)$ is itself the result of a maximization process, the envelope theorem applies to the derivatives calculated in E12.2. Show that the first of these $(\partial\pi^*/\partial P)$ provides an alternative way of computing the supply function for a profit/maximizing firm whereas the derivatives $\partial\pi^*/\partial v$ and $\partial\pi^*/\partial w$ provide a way of computing the demands for K and L. Explain why these input demand functions differ from those computed from the total cost function in Chapter 11 because now they allow output to vary (we will return to this distinction in Chapter 21).

E12.4

Show that for any two output prices, P_1 and P_2,

$$\pi^*(0.5P_1 + 0.5P_2, v, w) \le 0.5\pi^*(P_1, v, w) + 0.5\pi^*(P_2, v, w).$$

That is, show that the profit function is *convex* in output prices. *Hint:* Let $\overline{P} = 0.5P_1 + 0.5P_2$ and let $\overline{q}, \overline{K}$ and $\overline{L}$ be profit maximizing choices at $\overline{P}$. Explain why $\pi^*(P_1, v, w) \ge P_1\overline{q} - v\overline{K} - w\overline{L}$. Similarly, explain why $\pi^*(P_2, v, w) \ge P_2\overline{q} - v\overline{K} - w\overline{L}$. Now combine these statements.

E12.5

Use the results from E12.4 to show that a profit maximizing firm will prefer a fluctuating output price to one that is stabilized at the mean value of the fluctuating price. Explain this result intuitively using a graphic analysis of the firm's short-run supply curve.

E12.6

Analogously to the case of consumer's surplus, we can define the *producer's surplus* associated with a rise in output price as the extra profits generated by such a rise. Use the fact that

$$\frac{\partial\pi^*(P, w, v)}{\partial P} = q^*(P, w, v)$$

to show that the extra producer's surplus generated by a rise in output price from P_0 to P_1 can be found by integrating the supply function over this range. Interpret your results graphically using the firm's short-run supply curve.

REFERENCES

McFadden, D., "Cost, Revenue and Profit Functions," in M. Fuss and D. McFadden (Eds.), *Production Economics: A Dual Approach to Theory and Applications* (Amsterdam: North Holland, 1978) pp. 60–110.

Silberberg, E., *The Structure of Economics: A Mathematical Analysis* (New York: McGraw-Hill Book Company, 1978) pp. 263–274.

CHAPTER 13

Alternative Models of the Firm

In Chapter 12 we developed a rather simple model of a profit-maximizing firm. Although, as we shall see, this model is extremely useful in terms of generating testable hypotheses about firms' behavior, it has been criticized on a number of grounds. In this chapter we will look at a few of the issues that have arisen through attempts to develop alternative models of firm behavior. We begin by examining a simple alternative to profit maximization, revenue maximization, and then proceed to investigate more complex models that seek to represent contractual relationships among the individuals in a firm. In the final section of this chapter, we briefly examine issues that arise in modeling the behavior of not-for-profit firms.

REVENUE MAXIMI- ZATION

If we wish to continue to treat the firm as a single decision-making unit, there are relatively few alternatives to the profit-maximization hypothesis. Perhaps the most common such alternative is provided by the assumption of revenue maximization first developed by William J. Baumol in the 1960s.[1] In addition to the fact that this is a very simple hypothesis to model, several other observations suggest it may accurately capture some aspects of firms' behavior. Most important, when firms are uncertain about the demand curve they actually face or when they have no very reliable notion of the marginal costs of their output (as may be especially true in multiproduct firms), the decision to try to maximize sales may be a reasonable rule of thumb for assuring their long-term survival. Indeed, a number of management consulting firms stress to their clients the importance of maximizing their "market share" as a way of protecting themselves against the vagaries of the market.

Other pieces of evidence also suggest that revenue maximization may be a goal of firms. Executives of major corporations are often paid on the basis of the "size" (that is, total revenues) of their divisions. Indeed, some of the highest

---

[1] A clear statement of this hypothesis is found in W. J. Baumol, *Business Behavior, Value and Growth*, rev. ed. (New York: Harcourt, Brace & World, 1967), chap. 6.

Figure 13.1   *Revenue Maximization*

A firm that seeks to maximize total revenues will produce where marginal revenue is equal to zero (q^*). If the firm faces a minimum profit constraint, it may choose an output level between the profit-maximizing level (q^{**}) and q^*.

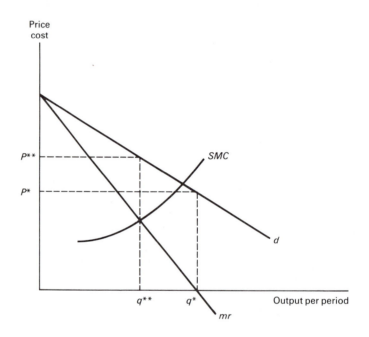

paid executives in the United States head very large (in sales) firms with mediocre records of profitability. Similarly, large firms may enjoy other advantages such as access to bank credit or favorable prices on raw materials that are more directly related to revenues than to profits. Governments also may be willing to treat large firms more favorably than small ones because they are major employers in the economy.

Graphic Analysis   A strictly revenue-maximizing firm would choose to produce that level of output for which marginal revenue is zero. That is, it should proceed to the point at which selling further units actually causes total revenues to fall. This choice is illustrated in Figure 13.1 For the firm that faces the demand curve[2] d, maximum revenues are obtainable by producing output level q^*. For $q < q^*$, mr is positive so selling more increases total revenues (though possibly not profits). For $q > q^*$, however, mr is negative so further sales actually reduce total

---

[2] We use a lower-case d to represent the demand curve facing the firm. We will use an upper-case D to represent the market demand curve. The marginal revenue curves associated with d and D are denoted by mr and MR, respectively.

revenues because of the price reductions that are required to get demanders to buy the good. Since we know from Chapter 12 that

$$mr = P\left(1 + \frac{1}{e_{q,P}}\right),$$ (13.1)

$mr = 0$ implies that $e_{q,P} = -1$: Demand will be unit elastic at q^*.

This revenue-maximizing choice might be contrasted to the output level that a profit-maximizing firm would choose q^{**}. At q^{**} marginal revenue equals short-run marginal cost (given by SMC in Figure 13.1). Increasing output beyond q^{**} would reduce profits since $mr < SMC$. Even though revenues continue to increase up to q^*, units of output beyond q^{**} bring in less than they cost to produce. Since mr is positive at q^{**}, Equation 13.1 shows that demand must be elastic ($e_{q,P} < -1$) at this point.

Constrained Revenue Maximization

A firm that chooses to maximize revenues is giving no attention to its costs nor to the profitability of the sales it is making. Indeed, it is quite possible that the output level q^* in Figure 13.1 may yield negative profits to the firm. Since, as we discussed briefly in Chapter 12 and will take up in more detail later in the application to this chapter, no firm can survive forever with extremely low profits, it may be more realistic to assume that firms must meet some minimum level of profitability from their activities. Hence, although they may be prompted to produce more than q^{**} because of a variety of motives for maximizing revenues, they may stop short of q^* because of the need to assure an acceptable level of profitability. They will, therefore, behave as constrained revenue maximizers and will opt for some output level between q^{**} and q^*.

Numerical Example

A simple numerical example of these issues can be developed from the linear demand relationship we studied in Chapter 12. To give the example concrete meaning, assume that the firm produces sidewalk slabs at a constant average and marginal cost of $4 each. The weekly demand for slabs facing the firm is given by

$$q = 100 - 10P.$$ (13.2)

As before, we can solve for total revenues as a function of q:

$$TR = Pq = 10q - \frac{q^2}{10}$$ (13.3)

and then find marginal revenue as

$$mr = \frac{dTR}{dq} = 10 - \frac{q}{5}.$$ (13.4)

Total revenues are maximized when $mr = 0$—that is, when $q = 50$. At an output of 50 slabs per week, Equation 13.3 shows that total revenue will be $250. Since slabs cost $4 each, the firm will have profits of $50 (= $250 − 50

× \$4) per week. If the firm wishes to maximize profits, it should produce where marginal revenue equals marginal cost:

$$mr = 10 - \frac{q}{5} = MC = 4 \qquad (13.5)$$

or $q = 30$. Although this level of output yields less in total revenues (\$210), total profits per week are nearly twice as large (\$90 = \$210 − 30 × \$4) as for the revenue-maximizing choice.

A minimum required profit goal of between \$50 and \$90 would yield an intermediate choice for this firm. Suppose, for example, that the firm's owners demanded they get at least \$80 per week as a return on their slab molds. Then the firm might seek to maximize total revenues subject to the constraint that

$$\pi = TR - TC = 10q - \frac{q^2}{10} - 4q = 80. \qquad (13.6)$$

Rearranging the terms of this constraint yields

$$q^2 = -60q + 800 = 0 \qquad (13.7)$$

or

$$(q - 40)(q - 20) = 0. \qquad (13.8)$$

Clearly, the solution $q = 40$ yields maximum revenues (\$240) from among the output options of 20 or 40 that yield at least \$80 in weekly profits.

Although we could explore other simple alternatives to profit maximization, the actual study of firm behavior has taken a different direction and stresses instead the complex nature of the relationships among the individuals involved. We now turn to examine some of this recent literature.

CONTRACTS WITHIN FIRMS

As we discussed briefly in Chapter 12, a firm is an organization that produces economic goods. In that process the activities of workers, managers, and suppliers of capital must be coordinated and controlled. This is accomplished through a series of contracts among these parties. In some cases the contracts may be explicitly written down—for example, the contract between the United Automobile Workers and General Motors runs for hundreds of pages. In many other instances, however, contracts may be in the form of implicit understandings about what the terms of employment are. Even though such contracts are not on paper, they may be very effective in assuring that the rights and responsibilities of the various parties are followed.

The modern study of the theory of the firm is primarily concerned with these various contracts. The firm itself is a legal entity (in the United States, firms are treated legally as individuals) that usually represents one side of the contract, and workers, managers, and capital suppliers represent the other side. The problem these parties face is to develop contracts that are desirable to everyone concerned. For example, contracts with workers must be desirable from the workers' point of view in terms of the wages paid and the working conditions provided, and desirable from the firm's point of view in terms of providing incentives for the workers to perform in a productive way.

The kinds of costs involved in developing such contracts vary a great deal among different types of firms, and as might be expected, a wide variety of contractual provisions may be encountered. Even if nothing is written down explicitly, the implicit understandings among individuals involved with a firm may be quite complex and, at times, seemingly nonsensical. An important aspect of the modern theory of the firm has been to try to understand why certain explicit or implicit contractual arrangements exist and how they affect the firm's operation.

Here we will examine three aspects of this topic. First, we ask about the organizational design of firms; that is, we briefly explore the factors that influence what firms look like. Next, we investigate some aspects of a firm's contracts with its workers. Finally, we examine managerial contracts and possible conflicts in the relationship between owners and managers.

ORGANIZA-TION OF FIRMS

The wide variety of existing firm types and sizes has prompted economists to speculate about the kinds of factors that might influence the organizational form chosen. Ronald Coase laid out the basic principles of these investigations in a famous 1937 article.[3] To Coase, firms were an alternative to the market-place as a way of organizing production. At one extreme, think of a situation in which all production is being carried out by individuals. A person who wanted to, say, produce an automobile would buy the parts from thousands of independent suppliers, assemble these parts, and then turn the car over to someone else to sell. All transactions in such a situation would be among individuals who would each be very specialized producers. At the alternative extreme, all production in an economy might take place inside a single vast firm. This firm would coordinate the production of all automobiles, all automobile parts, and everything else through non-market, command and control directives. In such a world there would be no need for any market transactions in intermediate goods.

To Coase, the location of an actual organization of production along this spectrum of possibilities was largely determined by cost considerations. Specifically, he argued that a firm's size and complexity would expand up to the point at which the costs involved in making additional transactions internally were exactly balanced by the costs involved in making the transactions through the market. In order to understand the size and scope of a firm's activities, we must therefore examine the relative significance of these various costs.

Advantages of the Market

Purchasing intermediate products in the marketplace offers a number of potential cost advantages to the firm. Because many firms buy from a single supplier, that supplier may be able to achieve economies of scale in production that

---

[3] R. H. Coase, "The Nature of the Firm," *Economica* (November 1937): 386–405.

would not be attainable if the firm tried to produce the input internally. For example, producers of personal computers (especially IBM "clones") purchase all of the principal internal electronics from one or two suppliers. Since electronic chip manufacturing involves substantial economies of scale whereas computer assembly does not, many computer producers are not integrated backward into the product chain.

Uncertainties in the demand for a firm's product may also provide a good reason for the firm to purchase its inputs in the market. Since the input supplier can sell to many firms, it may be able to maintain a fairly smooth flow of production even though sales to any one user may be quite erratic. Small convenience stores, for example, depend on outside firms to supply them with a wide range of items they sell only occasionally ("peg-board" items such as scissors, labels, or playing cards) whereas they may develop their own supply of regularly demanded items such as milk or deli sandwiches.

Finally, reliance on markets for inputs may permit the firm to utilize the pressures of competition to restrain costs. It may have the option to take its business elsewhere if a particular supplier becomes too costly. An integrated firm must instead try to keep its production costs down through various types of internal control mechanisms. Indeed, in some very large firms, competition between divisions may be purposely initiated to keep production costs in line. In many situations reliance on the marketplace serves this function automatically.

Advantages of Integration

Using the marketplace to acquire intermediate inputs for the firm also has many undesirable features, however. Purchasing such inputs from someone else requires that the firm undertake some type of transaction, which may have costs associated with it. Thus the firm must find a suitable provider, negotiate contract terms, and arrange for the goods to be delivered. All of these costs may be reduced (or entirely eliminated) if the firm decides to produce the input internally. Of course, internal production requires that the firm spend something for monitoring and controlling the production process. An independent provider would incur similar costs, however, and with internal production a firm may be more certain that production quality standards are met. Overall then, integration of the production process might be expected to enable the firm to obtain significant savings in transactions costs.

The need for specialized equipment provides a second possible rationale for expanding the types of functions carried on within the firm. If a firm must utilize a machine that is useful only to it (perhaps because the equipment must fit into a unique location or use a particular type of fuel), then it is probably less costly for the firm to buy than to try to locate another firm willing to make the investment. Only in relatively rare instances will a supplier firm invest in equipment that is only useful to one buyer since that puts the supplier in a very risky position. In such a case, the supplier can be viewed as a "hostage" of the purchasing firm and may have to make contract concessions to it during the equipment's lifetime. Therefore, in general, suppliers will not invest in such specialized equipment, and firms will usually make such purchases for themselves.

A final, related way in which a firm may enlarge the scope of its activities in order to minimize transactions costs concerns the hiring of workers with specialized skills. If workers must learn special skills that are uniquely valuable to one firm (for example, computer programmers who know the machine language for a particular line of computers), it may be more beneficial for the firm to develop long-term contractual relationships with these workers than to purchase their services from some other firm. In that way, as we shall see in the next section, the firm can structure employment contracts that give the workers an incentive to stay with the firm. If the workers were employed by an outside supplier, they might have fewer incentives to continue to use their specialized skills for the benefit of the final producer.

Size and Scope of the Firm

These considerations suggest that the size and scope of a firm's activities are an important subject for economic analysis.[4] Although it made sense to start our study of demand by defining the basic unit of analysis as the individual (or perhaps the family), defining the basic unit of analysis for supply decisions must necessarily involve some ambiguity. Ultimately, the definition of "the firm" is a fuzzy one that is determined by a constantly changing economic environment. Only a careful consideration of all the costs involved can provide an understanding of how the size of a firm changes over time. Still, at a given time, the firm is a legal entity with a fairly well-defined structure. Now we turn to examine some of the forces that shape the contractual nature of that structure.

CONTRACTS WITH WORKERS

Only about 20 percent of U.S. workers are represented by unions with collective bargaining agreements. The fraction of workers covered by such formal arrangements is somewhat higher in other western countries, but even in these other countries most workers are not subject to this sort of explicit contract. Still, virtually all employees have clear understandings with their employers about what their duties are and how they will be paid. In Chapter 22 we examine the theory of how wage levels are determined. Here we are not interested in the wage itself, but rather in explicit and implicit contracts and how they may affect the firm's costs and its supply decisions.

The Compensation Formula

In Chapter 12 (and in most other places in this book), we assumed that a firm's workers were paid a fixed hourly wage rate, w; that this rate of pay was determined in the labor market; and that it was independent of the worker's own efforts on the job and the overall success of the firm. A more generalized approach to the labor contract involves studying situations in which hourly compensation has several determinants. To do so, we define

---

[4]For a survey, see O. E. Williamson, "The Modern Corporation: Origins, Evolution, Attributes," *Journal of Economic Literature* (December 1981): 1537–1568.

Definition:	

Compensation Formula

The hourly compensation formula for one of a firm's workers is

$$\text{hourly pay} = w = w(k, s, \pi), \tag{13.9}$$

where k is a parameter determined in the market, s is the worker's own efforts, and (as before) π indicates the profits of the firm.

Our previous analysis represents a special case of Equation 13.9:

$$w(k, s, \pi) = \bar{w}, \tag{13.10}$$

where $\bar{w}$ is the market-determined wage. Other possibilities would include a pure profit-sharing system of compensation

$$w(k, s, \pi) = \frac{k\pi}{L}, \tag{13.11}$$

where k is a fixed percentage of the firm's profits that is to be divided among workers on the basis of hours worked (L). A hybrid compensation system could combine both wage and profit-sharing elements:

$$w(k, s, \pi) = \bar{w} + \frac{k\pi}{L}. \tag{13.12}$$

Other, more complex formulas might be hypothesized to represent the various compensation schemes that exist in actual firms. Some of these might depend on the individual worker's effort and productivity (s), but we will not examine that possibility explicitly here. Instead, we will look only at the simple profit-sharing case to provide an illustration of how the nature of the compensation formula might affect the firm's behavior.

The Profit-Sharing Case

For the profit-sharing case, hourly compensation is given by Equation 13.11. If, for simplicity, we assume the firm uses only labor inputs, its gross profits are given by its total revenues, Pq, since there are no costs other than the payment of a share of these revenues to labor. Net (after labor compensation) profits, π', are therefore given by

$$\pi' = (1 - k)Pq = (1 - k)Pf(L), \tag{13.13}$$

where $f(L)$ is the firm's (short-run) production function. The parameter k just shows how available revenues are split between workers and owners. If the firm wishes to maximize profits, it must choose labor inputs so as to maximize Equation 13.13. Assuming the firm is a price taker in the output market, this means

$$\frac{d\pi'}{dL} = (1 - k)P\frac{df(L)}{dL} = 0. \tag{13.14}$$

Consequently, the firm with a pure profit-sharing contract should expand labor input to the point at which labor's marginal physical productivity is zero ($f'(L) = 0$).[5] As long as a worker provides some additional output (and revenue), it makes sense for the firm to hire that worker. In this sense the profit-sharing firm acts as a revenue maximizer. The firm may be prevented from pursuing this strategy completely, however, if workers can earn higher wages elsewhere than they would get as a profit share when $f'(L) = 0$. In that case the firm will have an excess demand for workers at the prevailing employment level, a situation that has been extensively examined by Martin Weitzman and others.[6]

Using these same methods, it is possible to examine the consequences that other compensation formulas may have for the firm's behavior. Although competition in the labor market may ensure that, in the long run, workers earn about the same amount no matter which specific formula is used, the firm's short-run responses to price and other changes may be quite different under alternative compensation schemes. Some of the problems at the end of this chapter ask the reader to explore a few of these alternative compensation models.

Job-Specific Skills and Long-Term Contracts

As workers hold a job longer, they learn to do it better. Anyone who has ever started a new job knows very well the feeling of being totally confused and perplexed when trying to fit into a new employment situation. A new worker's productivity may be negative for the first few weeks as he or she asks so many questions and makes so many mistakes that total firm output may actually decline for awhile. Even after the chaos of orientation has ended, new workers may not be very productive until they have a chance to learn what the job entails and how they can work most effectively with those around them. In economic terms, any new worker must learn a set of *job-specific skills*, and that learning process will be time-consuming and costly.

Firms wish to reduce these costs as much as possible. The most direct way to do that is to adopt policies that encourage workers to stay with the firm. In Chapters 10–12 we were not concerned with this issue. Nothing in those chapters would have prevented a firm from hiring a different set of workers every hour as long as they all could be hired at the prevailing wage rate. In fact, however, such employee turnover would be very costly for the firm both because of the expenses involved in hiring new employees (such as the paperwork) and because of the low productivity of new employees. Instead, firms try to develop a longer term relationship with their employees.

---

[5] More generally, if market price depends on quantity sold, the firm should hire additional labor up to the point at which $mr \cdot f'(L) = 0$. If marginal revenue reaches 0 before $f'(L)$, the firm will be a revenue maximizer.

[6] See M. L. Weitzman, "Some Macroeconomic Implications of Alternative Compensation Systems," *The Economic Journal* (December 1983): 763–783. Weitzman claims that an economy based on share contracts would have much greater macroeconomic stability than one based on wage contracts.

Figure 13.2   *With Implicit Contracts, Output and Hiring Decisions May Be Less Flexible*

With no costs associated with changing labor input, a firm faced with a decline in price from P_2 to P_0 would reduce output from q_2 to q_0 and reduce labor input from L_2 to L_0. If there were an implicit contract between the workers and the firm, hiring might only fall to L_1, and output to q_1. This would still be the most profitable output level since costs associated with decreasing labor input further would exceed profits lost at q_1 (area *ABC*).

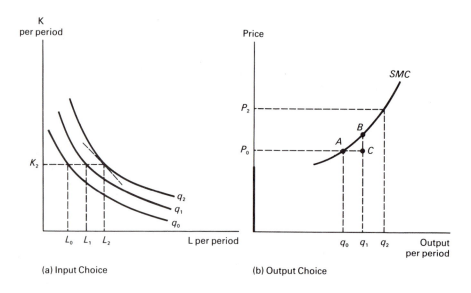

(a) Input Choice   (b) Output Choice

Employment Decisions

One consequence of such a long-term employment policy is that firms are reluctant to vary the number of workers they hire in response to temporary fluctuations in the demand for their products. They may make short-run decisions that are not exactly the same as those we examined in Chapter 11. Figure 13.2 illustrates such a situation: Panel (a) shows a price-taking firm's isoquant map, and (b) shows its short-run supply (and marginal cost) curve. Initially, the firm faces a market price of P_2 for its output and opts to produce at a level of q_2 per week as shown in Figure 13.2b. Assuming the firm has been producing q_2 for some time, it will have adjusted both its capital and labor inputs to their cost-minimizing levels K_2, L_2, as shown in Figure 13.2a.

Suppose now that the market price of this firm's product falls temporarily to P_0, perhaps because a recession temporarily reduces the demand for most goods. How will the firm respond to this decline? According to our discussion in Chapter 12, the firm would reduce output to q_0 and reduce its hiring of labor to L_0 since capital is fixed at K_2 in the short run. Under our previous assumptions, this temporary cutback in hiring could be accomplished by the firm with no special problems.

If workers have unique job-specific skills, however, reducing employment in this way may be costly for the firm. Once a worker is laid off, he or she may seek another job. Job-specific skills already acquired would be lost to the firm making the layoff. Even if the worker ultimately is hired back by this firm once the price returns to P_2, he or she may still need to readjust to the work process. For these reasons, the firm may hesitate to reduce employment immediately in response to temporary declines in demand. It may, instead, reassign workers to nonproduction activities (for example, cleaning up the stock room or doing preventive maintenance on machines), or it may continue to produce and add the surplus goods to inventory.

In all of these cases, the nature of the explicit or implicit contracts between workers and firms will make employment decisions far more complicated than our previous models assumed. A reduction of labor input to L_0 in Figure 13.2 may therefore be very costly, and some more modest steps may be taken instead. The firm could, for example, reduce hiring to L_1 and produce output level q_1. Such an output level would not provide maximum profits under our previous analysis of supply, but it may be more profitable than q_0 once all the costs associated with changing labor input are taken into account—that is, if the costs of reducing labor further exceed the profits lost by producing output level q_1 rather than q_0 (area ABC). Consequently, the firm's short-run supply (and hiring) decisions may be less responsive to temporary price changes than our simple model in Chapter 12 suggested.

Risk-Sharing in Labor Contracts

Labor contracts may expose both workers and firms to risks. Because the demand for a firm's product is subject to random influences, there may be periods when profits fall precipitously and, as we saw in the previous section, firms may try to cushion this decline by laying off workers. Even though firms and workers are subject to similar market risks, their attitudes toward these risks may be quite different. In Chapter 9 we saw that individuals will usually be risk averse. Hence we might expect that workers would prefer to adopt contractual arrangements that cushion fluctuations in their incomes. A firm's owners, on the other hand, may be able to diversify their investments among several opportunities and may therefore be neutral to risk from their investment in any one firm. They might therefore be willing to accept contractual arrangements that subject the firm's profits flow to somewhat greater variability than workers are willing to experience in their wages. Many conclusions in the modern theory of the firm are derived from this assumed difference in attitudes toward risk.

A Mathematical Model

A simple mathematical model of the contracting process can be used to illustrate these conclusions. Suppose a particular firm faces a possible falloff in its sales during some period and that the probability of this happening is k. The firm must decide on a wage policy that specifies how much each employed worker is paid (w) and how much each laid-off worker will be paid in unemployment benefits (s) if a recession occurs.[7] The firm employs L workers, L_1 of

---

[7]If these benefits were provided by the government (as is usually the case), we would have to change our analysis a bit. See the discussion that follows the mathematical development.

whom will be laid off in the event of a recession. Assuming the firm's expected revenues and extent of layoffs are unaffected by the type of wage contract it chooses, a profit-maximizing firm will be concerned only with the contract's expected costs (c):

$$c = (1 - k)wL + kw(L - L_1) + ksL_1. \tag{13.15}$$

That is, costs are equal to the expected value (see Chapter 9) of labor payments in recessionary and nonrecessionary situations.

Workers (or their bargaining representatives) wish to choose contractual terms that provide maximum utility for each possible level of the firm's costs. If we let $U(\ )$ represent the utility function for these workers, then expected utility is given by

$$\text{expected utility} = (1 - k)U(wL) + kU[w(L - L_1) + sL_1]. \tag{13.16}$$

The contracting problem now is to choose w and s to maximize Equation 13.16, subject to the constraint given by Equation 13.15. By considering all possible values for labor costs, all feasible, efficient contracts can be derived. To illustrate the properties of these contracts we set up the Lagrangian expression

$$\mathcal{L} = \text{expected utility} + \lambda(c_0 - c)$$

$$= (1 - k)U[wL] + kU[w(L - L_1) + sL_1] \tag{13.17}$$

$$+ \lambda\{c_0 - [(1 - k)wL + kw(L - L_1) + ksL_1]\},$$

where c_0 is some pre-assigned value for total labor costs. The first-order conditions for a constrained maximum for this contractual problem are

$$\frac{\partial \mathcal{L}}{\partial w} = (1 - k)U_n'L + kU_r'(L - L_1)$$

$$- \lambda[(1 - k)L + k(L - L_1)] = 0 \tag{13.18}$$

$$\frac{\partial \mathcal{L}}{\partial s} = kU_r'L_1 - \lambda kL_1 = 0$$

$$\frac{\partial \mathcal{L}}{\partial \lambda} = c_0 - (1 - k)wL + kw(L - L_1) + ksL_1 = 0,$$

where U_n' and U_r' represent the marginal utility of wage income in the nonrecessionary and recessionary situations, respectively. The second equation in 13.18 implies that $U_r' = \lambda$, and substitution of this into the first equation in 13.18 yields

$$(1 - k)U_n'L - (1 - k)U_r'L = 0 \tag{13.19}$$

or

$$U_n' = U_r'. \tag{13.20}$$

The marginal utility of wage income should be equal in the two possible demand states. But, assuming that workers are risk averse (see Chapter 9), this can only be achieved if income itself is equal in the two periods. And that can only be achieved under contracts in which $w = s$. For any given level of labor cost, the firm and its workers will reach contractual agreements under which the workers' incomes are completely protected against income fluctuations arising from the product market.

Of course, this conclusion arises directly from the very simplified model of the bargaining process we have assumed. A more complex representation of that process should take into account such factors as the following:

1. Workers may have valuable options for this unemployed time.
2. Unemployment benefits may be paid by the government, and the cost of these benefits may not be accurately reflected in the taxes that firms pay.
3. Wages and unemployment subsidies may be taxed at different rates.

In addition, any one firm's contract will be affected by competitive pressures from the labor market (since workers can choose to go elsewhere) and from the product market (since the probability of layoff, k, will affect the firm's costs). Economists have tried to develop contractual models that incorporate many of these features in the hope of better understanding why labor markets may not perform very well in certain circumstances.[8]

Other Issues in Labor Contracts

The forces that lead to long-term (explicit or implicit) labor contracts with major risk-sharing provisions also produce a number of other labor market results. These include seniority-based wage systems, employment bonuses based on firm performance (which are especially prevalent in Japan), and a variety of mandatory retirement provisions. An intriguing set of hypotheses have recently been developed around the possibility that some firms pay a higher wage than is actually required by the market in order to provide workers with an incentive to stay with the firm. Such an "efficiency wage" may also prompt workers to exert greater effort and may attract highly skilled workers from other firms. Paying a wage above what the market requires would by itself tend to raise costs, but, if it really did succeed in developing a more efficiently organized firm, it might actually be cost reducing. Although economists have built a number of models that reflect these possibilities, empirical evidence in support of them remains inconclusive.[9]

CONTRACTS WITH MANAGERS

In Chapter 12 we tended to treat the owner of a firm (that is, the owner of the firm's capital) and the manager of that firm as if they were the same person. This treatment makes the assumption of profit-maximizing behavior believable—a person who maximizes the profits in a firm that he or she owns will

[8] This literature is discussed in S. Rosen, "Implicit Contracts: A Survey," *Journal of Economic Literature* (September 1985): 1144–1175.

[9] One of the first economists to propose this efficient wage hypothesis was Joseph Stiglitz in "Wage Determination and Unemployment in L.D.C.'s: The Labor Turnover Model," *Quarterly Journal of Economics* (May 1974): 194–227.

succeed in making as much income as possible from this ownership. Then the process of profit maximization is consistent with the process of utility maximization we studied in Part II.

In many cases, however, managers do not actually own the firm for which they work. Rather, there is a separation between the ownership of the firm and the control of its behavior by hired managers. In this case, a manager acts as an *agent* for the owner.

Definition:

Agent

An agent is a person who makes economic decisions for another party; for example, the manager of a firm who is hired to act for the owner is an agent.

Conflicts in the Agent Relationship

Adam Smith understood the basic conflict between owners and managers. In *The Wealth of Nations,* he observed that "the directors of . . . companies, being the managers of other people's money than of their own, it cannot well be expected that they should watch over it with the same anxious vigilance with which [owners] watch over their own."[10] Using such famous British institutions as the Royal African Company, the Hudson's Bay Company, and the East India Company as examples, Smith went on to point out some of the consequences of management by nonowners. His observations provide an important starting point for the study of modern firms.

The principal issue raised by the existence of manager-agents is illustrated in Figure 13.3, which shows the indifference curve map of a manager's preferences between the firm's profits (which are of primary interest to the owners) and various benefits (such as fancy offices or travel in the corporate jet or helicopter) that accrue mainly to the manager.[11] This indifference curve map has the same shape as those in Part II on the presumption that both profits and benefits provide utility to the manager.

To construct the budget constraint that the manager faces in seeking to maximize his or her utility, assume first that the manager is also the owner of this firm. If the manager chooses to have no special benefits from the job, profits will be π_{max}. Each dollar of benefits received by the manager reduces these profits by one dollar. The budget constraint will have a slope of -1, and profits will reach zero when benefits total π_{max}.

Given this budget constraint, the owner-manager maximizes utility by opting for profits of π^* and benefits of B^*. Profits of π^*, while less than π_{max}, still represent maximum profits in this situation since any other owner-manager would also wish to receive B^* in benefits. That is, B^* represents a true cost

---

[10] Adam Smith, *The Wealth of Nations,* Modern Library ed. (New York: Random House, 1937), p. 700.

[11] Figure 13.3 is based on a figure presented in Michael C. Jensen and William H. Meckling, "Theory of the Firm: Managerial Behavior, Agency Costs and Ownership Structure," *Journal of Financial Economics* (October 1976): 305–360.

Figure 13.3   *Incentives for a Manager Acting as an Agent for a Firm's Owners*

If a manager were the sole owner of a firm, π^*, B^* would be chosen since this combination of profits and benefits provides maximum utility. If the manager only owns one-third of the firm, however, the perceived budget constraint will be flatter, and B^{**}, π^{**} will be chosen.

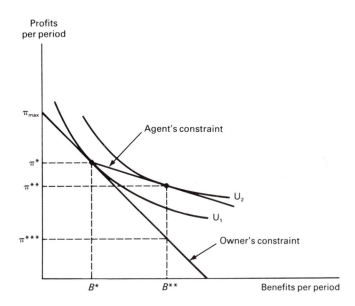

of doing business so, given these costs, the firm's manager really does maximize profits.

Now suppose that the manager is not the only owner of this firm. Instead, assume that, say, one-third of the capital of the firm is owned by the manager and the other two-thirds are owned by outside investors who play no role in operating the firm. In this case the manager will act as if he or she no longer faces a budget constraint that requires that one dollar of profits be sacrificed for each dollar of benefits. Now a dollar of benefits costs the manager only $.33 in profits since the other $.67 is effectively paid by the other owners in terms of reduced profits on their investment. Although the new budget constraint continues to include the point B^*, π^* (since the manager could still make the same decision a sole owner could), for benefits greater than B^* the slope of the budget constraint is only $-\frac{1}{3}$; profits in the manager's portion of the business decline by only $.33 for each dollar in benefits received. Given this new budget constraint, the manager would choose point B^{**}, π^{**} to maximize his or her utility. Being only a partial owner of the firm causes the manager to choose a lower level of profits and a higher level of benefits than would be chosen by a sole owner.

Point B^{**}, π^{**} is not really attainable by this firm. Although the cost of one dollar of benefits appears to be only \$.33 in profits for the manager, in reality, of course, the benefits cost one dollar. When the manager opts for B^{**} in benefits, the loss in profits (from π^* to π^{***}) is greater for the firm as a whole than for him or her personally. The firm's owners are harmed by having to rely on an agency relationship with the firm's manager. It appears that the smaller the fraction of the firm that is owned by the manager, the greater the distortions that will be induced by this relationship.

The situation illustrated in Figure 13.3 is representative of a variety of "principal-agent" problems that arise in economics. Whenever one person (the principal) hires another person (the agent) to make decisions, the motivation of this agent must be taken into account since the agent may make different decisions than the principal would. Examples of this relationship occur not only in the management of firms, but also in such diverse applications as hiring investment advisors (do they really put their clients' interests first?); relying on an automobile mechanic's assessment in ordering repairs; and buying a friend's clothes for him or her.

Management Contracts

The firm's owners would be unlikely to take the kind of behavior illustrated in Figure 13.3 lying down. They are being forced to accept lower profits than might be earned on their investments in exchange for manager-oriented benefits that provide no value to them personally. What can they do? Most obviously, they can refuse to invest in the firm if they know the manager will behave in this manner. In such a case the manager would have two options. First, he or she could go it alone and finance the company completely with his or her own funds. The firm would then simply return to the owner-manager situation in which B^*, π^* is the preferred choice of benefits and profits. Alternatively, the manager may obtain outside financing if the operation is too expensive to finance alone. In this case the manager must work out some sort of contractual arrangement with the would-be owners to induce them to invest.

One possible contract would be for the manager to agree to finance all of the benefits out of his or her share of the profits. This would make the would-be owners happy (since they would get the same level of profits no matter how many benefits the manager chose). But, when a dollar of benefits costs one dollar any choice of benefits greater than B^* will result in lower utility for the manager. In this situation, a manager who succumbed to the desire for benefits seemingly created by the agency relationship would actually be made worse off.

Writing a contract under which managers pay for benefits entirely out of their share of the profits is probably impossible for owners to do, anyway. Enforcing the provisions of such a contract would require constant supervision of the managers' activities—something the owners would prefer not to do because that would force them into a managerial role. Instead, they may try to develop less strict contracts that give managers an incentive to economize on benefits and thereby pursue goals closer to pure profit maximization. By offering such contract options as profit-sharing bonuses, stock option plans, and

Figure 13.4   *Possible Managerial Contracts*

The contract curve represents possible managerial contracts offered by the firm's owners to control the adverse incentives of the manager-agent relationship. Given these options, the manager will choose π_c, B_c if he or she cannot finance the business alone.

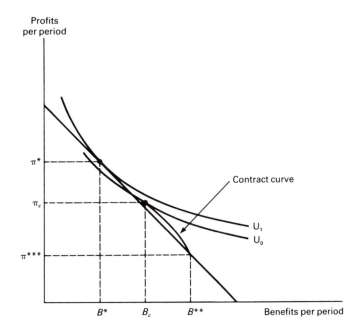

company-financed pensions, the owners may be able to give managers an incentive to be careful about the benefits they choose to take.

Graphing actual complex contract provisions such as stock options is probably impossible. A simplified view of this contracting process is illustrated in Figure 13.4. The contract curve shows the relationship between the benefits the manager receives and the amount of the firm's profits he or she gets to keep.

This curve lies outside the sole-owner budget constraint since the owners recognize that they cannot make the manager pay completely for his or her benefits because that would involve too much supervision. However, the slope of the contract curve is steeper than the agent's budget constraint shown in Figure 13.3 because the contract provisions do require a significant financial sacrifice by the manager for the benefits he or she takes. Given these contractual offerings, the manager chooses B_c, π_c as the best of the options available. Although this outcome requires the owners to sacrifice some of the profits they would receive if the firm were operated by a manager who behaved like a sole owner, it is preferable to a situation in which the manager is a pure agent. The contract represents a trade-off of some profit dollars for the assurance of better managerial performance.

As with labor contracts, the development of management contracts requires considerable give-and-take between the parties (owners and managers). The final agreement will be a compromise between the owners' desire to incorporate incentives that encourage profit-maximizing behavior and the costs involved in writing the contract and monitoring that behavior. Real-world management contracts may therefore be quite complex and offer a variety of incentives and sanctions.

NONPROFIT ORGANIZATIONS

Many firms are explicitly organized on a not-for-profit basis. Examples of such "firms" include government bureaucracies, most hospitals and schools, philanthropic foundations, and some labor-managed firms (for example, agricultural communes). For such organizations the hypothesis of profit maximization may be inappropriate, and some other specification of the firm's goals may be required. Although a complete discussion of these alternatives is outside the scope of this book, we shall present a few examples to indicate the analytical approaches that might be taken to study output decisions of such organizations.

Hospitals

There is considerable interest in comparing the behavior of hospitals that operate on a not-for-profit basis (the majority) to the behavior of profit-maximizing hospitals. A first step in this investigation is to decide what goal (or goals) a nonprofit hospital pursues. It might be hypothesized, for example, that, given the resources at its disposal, a hospital seeks to maximize the health status of the average citizen served; or that it maximizes the number of lives saved; or that it pursues some other health-oriented goal. A somewhat less philanthropic hypothesis has been proposed by J. P. Newhouse, who assumes that hospitals seek to maximize the utility of the doctors who govern them.[12] One implication of this hypothesis is that nonprofit hospitals will have a bias (relative to profit-maximizing hospitals) toward high-quality, high-technology care and away from "bargain" care (such as emergency room facilities). Some empirical data tend to support this hypothesis.

Regulatory Agencies

The rapid growth in government regulation of business in the early postwar years focused increased attention on the operations of agencies charged with this activity. An important set of investigations has attempted to identify precisely the agencies' goals and to measure the extent to which those goals have been met. For example, in one of the first investigations of this type, G. J. Stigler examined the goals of the U.S. Securities and Exchange Commission (SEC).[13] Two frequently mentioned goals of security market regulation were postulated: (1) the protection of "innocent" investors; and (2) the creation of an efficient securities market.

---

[12] J. P. Newhouse, "Toward a Theory of Nonprofit Institutions: An Economic Model of a Hospital," *American Economic Review* 60 (March 1970): 64–74.

[13] G. J. Stigler, "Public Regulation of the Securities Market," *Journal of Business* 37 (April 1964): 117–142.

Stigler examined a variety of data to determine if the SEC had any effect in its pursuit of these goals. After a series of careful analyses, the author concluded that no such effect could be detected. Given the substantial resources devoted to SEC activities, one must conclude either that the commission performed ineffectively or that it in fact pursued goals other than those postulated. The goals of other bureaucratic organizations would appear to be suitable for similar analyses.

Labor-Managed Firms

In a variety of organizations, workers make the principal production decisions. Agricultural and craft communes, Yugoslavian manufacturing plants, and (to some extent) university faculties are examples of this sort of management. Recent trends toward "worker participation" suggest that this mode of decision making will increase in importance. Economists have adopted two alternative approaches to the study of labor-managed firms. Under the first, workers are viewed as owning the firm's capital and (like any other owners of capital) desiring maximum profits from its use. Analyzing firms that operate in this way produces results concerning profit maximization that differ little from those analyzed elsewhere in this chapter. A rather different assumption adopted by some writers is that the labor-managed firm seeks to maximize the output (or, more properly, the "value added") per worker. In the terminology of Chapter 10, the firm will produce where the average product of labor is a maximum (at labor input L^{**} in Figure 10.1). Such decisions may differ substantially from those made by profit-maximizing firms, and the nature of the differences has been the subject of considerable analysis and controversy.[14]

As these three examples indicate, the study of nonprofit organizations is quite wide-ranging since it must address an enormous variety of enterprises. Clearly, no single hypothesis is capable of providing a foundation for modeling all such firms. Instead, some of the elements from our analysis of profit-maximizing firms (cost functions and contractual models, for example) must be adapted to specific institutional settings. We will not generally explore these applications here although, in the final part of the book, we will briefly examine some of the issues that arise in modeling the production of goods by the government.

SUMMARY

In this chapter we have tried to develop a somewhat broader picture of the nature of the firm and its decision-making process than was possible within the strict profit-maximization model in Chapter 12. As in any such modeling effort, the increase in descriptive realism we achieved in this chapter came at the cost of deriving far more complex and ambiguous models than the ones we

[14] For a summary, see J. Vanek, *The General Theory of Labor-Managed Market Economies* (Ithaca, N.Y.: Cornell University Press, 1970).

presented earlier. For most of the analysis of this book, we will rely on the simpler model of the profit-maximizing firm because this will permit us to devise fairly complete models of market interactions. Occasionally, however, we will point out some empirical observations that are not, at least on the surface, in accord with our basic model of firm behavior, and in these cases it will be useful to keep in mind the alternatives we have illustrated in this chapter:

- In situations of imperfect information, firms may opt for output decision rules that require less knowledge than does profit maximization. A particularly simple alternative is that of sales maximization in which the firm expands output to the point at which marginal revenue is equal to zero. In some cases, such decisions may be constrained by minimum profit requirements, however.
- Firms' contracts with their workers may be quite complex. They may, for example, be characterized by complicated compensation formulas and may incorporate provisions that encourage workers to stay with the firm. Such provisions may affect the way in which the firm makes short-run output decisions.
- Workers' contracts may also contain risk-sharing arrangements. If workers are risk averse but firms are not, it might be expected that optimal contracts would involve firms absorbing risks arising from uncertain demand in the product market.
- Contracts with managers will also reflect incentive issues. Because managers act as agents for the firm's owners, they may not always make decisions that are consistent with profit maximization. Contractual provisions may therefore be structured so as to bring profit-maximizing behavior and the manager's utility-maximizing behavior more closely into line.
- Nonprofit organizations pose difficult problems in modeling because their goals may be hard to define. Although cost and revenue concepts are clearly relevant to this modeling, the details of an applicable model will depend on the specific institutional setting.

Application

THE MARKET FOR FIRMS

In Chapter 13 we discussed the issue of developing labor and management contracts as evolving from bargaining between the parties involved with the firm. In this application, we take a somewhat broader view by considering the outside market pressures that affect these settlements. Specifically, we focus on the market for firms themselves, which has been termed the "market for corporate control" in recent economic discussions. Our general goal is to show how the workings of this market help to weed out inefficient, high-cost contractual arrangements in favor of more efficient ones.

Two other types of market pressures on firms should be mentioned. First, any firm must be attentive to the markets for the inputs it hires. Labor contracts that are distinctly inferior to those offered elsewhere will make it impossible for the firm to attract workers. Similarly, inferior management contracts will severely restrict the firm's ability to attract the managers it wishes to hire. The economic operations of these markets is a topic we take up in Part VII. Second, a firm must be attentive to the market for its product. If the firm's costs are too high, it may not be able to compete effectively with other producers. Competition in the product market is a powerful regulator of the firm's behavior, and we will study that topic extensively in Parts V and VI.

Profit Opportunities in the Market for Firms

The possible attractions of a would-be buyer of a firm are illustrated in Figure 13.5. The firm's short-run average and marginal cost curves are given by SAC and SMC as indicated in the figure.[15] With a market price of P^*, this firm will produce q^* and, since price exceeds average cost, earn a modest profit.

Assume now that a would-be buyer believes that this firm is currently rather inefficient and could be operated at lower cost if a new management team were installed. Specifically, assume this buyer believes that the firm could be operated with costs given by SAC' and SMC' if it were under new management. With these new costs, profits would be given by area $P^*E'BC'$ instead of P^*EAC. Such larger profits offer a major incentive for the potential buyer to proceed with plans to purchase the firm. If the firm is privately owned, an offer may be made directly to these owners. On the other hand, if ownership of the firm is spread widely over a large number of shareholders, the buyer may make a public offer to the shareholders.

Buying an entire firm is, of course, a more complex transaction than buying, say, a loaf of bread. Often considerable capital may be required to make the transaction, necessitating complex borrowing arrangements with banks and the accompanying legal formalities. Takeovers may also involve some explicit short-term costs, such as the relocation of the firm's headquarters or the departure of highly skilled employees who oppose the change. Existing management may make the purchase of their firm difficult by adopting various defensive ploys such as rigging the voting by shareholders or enlisting the government's assistance in opposing the takeover. As a result of these costs, it might be expected that only purchases that are quite profitable would proceed. Situations in which potential buyers would obtain only minor cost improvements over existing management would not produce sufficiently higher short-run profits to warrant incurring these costs. Instead, the normal workings of the marketplace (as we take up in the next part) will ensure that such inefficiencies are reduced over the long run.

Empirical Evidence on Takeovers

Evidence from merger and takeover activity in the late 1970s and early 1980s is consistent with this view. One extensive review of the research on this topic found that shareholders of firms that were acquired in this way experienced an increase of 20–30 percent in the value of their investments.[16] Unsuccessful takeover attempts, on the other hand, actually resulted in a small loss for existing shareholders, perhaps because managers spent real resources fighting off the takeover. It is possible that some of these gains from successful takeovers represent factors other than the lower operating costs illustrated in Figure 13.5. For example, as we will discuss in Chapter 18, some of these

---

[15] Figure 13.5 uses short-run curves because our discussion in Chapter 14 will show that cost inefficiencies are substantially eliminated over the longer term by competition in the market for goods.

[16] Michael C. Jensen and Richard S. Ruback, "The Market for Corporate Control: The Scientific Evidence," *Journal of Financial Economics* (March 1983): 5–50.

Figure 13.5   *Inefficient Costs Make the Firm a Takeover Candidate*

If the firm's costs (*SMC, SAC*) exceed those that a would-be buyer could achieve (*SMC', SAC'*), the firm may be acquired provided the increment to profits exceeds the costs of the acquisition.

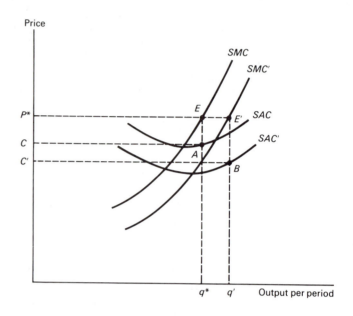

gains may reflect monopoly profits that are garnered by the larger firms that result from a merger. These mergers are extensively regulated by antitrust law, however, so such monopoly gains probably occur in only a few cases. It seems likely that a substantial portion of shareholders' profits do reflect some types of improved management efficiencies. The continuing strength of takeover activity in the United States indicates that the market for firms may be an important source of improvement in the overall performance of the U.S. economy.[17]

[17] For a discussion of several issues related to the market for corporate control, see U.S. Council of Economic Advisors to the President, "The Market for Corporate Control," Chapter 6 in *Economic Report of the President, 1985* (Washington, D.C.: U.S. Government Printing Office, 1985), pp. 187–216.

Corporate Raiders

"Corporate raiders" are individual investors who, primarily using borrowed funds, seek to take over the management of specific target firms. In recent years formerly obscure investors such as T. Boone Pickens, Carl Icahn, David Murdock, and Victor Posner have become widely known as their aggressive pursuit of various firms has made front-page news. The principal objection to these raiders appears to be the fear that they will "loot" the target company—that they are solely interested in making a quick profit and will then leave the company in shambles.

Both economic logic and the actual evidence contradict this villainous view of corporate raiders. In theoretical terms, raiders would seem to have no reason to destroy a firm. Presumably, they are purchasing a firm's assets because they believe the assets are worth more than their current value in the market. If the raider were really set on destroying the firm, some other potential buyer would step in to prevent this from happening.

An alternative view is that corporate raiders are performing a useful function by identifying poorly managed firms and promoting new management practices. For example, some observers argue that the persistent raids of T. Boone Pickens on various major oil companies has had the effect of making these firms think of themselves as two different businesses—owners of oil-producing properties and refiners of crude oil. By recognizing that many oil companies were poorly managing their crude oil reserves, Pickens was able to find a route to profitable acquisitions.

A 1985 study of the activities of six infamous corporate raiders by Clifford Holderness and

Dennis Sheehan reaches a similar conclusion.[18] Here the authors show that announcement of stock purchases by these six influential investors significantly raised the market value of target firms' shares, a finding inconsistent with the raider notion. The authors then examine possible reasons for this market reaction and conclude that a major portion can be attributed to the investors' ultimate involvement in managing the company. That is, the value of the corporation was increased by the raider's activities in some measure because the raider represented the promise of better management. Raiders are therefore an important component of the market for firms.

[18] Clifford G. Holderness and Dennis P. Sheehan, "Raiders or Saviors? The Evidence on Six Controversial Investors," *Journal of Financial Economics* (December 1985): 555–579.

SUGGESTED READINGS

Alchian, A. A., and Demsetz, H. "Production, Information Costs and Economic Organization." *American Economic Review* (December 1972): 777–795.

Interesting and easy-to-read survey of the firm's informational problems and how the organization of firms reflects solutions to them.

Arrow, K. J. *The Limits to Organization.* New York: W. W. Norton, 1974.

Brief and literate book about the limits between market and non-market transactions.

Coase, R. H. "The Nature of the Firm." *Economica* (1937): 386–405.

Early contribution to the contractual theory of the firm. Contains some interesting historical material.

Jensen, M. C., and Meckling, W. H. "Theory of the Firm: Managerial Behavior, Agency Costs and Ownership Structure." *Journal of Financial Economics* (October 1976): 305–360.

Basic article on the theory of agency. Presents several useful graphical techniques.

Marshak, T. A. "Organizational Design." In K. J. Arrow and M. D. Intriligator, eds., *Handbook of Mathematical Economics*, Vol. 3. Amsterdam: North Holland Publishing Co., 1986. Pp. 1359–1440.

Survey of the mathematical approach to organizational design. Illustrates formal methods for analyzing information flows in organizations.

Rosen, Sherwin. "Implicit Contracts: A Survey." *Journal of Economic Literature* (September 1985): 1144–1175.

Surveys the recent literature on implicit labor contracts in firms. Offers a fairly simple and readable model of layoff decisions and related issues.

Weitzman, M. L. "Some Macroeconomic Implications of Alternative Compensation Systems." *The Economic Journal* (December 1983): 763–783.

Contrasts wage and profit-sharing contracts with the main goal of studying macroeconomic performance. Provides the basis for Weitzman's paperback The Share Economy.

Williamson, O. E. "Transactions-Cost Economics: The Governance of Contractual Relations." *Journal of Law and Economics* (October 1979): 233–261.

Examination of the contractual nature of the firm with specific emphasis on enforcement of con- tracts. *Interesting discussion of the problem of asset specificity in production.*

Yellen, J. L. "Efficiency Wage Models of Unemployment." *American Economic Review* (May 1984): 200–205.

Interesting but brief survey of "efficiency wage models" and how they relate to the business cycle.

PROBLEMS

13.1

How do costs associated with hiring new employees affect the marginal revenue–marginal cost rule for profit maximization? Explain carefully why this effect might depend on whether short-run or long-run marginal costs are used. Why might a firm respond differently to temporary and permanent changes in the price of their product?

13.2

One way of modeling the way firms adjust their workforces is to use a "stock-adjustment model" that assumes the change in labor hired between week $t - 1$ and week t ($L_t - L_{t-1}$) is a fraction of the difference between what the firm wants to hire (L_t^*) and what it hired last week (L_{t-1}). That is

$$(L_t - L_{t-1}) = k(L_t^* - L_{t-1})$$

where k is some fraction less than one.

Suppose that a taxidermy shop has a short-run production function given by

$$q = \sqrt{L}$$

where q is the number of animals stuffed per week and L is hours of labor hired per week. Assume that the wage rate is $10 per hour and that short-run total costs are given by

$$STC = 200 + 10q^2$$

    a.   If the market price of q is $200 each, how many will be produced and how many workers will the firm wish to hire each week?

    b.   Suppose the firm starts in week 0 with 50 hours of workers' time used per week. If $k = 1/2$, how many workers will be hired in week 1? How many animals will be stuffed?

    c.   Answer part b for week 2.

    d.   Graph the firm's output and labor hiring decisions for weeks 0 to 5.

    e.   How many weeks will it take for the firm to get within one hour of the desired labor input?

13.3

United Airbags (A) and United Balloons (B) are two firms in the lighter-than-air parcel post business. For each the number of delivered packages per hour (q) is a simple function of the number of workers hired each hour (L):

$$q = L - .1L^2.$$

Wages of balloon pilots are determined by their opportunity costs of $4 per hour. Initially the competitive cost price of a delivered package is $10.

    a.   If firm A is a profit maximizer how many pilots will it hire?

b. If firm B wishes to adopt a revenue sharing formula that also yields $4 per hour to pilots and results in the same level of employment as for firm A, what share of revenues should it pay to its pilots?

c. Suppose the price of delivered packages falls to $5. What will happen to hiring at firm A?

d. If the price of delivered packages falls to $5 and firm B maintains the revenue sharing formula and employment levels calculated in part b, what will happen to pilots' wages? How might you expect firm B to adjust its contract to the lower price of delivered packages?

13.4
Suppose that a farm's production function for cabbage is given by

$$q = 2K^{1/2}L^{1/2},$$

and that in the short run, $K = 100$ and the farm must pay a rental rate of $1 per unit for capital.

a. Assuming that the farm manager can hire labor at a wage of $1, what will the farm's short-run supply curve (with q as a function of market price, P) for cabbage be? How much cabbage will be supplied at $P = $1? At $P = $2?

b. Suppose now that the farm is collectivized and becomes managed by the workers but that rental for capital equipment must still be paid (to the state). Assume that the workers are egalitarian and decide to share the excess of total revenues over capital cost equally and that they wish to maximize this average net revenue per worker. How will the collective farm's short-run output decisions depend on market price P? How much will be produced at $P = $1? At $P = $2? Can you explain this result intuitively?

13.5
Suppose that Mr. Entrepreneur is the only decision maker in his firm. The profits of this firm depend solely on the amount of time Mr. Entrepreneur spends on the job:

$$\pi = f(H),$$

where H is the number of hours on the job. However, Mr. E, who is a harsh boss, gets on everyone's nerves if he is around too long. Hence π reaches a maximum long before H reaches 24 hours per day. Suppose also that Mr. E has a utility function for profits and leisure ($L = 24 - H$) of the form

$$U = U(\pi, L).$$

a. In this situation, will the number of hours of work corresponding to profit maximization be the same number that maximizes Mr. E's utility? What special condition must hold for this to be true? Is this condition "reasonable?"

b. In fact, according to Marshall, profits (π) should be defined to exclude that portion of entrepreneurial income necessary to keep Mr. E in the business. Hence economic profits $= \pi' = \pi - w$, where w is the amount of income necessary to keep Mr. E in the business (that is, the wage to make him indifferent between working and staying home). Clearly, w depends on H.

c. With this new definition of profits, will the profit-maximizing position agree with Mr. E's utility-maximizing position? Show that in order for

this to be true, Mr. E must have indifference curves like those in problem 5.7—there is no income effect in the demand for hours worked.

13.6

Suppose the production function for high quality brandy is given by

$$q = \sqrt{K \cdot L}$$

where q is the output of brandy per week and L is labor hours per week. In the
short run K is fixed at 100, so the short-run production function is

$$q = 10\sqrt{L}.$$

  a. If capital rents for $10 each and wages are $5 per hour, show that short-
      run total costs are

$$STC = 1000 + .05q^2.$$

  b. Given the short-run total cost curve in part a, how much will the firm
      produce at a price of brandy of $20 per bottle? How many labor hours
      will be hired per week?

  c. Suppose that during recessions, the price of brandy falls to $15 per
      bottle. With this price, how much would the firm choose to produce
      and how many labor hours would be hired?

  d. Suppose that the firm believes that the fall in the price of brandy will
      last for only one week after which it will wish to return to the level of
      production in part a. Assume also that for each hour that the firm
      reduces its workforce below that described in part a, it incurs a cost of
      $1. If it proceeds as in part c, will it earn a profit or a loss? Explain.

  e. Is there some level of hiring other than that described in part c which
      will yield more profits for the firm during the temporary recession?

13.7

A hospital produces services that can be quantified in two dimensions: quantity
(Q) and quality (C). It faces infinitely elastic market demands for these aspects
of service: Prevailing prices are $P_Q = 10$, $P_C = 5$. The hospital's total costs are
given by

$$TC = 0.1Q^2 + 0.2C^2 - 125.$$

  a. If the hospital wishes to maximize profits, how much Q and C should
      be produced? What will profits be?

  b. Suppose that the hospital is managed by a nonprofit foundation. The
      utility of the foundation's president depends on the hospital outputs
      according to the function

$$U(Q, C) = \min (Q, C).$$

      If the hospital is now required to have the same total budget as in
      the profit-maximizing case, what levels of Q and C will be chosen to
      maximize the foundation president's utility? What will "profits" be in
      this case?

13.8

Managers often receive liberal severance pay provisions in their contracts (these are
sometimes called "golden parachutes"). Why would owners opt for such provisions? Once a manager is fired, he or she no longer can affect profits—so why
should owners pay managers anything in such a situation?

13.9

United Frisbee produces jeweled frisbees. The firm's short-run total costs are given by

$$STC = .01q^2 + 10,000$$

where q is the quantity of frisbees produced per week. Marginal costs are given by

$$SMC = .02q.$$

  a.   Suppose United can sell its frisbees at $30 each. How many will be produced and what will weekly profits be?
  b.   Suppose Ted Turnover, a famous corporate raider, can operate United at 3/4 the costs of the current management. What would the costs of the firm be in this situation? If frisbee prices remain at $30, how many would be produced and what would profits be?
  c.   How much more would Ted be willing to pay for United than would another buyer who could not achieve these cost efficiencies?

PART

V

Perfect Competition

In Parts II–IV we used the maximization hypothesis to develop models to explain the demand for goods by utility-maximizing individuals and the supply of goods by profit-maximizing firms. In this part we will bring these two strands of analysis together to describe the process by which prices are determined. We will focus only on one specific model of price determination, the perfectly competitive model. That model assumes a large enough number of demanders and suppliers of each good so that each must be a price taker. That is, each demander believes that he or she constitutes such a small part of the market that decisions about what to buy have no impact on market prices. Similarly, each firm believes that its supply decisions will not alter the price it receives for its output. Using these assumptions, we will develop and evaluate the complete competitive model of price determination—perhaps the most widely used model in economics. In Part VI we will illustrate some of the models that result from relaxing the strict price-taking assumptions of the competitive case, but in this part we assume price-taking behavior throughout.

Chapter 14, the first chapter in Part V, develops the familiar partial equilibrium model of price determination in competitive markets. The principal result is the Marshallian "cross" diagram of supply and demand that we first discussed in Chapter 1. This model illustrates a "partial" equilibrium view of price determination because it focuses only on a single market. In Chapter 14 we show how this limited focus permits a relatively detailed analysis of how such a single market operates. Especially important are the demonstration of the way in which market equilibria may differ between the short run and the long run and the discussion of how long-run forces severely constrain the types of outcomes that are possible.

Although the partial equilibrium competitive model is quite useful for studying a single market in detail, it is inappropriate for examining relationships between markets because it cannot illustrate precisely how changes in the equilibrium price in one market affect prices in other markets. To capture such cross-market effects requires the development of "general" equilibrium models—a topic we take up in Chapter 15. There we show how an entire economy can be viewed as a system of interconnected competitive markets that determine all prices simultaneously. We develop such a model and then use it to study some of the features of a competitive price system.

Chapters 14 and 15 have a primarily positive orientation: They seek to explain how perfectly competitive markets operate. Chapter 16, on the other hand, has a more normative, evaluative purpose. The chapter begins by describing what it means for an economy to allocate its available resources "efficiently" and then shows that, under certain circumstances, reliance on a perfectly competitive price system will achieve this result. Hence the analysis offers some support for Adam Smith's conception of the price system as an "invisible hand," directing resources to where they are most valued. But the chapter also offers some warnings about situations that may invalidate the connection between perfect competition and economic efficiency and briefly examines equity questions associated with competitive allocations.

Chapter 17, the final chapter in Part V, examines some additional questions about the operations of competitive markets with particular attention to the problem of transactions costs. The chapter shows how the existence of such costs may affect the equilibrium prices and quantities arrived at by competitive markets. Transactions costs may also affect the ways in which markets arrive at these equilibria, and Chapter 17 briefly addresses such dynamic questions.

In general, then, Part V provides a rather complete picture of the way in which competitive markets work. This fundamental model of price determination lies at the heart of much economic theorizing. In later parts we will use the model not only as a point of departure for developing additional applications based on alternative assumptions but also as a standard against which to evaluate other types of market outcomes.

CHAPTER 14

Partial Equilibrium Models of Competitive Price Determination

In this chapter we describe the familiar model of price determination under perfect competition originally developed by Alfred Marshall in the late nineteenth century. That is, we provide a fairly complete analysis of the supply-demand mechanism as it applies to a single market. This is perhaps the most widely used model for studies of the pricing of particular products, and a thorough knowledge of it is an important part of the economist's toolkit.

TIMING OF THE SUPPLY RESPONSE

In the analysis of competitive pricing, it is important to decide the length of time that is to be allowed for a *supply response* to changing demand conditions. The establishment of equilibrium prices will be different if we are talking about a very short period of time during which most inputs are absolutely fixed or if we are envisioning a very long-run process in which it is possible for new firms to enter an industry. For this reason it has been traditional in economics to discuss pricing in three different time periods: (1) very short run, (2) short run, and (3) long run. Although it is not possible to give these terms an exact chronological definition, the essential distinction being made concerns the nature of the supply response that is assumed to be possible. In the *very short run*, there is no supply response: Quantity supplied is absolutely fixed. In the *short run*, existing firms may change the quantity they are supplying, but no new firms can enter the industry. In the *long run*, new firms may enter an industry, thereby producing a very flexible supply response. In this chapter we will discuss each of these possibilities.

PRICING IN THE VERY SHORT RUN

In the very short run, or the *market period*, there is no supply response. The goods are already "in" the marketplace and must be sold for whatever the market will bear. In this situation, price acts only as a device to ration demand. Price will adjust to clear the market of the quantity that must be sold during the period. Although the market price may act as a signal to producers in future periods, it does not perform such a function in the current period because current period output is fixed. Figure 14.1 depicts this situation. Market demand is represented by the curve D. Supply is fixed at Q^*, and the price

Figure 14.1   *Pricing in the Very Short Run*

When quantity is absolutely fixed in the very short run, price acts only as a device to ration demand. With quantity fixed at Q^*, price P_1 will prevail in the market place if D is the market demand curve. At this price, individuals are willing to consume exactly that quantity available. If demand should shift upward to D', the equilibrium market price would rise to P_2.

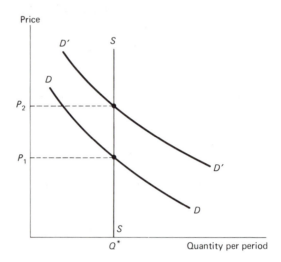

that clears the market is P_1. At P_1 individuals are willing to take all that is offered in the market. Sellers want to dispose of Q^* without regard to price (suppose that the good in question is perishable and will be worthless if it is not sold in the very short run). Hence P_1, Q^* is an equilibrium price-quantity combination. If demand should shift to D', the equilibrium price would increase to P_2, but Q^* would stay fixed since no supply response is possible. The *supply curve* in this situation, then, is a vertical straight line at output Q^*.

The analysis of the very short run is not particularly useful for most markets. Although such a theory may adequately represent some situations in which goods are perishable or must be sold on a given day (as in an auction for fresh fish), the far more usual case involves some degree of supply response to changing demand. It is usually presumed that a rise in price will bring additional quantity into the market. In the remainder of this chapter, we shall examine why firms may wish to increase their output levels in the short run in response to such a price increase. Before beginning our analysis, we should note that increases in quantity supplied need not come only from increased production. In a world in which some goods are durable (that is, last longer than a single period), current owners of these goods may supply them in increasing amounts to the market as price rises. For example, even though the supply of Rembrandts is absolutely fixed, we would not want to draw the market supply curve for these paintings as a vertical line, such as that shown in Figure 14.1.

As the price of Rembrandts rises, individuals and museums will become increasingly willing to part with them. From a market point of view, therefore, the supply curve for Rembrandts will have an upward slope, even though no new production takes place. A similar analysis would follow for many types of durable goods, such as antiques, used cars, back issues of the *National Geographic*, or corporate shares, all of which are in nominally "fixed" supply. Since we are more interested in examining how demand and production are related, we shall not analyze those cases in detail.

SHORT-RUN PRICE DETERMINATION

In short-run analysis the number of firms in an industry is fixed. It is assumed that firms do not have sufficient flexibility either to enter or to leave a given industry. However, those firms in the industry are able to adjust the quantity they are producing in response to changing conditions. They will do this by altering levels of employment for those inputs that can be varied in the short run, and we shall investigate this supply decision here. Before beginning the analysis, we should perhaps state explicitly the assumptions of this perfectly competitive model.

Definition:

Perfect Competition
A *perfectly competitive industry* is one that obeys the following assumptions:

1. There are a large number of firms, each producing the same homogeneous product.
2. Each firm attempts to maximize profits.
3. Each firm is a price taker: It assumes that its actions have no effect on market price.
4. Transactions are costless: Buyers and sellers incur no costs in making exchanges (for more on this assumption, see Chapter 17).

Now we will make use of these assumptions to study price determination in the short run.

Short-Run Market Supply Curve

In Chapter 12 we showed how to construct the short-run supply curve for a single profit-maximizing firm. To construct a market supply curve, we start by recognizing that the quantity of output supplied to the entire market in the short run is simply the sum of the quantities supplied by each firm. Since each firm uses market price to determine how much to produce, the total amount supplied to the market by all firms will obviously depend on price. This relationship between price and quantity supplied is called a *short-run market supply curve*. Figure 14.2 illustrates the construction of the curve. For simplicity assume two firms, A and B. The short-run supply (that is, marginal cost) curves for firms A and B are shown in Figures 14.2a and 14.2b. The market supply curve shown in Figure 14.2c is the horizontal sum of these two curves. For example, at a price of P_1, firm A is willing to supply q_1^A, and firm B is willing to supply q_1^B. Therefore at this price the total supply in the market is given by Q_1, which is equal to $q_1^A + q_1^B$. The other points on the curve are

Figure 14.2   *Short-Run Market Supply Curve*

The supply (marginal cost) curves of two firms are shown in (a) and (b). The market supply curve (c) is the horizontal sum of these curves. For example, at P_1 firm A supplies q_1^A, firm B supplies q_1^B, and total market supply is given by $Q_1 = q_1^A + q_1^B$.

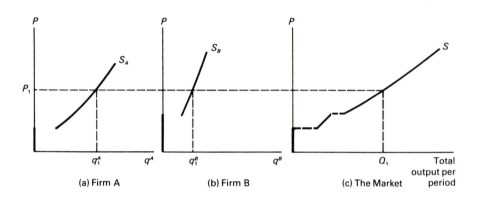

(a) Firm A   (b) Firm B   (c) The Market

constructed in an identical way. Because each firm's supply curve has a positive slope, the market supply curve will also have a positive slope. The positive slope reflects the fact that short-run marginal costs increase as firms attempt to increase their outputs.

Slope of the Short-Run Supply Curve

Although the construction shown in Figure 14.2 uses only two firms, actual market supply curves represent the horizontal summation of many firms' supply curves. Again the market supply curve will have a positive slope because of the positive slope in each firm's underlying marginal cost curve. In addition to this technical reason, there is an economic reason for the positive slope of market supply curves. As the firms in an industry attempt to expand production in the short run, they must hire additional (variable) inputs to do so. This action may cause the prices of inputs to be bid up as firms compete for those available. Such an increase in costs for each firm would shift marginal cost curves upward and would result in a more steeply sloped market supply curve. For example, a large expansion in the production of diamond jewelry in the short run would have the effect of bidding up the wages of diamond cutters as firms compete for their services. This *interaction effect* would increase firms' marginal costs, and it too must be considered when constructing the industry supply curve.[1]

Short-Run Supply Elasticity

One way of summarizing the responsiveness of the output of firms in an industry to higher prices is by the *short-run supply elasticity*. This measure shows how proportional changes in market price are met by changes in total

[1] Notice that the effect does not occur in constructing the individual firm's supply curve, since there the increased hiring of inputs is assumed to have no effect on input prices.

output. Consistent with the elasticity concepts developed in Chapter 7, this is defined as

---

Definition:

Short-Run Elasticity of Supply ($e_{S,P}$)

$$e_{S,P} = \frac{\text{percentage change in } Q \text{ supplied}}{\text{percentage change in } P} = \frac{\partial Q}{\partial P} \cdot \frac{P}{Q}. \qquad (14.1)$$

Since quantity supplied is an increasing function of price ($\partial Q/\partial P > 0$), the supply elasticity is positive. High values for $e_{S,P}$ imply that small increases in market price lead to a relatively large supply response by firms, since marginal costs do not rise steeply and input price interaction effects are small. Alternatively, a low value for $e_{S,P}$ implies that it takes relatively large changes in price to induce firms to change their output levels, since marginal costs rise rapidly or input price interaction effects are substantial.

Numerical
Example

In Chapter 11 we computed Hamburger Heaven's short-run total cost function as

$$STC = 4v + \frac{wq^2}{400}, \qquad (14.2)$$

and in Chapter 12 we used the short-run marginal cost function

$$SMC = \frac{2wq}{400} \qquad (14.3)$$

to construct the firm's short-run supply curve by equating price to SMC

$$P = SMC = \frac{2wq}{400} \qquad (14.4)$$

and solving for q:

$$q = \frac{200P}{w}. \qquad (14.5)$$

For the case $w = \$4$, this results in a simple linear supply function of the form

$$q = 50P. \qquad (14.6)$$

Now, assume there are 100 identical hamburger emporia in a particular city and let each firm's output be denoted as q_i ($i = 1 \ldots 100$). The supply function for each firm is now

$$q_i = 50P \quad (i = 1 \ldots 100), \qquad (14.7)$$

and the market supply function is given by

$$Q_s = \sum_{i=1}^{100} q_i = 100 \cdot (50P) = 5000P, \qquad (14.8)$$

where Q_s is the total quantity supplied to the market (as a function of market price faced by each firm, P). Notice that if the wage were to rise to $w = \$5$, each firm's supply function would be given by

$$q_i = 40P, \tag{14.9}$$

and the market supply function would be given by

$$Q_s = \sum q_i = 4000P. \tag{14.10}$$

At each price, fewer hamburgers would now be supplied.

Equilibrium Price
Determination

We are now ready to combine demand and supply curves to demonstrate the establishment of equilibrium prices in the market. Figure 14.3 shows this process. Looking first at Figure 14.3b, we see the market demand curve D (ignore D' for the moment) and the short-run supply curve S. The two curves intersect at a price of P_1 and a quantity of Q_1. This price-quantity combination represents an *equilibrium* between the demands of individuals and the costs of firms. At that point there is a precise balancing of the forces of supply and demand. Equilibrium will tend to persist from one period to the next unless one of the factors underlying the supply and demand curves should change. The equilibrium price P_1 serves two important functions. First, this price acts as a signal to producers by providing them with information with which to decide how much should be produced. In order to maximize profits, firms will produce that output level for which marginal costs are equal to P_1. In the aggregate, then, production will be Q_1. A second function of the price is to ration demand. Given the market price P_1, utility-maximizing individuals will decide how much of their limited incomes to devote to buying the particular good. At a price of P_1, total quantity demanded will be Q_1, and this is precisely the amount that will be produced. Hence we have

Definition:

Equilibrium Price
An *equilibrium price* is one for which the quantity demanded is precisely equal to the quantity supplied. At such a price there is no incentive for either demanders or suppliers to alter their behavior.

The implications of the equilibrium price (P_1) for a typical firm and for a typical individual are shown in Figures 14.3a and 14.3c, respectively. For the typical firm the price P_1 will cause an output level of q_1 to be produced. The firm earns a small profit at this particular price because short-run average total costs are covered. The demand curve d (ignore d' for the moment) for a typical individual is shown in Figure 14.3c. At a price of P_1, this individual demands $\bar{q}_1$. By adding up the quantities that each individual demands at P_1 and the quantities that each firm supplies, we can see that the market is in equilibrium. The market supply and demand curves provide a convenient way of making such a summation.

Figure 14.3   *Interactions of Many Individuals and Firms Determine Market Price in the Short Run*

Market demand curves and market supply curves are each the horizontal sum of numerous components. These market curves are shown in (b). Once price is determined in the market, each firm and each individual treat this price as a fixed parameter in their decisions. Although individual firms and persons are impotent in determining price, their interaction as a whole is the sole determinant of price. This is illustrated by a shift in an individual's demand curve to d'. This will not affect market price if only one individual reacts in this way. However, if everyone exhibits an increased demand, market demand will shift to D'; in the short run, price will rise to P_2.

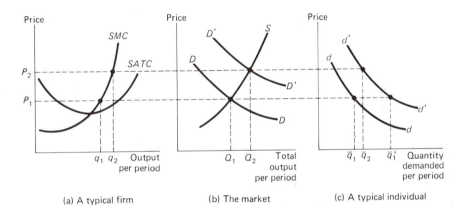

(a) A typical firm   (b) The market   (c) A typical individual

Market Reaction to a Shift in Demand

The three panels in Figure 14.3 can be used to show two important facts about short-run market equilibrium: the individual's "impotence" in the market and the nature of short-run supply response. First, suppose that a single individual's demand curve were to shift outward to d', as shown in Figure 14.3c. Since it was assumed that there are many demanders, this shift will have practically no effect on the market demand curve. Consequently, market price will be unaffected by the shift to d'; that is, price will remain at P_1. Of course, at this price, the person for whom the demand curve has shifted will consume more ($\overline{q}_1'$), as is shown in Figure 14.3c.[2]

If many individuals experience shifts outward in their demand curves, the entire market demand curve may shift. Figure 14.3b shows the new demand curve D'. The new equilibrium point will be at P_2, Q_2: At this point, supply-demand balance is reestablished. Price has increased from P_1 to P_2 in response

[2] It might properly be asked where the extra quantity $\overline{q}_1' - \overline{q}_1$ comes from, since nothing has happened to cause firms to change their output decisions. If, prior to the increase in demand, supply and demand were in balance, now there will be a shortage. The answer to this question lies in the extremely small magnitude that $\overline{q}_1' - \overline{q}_1$ represents when compared to the market as a whole. Since the effect on market price may only occur in the sixth decimal place (see some of the problems in this chapter), we can safely disregard it in our analysis.

to the demand shift. Notice also that the quantity traded in the market has increased from Q_1 to Q_2. The rise in price has served two functions. First, as in our previous analysis of the very short run, it has acted to ration demand. Whereas at P_1 a typical individual demanded $\overline{q}_1'$, now at P_2 only $\overline{q}_2$ is demanded. The rise in price has also acted as a signal to the typical firm to increase production. In Figure 14.3a the firm's profit-maximizing output level has increased from q_1 to q_2 in response to the price rise. That is what we mean by a *short-run supply response*: An increase in market price acts as an inducement to increase production. Firms are willing to increase production (and to incur higher marginal costs) because price has risen. If market price had not been permitted to rise (suppose, as described in the application to this chapter, that government price controls were in effect), firms would not have increased their outputs. At P_1 there would now be an excess (unfilled) demand for the good in question. If market price is allowed to rise, a supply-demand equilibrium can be reestablished so that what firms produce is again equal to what individuals demand at the prevailing market price. Notice also that at the new price P_2, the typical firm has increased its profits. This increasing profitability in the short run will be important to our discussion of long-run pricing later in this chapter.

SHIFTS IN SUPPLY AND DEMAND CURVES: A GRAPHIC ANALYSIS

In previous chapters we have analyzed many of the reasons why either a demand curve or a supply curve might shift. These reasons are briefly summarized in Table 14.1. It seems likely that these types of changes are constantly occurring in real-world markets. When either a supply curve or a demand curve does shift, equilibrium price and quantity will change as we illustrated in the previous numerical example. In this section we shall investigate graphically the relative magnitudes of such changes and show that the outcome depends on the shapes of the curves.

Shifts in Supply Curves: Importance of the Shape of the Demand Curve

Consider first a shift upward in the short-run supply curve for a good. Such a shift, for example, might have resulted from an increase in the prices of inputs used by firms to produce the good. Whatever the cause of the shift, it is important to recognize that the effect of the shift on the equilibrium level of P and Q will depend on the shape of the demand curve for the product. Figure 14.4

Table 14.1   *Reasons for Shifts in Demand or Supply Curves*

Demand Curves Shift because	Supply Curves Shift because
• Incomes change	• Input prices change
• Prices of substitutes or complements change	• Technology changes
• Preferences change	• Number of producers changes

Figure 14.4 *Effect of a Shift in the Short-Run Supply Curve*
Depends on the Shape of the Demand Curve

In (a) the shift upward in the supply curve causes price to increase only slightly whereas quantity declines sharply. This results from the elastic shape of the demand curve. In (b) the demand curve is inelastic; price increases substantially, with only a slight decrease in quantity.

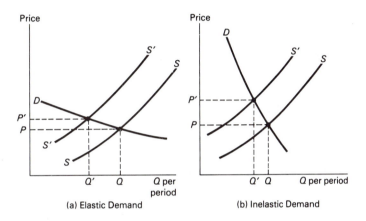

(a) Elastic Demand   (b) Inelastic Demand

illustrates two possible situations. The demand curve in Figure 14.4a is relatively price elastic; that is, a change in price substantially affects quantity demanded. For this case, a shift in the supply curve from S to S' will cause equilibrium price to rise only moderately (from P to P'), whereas quantity declines sharply (from Q to Q'). Rather than being "passed on" in higher prices, the increase in the firms' input costs is met primarily by a decrease in quantity (a movement down the firms' marginal cost curves) and only a slight increase in price.

This situation is reversed when the market demand curve is inelastic. In Figure 14.4b a shift in the supply curve causes equilibrium price to rise substantially, whereas quantity is little changed. The reason for this is that individuals do not reduce their demands very much if prices rise. Consequently, the shift upward in the supply curve is almost entirely passed on to demanders in the form of higher prices.

Shifts in Demand Curves: Importance of the Shape of the Supply Curve

In a procedure identical to that we just used, we can show that a given shift in a market demand curve will have different implications for P and Q, depending on the shape of the short-run supply curve. Two illustrations are shown in Figure 14.5. In Figure 14.5a the supply curve for the good in question is inelastic. In this situation a shift outward in the market demand curve will cause price to increase substantially. On the other hand, the quantity traded increases only slightly. Intuitively, what has happened is that the increase in demand (and in Q) has caused firms to move up their steeply sloped marginal cost curves. The concomitant large increase in price serves to ration demand.

Figure 14.5   *Effect of a Shift in the Demand Curve Depends on the Shape of the Short-Run Supply Curve*

In (a) supply is inelastic; a shift in demand causes price to increase greatly, with only a small concomitant increase in quantity. In (b), on the other hand, supply is elastic; price rises only slightly in response to a demand shift.

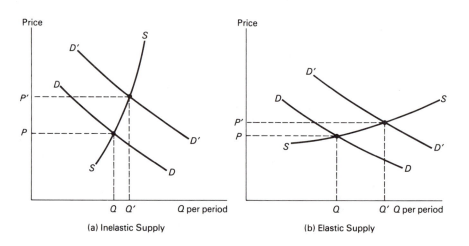

(a) Inelastic Supply   (b) Elastic Supply

Figure 14.5b shows a relatively elastic short-run supply curve. Such a curve would occur for an industry in which marginal costs do not rise steeply in response to output increases. For this case an increase in demand produces a substantial increase in Q. However, because of the nature of the supply curve, this increase is not met by great cost increases. Consequently, price rises only moderately.

These examples again demonstrate Marshall's observation that demand and supply simultaneously determine price and quantity. Recall his analogy from Chapter 1: Just as it is impossible to say which blade of a scissors does the cutting, so too is it impossible to attribute price solely to demand or to supply characteristics. Rather, the effect that shifts in either a demand curve or a supply curve will have depends on the shapes of both of the curves. Our numerical example illustrates some of these points.

Numerical Example

Continuing our hamburger example (just after you thought it was safe), suppose the hourly market demand for hamburgers in the city we have been studying is given by

$$Q_D = 10,000 - 5,000P. \tag{14.11}$$

To find the equilibrium price, we set quantity demanded equal to quantity supplied:

$$Q_D = 10,000 - 5,000P = Q_S = 5,000P \tag{14.12}$$

and solve for the price (P^*) that equates these two magnitudes:

$$10{,}000 = 10{,}000P \tag{14.13}$$

so

$$P^* = 1 \tag{14.14}$$

and

$$Q_D = Q_S = 5{,}000. \tag{14.15}$$

If the wage of hamburger workers were to rise to $5, the supply function would be

$$Q_S = 4{,}000P, \tag{14.16}$$

and the new market equilibrium would be

$$Q_D = 10{,}000 - 5{,}000P = Q_S = 4{,}000P$$

$$10{,}000 = 9{,}000P \tag{14.17}$$

$$P^* = 1.11 \tag{14.18}$$

$$Q^* = 4{,}444. \tag{14.19}$$

At the old price of $1, $Q_D = 5{,}000$ and $Q_S = 4{,}000$ so the rise to $1.11 restores equilibrium in two ways: (1) by increasing the quantity supplied; and (2) by reducing the quantity demanded. In this example these two responses are of approximately equal magnitude, but that need not be so. If the demand curve were flatter, for example, price would rise less, and a relatively larger portion of the quantity adjustment would be reflected in a move along the demand curve. Alternatively, if demand were steeper, there would be a greater rise in price, and more of the quantity change would arise from movement along the supply curve.[3]

A similar analysis would hold for an increase in demand. Suppose demand were to increase to

$$Q_D = 12{,}000 - 5{,}000P. \tag{14.20}$$

Assuming our original supply curve, the new market equilibrium would be

$$Q_D = 12{,}000 - 5{,}000P = Q_S = 5{,}000P$$

---

[3] The demand functions

$$Q_D = 15{,}000 - 10{,}000P \tag{i}$$

and

$$Q_D = 6{,}000 - 1{,}000P \tag{ii}$$

each have an equilibrium of $P^* = 1$, $Q^* = 5{,}000$ with the initial supply curve. The shift in supply results in a new equilibrium of $P^* = 1.071$, $Q^* = 4{,}284$ in case (i) but an equilibrium of $P^* = 1.20$, $Q^* = 4{,}800$ in case (ii).

or

$$P^* = 1.20 \tag{14.21}$$

$$Q^* = 6{,}000. \tag{14.22}$$

At the old price of \$1, $Q_D = 7{,}000$ and $Q_S = 5{,}000$ so the rise in price restores equilibrium by prompting an increase in quantity supplied and a reduction in quantity demanded. Again the relative change in price and quantity would be determined by the slopes of the curves, as we now illustrate with a general mathematical development.

MATHEMATICAL MODEL OF SUPPLY AND DEMAND

A general mathematical model of the supply-demand process can further illuminate the comparative statics of changing equilibrium prices and quantities. Suppose that the demand curve can be represented by

$$Q_D = D(P, \alpha), \tag{14.23}$$

where α is a parameter that allows us to shift the demand curve. It might represent consumer income, prices of other goods (this would permit the tying together of supply and demand in several related markets), or changing preferences. In general we expect $\partial D/\partial P = D_P < 0$, but $\partial D/\partial \alpha = D_\alpha$ may have any sign, depending precisely on what the parameter α means. Using this same procedure, we can write the supply relationship as

$$Q_S = S(P, \beta), \tag{14.24}$$

where β is a parameter that shifts the supply curve and might include such variables as input prices, technical changes, or (for a multiproduct firm) prices of other potential outputs. Here $\partial S/\partial P = S_P > 0$, but $\partial S/\partial \beta = S_\beta$ may have any sign. The model is closed by requiring that in equilibrium,[4]

$$Q_D = Q_S. \tag{14.25}$$

To analyze the comparative statics of this simple model, we write the total differentials of Equations 14.23 and 14.24 as

$$dQ_D = D_P \, dP + D_\alpha \, d\alpha$$

and $\tag{14.26}$

$$dQ_S = S_P \, dP + S_\beta \, d\beta.$$

---

[4]The model could be further modified to show how the equilibrium quantity supplied is to be allocated among the firms in the industry. If, for example, the industry is composed of n identical firms, the output of any one of them would be given by

$$q = \frac{Q}{n}.$$

In the short run, with n fixed, this would add little to our analysis. In the long run, however, n must also be determined by the model, as we show later in this chapter.

Since maintenance of equilibrium requires that

$$dQ_D = dQ_S,$$ (14.27)

we can solve these equations for the change in equilibrium price for any combination of shifts in demand (α) or supply (β). For example, suppose the demand parameter α were to change while β remains constant. Then, using the equilibrium condition (Equation 14.27), we have

$$D_P dP + D_\alpha d\alpha = S_P dP$$ (14.28)

or, manipulating terms a bit,

$$\frac{\partial P}{\partial \alpha} = \frac{D_\alpha}{S_P - D_P}.$$ (14.29)

Since the denominator of this expression is positive, the sign of $\partial P / \partial \alpha$ will be the same as the sign of D_α. If α represents consumer income (and the good in question is normal), D_α would be positive, and a rise in income would shift demand outward. This, as Equation 14.29 also indicates, would cause equilibrium price to rise, a result already reflected graphically in Figure 14.5.

An Elasticity Interpretation

Further algebraic manipulation of Equation 14.29 yields a more useful comparative statics result. Multiplying both sides of Equation 14.29 by α/P gives

$$e_{P,\alpha} = \frac{\partial P}{\partial \alpha} \cdot \frac{\alpha}{P} = \frac{D_\alpha}{S_P - D_P} \cdot \frac{\alpha}{P}$$ (14.30)

$$= \frac{D_\alpha \dfrac{\alpha}{Q}}{(S_P - D_P) \cdot \dfrac{P}{Q}} = \frac{e_{Q,\alpha}}{e_{S,P} - e_{Q,P}}.$$

Since the elasticities in this equation are frequently available from empirical studies, this equation can be a convenient way to make rough estimates of the effects of various events on equilibrium prices. As an example, suppose again that α represents consumer income and that there is interest in predicting how an increase in this parameter will affect the equilibrium price of, say, automobiles. Suppose empirical data suggest that $e_{Q,I} = e_{Q,\alpha} = 3.0$, $e_{Q,P} = -1.2$ (these figures are from Table 7.3) and assume that $e_{S,P} = 1.0$. Substituting these figures into Equation 14.30 yields

$$e_{P,\alpha} = \frac{e_{Q,\alpha}}{e_{S,P} - e_{Q,P}} = \frac{3.0}{1.0 - (-1.2)}$$ (14.31)

$$= \frac{3.0}{2.2} = 1.36.$$

The empirical elasticity estimates therefore suggest that each 1 percent rise in consumer incomes results in a 1.36 percent rise in the equilibrium price of automobiles. Estimates of other kinds of shifts in supply or demand can be similarly modeled by manipulating Equations 14.26 and obtaining estimates of the necessary parameters.

TAX INCIDENCE ANALYSIS

This mathematical model of supply and demand can also be used to illustrate some basic principles of tax incidence theory. That branch of the field of public finance is concerned with determining which segment of the economy bears the ultimate burden of a tax (which may be quite different from the agent charged statutorily with "paying" the tax). Examining the true incidence of some taxes is a very difficult question because many markets may be affected simultaneously. In the next chapter we will briefly discuss such a general equilibrium analysis of taxation. Here, however, we will analyze a very simple partial equilibrium incidence model as it applies to a "specific tax"; that is, a tax that is charged per unit of output of some commodity. Imposition of such a tax creates a "wedge" between the price paid by demanders and the price received by suppliers, and it is the effect of that wedge that we wish to analyze. Specifically, let t represent the per-unit amount of the tax; P_D, the price paid by demanders; and P_S, the price received by suppliers. Then assuming that before the tax $P_D = P_S$, now

$$P_D - P_S = t$$

and   (14.32)

$$dP_D - dP_S = dt.$$

Using this expression in the supply-demand system (Equations 14.26) gives

$$dQ_D = D_P dP_D$$

$$dQ_S = S_P dP_S = S_P(dP_D - dt)$$ (14.33)

$$dQ_D = dQ_S.$$

Simple algebraic manipulation of this system yields

$$\frac{dP_D}{dt} = \frac{S_P}{S_P - D_P}$$ (14.34)

and by multiplying the numerator and denominator of this expression by P/Q, we can write this derivative in elasticity terms as

$$\frac{dP_D}{dt} = \frac{e_{S,P}}{e_{S,P} - e_{Q,P}}.$$ (14.35)

A similar series of algebraic steps would lead to the result that

$$\frac{dP_S}{dt} = \frac{e_{Q,P}}{e_{S,P} - e_{Q,P}}.$$ (14.36)

Because of the signs of the elasticities, these calculations immediately provide the obvious results that

$$\frac{dP_D}{dt} \geq 0$$ (14.37)

Figure 14.6   *Tax Incidence Analysis*

Imposition of a specific tax of amount *t* per unit creates a "wedge" between the price consumers pay (P_D) and what suppliers receive (P_S). The extent to which consumers or producers pay the tax depends on the price elasticities of the demand and supply curves.

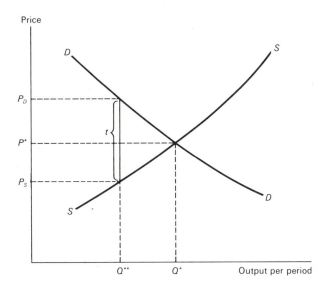

and

$$\frac{dP_S}{dt} \le 0.$$

More specifically, if $e_{Q,P} = 0$ (demand is perfectly inelastic), $dP_D/dt = 1$ and $dP_S/dt = 0$, so that the tax is fully paid by consumers. Alternatively, if demand is infinitely elastic ($e_{Q,P} = -\infty$), the full tax is paid by suppliers ($dP_S/dt = -1$). Similar polar cases can be calculated for alternative values of the supply elasticity, as can various intermediate cases in which the burden of the tax is shared by demanders and suppliers.

Graphic Analysis   Figure 14.6 illustrates this tax incidence analysis. Initially, the market is in equilibrium at P^*, Q^*. Imposition of a per-unit tax of t creates a divergence between the price paid by demanders (P_D) and the price received by suppliers (P_S), and in the process, quantity traded in the market declines to Q^{**}. In the figure it appears that the burden of the tax is shared approximately equally by demanders and suppliers, but that result stems from the similarity in demand and supply elasticities in the case pictured. Different distributions of the burden would result, depending on the values of the elasticities, as we showed in our mathematical representation of the incidence question.[5]

Transactions Costs

Although we have developed this discussion in terms of tax incidence theory, models incorporating a wedge between buyers' and sellers' prices have a number of other applications in economics. Perhaps the most important of these concern costs associated with making market transactions. In some cases these costs may be explicit. Most real estate transactions, for example, take place through a third-party broker, who charges a fee for the service of bringing buyer and seller together. Similar explicit transactions fees occur in the trading of stocks and bonds, boats and airplanes, and practically everything that is sold at auction. In all of these instances, buyers and sellers are willing to pay an explicit fee to an agent or broker who facilitates the transaction. In other cases transactions costs may be largely implicit. Individuals trying to purchase a used car, for example, will spend considerable time and effort reading classified advertisements and examining vehicles, and these activities amount to an implicit cost of making the transaction.

To the extent that transactions costs are on a per-unit basis (as they are in the real estate, securities, and auction examples), our previous taxation example applies exactly. From the point of view of the buyers and sellers, it makes little difference whether t represents a per-unit tax or a per-unit transactions fee, since the analysis of the fee's effect on the market will be the same. That is, the fee will be shared between buyers and sellers, depending on the specific elasticities involved. Trading volume will be lower than in the absence of such fees.[6] A somewhat different analysis would hold, however, if transactions costs were a lump-sum amount per transaction. In that case individuals would seek to reduce the number of transactions made, but existence of the charge would not affect the supply-demand equilibrium itself. For example, the cost of driving to the supermarket is mainly a lump-sum transaction cost on shopping for groceries. Existence of such a charge may not significantly affect the price of food items nor the amount of food consumed (unless it tempts people to grow their own), but the charge will cause individuals to shop less frequently, to buy larger quantities on each trip, and to hold larger inventories of food in their homes than would be the case in the absence of such a cost. A complete analysis of all of these possibilities would take us too far afield in the present chapter, but issues relating to the existence of transactions costs will recur at several places later in this part.

[5] This specific tax also involves an "excess burden" in that the loss of consumer surplus from its imposition exceeds the value of tax revenues collected.

[6] This analysis is restricted, however, by its failure to consider the benefits obtained from brokers. To the extent these services are valuable to the parties in the transaction, demand and supply curves will shift outward to reflect this value. Hence trading volume may actually expand with the availability of brokerage services, although the costs of such services will continue to create a wedge between sellers' and buyers' prices.

THE LONG RUN

We saw in Chapter 11 that in the long run, a firm may adapt all of its inputs to fit market conditions. For long-run analysis, therefore, we should use the firm's long-run cost curves, since these curves reflect flexibility in all inputs. A profit-maximizing firm that is a price taker will produce that output level for which price is equal to long-run marginal cost (MC). However, we must consider a second feature of the long run: the possibility of the entry of entirely new firms into the industry or the exit of existing firms from the industry. In mathematical terms we must allow the number of firms, n, to vary in response to economic incentives. The perfectly competitive model assumes that there are no special costs of entering or exiting from an industry. Consequently, new firms will be lured into any market in which (economic) profits are positive. Similarly, firms will leave any industry in which profits are negative. The entry of new firms will cause the short-run industry supply curve to shift outward, since there are now more firms producing than there were previously. Such a shift will cause market price (and industry profits) to fall. The process will continue until no firm contemplating entering the industry is able to earn a profit.[7] At that point, entry will cease and an equilibrium number of firms will be in the industry. A similar argument can be made for the case in which some of the firms in an industry are suffering short-run losses. Some firms will choose to leave the industry, and this will cause the supply curve to shift to the left. Market price will rise, thus restoring profitability to those firms remaining in the industry.

Equilibrium Conditions

For the purposes of this chapter, we shall assume that all the firms in an industry have identical cost curves; that is, no firm controls any special resources or technologies.[8] Because all firms are identical, the equilibrium long-run position requires that each firm earn exactly zero economic profits. In graphic terms the long-run equilibrium price must settle at the low point of each firm's long-run average total cost curve. Only at this point do the two equilibrium conditions $P = MC$ (which is required for profit maximization) and $P = AC$ (which is required for zero profit) hold. It is important to emphasize, however, that these two equilibrium conditions have rather different origins. Profit maximization is a goal of firms. The $P = MC$ rule therefore derives from the behavioral assumptions we have made about firms and is similar to the output decision rule used in the short run. The zero-profit condition is not a goal for firms. Firms obviously would prefer to have positive profits. The long-run operation

---

[7] Remember that we are using the economists' definition of profits here. These profits represent a return to the owner of a business in excess of that which is strictly necessary to keep him or her in the business. Hence, when we talk about a firm earning "zero" profits, we mean that no entrepreneurial income is being earned in excess of that which could be earned from alternative investments.

[8] If firms have different costs, very low-cost firms can earn positive long-run profits, and such extra profits will be reflected in the price of the resource that accounts for the firm's low costs. In this sense the assumption of identical costs is not very restrictive since an active market for the firm's inputs will insure that average costs (which include opportunity costs) are the same for all firms.

of the market, however, forces all firms to accept a level of zero economic profits ($P = AC$) because of the willingness of firms to enter and to leave an industry. Although the firms in a perfectly competitive industry may earn either positive or negative profits in the short run, in the long run only a level of zero profits will prevail. Hence we can summarize this analysis by

Definition:

Long-Run Competitive Equilibrium
A *perfectly competitive industry* is in *long-run equilibrium* if there are no incentives for profit-maximizing firms to enter or to leave the industry. This will occur when the number of firms is such that $P = MC = AC$ and each firm operates at the low point of its long-run average cost curve.

LONG-RUN EQUILIBRIUM: CONSTANT-COST CASE

In order to discuss long-run pricing in detail, we must make an assumption about how the entry of new firms into an industry affects the costs of firms' inputs. The simplest assumption we might make is that entry has no effect on the costs of those inputs. Under this assumption, no matter how many firms enter (or leave) an industry, each firm will retain the same set of cost curves with which it started. This assumption of constant input costs may not be tenable in many important cases, which we shall analyze in the next section. For the moment, however, we wish to examine the equilibrium conditions for a *constant-cost industry*.

Initial Equilibrium

Figure 14.7 demonstrates long-run equilibrium for an industry. For the market as a whole (Figure 14.7b), the demand curve is given by D and the short-run supply curve by SS. The short-run equilibrium price is therefore P_1. The typical firm (Figure 14.7a) will produce output level q_1, since at this level of output, price is equal to short-run marginal cost (SMC). In addition, with a market price of P_1, output level q_1 is also a long-run equilibrium position for the firm. The firm is maximizing profits, since price is equal to long-run marginal costs (MC). Figure 14.7a also implies a second long-run equilibrium property: Price is equal to long-run average costs (AC). Consequently, economic profits are zero, and there is no incentive for firms either to enter or to leave the industry. The market depicted in Figure 14.7 is therefore in both short-run and long-run equilibrium. Firms are in equilibrium because they are maximizing profits, and the number of firms is stable because economic profits are zero. This equilibrium will tend to persist until either supply or demand conditions change.

Responses to an Increase in Demand

Suppose now that the market demand curve in Figure 14.7b shifts outward to D'. If SS is the relevant short-run supply curve for the industry, then in the short run, price will rise to P_2. The typical firm, in the short run, will choose to produce q_2 and will earn profits on this level of output. In the long run, these profits will attract new firms into the market. Because of the constant-cost assumption, this entry of new firms will have no effect on cost curves: Costs of factors of production are not affected by the new firms that enter the industry. New firms will continue to enter the market until price is forced

Figure 14.7   *Long-Run Equilibrium for a Perfectly Competitive Industry: Constant-Cost Case*

An increase in demand from D to D' will cause price to rise from P_1 to P_2 in the short run. This higher price will create profits in the industry, and new firms will be drawn into the market. If it is assumed that the entry of these new firms has no effect on the cost curves of the firms in the industry, new firms will continue to enter until price is pushed back down to P_1. At this price, economic profits are 0. The long-run supply curve (LS) will therefore be a horizontal line at P_1. Along LS, output is increased by increasing the number of firms, each producing q_1.

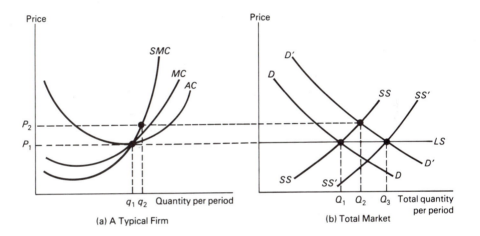

(a) A Typical Firm

(b) Total Market

down to the level at which there are again no pure economic profits. The entry of new firms therefore will shift the short-run supply curve to SS', where the equilibrium price (P_1) is reestablished. At this new long-run equilibrium, the price-quantity combination P_1, Q_3 will prevail in the market. The typical firm again will produce at output level q_1, although now there will be more firms than in the initial situation.

We have shown that the *long-run supply curve* for the constant-cost industry will be a horizontal straight line at price P_1. This curve is labeled LS in Figure 14.7b. No matter what happens to demand, the twin equilibrium conditions of zero long-run profits (since free entry is assumed) and profit maximization will ensure that no price other than P_1 can prevail in the long run.[9] For this reason, P_1 might be regarded as the "normal" price for this commodity. If the constant cost assumption is abandoned, however, the long-run supply curve need not be horizontal.

---

[9] These equilibrium conditions also point out what seems to be, somewhat imprecisely, an "efficient" aspect of the long-run equilibrium in perfectly competitive markets: The good under investigation will be produced at minimum average cost.

SHAPE OF THE LONG-RUN SUPPLY CURVE

Contrary to the short-run case, long-run analysis has very little to do with the shape of the (long-run) marginal cost curve. Rather, the zero-profit condition centers attention on the low point of the long-run average cost curve as the factor most relevant to long-run price determination. In the constant-cost case, the position of this low point does not change as new firms enter the industry. Consequently, only one price can prevail in the long run regardless of how demand shifts because the long-run supply curve is horizontal at this price. Once the constant-cost assumption is abandoned, this need not be the case. If the entry of new firms causes average costs to rise, the long-run supply curve will have an upward slope. On the other hand, if entry causes average costs to decline, it is even possible for the long-run supply curve to be negatively sloped. We shall now discuss these possibilities.

Increasing Cost Industry

The entry of new firms into an industry may cause the average costs of all firms to rise for several reasons. New and existing firms may compete for scarce inputs, thus driving up their prices. New firms may impose "external costs" on existing firms (and on themselves) in the form of air or water pollution. And new firms may place strains on governmental services (police forces, sewage treatment plants, and so forth), which may show up as increased costs for all firms. Figure 14.8 demonstrates market equilibrium in such an *increasing cost industry*. The initial equilibrium price is P_1. At this price the typical firm produces q_1, and total industry output is Q_1. Suppose now that the demand curve

---

Figure 14.8   *An Increasing Cost Industry Has a Positively Sloped Long-Run Supply Curve*

Initially, the market is in equilibrium at P_1, Q_1. An increase in demand (to D') causes price to rise to P_2 in the short run, and the typical firm produces q_2 at a profit. This profit attracts new firms into the industry. The entry of these new firms causes costs for a typical firm to rise to the levels shown in (b). With this new set of curves, equilibrium is reestablished in the market at P_3, Q_3. By considering many possible demand shifts and connecting all the resulting equilibrium points, the long-run supply curve (*LS*) is traced out.

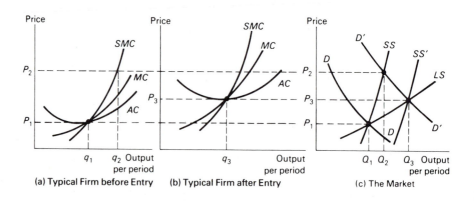

(a) Typical Firm before Entry   (b) Typical Firm after Entry   (c) The Market

for the industry shifts outward to D'. In the short run, price will rise to P_2, since this is where D' and the industry's short-run supply curve (SS) intersect. At this price the typical firm will produce q_2 and will earn a substantial profit. This profit then attracts new entrants into the market and shifts the short-run supply curve outward.

Suppose that this entry of new firms causes the cost curves of all firms to rise. The new firms may compete for scarce inputs, thereby driving up the prices of these inputs. A typical firm's new (higher) set of cost curves is shown in Figure 14.8b. The new long-run equilibrium price for the industry is P_3 (here $P_3 = MC = AC$), and at this price Q_3 is demanded. We now have two points $(P_1, Q_1$ and $P_3, Q_3)$ on the long-run supply curve. All other points on the curve can be found in an analogous way by considering all possible shifts in the demand curve. These shifts will trace out the long-run supply curve LS. Here LS has a positive slope because of the increasing cost nature of the industry. Notice that the LS curve is somewhat flatter than the short-run supply curves. This indicates the greater flexibility in supply response that is possible in the long run.

Decreasing Cost Industry

Not all industries exhibit constant or increasing costs. In fact, the entry of new firms may reduce the costs of firms in an industry. For example, the entry of new firms may provide a larger pool of trained labor from which to draw than was previously available, thus reducing the costs associated with the hiring of new workers. Similarly, the entry of new firms may provide a "critical mass" of industrialization, which permits the development of more efficient transportation and communications networks. Whatever the exact reason for the cost reductions, the final result is illustrated in the three panels of Figure 14.9. The initial market equilibrium is shown by the price-quantity combination P_1, Q_1 in Figure 14.9c. At this price the typical firm produces q_1 and earns exactly zero in economic profits. Now suppose that market demand shifts outward to D'. In the short run, price will increase to P_2 and the typical firm will produce q_2. At this price level, positive profits are being earned. These profits cause new entrants to come into the market. If this entry causes costs to decline, a new set of cost curves for the typical firm might resemble those shown in Figure 14.9b. Now the new equilibrium price is P_3; at this price, Q_3 is demanded. By considering all possible shifts in demand, the long-run supply curve, LS, can be traced out. This curve has a negative slope because of the decreasing cost nature of the industry. Therefore, as output expands, price falls. This possibility has been used as the basis for protective tariffs to shield new industries from foreign competition. It is assumed (only occasionally correctly) that the protection of the "infant industry" will permit it to grow and ultimately to compete at lower world prices.

Classification of Long-Run Supply Curves

Thus we have shown that the long-run supply curve for a perfectly competitive industry may assume a variety of shapes. The principal determinant of the shape is the way in which the entry of firms into the industry affects costs. The following definitions cover the various possibilities:

Figure 14.9   *A Decreasing Cost Industry Has a Negatively Sloped Long-Run Supply Curve*

Initially, the market is in equilibrium at P_1, Q_1. An increase in demand to D' causes price to rise to P_2 in the short run, and the typical firm produces q_2 at a profit. This profit attracts new firms to the industry. If the entry of these new firms causes costs for the typical firm to fall, a set of new cost curves might look like those in (b). With this new set of curves, market equilibrium is reestablished at P_3, Q_3. By connecting such points of equilibrium, a negatively sloped long-run supply curve (LS) is traced out.

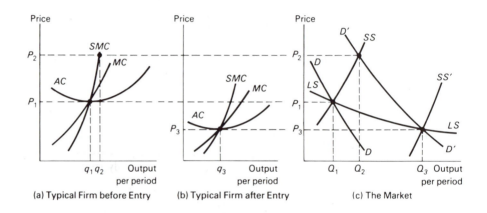

(a) Typical Firm before Entry   (b) Typical Firm after Entry   (c) The Market

---

Definitions:

Constant-, Increasing, and Decreasing Cost Industries
The shape of an industry supply curve is determined by one of three categories:

- *Constant cost*: Entry does not affect input costs; the long-run supply curve is horizontal at the long-run equilibrium price.
- *Increasing cost*: Entry increases input costs; the long-run supply curve is positively sloped.
- *Decreasing cost*: Entry reduces input costs; the long-run supply curve is negatively sloped.

Now we show how the shape of the long-run supply curve can be further quantified.

LONG-RUN ELASTICITY OF SUPPLY

The long-run supply curve for an industry incorporates information on both internal firm adjustments to changing prices and changes in the number of firms in response to profit opportunities. All of these supply responses are summarized in the following elasticity concept:

Long-Run Elasticity of Supply
The *long-run elasticity of supply* ($e_{LS,P}$) records the proportionate change in long-run industry output in response to a proportionate change in product price. Mathematically,

$$e_{LS,P} = \frac{\text{percentage change in } Q}{\text{percentage change in } P} = \frac{\partial Q}{\partial P} \cdot \frac{P}{Q}. \tag{14.38}$$

The value of this elasticity may be positive or negative, depending on whether the industry exhibits increasing or decreasing costs. In the constant-cost case, $e_{LS,P}$ is infinite, since industry expansions or contractions can occur without having any effect on product prices.

Empirical Estimates

It is obviously important to have good empirical estimates of long-run supply elasticities, because they indicate whether production can be expanded with only a slight increase in relative price (that is, supply is price elastic) or whether expansions in output can occur only if relative prices rise sharply (that is, supply is price inelastic). Such information can be used to assess the likely effect of shifts in demand on long-run prices and to evaluate alternative policy proposals intended to increase supply. Table 14.2 presents several long-run supply elasticity estimates. These relate primarily (though not exclusively) to natural resources because economists have devoted considerable attention to the implications of increasing costs of resource production.

The estimated elasticities for agricultural products are "acreage elasticities"; that is, they reflect how the number of acres planted in a particular crop responds to that crop's price. Assuming a constant yield per acre, these then can be translated directly into the supply elasticity concept defined in Equation 14.2. Although all of the reported elasticities are relatively low (less than 1), all are positive, indicating that increases in prices do lead to increases in output.

Two different types of supply elasticity are reported for natural resources in Table 14.2. For aluminum and chromium the figures refer to the relationship between annual production and market price. They show that the long-run supply of aluminum is nearly infinitely elastic at current market prices, since aluminum deposits are reasonably accessible given current technology. On the other hand, the supply elasticity for chromium is considerably lower, primarily because large price increases would be required to make existing deposits economically attractive.

For coal, natural gas, and oil, supply elasticities refer to the responsiveness of economically accessible reserves to price. In order to relate these elasticities directly to the notion of current production, one would also need a theory of firms' profit-maximizing output decisions from existing resource stocks.[10] The data show that coal reserves are far more price responsive than oil and natural

[10] For a brief discussion of such a theory, see Chapter 23, Appendix B.

Table 14.2   *Selected Estimates of Long-Run Supply Elasticities*

Agricultural acreage	
Corn	0.18
Cotton	0.67
Wheat	0.93
Aluminum	Nearly infinite
Chromium	0–3.0
Coal (eastern reserves)	15.0–30.0
Natural gas (U.S. reserves)	0.20
Oil (U.S. reserves)	0.76
Urban housing	
Density	5.3
Quality	3.8

Sources: Agricultural acreage—M. Nerlove, "Estimates of the Elasticities of Supply of Selected Agricultural Commodities," *Journal of Farm Economics* 38 (May 1956): 496–509. Aluminum and chromium—estimated from U.S. Department of Interior, *Critical Materials Commodity Action Analysis* (Washington, D.C.: U.S. Government Printing Office, 1975). Coal—estimated from M. B. Zimmerman, "The Supply of Coal in the Long Run: The Case of Eastern Deep Coal," MIT Energy Laboratory Report No. MITEL 75–021 (September 1975). Natural gas—based on estimate for oil (see text) and J. D. Khazzoom, "The FPC Staff's Econometric Model of Natural Gas Supply in the United States," *The Bell Journal of Economics and Management Science* (Spring 1971): 103–117. Oil—E. W. Erickson, S. W. Millsaps, and R. M. Spann, "Oil Supply and Tax Incentives," *Brookings Papers on Economic Activity* 2 (1974): 449–478. Urban housing—B. A. Smith, "The Supply of Urban Housing," *Journal of Political Economy* 40 (August 1976): 389–405.

gas reserves. That result derives primarily from the accessibility of the additional reserves and their geological features. Natural gas has a particularly low elasticity because it is usually found in conjunction with oil, but has a much lower value per well than does its associated oil. For example, at present market prices, the oil produced from the typical oil-gas well is worth four times the value of the gas produced from such a well. Hence the effect of an increase in the price of natural gas alone on drilling is only about one-fourth the effect of an increase in the price of oil.

The final estimates in Table 14.2 refer to two aspects of the supply of urban housing. They show that "more housing" can be produced in two ways: by increasing residential density while holding house quality constant and by increasing quality while holding density constant. Both of these output measures seem to be reasonably responsive to price.

COMPARATIVE STATICS ANALYSIS OF LONG-RUN EQUILIBRIUM

Earlier in this chapter we showed how to develop a simple comparative statics analysis of changing short-run equilibria in competitive markets. By using estimates of the long-run elasticities of demand and supply, exactly the same sort of analysis can be conducted for the long run as well. For example, it is a simple matter to show that in the long run in a constant-cost industry, the burden of a specific tax is borne entirely by consumers because long-run supply is infinitely elastic. In the increasing cost case, the burden of the tax would be shared by consumers and producers, with the respective shares being determined by the specific elasticities involved. In this case, however, the "producer's burden" of the tax should be interpreted differently than in the short-run case. In the short run, a tax-induced fall in the price received by suppliers results in a reduction in firms' short-term profits. Hence this share of the tax is paid by the firms' owners. In the long run, however, the zero-profit equilibrium condition holds. The reduction in supply price brought about by the tax reflects the falling price of some inputs in response to the reduction in the demand for their services as firms leave the industry. A part of the producers' burden of the tax therefore is passed on to those scarce resources that account for the positively sloped long-run supply curve. Consequently, to understand fully the true burden of the tax in the increasing cost case, one must also examine changing supply-demand patterns in the input market. In some cases capital owners will pay most of the producers' share of the tax (if the supply of capital to the industry is fairly inelastic and largely accounts for the industry's increasing costs). But in other cases workers or owners of other scarce resources may bear the producers' burden of the tax. To capture all of these effects, a general equilibrium model is required.

Industry Structure   One aspect of the changing long-run equilibria in a perfectly competitive market that would be obscured by using a simple supply-demand analysis is how the number of firms varies as market equilibria change. Because, as we will see in Part VI, the functioning of markets may in some cases be affected by the number of firms and because there may be direct public policy interest in entry and exit from an industry, some additional analysis seems required. In this section we will examine in detail determinants of the number of firms in the constant-cost case. Brief reference will also be made to the increasing cost case, and some of the problems for this chapter examine that case in more detail.

Shifts in Demand   Since the long-run supply curve for a constant-cost industry is infinitely elastic, analyzing shifts in market demand is particularly easy. If the initial equilibrium industry output is Q_0 and q^* represents the output level for which the typical firm's long-run average cost is minimized, then the initial equilibrium number of firms (n_0) is given by

$$n_0 = \frac{Q_0}{q^*}. \tag{14.39}$$

A shift in demand that changes equilibrium output to Q_1 will, in the long run, change the equilibrium number of firms to

$$n_1 = \frac{Q_1}{q^*}, \tag{14.40}$$

and the change in the number of firms is given by

$$n_1 - n_0 = \frac{Q_1 - Q_0}{q^*}. \tag{14.41}$$

That is, the change in the equilibrium number of firms is completely determined by the extent of the demand shift and by the optimal output level for the typical firm.

Input Costs

Even in the simple constant-cost industry case, analyzing the effect of an increase in an input price (and hence an upward shift in the infinitely elastic long-run supply curve) is relatively complicated. First, in order to calculate the fall in industry output, it is necessary to know both the extent to which minimum average cost is increased by the input price rise and how such an increase in the long-run equilibrium price affects total quantity demanded. Knowledge of the typical firm's average cost function and of the price elasticity of demand permits such a calculation to be made in a straightforward way. But an increase in an input price may also change the minimum average cost output level for the typical firm. Such a possibility is illustrated in Figure 14.10. Both the average and marginal costs have been shifted upward by the input price rise, but because average cost has shifted up by a relatively greater extent than the marginal cost, the typical firm's optimal output level has increased from q_0^* to q_1^*. If the relative sizes of the shifts in cost curves were reversed, however, the

Figure 14.10   *An Increase in an Input Price May Change Long-Run Equilibrium Output for the Typical Firm*

An increase in the price of an input will shift both average and marginal cost curves upward. The precise effect of these shifts on the typical firm's optimal output level (q^*) will depend on the relative magnitudes of the shifts.

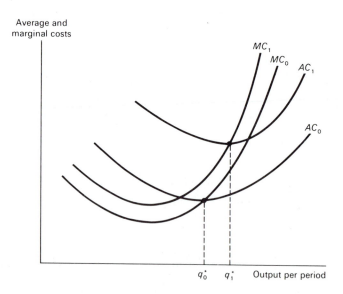

typical firm's optimal output level would have fallen.[11] Taking account of this change in optimal scale, Equation 14.41 becomes

$$n_1 - n_0 = \frac{Q_1}{q_1^*} - \frac{Q_0}{q_0^*} \qquad (14.42)$$

and a number of possibilities arise.

If $q_1^* \geq q_0^*$, the decline in quantity brought about by the rise in market price will definitely cause the number of firms to fall. However, if $q_1^* < q_0^*$, the result will be indeterminate. Industry output will fall, but optimal firm size also will fall, so that the ultimate effect on the number of firms depends on the relative magnitude of these changes. A decline in the number of firms still seems the most likely outcome when an input price rise causes industry output to fall, but an increase in n is at least a theoretical possibility.

SUMMARY

In this chapter we have developed a detailed model of competitive price determination in a single market. This model of supply and demand, which was first articulated by Alfred Marshall in the latter part of the nineteenth century, is at the heart of much of microeconomic analysis. Its principal properties include the following:

- In the short run, equilibrium prices are established by the interaction of what demanders are willing to pay (as reflected by the demand curve) and what firms are willing to produce (as reflected by the short-run supply curve). These prices are treated as fixed parameters in both demanders' and suppliers' decision-making processes.
- A shift in either demand or supply will cause the equilibrium price to change. The extent of such a change will depend on the slopes of the various curves and can be modeled using fairly simple comparative statics techniques.

---

[11] A simple mathematical proof would proceed as follows. Optimal output, q^*, is defined such that

$$AC(v, w, q^*) = MC(v, w, q^*).$$

Differentiating both sides of this expression, by, say, v, yields

$$\frac{\partial AC}{\partial v} + \frac{\partial AC}{\partial q^*} \cdot \frac{\partial q^*}{\partial v} = \frac{\partial MC}{\partial v} + \frac{\partial MC}{\partial q^*} \cdot \frac{\partial q^*}{\partial v};$$

but $\partial AC/\partial q^* = 0$, since average costs are minimized. By manipulating terms, we have

$$\frac{\partial q^*}{\partial v} = \frac{\frac{1}{\partial MC}}{\partial q^*} \left[\frac{\partial AC}{\partial v} - \frac{\partial MC}{\partial v} \right].$$

Since $\partial MC/\partial q > 0$ at the minimum AC, $\partial q^*/\partial v$ will be positive or negative, depending on the relative shifts in the AC and MC curves. For a more complete analysis see E. Silberberg, *The Structure of Economics* (New York: McGraw Hill Book Company, 1978), pp. 209–211.

- Taxes or other types of transactions costs create a wedge between the price demanders pay and what suppliers receive. Effects of such distortions can also be examined using comparative statics, partial equilibrium models of supply and demand.

- In the long run the number of firms is variable. The assumption of free entry and exit implies that the firms in a competitive industry will earn zero economic profits in the long run ($P = AC$). Since firms also seek maximum profits, the equality $P = MC = AC$ implies that firms will operate at the low points of their long-run average cost curves.

- The shape of the long-run supply curve depends on how entry and exit affect firms' input costs. In the constant-cost case, input prices do not change and the long-run supply curve is horizontal. If entry raises input costs, the long-run supply curve will have a positive slope.

- Changes in long-run market equilibrium will also change the number of firms. Precise predictions about the extent of these changes is made difficult by the possibility that the minimum average cost level of output may be affected by changes in input costs or by technical progress.

Application

PRICE CONTROLS AND SHORTAGES

In our model of competitive pricing in the long run, price increases played the crucial role of providing firms with the incentive to increase production in response to increases in demand. Governmental controls over prices may short-circuit this process and deter any long-run supply responses. That possibility is illustrated in Figure 14.11. Initially, the market is in equilibrium at the point P_1, Q_1, where the market demand curve, D, and the long-run supply curve, LS, intersect. Consider now the reaction to a shift in the market demand curve to D'. In the absence of price controls, price would rise to P_2 in the short run and firms would increase output to Q_2. Supply would increase further (to Q_3) in the long run as new firms enter the industry in response to profit possibilities. Imposition of price controls prevents both of these supply responses. If price is not allowed to rise above P_1, firms will continue to produce Q_1, even though demand has increased. At a price of P_1, individuals demand Q_4 (with the demand

curve D'), but only Q_1 is produced. Hence there is a shortage in the market, given by the distance $Q_4 - Q_1$. That shortage will persist as long as price controls continue to retard supply response. Notice that the shortage is exacerbated by the fact that more is demanded at the artificially low controlled price (Q_4) than would be demanded at the long-run market clearing price (Q_3).

The model depicted in Figure 14.11 therefore makes two predictions about the impact of price controls: (1) They will cause shortages; and (2) they will result in somewhat lower prices for those who are able to buy the good (for the increasing cost case illustrated in the figure). We will now examine two important cases, rent control and controls on the price of natural gas in the United States, where these predictions have been proved accurate.

Rent Controls

During World War II many U.S. cities adopted controls on rents in order to stop the increases in housing prices that were occurring as a result

Figure 14.11   *Price Controls Inhibit Supply Responses*

This market is initially in equilibrium at P_1, Q_1. A shift in demand to D' would cause price to rise to P_2 in the short run and to P_3 in the long run. Quantity would increase to Q_2 and Q_3, respectively. Price controls that held price at P_1 would inhibit this process, since firms would continue to supply Q_1. At P_1 there is a long-run shortage, given by $Q_4 - Q_1$.

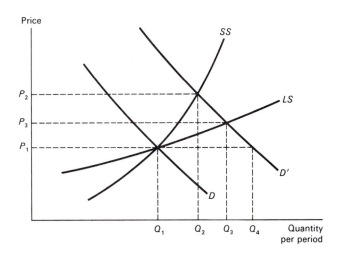

Table 14.3   *Waiting Time (in Months) for an Apartment in Stockholm*

Year	Wait	Year	Wait
1950	9	1955	23
1951	15	1956	30
1952	21	1957	35
1953	24	1958	40
1954	26		

Source: S. Rydenfelt, "Rent Control Thirty Years On" in *Verdict on Rent Control* (London: Institute for Economic Affairs, 1972), p. 65.

of rising demand. Many cities (notably New York) and several European countries still retain such controls. These are usually rationalized on the grounds that landlords (who are assumed to be rich) should not reap profits that occur as new demanders (who are assumed to be poor) enter a market. Regardless of whether such assertions are accurate (in many cases they are not), the economic implications of controls are clearly predicted by the competitive model: Shortages will result. Table 14.3 provides some evidence on such shortages in the city of Stockholm, Sweden, during the 1950s. The data show the average period (in months) that families had to wait to obtain an apartment. The data clearly show that this period lengthened greatly during the 1950s as postwar increases in income sharply increased the demand for housing and as rent controls retarded long-run supply responses. Existing tenants may have benefited from lower rents, but it is clear that substantial costs were imposed on families who had to wait more than three years to find a place of their own in which to live.

The effects of rent controls may show up in many other ways. In addition to the shortfall in the quantity of housing, the quality of housing may also deteriorate as landlords find it unprofitable to make repairs. For example, one study found that repair expenditures in 1967 on rent-controlled apartments in New York City averaged only about one-half of the expenditures on similar apartments that were not subject to rent controls.[12] "Elective" repairs (that is, those in excess of minimal requirements for health and safety) were particularly unlikely to be made in the rent-controlled apartments. Finally, tenants of rent-controlled apartments may sometimes find they can take advantage of their possession of a good for which there is excess demand. It is a common practice in some cities, for example, to require that new tenants pay "key money" to existing tenants for the right to take over their leases. Similarly, rent-controlled apartments are passed down among family members as if they were valuable heirlooms.

Natural Gas

A 1954 U.S. Supreme Court decision required the Federal Power Commission to begin regulating the wellhead price of natural gas sold through interstate pipelines in the United States. The effects of that decision were predicted at the time in a dissent by Justice William O. Douglas: "The effect is certain to be profound ... sales price determines profits and (these profits) have profound effects on the rate of production, the old wells that are continued in production, and the new ones explored."[13] By the mid-1970s, natural gas shortages induced by price controls were readily apparent. Many industries in the Northeast and North Central states were not able to obtain all the gas they wanted at prevailing prices and were forced to adopt more expensive and less suitable substitute fuels. Few natural gas utilities permitted hookups to new residential customers. By some estimates the shortfall of quantity supplied in 1977 was as high as 20 to 25 percent of total quantity demanded. In 1979 Congress adopted a program of "phased deregulation" for natural gas prices. Between the years 1979 to 1985 natural gas prices were permitted to rise in a series of stages from the controlled levels of $1.45 per 1000 cubic feet to market-clearing prices by 1985. Unfortunately, the years between 1979 and 1985 were quite volatile ones in world energy markets with prices at first rising rapidly, then falling precipitously. These wide swings imposed substantial strains on the bureaucratically determined price schedules for natural gas from "old" wells, and the market exhibited considerable inefficiencies during the period. By 1986, however, most prices were effectively decontrolled, and the chaos brought about by the 1954 Supreme Court decision, at least temporarily, came to an end.

---

[12] G. Sternlieb, *The Housing Dilemma* (New York: New York Housing and Development Administration, 1972), p. 202.

[13] *Phillips Petroleum Company* v. *Wisconsin*, 347 US 690, 1954.

SUGGESTED READINGS

Henderson, J. M., and Quandt, R. E. *Microeconomic Theory: A Mathematical Approach*, 3d ed. New York: McGraw-Hill Book Company, 1980. Chap. 6.

Covers much the same material as this chapter, with some useful algebraic examples. Also a nice discussion of futures markets.

Knight, F. H. *Risk, Uncertainty and Profit*. Boston: Houghton Mifflin Co., 1921. Chaps. 5 and 6.

Classic treatment of the role of economic events in motivating industry behavior in the long run.

Marshall, A. *Principles of Economics*, 8th ed. New York: Crowell-Collier and Macmillan Co., 1920. Book 5, chaps. 1, 2, and 3.

Classic development of the supply-demand mechanism.

Meade, J. E. "External Economies and Diseconomies in a Competitive Situation." *Economic Journal* 62 (March 1952): 54–67.

Early discussion of the notion of externalities in competitive markets in the long run.

Reynolds, L. G. "Cut-Throat Competition." *American Economic Review* 30 (December 1940): 736–747.

Critique of the notion that there can be "too much" competition in an industry.

Robinson, J. "What Is Perfect Competition?" *Quarterly Journal of Economics* 49 (1934): 104–120.

Critical discussion of the perfectly competitive assumptions.

Scherer, F. M. *Industrial Market Structure and Economic Performance*, 2d ed. Chicago: Rand McNally, 1980. Chaps. 2, 3, and 4.

Concise summary of the competitive model, with indications about how elements of that model enter into industrial organization theory.

Stigler, G. J. "Perfect Competition, Historically Contemplated." *Journal of Political Economy* 65 (1957): 1–17.

Fascinating discussion of the historical development of the competitive model.

PROBLEMS

14.1

Suppose that there are 100 identical firms in a perfectly competitive industry. Each firm has a short-run total cost curve of the form

$$C = \frac{1}{300} q^3 - 0.2q^2 + 4q + 10.$$

a. Calculate the firm's short-run supply curve with q as a function of market price (P).

b. On the assumption that there are no interaction effects among costs of the firms in the industry, calculate the short-run industry supply curve.

c. Suppose that market demand is given by $Q = -200P + 12,000$. What will be the short-run equilibrium price-quantity combination?

14.2

Suppose that there are 1,000 identical firms producing diamonds and that the total cost curve for each firm is given by

$$C = q^2 + wq,$$

where q is the firm's output level and w is the wage rate of diamond cutters.

a. If $w = 10$, what will be the firm's (short-run) supply curve? What is the industry's supply curve? How many diamonds will be produced at a price of 20 each? How many more diamonds would be produced at a price of 21?

b. Suppose that the wages of diamond cutters depend on the total quantity of diamonds produced and that the form of this relationship is given by

$$w = 0.002Q,$$

where Q represents total industry output, which is 1,000 times the output of the typical firm.

In this situation, show that the firm's marginal cost (and short-run supply) curve depends on Q. What is the industry supply curve? How much will be produced at a price of 20? How much more will be produced at a price of 21? What do you conclude about the shape of the short-run supply curve?

14.3
A perfectly competitive market has 1,000 firms. In the very short run, each of the firms has a fixed supply of 100 units. The market demand is given by

$$Q = 160,000 - 10,000P.$$

a.   Calculate the equilibrium price in the very short run.
b.   Calculate the demand schedule facing any one firm in this industry.
c.   Calculate what the equilibrium price would be if one of the sellers decided to sell nothing or if one seller decided to sell 200 units.
d.   At the original equilibrium point, calculate the elasticity of the industry demand curve and the elasticity of the demand curve facing any one seller.

Suppose now that in the short run, each firm has a supply curve that shows the quantity the firm will supply (q_i) as a function of market price. The specific form of this supply curve is given by

$$q_i = -200 + 50P.$$

Using this short-run supply response, answer questions (a) through (d) above.

14.4
Suppose the demand for Frisbees is given by

$$Q = 100 - 2P$$

and the supply by

$$Q = 20 + 6P.$$

a.   What will be the equilibrium price and quantities for Frisbees?
b.   Suppose the government levies a tax of $4 per Frisbee. Now what will be the equilibrium quantity, what price will consumers pay, and what price will firms receive? How is the burden of the tax shared by buyers and sellers?
c.   How would your answers to parts (a) and (b) change if the supply curve were instead

$$Q = 70 + P?$$

What do you conclude by comparing these two cases?

14.5
Wheat is produced under perfectly competitive conditions. Individual wheat farmers have U-shaped, long-run average cost curves that reach a minimum average cost of $3.00 per bushel when 1,000 bushels are produced.

a. If the market demand curve for wheat is given by

$$Q_D = 2,600,000 - 200,000P$$

where Q_D is the number of bushels demanded per year and P is the price per bushel, in long-run equilibrium what will be the price of wheat, how much total wheat will be demanded, and how many wheat farms will there be?

b. Suppose demand shifts outward to

$$Q_D = 3,200,000 - 200,000P.$$

If farmers cannot adjust their output in the short run, what will market price be with this new demand curve? What will the profits of the typical farm be?

c. Given the new demand curve described in part b, what will be the new long-run equilibrium? (That is, calculate market price, quantity of wheat produced, and the new equilibrium number of farms in this new situation.)

d. Graph your results.

14.6

A perfectly competitive industry has a large number of potential entrants. Each firm has an identical cost structure such that long-run average cost is minimized at an output of 20 units ($q_i = 20$). The minimum average cost is $10 per unit. Total market demand is given by

$$Q = 1,500 - 50P.$$

a. What is the industry's long-run supply schedule?

b. What is the long-run equilibrium price (P^*)? The total industry output (Q^*)? The output of each firm (q^*)? The number of firms? And the profits of each firm?

c. The short-run total cost curve associated with each firm's long-run equilibrium output is given by

$$C = 0.5q^2 - 10q + 200.$$

Calculate the short-run average and marginal cost curves. At what output level does short-run average cost reach a minimum?

d. Calculate the short-run supply curve for each firm and the industry short-run supply curve.

e. Suppose now that the market demand function shifts upward to $Q = 2,000 - 50P$. Using this new demand curve, answer part (b) for the very short run when firms cannot change their outputs.

f. In the short run, use the industry short-run supply curve to recalculate the answers to (b).

g. What is the new long-run equilibrium for the industry?

14.7

Suppose that the demand for stilts is given by

$$Q = 1,500 - 50P$$

and that the long-run total operating costs of each stilt-making firm in a competitive industry is given by

$$C = 0.5q^2 - 10q.$$

Entrepreneurial talent for stilt-making is scarce. The supply curve for entrepreneurs is given by

$$Q_S = 0.25w,$$

where w is the annual wage paid.

Suppose also that each stilt-making firm requires one (and only one) entrepreneur (hence the quantity of entrepreneurs hired is equal to the number of firms). Long-run total costs for each firm are hence given by

$$C = 0.5q^2 - 10q + w.$$

a.   What is the long-run equilibrium quantity of stilts produced? How many stilts are produced by each firm? What is the long-run equilibrium price of stilts? How many firms will there be? How many entrepreneurs will be hired, and what is their wage?

b.   Suppose that the demand for stilts shifts outward to

$$Q = 2428 - 50P.$$

Answer the questions posed in part (a).

c.   Sketch your results. Show the approximate shape of the long-run supply curve. Why does the curve have this shape?

14.8
In the long run, a specific tax imposed on a competitive decreasing cost industry will raise market price by more than the amount of the tax. Show why this is so and explain your result intuitively.

14.9
Suppose that the long-run total cost function for the typical mushroom producer is given by

$$TC = wq^2 - 10q + 100$$

where q is the output of the typical firm and w represents the hourly wage rate of mushroom pickers. Suppose also that the demand for mushrooms is given by

$$Q = -1,000P + 40,000$$

where Q is total quantity demanded and P is the market price of mushrooms.

a.   If the wage rate for mushroom pickers is $1, what will be the long-run equilibrium output for the typical mushroom picker?

b.   Assuming that the mushroom industry exhibits constant costs and that all firms are identical, what will be the long-run equilibrium price of mushrooms and how many mushroom firms will there be?

c.   Suppose the government imposed a tax of $3 for each mushroom picker hired (raising total wage costs, w, to $4). Assuming that the typical firm continues to have costs given by

$$TC = wq^2 - 10q + 100,$$

how will your answers to parts (a) and (b) change with this new, higher wage rate?

d.   How would your answers to (a), (b), and (c) change if market demand were instead given by

$$Q = -1,000P + 60,000?$$

CHAPTER 15

General Competitive Equilibrium

In Chapter 14 we examined how the forces of supply and demand interact to determine the price of a single commodity. Although that analysis is quite useful for illustrating the kinds of factors that influence market outcomes, it has one major limitation—it looks at only one market at a time. But we know from our prior analyses that in reality markets are highly interconnected. Pricing outcomes in one market will usually have effects in other markets, and these effects, in turn, will ripple throughout the economy, perhaps even to the extent of affecting the price-quantity equilibrium in the original market. For example, suppose individuals' preferences shift toward consuming poultry and away from consuming beef, perhaps because of health concerns. This will have the effect of shifting the demand curve for poultry outward and the demand curve for beef inward with the expected effects on the prices of these two goods. In our partial equilibrium analysis of Chapter 14 that would be, more or less, the end of the story. But, in a general equilibrium view of the many markets that constitute an economy, the story has just begun. Rising poultry prices may lure more firms into the business, and this entry of firms may raise prices for such inputs as grain, poultry farms, and chicken pluckers. Such changes in input prices will feed back into the poultry market by shifting the poultry supply curve. Similarly, declining prices of beef, besides affecting the demand for cowhands and other beef inputs, will also feed back into the poultry market by convincing some people that eating beef wasn't so bad after all.

The partial equilibrium models of Chapter 14 are clearly inadequate to analyze all of these effects. Instead, we need an economic model that permits us to view many markets simultaneously. Although the construction of such general equilibrium (multimarket) models has been of interest to economists for some time (indeed many of the tools we will present in this chapter were first developed in the nineteenth century), it was not until the advent of modern computer technology that it became possible to apply such models to actual market situations. In this chapter we will only make a few comments about these important innovations in economic model building since we will be more interested in developing the theory of general equilibrium price determination. Our application for this chapter does, however, explore some current computer applications of this theory.

PERFECTLY COMPETITIVE PRICE SYSTEM

The model we will develop in this chapter is primarily an elaboration of the supply-demand model that we presented in Chapter 14. Here we will assume that all markets are of the type described in that chapter and refer to such a set of markets as a *perfectly competitive price system*. The assumption is that there are some large number of homogeneous goods in this simple economy. Included in this list of goods are not only consumption items but also factors of production (whose pricing is described in Part VII). Each of these goods has an *equilibrium price*, established by the action of supply and demand.[1] At this set of prices, every market is cleared in the sense that suppliers are willing to supply that quantity which is demanded and consumers will demand that quantity which is supplied. We also assume that there are no transaction or transportation charges and that both individuals and firms have perfect knowledge of prevailing market prices.

Because of the zero transactions cost assumption, each good obeys the law of one price: A homogeneous good trades at the same price no matter who buys it or which firm sells it. If one good traded at two different prices, people would rush to buy the good where it was cheaper, and firms would try to sell all their output where the good was more expensive. These actions in themselves would tend to equalize the price of the good. In the perfectly competitive market, then, each good must have only one price. This is why we may speak unambiguously of *the* price of a good.

The perfectly competitive model assumes that people and firms react to prices in specific ways:

1. There are assumed to be a large number of people buying any one good. Each person takes all prices as given and adjusts his or her behavior to *maximize utility*, given the prices and his or her budget constraint. People may also be suppliers of productive services (for example, labor), and in such decisions they also regard prices as given.[2]
2. There are assumed to be a large number of firms producing each good, and each firm produces only a small share of the output of any one good. In making input and output choices, firms are assumed to operate to *maximize profits*. The firms treat all prices as given when making these profit-maximizing decisions.

---

[1]One aspect of this market interaction should be made clear from the outset. The perfectly competitive market only determines relative (not absolute) prices. In this chapter, we speak partly of relative prices. It makes no difference whether the prices of apples and oranges are $.10 and $.20, respectively, or $10 and $20. The important point in either case is that two apples can be exchanged for one orange in the market. In the final sections of the chapter, we will briefly examine the role of money and the determination of absolute prices.

[2]Since one price represents the wage rate, the relevant budget constraint is in reality a time constraint. This is the way we treat individuals' labor-leisure choices in Chapter 22.

Figure 15.1 *The Market for Wine and Several Related Markets*

Initially, the market for wine is in equilibrium (at P_1) as are the markets for grape pickers, cloth, and weavers. An increase in demand for wine will disturb these equilibria. Virtually all of the supply and demand curves will shift in the process of establishing a new general equilibrium.

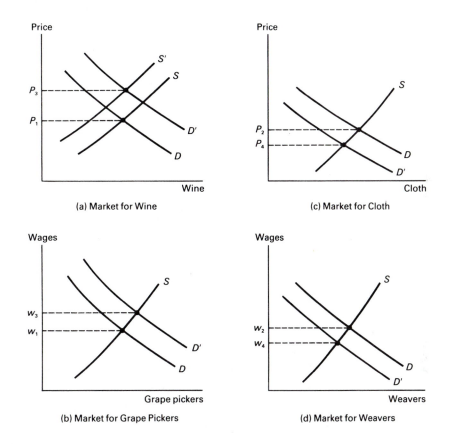

(a) Market for Wine

(c) Market for Cloth

(b) Market for Grape Pickers

(d) Market for Weavers

These various assumptions should be familiar since we have been making them throughout this book. Our purpose here is to show how an entire economic system operates when all markets work in this way.

AN ILLUSTRA-TION OF GENERAL EQUILIBRIUM

As a simple illustration of why a general equilibrium approach is needed, Figure 15.1 shows the market for one good, say, wine, and three other markets related to it: (1) the market for grape pickers; (2) the market for a related product, cloth; and (3) the market for weavers. Suppose that initially all of these markets are in equilibrium as shown by the original sets of supply and demand curves in the four panels of Figure 15.1. That is, the equilibrium price of wine is given by P_1, wages of grape pickers by w_1, the price of cloth by P_2, and the wages of weavers by w_2. Since these prices act to equate the amount supplied and demanded in each of these markets, the general equilibrium shown in Figure 15.1 will persist from period to period until something happens to change it.

Assume now that such a change does occur. Imagine a situation where the government announces that wine has been found to cure the common cold so everyone decides to drink more of it. An initial consequence of this discovery is that the demand for wine will shift outward to D′. In our previous analysis this shift would cause the price of wine to rise and that would be, more or less, the end of the story. Now, however, we wish to follow the repercussions of what has happened in the wine market into the other markets shown in Figure 15.1. A first possible reaction would be in the market for grape pickers. Since wine prices have risen, the demand for labor used to harvest grapes will rise, so the demand curve for labor in Figure 15.1b will shift to D′. This will tend to raise wages of grape pickers, which will, in turn, raise the costs of wine makers. The supply curve for wine (which, under perfect competition, just reflects wine makers' marginal costs) will shift to S′.

What happens to the market for cloth? Since people have an increased desire for wine, they may reduce their demands for cloth since wine makes them feel equally warm with less on. The demand for cloth will shift inward to D′ and cloth prices will fall. That will reduce the demand for weavers and the wage associated with that occupation will fall.

We could continue this story indefinitely. We could ask how the lower price of cloth affects the wine market. Or we could ask whether weavers discouraged by their falling wages might consider picking grapes, thereby shifting the labor supply curve in Figure 15.1b outward. To follow this chain of events further would add little to our story. Eventually, we would expect all four markets in Figure 15.1 to reach a new equilibrium such as that illustrated by the new supply-demand intersections in the figure. Once all the repercussions have been worked out, the final result would be a rise in wine prices (to P_3), a rise in the wages of grape pickers (to w_3), a fall in cloth prices (to P_4), and a fall in the wages of weavers (to w_4). This is what we mean then by a smoothly working system of perfectly competitive markets. Following any disturbance, all of the markets eventually reestablish a new set of equilibrium prices at which quantity demanded is equal to quantity supplied in each market.[3]

A SIMPLE GRAPHICAL MODEL OF GENERAL EQUILIBRIUM

Unfortunately, the model illustrated in Figure 15.1 is not a very precise one since we shifted the various curves more or less arbitrarily to arrive at the new equilibrium. To develop a precise mathematical statement of the model would be quite cumbersome, however, and would require at least eight equations (to represent the supply and demand functions in each market) to determine the four equilibrium prices and four equilibrium quantities in the figure. To avoid the burden of introducing all of this notation, we will instead describe a very

---

[3] Actually, the question of whether many markets can establish a set of prices that brings equilibrium to each of them is a major and difficult theoretical question that we take up later in this chapter.

simple graphical model of general equilibrium involving only two goods, which we will call X and Y. This model will prove to be very useful because it incorporates many of the features of far more complex general equilibrium representations of the economy. We will make extensive use of the model in later chapters.

General Equilibrium Demand

Ultimately, demand patterns in an economy are determined by individuals' preferences. For our simple model we will assume that all individuals have identical preferences, which can be represented by an indifference curve map[4] defined over quantities of the two goods, X and Y. The benefit of this approach for our purposes is that this indifference curve map (which is identical to the ones used in Chapters 3–6) shows how individuals rank consumption bundles containing both goods. These rankings are precisely what we mean by "demand" in a general equilibrium context. Of course, we cannot actually illustrate which bundles of commodities will be chosen until we know the budget constraints that demanders face. Since incomes are generated as individuals supply labor, capital, and other resources to the production process, we must delay this illustration until we have examined the forces of production and supply in our model.

General Equilibrium Supply

Developing a notion of general equilibrium supply in this two-good model is a somewhat more complex process than describing the demand side of the market since we have not thus far illustrated production and supply of two goods simultaneously. Our approach is to use the familiar production possibility curve (see Chapter 1) for this purpose. By detailing the way in which this curve is constructed, we can also use this construction to examine the ways in which markets for outputs and inputs are related.

Edgeworth Box Diagram

Construction of the production possibility curve for two outputs (X and Y) begins with the assumption that there are fixed amounts of capital and labor inputs that must be allocated to the production of the two goods. As our discussion of exchange in Chapter 8 indicated, the possible allocations of these inputs can be illustrated with an Edgeworth box diagram with dimensions given by the amounts of capital and labor available.

In Figure 15.2 the length of the box represents total labor-hours and the height of the box represents total capital-hours. The lower left-hand corner of the box represents the "origin" for measuring capital and labor devoted to production of good X. The upper right-hand corner of the box represents the

[4]There are some technical problems in using a single indifference curve map to represent the preferences of an entire community of individuals. In this case the marginal rate of substitution (that is, the slope of the community indifference curve) will depend on how the available goods are distributed among individuals: The increase in total Y required to compensate for a one unit reduction in X will depend on which specific individual(s) the X is taken from. Although we will not discuss this issue in detail here, it has been widely examined in the international trade literature. For an early example, see Tibor de Scitovszky, "A Reconsideration of the Theory of Tariffs," *Review of Economic Studies* (Summer 1942): 89–110.

Figure 15.2 *Construction of an Edgeworth Box Diagram for Production*

The dimensions of this diagram are given by the total quantities of labor and capital available. Quantities of these resources devoted to *X* production are measured from origin O_x; quantities devoted to *Y* are measured from O_Y. Any point in the box represents a fully employed allocation of the available resources to the two goods.

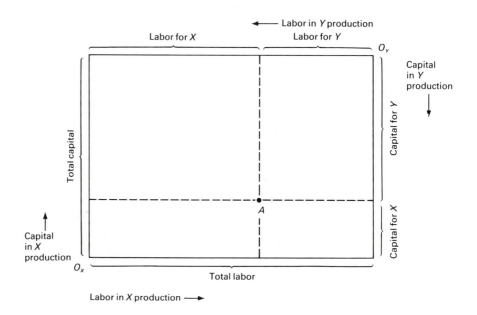

origin for resources devoted to *Y*. Using these conventions, any point in the box can be regarded as a fully employed allocation of the available resources between goods *X* and *Y*. Point *A*, for example, represents an allocation in which the indicated number of labor hours are devoted to *X* production together with a specified number of hours of capital. Production of good *Y* uses whatever labor and capital are "left over." Point *A* in Figure 15.2, for example, also shows the exact amount of labor and capital used in the production of good *Y*. Any other point in the box has a similar interpretation. Thus the Edgeworth box shows every possible way the existing capital and labor might be used to produce *X* and *Y*.

Efficient Allocations

As in Chapter 8, many of the allocations shown in Figure 15.2 are technically inefficient in that it is possible to produce both more *X* and more *Y* by shifting capital and labor around a bit. In our model we assume that competitive markets will not exhibit such inefficient input choices (for reasons we will explore in more detail in the next chapter). Hence we wish to discover the efficient allocations in Figure 15.2 since these illustrate the actual production outcomes in this model. To do so, we introduce isoquant maps for good *X* (using O_X as

Figure 15.3   *Edgeworth Box Diagram of Efficiency in Production*

This diagram adds production isoquants for X and Y to Figure 15.2. It then shows technically efficient ways to allocate the fixed amounts of K and L between the production of the two outputs. The line joining O_X and O_Y is the locus of these efficient points. Along this line the *RTS* (of L for K) in the production of good X is equal to the *RTS* in the production of Y.

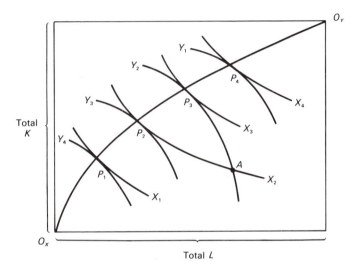

the origin) and good Y (using O_Y as the origin) as shown in Figure 15.3. In this figure it is clear that the arbitrarily chosen allocation A is inefficient.

With capital (K) and labor (L) allocated in this way, Y_2 is produced together with X_2. By moving along the Y_2 isoquant to P_3, we can hold Y output constant and increase X output to X_3. Thus point A was not an efficient allocation since we were able to increase output of one good (X) without decreasing output of the other good (Y). Although both point A and point P_3 represent fully employed allocations of the available resources, the allocation at point P_3 results in good X using more capital and less labor whereas Y uses more labor and less capital than at point A.

The efficient allocations in Figure 15.3 are those such as P_1, P_2, P_3, and P_4 where the isoquants are tangent to each other. At any other points in the box diagram, the two goods' isoquants will intersect, and we can show inefficiency as we did for point A. At the points of tangency, however, this kind of unambiguous improvement cannot be made. In going from P_2 to P_3, for example, more X is being produced, but at the cost of less Y being produced, so P_3 is not "more efficient" than P_2—both of the points are efficient. Tangency of the isoquants for good X and good Y implies that their slopes are equal. That is, the *RTS* of capital for labor is equal in X and Y production. In the next chap-

446   Part V   Perfect Competition

Figure 15.4   *Production Possibility Frontier*

The production possibility frontier shows the alternative combinations of X and Y that can be efficiently produced by a firm with fixed resources. The curve can be derived from Figure 15.3 by varying inputs between the production of X and Y while maintaining the conditions for efficiency. The slope of the production possibility curve is called the rate of product transformation (*RPT*).

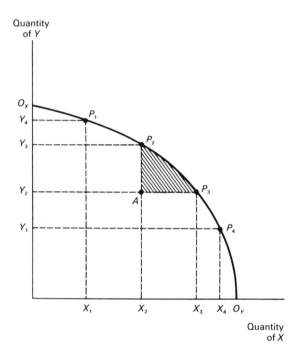

ter, we will show how competitive input markets will lead firms to make such efficient input choices.

The curve joining O_X and O_Y that includes all of these points of tangency therefore shows all of the efficient allocations of capital and labor. Points off this curve are inefficient in that unambiguous increases in output can be obtained by reshuffling inputs between the two goods. Points in O_X, O_Y are all efficient allocations, however, because more X can be produced only by cutting back on Y production and vice versa.

Production Possibility Frontier

The efficiency locus in Figure 15.3 shows the maximum output of Y that can be produced for any preassigned output of X. We can use this information to construct a *production possibility frontier*, which shows the alternative outputs of X and Y that can be produced with the fixed capital and labor inputs. In Figure 15.4 the O_X, O_Y locus has been taken from Figure 15.3 and transferred onto a graph with X and Y outputs on the axes. At O_X, for example, no resources are devoted to X production; consequently, Y output is as large as is possible with the existing resources. Similarly, at O_Y, the output of X is as large as possible. The other points on the production possibility frontier (say, P_1, P_2, P_3, P_4) are derived from the efficiency locus in an identical way. Hence we have derived the following:

Definition:

Production Possibility Frontier
The *production possibility frontier* shows those alternative combinations of two outputs that can be produced with fixed quantities of inputs if those inputs are employed efficiently.

Rate of Product Transformation

The slope of the production possibility frontier shows how X output can be substituted for Y output when total resources are held constant. For example, for points near O_X on the production possibility frontier, the slope is a small negative number, say, $-\frac{1}{4}$, implying that by reducing Y output by 1 unit, X output could be increased by 4. Near O_Y, on the other hand, the slope is a large negative number, say, -5, implying that Y output must be reduced by 5 units to permit the production of one more X. The slope of the production possibility frontier, then, clearly shows the possibilities that exist for trading Y for X in production. The negative of this slope is called the *rate of product transformation* (*RPT*). That is,

---

Definition:

Rate of Product Transformation
The *rate of production transformation* (*RPT*) between two outputs is the negative of the slope of the production possibility frontier for those outputs. Mathematically,

$$RPT \quad \text{(of } X \text{ for } Y) \quad = \; -\text{slope of production possibility frontier}$$

$$= \; -\frac{dY}{dX} \quad \text{(along } O_X, O_Y). \tag{15.1}$$

The *RPT* records how X can be technically traded for Y while continuing to keep the available productive inputs efficiently employed.

Shape of the Production Possibility Frontier

The production possibility frontier illustrated in Figure 15.4 exhibits an increasing *RPT*. For output levels near O_X, relatively little Y must be sacrificed to obtain one more X ($-dY/dX$ is small). Near O_Y, on the other hand, additional X may be obtained only by substantial reductions in Y output ($-dY/dX$ is large). In this section we shall show why this concave shape might be expected to characterize most production situations.

A first step in that analysis is to recognize that *RPT* is equal to the ratio of the marginal cost of X (MC_X) to the marginal cost of Y (MC_Y). Intuitively, this result is obvious. Suppose, for example, that X and Y are produced only with labor. If it takes 2 labor-hours to produce one more X, we might say that MC_X is equal to 2. Similarly, if it takes only 1 labor-hour to produce an extra

Y, MC_Y is equal to 1. But, in this situation it is clear that the RPT is 2: Two Y must be forgone to provide enough labor so that X may be increased by 1 unit. Hence the RPT is indeed equal to the ratio of the marginal costs of the two goods.

More formally, suppose that the costs (say, in terms of the "disutility" experienced by factor suppliers) of any output combination are denoted by $C(X, Y)$. Along the production possibility frontier, $C(X, Y)$ will be constant since the inputs are in fixed supply. Hence we can write the total differential of the cost function as

$$dC = \frac{\partial C}{\partial X} \cdot dX + \frac{\partial C}{\partial Y} \cdot dY = 0 \qquad (15.2)$$

for changes in X and Y along the production possibility frontier. Manipulating Equation 15.2 yields

$$RPT = -\frac{dY}{dX} \quad \text{(along } O_X, O_Y\text{)} \quad = \frac{\partial C/\partial X}{\partial C/\partial Y} = \frac{MC_X}{MC_Y}, \qquad (15.3)$$

which was precisely what we wished to show: The RPT is a measure of the relative marginal costs of the two goods.

To demonstrate reasons why the RPT might be expected to rise for clockwise movements along the production possibility frontier, we can proceed by showing why the ratio of MC_X to MC_Y should rise as X output expands and Y output contracts. We first present two relatively simple arguments that apply only to special cases; then we turn to a more sophisticated general argument.

Diminishing Returns

The most common rationale offered for the concave shape of the production possibility frontier is the assumption that both goods are produced under conditions of diminishing returns. Hence, increasing the output of good X will raise its marginal cost, whereas decreasing the output of Y will reduce its marginal cost. Equation 15.3 then shows that the RPT will increase for movements along the production possibility frontier from O_X to O_Y. A problem with this explanation, of course, is that it applies only to cases in which both goods exhibit diminishing returns to scale, and that assumption is at variance with the theoretical reasons for preferring the assumption of constant or even increasing returns to scale we have mentioned elsewhere in this book.

Specialized Inputs

If some inputs were "more suited" for X production than for Y production (and vice versa), the concave shape of the production frontier also could be explained. In that case, increases in X output would require drawing progressively less suitable inputs into the production of that good. Marginal costs of X therefore would rise. Marginal costs for Y, on the other hand, would fall as smaller output levels for Y would permit the use of only those inputs most suited for Y production. Such an argument might apply, for example, to a farmer with a variety of types of land under cultivation in different crops. In trying to increase the production of any one crop, the farmer would be forced to grow it on increasingly unsuitable parcels of land. Although this type of specialized input assumption has considerable importance in explaining a variety of real-world phenomena, it is nonetheless at variance with our general assumption of homogeneous factors of production. It cannot serve as a fundamental explanation for concavity.

Differing Factor Intensities

Even if inputs are homogeneous and production functions exhibit constant returns to scale, the production possibility frontier will be concave if goods X and Y use inputs in different proportions.[5] In the production box diagram of Figure 15.3, for example, good X is *capital intensive* relative to good Y. That is, at every point along the $O_X O_Y$ contract curve, the ratio of K to L in X production exceeds the ratio of K to L in Y production: The bowed curve $O_X O_Y$ is always above the main diagonal of the Edgeworth box. If, on the other hand, good Y had been relatively capital intensive, the $O_X O_Y$ contract curve would have been bowed downward below the diagonal. Although a formal proof that unequal factor intensities result in a concave production possibility frontier will not be presented here, it is possible to suggest intuitively why that occurs. Consider any two points on the frontier $O_X O_Y$ in Figure 15.4—say, P_1 (with coordinates X_1, Y_4) and P_3 (with coordinates X_3, Y_2). One way of producing an output combination "between" P_1 and P_3 would be to produce the combination

$$\frac{X_1 + X_3}{2}, \frac{Y_4 + Y_2}{2}.$$

Because of the constant returns-to-scale assumption, that combination would be feasible and would fully utilize both factors of production. The combination would lie at the midpoint of a straight-line chord joining points P_1 and P_3. Although such a point is feasible, it is not efficient, as can be seen by examining points P_1 and P_3 in the box diagram of Figure 15.3. Because of the bowed nature of the contract curve, production at a point midway between P_1 and P_3 would be off the contract curve: Producing at a point such as P_2 would provide more of both goods. The production possibility frontier in Figure 15.3 therefore must "bulge out" beyond the straight line $P_1 P_3$. Since such a proof could be constructed for any two points on $O_X O_Y$, we have shown that the frontier is concave; that is, the *RPT* increases as the output of good X increases. When production is reallocated in a northeast direction along the $O_X O_Y$ contract curve (in Figure 15.3), the capital-labor ratio decreases in the production of *both* X and Y. Since good X is capital intensive, this change raises MC_X. On the other hand, since good Y is labor intensive, MC_Y falls. Hence the relative marginal cost of X (as represented by the *RPT*) rises.

---

[5] If, in addition to homogeneous factors and constant returns to scale, each good also used K and L in the same proportions under optimal allocations, then the production possibility frontier would be a straight line.

Opportunity Cost   The reason we have devoted so much of this chapter to the concept of the production possibility frontier is that it is the single most important tool for studying issues that arise in analyzing the production of two goods simultaneously. The curve demonstrates that there are many possible efficient combinations of the two goods and that producing more of one good necessitates cutting back on the production of some other good. This is precisely what economists mean by the term *opportunity cost*. The cost of producing more X can be most readily measured by the reduction in Y output that this entails. The cost of one more unit of X therefore is best measured as the *RPT* (of X for Y) at the prevailing point on the production possibility frontier. This then is our general formulation of the supply concept.

Determination of Equilibrium Prices   Given these notions of demand and supply in our simple two-good economy, we can now illustrate how equilibrium prices are determined. Figure 15.5 shows the production possibility frontier for the economy (PP), and the set of indifference curves represents individuals' preferences for these goods. First,

Figure 15.5   *Determination of Equilibrium Prices*

With a price ratio given by P_X/P_Y, firms will produce X_1, Y_1; society's budget constraint will be given by line C. With this budget constraint, individuals demand X'_1 and Y'_1; that is, there is an excess demand for good X ($X'_1 - X_1$), and an excess supply of good Y ($Y_1 - Y'_1$). The workings of the market will move these prices toward their equilibrium levels P^*_X, P^*_Y. At those prices, society's budget constraint will be given by line C^*, and supply and demand will be in equilibrium. The combination X^*, Y^* of goods will be chosen.

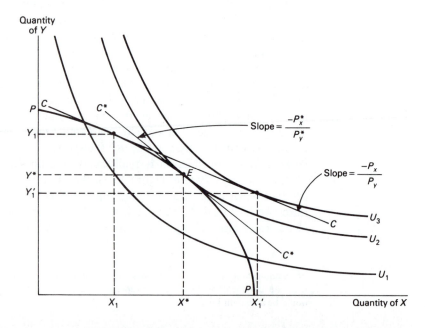

consider the price ratio P_X/P_Y. At this price ratio, firms will choose to produce the output combination X_1, Y_1. Profit-maximizing firms will choose the more profitable point on PP. At X_1, Y_1 the ratio of the two goods' prices (P_X/P_Y) is equal to the ratio of the goods' marginal costs (the RPT) so profits are maximized there. On the other hand, given this budget constraint (line C)[6] individuals will demand X_1', Y_1'. Consequently, with these prices, there is an excess demand for good X (individuals demand more than is being produced) whereas there is an excess supply of good Y. The workings of the marketplace therefore will cause P_X to rise and P_Y to fall. The price ratio P_X/P_Y will rise; the price line will take on a steeper slope. Firms will respond to these price changes by moving clockwise along the production possibility frontier; that is, they will increase their production of good X and decrease their production of good Y. Similarly, individuals will respond to the changing prices by substituting Y for X in their consumption choices. These actions of both firms and individuals, then, serve to eliminate the excess demand for X and the excess supply of Y as market prices change.

Equilibrium is reached at X^*, Y^* with a price ratio of P_X^*/P_Y^*. With this price ratio,[7] supply and demand are equilibrated for both good X and good Y. Given P_X and P_Y, firms will produce X^* and Y^* in maximizing their profits. Similarly, with a budget constraint given by C^*, individuals will demand X^* and Y^*. The operation of the price system has cleared the markets for both X and Y simultaneously. This figure therefore provides a "general equilibrium" view of the supply-demand process for two markets working together. For this reason we will make considerable use of this figure in our subsequent analysis.

Numerical Example

This general equilibrium model of price determination can be illustrated with a simple numerical example. Suppose the production possibility frontier for X and Y is represented by the quarter ellipse:

$$X^2 + 4Y^2 = 200 \tag{15.4}$$

and that the communities' preferences can be represented by

$$\text{utility} = U(X, Y) = \sqrt{XY}. \tag{15.5}$$

To determine the equilibrium price ratio in this situation, we first calculate the slope of the production possibility frontier (the RPT) as

$$2X \cdot dX + 8Y \cdot dY = 0 \tag{15.6}$$

or

---

[6] It is important to recognize why the budget constraint has this location. Since P_X and P_Y are given, the value of total production is $P_X \cdot X_1 + P_Y \cdot Y_1$. This is the value of "GNP" in the simple economy pictured in Figure 15.5. It is also, therefore, the total income accruing to people in society. Individuals' budget constraint therefore passes through X_1, Y_1 and has a slope of $-P_X/P_Y$. This is precisely the budget constraint labeled C in the figure.

[7] Notice again that competitive markets only determine equilibrium relative prices. Determination of the absolute price level requires the introduction of money into this barter model.

$$RPT = -\frac{dY}{dX} = \frac{X}{4Y}. \tag{15.7}$$

Under perfect competition, profit-maximizing firms will equate this ratio of marginal costs to the price ratio P_X/P_Y:

$$RPT = \frac{X}{4Y} = \frac{P_X}{P_Y}. \tag{15.8}$$

For consumers, utility maximization requires that

$$MRS = \frac{Y}{X} = \frac{P_X}{P_Y} \tag{15.9}$$

as we have shown in many previous numerical examples. Equilibrium requires that firms and individuals face the same price ratio,

$$RPT = \frac{X}{4Y} = \frac{P_X}{P_Y} = \frac{Y}{X} = MRS \tag{15.10}$$

or

$$X^2 = 4Y^2, \tag{15.11}$$

and that this common equilibrium be on the production possibility frontier (Equation 15.4). Therefore

$$X^2 + 4Y^2 = 2X^2 = 200, \tag{15.12}$$

or

$$X^* = 10$$

and $\qquad\qquad\qquad\qquad\qquad\qquad\qquad\qquad\qquad\qquad$ (15.13)

$$Y^* = 5$$

are the equilibrium outputs of X and Y. With these outputs we can use Equation 15.9 to calculate

$$\frac{P_X^*}{P_Y^*} = \frac{5}{10} = \frac{1}{2}. \tag{15.14}$$

In equilibrium, the relative price of good X is ½ (alternatively, the relative price of Y is 2). If we choose arbitrarily to let $P_X^* = 1$, then $P_Y^* = 2$ and the total value of output is

$$P_X^* \cdot X^* + P_Y^* \cdot Y^* = 1 \cdot 10 + 2 \cdot 5 = 20. \tag{15.15}$$

In this problem the communities' utility is $\sqrt{50}$, which also happens to be the largest value attainable given the constraints imposed by the production possibilities—an observation we will explore more fully in the next chapter.

Comparative Statics Analysis of General Equilibrium

The equilibrium price ratio P_X^*/P_Y^* illustrated in Figure 15.5 will tend to persist until either preferences or production technologies change. Ultimately, therefore, the competitively determined price ratio reflects these two basic economic forces. If preferences were to shift, say, toward good X, P_X/P_Y would rise,

Figure 15.6 *Effects of Technical Progress in X Production*

Technical advances that lower marginal costs of X production will shift the production possibility frontier. This will generally create income and substitution effects that cause the quantity of X produced to increase (assuming X is a normal good). Effects on the production of Y are ambiguous since income and substitution effects work in opposite directions.

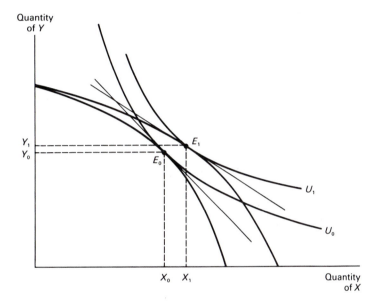

and a new equilibrium would be established by a clockwise move along the production possibility curve. More X and less Y would be produced to meet these changed preferences. Similarly, technical progress in the production of good X would shift the production possibility curve outward as illustrated in Figure 15.6. This would tend to lower the relative price of X and increase the quantity of X consumed (assuming X is a normal good). In the figure the quantity of Y consumed also increases as a result of the income effect arising from the technical advance; but a slightly different drawing of the figure could have reversed that result if the substitution effect had been dominant.

In general then our simple general equilibrium model reinforces Marshall's observations about the importance of both supply and demand forces in the price determination process. But, by providing an explicit connection between the markets for both goods, the general equilibrium model makes it possible to examine more complex questions about market relationships—a use we will now illustrate with a specific historical example.

Figure 15.7   *Analysis of the Corn Laws Debate*

Reduction of tariff barriers on grain would cause production to be reallocated from point *E* to point *A*. Consumption would be reallocated from *E* to *B*. If grain production is relatively capital intensive, the relative price of capital would fall as a result of these reallocations.

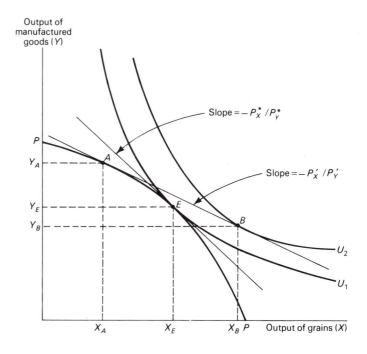

GENERAL
EQUILIBRIUM
MODELING
AND THE
CORN LAWS
DEBATE

High tariffs on grain imports were imposed by the British government following the Napoleonic wars. Debate over the effects of these "corn laws" dominated the analytical efforts of economists between the years 1829 and 1845. A principal focus of the debate concerned the effect that elimination of the tariffs would have on factor prices, a question that continues to have relevance today, as we will see. In this section we present a simple general equilibrium analysis of the corn laws question using the model we have developed.

The production possibility frontier in Figure 15.7 shows those combinations of grain (X) and manufactured goods (Y) that could be produced by British factors of production. Assuming (somewhat contrary to actuality) that the corn laws completely prevented trade, market equilibrium would be at E with the domestic price ratio given by P_X^*/P_Y^*. Removal of the tariffs would reduce this price ratio to P_X'/P_Y'. Given that new ratio, Britain would produce combination A and consume combination B. Grain imports would amount to $X_B - X_A$, and these would be financed by export of manufactured goods equal to $Y_A - Y_B$. Overall utility for the typical British consumer would be increased by the opening of trade. Use of the production possibility diagram therefore demonstrates the implications relaxing the tariffs would have for the production of both goods.

Trade and Input Prices

By referring back to the Edgeworth production box diagram that lies behind the production possibility frontier (Figure 15.3), it is also possible to analyze the effect of tariff reductions on factor prices. The movement from point E to point A in Figure 15.7 is similar to a movement from P_3 to P_1 in Figure 15.3 where production of X is decreased and production of Y is increased by such a move. Figure 15.3 also records the reallocation of capital and labor made necessary by such a move. If we assume that grain production is relatively capital intensive, the movement from P_3 to P_1 causes the ratio of K to L to rise in both industries.[8] This in turn will cause the relative price of capital to fall (and the relative price of labor to rise). Hence we conclude that repeal of the corn laws would be harmful to capital owners (that is, landlords) and helpful to laborers. It is not surprising that landed interests fought repeal of the laws.

Political Support for Trade Policies

The possibility that trade policies may affect the relative incomes of various factors of production continues to exert a major influence on political debates about such policies. In the United States, for example, exports tend to be intensive in their use of skilled labor whereas imports tend to be intensive in unskilled labor input. By analogy to our discussion of the corn laws, therefore, it might be expected that further movements toward free trade policies would result in rising relative wages for skilled workers and in falling relative wages for unskilled workers. It is not surprising therefore that unions representing skilled workers (the Machinists or the Petroleum and Atomic Workers) tend to favor free trade whereas unions of unskilled workers (those in textiles, shoes, and related businesses) tend to oppose it. Trade policy is clearly one area where economic interests exert a major influence on the political positions taken.

EXISTENCE OF GENERAL EQUILIBRIUM PRICES

In prior sections we have more or less assumed that competitive markets can reach an equilibrium in which the forces of supply and demand are balanced in all markets simultaneously. But, given the assumptions we have made, such a simultaneous solution is by no means assured. Beginning with the nineteenth-century investigations by Leon Walras, economists have used increasingly sophisticated tools to examine whether a set of prices that equilibrates all markets exists and, if so, how this set of prices can be found. In this section we will explore some aspects of this question. Since modern general equilibrium theory is perhaps the most sophisticated area of microeconomics in terms of the level of mathematics employed, the intention here is to give some flavor of the type of analysis used without needlessly complicating the text.

A Simple Mathematical Model

The essential aspects of the modern solution to the Walrasian problem can be demonstrated for the case where no production takes place. Suppose that there are n goods, in absolutely fixed supply, in this economy and that they are

---

[8] In the corn laws debate, attention centered on the factors land and labor. For convenience, here we shall identify "land" as being synonymous with capital.

distributed in some way among the individuals in society. Let S_i ($i = 1, \ldots,$ n) be the total supply of good i available, and let the price of good i be represented by P_i ($i = 1, \ldots, n$). The total demand for good i depends on all the prices, and this function represents the sum of the individuals' demand functions for good i. This total demand function is denoted by

$$D_i(P_1, \ldots, P_n) \tag{15.16}$$

for $i = 1, \ldots, n$.

Since we are interested in the whole set of prices $P_1, \ldots, P_n$, it will be convenient to denote this whole set by P. Hence the demand functions can be written as

$$D_i(P). \tag{15.17}$$

Walras' problem then can be stated formally as: Does there exist an *equilibrium set of prices* (P^*) such that

$$D_i(P^*) = S_i \tag{15.18}$$

for all values of i? The question posed by Walras is whether a set of prices exists for which supply is equal to demand *in all markets simultaneously*.

Excess Demand Functions

In what follows it will be more convenient to work with excess demand functions for good i at any set of prices (P), which is defined to be[9]

$$ED_i(P) = D_i(P) - S_i. \tag{15.19}$$

Using this notation, the equilibrium conditions can be rewritten as

$$ED_i(P^*) = D_i(P^*) - S_i = 0. \tag{15.20}$$

This condition states that at the equilibrium prices, excess demand is to be equal to zero in all markets.[10]

Walras himself noted several interesting features about the system of Equation 15.20. First, it can be assumed that demand functions (and hence the excess demand functions) are *homogeneous of degree 0*. If all prices were to double (including the wages of labor), the quantity demanded of every good would remain unchanged. A second assumption made by Walras was that the demand functions (and therefore the excess demand functions) are *continuous*: If prices were to change by only a small amount, quantities demanded would change by only a small amount. This and the previous assumption are both direct results of the theory of consumer behavior that was presented in Part II.

---

[9] Although we will not do so, supply behavior can be introduced here by making S_i depend on P also.

[10] This equilibrium condition will be amended slightly below.

Walras' Law

A final observation that Walras made is that the n excess demand functions are not independent of one another. The equations are related by the formula

$$\sum_{i=1}^{n} P_i \cdot ED_i(P) = 0. \qquad (15.21)$$

Equation 15.21 is usually called *Walras' law*. The equation states that the "total value" of excess demand is zero at *any* set of prices. There can be neither excess demand for all goods together nor excess supply. Proving Walras' law is a simple matter, although it is necessary to introduce some cumbersome notation. The proof rests on the fact that each individual in the economy is bound by a budget constraint. A simple example of the proof is given in the footnote;[11] the generalization of this proof is left to the reader.

Walras' law, it should be stressed, holds for any set of prices, not just for equilibrium prices. The law can be seen to apply trivially to an equilibrium set of prices, since each of the excess demand functions will be equal to zero at this set of prices. Walras' law shows that the equilibrium conditions in n markets are not independent. We do not have n independent equations in n unknowns (the P's). Rather, Equation 15.20 represents only $(n-1)$ independent equations, and hence we can hope to determine only $(n-1)$ of the prices. But this is what would have been expected in view of the homogeneity property of the demand functions. We can hope to determine only equilibrium *relative prices*; nothing in this model permits the derivation of absolute prices.

Walras' Proof of the Existence of Equilibrium Prices

Having recognized these technical features of the system of excess demand equations, Walras turned to the question of the existence of a set of equilibrium

---

[11] Suppose that there are two goods (A and B) and two individuals (Smith and Jones) in society. Let D_A^s, D_B^s, S_A^s, S_B^s be Smith's demands and supplies of A and B and use a similar notation for Jones's demands and supplies. Smith's budget constraint may be written as

$$P_A D_A^s + P_B D_B^s = P_A S_A^s + P_B S_B^s$$

or

$$P_A (D_A^s - S_A^s) + P_B (D_B^s - S_B^s) = 0$$

or

$$P_A ED_A^s + P_B ED_B^s = 0,$$

where ED_A^s and ED_B^s represent the excess demand of Smith for A and B, respectively.

A similar budget constraint holds for Jones:

$$P_A ED_A^J + P_B ED_B^J = 0,$$

and therefore letting ED_A and ED_B represent total excess demands for A and B, it must be the case that

$$P_A \cdot (ED_A^s + ED_A^J) + P_B \cdot (ED_B^s + ED_B^J) = P_A \cdot ED_A + P_B \cdot ED_B = 0.$$

This is Walras' law exactly as it appears in Equation 15.21.

(relative) prices. He tried to establish that the n equilibrium conditions of Equation 15.20 were sufficient, in this situation, to ensure that such a set of prices would in fact exist, and therefore that the exchange model had a consistent theoretical framework. A first indication that this existence of equilibrium prices might be assured is provided by a simple counting of equations and unknowns. The market equilibrium conditions provide $(n - 1)$ *independent* equations in $(n - 1)$ unknown relative prices. Hence the elementary algebra of solving simultaneous linear equations suggests that an equilibrium solution might exist.

Unfortunately, as Walras recognized, the act of solving for equilibrium prices is not nearly as simple a matter as counting equations and unknowns. First, the equations are not necessarily linear. Hence the well-known conditions for the existence of solutions to simultaneous linear equations do not apply in this case. Second, from consideration of the economics of the problem, it is clear that all the equilibrium prices must be nonnegative. A negative price has no meaning in the context of this problem. To attack these two difficulties, Walras developed a very difficult and tedious proof, which involved solving for equilibrium prices in a series of successive approximations. Without presenting Walras' proof in detail, it is instructive to see how he approached the problem.

Start with some initial, arbitrary set of prices. Holding the other $(n - 1)$ prices constant, find the equilibrium price in the market for good 1. Call this "provisional" equilibrium price P_1'. Now, holding P_1' and the other $(n - 2)$ prices constant, solve for the equilibrium price in the market for good 2. Call this price P_2'. Notice that in changing P_2 from its initial position to P_2', the price initially calculated for market 1 need no longer be an equilibrium price. This is a reflection of the fact that the system of equations is indeed simultaneous. Using the provisional prices P_1' and P_2', solve for a provisional P_3'. The proof proceeds in this way until a complete set of provisional relative prices has been calculated.

In the second iteration of Walras' proof, $P_2', \ldots, P_n'$ are held constant while a new equilibrium price is calculated for the first good. Call this new provisional price P_1''. Proceeding as outlined above, an entire new set of provisional relative prices $(P_1'', \ldots, P_n'')$ can be calculated. The proof continues to iterate in this way until a reasonable approximation to a set of equilibrium prices is achieved.

The importance of Walras' proof is its ability to demonstrate the simultaneous nature of the problem of finding equilibrium prices. It is, however, a cumbersome proof and cannot be reproduced easily here. More recent work has utilized some relatively simple tools of advanced mathematics to demonstrate the existence of equilibrium prices in a formal and elegant way. In order to demonstrate such a proof, one advanced mathematical theorem must be discussed in detail.

Brouwer's Fixed-Point Theorem

Since this section must of necessity be purely mathematical, it is perhaps best to plunge right in by stating Brouwer's theorem:

> Any continuous mapping $[F(X)]$ of a closed, bounded, convex set into itself has at least one fixed point (X^*) such that $F(X^*) = X^*$.

Figure 15.8   *A Graphic Illustration of Brouwer's Fixed-Point Theorem*

Since any continuous function must cross the 45° line somewhere in the unit square, this function must have a point for which $f(x^*) = x^*$. This point is called a "fixed point."

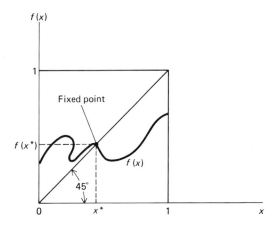

Before analyzing this theorem on a word-by-word basis, perhaps an example will aid in understanding the terminology. Suppose that $f(x)$ is a continuous function defined on the interval $[0, 1]$ and that $f(x)$ takes on values also on the interval $[0, 1]$. This function then obeys the conditions of Brouwer's theorem; it must be the case that there exists some x^* such that $f(x^*) = x^*$. This fact is demonstrated in Figure 15.8. It is clear from this figure that any function, as long as it is continuous (as long as it has no "gaps"), must cross the 45° line somewhere. This point of crossing is a *fixed point*, since f maps this point (x^*) into itself.

To study the more general meaning of the theorem, it is first necessary to define the terms "mapping," "closed," "bounded," and "convex." Definitions of these concepts will be presented in an extremely intuitive, nonrigorous way, because the costs of mathematical rigor greatly outweigh its possible benefits for the purposes of this book.

A *mapping* is simply a rule that associates the points in one set with points in another (possibly the same) set. The most commonly encountered mappings are those that associate one point in n-dimensional space with some other point in n-dimensional space. Suppose that F is the mapping we wish to study. Then let X be a point for which the mapping is defined: The mapping associates X with some other point $Y = F(X)$. If a mapping is defined over a subset of an n-dimensional space (S), and if every point in S is associated (by the rule F) with some other point in S, the mapping is said to map S *into* itself. In Figure 15.8 the function f maps the unit interval into itself. A mapping is *continuous* if points that are "close" to each other are mapped into other points that are "close" to each other.

The *Brouwer fixed-point theorem* considers mappings defined on certain kinds of sets. These sets are required to be closed, bounded, and convex. Perhaps the simplest way to describe such sets is to say that they look like (*n*-dimensional analogies of) soap bubbles. They are *closed* in the sense that they contain their boundaries; the sets are *bounded* because none of their dimensions is infinitely large; and they are *convex* because they have no "holes" in them. A technical description of the properties of such sets can be found in any elementary topology book.[12] For our purposes, however, it is only necessary to recognize that Brouwer's theorem is intended to apply to certain types of conveniently shaped sets. In order to use the theorem to prove the existence of equilibrium prices, therefore, we must first describe the set of points that has these desirable properties.

Proof of the Existence of Equilibrium Prices

The key to applying Brouwer's theorem to the exchange model just developed is to choose a suitable way for "normalizing" prices. Since only relative prices matter in the exchange model, it is convenient to assume that prices have been defined so that the sum of all prices is 1. Mathematically, for any arbitrary set of prices $(P_1, \ldots, P_n)$, we instead can deal with *normalized* prices of the form[13]

$$P'_i = \frac{P_i}{\sum_{i=1}^{n} P_i}. \tag{15.22}$$

These new prices will retain their original relative values ($P'_i/P'_j = P_i/P_j$) and will sum to 1:

$$\sum_{i=1}^{n} P'_i = 1. \tag{15.23}$$

Because of the homogeneity of degree 0 of all the excess demand functions, this kind of normalization always can be made. Hence, for the remainder of this proof, it will be assumed that the feasible set of prices (call this set S) is composed of all possible combinations of n nonnegative numbers that sum to 1. To avoid complex notation, we shall drop the special symbols we have been using for such prices.

This set, S, is the one to which we can apply Brouwer's theorem. The set S is closed, bounded, and convex.[14] To apply Brouwer's theorem, it is necessary

[12] For a development of the mathematics used in general equilibrium theory, see G. Debreu, *Theory of Value* (New York: John Wiley & Sons, 1959), chap. 1.

[13] One additional assumption must be made here; that is, at least one of the prices is nonzero. In economic terms this means that at least one good is scarce. Without this assumption a normalization of prices would not be possible.

[14] In two dimensions the set simply would be a straight line joining the coordinates (0, 1) and (1, 0). In three dimensions the set would be a triangular-shaped plane with vertices at (0, 0, 1), (0, 1, 0), and (1, 0, 0). It is easy to see that each of these sets is closed, bounded, and convex.

to define a continuous mapping of S into itself. By a judicious choice of this mapping, it is possible to show that the fixed point dictated by the theorem is in fact a set of equilibrium relative prices.

Free Goods

Before demonstrating the details of the proof, it is necessary to redefine what is meant by an "equilibrium set of prices." We do not really require that excess demand be equal to zero in every market for an equilibrium. Rather, goods may exist for which the markets are in equilibrium but for which the available supply exceeds demand; there is negative excess demand. For this to be the case, however, it is necessary that the price of this particular good be zero. Hence the equilibrium conditions of Equation 15.20 may be rewritten to take account of such *free goods*:

$$ED_i(P^*) = 0 \quad \text{for } P_i^* > 0$$

$$ED_i(P^*) \leq 0 \quad \text{for } P_i^* = 0$$

(15.24)

Notice that such a set of equilibrium prices continues to obey Walras' law.

Mapping the Set of Prices into Itself

Using this definition of equilibrium and remembering that prices have been normalized to sum to 1, it is now possible to construct a continuous function that transforms one set of prices into another. The function to be defined builds on the Walrasian idea that in order to achieve equilibrium, prices of goods that are in excess demand should be raised whereas those in excess supply should have their prices lowered. Hence, define the mapping $F(P)$ for any (normalized) set of prices, P, such that the ith component of $F(P)$, denoted by $F^i(P)$, is given by

$$F^i(P) = P_i + ED_i(P)$$

(15.25)

for all i. The mapping then performs the necessary task of appropriately raising and lowering prices. If, at P_i, good i is in excess demand $[ED_i(P) > 0]$, the price P_i is raised, whereas if excess demand is negative, P_i is reduced. Because the excess demand functions are assumed to be continuous, this mapping also will be continuous. Two problems with the mapping of Equation 15.25 remain. First, nothing ensures that the new prices will be nonnegative. Hence the mapping must be redefined to be

$$F^i(P) = \text{Max } [P_i + ED_i(P), 0]$$

(15.26)

for all i. The term "Max" here simply means that the new prices defined by the mapping F must be either positive or zero; prices are not allowed to go negative. The mapping of Equation 15.26 is also continuous.

A second problem with the mapping of Equation 15.26 is that the recalculated prices are not necessarily normalized; they will not sum to 1. It would be a simple matter, however, to normalize these new prices so that they do sum to 1.[15] To avoid introducing additional notation, assume that this normalization has been done and therefore that

$$\sum_{i=1}^{n} F'(P) = 1. \tag{15.27}$$

Application of Brouwer's Theorem

With this normalization, then, F satisfies the conditions of the Brouwer fixed-point theorem. It is a continuous mapping of the set S into itself. Hence there exists a point (P^*) that is mapped into itself. For this point,

$$P_i^* = \text{Max} \; [P_i^* + ED_i(P^*), 0] \tag{15.28}$$

for all i.

But this says that P^* is an equilibrium set of prices: for $P_i^* > 0$,

$$P_i^* = P_i^* + ED_i(P^*)$$

or   (15.29)

$$ED_i(P^*) = 0;$$

and for $P_i^* = 0$,

$$P_i^* + ED_i(P^*) \le 0$$

or   (15.30)

$$ED_i(P^*) \le 0.$$

Therefore it has been shown that the set of excess demand functions does in fact possess an equilibrium solution consisting of nonnegative prices. The simple exchange model developed here is consistent in that the market supply and demand functions necessarily have a solution. The homogeneity and con-

---

[15] In order to accomplish this normalization, it is first necessary to show that not all of the transformed prices will be zero; it is necessary to show that $P_i + ED_i(P) > 0$ for some i. This can be proved by contradiction. Assume that $P_i + ED_i(P) \le 0$ for all i. Multiply this expression by P_i and sum over all values of i, giving

$$\sum_{i=1}^{n} P_i^2 + \sum_{i=1}^{n} P_i ED_i(P) \le 0.$$

But

$$\sum_{i=1}^{n} P_i ED_i = 0$$

by Walras' law. Hence

$$\sum_{i=1}^{n} P_i^2 \le 0$$

and this implies that $P_i = 0$ for all i. However, we have already ruled out this situation (see footnote 13), and therefore we have proved that at least one of the transformed prices must be positive.

tinuity properties of the demand functions and the ability of Walras' law to tie together supply and demand are jointly responsible for this result.[16]

Generalizations

Although this proof is a relatively old one in the field of general equilibrium analysis, it does exhibit features of much of the more recent literature in this field. In particular, practically all modern proofs use Walras' law and rely on some type of fixed-point theorem. More recent work has tended to focus on ways in which the proof of the existence of general equilibrium prices can be generalized to situations involving more complex supply assumptions and on how equilibrium prices can actually be computed. In later chapters of this book, we will examine some of these alternative supply assumptions such as cases of imperfect competition and problems caused by "public goods" (which we define in the next chapter). The application to this chapter illustrates how the capacity of modern computers can be used to solve large-scale equilibrium pricing problems that seek to examine the impact of taxes on the economy and other issues. In addition, the Extensions to this chapter show some of the ways in which this existence proof can be applied to different types of markets.

MONEY IN GENERAL EQUILIBRIUM MODELS

Thus far in this chapter, we have showed how competitive markets can establish a set of relative prices at which all markets are in equilibrium simultaneously. At several places we stressed that such competitive market forces determine only relative, not absolute, prices and that to examine how the absolute price level is determined we must introduce money into our models. Although a complete examination of this topic is more properly studied as part of macroeconomics, here we can briefly explore some questions of the role of money in a competitive economy that relate directly to microeconomics.

Nature and Function of Money

Money serves two primary functions in any economy: (1) It facilitates transactions by providing an accepted medium of exchange; and (2) it acts as a store of value so that economic actors can better allocate their spending decisions over time. Any commodity can serve as "money" provided it is generally accepted for exchange purposes and is durable from period to period. Today most economies tend to use government-created (fiat) money because the costs associated with its production (e.g., printing paper with portraits of past or present rulers or keeping records on magnetic tape) are very low. In earlier times, however, commodity money was common with the particular good chosen ranging from the familiar (gold and silver) to the obscure and even bizarre (sharks' teeth or, on the island of Yap, large stone wheels). Societies probably choose the particular form that their money will take as the result of a wide variety of economic, historical, and political forces.

---

[16] The proof used in this section represents a simplified (and considerably vulgarized) version of a proof first presented by J. Kemeny and J. L. Snell, *Mathematical Models in the Social Sciences* (New York: Blaisdell Publishing Co., 1962), pp. 35–41.

Money as the Accounting Standard

One of the most important functions usually played by money is to act as an accounting standard or *numéraire*. In the previous section we showed that a competitive market system for n goods can generally arrive at an equilibrium set of prices $(P_1, \ldots P_n)$ at which all markets are in equilibrium. But these prices are unique only up to a common multiple since market forces of demand and supply can only determine relative, not absolute, prices. In principle any good (say, good k) could be chosen as an accounting standard, and we could always refer to the prices of the other $n - 1$ goods in terms of this good:

$$P_1' = \frac{P_1}{P_k}$$

$$P_2' = \frac{P_2}{P_k} \tag{15.31}$$

$$P_n' = \frac{P_n}{P_k}.$$

Since it is always true that

$$\frac{P_i}{P_j} = \frac{P_i/P_k}{P_j/P_k} = \frac{P_i'}{P_j'} \tag{15.32}$$

for any pair of goods, i and j, relative prices will be unaffected by which good (or possibly basket of goods) is chosen as the accounting standard. For example, if one apple (good i) exchanges for two plums (good j),

$$\frac{P_i}{P_j} = \frac{2}{1}, \tag{15.33}$$

and it makes little difference how those prices are quoted. If, for example, a society chooses clams as a unit of account, an apple might exchange for four clams and a plum for two clams. Then, if we let clams be the *numéraire* good k,

$$\frac{P_i'}{P_j'} = \frac{P_i/P_k}{P_j/P_k} = \frac{4}{2} = \frac{2}{1} = \frac{P_i}{P_j}. \tag{15.34}$$

We could change from counting in clams to counting in sharks' teeth (good 1) by knowing that ten sharks' teeth exchange for one clam. Then the price of our goods in sharks' teeth would be

$$P_i'' = \frac{P_i}{P_k} \cdot \frac{P_k}{P_1} = 4.10 = 40$$

and

$$P_j'' = \frac{P_i}{P_k} \cdot \frac{P_k}{P_1} = 2.10 = 20, \tag{15.35}$$

and one apple (which costs 40 teeth) would still exchange for 2 plums, which cost 20 teeth each.

Of course, using clams or sharks' teeth is not very common. Instead, societies usually adopt money as their accounting standard. An apple might exchange for half a piece of paper picturing George Washington (i.e., $.50) and a plum for one-fourth of such a piece of paper ($.25). Thus, with this monetary standard, the relative price remains two for one. Choice of an accounting standard does not, however, necessarily dictate any particular absolute price level. An apple might exchange for four clams or four hundred, but, as long as a plum exchanges for half as many clams, relative prices will be unaffected by the absolute level that prevails. But absolute price levels are obviously important, especially to individuals who wish to use money as a store of value. A person with a large investment in clams obviously cares about how many apples they will buy. Although a complete theoretical treatment of the price level issue is beyond the scope of this book, we do offer some brief comments on it here.

Commodity Money

In an economy where money is produced in a way similar to any other good (gold is mined, clams are dug, or sharks are caught), the relative price of money is determined like any other relative price—by the forces of demand and supply. Economic forces that affect either the demand or supply of money will also affect these relative prices. For example, Spanish importation of gold from the New World during the fifteenth and sixteenth centuries greatly expanded gold supplies and caused the relative price of gold to fall. That is, the prices of all other goods rose relative to that of gold—there was general inflation in the prices of practically everything in terms of gold. Similar effects would arise from changes in any factor that affected the equilibrium price for the good chosen as money.

Fiat Money and the Classical Dichotomy

For the case of fiat money produced by the government, the analysis can be extended a bit. In this situation the government is the sole supplier of money and can generally choose how much it wishes to produce.[17] What effects will the level of money production have on the real economy? In general, the situation would seem to be identical to that for commodity money. A change in money supply will disturb the general equilibrium of all relative prices, and, although it seems likely that an expansion in supply will lower the relative price of money (that is, result in an inflation in the money prices of other goods), any more precise prediction would seem to depend on the results of a detailed general equilibrium model.

Beginning with David Hume, however, classical economists argued that money (especially fiat money) differs from other economic goods and should be considered to be outside the real economic system of demand, supply, and relative price determination. In this view the economy can be dichotomized into a real sector in which relative prices are determined and a monetary sector where the absolute price level (that is, the value of fiat money) is set. Money,

---

[17]By being a monopoly supplier of money (which is produced at low cost), the government may make long-run profits from its seigniorage activities.

therefore, acts only as a "veil" for real economic activity—the quantity of money available has no effect on the real sector.

Unfortunately, developing general equilibrium models that exhibit the classical dichotomy between monetary and real sectors presents some conceptual difficulties. If preferences for money are treated like those for any other good (since money makes transactions easier, it also yields utility), then only special types of preferences result in the classical dichotomy. Specifically, if individuals' marginal rates of substitution (MRS) between any two real commodities are assumed to be independent of the quantity of money they have (and a similar assumption is made about firms' rates of product transformation between these goods), then relative prices determined by the forces of supply and demand will be independent of the quantity of money in circulation. In the absence of such assumptions, however, individuals' relative preferences and firms' relative productive abilities will be affected by the quantity of money, and the classical dichotomy will not exist. Some of the problems at the end of this chapter explore these various possibilities.

A limiting case of these special assumptions about preferences and technology is that the quantity of money has no effect on real forces—that is, the quantity of money in circulation does not enter either individuals' utility functions or firms' production functions. So why do individuals and firms use money? One possible assumption is that these actors "need" money to make transactions even though money *per se* yields no utility or productivity. If, for example, there are two nonmonetary goods (X and Y) in the economy, total transactions per period are given by $P_X^* X^* + P_Y^* Y^*$ (where P_X^* and P_Y^* are equilibrium prices associated with the equilibrium quantities X^* and Y^*). Conducting these transactions requires that a certain fraction (say, α) of their total value be available as circulating money. The demand for money is therefore

$$D_M = \alpha(P_X^* X^* + P_Y^* Y^*), \tag{15.36}$$

and monetary equilibrium requires that

$$D_M = S_M, \tag{15.37}$$

where S_M is the quantity of money supplied by the government.

A doubling of the money supply would throw this system into disequilibrium; at the prior equilibrium level of transactions for X and Y, there would now be an excess supply of money and according to Walras' law (Equation 15.21), this would be balanced by a net excess demand for goods.

Equilibrium could be restored in this economy by a precise doubling of equilibrium nominal prices. This would double the transactions demand for money, but, because relative prices would be unchanged, it would not alter equilibrium quantities of X and Y:

$$D_M' = \alpha(2P_X^* X^* + 2P_Y^* Y^*)$$

$$= 2\alpha(P_X^* X^* + P_Y^* Y^*) \tag{15.38}$$

$$= 2D_M.$$

In this system, therefore, nominal equilibrium prices are proportional to the money supply, and the classical dichotomy is complete.[18] Money is truly a veil—it has no effect on the real economy.

Whether the classical dichotomy between the real and monetary sectors actually holds in the real world is an empirical question that cannot be resolved on theoretical grounds alone. Although there are ways of incorporating a monetary sector into the standard competitive model of general equilibrium that preserve the dichotomy, these are somewhat artificial and rely on rather restrictive assumptions. Discovering whether they still represent a reasonable approximation of the behavior of the economy (especially over the long term) is an important unresolved issue in macroeconomics.

SUMMARY

In this chapter we have showed how the partial equilibrium model of competitive price determination that we developed in Chapter 14 can be generalized to represent multiple markets. The principal complication encountered in making this generalization is the need to take into account relationships among many markets for different goods and factors of production. Our examination of such issues reached the following conclusions:

- Simple Marshallian models of supply and demand in several markets may not in themselves be adequate for addressing general equilibrium questions because they do not provide a direct way of tying the markets together and illustrating the feedback effects that occur when market equilibria change.
- A simple general equilibrium model of relative price determination for two goods can be developed using an indifference curve map to represent demands for the goods and the production possibility frontier to represent supply. This model is useful for examining comparative statics questions in a general equilibrium context.
- Construction of the production possibility frontier from the Edgeworth box diagram also permits an integration of factor markets into a simple general equilibrium model. The shape of the production possibility frontier illustrates how reallocating factors of production among outputs affects the marginal costs associated with producing those outputs. Specifically, the slope of the production possibility frontier—the rate of product transformation—measures the ratio of the two goods' marginal costs.

---

[18] This leads directly to the Quantity Theory of the Demand for Money, first suggested by Hume:

$$D_M = \frac{1}{V} \cdot P \cdot Q,$$

where D_M is the demand for money, V is the velocity of monetary circulation ($= 1/\alpha$ in our model), P is the overall price level, and Q is a measure of the quantity of transactions (often approximated by real GNP).

- Whether a set of competitive prices exists that will equilibrate many markets simultaneously is a complex theoretical question. Such a set of prices will generally exist if demand and supply functions are suitably continuous and if Walras' law (which requires that net excess demand be zero at any set of prices) holds.
- Incorporating money into a general equilibrium model is a major focus of macroeconomic research. In some cases such monetary models will exhibit the classical dichotomy in that monetary forces will have no effect on relative prices observed in the "real" economy. These cases are rather restrictive, however, so the extent to which the classical dichotomy holds in the real world remains an unresolved issue.

Application

USING A COMPUTER TO MODEL THE IMPACT OF TAXES

Chapter 14 illustrated how the competitive model might be used to analyze the impact of taxes on a single market. A primary shortcoming of that approach is that it does not allow a very complete description of the various effects a tax may have. For example, we showed that an excise tax on a good is paid partly by consumers and partly by firms, with the respective shares being determined by elasticities of demand and supply. This conclusion tells us very little about who really bears the burden of the tax. We have no idea how that burden is shared among different consumers of the good, nor do we know who finally pays the firms' share (it could be owners of the firms, workers in the firms, or some combination of the two). Simple models of supply and demand are just not detailed enough to answer such questions.

The development of large-scale computers and sophisticated programs for modeling the economy has changed this situation dramatically. Now it is possible to use general equilibrium models of the economy to obtain very detailed appraisals of the impact of taxes. Some of these models divide the economy into as many as 50 or more industries and equally as many different types of consumers. A graphic representation of such models might look like Figure

15.1 but with more than 100 different markets represented. Coping with the information necessary to compute equilibrium prices in all of these markets without a computer would be impossible. Using the speed and capacity of modern computers makes it a fairly simple process.

These large general equilibrium models of the economy have yielded major and sometimes surprising conclusions about the effects of taxes on an economy. Generally, these effects are bigger than have usually been discovered using partial equilibrium methods.[19] One study of the entire tax system of the United Kingdom, for example, concluded that distortions introduced by that system resulted in a loss of consumer surplus of 6 to 9 percent of total gross national product. The taxes also caused a transfer of nearly one-quarter of all income from high-income to low-income households. The study found that the British tax system imposed particularly heavy costs on its manufacturing industries—perhaps providing an explanation for recent poor industrial performance in that country. Studies of the U.S. tax system tend to

---

[19] For a summary of many of these models, see John B. Shoven and John Whalley, "Applied General Equilibrium Models of Taxation and International Trade," *Journal of Economic Literature* (September 1984): 1007–1051.

reach similar, though perhaps not so dramatic, conclusions. For example, some authors have reported that, at the margin, the U.S. tax system involves large losses of consumer surplus. Collecting one dollar in extra taxes imposes very large costs (perhaps as much as two dollars) on people who pay them. These studies suggest that moving to simpler tax schemes, such as a flat rate consumption tax, would reduce these losses substantially.

SUGGESTED READINGS

Arrow, K. J., and Hahn, F. *General Competitive Analysis.* San Francisco: Holden-Day, 1971. Chaps. 1, 2, and 4.

Sophisticated mathematical treatment of general equilibrium analysis. Each chapter has a good literary introduction.

Debreu, G. "Existence of Competitive Equilibrium." In K. J. Arrow and M. D. Intriligator, eds., *Handbook of Mathematical Economics*, Vol. 2. Amsterdam: North Holland Publishing Co., 1982. Pp. 697–743.

Fairly difficult survey of existence proofs based on fixed-point theorems. Contains a comprehensive set of references.

Debreu, G. *Theory of Value.* New York: John Wiley & Sons, 1959.

Basic reference, difficult mathematics. Does have a good introductory chapter on the mathematical tools used.

Johnson, H. G. *The Two-Sector Model of General Equilibrium.* Chicago: Aldine-Atherton, 1971.

Complete geometric treatment of two-good, two-input models.

Quirk, J., and Saprosnik, R. *Introduction to General Equilibrium Theory and Welfare Economics.* New York: McGraw-Hill Book Company, 1968.

Basic text on general equilibrium. Quite readable, heavy mathematics kept to a minimum.

Scarf, H. E. "The Computation of Equilibrium Prices: An Exposition." In K. J. Arrow and M. D. Intriligator, eds., *Handbook of Mathematical Economics*, Vol. 2. Amsterdam: North Holland Publishing Co., 1982. Pp. 1007–1061.

Illustrates Scarf's algorithm for computing equilibrium prices. This method is widely used in computer modeling.

Shoven, J. B., and Whalley, J. "Applied General Equilibrium Models of Taxation and International Trade." *Journal of Economic Literature* (September 1984): 1007–1051.

Good survey of applications of large-scale general equilibrium models. Nice discussion of the theoretical foundations of the models and how these affect the results obtained.

PROBLEMS

15.1

Suppose the production possibility frontier for cheeseburgers (C) and milkshakes (M) is given by

$$C + 2M = 600.$$

a. Graph this function.

b. Assuming that people prefer to eat two cheeseburgers with every milkshake, how much of each product will be produced? Indicate this point on your graph.

c. Given that this fast food economy is operating efficiently, what price ratio (P_C/P_M) must prevail?

15.2

Suppose the production possibility frontier for guns (X) and butter (Y) is given by

$$X^2 + 2Y^2 = 900.$$

a. Graph this frontier.
b. If individuals always prefer consumption bundles in which $Y = 2X$, how much X and Y will be produced?
c. At the point described in Part (a) what will be the RPT and hence what price ratio will cause production to take place at that point? (This slope should be approximated by considering small changes in X and Y around the optimal point.)
d. Show your solution on the figure from Part (a).

15.3

Suppose an economy produces only two goods, X and Y. Production of good X is given by

$$X = K_X^{1/2} L_X^{1/2}$$

where K_X and L_X are the inputs of capital and labor devoted to X production. The production function for good Y is given by

$$Y = K_Y^{1/3} L_Y^{2/3}$$

where K_Y and L_Y are the inputs of capital and labor devoted to Y production. The supply of capital is fixed at 100 units and the supply of labor is fixed at 200 units. Hence, if both units are fully employed,

$$K_X + K_Y = K_T = 100$$

$$L_X + L_Y = L_T = 200.$$

Using this information complete the following questions.
a. Show how the capital-labor ratio in X production ($K_X/L_X = k_X$) must be related to the capital-labor ratio in Y production ($K_Y/L_Y = k_Y$) if production is to be efficient.
b. Show that the capital-labor ratios for the two goods are constrained by

$$\alpha_X k_X + (1 - \alpha_X)k_Y = \frac{K_T}{L_T} = \frac{100}{200} = \frac{1}{2}$$

where α_X is the share of total labor devoted to X production [that is, $\alpha_X = L_X/L_T = L_X(L_X + L_Y)$].
c. Use the information from parts (a) and (b) to compute the efficient capital-labor for good X for all values of α_X between 0 and 1.
d. Graph the Edgeworth Production Box for this economy and use the information from part (c) to develop a rough sketch of the production contract curve.
e. Which good, X or Y, is capital-intensive in this economy? Explain why the production possibility curve for the economy is concave.
f. Calculate the mathematical form of the production possibility frontier for this economy (this calculation may be rather tedious!). Show that, as expected, this is a concave function.

15.4

The purpose of this problem is to examine the relationship among returns-to-scale, factor intensity, and the shape of the production possibility frontier.

Suppose there are fixed supplies of capital and labor to be allocated between the production of good X and good Y. The production function for X is given by

$$X = K^\alpha L^\beta$$

and for Y by

$$Y = K^\gamma L^\delta$$

where the parameters α, β, γ, δ will take on different values throughout this problem.

Using either intuition, a computer, or a formal mathematical approach, derive the production possibility frontier for X and Y in the following cases:

 a. $\alpha = \beta = \gamma = \delta = \frac{1}{2}$.
 b. $\alpha = \beta = \frac{1}{2}, \gamma = \frac{1}{3}, \delta = \frac{2}{3}$.
 c. $\alpha = \beta = \frac{1}{2}, \gamma = \delta = \frac{2}{3}$.
 d. $\alpha = \beta = \gamma = \delta = \frac{2}{3}$.
 e. $\alpha = \beta = .6, \gamma = .2, \delta = 1.0$.
 f. $\alpha = \beta = .7, \gamma = .6, \delta = .8$.

Do increasing returns to scale always lead to a convex production possibility frontier? Explain.

15.5

The country of Podunk produces only wheat and cloth, using as inputs land and labor. Both are produced by constant returns to scale production functions. Wheat is the relatively land-intensive commodity.

 a.   Explain in words, or with diagrams, how the price of wheat relative to cloth (p) determines the land-labor ratio in each of the two industries.
 b.   Suppose that p is given by external forces (this would be the case if Podunk were a "small" country trading freely with a "large" world). Show, using the Edgeworth box, that if the supply of labor increases in Podunk, the output of cloth will rise and the output of wheat will fall.

15.6

Suppose two individuals (Smith and Jones) each have 10 hours of labor to devote to producing either ice cream (X) or chicken soup (Y). Smith's utility function is given by

$$U_S = X^{.3} Y^{.7}$$

whereas Jones's is given by

$$U_J = X^{.5} Y^{.5}.$$

The individuals do not care whether they produce X or Y and the production function for each good is given by

$$X = 2L$$
$$Y = 3L$$

where L is the total labor devoted to production of each good. Using this information

 a.   What must the price ratio, P_X/P_Y, be?
 b.   Given this price ratio how much X and Y will Smith and Jones demand? (Hint: Set the wage equal to one here.)
 c.   How should labor be allocated between X and Y to satisfy the demand calculated in part b?

15.7

Suppose there are only 3 goods $(X_1, X_2,$ and $X_3)$ in an economy and that the excess demand functions for X_2 and X_3 are given by

$$ED_2 = -3P_2/P_1 + 2P_3/P_1 - 1$$

$$ED_3 = 4P_2/P_1 - 2P_3/P_1 - 2$$

    a.   Show that these functions are homogeneous of degree zero in P_1, P_2, and P_3.

    b.   Use Walras' law to show that if $ED_2 = ED_3 = 0$, ED_1 also must be 0. Can you also use Walras' law to calculate ED_1?

    c.   Solve this system of equations for the equilibrium relative prices P_2/P_1 and P_3/P_1. What is the equilibrium value for P_3/P_2?

15.8

Use the simple two-good model of general equilibrium pricing developed in this chapter to illustrate a situation in which there will be two equilibrium price ratios by relaxing the assumption that the production possibility frontier is concave. Explain your result intuitively.

15.9

Return to Problem 15.6 and now assume that Smith and Jones conduct their exchanges in paper money. The total supply of such money is $60 and each individual wishes to hold a stock of money equal to ¼ of the value of transactions made per period.

    a.   What will the money wage rate be in this model? What will the nominal prices of X and Y be?

    b.   Suppose the money supply increases to $90. How will your answers to part a change? Does this economy exhibit the classical dichotomy between its real and monetary sectors?

EXTENSIONS

GENERALIZED NOTIONS OF GENERAL EQUILIBRIUM

Our proof of the existence of a general equilibrium set of prices can be extended in many ways. Since the theorem applies to any n "goods," the most direct generalizations can be obtained through suitable redefinitions of the notion of a "good." For example, a model that incorporates a spatial dimension to general equilibrium price determination can be constructed by labeling goods as X_{ir} where i (= 1 . . . k) is used to index specific kinds of goods and r (= 1 . . . j) is used to index locations. Here n = i · r and identical commodities available at different locations can be treated as different goods (a bushel of wheat in Omaha is a different good from a bushel in Toronto). Similarly, goods available in different time periods could be denoted by X_{it} (where t = 1 . . . T) to indicate that a bushel of wheat delivered today is a different commodity than one delivered next year. More generally we could denote a good by X_{is} (s = 1 . . . S) where s would index "states-of-the-world" (see Chapter 9) which might include not only differences in location or timing, but also in "environmental" factors such as whether it is raining or whether the country is in recession. Here we will examine some issues that arise in describing the nature of equilibrium in such an extended set of markets. Since our treatment must be cursory, the interested reader is directed to the references for more detail.

E15.1

Consider the nature of equilibrium in spatially separated markets. What relationship must hold between P^*_{ij} and P^*_{ik}—that is, what relationship must hold between equilibrium prices for the same good at different locations? Can such price differences exceed transportation costs between the markets? Can the existence theorem presented in Chapter 15 be generalized to show that this type of equilibrium must exist, or does the issue of movement of goods among markets make the existence of equilibrium less likely?

E15.2

In the context of intertemporal general equilibrium goods are traded in both current ("spot") and *futures markets*. Trading in the futures markets is not for goods themselves but rather for contracts that promise to deliver these goods in future periods. Such a contract might promise one bushel of corn at a date one year in the future, for example. A buyer of such a contract would then be entitled to the bushel of corn on that date whereas the seller of the contract would be obligated to deliver the corn. Assuming all goods are perishable, what relationships exist between the futures market for a good (i.e. "corn in one year") and the spot market for that good in the future (the actual market for corn in one year)? Can the quantity of futures contracts exceed the actual quantity of a good available in the future? If so, how are futures contracts settled? What current budget constraints affect buyers and sellers of futures contracts? How does the budget constraint operate in the future? How do expected future spot prices for a good affect current futures prices for that good? Must they necessarily agree?

E15.3

How would the presence of durable goods (goods that last several periods) affect futures markets? Would the presence of a monetary asset that paid a certain interest rate affect the relationship between the spot price, P_{it}, and the futures price, P_{it+1}, for a durable good? How would expectations about the spot price of good i in period $t + 1$ affect this relationship? Would these relationships for durable goods hold also for perishable goods?

E15.4

In Chapter 9 we discussed the notion of a contingent commodity—a contract that promises to deliver a particular good only if a specific state of the world occurs. Would you expect there to be a complete set of markets for such contingent commodities? What factors might prevent the emergence of such markets? Provide some actual examples of potential contingent markets that do not exist.

E15.5

Suppose there are n goods (which may include futures contracts or contracts on contingent commodities in the future), but that current markets exist for only a subset of these goods.

    a.   Describe how the existence proof might be modified to show the existence of equilibrium prices in this subset of markets contingent on expected future prices for the goods for which no current markets exist.

    b.   Explain why the equilibrium described in part a will be affected by changing expectations about future prices of goods not currently traded.

c.   Given these observations, would you expect the temporary equilibria described in part a to be (intertemporally) efficient?

REFERENCES

Arrow, K. J., and F. H. Hahn, *General Competitive Analysis* (San Francisco: Holden-Day, Inc., 1971), Chapter 6.

Debreu, G., *Theory of Value* (New York: Wiley, 1959).

Radner, R., "Equilibrium Under Uncertainty," in K. J. Arrow and M. D. Intriligator (Eds.), *Handbook of Mathematical Economics*, Vol. 2 (Amsterdam: North Holland, 1982).

CHAPTER 16

The Efficiency of Perfect Competition

Although most people recognize the equilibrium properties of the competitive price system (after all, prices usually do not fluctuate widely from day-to-day), they see little overall pattern to the resulting allocation of resources. The relationships described by the competitive model presented in the previous chapter are so complex that it is hard to believe that any desirable outcome will emerge from the chaos. This view provides an open-ended rationale to tinker with the system—since the results of market forces are chaotic, surely human societies can do better through careful planning.

It took the genius of Adam Smith to challenge this view, which was probably the prevalent one in the eighteenth century. To Smith, the competitive market system represented the polar opposite from chaos. Rather, it provided a powerful "invisible hand" that assured that resources would find their way to where they were most valued, thereby enhancing the "wealth" of the nation. In Smith's view, reliance on the economic self-interest of individuals and firms would result in a (perhaps surprisingly) desirable social outcome.

Smith's initial insights gave rise to modern welfare economics. Specifically, his widely quoted "invisible hand" image provided the impetus for what is now called the "fundamental theorem" of welfare economics—that there is a close correspondence between the efficient allocation of resources and the competitive pricing of these resources. In this chapter we will investigate this correspondence in some detail. We begin by defining economic efficiency in a variety of contexts. These definitions, all of which draw on the work of the nineteenth-century economist Vilfred Pareto, have already been described briefly in earlier chapters; our goal here is to draw these discussions together and illustrate their underlying similarities.

There are two general ways in which it might be possible to achieve the kind of efficient allocation of resources we will describe: through comprehensive economic planning or through decentralized decision making that responds to economic incentives. Although we briefly describe some of the information problems associated with central planning, for the major part of this chapter we focus on competitive markets as decentralized allocational devices. We show that, under certain conditions, competitive market allocations will be efficient in the sense defined by Pareto. The competitive market has a remarkable ability to assimilate information from both demanders and suppliers and to coordinate their actions into a coherent overall pattern. Thus Smith's invisible hand exerts a powerful force in directing resources to their most valuable use.

Some of the most interesting aspects of the relationship between efficiency and competitive markets, however, concern situations in which the theorem fails. In the final sections of this chapter we provide a brief catalog of such possible failures. Each of these suggests a number of analytical issues that we will take up in detail in later chapters.

PARETO EFFICIENCY

In Chapter 8 we introduced Pareto's definition of economic efficiency. Although that definition was developed for an exchange economy in which no production takes place, it can also serve as a more general basis for our analysis in this chapter:

Definition:

Pareto Efficient Allocation

An allocation of resources is Pareto efficient if it is not possible (through further reallocations) to make one person better off without making someone else worse off.

The Pareto definition then identifies particular allocations as being "inefficient" if unambiguous improvements are possible. In Chapter 8 we showed how Pareto efficient allocations in an exchange economy could be illustrated in an Edgeworth box diagram and how reliance on competitive equilibrium prices might allow individuals to reach such allocations. Here we are interested in generalizing this analysis to include production.

EFFICIENCY IN PRODUCTION

In simple terms, an economy is efficient in production if it is on its production possibility frontier. Formally, we can use Pareto's terminology to define

Definition:

Productive Efficiency

An allocation of resources is efficient in production (or "technically efficient") if no further reallocation would permit more of one good to be produced without necessarily reducing the output of some other good.

As for Pareto efficiency itself, it is perhaps easiest to grasp this definition by studying its converse—an allocation would be inefficient if it were possible to move existing resources around a bit and get additional amounts of one good and no less of anything else. With technically efficient allocations, no such unambiguous improvements are possible. The trade-offs among outputs necessitated by movements along the production possibility frontier reflect the technically efficient nature of all of the allocations on the frontier.

Technical efficiency is an obvious precondition for overall Pareto efficiency. Suppose resources were allocated so that production was inefficient; that is, production was occurring at a point inside the production possibility frontier. It would then be possible to produce more of at least one good and no less of anything else. This increased output could be given to some lucky person making him or her better off (and no one else worse off). Hence inefficiency in production is also Pareto inefficiency. As we shall see in the next section, however, technical efficiency does not guarantee Pareto efficiency. An economy can be efficient at producing the wrong goods—devoting all available resources to producing left shoes would be a technically efficient use of those resources, but surely some Pareto improvement could be found in which everyone would be better off. Before discussing this issue, however, we must examine the conditions required for productive efficiency more thoroughly.

A discussion of efficiency in production and its relationship to the production possibility frontier is somewhat more complex than our simple presentation in Chapter 15 might imply. Because the economy is divided into many firms, we must be concerned not only with the ways in which a single firm uses its resources (as we essentially were in the previous chapter), but also with how resources are allocated among firms. To facilitate this examination, we will break the question down into three separate issues: (1) resource allocation within a single firm; (2) allocation of productive resources among firms; and (3) coordination of firms' output choices. Results for each of these issues will be summarized by a general "Allocation Rule." All of these rules must hold to ensure productive efficiency.

Efficient Choice of Inputs for a Single Firm

In Chapter 15 we examined the situation of a firm having fixed inputs of capital and labor. There we showed that the firm will have allocated these inputs efficiently if they are fully employed and if the rate of technical substitution (RTS) between capital and labor is the same for every output the firm produces. Previously, we developed a detailed graphical proof of this assertion; here we will use a mathematical approach. Assume the firm produces two goods, X and Y, and that the total available inputs of capital and labor are given by $\overline{K}$ and $\overline{L}$. The production function for good X is given by

$$X = f(K_X, L_X), \tag{16.1}$$

where K_X and L_X are capital and labor devoted to X production. If we assume full employment, $K_Y = \overline{K} - K_X$, $L_Y = \overline{L} - L_X$, and the production function for good Y is

$$Y = g(K_Y, L_Y) = g(\overline{K} - K_X, \overline{L} - L_X). \tag{16.2}$$

Technical efficiency requires that X output be as large as possible for any predetermined value of Y output (say, $\overline{Y}$). Setting up the Lagrangian expression for this constrained-maximum problem yields

$$\mathcal{L} = f(K_X, L_X) + \lambda[\overline{Y} - g(\overline{K} - K_X, \overline{L} - L_X)]. \tag{16.3}$$

Differentiation with respect to K_X, L_X, and λ gives the following first-order conditions for a constrained maximum:

$$\frac{\partial \mathscr{L}}{\partial K_X} = f_K + \lambda g_K = 0$$

$$\frac{\partial \mathscr{L}}{\partial L_X} = f_L + \lambda g_L = 0 \tag{16.4}$$

$$\frac{\partial \mathscr{L}}{\partial \lambda} = \overline{Y} - g(\overline{K} - K_X, \overline{L} - L_X) = 0.$$

Moving the terms in λ to the right-hand side of the first two of these equations, we have

$$\frac{f_K}{f_L} = \frac{g_K}{g_L}, \tag{16.5}$$

and, using the result (from Chapter 10) that the *RTS* is the ratio of the inputs' marginal productivities, that implies[1]

$$RTS_X \quad (K \text{ for } L) = RTS_Y \quad (K \text{ for } L). \tag{16.6}$$

This result makes intuitive sense. Suppose a firm had 100 labor hours and 200 machine hours to devote to the production of frisbees and galoshes. Suppose it (mistakenly, as it turns out) allocated half of each input to each output. Assume that with $50L$ and $100K$ the *RTS* in frisbee production is 2, but that the *RTS* in galoshes production is 1. The same number of frisbees can then be produced with $51L$ and $98K$, and the same galoshes production can be accomplished with $49L$ and $101K$. Under this alternative allocation, there is one extra machine hour that, assuming f_K and g_K are not zero, could be used to produce more of one of the goods. Hence, the initial allocation was inefficient, and, since these numbers were purely arbitrary, any allocation in which the *RTS*'s differ must also be inefficient. We can therefore summarize our discussion by

> Allocation Rule 1. A firm with fixed resources has allocated those resources efficiently if it has them fully employed and if the *RTS* between the inputs is the same for every output the firm produces.

Efficient Allocation of Resources among Firms

Resources must also be allocated in some efficient way among firms in order to ensure overall productive efficiency. Intuitively, resources should be allocated to those firms where they can be most efficiently used. More precisely, the condition for efficient allocation is given by

> Allocation Rule 2. If production is to be efficient, resources should be allocated so that the marginal physical product of any resource in the pro-

---

[1] All of these results hold only for an interior maximum in which both inputs are actually used to produce both goods. If that were not the case, these first-order conditions would have to be amended.

duction of a particular good is the same no matter which firm produces that good.

A mathematical proof of this rule is straightforward. Suppose that there are two firms producing the same good (X) and that their production functions are given by $f_1(K_1, L_1)$ and $f_2(K_2, L_2)$. Assume also that total supplies of capital and labor are given by $\overline{K}$ and $\overline{L}$. The allocational problem is then to maximize

$$X = f_1(K_1, L_1) + f_2(K_2, L_2), \tag{16.7}$$

subject to the constraints

$$K_1 + K_2 = \overline{K} \tag{16.8}$$
$$L_1 + L_2 = \overline{L}.$$

Upon substituting the constraints into Equation 16.7, the maximization problem becomes

$$X = f_1(K_1, L_1) + f_2(\overline{K} - K_1, \overline{L} - L_1). \tag{16.9}$$

First-order conditions for a maximum are

$$\frac{\partial X}{\partial K_1} = \frac{\partial f_1}{\partial K_1} + \frac{\partial f_2}{\partial K_1} = \frac{\partial f_1}{\partial K_1} - \frac{\partial f_2}{\partial K_2} = 0$$
$$\tag{16.10}$$
$$\frac{\partial X}{\partial L_1} = \frac{\partial f_1}{\partial L_1} + \frac{\partial f_2}{\partial L_1} = \frac{\partial f_1}{\partial L_1} - \frac{\partial f_2}{\partial L_2} = 0$$

or

$$\frac{\partial f_1}{\partial K_1} = \frac{\partial f_2}{\partial K_2}$$

and

$$\frac{\partial f_1}{\partial L_1} = \frac{\partial f_2}{\partial L_2}, \tag{16.11}$$

as was to be shown.

Figure 16.1 provides a graphic proof. The figure shows the marginal productivity of labor curves for two firms, both producing the same output. Suppose that the initial allocation of labor between the firms has L_1 workers working for firm 1 and L_2 for firm 2. From the figure, we can see that the marginal productivity of labor in firm 1 exceeds that in firm 2. Allocation Rule 2 suggests that labor therefore should be transferred from firm 2 to firm 1. Suppose that only 1 worker is so transferred. The effects of this transfer are shown in the figure. The reduction in output in firm 2 is shown by the shaded area in Figure 16.1b. If this worker is added to the labor force for firm 1, output will expand by the shaded area in Figure 16.1a. It is clear that output has been increased by this transfer: The shaded area in Figure 16.1a is larger than that in Figure 16.1b. The transfer of labor also serves to equilibrate the marginal

Figure 16.1   *Equality of Marginal Products Is Required for Efficiency*

When marginal productivities in the production of a single good differ between firms, output of the good can be increased by reallocating labor. In the figure, moving one worker from firm 2 to firm 1 increases output. Such a reallocation should continue until the marginal productivities are equal.

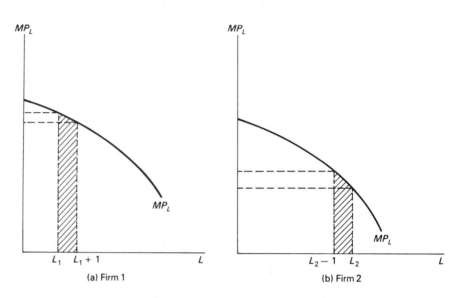

(a) Firm 1   (b) Firm 2

product of labor between the firms. The additional worker in firm 1 causes labor's marginal product to fall, whereas firm 2 now has fewer workers and, consequently, their marginal productivity has risen. The transfer of labor should continue until the equality required by Allocation Rule 2 is achieved. The available stock of labor (or capital) should be reallocated until a situation is reached in which marginal productivities do not differ among firms.

Efficient Choice of Output by Firms   Even though resources may be efficiently allocated both within a firm and among all firms, there is still one other condition of efficient production that must be obeyed: Firms must produce efficient combinations of outputs. Roughly speaking, firms that are good at producing hamburgers should produce hamburgers and those good at producing cars should produce cars. The necessary conditions for efficient choices of outputs are summarized in

> Allocation Rule 3. If two (or more) firms produce the same outputs, they must operate at those points on their respective production possibility frontiers at which their rates of product transformation are equal.

Consider two firms (A and B) that each produce both cars and trucks. Let their production possibility curves be given by those in Figure 16.2. Suppose that firm A chooses to produce at a point, P_1^A (100 cars and 50 trucks), where

Figure 16.2   *Graphic Demonstration of Allocation Rule 3*

If two firms' rates of product transformation differ, total output can be increased by moving these firms toward equalization of those rates. In the figure firm A is relatively efficient at producing cars, and firm B is relatively efficient at producing trucks. If each firm were to specialize in its efficient product, total output could be increased.

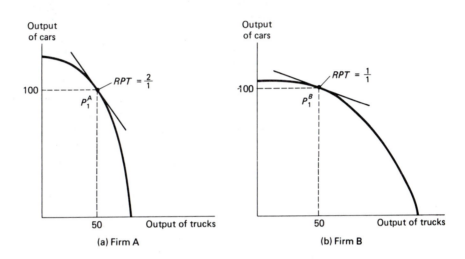

(a) Firm A   (b) Firm B

its RPT (of trucks for cars) is $2/1$. At this point, firm A must give up 2 cars if it is to produce one more truck. Suppose also that firm B chooses to produce 100 cars and 50 trucks but that at this point its RPT (of trucks for cars) is $1/1$. In this case productive efficiency can be improved by having firm A produce more cars (since it is relatively efficient in this) and firm B produce more trucks. For example, firm A could produce 102 cars and 49 trucks, whereas B could move to producing 99 cars and 51 trucks. By this reordering of production, the total output of cars has been increased without decreasing the total output of trucks. Hence the initial choices of firms A and B were inefficient. Only if Allocation Rule 3 holds is it impossible to make such a beneficial reallocation. This result is particularly interesting in that it shows that output may be increased, even if the inputs to each firm are fixed, by having firms produce the "correct" output combinations.

Theory of Comparative Advantage

One of the most important applications of Allocation Rule 3 is in the study of international trade, where it is used as the basis for the *theory of comparative advantage*. This theory was first proposed by Ricardo, who argued that countries should specialize in producing those goods of which they are relatively more efficient producers.[2] The countries then should trade with the rest of the

---

[2]See D. Ricardo, *The Principles of Political Economy and Taxation* (1817; reprint ed., London: J. M. Dent and Son, 1965), pp. 81–93.

world to obtain needed commodities. If countries do specialize in this way, total world production will be greater than if each country tried to produce a balanced bundle of goods. To demonstrate this fact, let us look again at Figure 16.2. Now we can take the two production possibility curves to represent those of two different countries with fixed resources. Points P_1^A and P_1^B may represent the countries' pretrade production choices. Since the *RPT* differs between the two countries, world output could be increased by having country A produce more cars and country B produce more trucks. The countries should proceed to specialize in this way until their *RPT*'s are equilibrated.[3] With country A specializing in car production, it can trade with country B to get the trucks it needs; similarly, B can trade with A for cars. Because total world output has been increased as a result of specialization, both countries will now be better off. This is the logic that provides intellectual support for the belief that "free trade is the best policy." It is important to note that the analysis uses only information about the product transformation rates between the two goods in each country, not about marginal productivity differences between countries. It is possible that a country could have an "absolute" advantage in the production of every good (in the sense that its marginal productivity of labor in the production of *every* good exceeded that of its trading partner), but such a country would still benefit from specialization and trade. For Allocation Rule 3, the important differences are in comparative, not absolute, advantages.[4]

---

[3] Actually, in Ricardo's examples the production possibility frontiers of the two countries were assumed to be straight lines. Hence the *RPT* was assumed constant over all possible output combinations. However, *RPT*'s were assumed to differ between the countries. In this situation both countries should completely specialize in production. Consider the following simple example. Suppose (following Ricardo) that there are two goods, wine and cloth, produced by two countries, say, Portugal and England. Suppose that the *RPT* (of cloth for wine) in Portugal is 2: Portugal always can trade 2 units of wine for 1 unit of cloth in production. On the other hand, suppose that the *RPT* in England is 1. Consequently, England has a comparative advantage in cloth production, whereas Portugal has a comparative advantage in wine production. Suppose, prior to trade, that England produces 100 units of cloth and 100 units of wine. It is easy to show that England can be made better off by shifting its output mix toward producing more cloth. If England were to produce one less unit of wine and one more unit of cloth, it could then trade this unit of cloth with Portugal for 2 units of wine. Consumption then would be 100 units of cloth and 101 units of wine—an improvement over the pretrade position. In fact, because the *RPT*'s are assumed to be constant, England should completely specialize in cloth production. By producing 200 units of cloth, it can trade 100 of these with Portugal for 200 units of wine. With complete specialization, then, England can consume 100 units of cloth and 200 units of wine. In the example in the text, such complete specialization would not take place because the production possibility curves are concave; that is, marginal costs begin to rise as specialization proceeds. Both countries therefore will continue to produce some of each good. In the real world, however, complete specialization is possible if equalizing *RPT*'s leads to allocations on the axes of a country's production possibility frontier or if demand patterns are especially skewed toward certain goods.

[4] Of course, Allocation Rule 2 suggests that world output also can be increased by transferring resources from countries in which the marginal productivities of factors of production are low to those in which marginal productivities are high. Although such international movements of labor and capital do take place, the flows generally are not of sufficient magnitude to equalize marginal productivities.

Lerner's Rule

The three allocation rules in the previous sections may be difficult to remember. They can be conveniently summarized in one equation: *Lerner's rule.*[5] Consider any firm, say, firm A. This firm is characterized by a *transformation function*, which states the technical relationship between the firm's inputs and its outputs. The function can be written in implicit form as

$$T^A(X_1^A, X_2^A, \ldots, X_n^A) = 0, \tag{16.12}$$

where some of the X's are inputs and some are outputs. All Equation 16.12 says is that there is some function relating these inputs and outputs. The production functions studied in Chapter 10 are a special case of a transformation function that has only one output. Here we are generalizing to allow for multi-product firms. Similarly, any other firm (B) also will have a (possibly different) transformation function relating its inputs and outputs in the form

$$T^B(X_1^B, X_2^B, \ldots, X_n^B) = 0. \tag{16.13}$$

Consider allocating any two X's, say, X_1 and X_2, efficiently between firms A and B when the levels of the other X's are held constant for each firm. Lerner's rule states that the rate of trade-off between X_1 and X_2 should be the same for both firms if these goods are to be allocated efficiently. Mathematically, this can be summarized as

$$\frac{dX_1^A}{dX_2^A} = \frac{dX_1^B}{dX_2^B}. \tag{16.14}$$

Allocation Rules 1, 2, and 3 are special cases of Equation 16.14. For example, if X_1 is an output and X_2 is an input, the equation states that the marginal physical product of X_2 in the production of X_1 should be equal for the two firms. This is exactly what was required by Rule 2. If X_1 and X_2 are both outputs, Equation 16.14 says that the *RPT* (of X_2 for X_1) should be equal for the two firms. This is Rule 3. Finally, if X_1 and X_2 are both inputs, the equation says that the *RTS* (of X_2 for X_1) should be equal between any two firms in the production of any output. Rule 1 then is simply a special case of this more general requirement.

Lerner's rule summarizes all the necessary rules for productive efficiency. Only if rates of trade-off are identical for all firms will production be efficient;[6] that is, all of these rules are required to assure that production occurs on the production possibility frontier. Impediments in an economy that hinder the equating of these rates of trade-off can make such efficiency impossible to achieve.

---

[5] Named for Abba P. Lerner, who carefully laid out the rules for efficiency in production in his book *The Economics of Control: Principles of Welfare Economics* (New York: Macmillan Co., 1944).

[6] Again the reader should be reminded that such equalities are required only for interior solutions. For corner solutions, trade-off rates may differ, even if resources are allocated efficiently. Some of the problems in this chapter illustrate this fact.

EFFICIENCY IN PRODUCT MIX

As we have already pointed out, for production to be efficient is not a sufficient condition for Pareto efficiency. The right mix of goods must also be produced. It does little good for an economy to be an efficient producer of yo-yos and xylophones if no one wants these goods. In order to assure Pareto efficiency, we need some way to tie individuals' preferences and production possibilities together. The condition necessary to ensure that the right goods are produced is that the *marginal rate of substitution* for any two goods (these rates should be identical for all individuals if we are to have efficiency in exchange—see Chapter 8) must be *equal* to the *rate of product transformation* of the two goods (these rates are identical for all firms by Allocation Rule 3). Simply phrased, the psychological rate of trade-off between the two goods in people's preferences must be equal to the rate at which they can be traded off in production.

For example, if individuals were willing to trade 2 apples for 1 orange, but resources were allocated so that 1 apple could be traded for 1 orange in production, conditions would not be efficient. Too few oranges would be produced, since individuals would be placing a relatively higher valuation on oranges than their opportunity cost in production. To grow 1 additional orange, it would be necessary to cut back the apple harvest by 1. But individuals would be willing to sacrifice 2 apples for another orange. Consequently, they would be better off to the extent of 1 apple. As in the other examples comparing trade-off rates in this book, any time the rate at which individuals are willing to trade differs from the rate at which they can technically trade, a beneficial reallocation can be made.

A Graphic Proof

Figure 16.3 illustrates the requirement for efficiency in production and exchange for a very simple case. It assumes that in this society there are only two goods (X and Y) being produced and that there is only one individual (Robinson Crusoe?) or perhaps many individuals with identical preferences. Those combinations of X and Y that can be produced are given by the production possibility frontier PP. Any point on PP represents a point of efficient production. By superimposing the individual's indifference map on Figure 16.3, however, we see that only one point on PP provides maximum utility. This point of maximum utility is at E, where the curve PP is tangent to the individual's highest indifference curve, U_2. At this point of tangency, the individual's MRS (of X for Y) is equal to the technical RPT (of X for Y); hence this is the required condition for overall efficiency. Notice that point E is preferred to every other point that is efficient in a productive sense. In fact, for any point (other than point E) such as F on the curve PP, there exist points that are inefficient but that are preferred to F. In Figure 16.3 the "inefficient" point G is preferred to the "efficient" point F. It would be preferable from the individual's point of view to produce inefficiently rather than be forced to produce the "wrong" combination of goods in an efficient way. Point E (which is efficiently produced) is superior to any such "second-best" solutions. We shall return later in this chapter to investigate why it might be desirable to choose points such as G.

Figure 16.3   *Efficiency in Product Mix in a Robinson Crusoe Economy*

In a single-person economy, the curve *PP* represents those combinations of *X* and *Y* that can be produced. Every point on *PP* is efficient in a production sense. However, only the output combination at point *E* is a true utility maximum for the individual. At *E* the individual's *MRS* is equal to the rate at which *X* can technically be traded for *Y* (*RPT*).

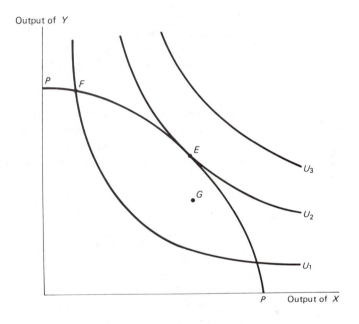

A Mathematical Proof

To demonstrate this result mathematically, assume there are only two goods (X and Y) and one individual in society (again Robinson Crusoe) whose utility function is given by $U(X, Y)$. Assume also that this society's production possibility frontier can be written in implicit form as $T(X, Y) = 0$. Robinson's problem is to maximize utility subject to this production constraint. Setting up the Lagrangian expression for this problem yields

$$\mathcal{L} = U(X, Y) + \lambda[T(X, Y)], \tag{16.15}$$

and the first-order conditions for an interior maximum are

$$\frac{\partial \mathcal{L}}{\partial X} = \frac{\partial U}{\partial X} + \lambda \frac{\partial T}{\partial X} = 0$$

$$\frac{\partial \mathcal{L}}{\partial Y} = \frac{\partial U}{\partial Y} + \lambda \frac{\partial T}{\partial Y} = 0 \tag{16.16}$$

$$\frac{\partial \mathcal{L}}{\partial \lambda} = T(X, Y) = 0.$$

Combining the first two of these equations yields

$$\frac{\partial U/\partial X}{\partial U/\partial Y} = \frac{\partial T/\partial X}{\partial T/\partial Y} \tag{16.17}$$

or

$$MRS \quad (X \text{ for } Y) = -\frac{\partial Y}{\partial X} \quad (\text{along } T) = RPT \quad (X \text{ for } Y), \tag{16.18}$$

as Figure 16.3 illustrated. We have shown that only if individuals' preferences are taken into account will resources be allocated in a Pareto efficient way. Without such an explicit reference to preferences, it would be possible, by reallocating production, to raise at least one person's utility without reducing anyone else's.

COMPETITIVE PRICES AND EFFICIENCY

The essence of the relationship between perfect competition and the efficient allocation of resources can be summarized in a very simple way. Attaining a Pareto efficient allocation of resources has been shown to require that (except when corner solutions occur) the rate of trade-off between any two goods, say, X and Y, should be the same for all economic agents. In a perfectly competitive economy the ratio of the price of X to the price of Y provides this common rate of trade-off to which all agents will adjust. Because prices are treated as fixed parameters in both individuals' utility-maximizing decisions and firms' profit-maximizing decisions, all trade-off rates between X and Y will be equalized to the rate at which X and Y can be traded in the market (P_X/P_Y). Since all agents face the same prices, all trade-off rates will be equalized and an efficient allocation will be achieved. In Chapter 8 we showed how the establishment of equilibrium prices can lead to efficient exchange. Now we integrate production into that discussion.

Efficiency in Production

To show that competitive pricing can lead to efficiency in production, we shall examine the three allocation rules developed earlier in this chapter. Allocation Rule 1 requires that a firm have identical rates at which it can trade one input for another (the rate of technical substitution, RTS) in all those outputs that it produces. But this is assured by the existence of perfectly competitive markets for inputs. In minimizing costs the firm will equate the RTS between any two inputs, say, labor and capital, to the ratio of their competitive rental prices (w/v). This will be true for any output that the firm happens to produce; hence the firm will be equating all its RTS's to the common price ratio w/v. In this way, without any external direction, the firm will be led to adopt efficient input proportions in a decentralized way.

Allocation Rule 2 will hold for a similar reason. This rule requires that every firm that produces a particular good, say, X, has identical marginal productivities of labor in the production of X. In Chapter 12 we showed that a profit-maximizing firm will hire additional units of any input (say, labor) up to the point at which its marginal contribution to revenues is equal to the marginal cost of hiring the input (see Equation 12.25). If we let P_X represent the price of the good being sold and f^1 and f^2 represent the production functions for two firms that produce X, then profit maximization requires that

$$P_X f_L^1 = w$$

and   (16.19)

$$P_X f_L^2 = w.$$

Since both firms face both the same price for X and the same competitive wage rate, these equations imply

$$f_L^1 = f_L^2.$$ (16.20)

Consequently, every firm will have the same marginal productivity of labor in the production of X. The market has succeeded in bringing about an efficient allocation of inputs among firms.

Finally, Allocation Rule 3 requires that the rate of product transformation (RPT—this is the rate at which one output can be traded for another in production) between any two goods, say, X and Y, be the same for all firms. That a perfectly competitive price system will ensure this can be most easily shown by recalling (from Chapter 15) that the RPT (of X for Y) is equal to the ratio of the marginal cost of X (MC_X) to that of Y (MC_Y). But each profit-maximizing firm will produce that output level for which marginal cost is equal to the market price. Therefore, for every firm, $P_X = MC_X$ and $P_Y = MC_Y$, and hence $MC_X/MC_Y = P_X/P_Y$ for all firms. Allocation Rule 3 is therefore satisfied.[7]

This discussion demonstrates that the profit-maximizing, decentralized decisions of many firms can achieve efficiency in production without any central direction. Competitive market prices act as signals to unify the multitude of decisions that firms make into one coherent, efficient pattern. Relying on the self-interest of entrepreneurs is a theoretically plausible way of prompting the production sector to act efficiently. Of course, as we discuss in our application on socialist pricing, the gap between theoretical plausibility and real-world performance may sometimes be quite large.

Efficiency in Product Mix

Proving that perfectly competitive markets lead to efficiency in the relationship between production and preferences is also straightforward. Since the price ratios quoted to consumers are the same ratios that the market presents to firms, the MRS shared by all individuals will be identical to the RPT that is shared by all firms. This will be true for any pair of goods. Consequently, an efficient mix of goods will be produced. Again notice the two important func-

---

[7] An interesting example of the ability of a perfectly competitive price system to satisfy Allocation Rule 3 occurs in the theory of international trade. If world prices are set by the supply-demand mechanism, and if all markets are competitive, each country's RPT will be equated to these prevailing world prices. But this will ensure that world production is allocated efficiently among countries. Each country will specialize in producing those goods of which it is a relatively efficient producer. This "theorem" forms the basis for most free trade arguments founded on principles of comparative advantage.

Figure 16.4 *Competitive Equilibrium and Efficiency in Output Mix*

Although all of the output combinations on *PP* are technically efficient, only combination X^*, Y^* is Pareto optimal. A competitive equilibrium price ratio of P_x/P_y will lead this economy to this Pareto efficient solution (see also Figure 15.5).

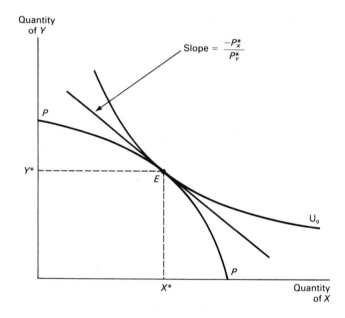

tions that market prices perform. First, they assure that supply and demand will be equalized for all goods. If a good were produced in too great amounts, a market reaction would set in (its price would fall) that would cut back on the production of the good and shift resources into other employment. The equilibrating of supply and demand in the market therefore assures that there will be neither excess demand nor excess supply. Second, equilibrium prices provide market trade-off rates for both firms and individuals to use as parameters in their decisions. Because these trade-off rates are identical for both firms and individuals, efficiency is assured.

A Graphic Proof   Our discussion of general equilibrium modeling in Chapter 15 provides precisely the tools required to show this result graphically. Figure 16.4 repeats Figure 15.5, but now we are more interested in the efficiency properties of the general equilibrium solution illustrated. Given the production possibility frontier *PP* and preferences represented by the indifference curves, it is clear that X^*, Y^* represents the efficient output mix (compare this figure to Figure 16.3). Possibly X^*, Y^* could be decided upon in a centrally planned economy if the planning board had adequate information about production possibilities and individuals' preferences. Alternatively, as we showed in Chapter 15, reliance on competitive markets and the self-interest of firms and individuals will also lead to this allocation. Only with a price ratio of P_X^*/P_Y^* will supply and demand be in equilibrium in this model, and that equilibrium will occur at the efficient product mix, E. Smith's invisible hand ensures not only that production is technically efficient (that output combinations lie on the production possibility frontier), but also that the forces of supply and demand lead to the Pareto efficient output combination. More complex models of competitive equilibrium price determination reach essentially the same conclusion.[8] Similarly, reversing all the arguments we have made would show that any Pareto efficient allocation can be attained through suitably chosen competitive equilibrium prices. This duality between pricing and allocation is examined in the context of linear programming problems in the appendix to this chapter. Overall, then, our demonstration of the "fundamental theorem" of welfare economics is complete. In the remainder of this chapter and more generally, in the remainder of this book, we will examine the lessons and limitations of this theorem.

Laissez-Faire Policies

In its most dogmatic expression, the correspondence between competitive equilibrium and Pareto efficiency provides "scientific" support for the laissez-faire position taken by many economists. For example, Smith's assertion that

> . . . the natural effort of every individual to better his own condition, when suffered to exert itself with freedom and security, is so powerful a principle that it is alone, and without any assistance, not only capable of carrying on the society to wealth and prosperity, but of surmounting a hundred impertinent obstructions with which the folly of human laws too often encumbers its operations . . .[9]

has been shown to have considerable validity. Again, as Smith noted, it is not the "public spirit" of the baker that provides bread for individuals' consumption. Rather, bakers (and other producers) operate in their own self-interest in responding to market signals. Individuals also respond to these signals in deciding how to allocate their incomes. Government intervention in this smoothly functioning process may only result in a loss of Pareto efficiency.

Such a sweeping conclusion, of course, vastly overstates the general applicability of the simple model we have been using. No one should attempt to draw policy recommendations from a theoretical structure that pays so little attention to institutional details in the real world. Still, the efficiency properties of the competitive system do provide a benchmark, a place to start to examine reasons why competitive markets may fail. Two general types of failures might be identified. First, even within the rigid confines of the perfectly competitive model, markets may fail to attain efficient equilibrium prices. Reasons for this

---

[8] See, for example, K. J. Arrow and F. H. Hahn, *General Competitive Analysis* (San Francisco: Holden-Day, 1971), chapters 4 and 5.

[9] A. Smith, *The Wealth of Nations* (New York: Random House, Modern Library ed., 1937), p. 508.

are largely theoretical in origin and relate to the informational requirements implicit in the competitive model. In Chapter 17 we will examine some of these theoretical difficulties.

Once the basic competitive assumptions that are made in Chapter 15 are abandoned, an even larger number of issues arise. We now turn to a brief cataloging of these issues.

EFFECTS OF DEPARTURES FROM THE COMPETITIVE ASSUMPTIONS

Although the number of departures from perfect competition that we might discuss is practically infinite, they can be classed into three general groupings that include most of the interesting cases: (1) imperfect competition, (2) externalities, (3) public goods. A fourth set of issues about the desirability of perfect competition, distributional considerations, are also sometimes mentioned, although such considerations do not directly affect the relationship between perfect competition and efficiency. In this section we shall discuss each of these questions separately.

Imperfect Competition

We shall use the term "imperfect competition" in a broad sense to include all those situations in which economic agents exert some market power in determining price. In this case, as the analysis of Chapter 12 illustrated, these agents will take such effects into account in their decisions. A firm that faces a downward-sloping demand curve for its product, for example, will recognize that the marginal revenue from selling one more unit is less than the market price of that unit. Since it is the marginal return to its decisions that motivates the profit-maximizing firm, marginal revenue rather than market price becomes the important magnitude. Market prices no longer carry the informational content required to achieve Pareto efficiency. Other cases of market power result in similar informational shortcomings.

As an example, consider the efficiency conditions diagrammed in Figure 16.5. Point E represents an efficient allocation in that, at this point, the MRS (of X for Y) is equal to the RPT (of X for Y). A perfectly competitive price ratio of P_X^*/P_Y^* could generate this allocation. Suppose, instead, that one of the goods, say, X, is produced under imperfectly competitive conditions whereas Y is produced under conditions of perfect competition. For good X, therefore, $MR_X < P_X^*$ whereas for Y, $MR_Y = P_Y^*$. The profit-maximizing output choice, then, is that combination of X and Y for which

$$RPT \quad (X \text{ for } Y) = \frac{MC_X}{MC_Y} = \frac{MR_X}{P_Y^*} < \frac{P_X^*}{P_Y^*} = MRS \quad (\text{of } X \text{ for } Y), \quad (16.21)$$

where the inequality holds because of the presence of imperfect competition in the market for good X. But that will entail a choice of outputs such as that represented by point B, with less X and more Y being produced than is optimal, given the existing tastes and technology. Although production is efficient at B and supply and demand are in equilibrium, the price system has no longer led to a Pareto efficient outcome.

A similar proof would hold for other circumstances in which markets are imperfectly competitive. Market power by an agent creates a divergence be-

Figure 16.5   *The Production of Good X under Imperfect Competition Prevents Efficiency in Production and Exchange*

If good *X* is produced under imperfect competition, the profit-maximizing firm will choose that output combination for which the *RPT* (of *X* for *Y*) is equal to MR_X/P_Y; this will be less than the ratio of these goods' market prices (P_X^*/P_Y^*). Production will take place at a point such as *B*, where the *RPT* is less than the individuals' marginal rates of substitution. Too little *X* will be produced as a result of imperfect competition in its market.

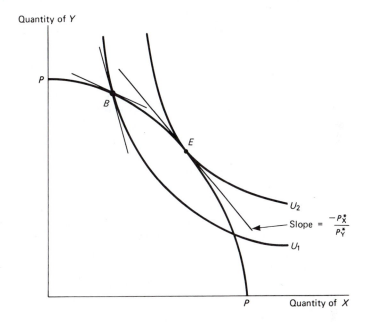

tween market price and the marginal figure that is relevant to the agent's decisions. Because of this divergence, market prices will not carry the appropriate information about relative marginal costs. The workings of the price system will be distorted, and an optimal allocation of resources cannot be achieved. In Part VI we will examine a number of models of imperfectly competitive markets in which such distortions occur.

The importance for allocational efficiency of having market prices accurately reflect marginal costs cannot be overstated. It is this condition (or a slight generalization of it, which will be taken up shortly) that directly ties together individuals' demands and the decisions of firms. When *P = MC*, what individuals are willing to pay for a good at the margin is exactly what it costs to produce that good. When the equality fails to hold, demands and productive technologies are not properly tied together; consequently, resources are not efficiently allocated. Many real-world applications of the principle of economic efficiency focus on bringing market prices into line with marginal costs.

Externalities

The competitive price system can also fail to allocate resources efficiently when there are interactions among firms and individuals that are not adequately reflected in market prices. Examples of such occurrences are numerous. Perhaps the most common one is the case of a firm that pollutes the air with industrial smoke and other debris. Such a situation is termed an *externality*: It is an interaction between the firm's level of production and individuals' well-being that is not accounted for by the price system. A more complete discussion of the nature of externalities will be presented in Chapter 24, but here we can describe why the presence of such nonmarket interactions interferes with the ability of the price system to allocate resources efficiently.

The conditions for Pareto efficiency must be redefined in a "social" sense when we recognize the possibility of externalities. For example, we would say that the *social rate of product transformation* (the rate at which society can transform one good into another) must be equal to the *social marginal rate of substitution* (the rate at which society is willing to trade one good for another) for there to be an optimal allocation of resources. The problem that arises in the presence of externalities is that economic agents pay attention to only *private* rates of transformation and substitution in their decisions. If private and social rates diverge, the perfectly competitive price system will not generate an efficient allocation.

As an application of this logic, imagine two goods in an economy, say, steel and balloons. Assume that the private marginal cost of balloons (MC_B) is identical to the social marginal cost (SMC_B); in other words, there are no externalities in balloon production. On the other hand, suppose that the production of steel entails the pollution of water and air, thereby imposing costs (such as having dirty clothes or having pollutants in drinking water) on society in addition to production costs. Hence the social marginal cost of steel (SMC_S) exceeds the private marginal cost of steel (MC_S). The social rate of product transformation of steel for balloons ($SRPT$) is then defined as

$$SRPT = \frac{SMC_S}{SMC_B}. \qquad (16.22)$$

As before, the rate at which society can transform balloons into steel is given by the ratio of these goods' (social) marginal costs. It is easy to see that this rate will exceed the private rate of product transformation (RPT):

$$SRPT = \frac{SMC_S}{SMC_B} > RPT = \frac{MC_S}{MC_B} \qquad (16.23)$$

because of the externalities associated with steel production (that is, because $SMC_S > MC_S$). Equation 16.23 says that the rate at which society can trade steel for balloons exceeds the rate at which they can be traded privately. In giving up 1 ton of steel production, additional resources for balloon production come from two sources: those resources that were previously used in steel production and those that were used in combating the effects of air and water pollution. The social RPT records the additional balloons that can be produced with the resources from both those sources. From the firm's point of view, however, the *RPT* reflects only the shifting of those resources that move directly from steel production into balloon production: The external effects are ignored in a firm's private decisions.

In this example, the required condition for efficiency is that

$$SRPT \quad \text{(of steel for balloons)} = SMRS \quad \text{(of steel for balloons)}, \quad \textbf{(16.24)}$$

where *SMRS* is the social marginal rate of substitution of steel for balloons (which is assumed to be equal to the private rate). The price system, by relying on the private motivation of firms, will generate an allocation in which

$$RPT \quad \text{(of steel for balloons)} = \frac{P_S}{P_B} < SMRS \quad \text{(of steel for balloons)}. \quad \textbf{(16.25)}$$

Since the social and private rates of product transformation differ, that allocation will not obey the conditions for a Pareto optimal allocation. The private market will tend to produce too much steel and too few balloons. In such a situation decentralized decisions, because they ignore externalities, have led to an inefficient allocation of resources.

Public Goods

A third possible failure of the price system to yield an optimal allocation of resources is related to the problem of externalities and stems from the existence of goods that must be provided on a "nonexclusive" basis. Such goods include national defense, inoculations against infectious diseases, criminal justice, and pest control. The distinguishing feature of these goods is that they provide benefits to all individuals: Once the goods are produced, it is impossible (or at least very costly) to exclude anyone from benefiting from them. Consequently, there is an incentive for each individual to adopt the position of a "free rider" by refusing to pay for the good in the hope that others will purchase it and thereby provide benefits to all. The pervasive nature of this incentive will ensure that resources are underallocated to nonexclusive goods. To avoid this underallocation, communities (or nations) may decide to have the government produce nonexclusive goods and finance this production through compulsory taxation. For that reason, nonexclusive goods frequently are termed *public goods*. In Chapter 24 we shall treat in detail the problems raised by the existence of such goods.

Distributional Considerations

A final potential difficulty with a competitive equilibrium is that the distribution of utilities (or incomes) that it generates among individuals, although efficient, may be regarded as unfair or inequitable by many members of a society. Nothing in the competitive model ensures "fairness"; indeed the precise meaning attached to that term may be quite ambiguous with different people holding widely divergent views. Still, as A. K. Sen (and many other economists) has pointed out, a perfectly competitive economy may be efficient in the Pareto sense "even when some people are rolling in luxury and others are near starvation as long as the starvers cannot be made better off without cutting into the pleasures of the rich. . . . In short, a society or an economy can be Pareto optimal and still be perfectly disgusting."[10]

To state the distributional problem, however, is not to find an acceptable solution to it. Individuals may hold various opinions about what the distribution of utility in society should be, and mechanisms to alter the market-generated distribution may be quite problematic as to their overall effects. The subject of welfare and distribution therefore is a quite complex one, and we shall return to examine it as one focus of our discussion of social choice in Chapter 25, the final chapter of this book.

THEORY OF THE SECOND BEST

These four issues about the relationship between perfect competition and Pareto efficiency arise in all economies. It is tempting to reason that a competitive price system would be Pareto optimal in those sectors of the economy in which the three allocational problems are unimportant. By using the price system in these sectors, the Pareto rules for allocational efficiency would be satisfied there; this would be a *second-best* solution to the allocational problem. Unfortunately, this intuitive answer to the problem of finding a second-best solution is not correct. In a 1956 article R. G. Lipsey and K. Lancaster addressed themselves to this general question and reached an essentially negative conclusion.[11] If certain constraints within the economic system prevent some of the Pareto conditions from holding, then, given these constraints, it generally will not be desirable to have the optimum conditions hold elsewhere. It is not true that having more (but not all) of the optimum conditions hold is necessarily superior to having fewer hold. One must analyze each individual situation and calculate optimal departures from perfect competition rather than adopting a simple piecemeal prescription.

Although a technical proof of the assertions made by Lipsey and Lancaster is rather difficult, the basic point can be made using a simple graphic argument. Suppose that society's production possibilities for two goods are represented by the frontier *PP* in Figure 16.6 and that preferences are given by the indifference curves. Assume also that there is a constraint in the economic system that makes the true optimal point (*E*) unattainable. Let this constraint be represented by the line *AB*; combinations of goods to the northeast of line *AB* cannot be achieved because of the constraint. Society's optimization problem is to maximize welfare (as represented by the indifference curves), subject to the constraint *AB*. The figure makes clear that this optimal point need not be on the *PP* frontier; the point *C* is definitely preferable to the technically efficient point *D*. This, then, demonstrates the principal negative result of the theory of the second best: If all the conditions for a Pareto optimum cannot be satisfied, it is not necessarily true that fulfilling some of them is the best policy. Rather the allocational problem must be approached as a problem in

[10] A. K. Sen, *Collective Choice and Social Welfare* (San Francisco: Holden-Day, 1970), p. 22.

[11] R. G. Lipsey and K. Lancaster, "The General Theory of Second Best," *Review of Economic Studies* 24 (1956–1957): 11–32.

Figure 16.6 *Graphic Demonstration of the Theory of the Second Best*

In the diagram the constraint *AB* prevents the optimal point *E* from being achieved. It is not true that, given this constraint, a society should strive for productive efficiency. Points such as *C* are preferred to those efficient points, such as *D*, which are obtainable. Second-best points are therefore not necessarily efficient points.

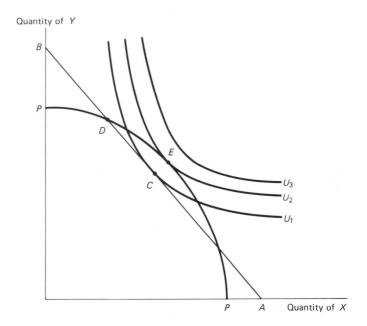

constrained optimization. With complete knowledge of society's preferences and technology, it may in fact be possible to derive some optimal departures from perfectly competitive pricing.[12]

SUMMARY

In this chapter we have formalized Adam Smith's initial conjectures about the efficient properties of the "invisible hand" of competitive market forces. The equivalence between Pareto efficient allocations and perfectly competitive equilibria is the principal discovery of modern welfare economics. It provides the point of departure into practically all areas of normative, policy-oriented economics. Several major points were illustrated in our development of this fundamental relationship:

[12] For a general theoretical discussion, see W. J. Baumol and D. F. Bradford, "Optimal Departures from Marginal Cost Pricing," *American Economic Review* (June 1970): 265–283.

- Pareto's definition of an efficient allocation of resources—that no one person can be made better off without making someone else worse off—provides the basic focus for normative welfare theory. Because the definition stresses unambiguous improvements in welfare, it does not require interpersonal comparisons of well-being.

- Productive or technical efficiency is a necessary though not sufficient condition for Pareto efficiency. Achieving technical efficiency (that is, being on the production possibility frontier) requires that three marginal allocation rules hold: (1) equality of rates of technical substitution across different outputs; (2) equality of marginal productivities among firms; and (3) equality of rates of product transformation across firms.

- Pareto efficiency requires both productive efficiency and efficiency in the choice of output mix. This latter goal can be attained by choosing that technically efficient output combination for which the rate of product transformation between any two goods is equal to individuals' marginal rate of substitution for these goods.

- Reliance on competitive equilibrium prices will yield a technically efficient allocation of resources because profit-maximizing firms will make choices that are consistent with the three marginal allocation rules.

- Existence of competitive equilibrium prices for outputs will also result in an efficient output mix. By so doing, the correspondence between Pareto efficiency and competitive equilibria is made complete.

- Informational difficulties may prevent the establishment of Pareto efficient equilibrium prices (see Chapter 17). Such violations of the competitive assumptions as imperfect competition, externalities, or the existence of public goods may also distort the allocation of resources away from Pareto efficiency.

- The general theory of the second best suggests caution in applying the correspondence between Pareto efficiency and competitive prices on a piecemeal basis.

Application

LANGE MODEL OF SOCIALIST PRICING

One of the more interesting (and important) issues to which the efficiency properties of a perfectly competitive price system have been applied is the problem of planning in a socialist economy. Early writers on this subject claimed that an efficient allocation of resources would be impossible to achieve in a socialist state because of the vast amount of information and infinite computations that would be necessary. It was argued that no central planning board could possibly assimilate all the information that the price system provides in a market economy; without the free operation of a market, resource allocation would be hopelessly inefficient. These views were challenged by the Polish economist Oscar Lange in a series of articles in the late 1930s.[13] Lange suggested that a social-

[13] The principal article appears in edited form in O. Lange, *On the Economic Theory of Socialism* (New York: McGraw-Hill Book Company Paperbacks, 1964; originally published by the University of Minnesota Press).

ist economy could achieve an efficient allocation of resources (at least in theory) by utilizing the desirable properties of markets in
permitting decentralized decision making, while
at the same time having social ownership of the
means of production. Because an examination
of Lange's proposals illustrates as much about
the problems of resource allocation in a market
economy as it does about resource allocation in
a centrally planned one, we shall outline his
scheme in some detail and then present some
evidence on its operation in practice.

Socialist Price Setting

Under Lange's system the central planning
board is charged with setting prices that are to
be regarded by all economic agents as fixed.
Individuals are free to make consumption decisions given these prices, and presumably they
will do so in a utility-maximizing way. Firm
managers are under strict orders to minimize
the costs of producing any level of output and
are to produce that output for which price
equals marginal cost. In other words, they are
to approximate the decisions that managers of
perfectly competitive firms would make in order
to maximize profits even though the firms are
effectively owned by the state. What Lange's
model attempts to do is to approximate the
efficient features of the perfectly competitive
model.

From a theoretical viewpoint there are at
least three interesting theoretical questions that
we might raise about the Lange model: How is
equilibrium between supply and demand assured? How are factor supplies regulated? How
are possible externalities treated?

Equilibrium between Supply
and Demand

The first of these problems is perhaps the most
important. If the central planning board sets
nonequilibrium prices, chaos is certain to result. A price set too high will mean that an excess supply of the good in question will be
produced. Similarly, a price set below equilibrium will have the result of bringing about

long shopping queues and other manifestations
of excess demand. In a market economy such
problems are avoided by relying on the interactions of supply and demand to establish equilibrium price. Because this market interaction
would not take place in a planned economy,
the central planning board is under a strict man-
date to raise prices of those goods in excess demand and lower the prices of those that are being oversupplied. It is hoped that, by closely
observing inventories and other indicators of
market equilibrium, the central planning board
would be able to adjust prices so as to respond
to any possible discrepancies between supply
and demand. Ideally, the board should be free
from political constraints in its setting of prices.

Factor Supplies

In the Lange model, labor is allocated in the
same manner that is assumed to operate in a
market economy. Wage rates are set by the central planning board, and individuals make their
occupational choices based on those rates. Similarly, firms demand labor based on the marginal
productivity principle because of the requirement that they "maximize profits." The board
must be careful to set equilibrium wage rates.

It is in the supply of capital that Lange's solution differs markedly from the perfectly competitive model. Since capital is not privately owned
in a socialist economy, no rental payments are
made to individuals. Individuals therefore have
no incentive to own capital, so the central planning board is charged with the responsibility of
deciding how much output to withhold from
current production for purposes of capital accumulation. Firms are, however, charged an
"efficient" rental rate for the capital equipment
they use in order to ensure that the available
supply of capital is allocated among firms in an
efficient way.

Externalities

To deal with externalities, Lange proposed a final ingenious solution to the problem of achieving an efficient allocation of resources. His suggestion was that external costs of production

should be imposed (in the form of taxes) on the responsible firms. This would shift the firms' marginal cost curves up and would reduce the quantities they were willing to supply at the prevailing price. Then a shortage would appear in the market at the current price, and the central planning board would respond to this excess demand by raising prices. Finally, this action would presumably cut back on the demand for those products that are produced with harmful external side effects. Lange's suggestion ensures an allocation of resources that adequately reflects true social costs. We shall see in Chapter 24 that a similar solution might be desirable in a capitalist economy as well.

Market Socialism in Practice

Although Lange's model of market socialism is primarily a theoretical construction, it has had important influences on many economic reforms in socialist economies. Prominent examples of such reform measures include the development of relatively free labor markets in Yugoslavia, deregulation of pricing for smaller firms in Hungary, and the encouragement of export-oriented entrepreneurship in some provinces in China. In none of these cases, however, is the Lange model employed in its strict form. Powerful central bureaucracies continue to exercise considerable control over price setting, and, contrary to Lange's procedures, supply-demand imbalances continue to persist in many markets. Government officials involved in price setting are, not surprisingly, more interested in pursuing their own political goals than in following the mechanical rules the Lange model requires.[14] Similarly, firms' managers often find

they must pursue a variety of goals in addition to maximization of profits (e.g., maintenance of employment) so the types of behavior required in the Lange model become diluted. Since the types of mechanisms that enforce profit maximization in competitive markets are weakened under socialism (firms can obtain long-term subsidies, for example), managers may be somewhat freer to address these other goals without fiscal repercussions. Overall, then, any study of market socialism in practice must start with a realistic appraisal of the institutional constraints that arise in applying the Lange model.

These comments are especially relevant to recent economic reform movements in the Soviet Union. Although such reforms have a long intellectual history,[15] most recent activity stems from the "Gorbachev reforms" first put forth in detail in June 1987. These reforms give smaller enterprises considerably more leeway in setting prices than was true in the past and permit an increase in the role of the legal private sector, especially in agriculture. In principle, such reforms could lead to a dual-sector Lange-type model in which a system of private markets coexists with a sector operating under principles of market socialism. But, under the Gorbachev plans, the state retains considerable control over both of these sectors so the possibilities for political intervention remain significant. The slowdown in Soviet economic growth during the years after 1975 provides a considerable impetus to improve matters through economic reform, however, so the ultimate evolution of this dual system remains unclear.[16]

---

[14] For a discussion of these issues in the Hungarian context, see J. Kornai, "The Hungarian Reform Process," *Journal of Economic Literature* (December 1986): 1725–1728, especially.

[15] For an application of Lange's ideas, see E. G. Liberman, "The Plan, Profits, and Processes" in A. Nove and D. M. Nutti, eds., *Socialist Economics: Selected Readings* (Middlesex: Penguin Books, 1962), pp. 309–318.

[16] See G. Ofer, "Soviet Economic Growth: 1929–1985," *Journal of Economic Literature* (December 1987): 1767–1833.

SUGGESTED READINGS

Arrow, K. J., and Hahn, F. H. *General Competitive Analysis.* San Francisco: Holden-Day, 1972. Chaps. 1 and 2.

Comprehensive treatment of the efficiency of perfect competition. Heavy going in spots, but many literary sections too.

Bator, F. M. "The Anatomy of Market Failure." *Quarterly Journal of Economics* 72 (August 1958): 351–379.

Good graphical and simple mathematical treatment of reasons for market failure.

Bator, F. M. "The Simple Analytics of Welfare Maximization." *American Economic Review* (March 1957): 22–59.

Good graphical integration of productive and exchange efficiency.

Feldman, A. *Welfare Economics and Social Choice Theory.* Amsterdam: Martinus Nijhoff, 1980.

First two chapters give a good summary of efficiency notion in general equilibrium models.

Koopmans, T. C. *Three Essays on the State of Economic Science.* New York: McGraw-Hill Book Company, 1957.

Uses activity analysis to develop several efficiency notions.

Russell, R. R., and Wilkinson, M. *Microeconomics: A Synthesis of Modern and Neoclassical Theory.* New York: John Wiley & Sons, 1979. Chaps. 15, 16, and 17.

Good treatment of efficiency issues. Notation sometimes hard to follow, however.

Sen, A. K. *Collective Choice and Social Welfare.* San Francisco: Holden-Day, 1970. Chaps. 1 and 2.

Basic reference on social choice theory. Early chapters have a good discussion of the meaning and limitations of the Pareto efficiency concept.

PROBLEMS

16.1

Suppose that Robinson Crusoe produces and consumes fish (F) and coconuts (C). Assume that during a certain period he has decided to work 200 hours, and is indifferent as to whether he spends this time fishing or gathering coconuts. Robinson's production for fish is given by

$$F = \sqrt{L_F}$$

and for coconuts by

$$C = \sqrt{L_C}$$

where L_F and L_C are the number of hours spent fishing or gathering coconuts. Consequently,

$$L_C + L_F = 200.$$

Robinson Crusoe's utility for fish and coconuts is given by

$$\text{utility} = \sqrt{F \cdot C}.$$

a. If Robinson cannot trade with the rest of the world, how will he choose to allocate his labor? What will the optimal levels of F and C be? What will his utility be? What will be the *RPT* (of fish for coconuts)?

b. Suppose now that trade is opened and Robinson can trade fish and coconuts at a price ratio of $P_F/P_C = 2/1$. If Robinson continues to produce the quantities of F and C in part (a), what will he choose to consume, given the opportunity to trade? What will his new level of utility be?

c. How would your answer to part (b) change if Robinson adjusts his production to take advantage of the world prices?

d. Graph your results for parts (a), (b), and (c).

16.2

In an economy with two individuals (A and B), use the Edgeworth box diagram to discuss the results of exchange in the following situations.

   a.   Neither individual cares about the other's utility.

   b.   A is altruistic and gains some utility from B's welfare.

   c.   A is envious and loses utility as B is made better off.

16.3

Consider an economy with just one technique available for the production of each good:

Good	Food	Cloth
Labor per unit output	1	1
Land per unit output	2	1

   a.   Suppose that land is unlimited, but labor equals 100. Write and sketch the production possibilities frontier.

   b.   Suppose that labor is unlimited but land equals 150. Write and sketch the production possibilities frontier.

   c.   Suppose that labor equals 100 and land equals 150. Write and sketch the production possibilities frontier. (Suggestion: What are the intercepts of the production possibilities frontier? When is land fully employed? Labor? Both?)

   d.   Explain why the production possibility frontier of part (c) is concave.

   e.   Sketch the relative price of food as a function of its output in case (c).

   f.   If consumers insist on trading 4 units of food for 5 units of cloth, what is the relative price of food? Why?

   g.   Explain why production is exactly the same at a price ratio of $P_F/P_C = 1.1$ as at $P_F/P_C = 1.9$.

   h.   Suppose that capital is also required for producing food and clothing and that capital requirements per unit of food are 0.8 and per unit of clothing are 0.9. There are 100 units of capital available. What is the production possibilities curve in this case? Answer part (e) for this case.

16.4

In the country of Ruritania there are two regions, A and B. Two goods (X and Y) are produced in both regions. Production functions for region A are given by

$$X_A = \sqrt{L_{XA}}$$

$$Y_A = \sqrt{L_{YA}}.$$

L_X and L_Y are the quantity of labor devoted to X and Y production, respectively. Total labor available in region A is 100 units. That is,

$$L_X + L_Y = 100.$$

Using a similar notation for region B, production functions are given by

$$X_B = \frac{1}{2}\sqrt{L_X}$$

$$Y_B = \frac{1}{2}\sqrt{L_Y}$$

There are also 100 units of labor available in region B:

$$L_X + L_Y = 100.$$

a. Calculate the production possibility curves for regions A and B.
b. What condition must hold if production in Ruritania is to be allocated efficiently between regions A and B (assuming that labor cannot move from one region to the other)?
c. Calculate the production possibility curve for Ruritania (again assuming that labor is immobile between regions). How much total Y can Ruritania produce if total X output is 12?

Hint: A graphic analysis may be of some help here.

16.5

The country of Extremum produces only skis (S) and water skis (W), using capital (K) and labor (L) as inputs. The production function for both S and W are fixed proportions. It takes 2 units of labor and 1 unit of capital to produce a pair of skis. Water skis, on the other hand, require 1 unit of labor and 1 unit of capital. If the total supply of labor in Extremum is 150 units and the total supply of capital is 100 units, construct the production possibility curve for this economy. Are all inputs fully employed at every point on the production possibility curve? How do you explain any unemployment that might exist?

16.6

Suppose that all of the firms in Utopia obey the Pareto conditions for efficiency except General Widget (GW). That firm has a monopoly in production of widgets and is the only hirer of widget makers in the country. Suppose that the production function for widgets is

$$Q = 2L$$

(where L is the number of widget makers hired). If the demand for widgets is given by

$$P = 100 - Q$$

and the supply curve of widget makers by

$$w = 20 + 2L,$$

how many widgets should WG produce in order to maximize profits? At that output, what will L, w, and P be? How does this solution compare to that which would prevail if GW behaved in a competitive manner? Can you evaluate the gain to society of having GW be competitive?

16.7

Develop a graphic example of how either non-convex indifference curves or a non-concave production possibility frontier may yield supply demand equilibria that are inefficient. Discuss whether such inefficient equilibria would be stable.

Appendix to Chapter 16

Linear Programming, Pricing of Inputs, and Duality

This appendix has two basic purposes: to introduce the mathematical tool of linear programming and to use this tool to demonstrate some additional relationships between the efficient use of resources and the pricing of those resources. Of course, a detailed treatment of linear programming is beyond the scope of this book, and therefore our analysis must be brief.[1] We shall examine only one specific example of linear programming techniques. In this example, an economy is assumed to have fixed amounts of various productive inputs and must choose how to allocate these to the production of two goods, cars and small trucks. In order to avoid introducing demand conditions, we shall assume that the prices of the two goods remain constant throughout our analysis. More specifically, we shall assume that the price of trucks (P_T) is $8,000 each and that the price of cars (P_C) is $10,000 each. The sole goal of the central planner in our simple economy is to allocate the available resources to car and truck production so that the total value of output is as large as possible. That is, the goal is to choose car output (C) and truck output (T) so that

$$\text{total value} = TV = P_T \cdot T + P_C \cdot C$$
$$= 8{,}000 \cdot T + 10{,}000 \cdot C$$

(16A.1)

is as large as possible given available resources.

Before we approach the solution to this problem through the use of linear programming, it may be useful first to demonstrate the general kind of solution we might derive by applying the tools we have presented earlier. The most direct way to proceed is by using a graphic analysis. In Figure 16A.1 we have drawn the production possibility frontier for the economy. The curve PP represents those combinations of cars and trucks that can be produced given the inputs available. Our goal now is to choose that point on the PP frontier that provides maximum revenues. This maximization process is shown in the figure. The several parallel straight lines (labeled TV_1, TV_2, TV_3) record those combinations of cars and trucks that provide equal value. The combinations lying along TV_3 provide more in total value than do those on TV_2, which in turn provide more value than do those on TV_1. The slope of these lines is given by $-P_T/P_C$ ($= -8{,}000/10{,}000 = -4/5$), since this ratio of prices tells how cars can be traded for trucks in the market while keeping total revenue constant. The total value of cars and trucks produced is as large as possible when output combination C^*, T^* is chosen. This combination produces total revenues of TV_2, and it is the only combination that is capable of providing this amount:

---

[1] For an interesting though fairly difficult survey of linear programming techniques, see R. Dorfman, P. A. Samuelson, and R. M. Solow, *Linear Programming and Economic Analysis* (New York: McGraw-Hill Book Company, 1958).

Figure 16A.1   *Value Maximization in a Hypothetical Economy*

PP represents the feasible combinations of cars and trucks that can be produced with available resources. If a central planner wishes to maximize the total value of production (*TV*), the combination *C**, *T** should be produced. At this output combination the *RPT* (of trucks for cars) is equal to the ratio of these goods' prices (P_T/P_C).

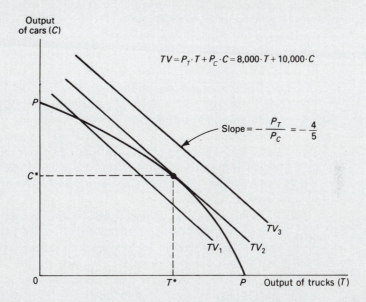

Output of cars (*C*)

$$TV = P_T \cdot T + P_C \cdot C = 8{,}000 \cdot T + 10{,}000 \cdot C$$

Slope $= -\dfrac{P_T}{P_C} = -\dfrac{4}{5}$

TV_1 TV_2 TV_3

Output of trucks (*T*)

All other feasible output combinations on *PP* provide less total value than does this optimal choice. At *C**, *T** the production possibility frontier is exactly tangent to the total value line *TV*$_2$. This is the type of result that should by now be familiar. At the optimal point, the rate at which cars technically can be traded for trucks is equal to the rate at which these two goods can be traded in the market. In other words, the rate of product transformation (of trucks for cars) is equal to the price ratio P_T/P_C.

We shall now turn to an examination of the way in which this same problem might be solved by linear programming techniques. We shall see that these techniques provide not only an answer that is qualitatively very similar to what we just derived but also additional insights into the resource allocation questions raised by the problem.

A LINEAR PRO-GRAMMING STATEMENT OF THE PROBLEM

Linear programming is a mathematical technique that is particularly suited to solving the problem we have stated. The technique was developed as a systematic way to find the maximum values of linear functions (such as Equation 16A.1) when the variables in these functions (that is, *C* and *T*) are constrained in the values they can take on by other linear functions. In order to show how this technique works, we must first examine the factors in the economy that constrain the output choices that are feasible. There are two types of con-

Table 16A.1   *Resources and Technology in a Hypothetical Economy*

Resource	Total Available	Required to Produce 1 Truck	Required to Produce 1 Car
Labor	720 labor-hours	1 labor-hour	2 labor-hours
Machines	900 machine-hours	3 machine-hours	1 machine-hour
Steel	1,800 tons	5 tons	4 tons

straints present in any productive economy: Total quantities of various inputs are fixed, and certain technological rules (that is, production functions) must be followed in turning these inputs into outputs. For the purposes of our car-truck example, we shall assume that there are only three possible inputs: labor, machines, and steel. The quantities of these inputs that are assumed to be available are shown in the second column of Table 16A.1. No production plan can be implemented that uses more than 720 labor-hours, 900 machine-hours, or 1,800 tons of steel.

Table 16A.1 also indicates the amounts of each of these inputs that are required to produce one car or one truck. It takes 1 labor-hour, 3 machine-hours, and 5 tons of steel to build a truck; it takes 2 labor-hours, 1 machine-hour, and 4 tons of steel to build a car. Notice that the production techniques shown in Table 16A.1 are of the fixed-proportions type: No substitution between inputs is possible. This kind of "linear" technology is one characteristic of most linear programming problems.

We are now in a position to examine the constraints that the availability of inputs places on the combinations of cars and trucks that can be produced. If we again let C represent the number of cars to be produced and T the number of trucks, then the first line of Table 16A.1 records the fact that all possible choices of T and C must obey the constraint

$$1 \cdot T + 2 \cdot C \le 720. \qquad (16A.2)$$

That is, the quantity of labor employed in truck production (remember, it takes 1 labor-hour to build one truck) plus the quantity employed in car production (that is, 2 labor-hours per car) cannot exceed the 720 labor-hours available. Equation 16A.2 might be called the "labor-hours" constraint in production.

Similar constraints exist for machines and for steel. The machine-hour constraint is

$$3 \cdot T + 1 \cdot C \le 900, \qquad (16A.3)$$

and the steel constraint is

$$5 \cdot T + 4 \cdot C \le 1,800. \qquad (16A.4)$$

These constraints record that no more machines or steel may be used than are available.

Figure 16A.2   *Construction of the Production Possibility Frontier for the Linear Programming Problem*

The heavy line in this diagram is the production possibility frontier for cars and trucks implied by the input constraints. It is the perimeter of the set of output combinations that satisfies all the constraints.

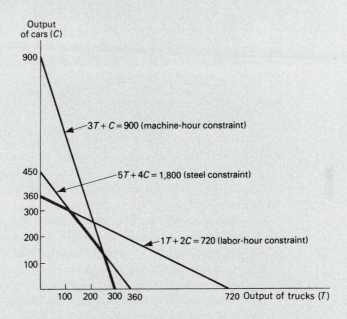

Given the three input constraints, our problem now is to find values of T and C that satisfy these constraints and make the total value of output (TV),

$$TV = 8,000 \cdot T + 10,000 \cdot C, \tag{16A.5}$$

as large as possible. That, then, is our linear programming problem.

Construction of the Production Possibility Frontier

One possible (and very time-consuming but simple) solution to the problem would be to enumerate all the combinations of C and T that satisfy the constraints, calculate the total value of each of these, and choose the one with the largest value. A far more efficient procedure makes use of graphic techniques. Figure 16A.2 graphs the three resource constraints. Since any feasible combination of C and T must satisfy *all* three constraints, we are interested only in those points in the diagram that fall on or below all three lines. The heavy line in Figure 16A.2 indicates the outer perimeter of such feasible choices. Points on or inside this curve can be produced.

For example, should the central planner in the economy decide to produce only cars, the heavy line indicates that 360 could be produced. In producing only cars, the economy "runs out" of labor-hours first (there is enough steel to produce 450 cars and enough machines to produce 900 cars). For trucks, on

---

Figure 16A.3   *Maximization of Revenue in the Linear Program*

By superimposing several lines of equal revenue on the production possibility frontier, the point of maximum revenue can be found. This point occurs where the labor-hour and steel constraints intersect.

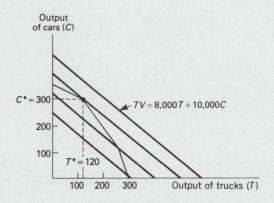

Linear Programming Solution of the Problem

the other hand, the binding constraint is machine availability. There are only enough machines to build 300 trucks if only trucks are built. Other combinations of cars and trucks on or inside the heavy line in Figure 16A.2 similarly satisfy all the constraints. The curve is in fact the production possibility frontier for the simple economy we have described. Notice that even though the production functions used here are of a fixed-proportion, constant returns-to-scale type, the production possibility frontier is concave because the two goods use the various inputs in different proportions.

We can now use the production possibility frontier we derived in Figure 16A.2 to solve our maximum value problem in much the same way that the problem was solved in Figure 16A.1. Figure 16A.3 shows the production possibility frontier together with several lines of equal revenue. From the figure we can see that the value-maximizing point is that output combination, C^*, T^*, where the labor-hour constraint and the steel constraint intersect.[2] (You should refer back to Figure 16A.2 to check that these are indeed the constraints that intersect at C^*, T^*.) Solving the two constraints for C^* and T^* gives

$$1T + 2C = 720 \text{ (labor-hour constraint)}$$
$$5T + 4C = 1{,}800 \text{ (steel constraint)}$$

(16A.6)

---

[2]This point in a sense satisfies the rule that the *RPT* should equal the ratio P_T/P_C. The *RPT* along the labor-hour constraint is $-\frac{1}{2}$; along the steel constraint the *RPT* is $-\frac{5}{4}$. The vertex at C^*, T^* includes all slopes between $-\frac{1}{2}$ and $-\frac{5}{4}$. But the ratio $-P_T/P_C$ is given by $-\frac{4}{5}$, which lies between these two values. Hence C^*, T^* is the revenue-maximizing point. In linear programming problems the optimal solution will usually occur at vertices, such as the one illustrated.

or, from the labor-hour constraint,

$$T = 720 - 2C.$$

Therefore, by substitution into the steel constraint,

$$5(720) - 10C + 4C = 1,800$$
$$-6C = -1,800.$$

Hence our optimal solution is

$$C^* = 300$$

and   (16A.7)

$$T^* = 120.$$

That means that 120 trucks should be produced along with 300 cars. The revenue provided by these outputs is $3,960,000; this is the maximum value possible given the resource constraints. Notice that at this production level not all the available machine-hours are being used. Production of 300 cars and 120 trucks requires only 660 machine-hours, whereas 900 are available. The observation that at the value-maximizing output level there are unused machines has important implications for the pricing of machines, as we shall now demonstrate.

DUALITY AND THE PRICING OF INPUTS

Thus far we have said nothing about the price of inputs in this linear programming problem. The economy had the inputs on hand and set about the task of maximizing the value of its output. A linear programming problem that is related to the *primal* problem above is the *dual* linear programming problem of finding input prices associated with the optimal choice of C and T. Formally, these dual input prices solve the following linear programming problem.

Minimize

$$M = 720P_L + 900P_K + 1,800P_S,   \text{(16A.8)}$$

subject to

$$P_L + 3P_K + 5P_S \geq 8,000$$
$$2P_L + P_K + 4P_S \geq 10,000,   \text{(16A.9)}$$

where P_L, P_K, and P_S are the (nonnegative) per-unit prices of labor, capital, and steel. This dual problem can be given an economic interpretation. We are asked to find prices for the inputs that minimize the total value of all inputs available but that also have the property that neither the production of cars nor the production of trucks earns a pure profit (this is stated by the inequalities of Equation 16A.9 of the dual). For example, the first inequality says that the costs of producing one truck (that is, the cost of 1 labor-hour, 3 machine-hours, and 5 tons of steel) should not be less than the price of a truck. If constraints such as those of Equation 16A.9 were not imposed, the minimization problem could be trivially solved by setting $P_L = P_K = P_S = 0$.

Without going into formal detail, it should be clear that the dual problem is related in some way to the original problem. All the parameters that appeared in the primal problem also appear in the dual but in different places. In particular, notice that quantities that appeared in the original constraints now appear as coefficients in the dual objective function (M) and vice versa. Also, the constraints of the primal problem seem to have been "turned on their side" in the dual.

A graphic solution to the dual linear programming problem will not be presented here because it would require a three-dimensional graph. It must be taken on faith that the solution to the dual program turns out to be

$$P_L = \$3,000$$

$$P_K = \$0 \tag{16A.10}$$

$$P_S = \$1,000.$$

These are the prices of L, K, and S that minimize 16A.8 and obey the two constraints given by Equation 16A.9. The reader may wish to check to see that this is indeed true.

There are several important features to be noted about this solution.

1. With these input prices the inequalities in Equation 16A.9 are exactly satisfied. Neither good is produced at a loss. Hence both goods can be produced in the economy.
2. The value of M with these input prices is \$3,960,000. It is no coincidence that this is identical to the maximum value for TV that we found in the primal problem. Such a relationship holds between the primal and the dual solutions of all linear programs. Here this equality resembles the income-output identity in the National Income and Product Accounts. The total value of output is equal to the total value of inputs.
3. The input that was not a binding constraint in the primal problem (machine-hours) is given a price of \$0 in the dual problem. This result tells economists that adding machines in this economy would have no effect on the value of output. On the other hand, since labor and steel are the inputs that prevent output from being increased, these inputs are given positive prices. The values given in Equations 16A.10 for P_L and P_S indicate how much extra value would be provided by one more unit of these inputs. The reader may wish to show, for example, that an increase in labor by 1 unit will cause the total of output to increase by \$3,000 (if we allow the economy to produce fractional parts of cars and trucks).[3]

Further Observations on Duality

These linear programming problems clearly demonstrate the relationship between the optimal choice of outputs and the correct choice of input prices. The optimal allocation of a fixed amount of inputs to the production of a variety

[3] The firm will produce ⅚ of an additional car in this situation but will cut truck production by ⅔ of a truck. Consequently, total revenue is changed by ⅚ · 10,000 − ⅔ · 8,000, which is \$3,000.

of possible outputs has as its associated dual problem the optimal pricing of those available inputs. The solution of one problem is equivalent to the solving of the other.[4] This relationship has been used widely. For example, the computation of factor prices from a linear programming model can be very useful for economic planning in less-developed economies because such "shadow prices" can provide information about how important certain inputs are. Occasionally, however, such computed prices may differ greatly from the actual prices of the inputs. For example, there are institutional reasons (labor unions, minimum wages, and so forth) why some groups of workers may have high wages, even though labor is an overabundant resource in the particular country. On the other hand, linear programming models may suggest that the "real" value of labor is rather low. Planners therefore should adopt productive techniques that utilize labor to a greater extent than would seem economically warranted by looking only at market wage rates.

In a similar way linear programming has been used by corporations in order to make more efficient management decisions. One such use arises when a firm wishes to decentralize its decision making. To do so, the firm often divides its operations among several "profit centers," which are responsible for all production decisions within a specific area. One problem with which the management of such decentralized firms must contend is how to charge each profit center for the general company inputs (such as plant and equipment, administrative staff, and advertising staff) that it uses. Only by correctly choosing the bookkeeping prices of these inputs can the firm's management be sure that the decisions of the manager of each profit center will produce desirable overall results. Linear programming has been used extensively for calculating the prices of such intracompany resources.

Of course, these two examples merely hint at the huge number of applications that linear programming has had. Others include such widely different applications as the planning of natural gas pipelines and railway yards, investigating the optimal portfolio of stocks for a mutual fund to own, and studying the movement of seasonal labor forces in Africa. In many of these applications a linear program's duality features are utilized.

SUGGESTED READINGS

Beals, R. E.; Levy, M. B.; and Moses, L. N. "Rationality and Migration in Ghana." *Review of Economics and Statistics* 49 (November 1967): 480–486.

Uses linear programming methods to estimate implicit wage rates for seasonal migrants.

[4]Linear programming problems may not always have solutions. If a linear programming problem and its associated dual have "feasible" solutions (solutions that satisfy the constraints of the problems), then they each have optimal solutions that have the qualitative properties listed above. For an elegant and concise discussion of the relationship between primal and dual linear programming problems with applications to a variety of allocational problems, see D. Gale, *The Theory of Linear Economic Models* (New York: McGraw-Hill Book Company, 1960).

Dorfman, R. "Mathematical or 'Linear' Programming: A Nonmathematical Exposition." *American Economic Review* 43 (December 1953): 797–825.

Very good, readable survey of linear methods.

Dorfman, R.; Samuelson, P. A.; and Solow, R. M. *Linear Programming and Economic Analysis.* New York: McGraw-Hill Book Company, 1958.

Basic reference on linear programming. Has several interesting economic applications together with a discussion of more advanced methods.

Farrar, D. E. *The Investment Decision under Uncertainty.* Englewood Cliffs, N.J.: Prentice-Hall, 1962.

Use of linear programming to derive optimal investment portfolios.

Gale, D. *The Theory of Linear Economic Models.* New York: McGraw-Hill Book Company, 1960.

Advanced text with very elegant proofs.

Glicksman, A. M. *An Introduction to Linear Programming and the Theory of Games.* New York: John Wiley & Sons, 1963.

Nice, low-level introduction. Good discussion of the simplex method of solution.

Hicks, J. R. "Linear Theory." *Economic Journal* 70 (December 1960): 671–709.

Very readable survey article.

Waverman, L. "The Preventive Tariff and the Dual in Linear Programming." *American Economic Review* 62 (September 1972): 620–629.

Use of linear programming to evaluate the costs of a tariff on imported goods.

CHAPTER 17

Information and Competitive Equilibrium

Thus far, our model of competitive equilibrium price determination has assumed that economic actors have complete information. Specifically, both demanders and suppliers were assumed to know the prices of all available goods and to use those prices in making allocational decisions. As we pointed out in Chapter 9, however, such a complete degree of knowledge is unlikely to exist in the real world. Acquiring information about the prices and other characteristics of economic goods is a costly activity. It is also an activity at which some individuals may be more efficient than others—a trained auto mechanic is in a much better position to judge the value of a used car than is an economics professor, for example. We might, therefore, expect actual market information to be both imperfect and unevenly distributed. In this chapter we will examine some of the theoretical consequences of such informational inequalities. Our coverage parallels the analysis of Chapters 15 and 16. That is, we begin by examining some of the ways in which the existence of imperfect information might affect the ability of markets to establish equilibrium prices. We also discuss some of the ways in which nonequilibrium prices might occur. Finally, we ask whether equilibrium prices that are established in the presence of imperfect information will have the same efficiency properties as those in the simple models of the previous chapter.

ESTABLISHING COMPETITIVE EQUILIBRIUM PRICES

One of the most difficult informational problems faced by any competitive market is how an equilibrium price is discovered. What market signals do suppliers and demanders use to adjust their behavior toward equilibrium? Are temporary, nonequilibrium prices relied upon to make such decisions, or are other mechanisms available? In mathematical terms, suppose the competitive market price for some commodity starts at an arbitrary price, say, P_0. We know from Chapter 15 that for most such markets there exists an equilibrium price, P^*, for which

$$D(P^*) = S(P^*), \tag{17.1}$$

where D and S are the demand and supply functions for the good. Now we wish to examine how market price moves from P_0 to P^*. We begin with some theoretical answers proposed by economists, then turn to examine briefly some of the informational issues that arise in applying these theoretical suggestions.

The Impartial Auctioneer and Recontracting

To explain the movement of price to its equilibrium level, some economists have relied on the fictitious notion of an *impartial auctioneer*. The auctioneer is charged with calling out prices and recording the actions of buyers and sellers. Only when the auctioneer calls a price for which the quantity demanded is identical to that which is supplied will trading be permitted to take place. Presumably, the auctioneer will use information about the market supply and demand curves to guide the pricing decisions, but precise rules for this operation are seldom spelled out.

Although some markets do operate with actual auctioneers (the market for antiques is a good example), in general, no such agents are involved in price determination. Numerous attempts have, therefore, been made to give this fictional concept a behavioral interpretation. One such interpretation is the idea of *recontracting* in which buyers and sellers are assumed to enter into provisional contracts before the exchange of goods actually takes place. Each of these provisional contracts is voided if it is discovered that at the agreed-upon price, the market is not in equilibrium. Only when market-clearing prices for all markets are discovered will exchange take place. Recontracting is then a form of haggling over price, and price determination should therefore be regarded as one aspect of contract theory.

Walrasian Price Adjustment

A second suggestion, which is similar to recontracting, was proposed by Walras.[1] In this scheme equilibrium prices are a goal toward which the market gropes. Changes in price are motivated by information from the market about the degree of *excess demand* at any particular price. Mathematically, the Walrasian adjustment mechanism specifies that the change in price over time is given by

$$\frac{dP}{dt} = k[D(P) - S(P)] = k[ED(P)] \qquad k > 0, \tag{17.2}$$

where $ED(P)$ represents excess demand at price P. Equation 17.2 says that price will increase if there is positive excess demand and will decrease if excess demand is negative. Such a mechanism is called a *tâtonnement* ("groping") *process*. This mechanism is pictured graphically in Figure 17.1. For any price above the equilibrium price (P^*), the *tâtonnement* process operates to lower price. Similarly, for prices less than P^* the process raises price. In Figure 17.1a the equilibrium price P^* is *stable*; there are forces that move P toward P^*. This may not always be the case, however, as Figure 17.1b illustrates. In this case the *tâtonnement* rule causes price to move away from its equilibrium level.

---

[1] L. Walras, *Elements of Pure Economics*, trans. W. Jaffee (Homewood, Ill.: Richard D. Irwin, 1954).

Figure 17.1 *Two Possible Supply-Demand Configurations and Their Walrasian Stability*

The Walrasian definition of stability specifies that prices will adjust in response to excess demand. If at some price, quantity demanded exceeds quantity supplied, price is assumed to rise. Conversely, if quantity demanded is less than that supplied, price falls. In (a) these rules ensure that the equilibrium price P^* will be stable. Starting anywhere, there are forces moving price toward P^*. This is not true for the supply-demand configuration shown in (b). There the Walrasian mechanism will cause price to move away from P^*.

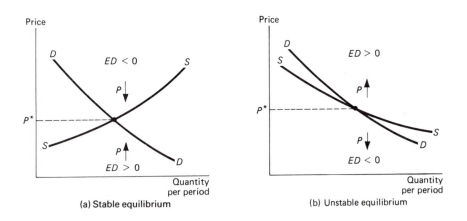

(a) Stable equilibrium   (b) Unstable equilibrium

It is easy to see that if the supply curve has a positive slope, the equilibrium price P^* is stable.

Another way to see the Walrasian result is to examine the excess demand function, $ED(P)$. Three possible shapes for the excess demand function are shown in Figure 17.2. For each of these shapes equilibrium prices exist at those points where excess demand equals 0. In Figure 17.2a the equilibrium price P_1 is a stable equilibrium in the Walrasian sense. If price initially starts above P_1, the Walrasian process will tend to move it downward toward P_1. Similarly, if the initial price is less than P_1, it will be adjusted upward. The excess demand function in Figure 17.2b is unstable. The Walrasian process will tend to move price in the wrong direction. In Figure 17.2c there are multiple equilibria: P_1, P_2, and P_3 all cause excess demand to be 0. However, only P_1 and P_3 are stable in the Walrasian sense. There are no forces moving price toward P_2 (although if price started exactly at P_2, it would stay at this equilibrium position).

A Mathematical Derivation

In mathematical terms the Walrasian price adjustment procedure reflected in Equation 17.2 is a differential equation. To study the (local) behavior of such an equation in the vicinity of an equilibrium price, it is possible to use a Taylor approximation[2] of the form

---

[2]For a discussion of this approximation, see footnote 12 of Chapter 9.

Figure 17.2 *Using Excess Demand Curves to Show Walrasian Stability*

Using the excess demand function $[ED(P) = D(P) - S(P)]$, we can investigate the stability of various equilibrium prices that occur whenever $ED(P) = 0$. However, only if the slope of the excess demand curve is negative $[ED'(P) < 0]$ at the equilibrium point will the Walrasian adjustment mechanism ensure stability. Notice, for example, that in (c) stable and unstable equilibria alternate.

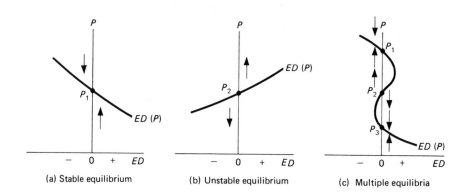

(a) Stable equilibrium   (b) Unstable equilibrium   (c) Multiple equilibria

---

$$\frac{dP}{dt} \cong k[ED'(P^*)] \cdot (P - P^*). \tag{17.3}$$

This equation is a simple first-order differential equation. An important theorem in the theory of such equations is that their solutions have the same stability properties as do the nonlinear equations that they approximate (Equation 17.2). Hence, for the purpose of our analysis of stability, we can study Equation 17.3, which is considerably easier to solve. Indeed the general solution to this type of equation will be of the form[3]

$$P(t) = (P_0 - P^*)e^{kED'(P^*)t} + P^*, \tag{17.4}$$

where P_0 represents the initial price at time, $t = 0$. For this system to be stable (that is, for $P(t)$ to approach P^* as t gets large), it must be the case that $ED'(P^*) < 0$. In words, an increase in price must reduce excess demand, and a fall in price must increase excess demand. This is the result illustrated in Figure 17.2. Some numerical examples are provided in the problems to this chapter.

Marshallian Quantity Adjustment

The adjustment process we have just discussed views price as the motivating force in the adjustment of markets to equilibrium. Individuals and firms respond to price changes by moving along their respective demand and supply

---

[3] For an introduction to differential equations, see A. Chiang, *Fundamental Methods of Mathematical Economics*, 2d ed. (New York: McGraw-Hill Book Company, 1974), chap. 14. For a more detailed treatment, see L. S. Pontryagin, *Ordinary Differential Equations* (Reading, Mass.: Addison-Wesley Publishing Co., 1962).

Figure 17.3 *Marshallian Quantity Adjustment*

Under Marshallian adjustment, a difference between demand and supply prices sets up incentives for economic agents to alter output levels. If demand price exceeds supply price ($ED^{-1} > 0$), Q will rise. If supply price exceeds demand price ($ED^{-1} < 0$), Q will fall. The adjustment mechanism shown in the figure is stable, since Q converges to Q^*.

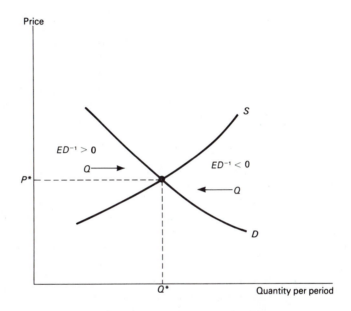

curves until an equilibrium price-quantity combination is reached. A somewhat different picture of the adjustment process was suggested by Marshall in his classic *Principles of Economics*.[4] There Marshall theorized that individuals and firms should be viewed as adjusting quantity in response to imbalances in quantities demanded and supplied and that price changes follow from these changes in quantity. If we let $D^{-1}(Q)$ represent the price that demanders are willing to pay for each quantity and $S^{-1}(Q)$ represent the price that suppliers require for each quantity (that is, their marginal cost), then the Marshallian adjustment mechanism can be represented by

$$\frac{dQ}{dt} = k[D^{-1}(Q) - S^{-1}(Q)] = k[ED^{-1}(Q)] \qquad k > 0. \qquad (17.5)$$

In words, movements in quantity toward equilibrium are motivated by discrepancies between the price individuals are willing to pay and the price firms wish to receive. When those two figures coincide, quantity adjustment ceases.

Quantity adjustment is illustrated in Figure 17.3. For quantities below equilibrium (Q^*), demand price exceeds supply price. Quantity produced and con-

[4]A. Marshall, *Principles of Economics*, 8th ed. (London: Macmillan & Co., 1920), pp. 287–288.

sumed therefore increases. For quantities above equilibrium, supply price exceeds demand price, providing incentives for quantity reduction. As was the case for the price-adjustment mechanism pictured in Figure 17.1a, the Marshallian mechanism pictured in Figure 17.3 implies that the price-quantity equilibrium is a stable one. Starting from any initial position, forces come into play that move economic agents toward equilibrium. The precise mechanism by which the movement comes about, however, differs between the Walrasian and Marshallian models.

Transactions and Information Costs

The Walrasian and Marshallian adjustment processes (Equations 17.2 and 17.5) represent mathematically elegant solutions to the market adjustment problem. But these solutions are largely devoid of economic content. Contrary to the other theoretical developments in this book, these adjustment processes do not represent any sort of optimizing behavior by economic agents. Rather, the differential equations have been plucked, more or less, out of the air. To develop a behaviorally oriented theory of market adjustment, one must examine the costs involved in reaching market equilibrium and illustrate how economic actions will seek to minimize those costs.

As a simple example, consider the question of whether market adjustments will be primarily of the Walrasian (price) or Marshallian (quantity) type. Presumably, the choice will be dictated by the types of transactions and information costs involved. If prices can easily be changed (say, by switching price tags) and if information about changed prices is readily disseminated among buyers and sellers, Walrasian price adjustment may predominate. Important examples are provided by auctions. In these cases, the auctioneer calls out tentative prices and can readily perceive how demanders react to them. Even in this simple case, however, a would-be buyer faces difficult decision problems because he or she does not know precisely what rival bidders will do. Whether a particular bidding sequence reaches a true equilibrium price for the item being auctioned may depend on the kinds of information shared by bidders (how much do they know about a potential oil-producing tract, for example) and on the bidding strategies used by the parties.[5]

Market situations that have characteristics markedly different from auctions may be more likely to exhibit Marshallian quantity adjustment. If prices are difficult to alter (perhaps because they are specified in long-term contracts) and if the quantity traded can be changed with little cost (say, by using inventory stockpiles), the information necessary to reach an equilibrium will come mainly from quantity flows. Macroeconomics frequently uses such observations, for example, to explain why employment rather than wage rates tends to adjust to cyclical fluctuations in demand.

Ultimately, however, such speculation about the choice of adjustment mechanism is largely beside the point because neither the Walrasian nor the

---

[5]Prices set by auction are "equilibrium prices" in the sense that the good to be sold actually changes hands. But they may not represent an equilibrium in the sense that buyers' and sellers' decisions are, after the fact, optimal. For a discussion of the theory of auctions, see R. P. McAfee and J. McMillan, "Auctions and Bidding," *Journal of Economic Literature* (June 1987): 699–738.

Marshallian mechanisms reflect actual behavior by economic agents. To devise behavioral models requires the adoption of the principle that some agent (typically the firm) sets a price and then adjusts that price in response to experience. Some general models of this type have been developed based on assumed patterns of search behavior by demanders (who are looking for bargains), but these models are too specialized to examine here.[6] Instead we will move on to more tractable representations of the price determination process.

DISEQUILIB-RIUM PRICING

One problem that interferes with the specification of a realistic adjustment process is that the traditional model pictures supply and demand decisions as being made simultaneously. There are two equations (the supply and demand functions) to be solved simultaneously for two unknowns (price and quantity). The theory offers no guidance on how demanders or suppliers behave in disequilibrium situations. If the simultaneity assumption could be relaxed (by assuming, say, that supply decisions are made first), this problem would be simplified. For example, if firms based their current output decisions on the market price occurring in the previous period, then output in the current period could be regarded as fixed; there would be no current-period supply response. The analysis of pricing in the "very short run" would then be the relevant model to study. The mechanisms for pricing in such situations are relatively well understood (auctions are the primary example): Here price acts only as a rationing device for demand; it has no influence on production in the current period. In the next period, the market price established in this period will be the one relevant to output decisions; thus there is some (lagged) response of output to price changes.

A Formal Model

These ideas can be shown most clearly by a simple *cobweb model* of price determination. Suppose that firms' supply decisions in period t depend linearly on the market price that prevailed in period $t - 1$:

$$\text{supply in period } t = Q_t^S = a + bP_{t-1}. \tag{17.6}$$

The total quantity supplied is then sold in the market for whatever it will bring. Market demand depends on current price:

$$\text{demand in period } t = Q_t^D = c - dP_t; \tag{17.7}$$

and equilibrium in the market at time t necessitates that

$$Q_t^S = Q_t^D. \tag{17.8}$$

This view of the market assumes the following sequence of events: Firms decide on Q_t^S by referring to P_{t-1}; demanders (perhaps by auction) bid for Q_t^S and in so doing establish P_t. Firms' output decisions in period $t + 1$ are then based on P_t. An equilibrium price in this system is one that will be repeated each

---

[6] For a survey, see F. Hahn, "Stability," in K. J. Arrow and M. D. Intriligator, eds., *Handbook of Mathematical Economics*, vol. 2 (Amsterdam: North Holland Publishing Co., 1982), Chap. 16.

period: $P^* = P_t = P_{t-1}$. This equilibrium price can be found by setting $Q_t^S = Q_t^D$:

$$a + bP_{t-1} = c - dP_t, \qquad (17.9)$$

or at an equilibrium price, P^*:

$$a + bP^* = c - dP^*$$

and   (17.10)

$$P^* = \frac{c - a}{b + d}.$$

*A General
Solution*

Also, any price, P_t, can be "predicted" from the market-clearing Equation 17.9 by

$$P_t = -\frac{b}{d} P_{t-1} + \frac{c - a}{d}. \qquad (17.11)$$

Hence, for any arbitrary initial price P_0,

$$P_1 = -\frac{b}{d} P_0 + \frac{c - a}{d}$$

$$P_2 = -\frac{b}{d} P_1 + \frac{c - a}{d}$$

$$= \left(-\frac{b}{d} \right)^2 P_0 + \frac{c - a}{d} \left[1 + \left(-\frac{b}{d} \right) \right]$$

and by repeated substitution,

$$P_t = \left(-\frac{b}{d} \right)^t P_0$$

$$+ \frac{c - a}{d} \left[1 + \left(-\frac{b}{d} \right) + \left(-\frac{b}{d} \right)^2 + \cdots + \left(-\frac{b}{d} \right)^{t-1} \right]. \qquad (17.12)$$

Therefore[7]

$$P_t = \left(-\frac{b}{d} \right)^t P_0 + \frac{c - a}{d} \left\{ \frac{d}{b + d} \left[1 - \left(-\frac{b}{d} \right)^t \right] \right\} \qquad (17.13)$$

$$= \left(P_0 - \frac{c - a}{b + d} \right) \left(-\frac{b}{d} \right)^t + \frac{c - a}{b + d}.$$

---

[7]This line is a result of the mathematical formula:

$$\frac{1}{1 - X} = 1 + X + X^2 + \cdots + X^n + \cdots.$$

Let $X = -b/d$. Therefore $1/(1 - X) = d(b + d)$.

Figure 17.4   *Cobweb Model of Price Determination*

In the cobweb model of lagged response to price by firms, a theory of nonequilibrium pricing can be established. Whether these prices will approach an equilibrium price level will depend on the relative slopes of the demand and supply curves. In the configuration shown in (a), convergence will take place, whereas in (b) it will not. A third possibility (not shown) would be for the supply and demand curves to have slopes so that the price perpetually oscillates about P^*.

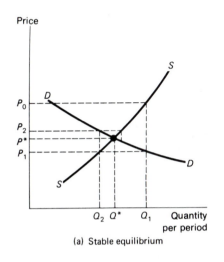

(a) Stable equilibrium

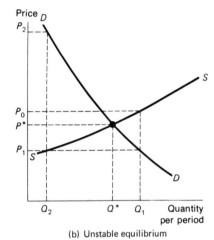

(b) Unstable equilibrium

Finally, then, by substitution of the equilibrium price, P^*, from Equation 17.10:

$$P_t = (P_0 - P^*) \left(-\frac{b}{d} \right)^t + P^*. \tag{17.14}$$

This equation shows the time pattern of prices (P_t) starting from any initial position. We wish to know if P_t approaches P^*.

Stability of the Cobweb Model

Equation 17.14 says that market price will oscillate around P^* [since the factor $(-b/d)^t$ is alternatively positive and negative]. P_t will approach P^* provided that $(-b/d)^t$ goes to 0 for large values of t. This will be the case if $b/d < 1$ or, equivalently, if $b < d$. On the other hand, if $b > d$, the price oscillations will become wider over time. These two possibilities are illustrated in the "cobweb" supply-demand graphs in Figure 17.4. The demand curve in Figure 17.4a is flat relative to the supply curve $(b < d)$.[8] This means that any initial price (say, P_0)

[8]The reader should be warned that the demand and supply curves are expressed here with the dependent variable on the horizontal axis rather than in the "usual" way of having the dependent variable on the vertical axis. Consequently, somewhat more care must be employed in thinking about what the words "flat" and "steep" imply.

will ultimately converge to P^*. The sequence of events depicted in this diagram would be as follows: P_0 dictates the amount supplied in period 1 (Q_1); this determines period 1's price (P_1) by reference to the demand curve; P_1 then is used in firms' decisions to set Q_2; and the process is repeated. From the diagram it is clear that the market price will work its way toward P^*. In Figure 17.4b, however, this does not happen. Here the oscillations of price are explosive, since $d > b$. The reason for this is that demand is relatively inelastic. Hence prices change rather greatly in response to quantity changes. But these price changes interact with a fairly elastic supply curve to produce even greater quantity changes, and the whole process quickly becomes explosive.[9]

Price Expectations: Rational and Otherwise

The regularly oscillating prices of the cobweb model are a clear indication of the model's excessive simplicity. It would take an extreme lack of sophistication on the part of both buyers and sellers not to recognize the pattern in price movements. And once such patterns were recognized, it seems clear that economic agents would take them into account in their decisions. To examine some of the issues that arise in modeling such expectations about price, assume (as in the cobweb model) that demanders respond to the current market price, which is known with certainty, but that suppliers must respond only to what they expect the market price to be. Hence, demand is given by

$$Q_t^D = c - dP_t \qquad (17.15)$$

and supply by

$$Q_t^S = a + bE(P_t), \qquad (17.16)$$

where $E(P_t)$ is what suppliers expect market price to be at time t.[10]

The behavior of this model obviously will depend on how suppliers form price expectations. If, for example, suppliers are myopic and always expect the price in period $t - 1$ to prevail in period t, we would have

$$E(P_t) = P_{t-1}, \qquad (17.17)$$

and the model would reduce to the cobweb case studied previously. A more sophisticated supplier might use the entire past history of a good's price to predict its level in period t:

$$E(P_t) = f(P_{t-1}, P_{t-2}, \dots, P_{t-n}), \qquad (17.18)$$

but this too might give rise to some more complex types of oscillating behavior.

[9] A third possibility would be that $b = d$. In this case $-b/d = -1$, and market price would oscillate perpetually about P^*.

[10] This supply equation is a special case of a supply function of the form $Q_t^S = f(P_t \mid I_{t-1})$, where P_t is a random variable whose subjective distribution depends on the information available to the firm at time $t - 1$ (that is, I_{t-1}). In general, I_{t-1} will be to some degree under the firm's control. That is, it can invest in information acquisition in period $t - 1$ to provide a more accurate picture of the likely distribution of prices in period t. We will not examine that process here, however.

A particularly intriguing hypothesis about the formation of price expectations was proposed by Muth in the early 1960s.[11] He suggested that one (and perhaps the only) method of forming expectations that is consistent with general optimizing behavior is to make such expectations on a "rational" basis by incorporating all available information about the market in question. Specifically, a supplier who knew the precise forms of the demand and supply curves could calculate the equilibrium price

$$P^* = \frac{c - d}{b + a} \tag{17.19}$$

and then use this to form the price expectation

$$E(P_1) = P^* = \frac{c - d}{b + a}. \tag{17.20}$$

Using this expected price, supply will be at its equilibrium level, and the market will be free of the fluctuations observed in the cobweb model. In the absence of any other information or transactions costs, equilibrium will be established instantly.

The information requirements for the rational expectations solution are quite severe. Not only must the supplier know the precise values of the economic parameters a, b, c, and d, but it must also be assumed that no other random influences affect the supply or demand relationships. Models that relax both of these assumptions have been developed, principally in the field of macroeconomics.[12] As might be expected, the results of the rational expectations approach are not so simple once more realistic assumptions are employed, but the approach has revolutionized economists' thinking about expectations.[13]

INFORMATION AND PARETO EFFICIENCY

Existence of imperfect information may not only affect the ability of markets to establish equilibrium prices, but it may also call into question the correspondence between competitive prices and Pareto efficiency. Our proof of the efficiency of competitive prices assumed that these equilibrium prices were known to all economic actors. If some actors are not fully informed about prevailing prices or (what amounts to the same thing) if information about product quality is not freely available, Adam Smith's invisible hand may not be very effective. Incorrect decisions based on faulty information about price or quality can result in inefficient allocations.

---

[11] John Muth, "Rational Expectations and the Theory of Price Movements," *Econometrica* (July 1961): 315–335.

[12] See, for example, T. Sargent and N. Wallace, "Rational Expectations and the Theory of Economic Policy," *Journal of Monetary Economics* (April 1976): 169–183.

[13] In the theory of financial markets, for instance, the rational expectations notion leads to the "efficient market hypothesis"—that the current market price of an asset reflects all available information about that asset so that any future price movements must depend on the random and unpredictable arrival of new information.

A vast number of economic models seek to explore the consequences of imperfect information about prices. Here we will briefly review some of these models that are based on a competitive framework (that is, models with large numbers of buyers and sellers). In Chapter 19 we will return to the topic of information when we examine product differentiation in markets with relatively few producers.

Asymmetric Information and Adverse Selection

One of the first formal models to incorporate imperfect information into a competitive framework was an examination of the market for used cars by G. A. Akerlof.[14] Although as we shall see, this model applies to any situation in which buyers and sellers of a good have differing ("asymmetric") amounts of information, it has come to be known as the "lemons model" because of its association with poor-quality cars. To develop his model, Akerlof assumed that used cars come in a number of qualities, say, n. Each of these qualities has a price associated with it ($P_1 \ldots P_n$) representing the value these cars would have to buyers and sellers in a fully informed situation. The asymmetry in information in this problem arises from the fact that sellers of used cars have much more experience with their cars than do would-be buyers. Specifically, Akerlof assumed that sellers know precisely the value of the car they wish to sell, but buyers have no way of knowing a car's quality until they own it. Buyers base their evaluation of cars on the average quality of all cars available, $\overline{P}$. In equilibrium, therefore, the price of used cars will be $\overline{P}$ and the quantity supplied, Q_S, will be given by

$$Q_S = \sum_{P_i < \overline{P}} S_i(P_i), \qquad (17.21)$$

where S_i is the supply of cars of quality P_i, and the sum is taken only over qualities less than $\overline{P}$. For better quality cars, $P_i > \overline{P}$, a would-be seller would rather hold on to his or her car since it is worth more than (poorly informed) demanders are willing to pay. In this equilibrium then, supply equals demand, but buyers are ultimately unsatisfied since the average quality of used cars traded is less than they expect, $\overline{P}$—only the poor-quality cars are brought to the market so the average quality of cars traded is lower than the overall average of the entire stock of used cars.

The inefficiency of Akerlof's lemons model arises from the fact that some Pareto optimal transactions do not occur. Both buyers and sellers would be willing to trade at a price in excess of $\overline{P}$ for a high-quality car. But the seller has no way to convince the buyer that his or her car is not a lemon. Indeed, matters may even deteriorate further if buyers learn over time that average quality falls short of $\overline{P}$ and drop their price offers accordingly. In this case, supply and quality will (according to Equation 17.21) fall even further, and an even larger number of Pareto optimal trades will be forgone.

---

[14]G. A. Akerlof, "The Market for Lemons: Quality Uncertainty and the Market Mechanism," *Quarterly Journal of Economics* (August 1970): 485–500.

In formal terms, the lemons problem is one example of adverse selection in the marketplace:

Definition:	

Adverse Selection
When buyers and sellers have asymmetric information about product quality, market outcomes will exhibit adverse selection—the quality of goods traded will be biased to favor the actor with better information.

Adverse selection in the used car market is mirrored in most other markets for used durable goods. Indeed, in some cases (trading between individuals in precious gems, for example) the problem may be so severe as to foreclose practically all exchanges. The problem arises in insurance markets when buyers of health or life insurance know more about their own health than do sellers of such insurance. In this case, only high-risk individuals may choose to buy insurance since those who know they are low risk may find insurance too costly. In markets for inputs, adverse selection may be manifested if firms are less able to judge productivity than is the inputs' supplier. Especially productive workers may have no way to illustrate their skills to would-be hirers and may turn down job offers based on employers' perceptions of the average skills of only "typical" workers. In all of these cases, therefore, informational asymmetries may cause competitively determined prices to depart from Pareto optimality.

Acquisition and Provision of Information

In many situations, however, these conclusions drawn from the lemons model may be premature since they take no account of possible actions by market participants to improve information flows. The inefficiency inherent in the adverse selection outcomes provides a powerful incentive for economic actors to acquire information. It might, therefore, be expected that Smith's invisible hand would also be operating in the market for information. In the used car case, for example, potential buyers might spend both time and money to appraise used cars they are considering. Sellers might also attempt to provide information by showing maintenance records or by offering limited warranties. That is, they will attempt to "signal" the quality of the car they wish to sell. Of course, as any used car buyer knows, such information may not always be accurate (one might, for example, question a ten-year-old car with 45,000 miles on the odometer).

The lemons example, therefore, suggests that information about product quality can be acquired and provided in many different ways and that such information may not always be perfectly accurate. To develop models of how competitive markets operate in such situations is very difficult, and there are no universally accepted results. To illustrate some of the problems in building such models, consider the comparatively simple question of how a market equilibrium should be defined. Suppose the quantity demanded of a product can be represented by

$$\text{quantity demanded} = D(P, \alpha), \tag{17.22}$$

where α is the information used by the demander in making his or her decisions. Similarly, supply can be represented by

$$\text{quantity supplied} \; = \; S(P, \beta), \tag{17.23}$$

where β is the supplier's information set. As before, an equilibrium occurs where

$$D(P^*, \alpha) \; = \; S(P^*, \beta), \tag{17.24}$$

where P^* is the equilibrium price for this good given the information sets α and β. But these information sets themselves are not exogenously determined. Rather, as the used car example suggests, they are determined endogenously as part of demanders' and suppliers' overall decision processes. Furthermore, since the market equilibrium price, P^*, reflects these information sets, rational actors may draw additional information from this price itself. That is, actors may, to some extent, judge quality by price. A rational buyer of expensive cameras, for example, might reason that current prices reflect actual quality differences so he or she need not gain any more information before making a purchase. The fact that other buyers have read *Consumers' Report* is already reflected in the market price. If everyone adopts this position, however, there will not be sufficient pressure on the demand side of the market to assure that the assumption of efficient pricing is valid.

In these situations, then, the concept of market equilibrium is a complex one. It is possible to develop models in which no such equilibrium exists or in which multiple equilibria exist.[15] Given the current state of information theory, it is not possible to state with any certainty which of these models can be considered to be of general validity. Empirical testing of the models is in its infancy.

Equilibrium and Pareto Efficiency

Because of these complexities in defining market equilibria in cases of imperfect information, it is not surprising that there are no fundamental results about the nature of Pareto optimal allocations in such situations.[16] It is clear that equilibrium allocations with imperfect information will generally be Pareto inferior to allocations with perfect information (as the lemons model suggests), but that conclusion is not an especially interesting one. That information is imperfect and costly to acquire is a fact of nature in all economic organizations. The relevant allocational question is which mechanisms produce Pareto efficient results from among all those that operate within a given informational environment. In the language of Chapter 16, Pareto efficiency with imperfect information must be approached as a problem in "second-best" allocations. The informational environment poses a series of constraints on any

[15] For a discussion, see J. E. Stiglitz, "The Causes and Consequences of the Dependence of Quality on Price," *Journal of Economic Literature* (March 1987): 1–48.

[16] Some formal models have been developed by assuming competitive markets exist in all possible contingent commodities (see Chapter 9). But existence of such a complete set of markets in the real world is doubtful. For a theoretical discussion, see K. J. Arrow and F. H. Hahn, *General Competitive Analysis* (San Francisco: Holden-Day, 1971), pp. 122–126.

economic system, and Pareto efficiency must be defined subject to these constraints. Competitive markets incorporate powerful incentives both to generate and to reveal information. But their Pareto efficiency in a variety of imperfect information contexts has not been clearly demonstrated.

SUMMARY

In this chapter we have examined how the perfectly competitive market structure performs in situations of limited information. The general purpose of this examination was to explore the limits that should be placed on interpretations of the fundamental correspondence between competitive equilibria and Pareto efficient allocations. We showed that extending this correspondence to situations involving imperfect information raised many complex questions:

- Information costs may determine how markets adjust to new equilibrium configurations and the time that such adjustments require. For example, whether Walrasian (price) or Marshallian (quantity) adjustment dominates will be importantly influenced by transactions and information costs.
- In some models of market adjustment, disequilibrium prices may occur. The path by which such prices approach equilibrium can be importantly affected by the information available and by how expectations are based on that information.
- With asymmetric information, adverse selection may result in Pareto inefficient allocations, at least in models with no information acquisition possibilities.
- In general, economic actors will wish to acquire and to signal information about market transactions in which they participate. Equilibrium prices (if they exist) will incorporate prevailing information levels and may themselves be sources of information to market participants.

Application

DISPERSION OF RETAIL PRICES

Imperfect information and transactions costs may result in market situations that appear to be out of equilibrium, but in fact are quite stable. One example is the widely differing prices in a market for a seemingly homogeneous product. When information is costly, a potential buyer may choose not to check all the possible sellers for the lowest price, but may instead adopt relatively simple low-cost search procedures such as shopping at a customary outlet. In this situation then, market forces that tend to assert the law of one price will be weakened, and a degree of dispersion (that is, price differences among sellers) can persist indefinitely.[17]

[17] For an elegant theoretical analysis of price searching and price dispersions, see G. J. Stigler, "The Economics of Information," *Journal of Political Economy* (June 1961): 213–225.

Retail Gasoline Prices

An illustration of this sort of situation was provided in a 1976 study of gasoline prices by H. Marvel.[18] In that study the author examined the dispersion of prices for regular-grade gasoline in 20 U.S. cities. He found that the average observed price range within the cities was nearly 5 cents per gallon and that, in some instances, ranges as wide as 20 cents per gallon seemed quite compatible with market equilibrium.

Perhaps more interestingly, Marvel found that the degree of price dispersion in particular cities seemed to be associated with the costs and benefits of price information to consumers. For example, cities in which gasoline use was relatively greater tended to have less price dispersion possibly because drivers in such cities had greater incentives to seek out low prices. Similarly, cities that required gas stations to post prices that were readable from the highway tended to have smaller price dispersions, probably because such price posting provided simple price information to passing motorists.

[18] Howard Marvel, "The Economics of Information and Retail Gasoline Price Behavior," *Journal of Political Economy* (October 1976): 1033–1059.

Advertising of Prices

Price advertising can have a similar effect of providing information and reducing price dispersion. Such effects have been found for products such as eyeglasses and prescription drugs where some states permit price advertising and others do not. Similarly, states that ban price advertising for lawyers' and physicians' services (using the rationale that such advertising is "unprofessional") tend to have both higher average prices and a wider dispersion in prices than do states that permit advertising. Heavy price advertising of "big ticket" durable goods (televisions, refrigerators, dishwashers and so forth) by discount chains probably has the same effect although some dispersion in prices may remain if different retailers provide different amounts of post-sale service to their customers.

In markets with perfect information, price differences for a homogeneous product are Pareto inefficient. Additional trades between low-price-receiving sellers and high-price-paying buyers would improve the allocation of resources. But, in the examples discussed here, remaining price dispersions may reflect imperfect information, and they can be reduced only through more information acquisition. If the gains to such acquisition (better exchange) do not exceed its costs, the dispersion might represent an efficient market outcome.

SUGGESTED READINGS

Akerlof, G. A. "The Market for Lemons: Quality Uncertainty and the Market Mechanism." *Quarterly Journal of Economics* (August 1970): 488–500.

Early demonstration of the inefficiency of asymmetric information. Suggests many additional applications of the model.

Arrow, K. J. "Limited Knowledge and Economic Analysis." *American Economic Review* 64 (March 1974): 1–10.

Arrow's AEA presidential address about the need to develop further the economic theory of information.

Grossman, S., and Stiglitz, J. "On the Impossibility of Informationally Efficient Markets." *American Economic Review* (June 1980): 393–408.

Illustrates some difficulties in defining equilibrium in markets with efficient acquisition of information and where market prices incorporate all available information.

Harlow, A. A. "The Hog Cycle and the Cobweb Theorem." *Journal of Farm Economics* 42 (November 1960): 842–853.

Classic study of the "corn-hog" cycle in agricultural markets.

McCallum, B. T. "Competitive Price Adjustments: An Empirical Study." *American Economic Review* 64 (March 1974): 56–65.

Interesting study of inventory behavior by the lumber industry and its implications for price adjustment models.

Phelps, E. S., et al. *Microeconomic Foundations of Employment and Inflation Theory.* New York: W. W. Norton & Co., 1970.

Collection of articles about the importance of market dynamics to macroeconomic questions.

Spence, M. *Market Signalling.* Cambridge, Mass.: Harvard University Press, 1974.

Examines the consequences of markets in which information is imperfect and where participants try to signal product quality. Many applications, especially to the labor market.

Stigler, G. J. "The Economics of Information." *Journal of Political Economy* 69 (June 1961): 213–225.

First detailed study of the economics of price-searching behavior.

PROBLEMS

17.1

If the demand curve has a negative slope and the supply curve has a positive slope, the equilibrium price is stable under both Walrasian and Marshallian adjustment. Use a graphic analysis to show that for the case where both demand and supply curves have negative slopes, the equilibrium price will be stable under one method of adjustment, but unstable under the other.

17.2

Suppose that the market demand for a particular product is given by

$$Q_D = -2P + 13$$

and the industry supply curve by

$$Q_S = 2P^2 - 12P + 21.$$

What are the equilibrium prices for this market? Which of these prices is stable by the Walrasian criterion?

17.3

Suppose that the demand curve for corn at time t is given by

$$Q_t = 100 - 2P_t$$

and that supply in period t is given by

$$Q_t = 70 + E(P_t)$$

where $E(P_t)$ is what suppliers expect the price to be in period t.

a.   If in equilibrium $E(P_t) = P_t$, what are the price and quantity of corn in this market?

b.   Suppose that suppliers are myopic and use last period's price as their expectation of this year's price (that is, $E(P_t) = P_{t-1}$). If the initial market price of corn is $8, how long will it take for price to get within $.25 of the equilibrium price?

c.   If farmers have "rational" expectations, how would they choose $E(P_t)$?

17.4

Under the assumptions of part b of problem 17.3, solve explicitly for P_t as a function of the initial price, P_0, and time. Graph this relationship and show that the oscillations about the equilibrium price are damped. Suppose the supply function were instead given by

$$Q_t = 50 + 3P_{t-1}.$$

Would the equilibrium price now be stable?

17.5

The used car supply in Metropolis consists of 10,000 cars. The value of these cars ranges from $5,000 to $15,000 with exactly one car being worth each dollar amount between these two figures. Used car owners are always willing to sell their cars for what they are worth. Demanders of used cars in Metropolis have no way of telling the value of a particular car. Their demand depends on the average value of cars in the market ($\bar{P}$) and on the price of the cars themselves (P) according to the equation

$$Q = 1.5\bar{P} - P$$

a. If demanders base their estimate of $\bar{P}$ on the entire used car market, what will its value be and what will be the equilibrium price of used cars?

b. In the equilibrium described in part a, what will be the average value of used cars actually traded in the market?

c. If demanders revise their estimate of $\bar{P}$ on the basis of the average value of cars actually traded, what will be the new equilibrium price of used cars? What is the average value of cars traded now?

d. Is there a market equilibrium in this situation at which the actual value of $\bar{P}$ is consistent with supply-demand equilibrium at a positive price and quantity?

17.6

A market is "informationally efficient" if *all* available information is instantly and costlessly incorporated into the price of a good.

a. Explain why it is impossible to predict the arrival of new information in such a market.

b. Is it possible to earn private gains from information acquisition in this type of market? What is the optimal information acquisition strategy?

c. In view of your analysis in part b, under what circumstances do you think a market will be informationally efficient?

17.7

The "Random Walk" hypothesis of the pricing of share prices assumes that these prices move randomly in ways that are totally unpredictable.

a. Explain the relationship between the Random Walk hypothesis and the concept of informational efficiency defined in Problem 17.6.

b. If share prices do follow a random walk, what do stock market advisers do and why are they paid so highly? Do the high salaries of such advisers tend to cast doubt on the Random Walk hypothesis?

PART
VI

Models of Imperfect Competition

One of the most important assumptions made throughout Part V was that both suppliers and demanders were price takers. All economic actors were assumed to exert no influence on prices, and therefore prices were treated as fixed parameters in their decisions. This behavioral assumption was crucial to most of our analysis, especially that related to the efficiency properties of the competitive price system. In this part we will explore the consequences of dropping the price-taking assumption for suppliers of goods. For most of our presentation, we will continue to assume that demanders are price takers on the presumption that in many important cases there are so many demanders of a good that no one of them has any influence on prices. But, as we shall demonstrate, such an assumption is frequently inappropriate for supplier behavior. Many markets are dominated by only a few sellers. In some cases there may be only one supplier together with major barriers that prevent others from entering the marketplace. Such circumstances raise doubts about the price-taker assumption since suppliers will

find that their actions do indeed have some influence on market prices. It would, for example, be particularly naïve to assume that the managers of General Motors make decisions on the assumption that these decisions cannot affect the market price of automobiles. Instead, models of supplier behavior that assume the firm can influence prices by deciding the types and quantities of cars it will make would seem to provide a better explanation of how the automobile market works. In this part we will examine such models.

We begin our examination of imperfect competition in Chapter 18 with the case of a single supplier of a good. Such a supplier is called a *monopoly*. This supplier faces the entire market demand curve for its product and can choose to operate at any point on that demand curve. That is, the monopoly supplier can choose whatever price-quantity combination on the demand curve it finds most profitable. Its activities are constrained only by the nature of the demand curve for its product, not by the behavior of rival producers. This then is the polar opposite case from perfect competition in which the existence of many suppliers enforces price-taking behavior on any one firm. In Chapter 18 we will show that, as was true for perfect competition in Part V, it is possible to analyze this case rather completely. We also show in detail why the presence of monopoly results in an allocation of resources that is inefficient in the Pareto sense and illustrate some of the issues that arise in attempting to regulate monopoly in a way that mitigates these inefficiencies.

In Chapter 19 we move from the relatively simple case of monopoly to market structures involving a "few" firms. As we shall see, adding additional suppliers (even if we only restrict ourselves to two-firm models of duopoly) makes matters much more complicated. In such cases any one firm does not face the total market demand curve, but, rather, faces a demand curve for its own output that will have properties determined in part by its rivals' behavior—the demand curve for GM cars depends in part on what Ford and Toyota do. To develop a realistic model, therefore, requires that some assumption be made about how one firm believes its rivals behave. Besides exploring some simple models of this type, Chapter 19 also examines situations in which one firm's product is slightly different from that being produced by its rivals. Since many imperfectly competitive markets are characterized by such *differentiated products* (Pontiacs and Toyotas are not identical goods), this type of model has many applications to the real world.

The issues of intrafirm rivalry and product differentiation introduced in Chapter 19 can also be approached formally as applications of the economic *theory of games*. In Chapter 20 we provide a brief introduction to some of the tools used in that field. We show how many strategic situations can be interpreted in game-theoretic terms and illustrate how the notion of market equilibrium has analogies in some game-theoretic models. Since concepts drawn from game theory are encountered in many areas of microeconomic theory, Chapter 20 provides important background material for further study.

CHAPTER 18

Models of Monopoly Markets

The market for a particular good is described as a monopoly if there is only one producer of the good. This single firm faces the entire market demand curve. Using its knowledge of this demand curve, the monopoly makes a decision on how much to produce. Unlike the perfectly competitive firm's output decision (which has no effect on market price), the monopoly's output decision will, in fact, determine the good's price. In this sense monopoly markets and markets characterized by perfect competition are polar opposite cases.

At times we will treat monopolies as having the power to set price, and in a sense, monopolies do have this power. Technically, a monopoly can choose that point on the market demand curve at which it prefers to operate. It may choose either market price or quantity, but not both. In this chapter it will usually be convenient for us to assume that monopolies choose the quantity of output that maximizes profits and then settle for the market price that that output level yields. It would be a simple matter to rephrase the discussion in terms of price setting, and in some places we shall do so. Given these conventions, we have

---

Definition:

Monopoly Market
A market is a *monopoly* if there is only one supplier. This firm may choose to produce at any point on the market demand curve.

BARRIERS TO ENTRY

The reason a monopoly exists is that other firms find it unprofitable or impossible to enter the market. *Barriers to entry* are therefore the source of all monopoly power. If other firms could enter a market, it would, by definition, no longer be a monopoly. There are two general types of barriers to entry: technical barriers and legal barriers.

Technical Barriers to Entry

A primary technical barrier is that the production of the good in question may exhibit decreasing marginal (and average) costs over a wide range of output levels. The technology of production is such that relatively large-scale firms are efficient. In this situation one firm may find it profitable to drive others out of the industry by price cutting. Similarly, once a monopoly has been established, entry will be difficult because any new firm must produce at relatively low levels of output and therefore at relatively high average costs. It is important to stress that the range of declining costs need only be "large" relative to the market in question. Declining costs on some absolute scale are not necessary. For example, the production and delivery of concrete does not exhibit declining marginal costs over a broad range of output when compared to the total U.S. market. However, in any particular small town, declining marginal costs may permit a monopoly to be established. The high costs of transportation in this industry tend to isolate one market from another.

Another technical basis of monopoly is special knowledge of a low-cost productive technique. But the problem for the monopoly that fears entry is keeping this technique uniquely to itself. When matters of technology are involved, this may be extremely difficult, unless the technology can be protected by a patent (see below). Ownership of unique resources, such as mineral deposits or land locations, or the possession of unique managerial talents may also be a lasting basis for maintaining a monopoly.

Legal Barriers to Entry

Many pure monopolies are created as a matter of law rather than as a matter of economic conditions. One important example of a government-granted monopoly position is in the legal protection of a productive technique by a patent. Xerox machines and Polaroid cameras are the most notable examples of highly successful products that were protected from competition (for a while) by a labyrinth of patents. Because the basic technology for these products was uniquely assigned to one firm, a monopoly position was established. The defense made of such a governmentally granted monopoly position is that the patent system makes innovation more profitable and therefore acts as an incentive to technical progress. Whether the benefits of such innovative behavior exceed the costs of having technological monopolies is an open question.[1]

A second example of a legally created monopoly is the awarding of an exclusive franchise to serve a market. These franchises are awarded in cases of public utility (gas and electric) service, communications services, the post office, some television and radio station markets, and a variety of other situations. The argument usually put forward in favor of creating these franchised monopolies is that having only one firm in the industry is somehow "more desirable" than permitting open competition. In that this rationale has an economic basis, the

---

[1] Some economists have argued that inventors should be rewarded directly by the government and that the invention should then be made available to all firms at no cost. Ideally, the prize to inventors would provide the incentive the patent system currently gives without creating the monopolies that arise under patents. In practice, it would be very difficult to decide how much a particular invention is "worth."

one usually proposed is that the industry in question is a *natural monopoly*: Average cost is diminishing over a broad range of output levels, and minimum average cost can be achieved only by organizing the industry as a monopoly. The public utility and communications industries are often considered to be good examples of such natural monopolies. Certainly, that does appear to be the case for local electricity and telephone service where a given network probably exhibits declining average cost up to the point of universal coverage. But recent deregulation actions in long distance telephone service and suggestions for similar reforms in electricity generation suggest that even for these industries the natural monopoly rationale may not be all-inclusive. In other cases, franchises may be based largely on political rationales. This seems to be true for the postal service in the United States and for a number of nationalized industries (airlines, radio and television, banking) in other countries.

Creation of Barriers to Entry

Although some barriers to entry may be independent of the monopolist's own activities, other barriers may result directly from those activities. For example, firms may develop unique products or technologies and take extraordinary steps to keep these from being copied by competitors. Or firms may buy up unique resources to prevent potential entry. The De Beers cartel, for example, controls a high fraction of the world's diamond mines. Finally, a would-be monopolist may enlist government aid in devising barriers to entry. It may lobby for legislation that restricts new entrants so as to "maintain an orderly market" or for health and safety regulations that raise potential entrants' costs. Because the monopolist has both special knowledge of its business and significant incentives to pursue these goals, it may have considerable success in creating such barriers to entry.

The attempt by a monopolist to erect barriers to entry may involve real resource costs. Maintaining secrecy, buying unique resources, and engaging in political lobbying are all costly activities. A full analysis of monopoly should involve not only questions of cost minimization and output choice (as under perfect competition) but also an analysis of profit-maximizing entry barrier creation. However, we will not provide a detailed investigation of such questions here.[2] Instead we will generally assume that the monopolist can do nothing to affect barriers to entry and that the firm's costs are therefore similar to what a competitive firm's costs would be. At times, however, we will mention some of the complications raised by the possibility of expenditures incurred to create barriers to entry.

PROFIT MAXI-MIZATION AND OUTPUT CHOICE

In order to maximize profits, a monopoly will choose to produce that output level for which marginal revenue is equal to marginal cost. Since the monopoly, in contrast to a perfectly competitive firm, faces a negatively sloped market demand curve, marginal revenue will be less than price. To sell an additional unit, the monopoly must lower its price on all units to be sold if it is to gen-

---

[2] For a simple treatment, see R. A. Posner, "The Social Costs of Monopoly and Regulation," *Journal of Political Economy* 83 (August 1975): 807–827.

Figure 18.1 *Profit Maximization and Price Determination in a Monopoly Market*

A profit-maximizing monopolist produces that quantity for which marginal revenue is equal to marginal cost. In the diagram this quantity is given by Q^*, which will yield a price of P^* in the market. Monopoly profits can be read as the rectangle P^*EAC.

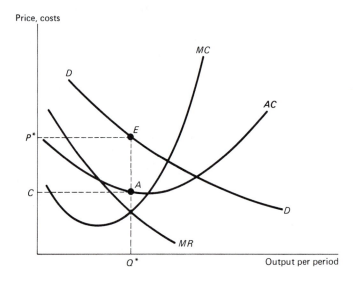

erate the extra demand necessary to absorb this marginal unit. The profit-maximizing output level for a firm is then the level Q^* in Figure 18.1. At that level marginal revenue is equal to marginal costs, and profits are maximized.

If a firm produced slightly less than Q^*, profits would fall, since the revenue lost from this cutback (MR) would exceed the decline in production costs (MC). A decision to produce more than Q^* also would lower profits, since the additional costs from increasing production exceed the incremental revenues yielded by selling the extra output in the market. Consequently, profits are at a maximum at Q^*, and a profit-maximizing monopoly will choose this output level.

Given the monopoly's decision to produce Q^*, the demand curve D indicates that a market price of P^* will prevail. This is the price that demanders as a group are willing to pay for the output of the monopoly. In the market, an equilibrium price-quantity combination of P^*, Q^* will be observed.[3] Assuming $P^* > AC$, this output level will be profitable, and the monopolist will have no incentive to alter output levels unless demand or cost conditions change. Hence we can conclude

---

[3]This combination will be on an elastic section of the demand curve as long as $MC > 0$. This will be true because $MC > 0$ implies that for a profit maximum, $MR > 0$. Hence $e_{Q,P} < -1$, since we have shown that $MR = P(1 + 1/e_{Q,P})$.

Optimization Principle:	

Monopolist's Output

A monopolist will choose to produce that output for which marginal revenue equals marginal cost. Since the monopolist faces a downward-sloping demand curve, market price will exceed both marginal revenue and the firm's marginal cost at this output level.

Monopoly Profits

Total profits earned by the monopolist can be read directly from Figure 18.1. These are shown by the rectangle P^*EAC and again represent the profit per unit (price minus average cost) times the number of units sold. These profits will be positive if market price exceeds average total cost. If $P^* < AC$, however, the monopolist can only operate at a long-term loss and will decline to serve the market.

Since no entry is possible into a monopoly market, the monopolist's positive profits can exist even in the long run. For this reason some authors refer to the profits that a monopoly earns in the long run as *monopoly rents*. These profits can be regarded as a return to that factor that forms the basis of the monopoly (a patent, a favorable location, or a dynamic entrepreneur, for example); hence another possible owner might be willing to pay that amount in rent for the right to the monopoly. The potential for profits is the reason why some firms pay other firms for the right to use a patent and why concessioners at sporting events (and on some highways) are willing to pay for the right to the concession. To the extent monopoly rights are given away at below their true market value (as in radio and television licensing), the wealth of the recipients of those rights is increased.

Although a monopoly may earn positive profits in the long run,[4] the size of such profits will depend on the relationship between the monopolist's average costs and the demand for its product. Figure 18.2 illustrates two situations in which the demand, marginal revenue, and marginal cost curves are rather similar. But average costs in Figure 18.2a are considerably lower than Figure 18.2b. Although the profit-maximizing decisions are similar in the two cases, the level of profits ends up being quite different. In Figure 18.2a the monopolist's price (P^*) exceeds the average cost of producing Q^* (labeled AC^*) by a large extent, and significant profits are obtained. In Figure 18.2b, however, $P^* = AC^*$ and the monopoly earns zero economic profits, the largest amount possible in this case. Hence large profits from a monopoly are not inevitable, and the actual extent of economic profits may not always be a good guide to the significance of monopolistic influences in a market.

There Is No Monopoly Supply Curve

In the theory of perfectly competitive markets we presented earlier, it was possible to speak of an industry supply curve. We constructed this curve by allowing the market demand curve to shift and observing the supply curve that was

---

[4]As in the competitive case, the profit-maximizing monopolist would be willing to produce at a loss in the short run as long as market price exceeds average variable cost.

Figure 18.2 *Monopoly Profits Depend on the Relationship between the Demand and Average Cost Curves*

Both of the monopolies in this figure are equally "strong," if by this we mean they produce similar divergences between market price and marginal cost. However, because of the location of the demand and average cost curves, it turns out that the monopoly in (a) earns high profits whereas that in (b) earns no profits. Consequently, the size of profits is not a measure of the strength of a monopoly.

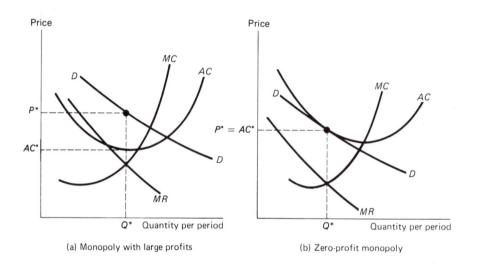

(a) Monopoly with large profits   (b) Zero-profit monopoly

traced out by the series of equilibrium price-quantity combinations. This type of construction is not possible for monopolistic markets. With a fixed market demand curve, the supply "curve" for a monopoly will be only one point, namely, that price-quantity combination for which $MR = MC$. If the demand curve should shift, the marginal revenue curve would also shift, and a new profit-maximizing output would be chosen. However, connecting the resulting series of equilibrium points on the market demand curves would have little meaning. This locus might have a very strange shape, depending on how the market demand curve's elasticity (and its associated MR curve) changes as the curve is shifted. In this sense the monopoly firm has no well-defined "supply curve." In some of the problems to this chapter, we examine how the equilibrium in a monopoly market shifts when cost or demand conditions change.

Numerical Example

Suppose the annual market for Olympic-quality frisbees (Q) has a demand curve of the form

$$Q = 2000 - 20P \tag{18.1}$$

or

$$P = 100 - \frac{Q}{20} \tag{18.2}$$

and that the costs of a monopoly frisbee producer are given by

$$TC = .05\,Q^2 + 10{,}000 \tag{18.3}$$

and

$$AC = .05\,Q + \frac{10{,}000}{Q}. \tag{18.4}$$

To maximize profits, this producer chooses that output level for which $MR = MC$:

$$P \cdot Q = 100Q - \frac{Q^2}{20} \tag{18.5}$$

so

$$MR = 100 - \frac{Q}{10} = MC = .1Q \tag{18.6}$$

and

$$Q^* = 500 \qquad P^* = 75; \tag{18.7}$$

with this output level

$$AC = .05(500) + \frac{10{,}000}{500} = 45, \tag{18.8}$$

and profits are given by

$$\pi = (P^* - AC) \cdot Q^* = (75 - 45) \cdot 500 = 15{,}000. \tag{18.9}$$

Notice that at this equilibrium there is a large gap between price (75) and marginal cost ($MC = .1Q = 50$). As long as entry barriers prevent a new firm from producing Olympic-quality frisbees, however, this gap and the positive economic profits reported in Equation 18.9 can persist indefinitely.

MARKET SEPARATION AND PRICE DISCRIMINATION

It sometimes may be the case that a firm will have a monopolistic position in different markets for the same good. If these markets are effectively separated so that buyers cannot shift from one market to the other, the monopolist may be able to increase profits further by practicing *price discrimination*. The profit-maximizing decision would be to produce that quantity in each market for which marginal revenue equals marginal cost. This may lead to different prices for the same good in the two markets; if the markets are effectively separated, these price differentials can persist.

Graphic Proof for Two Markets

Price discrimination in two markets is shown graphically in Figure 18.3. The figure is drawn so that the market demand (and marginal revenue) curves in two separated markets share the same vertical axis. For simplicity it also assumes that marginal cost is constant over all levels of output. The profit-maximizing decision for the monopoly is to produce Q_1^* in the first market and Q_2^* in the second market. The prices in these two markets will then be given

---

Figure 18.3   *Separated Markets Raise the Possibility of Price Discrimination*

If two markets are separate, a monopolist can maximize profits by selling his or her product at different prices in the two markets. This would entail choosing that output for which $MC = MR$ in each of the markets. The diagram shows that the market which has a less elastic demand curve will be charged the higher price by the price discriminator.

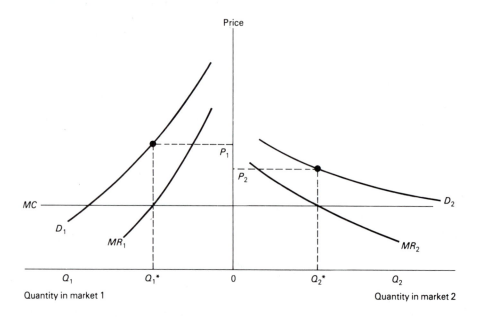

by P_1 and P_2, respectively. It is clear from the figure that the market with the less inelastic demand curve will have the higher price in this price-discriminating example. The price-discriminating monopolist will charge a higher price in that market in which quantity purchased is less responsive to price changes. Although the analysis in Figure 18.3 assumes that marginal costs are constant, an identical result would hold in the more realistic case of increasing marginal costs, as we now show.

A Mathematical Development

To derive these results mathematically, let Q_1 and Q_2 be the quantities sold in the two markets and let total profits in these markets be given by

$$\pi(Q_1,\ Q_2) = R_2(Q_1) + R_2(Q_2) - TC(Q_1 + Q_2). \qquad (18.10)$$

The first-order conditions for a maximum are

$$\frac{\partial \pi}{\partial Q_1} = \frac{\partial R_1}{\partial Q_1} - \frac{\partial TC}{\partial Q_1} = 0$$

$$\frac{\partial \pi}{\partial Q_2} = \frac{\partial R_2}{\partial Q_2} - \frac{\partial TC}{\partial Q_2} = 0 \qquad (18.11)$$

or

$$MR_1 = \frac{\partial R_1}{\partial Q_1} = \frac{\partial TC}{\partial Q_1} = MC = \frac{\partial TC}{\partial Q_2} = \frac{\partial R_2}{\partial Q_2} = MR_2, \qquad (18.12)$$

since costs of production are the same no matter to which market the output is supplied. Hence marginal revenue in the two markets must be the same for profit maximization.

We now can use this equality of marginal revenue to derive the relationship between prices in the two markets. Using Equation 12.13 we have

$$MR_1 = P_1 \left(1 + \frac{1}{e_1}\right) \qquad (18.13)$$

and

$$MR_2 = P_2 \left(1 + \frac{1}{e_2}\right), \qquad (18.14)$$

where e_1 and e_2 are the price elasticities of demand in markets 1 and 2, respectively. So, by Equation 18.12,

$$P_1 \left(1 + \frac{1}{e_1}\right) = P_2 \left(1 + \frac{1}{e_2}\right) \qquad (18.15)$$

or

$$\frac{P_1}{P_2} = \frac{\left(1 + \dfrac{1}{e_1}\right)}{\left(1 + \dfrac{1}{e_2}\right)}. \qquad (18.16)$$

If $e_1 > e_2$ (market 2 has a more price elastic demand, remember that $e_{Q,P}$ is negative), P_1 will exceed P_2. Only if the demand elasticities are equal will identical prices be observed. For the more general case in which marginal costs also differ between the markets (for example, because of differences in transport costs), a relationship similar to Equation 18.16 would hold for the *gap* between price and marginal cost, with this gap being larger in the less elastic market.

Numerical
Example

Returning to our numerical example, suppose that the demand for Olympic-quality frisbees can be separated into a domestic component:

$$Q_1 = 1,200 - 10P_1 \qquad (18.17)$$

and a foreign component

$$Q_2 = 800 - 10P_2. \qquad (18.18)$$

At any price foreign demand is more elastic than domestic demand (at $P = 70$, $e_1 = -1.4$, $e_2 = -7.0$, for example), perhaps because foreign imitations of these high-quality frisbees are more readily available. Solving for marginal revenue as before, we have

$$MR_1 = 120 - \frac{Q_1}{5}$$

$$MR_2 = 80 - \frac{Q_2}{5},$$

(18.19)

and using the conditions for a profit maximum (Equation 18.12) gives

$$MR_1 = 120 - \frac{Q_1}{5} = MC = .1(Q_1 + Q_2)$$

$$= MR_2 = 80 - \frac{Q_2}{5}.$$

(18.20)

Some algebraic manipulation of these equations yields

$$Q_1^* = 350 \qquad P_1^* = 85$$

$$Q_2^* = 150 \qquad P_2^* = 65.$$

(18.21)

As would be expected from our theoretical development, the price-discriminating frisbee producer charges a higher price to the domestic market where demand is less elastic. Profits are now given by

$$\pi = (P_1^* - AC)Q_1^* + (P_2^* - AC)Q_2^*$$

$$= (85 - 45) \cdot 350 + (65 - 45) \cdot 150$$

$$= 14,000 + 3,000 = 17,000,$$

(18.22)

a 2,000 improvement over the profits obtained with a single-price policy. Notice that most of the profits in this case come from the (relatively less elastic) domestic market.

Perfect Price Discrimination

Generalizing this analysis of price discrimination to many separate markets is straightforward. The firm should choose a quantity (or price) in each market at which marginal revenue equals marginal cost. A limiting case would be for the monopoly to charge a different price to each buyer. If the monopoly can identify the maximum price each buyer is willing to pay and prevent him or her from obtaining the good elsewhere, this can be a very profitable strategy.

The perfect price discrimination procedure is illustrated in Figure 18.4. The monopoly sells its first Q_1 units of output to buyers who are willing to pay P_1 for it. Then $Q_2 - Q_1$ units of output are sold at a price of P_2 to buyers who are willing to pay somewhat less than those in the first group. As long as an incremental group of buyers is willing to pay more for some of the monopolist's output than the marginal cost of producing it, profits can be increased further by serving this group. The firm will decline to serve any group willing to pay less than marginal cost, however. Hence, the perfect price discriminator will produce output level Q^* in Figure 18.4, and the price paid by the marginal buyer will be equal to marginal cost. Total revenues received by the perfect

Figure 18.4   *Perfect Price Discrimination*

Under perfect price discrimination, the monopoly charges a different price to each buyer. It sells Q_1 units at P_1, $Q_2 - Q_1$ units at P_2, and so forth. In this case the firm will produce Q^*, and total revenues will be DEQ^*0.

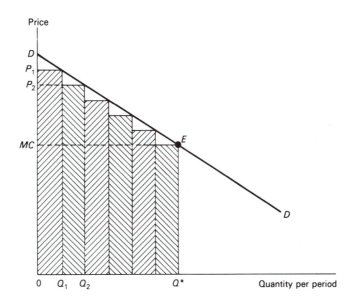

price-discriminating monopolist will be given by the entire shaded area DEQ^*0. In this situation the monopolist has extracted all of the consumer surplus (see Chapter 5) available with this market demand curve.

Numerical Example

Since relatively few Olympic-quality frisbees are sold, the monopolist may find it possible to discriminate perfectly among world-class flippers. In this case it will choose to produce that quantity for which the marginal buyer pays exactly the marginal cost of a frisbee:

$$P = 100 - \frac{Q}{20} = MC = .1Q. \qquad (18.23)$$

Hence

$$Q^* = 666$$

and, at the margin, price and marginal cost are given by

$$P = MC = 66.7. \qquad (18.24)$$

To find total profits in this perfect price discrimination case, we must compute total revenues as

$$TR = \int_0^{Q^*} P(Q)\,dQ = 100Q - Q^2/40 \Big|_0^{666} \tag{18.25}$$

$$= 55,511$$

and total costs as

$$TC = .05\,Q^2 + 10,000 = 32,178. \tag{18.26}$$

Total profits are given by

$$\pi = TR - TC = 23,333, \tag{18.27}$$

which again represents a substantial increase over the single-price and two-price policies.

Conditions for Successful Price Discrimination

By considering the possibility that a monopoly may adopt multiple prices for its product, we have developed the following definition:

Definition:

Price Discrimination

A monopoly may be able to practice *price discrimination* by charging different prices in separated markets in order to maximize profits. As a limiting case, the monopoly may be able to practice *perfect price discrimination* by charging different prices to each buyer.

The assumption that markets are separated is crucial to the monopolist's ability to practice this sort of behavior—it must be able to identify which buyer belongs to which market and prevent buyers in the high-priced market from moving to the lower-priced one. In some cases this separation may be spatial. For example, book publishers tend to charge higher prices in the United States than abroad because foreign markets are more competitive and subject to illegal copying. In this case the oceans enforce market separation since few people would travel abroad simply to buy books. Such a discriminatory policy would not work if transportation costs were low, however. As chain stores that charge different prices in different parts of town have discovered, people will flock to where the bargains are.

Price discrimination by time of sale may also be possible. Late night or afternoon showings of motion pictures are usually cheaper than evening shows. Discriminating against those who wish to attend prime-time shows succeeds because the good being purchased cannot be resold later. A firm that tried to sell toasters at two different prices during the day might discover itself to be in competition with savvy customers who bought when the price was low and undercut the firm by selling to other customers during high-price periods. If customers themselves can alter when they shop, a discriminatory policy may not work. A firm that offers lower post-Christmas prices may find its pre-Christmas business facing stiff competition from those sales.

Finally, of course, the practice of price discrimination requires monopoly power. Because the discriminator chooses an output level for which price exceeds marginal (and perhaps average) cost, potential competitors may be encouraged to enter the market. Prior to deregulation, for example, airlines practiced a number of discriminatory policies in their pricing. The goal of such policies as advance ticket purchase requirements and minimum stay provisions was to differentiate between business travelers (who had relatively inelastic demands) and discretionary travelers. The large profits being made from business travel could not persist in an era of greater competition as new airlines sought to enter this market.

MONOPOLY AND RE-SOURCE ALLOCATION

In Chapter 16 we showed that the presence of monopoly can destroy the efficiency properties of a competitive price system. Because a monopoly can affect market prices, it may be in its interest to restrict output in order to attain higher profits than are available at competitive prices. In this section we will offer a somewhat more complete analysis of this distortion using the partial equilibrium model of monopoly.

A Graphic Analysis

Figure 18.5 shows a simple linear demand curve for a product that is produced under constant marginal and average costs.[5] If this market were competitive, output would be Q^*—that is, production would occur where price is equal to marginal cost. Under a simple single-price monopoly, output would be Q^{**} since this is the level of production for which marginal revenue is equal to marginal cost. The restriction in output from Q^* to Q^{**} represents the misallocation brought about through monopolization. This is the result we showed previously in Figure 16.5. The total value of resources released by this output restriction is shown in Figure 18.5 as area AEQ^*Q^{**}. As we discussed previously, transferring these inputs elsewhere will cause these other goods to be overproduced relative to their Pareto efficient levels.

The restriction in output from Q^* to Q^{**} involves a total loss in consumer surplus of $P^{**}BEP^*$. Part of this loss is captured by the monopoly as profits. These profits are measured by $P^{**}BAP^*$, and they reflect a transfer of income from consumers to the firm. Whether such a transfer is regarded as desirable depends on prevailing societal norms about whether consumers or the monopoly are more deserving of such gains. As for any transfer, difficult issues of equity arise in attempting to assess social desirability. There is no ambiguity about the loss in consumers' surplus given by area BEA, however, since this loss is not transferred to anyone. It is a pure "deadweight" loss and represents the principal measure of the allocational harm of the monopoly.

To illustrate the nature of this deadweight loss, consider our numerical frisbee example. For a simple, single-price monopoly we calculated an equilib-

---

[5] Here we use the usual Marshallian demand curve on the presumption that income effects are relatively unimportant for the market we are analyzing. If income effects were significant, our analysis would be more formally correct if we used an income-compensated demand curve instead.

Figure 18.5   *Allocational and Distributional Effects of Monopoly*

Monopolization of this previously competitive market would cause output to be reduced from Q^* to Q^{**}. Consumer expenditures and productive inputs worth AEQ^*Q^{**} are reallocated into the production of other goods. Consumer surplus equal to $P^{**}BAP^*$ is transferred into monopoly profits. There is a deadweight loss given by BEA.

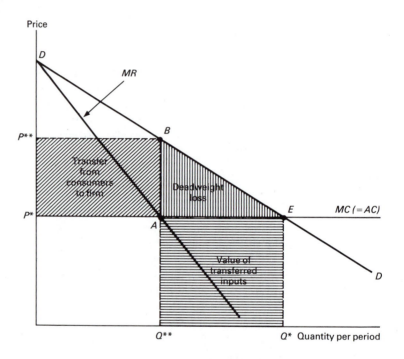

rium price of $75 and a marginal cost of $50. This gap between price and marginal cost is an indication of the efficiency-improving trades that are forgone through monopolization. Undoubtedly, there is a would-be buyer who is willing to pay, say, $60 for an Olympic frisbee, but not $75. A price of $60 would more than cover all of the resource costs involved in frisbee production, but the presence of the monopoly prevents such a mutually beneficial transaction between frisbee users and frisbee makers. For this reason, simple monopoly clearly does not lead to a Pareto optimal allocation of resources. Economists have made many attempts to estimate the overall cost of these deadweight losses in actual monopoly situations. In the application to this chapter we will examine some of these estimates.

Resource Allocation and Price Discrimination

Adoption of price discrimination policies by a monopoly may reduce deadweight losses. Although such policies will result in a larger transfer of consumer surplus into monopoly profits, Pareto inefficiency may be reduced. The most extreme case of this somewhat surprising result occurs in the case of perfect price discrimination. In this situation there are no deadweight losses since at the margin, price is equal to marginal cost. In Figure 18.5 the output for both a competitive market and for a perfect price discriminator would be Q^*. With the perfect price discriminator, all potential consumer surplus (area DEP^*) would be converted into monopoly profits so there would be no deadweight loss. Thus, since the competitive level of output is being produced, Pareto criteria cannot be used to determine the desirability of this allocation of resources. Instead, whether the perfect price discriminator is socially desirable will depend on whether the transfer from consumer surplus into monopoly profits is considered equitable. One case that is alleged to be both efficient and equitable is the practicing of price discrimination by rural physicians. Under a single-price policy, physicians might refuse to live in rural areas. But with price discrimination they can convert enough consumer surplus into their own incomes to make rural areas competitive with potential urban locations. Consumers are no worse off under such a policy than they would be without physician services and may even be better off if the physician is not a perfect discriminator.

REGULATION OF MONOPOLIES

The regulation of monopolies is an important subject in applied economic analysis. The utility, communications, and transportation industries are highly regulated in most countries, and devising regulatory procedures that cause these industries to operate in a desirable way is an important practical problem. Here we will examine a few aspects of the regulation of monopolies that relate to pricing policies.

Marginal Cost Pricing and the Natural Monopoly Dilemma

By analogy to the perfectly competitive case, many economists believe that it is important for the prices charged by regulated monopolies to reflect marginal costs of production accurately. In this way the deadweight loss from monopolies is minimized. The principal problem raised by an enforced policy of marginal cost pricing is that it may require true natural monopolies to operate at a loss. Natural monopolies, by definition, exhibit decreasing average costs over a broad range of output levels. The cost curves for such a firm might look like those shown in Figure 18.6. In the absence of regulation the monopoly would produce output level Q_A and receive a price of P_A for its product. Profits in this situation are given by the rectangle $P_A ABC$. A regulatory agency might instead set a price of P_R for the monopoly. At this price, Q_R is demanded, and the marginal cost of producing this output level is also P_R. Consequently, marginal cost pricing has been achieved. Unfortunately, because of the declining nature of the firm's cost curves, the price P_R (= marginal cost) falls below average costs. With this regulated price, the monopoly must operate at a loss of $GFEP_R$. Since no firm can operate indefinitely at a loss, this poses a dilemma for the regulatory agency: Either it must abandon its goal of marginal cost pricing, or the government must subsidize the monopoly forever.

Two-Tier Pricing Systems

One way out of the marginal cost pricing dilemma is the implementation of a two-part pricing system. Under such a system the monopoly is permitted to charge some users a high price while maintaining a low price for marginal

Figure 18.6   *Price Regulation for a Decreasing Cost Monopoly*

Because natural monopolies exhibit decreasing costs, marginal costs fall below average costs. Consequently, enforcing a policy of marginal cost pricing will entail operating at a loss. A price of P_R, for example, will achieve the goal of marginal cost pricing but will necessitate an operating loss of $GFEP_R$.

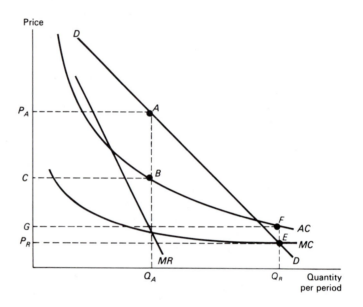

users. In this way the demanders paying the high price in effect subsidize the losses of the low-price customers. Such a pricing scheme is shown in Figure 18.7. Here the regulatory commission has decided that some users will pay a relatively high price, P_1. At this price, Q_1 is demanded.[6] Other users (presumably those who would not buy the good at the P_1 price) are offered a lower price, P_2. This lower price generates additional demand of $Q_2 - Q_1$. Consequently, a total output of Q_2 is produced at an average cost of A. With this two-part pricing system, the profits on the sales to high-price demanders (given by the rectangle P_1DBA) balance the losses incurred on the low-priced sales ($BFEC$). Furthermore, for the "marginal user," the marginal cost pricing rule is being followed: It is the "intramarginal" user who subsidizes the firm so that it does not operate at a loss. Although in practice it may not be so simple to establish pricing schemes that maintain marginal cost pricing and cover oper-

---

[6] Under some marginal cost pricing schemes, the intramarginal users are treated as paying both the fixed and the variable component of average costs whereas marginal users pay only for variable marginal costs. More recently, however, it has been argued that (peak-period) "marginal users" should pay capital costs, since it is their incremental demands that create the need for additional production capacity. For a summary, see "Symposium on Peak Load Pricing," *The Bell Journal of Economics and Management Science* 7 (Spring 1976): 197–248.

Figure 18.7   *Two-Part Pricing Schedule*

By charging a high price (P_1) to some users and a low price (P_2) to others, it may be possible for a regulatory commission to (1) enforce marginal cost pricing and (2) create a situation where the profits from one class of user (P_1DBA) subsidize the losses of the other class ($BFEC$).

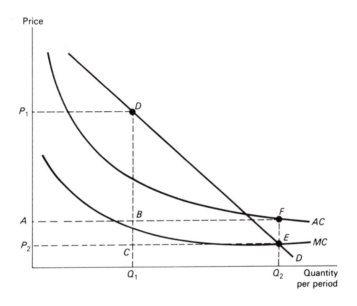

ating costs, many regulatory commissions do use multipart tariff schedules that intentionally discriminate against some users to the advantage of others.

Rate of Return Regulation

Another approach to devising monopoly pricing schemes that is followed in many regulatory situations is to permit the monopoly to charge a price above average cost that is sufficient to earn a "fair" rate of return on investment. Much analytical effort is then devoted to defining the "fair" rate concept and to developing ways in which it might be measured. From an economic point of view, some of the most interesting questions about this procedure concern how the regulatory activity affects the firm's input choices. If, for example, the rate of return allowed to firms exceeds what owners might obtain under competitive circumstances, there will be an incentive to use relatively more capital input than would truly minimize costs. Or if regulators typically delay in making rate decisions, firms may be given incentives to minimize costs that would not otherwise exist. We will now briefly examine a formal model of such possibilities.[7]

---

[7]This model is based on H. Averch and L. L. Johnson, "Behavior of the Firm under Regulatory Constraint," *American Economic Review* (December 1962): 1052–1069.

A Formal Model   Suppose a regulated utility has a production function of the form

$$Q = f(K, L). \tag{18.28}$$

This firm's actual rate of return on capital is then defined as

$$s = \frac{Pf(K, L) - wL}{K}, \tag{18.29}$$

where P is the price of the firm's output (which depends on Q) and w is the wage rate for labor. If s is constrained by regulation to be equal to, say, $\bar{s}$, then the firm's problem is to maximize profits

$$\pi = Pf(K, L) - wL - vK \tag{18.30}$$

subject to this regulatory constraint. Setting up the Lagrangian expression for this problem yields

$$\mathcal{L} = Pf(K, L) - wL - vK + \lambda[wL + \bar{s}K - Pf(K, L)]. \tag{18.31}$$

Notice that if $\lambda = 0$, regulation is ineffective and the monopoly behaves like any profit-maximizing firm. If $\lambda = 1$, Equation 18.31 reduces to

$$\mathcal{L} = (\bar{s} - v)K, \tag{18.32}$$

which, assuming $\bar{s} > v$ (which it must be if the firm is not to earn less than the prevailing rate of return on capital elsewhere) means that this monopoly will hire infinite amounts of capital—an implausible result. Hence, $0 < \lambda < 1$. The first-order conditions for a maximum are

$$\frac{\partial \mathcal{L}}{\partial L} = Pf_L - w + \lambda(w - Pf_L) = 0$$

$$\frac{\partial \mathcal{L}}{\partial K} = Pf_K - v + \lambda(\bar{s} - Pf_K) = 0 \tag{18.33}$$

$$\frac{\partial \mathcal{L}}{\partial \lambda} = wL + \bar{s}K - Pf(K, L) = 0.$$

The first of these conditions implies that the regulated monopoly will hire additional labor input up to the point at which $Pf_L = w$—a result that holds for any profit-maximizing firm. For capital input, however, the second condition implies

$$(1 - \lambda)Pf_K = v - \lambda\bar{s} \tag{18.34}$$

or

$$Pf_K = \frac{v - \lambda\bar{s}}{1 - \lambda} = v - \frac{\lambda(\bar{s} - v)}{1 - \lambda}. \tag{18.35}$$

Since $\bar{s} > v$ and $\lambda < 1$, Equation 18.35 implies

$$Pf_K < v. \tag{18.36}$$

The firm will hire more capital (and achieve a lower marginal productivity of capital) than it would under unregulated conditions. "Overcapitalization" may therefore be a regulatory-induced misallocation of resources for some utilities.

Although we shall not do so here, it is possible to examine other regulatory questions using this general analytical framework.[8] Since knowing how firms will respond to various cost or environmental constraints has direct relevance to the adoption of regulatory policies, this type of examination is used in a wide variety of contexts.

DYNAMIC VIEWS OF MONOPOLY

Our analysis in this chapter has made two major arguments against monopolies. The first uses a static analysis to show that the allocational effects of monopolies are harmful: Too few resources are devoted to the production of a good for which the supply is monopolized. The second argument is somewhat more ambiguous but is probably more important from a policy perspective: Monopolies may have undesirable distributional effects. The monopolization of a market creates the possibility for substantial transfers into monopoly profits, and these profits may accrue to relatively rich owners at the expense of relatively poor consumers. This distributional argument reinforces the allocational argument and provides the basis for the notion that monopolies are an unambiguous evil. Such a conclusion, however, is not shared by all economists. Some writers, most notably J. A. Schumpeter, have stressed the beneficial role that monopoly profits can play in the process of economic development.[9] In this section we shall briefly review some of the suggestions about the possible beneficial aspects of monopolies that have been made.

Authors who discuss the possible benefits of monopolies tend to take a dynamic view of the economic process. They place considerable emphasis on innovation and the ability of particular types of firms to achieve technical advances. In this context the profits that monopolistic firms earn play an important role. Profits provide funds that can be invested in research and development. Whereas perfectly competitive firms must be content with a normal return on invested capital, monopolies have "surplus" funds with which to undertake the risky process of research. More important, perhaps, the possibility of attaining a monopolistic position, or the desire to maintain such a position, provides an important incentive to keep one step ahead of potential competitors. Innovations in new products and cost-saving production techniques may be integrally related to the possibility of monopolization. Without such a monopolistic position the full benefits of innovation could not be obtained by the innovating firm.

Schumpeter stresses the point that the monopolization of a market may make it less costly for a firm to plan its activities. Being the only source of

---

[8] For some examples, see E. E. Bailey, *Economic Theory of Regulatory Constraint* (Lexington, Mass.: D. C. Heath, 1973).

[9] See, for example, J. A. Schumpeter, *Capitalism, Socialism, and Democracy,* 3d ed. (New York: Harper & Row, 1950), especially chap. 8.

supply for a product eliminates many of the contingencies that a firm in a competitive market must face. For example, a monopoly may not have to spend as much on selling expenses (advertising, brand identification, and visiting retailers, for example) as would be the case in a more competitive industry. Similarly, a monopoly may know more about the specific demand curve for its product and may more readily adapt to changing demand conditions.

Of course, whether any of these purported benefits of monopolies outweigh their allocational and distributional disadvantages is an empirical question. Issues of innovation and cost savings cannot be answered by recourse to *a priori* arguments. Detailed investigation of real-world markets is a necessity.

SUMMARY

In this chapter we have examined models of markets in which there is only a single, monopoly supplier. Unlike the competitive case that we investigated in Part V, monopoly firms do not exhibit price-taking behavior. Instead, the monopolist can choose the price-quantity combination on the market demand curve that is most profitable. A number of consequences then follow from this market power:

- The most profitable level of input for the monopolist is that one for which marginal revenue is equal to marginal cost. At this output level, price will exceed marginal cost. The profitability of the monopolist will depend on the relationship between price and average cost.
- A monopoly may be able to increase its profits further through price discrimination—that is, charging different prices in separated markets that are unrelated to differences in costs. The price-discriminating monopolist will charge a higher price in markets in which demand is relatively less elastic. The ability of the monopoly to practice price discrimination depends on its ability to keep markets separated.
- In the limiting case, a monopoly may be able to practice perfect price discrimination by charging a different price to each buyer. With perfect price discrimination, the monopoly will serve any buyer who is willing to pay at least the marginal cost of producing a good.
- Relative to perfect competition, monopoly involves a loss of consumer surplus for demanders. Some of this is transferred into monopoly profits whereas some of the loss in consumer supply represents a deadweight loss of overall economic welfare. It is a sign of Pareto inefficiency.
- Governments often choose to regulate natural monopolies (firms with diminishing average costs over a broad range of output levels). The type of regulatory mechanisms adopted can affect the behavior of the regulated firm.

Application

MEASURING THE SOCIAL COSTS OF MONOPOLY

Arnold Harberger was one of the first economists to use the kind of analysis we developed in this chapter to try to estimate the allocational losses from monopolization of markets in the U.S. economy.[10] Harberger's method was rather simple. First, he assembled cost and profit data for 73 different industries. For each industry he estimated the percentage by which price exceeded average cost. This is equivalent to measuring the distance $P^{**} - P^*$ in Figure 18.5. For example, Harberger found that prices in the cement industry exceed average costs by 8.4 percent. Next Harberger calculated the expansion in demand $(Q^* - Q^{**})$ that would occur by lowering prices to the competitive level. Assuming an elasticity of demand for cement of -1.0, the quantity of cement demanded would be increased by 8.4 percent if competitive prices prevailed. Using those two figures, the author then calculated the area of the triangle BEA,

$$\frac{1}{2(P^{**} - P^*)(Q^* - Q^{**})},$$

as a measure of the welfare loss from partial monopoly in the cement industry. For this case the loss amounted to $420,000 for the period under investigation (1924 to 1928). By making similar calculations for the other 72 industries in his sample, Harberger concluded that the total welfare loss from monopolies was about $150 million. This amounted to about 0.1 percent of Gross National Product during the period.

Most economists were quite surprised by the relatively modest level of distortion that Harberger calculated. Both the legal and the rhe-

torical emphasis given to antimonopoly activity would seem to indicate that monopolistic distortions had a much greater quantitative importance. Of course, there has been considerable controversy over Harberger's methods, and they are by no means widely accepted by economists. Several more recent studies of the same subject, however, have failed to refute the impression that the overall welfare loss from monopolies is a relatively small percentage of total output. For example, in a 1974 article by J. J. Siegfried and T. K. Tiemann, the authors showed that in 1963 monopolistic distortions again amounted to less than 0.1 percent of national income.[11] Three industries—motor vehicles, plastics, and petroleum refining and extraction—accounted for more than 60 percent of the total value of monopolistic distortions. Even in those industries, however, the authors express some doubt that there is much to be gained by pursuing some type of antimonopoly policy.

Some economists believe that these types of calculations substantially understate the social costs of monopolies because they take no account of possible differences in costs between monopolies and competitive firms that may arise from entry-restricting activities of the monopolist. Taking account of such differences, it is claimed, may substantially reverse the conclusion that the allocational costs of monopolies are small. For example, a 1978 study by K. Cowling and D. C. Mueller tried to estimate that portion of firms' costs that went toward creating monopolistic profits.[12] From those es-

[10] A. Harberger, "Monopoly and Resource Allocation," *American Economic Review* 44 (May 1954): 77–87.

[11] J. J. Siegfried and T. K. Tiemann, "The Welfare Cost of Monopoly: An Inter-Industry Analysis," *Economic Inquiry* 12 (June 1974): 190–202.

[12] K. Cowling and D. C. Mueller, "The Social Cost of Monopoly Power," *Economic Journal* 88 (December 1978): 727–748.

timates the authors calculated that monopolistic distortions may have represented as much as 13 percent of U.S. GNP in 1973. Estimates of such distortions were particularly large for automobile companies (they amounted to more than $1 billion for General Motors) and for household products companies (nearly $500 million each for Unilever and Procter & Gamble). Allocational costs were also significant for some highly regulated firms such as AT&T and Pacific Telephone and Telegraph, possibly because of expenditures made by those companies in an attempt to influence regulatory outcomes.

These estimates are controversial, however, because of the arbitrariness necessarily involved in deciding which costs are really related to seeking a monopolistic position. For example, Cowling and Mueller included *all* advertising costs in that category, though they admit that some portion of such expenditures is probably unrelated to monopolistic goals and may instead provide useful information to consumers. Similar ambiguities arise in judging attempts of some firms to differentiate their products from those of their competitors. We will take up this topic in the next chapter.

SUGGESTED READINGS

Averch, H., and Johnson, L. L. "Behavior of the Firm under Regulatory Constraint." *American Economic Review* 52 (1962): 1052–1069.

Article introducing the idea of firm behavior with a regulatory constraint. Very readable.

Coase, R. H. "Some Notes on Monopoly Price." *Review of Economic Studies* 5 (1937–1938): 17–31.

Early thoughts about the sustainability of a monopolist's price.

Harberger, A. "Monopoly and Resource Allocation." *American Economic Review* 44 (May 1954): 77–87.

Empirical estimate of the deadweight loss from monopoly in the 1920s.

Kessel, R. A. "Price Discrimination in Medicine." *Journal of Law and Economics* 1 (October 1958): 20–53.

Interesting development of the hypothesis that doctors widely engage in price discrimination.

Posner, R. A. "The Social Costs of Monopoly and Regulation." *Journal of Political Economy* 83 (1975): 807–827.

An analysis of the probability that monopolies may spend resources on creation of barriers to entry and therefore may have higher costs than perfectly competitive firms.

Schumpeter, J. A. *Capitalism, Socialism and Democracy*, 3d ed. New York: Harper & Row, 1950.

Classic defense of the role of the entrepreneur and economic profits in the economic growth process.

Stigler, G. J. "The Theory of Economic Regulation." *The Bell Journal of Economics and Management Science* 2 (Spring 1971): 3.

Early development of the "capture" hypothesis of regulatory behavior—that the industry captures the agency supposed to regulate it and uses that agency to enforce entry barriers and further enhance profits.

PROBLEMS

18.1

A monopolist can produce at constant average and marginal costs of $AC = MC = 5$. The firm faces a market demand curve given by $Q = 53 - P$.

  a. Calculate the profit-maximizing price-quantity combination for the monopolist. Also calculate the monopolist's profits.

  b. What output level would be produced by this industry under perfect competition (where price = marginal cost)?

  c. Calculate the consumer's surplus obtained by consumers in case (b).

Show that this exceeds the sum of the monopolist's profits and the consumer's surplus received in case (a). What is the value of the "deadweight loss" from monopolization?

18.2

A monopolist faces a market demand curve given by

$$Q = 70 - P.$$

a. If the monopolist can produce at constant average and marginal costs of $AC = MC = 6$, what output level will the monopolist choose in order to maximize profits? What is the price at this output level? What are the monopolist's profits?

b. Assume instead that the monopolist has a cost structure where total costs are described by

$$TC = .25Q^2 - 5Q + 300$$

With the monopolist facing the same market demand and marginal revenue, what price-quantity combination will be chosen now to maximize profits? What will profits be?

c. Assume now that a third cost structure explains the monopolist's position with total costs given by

$$TC = .333Q^3 - 26Q^2 + 695Q - 5,800$$

Again, calculate the monopolist's price-quantity combination that maximizes profits. What will profit be? [*Hint:* set $MC = MR$ as usual and use the Quadratic Formula or simple factoring to solve the second order equation for Q.]

d. Graph the market demand curve, the MR curve, and the three marginal cost curves from parts a, b, and c. Notice that the monopolist's profit-making ability is constrained by 1) the market demand curve (along with its associated MR curve), and 2) the cost structure underlying production.

18.3

A single firm monopolizes the entire market for widgets and can produce at constant average and marginal costs of

$$AC = MC = 10.$$

Originally, the firm faces a market demand curve given by

$$Q = 60 - P$$

a. Calculate the profit-maximizing price-quantity combination for the firm. What are the firm's profits?

b. Now assume that the market demand curve shifts outward (becoming steeper) and is given by

$$Q = 45 - .5P$$

What is the firm's profit-maximizing price-quantity combination now? What are the firm's profits?

c. Instead of the assumptions of part b, assume that the market demand curve shifts outward (becoming flatter) and is given by

$$Q = 100 - 2P.$$

What is the firm's profit-maximizing price-quantity combination now? What are the firm's profits?

d. Graph the three different situations of parts a, b, and c. Using your results, explain why there is no real supply curve for a monopoly.

18.4

Suppose that the market for hula hoops is monopolized by a single firm.

a. Draw the initial equilibrium for such a market.

b. Suppose now that the demand for hula hoops shifts outward slightly. Show that, in general (contrary to the competitive case), it will not be possible to predict the effect of this shift in demand on the market price of hula hoops.

c. Consider three possible ways in which the price elasticity of demand might change as the demand curve shifts—it might increase, it might decrease, or it might stay the same. Consider also that marginal costs for the monopolist might be rising, falling, or constant in the range where $MR = MC$. Consequently there are nine different combinations of types of demand shifts and marginal cost slope configurations. Analyze each of these to determine for which it is possible to make a definite prediction about the effect of the shift in demand on the price of hula hoops.

18.5

Suppose that a monopoly market has a demand function in which quantity demanded depends not only on market price (P) but also on the amount of advertising the firm does (A, measured in dollars). The specific form of this function is

$$Q = (20 - P)(1 + 0.1A - 0.01A^2).$$

The monopolistic firm's cost function is given by

$$TC = 10Q + 15 + A.$$

a. Suppose that there is no advertising ($A = 0$). What output will the profit-maximizing firm choose? What market price will this yield? What will be the monopoly's profits?

b. Now let the firm also choose its optimal level of advertising expenditure. In this situation, what output level will be chosen? What price will this yield? What will the level of advertising be? What are the firm's profits in this case?

Hint: Part (b) can be worked out most easily by assuming that the monopoly chooses the profit-maximizing price rather than quantity.

18.6

Suppose that a monopoly produces its output in several different plants and that these plants have differing cost structures. How should the firm decide how much total output to produce? How should it distribute this output among its plants in order to maximize profits?

18.7

Suppose that a monopoly can produce any level of output it wishes at a constant marginal (and average) cost of $5 per unit. Assume that the monopoly sells its goods in two different markets which are separated by some distance. The demand curve in the first market is given by

$$Q_1 = 55 - P_1,$$

and the demand curve in the second market is given by

$$Q_2 = 70 - 2P_2.$$

    a.   If the monopolist can maintain the separation between the two markets, what level of output should be produced in each market and what price will prevail in each market? What are total profits in this situation?

    b.   How would your answer change if it only cost demanders $5 to transport goods between the two markets? What would be the monopolist's new profit level in this situation?

    c.   How would your answer change if transportation costs were 0?

18.8

Suppose a perfectly competitive industry can produce widgets at a constant marginal cost of $10 per unit. Monopolized marginal costs rise to $12 per unit because $2 per unit must be paid to lobbyists to retain the widget producers' favored position. Suppose the market demand for widgets is given by

$$Q_D = 1,000 - 50P.$$

    a.   Calculate the perfectly competitive and monopoly outputs and prices.

    b.   Calculate the total loss of consumer surplus from monopolization of widget production.

    c.   Graph your results.

18.9

Use the concept of consumer's surplus introduced in Chapter 5 to show that imposition of a specific tax in a perfectly competitive industry involves a deadweight loss similar to that shown for the case of a monopoly.

CHAPTER 19

Pricing in Imperfectly Competitive Markets

In this chapter we examine the theory of price determination in markets that fall between the polar extremes of perfect competition and monopoly.[1] Although no single model can be used to explain all possible forms of such imperfect competition, we will examine a few of the basic elements that are common to many of the models that are in current use. To that end we will focus on three specific topics: (1) pricing of homogeneous goods in oligopolistic markets in which there are relatively few firms; (2) product differentiation in oligopolistic markets; and (3) the effect that entry and exit possibilities have on long-run outcomes in imperfectly competitive markets. In a sense then, this chapter concerns how the stringent assumptions of the perfectly competitive model can be relaxed and what the results of changing those assumptions are. For this study, the perfectly competitive model provides a useful benchmark since departures from the competitive norm may involve efficiency losses. Two specific criteria we will use in this comparison are (1) whether prices under imperfect competition equal marginal costs and (2) whether, in the long run, production occurs at minimum average cost. We will see that often imperfectly competitive markets will lack one or both of these desirable features of perfect competition.

Because the theory of imperfect competition does not yield results that are as precise and well-defined as do the theories of perfect competition and monopoly, much of the literature on the subject is descriptive and empirical rather than strictly analytical. This field of "industrial organization" has grown rapidly in recent years and provides a number of insights into behavior in complicated real-world market structures. Although, in keeping with the general spirit of this book, the present chapter is primarily analytical, the final sections offer a brief glimpse of some of the other types of research in industrial organization.

[1]The organization of this chapter benefited greatly from helpful suggestions by Professor Takeo Nakao of Doshisha University, Kyoto, Japan.

**PRICING
UNDER
HOMO-
GENEOUS
OLIGOPOLY**

In this section we will examine the general theory of price determination in markets in which relatively few firms produce a single homogeneous product. As before, we will assume that the market is perfectly competitive on the demand side; that is, there are assumed to be many demanders, each of whom is a price taker. We will also assume that there are no transactions or information costs, so that the good in question obeys the law of one price and we may speak unambiguously of *the* good's price. Later in this chapter we will relax this assumption when we consider product differentiation. Finally, in this section we will assume that there are a fixed number of n identical firms (where n is taken to be a relatively small number). Later, we will consider a specific numerical example of duopoly (in which $n = 2$), but for the moment there is no reason to restrict our analysis to any specific number, since the method of analysis will not for the most part depend on what n happens to be. Throughout this section we will assume that n is fixed, but later in the chapter we will allow n to vary through entry and exit in response to firms' profitability.

*Basic Structure
of the Model*

The output of each firm in our model will be denoted by q_i $(i = 1 \ldots n)$. Since firms generally are assumed to be identical, symmetry in costs will usually require that these outputs are all equal, although it would be a simple matter to allow for some differences among firms. The inverse demand function for the good being examined will be denoted by $f(Q)$, and this shows the price, P, that demanders as a group are willing to pay for any particular level of industry output. That is,

$$P = f(Q) = f(q_1 + q_2 + \cdots + q_n). \qquad (19.1)$$

Each firm's decision problem is to maximize its own profits (π_i), given this market price of the good and the firm's total costs, which are denoted by $TC_i(q_i)$. Hence the firm's goal is to maximize

$$
\begin{aligned}
\pi_i &= Pq_i - TC_i(q_i) \\
&= f(Q)q_i - TC_i(q_i) \qquad (19.2) \\
&= f(q_1 + q_2 + \cdots + q_n)q_i - TC_i(q_i).
\end{aligned}
$$

Most of the issues to be discussed in this section ultimately center around how firms are assumed to make this profit-maximizing output choice. In perhaps overly simple mathematical terms, the results will depend on precisely what is assumed about how Equation 19.2 is to be differentiated to solve for a profit maximum.

Four possible models will be examined here. These are summarized in the definitions on page 561. We will see that these different models yield rather different results and that equilibria arising from the conjectural variations model are generally indeterminate except in a few special cases.

Definitions:

Oligopoly Pricing Models
Quasi-competitive model: Assumes price-taking behavior by all firms (P is treated as fixed).
Cartel model: Assumes firms can collude perfectly in choosing industry output.
Cournot model: Assumes that firm i treats firm j's output as fixed in its decisions ($\partial q_j / \partial q_i = 0$).
Conjectural variations model: Assumes that firm j's output will respond to variations in firm i's output ($\partial q_j / \partial q_i \neq 0$).

Quasi-Competitive Model

As was the case under perfect competition, each firm in the quasi-competitive model is a price taker. That is, each firm assumes (probably incorrectly) that its decisions will not affect market price. In this case the first-order condition for profit maximization is that

$$\frac{\partial \pi_i}{\partial q_i} = P - \frac{\partial TC_i(q_i)}{\partial q_i} = 0 \tag{19.3}$$

or

$$P = MC_i(q_i) \qquad (i = 1, n). \tag{19.4}$$

These n supply equations, together with the market-clearing demand equation,

$$P = f(Q) = f(q_1 + q_2 + \cdots + q_n), \tag{19.5}$$

will assure that this market arrives at the short-run competitive solution. That solution is illustrated for the case of constant marginal costs as point C in Figure 19.1. Even though n may be a small number, the assumption of price-taking behavior in this case results in a competitive outcome.

Cartel Model

Of course, the assumption of price-taking behavior may be particularly inappropriate in oligopolistic industries in which each firm recognizes that its decisions have an obvious effect on price. An alternative assumption would be that firms as a group recognize that they can affect price and manage to coordinate their decisions so as to achieve monopoly profits. In this case the cartel acts as a multiplant monopoly and chooses $q_1, q_2, \ldots, q_n$ so as to maximize total industry profits.

$$\pi = PQ - [TC_1(q_1) + TC_2(q_2) + \cdots + TC_n(q_n)] \tag{19.6}$$

$$= f(q_1 + q_2 + \cdots + q_n)[q_1 + q_2 + \cdots + q_n] - \sum_{i=1}^{n} TC_i(q_i) \tag{19.7}$$

The first-order conditions for a maximum are that

$$\frac{\partial \pi}{\partial q_i} = P + (q_1 + q_2 + \cdots + q_n) \frac{\partial P}{\partial q_i} - MC_i(q_i) = 0 \tag{19.8}$$

$$= MR(Q) - MC_i(q_i) = 0, \tag{19.9}$$

since total revenue depends on the sum of all cartel members' output levels and marginal revenue is the same no matter whose output level is changed. Hence

Figure 19.1   *Alternative Solutions to the Oligopolistic Pricing Problem*

Market equilibrium under an oligopoly can occur at many points on the demand curve. In this figure (which assumes that marginal costs are constant over all output ranges), the quasi-competitive equilibrium occurs at point *C*, the cartel equilibrium at point *M*, and the Cournot solution at point *A*. Many other solutions may occur between points *M* and *C*, depending on the specific assumption made about firms' strategic interrelationships.

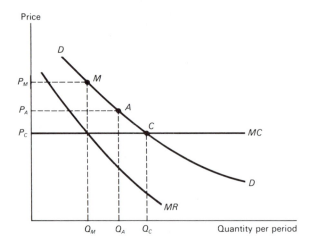

at the profit-maximizing point this common marginal revenue will be equated for each firm's marginal production cost. Assuming these marginal costs are equal and constant for all firms, the output choice is indicated by point *M* in Figure 19.1. Because this coordinated plan requires a specific output level for each firm, the plan will also dictate how monopoly profits earned by the cartel are to be shared. In the aggregate these profits will be as large as possible, given the market demand curve and the industry's cost structure.

There are three problems with this cartel solution. First, and most obviously, such monopolistic decisions may be illegal. In the United States, for example, Section I of the Sherman Act (1890) outlaws "conspiracies in restraint of trade," so would-be cartel members may expect a visit from the FBI. Similar laws exist in many other countries. A second problem with the cartel solution is that it requires that a considerable amount of information be available to the directors of the cartel—specifically, they must know the market demand function and each firm's marginal cost function. This information may be costly to obtain, and some cartel members may be reluctant to provide it. Finally, and most important, the cartel solution may be fundamentally unstable. Since each cartel member will produce an output level for which $P > MC_i$, each will have an incentive to expand output. If the directors of the oligopoly are not able to police such "chiseling," the monopolistic solution may collapse. The difficulties of the OPEC cartel in dictating output levels to its members during the mid-

1980s attest to these problems. Hence we now turn to examine solutions based only on each individual firm's decisions.

Cournot Solution   One of the first researchers to develop a model of markets containing few firms was the French economist Augustin Cournot, who presented a formal analysis of duopoly behavior in 1838.[2] In our notation Cournot assumed that each firm recognizes that its own decisions about q_i affect price but that any one firm's output decisions do not affect those of any other firm. That is, each firm recognizes that $\partial P/\partial q_i \neq 0$ but assumes that $\partial q_j/\partial q_i = 0$ for all $j \neq i$. Using these assumptions, the first-order conditions for a profit maximum in our model are

$$\frac{\partial \pi_i}{\partial q_i} = P + q_i \frac{\partial P}{\partial q_i} - MC_i(q_i) = 0 \tag{19.10}$$

(for all $i = 1, n$). Notice from this equation that the firm assumes that changes in q_i affect its total revenue only through their direct effect on the market price of its own sales. Hence the equation differs both from the cartel solution (where the effect of a change in price on total industry revenues is taken into account—see Equation 19.8) and from the conjectural variations case, to be discussed next, in which indirect effects of firm i's output on firm j's output are taken into account. In general the n equations in 19.10, together with the market-clearing demand Equation 19.5, will permit an equilibrium solution for the variables $q_1, q_2, \ldots, q_n$ and P. An examination of the profit-maximizing Equation 19.10 shows that as long as marginal costs are increasing (as they generally must be for a true profit maximum), each firm's output in the Cournot solution will exceed the cartel output, since the "firm-specific" marginal revenue in that equation is larger than the market–marginal revenue notion in Equation 19.8. On the other hand, the firm's output will fall short of the competitive output since the term $q_i \cdot \partial P/\partial q_i$ in Equation 19.10 is negative. Market equilibrium will therefore occur at a point such as A in Figure 19.1. At this point price exceeds marginal cost, but output is higher and industry profits lower than in the monopoly case.

In general it might also be supposed that the greater the number of firms in the industry, the closer the equilibrium point will be to the competitive point C. With a larger number of firms the term $q_i \cdot \partial P/\partial q_i$ in Equation 19.10 tends to approach zero, and the equation therefore comes to resemble the quasi-competitive solution represented by Equation 19.4. For an example of this limit property of the Cournot model, see the numerical example in the next section.[3]

[2] A. Cournot, *Researches into the Mathematical Principles of the Theory of Wealth*, trans. N. T. Bacon (New York: Macmillan Co., 1897).

[3] For a formal discussion of these issues, see J. Friedman, "Oligopoly Theory," in K. J. Arrow and M. D. Intriligator, eds., *Handbook of Mathematical Economics*, vol. 2 (Amsterdam: North Holland Publishing Co., 1982).

*Conjectural
Variations Model*

So far our models of oligopolistic price determination have not allowed for strategic interactions among firms. In markets with few firms, that is a particularly untenable assumption. Ford must obviously take some account of how General Motors will respond to its pricing and output decisions; all other computer companies must worry about what IBM will do; and members of the OPEC cartel must be concerned with new oil exploration throughout the world. The problem faced by economic theorists is how to capture these strategic considerations in some sort of tractable analytical model. One approach relies on the tools of modern game theory to examine strategic choices in a simplified setting. In Chapter 20 we will develop some of these tools and illustrate how they can be applied to the analysis of duopolistic markets. Here we explore some of the ways in which strategic concerns can be integrated into the models we have already developed.

The primary way of building strategic concerns into our model is by considering the assumptions that might be made by one firm about other firms' behavior. In mathematical terms we wish to examine the possible assumptions that firm i might make about how its decisions might affect those of firm j. Specifically, for each firm i we are concerned with the assumed value of the derivative $\partial q_j / \partial q_i$ for all firms j other than firm i itself. Because the value of this derivative will be speculative, models based on various assumptions about its value are termed "conjectural variations" models; that is, they are concerned with firm i's "conjectures" about firm j's output variations.

Thus far in our models we have assumed that $\partial q_j / \partial q_i = 0$ for all $j \neq i$. We therefore have assumed no strategic interaction among firms. Once this assumption is relaxed, each firm's profit-maximizing decision becomes very complex. Now the first-order condition for maximizing Equation 19.2 becomes

$$\frac{\partial \pi_i}{\partial q_i} = P + q_i \left[\frac{\partial P}{\partial q_i} + \sum_{j \neq i} \frac{\partial P}{\partial q_j} \cdot \frac{\partial q_j}{\partial q_i} \right] - MC_i(q_i) = 0. \qquad (19.11)$$

That is, the firm must now not only be concerned with how its own output affects market price directly but also must consider how variations in its own output will affect market price through their effect on other firms' output decisions. Because any number of plausible assumptions might be made about such responses, there is no generally accepted theory of the type of equilibrium that is likely to emerge from the responses given by Equation 19.11. A few interesting models have been developed for the duopoly case, and we will demonstrate a simple numerical example of these later in this chapter. And in the next section we will examine a particular formulation of Equation 19.11 that yields a simple "price leadership" model. But these two examples are quite specific cases that fail to capture all of the intricacies that may occur in the conjectural variations model in its full generality.

Some authors have adopted a more descriptive approach to the study of pricing in oligopolistic markets where strategic interactions are important. Others have argued that such strategic considerations may be of second-order importance and that the quasi-competitive model (in which all firms are essen-

Figure 19.2 *Formal Model of Price Leadership Behavior*

The curve $D'D'$ shows the demand curve facing the price leader; it is derived by subtracting what is produced by the competitive fringe of firms (SC) from market demand (DD). Given $D'D'$, the firm's profit-maximizing output level is Q_L, and a price of P_L will prevail in the market.

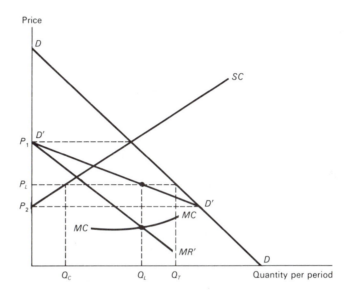

tially price takers) is a sufficiently good approximation to reality. Some of this debate will be summarized in our discussion of the field of industrial organization at the end of this chapter.

Price Leadership Model

One tractable form of the conjectural variations model is based on the assumption that the market in question is composed of a single price leader and a fringe of quasi-competitive competitors. Assuming that the leader is firm 1, a mathematical representation of this market would include a price-taking reaction such as that given by Equation 19.4 for firms $2 \ldots n$, with only firm 1 requiring a complex reaction function of the type given by Equation 19.11. A graphical analysis of such a market is provided by Figure 19.2. The demand curve in the figure represents the total demand curve for the industry's product, and the supply curve SC represents the supply decisions of all the $n - 1$ firms in the competitive fringe. It is simply the horizontal sum of their marginal cost curves. Using these two curves, the demand curve ($D'D'$) facing the industry leader is derived as follows. For a price of P_1 or above, the leader will sell nothing, since the competitive fringe would be willing to supply all that is demanded. For prices below P_2 the leader has the market to itself, since the fringe is not willing to supply anything. Between P_2 and P_1 the curve $D'D'$ is constructed by subtracting what the fringe will supply from total market demand; that is, the leader gets that portion of demand not taken by the fringe firms.

Given the demand curve $D'D'$, the leader can construct its marginal revenue curve (MR') and then refer to its own marginal cost curve (MC) to determine the profit-maximizing output level, Q_L. Market price then will be P_L. Given that price, the competitive fringe will produce Q_C, and total industry output will be $Q_T (= Q_C + Q_L)$.

Of course, this model does not answer such important questions as how the price leader in an industry is chosen or what happens when a member of the fringe decides to challenge the leader for its position and profits. But the model does illustrate one tractable example of the conjectural variations model that may explain pricing behavior in some instances. For example, it has been argued that the model may offer an appropriate explanation for pricing in such markets as those for prime commercial loans (here the major money center banks are the "leaders"), standardized steel products (U.S. Steel is the leader), and, perhaps, the OPEC cartel (where Saudi Arabia by virtue of politics and geology can play the role of leader). Of course, all such purported examples require substantial empirical investigation to determine the validity and scope of this model.

Generalizations

Overall then it is clear that even in the simple case of a homogeneous product, considerable indeterminacy arises about the nature of market equilibrium under an oligopoly. Prices actually observed will depend on strategic interactions among firms, and these interactions in turn will depend on the degree of information available to firms and on the methods firms choose to cope with uncertainty. In general the quasi-competitive and cartel solutions will provide the limits within which equilibrium will occur. The Cournot equilibrium represents one such interior point. But many other such equilibria are possible, depending on the assumptions made.

Two additional types of questions have been raised about the nature of oligopolistic equilibrium. First are questions about how the final equilibrium depends on n, the number of firms. In general there is a presumption that as n increases, the oligopolistic equilibrium will approach the competitive solution. In mathematical terms it seems likely that the effects that variations in a single firm's output have on market prices (see Equation 19.11 for a full statement of those effects) will get smaller as n expands. So, at least in the limit, price-taking behavior will dominate. But there is no general answer to the question of "how large" an n is required for equilibria to be "reasonably close" to the competitive solution. As always in the oligopoly case, it depends on the strategic assumptions made.

A second set of questions about oligopoly pricing concerns how the equilibrium may change from period to period. In this section we have examined only single-period models, so there is no opportunity for firms to learn about their competitors' actions. In a multiperiod analysis, however, firms would obtain some feedback from the market about their rivals' actions and might utilize

Figure 19.3   *Solutions to the Duopoly Problem*

Given the demand curve $Q = 120 - P$, the points M, A, S, and C represent, respectively, the cartel, Cournot, Stackelberg, and quasi-competitive solutions to the duopoly problem.

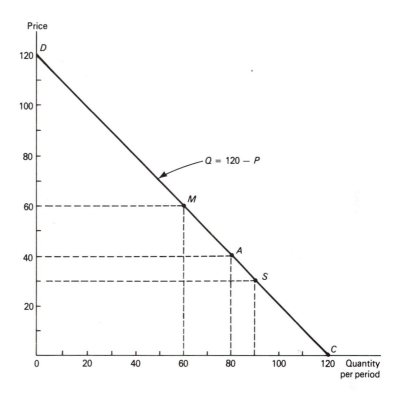

that information in subsequent periods. Several oligopolistic pricing models of this type have been developed, but we shall not examine these here.[4]

NUMERICAL EXAMPLES OF DUOPOLY

As a numerical example of some of these ideas, we will consider a very simple case in which there are no production costs and only two firms. Here each firm might be assumed to have a large quantity of a costless good (say, water from a spring—an example used by Cournot in the nineteenth century) in its own possession, and the problem is how much to provide to the market. The demand for the commodity is given by the linear demand curve

$$Q = q_1 + q_2 = 120 - P \tag{19.12}$$

and is illustrated in Figure 19.3. We will now examine various market equilibria along this demand curve.

[4] For a summary, see J. Friedman, "Oligopoly Theory."

Quasi-Competitive Solution

Since each firm has zero marginal costs, the quasi-competitive solution will result in a market price of zero. Total demand will be 120. In this particular example the division of this output between the two firms is indeterminate since marginal costs are constant over all output ranges. The quasi-competitive output level is indicated by point C in Figure 19.3.

Cartel Solution

The cartel solution to this example can be found by maximizing total industry revenue (and profits):

$$\pi = PQ = 120Q - Q^2. \tag{19.13}$$

The first-order condition for a maximum is

$$\frac{\partial \pi}{\partial Q} = 120 - 2Q = 0$$

or

$$Q = 60$$
$$P = 60 \tag{19.14}$$
$$\pi = 3600.$$

Again the precise division of these output levels and profits among the firms in the industry is indeterminate. The monopolistic cartel solution is indicated by point M in Figure 19.3.

Cournot Solution

From Equation 19.12 it is easy to see that the two firms' profits are given by

$$\pi_1 = Pq_1 = (120 - q_1 - q_2)q_1 = 120q_1 - q_1^2 - q_1q_2$$
$$\pi_2 = Pq_2 = (120 - q_1 - q_2)q_2 = 120q_1 - q_2^2 - q_1q_2. \tag{19.15}$$

Assuming that $\partial q_1/\partial q_2 = \partial q_2/\partial q_1 = 0$, the first-order conditions for a maximum are

$$\frac{\partial \pi_1}{\partial q_1} = 120 - 2q_1 - q_2 = 0$$
$$\frac{\partial \pi_2}{\partial q_2} = 120 - 2q_2 - q_1 = 0. \tag{19.16}$$

These two "reaction functions" can be solved simultaneously for the equilibrium values of q_1 and q_2 to yield

$$q_1 = q_2 = 40$$
$$P = 120 - (q_1 + q_2) = 40 \tag{19.17}$$
$$\pi_1 = \pi_2 = Pq_1 = Pq_2 = 1600.$$

More will be supplied under the Cournot assumptions than under the cartel case, and industry profits (3200) will be somewhat lower than when output decisions are fully coordinated. This Cournot solution is denoted by point A

in Figure 19.3. In this particular case it is easy to show that as more firms are introduced into the analysis, the equilibrium moves toward the competitive point.[5] For a somewhat more realistic case that also yields that solution, see problem 19.2.

Stackelberg Leadership Solution

The assumption of a constant marginal cost makes the price leadership model developed previously inappropriate for this simple problem. In this case the "competitive fringe" would simply take the entire market by pricing at marginal cost (here zero), with no room left in the market for the price leader. There is, however, the possibility for a different type of strategic leadership, a possibility first recognized by the German economist Heinrich von Stackelberg.[6] Von Stackelberg examined the consequences of assuming that one firm (say, firm 1) recognized how the other firm makes its output decisions. That is, he assumed that firm 1 knows (from Equation 19.16) that firm 2 chooses q_2 so that

$$q_2 = \frac{120 - q_1}{2}. \tag{19.18}$$

Firm 1 can now calculate the conjectural variation,

$$\frac{\partial q_2}{\partial q_1} = -\frac{1}{2}, \tag{19.19}$$

and firm 1's profit-maximization problem must be rewritten to take account of this reaction:

$$\pi_1 = Pq_1 = 120q_1 - q_1^2 - q_1 q_2 \tag{19.20}$$

and

$$\frac{\partial \pi_1}{\partial q_1} = 120 - 2q_1 - q_1 \frac{\partial q_2}{\partial q_1} - q_2 = 0$$

$$= 120 - \frac{3}{2} q_1 - q_2 = 0. \tag{19.21}$$

---

[5] With n firms Equation 19.16 becomes

$$\frac{\partial \pi_i}{\partial q_i} = 120 - 2q_i - \sum_{j \neq i} q_j = 0 \qquad (i = 1, n).$$

Assuming, by symmetry, that all the q's are equal to $\bar{q}$, we have

$$\frac{\partial \pi_i}{\partial q_i} = 120 - (n + 1)\bar{q} = 0.$$

Hence $\bar{q} = 120/(n + 1)$ and total output $= n\bar{q} = [n/n + 1] (120)$, which approaches 120 (the competitive output) for large values of n.

[6] H. von Stackelberg, *The Theory of the Market Economy*, trans. A. T. Peacock (New York: Oxford University Press, 1952).

Solving this equation simultaneously with firm 2's reaction function (Equation 19.18) yields the following equilibrium values:

$$q_1 = 60$$

$$q_2 = 30$$

$$P = 120 - (q_1 + q_2) = 30 \qquad (19.22)$$

$$\pi_1 = Pq_1 = 1800$$

$$\pi_2 = Pq_2 = 900.$$

Firm 1 has been able to increase its profits by using its knowledge of firm 2's reactions. Firm 2's profits have been seriously eroded in the process. This solution is shown as point S on the demand curve presented in Figure 19.3.

One ambiguous feature of the Stackelberg model is how to decide which firm will be the leader and which the follower. If each firm assumes that the other is a follower, each will produce 60 and will be disappointed at the final outcome (with total output of 120, market price, in the present example, will fall to zero). On the other hand, if each acts as a follower, the situation will revert to the Cournot equilibrium discussed in the previous section. This equilibrium, however, is unstable: Each firm can perceive the benefits of being a leader and may try to choose its output accordingly. In Chapter 20 we will examine this situation again because it is representative of a number of problems in the theory of games.

PRODUCT DIFFEREN- TIATION

Up to this point we have been assuming that the oligopolistic firms we have been examining produce a homogeneous output. Demanders therefore were assumed to be indifferent about which firm's output they bought, and the law of one price was assumed to hold in the market. Such an assumption is widely at variance with many real-world markets. Firms often devote considerable resources to differentiating their products from those of their competitors through such devices as quality and style variations, warranties and guarantees, special service features, and product advertising. All of these activities require firms to employ additional resources, and firms will choose to do so if profits are thereby increased. Such attempts at product variation also will result in a relaxation of the law of one price, since now the market will consist of goods that vary from firm to firm and demanders may have preferences about which supplier to patronize. That possibility introduces a certain fuzziness into what we mean by the "market for a good," since now there are many closely related, but not identical, products being produced. For example, once it is recognized that toothpaste brands vary somewhat from supplier to supplier, should we consider all these products to be in the same market? Or should we differentiate, say, among fluoridated products, gels, striped toothpaste, smokers' toothpaste, and so forth? Or, consider the problem of spatial differentiation. Since demanders will be closer to some sellers than to others, they may view nearby sellers more favorably because buying from them involves lower transportation charges. Here we will assume that the market is composed of n

firms, each producing a slightly different product, but that these products can usefully be considered a single product group. This notion can be made more precise by

---

Definition:

Product Group
The outputs of a set of firms constitute a *product group* if the substitutability in demand among the products (as measured by the cross-price elasticity) is very high relative to the substitutability between those firms' outputs and other goods generally.

Although this definition has its own ambiguities (arguments about the definition of a product group often dominate antitrust proceedings, for example), it should suffice for our purposes.[7] Now we will proceed to offer a formal but simplified analysis of pricing within the market for such a product group.

Firms' Choices   Again we will assume that there are n firms competing in a particular product group. Now, however, each firm can choose the amount it spends on attempting to differentiate its product from those of its competitors. We will denote the resources used by the ith firm for this purpose by z_i, which might include spending on special options, quality, brand advertising, or moving to a favorable location. The firm's costs now are given by

$$\text{total costs} = TC_i(q_i, z_i). \tag{19.23}$$

Because there are n slightly different goods in the product group, we must allow for the possibility of different market prices for each of these goods. Such prices will be denoted by $P_1, \ldots, P_n$ (although some of these may be equal). The demand facing the ith firm shows how price received depends on quantity produced by that firm (q_i), on prices being charged by all other firms (P_j for $j \neq i$), and on the ith firm's and all other firms' attempts to differentiate their products (z_j, $j = 1 \ldots n$). In its most general form then,

$$P_i = g(q_i, P_j, z_i, z_j), \tag{19.24}$$

where the terms P_j and z_j are intended to include all other prices and differentiation activities, respectively. Presumably, $\partial g / \partial q_i \leq 0$, $\partial g / \partial P_j \geq 0$, $\partial g / \partial z_i \geq 0$, and $\partial g / \partial z_j \leq 0$. That is, the demand curve facing the individual firm is downward sloping and is shifted outward by price increases by its competitors. Product differentiation activities by the ith firm may also shift demand outward, whereas such activities by competitors will shift demand inward.

The ith firm's profits are given by

$$\pi_i = P_i q_i - TC_i(q_i, z_i), \tag{19.25}$$

---

[7] A more precise definition might be built around the "attribute" concept introduced in Chapter 6. Under this approach, goods that share a common set of attributes would constitute a product group.

and in the simple case where $\partial z_j / \partial q_i$, $\partial z_j / \partial z_i$, $\partial P_j / \partial q_i$, and $\partial P_j / \partial z_i$ are all zero, the first-order conditions for a maximum are

$$\frac{\partial \pi_i}{\partial q_i} = P_i + q_i \frac{\partial P_i}{\partial q_i} - \frac{\partial TC_i}{\partial q_i} = 0 \tag{19.26}$$

$$\frac{\partial \pi_i}{\partial z_i} = q_i \frac{\partial P_i}{\partial z_i} - \frac{\partial TC_i}{\partial z_i} = 0. \tag{19.27}$$

Equation 19.26 is again simply a restatement of the marginal revenue equals marginal cost condition for a profit maximum. Equation 19.27 shows that, as for any input, additional differentiation activities should be pursued up to the point at which the additional revenues they generate are equal to their marginal costs.

Market Equilibrium

Although this description of firms' choices seems straightforward, these choices are actually quite complex. Since the demand curve facing any one firm depends on the prices and product differentiation activities of its competitors, that demand curve may shift frequently, and its position at any particular time may only be partly understood. As in the Cournot model, the firm must make some assumptions in order to make decisions. And, as in the conjectural variations model, whatever one firm decides to do may affect its competitors' actions. Hence the differentiated oligopoly model poses even more complex strategic issues than did the models we examined for the homogeneous good case. Not surprisingly, few definitive conclusions can be reached about the nature of the market equilibria that result from such a situation. Two very general conclusions might be mentioned, however. First, because of the differentiated nature of goods in the product group, price-taking behavior is unlikely. Each firm will believe that its activities have some effect on the price of its product. Price will exceed marginal revenue and marginal cost, and there may be some allocational inefficiency. Second, because of the uncertain demand facing each firm, information costs may be quite high. Therefore firms may opt for strategies that economize on such costs. For example, they may adopt relatively simple "rules of thumb" in their decisions, such as adopting markup pricing (Chapter 12) or aiming for a target market share (Chapter 13) based on historical patterns. As a result of these types of behavior, market equilibria may be somewhat more stable over time than might at first be suggested by the complexities and uncertainties of the problem. Indeed it is possible that both prices and product types may converge around some median values, so that the homogeneous oligopoly models become appropriate. For example, product attributes may come to approximate those desired by the "typical" consumer, since any firm that departs very far from producing such a good may find itself outflanked by competitors. The tendency of television networks to produce the same types of shows and of political candidates to gravitate to the middle of the road in their positions are probably the most familiar instances of such behavior, but other occurrences come readily to mind. However, the condi-

Figure 19.4 *Spatial Differentiation and Pricing*

Ice cream stands are located at points A and B along a linear beach of length L. In equilibrium, consumers to the left of E will patronize stand A, those to the right will patronize stand B. Different prices will prevail at the two stands. If the stands can relocate, they will move to the center of the beach.

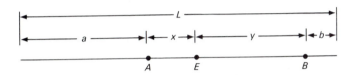

tions under which this may happen have not as yet been clearly identified.[8] The following example illustrates the phenomenon for a particularly graphic case.

Numerical Example of Spatial Differentiation

To develop a simple model of product differentiation, consider the case of ice cream stands located on a beach—a problem first studied by H. Hotelling in the 1920s.[9] Figure 19.4 shows this (linear) beach together with two ice cream stands located at points A and B. Assume demanders are located uniformly along the beach, one at each unit of length, and that each buys exactly one ice cream cone per period. Ice cream cones are assumed to be costless to produce, but carrying them back to one's beach umbrella results in a cost c per unit of distance traveled (since the ice cream melts). If we let P_A be stand A's price and P_B be stand B's price, a person located at point E will be indifferent between stands A and B if

$$P_A + cx = P_B + cy. \tag{19.28}$$

As Figure 19.4 shows,

$$a + x + y + b = L, \tag{19.29}$$

where L is the length of the beach. The coordinate of point E is therefore

$$x = \frac{P_B - P_A + cy}{c} \tag{19.30}$$

$$= \frac{P_B - P_A}{c} + L - a - b - x \tag{19.31}$$

[8] For a brief survey of the literature on markets with imperfect information, see M. Rothschild, "Models of Market Organization with Imperfect Information: A Survey," *Journal of Political Economy* (November–December 1973): 1283–1308.

[9] H. Hotelling, "Stability in Competition," *The Economic Journal* (January 1929): 41–57.

or

$$x = \frac{1}{2}\left\{L - a - b + \frac{P_B - P_A}{c}\right\}$$

(19.32)

and

$$y = \frac{1}{2}\left\{L - a - b + \frac{P_A - P_B}{c}\right\}.$$

(19.33)

Profits for the two firms are

$$\pi_A = P_A(a + x) = \frac{1}{2}(L + a - b)P_A + \frac{P_A P_B - P_A^2}{2c}$$

(19.34)

and

$$\pi_B = P_B(b + y) = \frac{1}{2}(L - a + b)P_B + \frac{P_A P_B - P_B^2}{2c}.$$

(19.35)

Each firm will choose its own price so as to maximize profits:

$$\frac{\partial \pi_A}{\partial P_A} = \frac{1}{2}(L + a - b) + \frac{P_B}{2c} - \frac{P_A}{c} = 0$$

$$\frac{\partial \pi_B}{\partial P_B} = \frac{1}{2}(L - a + b) + \frac{P_A}{2c} - \frac{P_B}{c} = 0.$$

(19.36)

These can readily be solved for

$$P_A = c\left(L + \frac{a - b}{3}\right)$$

$$P_B = c\left(L - \frac{a - b}{3}\right).$$

(19.37)

In general, these prices will depend on the precise location of the two stands and will differ from each other. Assume that the beach is 100 yards long, $a = 40$ yards, $b = 10$ yards, and $c = \$.01$ per yard, then

$$P_A = .01\left(100 + \frac{30}{3}\right)$$

$$= \$1.10$$

(19.38)

$$P_B = .01\left(100 - \frac{30}{3}\right)$$

$$= \$.90.$$

These price differences arise only from the locational aspects of this problem since cones themselves are costless. Because A is somewhat more favorably located than B, it can charge a higher price for its cones without losing too much business to B. Using Equation 19.32 shows

$$x = \frac{1}{2}(100 - 40 - 10 - 20) = 15 \qquad (19.39)$$

so that stand A sells 55 cones (despite its higher price) whereas B sells only 45.

At point E a consumer is indifferent between walking 15 yards to A and paying \$1.10 or walking 35 yards to B and paying \$.90. The solution is inefficient in that a consumer slightly to the right of E would incur a shorter walk by patronizing A, but chooses B because of A's power to set higher prices.

Perhaps the most interesting insights from Hotelling's model arise if we assume the stands can change their locations at zero cost. In this case B would move to just slightly to the right of A and capture 60 percent of the market. If A would then leapfrog B and regain the dominant position, ultimately both firms would move to the center of the beach, and each would get half the market, just as political candidates move to the center of the policy spectrum. The inefficiency in this situation arises because total transport costs would be minimized if the stands were located 25 yards from each end of the beach, but this efficient solution is unstable under duopoly.[10]

ADVERTISING AND RESOURCE ALLOCATION

Because of its economic importance and controversial nature, advertising has been somewhat more intensively examined by economists than other aspects of behavior in differentiated oligopoly markets have been. These analyses have included theoretical studies of advertising and resource allocation, empirical studies of the effect of advertising on the demands for specific products, and legal investigations of what should be done about false advertising claims.[11] Here we will examine only the allocational issue. Specifically, we will investigate two arguments that suggest that in an unregulated market, resources may be overallocated to the provision of advertising messages.

The first of these analyses starts with the observation that the "market" for advertising messages is not separated from the market for the good being advertised. When someone purchases a box of laundry soap, he or she also pays for the advertising messages that the soap maker provides. In other words, a good and its associated advertising are *joint products*. This technical property of the way in which advertising messages are supplied may cause too many messages to be produced. As we have seen, firms will produce additional advertising messages up to the point at which the marginal revenue brought from the additional demand generated by a message is equal to the message's cost. This additional revenue being generated reflects individuals' willingness to pay

---

[10] Total walking costs to A are

$$\int_0^a z\,dz + \int_0^x z\,dz = (a^2 + x^2)/2.$$

Similarly, costs of walking to B are $(b^2 + y^2)/2$. The sum of these is minimized when

$$a = x = b = y = L/4.$$

[11] Some of these analyses (together with a wealth of empirical information) are reviewed in R. Schmalensee, *The Economics of Advertising* (Amsterdam: North Holland Publishing Co., 1972), chap. 1.

for both the goods being bought and for the information provided by the advertising message itself. Looking at the advertising message alone, it is clear that individuals must be evaluating it at less than its production cost (since the good itself must have some value). If the information contained in the advertisement had been marketed separately, its market price would not have exceeded its production cost. The fact of joint production may cause too many advertising messages to be produced.

The second observation that suggests that there may be too much advertising derives from a distinction (first made by A. Marshall) between *constructive* and *combative* advertising. Constructive advertising conveys useful information and by so doing may increase the total demand for a product. Combative advertising, on the other hand, merely reflects competition among different brands for a share of a fixed market. This kind of advertising is "defensive" in that any one firm is forced to do it because all the others do (see Chapter 20 for a model of this process). An across-the-board reduction of advertising by all firms would not affect total demand at all, whereas a reduction by any one firm would be harmful to that firm. A reduction in such combative advertising would free resources that could be productively employed elsewhere. In this sense there may again be too much advertising.

Although these arguments are suggestive, a number of contrary points also have been raised. Advertising provides information to consumers, usually without cost. Hence it has some attributes of a "public good," and as we shall show in Chapter 24, resources may be *underallocated* to such goods. Advertising also may have competitive effects on industry structure if the ability to promote a new firm's product reduces barriers to entry created by entrenched brands. For example, the highly successful Volkswagen advertising campaign of the early 1960s may have contributed significantly to opening the U.S. market to imports of small cars. To the extent that there are economies of scale in producing advertising messages, however, these pro-competitive effects may be mitigated by cost advantages that will be enjoyed by existing, larger firms. So, there is no general answer to the questions of whether advertising helps or hinders competition and whether an appropriate level of resources will be devoted to producing advertising messages. A full evaluation will depend on the specific market circumstances.

ENTRY

The possibility of new firms entering an industry plays an important part in the development of the theory of perfectly competitive price determination. That possibility assures that any long-run profits will be eliminated by new entrants and that firms will produce at the low points of their long-run average cost curves. Under conditions of oligopoly, the first of these forces continues to operate. To the extent that entry is possible, long-run profits are constrained. If entry is completely costless, long-run economic profits will be zero (as in the competitive case).

Zero-Profit Equilibrium

Whether firms in an oligopolistic industry with free entry will be directed to the low point of their average cost curves depends on the nature of the demand curve facing them. If firms are price takers, the analysis given for the competi-

Figure 19.5   *Entry Reduces Profitability in an Oligopoly*

Initially, the demand curve facing the firm is *dd*. Marginal revenue is given by *mr*, and q^* is the profit-maximizing output level. If entry is costless, new firms attracted by the possibility for profits may shift the firm's demand curve inward to $d'd'$, where profits are zero. At output level q', average costs are not a minimum, and the firm exhibits excess capacity given by $qm - q'$.

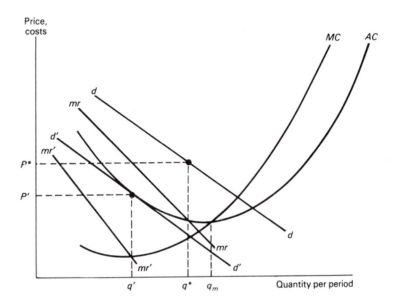

tive case carries over directly: Since $P = MR = MC$ for profit maximization with price taking and since $P = AC$ if entry is to result in zero profits, production will take place where $MC = AC$ (that is, at minimum average cost).

If oligopolistic firms have some control over the price they receive (perhaps because each produces a slightly differentiated product), each firm will face a downward-sloping demand curve and the competitive analysis will not hold. Entry still may reduce profits to zero, but now production at minimum average cost is not assured. This situation is illustrated in Figure 19.5. Initially, the demand curve facing the firm is given by *dd* and economic profits are being earned. New firms will be attracted by these profits, and their entry will shift *dd* inward (because there are now a larger number of firms to contend with a given market demand curve). Indeed, entry can reduce profits to zero by shifting the demand curve to $d'd'$. The level of output that maximizes profits with this demand curve (q') is not, however, the same as that level at which average costs are minimized (q_m). Rather, the firm will produce less than that "efficient" output level and will exhibit "excess capacity," given by $q_m - q'$. Some economists have hypothesized that this outcome characterizes industries such as service stations, convenience stores, and fast-food franchisers, where product differentiation is prevalent but entry is relatively costless.[12]

*Contestable
Markets and
Industry Structure*

The conclusion that the zero-profit equilibrium pictured in Figure 19.5 is sustainable in the long run has been challenged recently by several economists.[13] They argue that the model neglects the effects of *potential entry* on market equilibrium by focusing only on the behavior of actual entrants. They therefore reintroduce to economics the distinction, first made by H. Demsetz, between competition *in* the market and competition *for* the market by showing that the latter concept provides a more appropriate perspective for analyzing the free entry assumption.[14] Within this broader perspective the "invisible hand" of competition becomes even more constraining on firms' behavior, and perfectly competitive equilibria are more likely to emerge.

The expanded examination of entry begins by defining a "perfectly contestable market."

Definition:

Perfectly Contestable Market
A market is *perfectly contestable* if entry and exit are absolutely free. Equivalently, a perfectly contestable market is one in which no outside potential competitor can enter by cutting price and still make profits (since if such profit opportunities existed, potential entrants would take advantage of them).

A perfectly contestable market then drops the perfectly competitive assumption of price-taking behavior but expands a bit upon the concept of free entry by permitting potential entrants to operate in a hit-and-run manner, snatching up whatever profit opportunities are available. Such an assumption, as we will point out below, is not necessarily accurate in many market situations, but it does provide a different starting place for a simplified theory of pricing.

The equilibrium illustrated in Figure 19.5 is unsustainable in a perfectly contestable market, provided that two or more firms are already in the market. In such a case a potential hit-and-run entrant could turn a quick profit by taking all the first firm's sales by selling q' at a price slightly below P' and making up for the loss this would entail by selling a further marginal increment in output to the other firm(s)' customers at a price in excess of marginal cost. That is, because the equilibrium in Figure 19.5 has $P > MC$, it permits a would-be

---

[12] This analysis was originally developed by E. H. Chamberlin, *The Theory of Monopolistic Competition* (Cambridge, Mass.: Harvard University Press, 1950). The resulting model of free entry but slightly differentiated products is sometimes referred to as "monopolistic competition." For additional discussion of the model see the Extensions at the end of this chapter.

[13] See W. J. Baumol, "Contestable Markets: An Uprising in the Theory of Industry Structure," *American Economic Review* (March 1982): 1–19, and W. J. Baumol, J. C. Panzar, and R. D. Willig, *Contestable Markets and the Theory of Industry Structure* (San Diego, Calif.: Harcourt Brace Jovanovich, 1982).

[14] H. Demsetz, "Why Regulate Utilities?" *Journal of Law and Economics* (April 1968): 55–65.

Figure 19.6   *Perfect Contestability and Industry Structure*

In a perfectly contestable market, equilibrium requires that $P = MC = AC$. The number of firms is completely determined by market demand (Q^*) and by the output level that minimizes average cost (q^*).

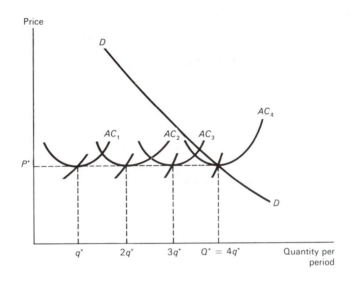

entrant to take away one zero-profit firm's market and encroach a bit on other firms' markets where, at the margin, profits are attainable. The only type of market equilibrium that would be impervious to such hit-and-run tactics would be one in which firms earn zero profits and price at marginal costs. And as we saw in Chapter 14, this requires that firms produce at the low points of their long-run average cost curves where $P = MC = AC$. Even in the absence of price-taking behavior in markets with relatively few firms, perfect contestability provides an "invisible hand" that guides market equilibrium to a competitive-type result.

This perfectly contestable analysis can be taken one step further by showing how industry structure is determined. If, as in Chapter 14, we let q^* represent that output level for which average costs are minimized and Q^* represent the total market demand for the commodity when price equals minimal average cost, then the equilibrium number of firms in the industry is given by

$$n = \frac{Q^*}{q^*} \tag{19.40}$$

and contrary to the perfectly competitive case, this number may be relatively small. In Figure 19.6, for example, exactly four firms fulfill the market demand for Q^*, and the perfectly contestable assumption will ensure competitive behavior, even though these firms may recognize strategic relationships among themselves. The ability of potential entrants to seize any possible opportunities for profit sharply constrains the types of behavior that are possible and thereby provides a determinate equilibrium market structure.

Barriers to Entry   All of the analysis presented so far in this section has been predicated on the assumptions of free entry and exit. When various barriers prevent such flexibility, these results must be modified. Possible barriers to entry in the oligopoly case include many of those already discussed in connection with monopoly in the previous chapter. They also include those arising specifically out of some features of oligopolistic markets. Product differentiation, for example, may raise entry barriers by promoting strong brand loyalty. Or producers may so proliferate their brands that no room remains for would-be entrants to do anything different (this has been alleged to be true in the ready-to-eat breakfast cereal industry). The possibility of strategic pricing decisions may also deter entry if existing firms can convince firms wishing to enter that it would be unprofitable to do so. Firms may, for a time, adopt lower, entry-deterring prices in order to accomplish this goal, with the intent of raising prices once potential entrants disappear (assuming they do).

Finally, the completely flexible type of hit-and-run behavior assumed in the contestable markets theory may be subject to two other types of barriers in the real world. First, some types of capital investments made by firms may not be reversible. A firm cannot build an automobile assembly plant for a week's use and then dismantle it at no loss. In this case there are exit costs that will make recurrent raids on the industry unprofitable. Of course, in other cases, such as the trucking industry, capital may be easily rented for short periods and exit will then pose few costs. Second, the contestable markets model requires that quantity demanded respond instantly to price differentials. If, instead, demanders only switch slowly to a new product, potential entrants cannot attain market penetration quickly, and their ability to discipline firms in the market will be constrained.[15] The importance of all such restrictions for market behavior is ultimately an empirical question.

INDUSTRIAL ORGANIZATION THEORY   Thus far in this chapter we have been primarily concerned with a formal analysis of price determination in oligopolistic markets. Although this analysis has offered a number of insights into the behavior of such markets, we have also seen that it is very difficult to capture in a formal way all of the factors that may affect market outcomes. In recent years research in the field of industrial organization has expanded rapidly in an effort to provide details on those aspects of market behavior that are not easily captured by formal models. In this concluding section, we will briefly examine some of this analysis. The applied example at the end of this chapter also provides an illustration of how the tools of industrial organization are used in the field of antitrust.

---

[15] For some additional criticisms of this type, see M. Spence, "Contestable Markets and the Theory of Industrial Structure," *Journal of Economic Literature* (September 1983): 981–990.

It is customary to divide industrial organization analysis into three topics: (1) market structure; (2) firm conduct; and (3) economic performance.[16] The first of these is concerned with describing the industry: How many firms are there? What types of products are produced? Are there increasing returns to scale? Are there significant barriers to entry? Understanding such facts is a necessary precondition for analyzing firm conduct, the second basic topic in industrial organization theory. That topic concerns such matters as firms' output and price decisions, product differentiation, advertising, investment decisions, research activities, and so forth. That is, the topic investigates what firms do. Finally, the "performance" aspect of industrial organization theory is concerned with appraising the desirability of particular markets. Criteria used in that appraisal include questions of economic efficiency, distributional equity, and the long-term growth of the industry. We now turn to examine each of the three topics in somewhat greater detail.

Market Structure   Perhaps the most important types of information on market structure are those that concern the number, size, and general concentration of the firms in an industry. A representative selection of these data is illustrated in Table 19.1 for the year 1977 (the most recent available, unfortunately). Of particular interest to industrial organization economists are the "concentration ratios," the percentages of total domestic shipments produced by the 4, 8, 20, and 50 largest firms. The figures indicate, for example, that production of motor vehicles, cigarettes, and organic fibers are all highly concentrated, with 4-firm concentration ratios of around 80 or higher. On the other hand, industries such as commercial printing, bottled soft drinks, and sawmills have a low concentration of production, with less than half of industry output being produced by the 50 largest firms. Hence there appears to be a great variety among the structures prevalent in U.S. industries.

Unfortunately, the types of data on industry concentration that are illustrated in Table 19.1 suffer from a number of shortcomings. Imports are not reflected in the data, for example, and this may lead to a distorted picture of the degree of competition in industries (such as automobiles), where competition from foreign goods is strong. Similarly, the data presented are quite aggregated, and they may obscure concentration patterns in more narrowly defined markets. For example, the "toilet preparations" industry appears to be relatively unconcentrated on the basis of the data in the table, although some sectors of this market (such as toothpaste production) are very concentrated indeed. And many other problems of interpretation may arise from the specific details of the industry in question. The low concentration in soft drinks, for example, becomes more problematic when it is recognized that many of the local bottlers represented in the data operate under exclusive area-wide licenses from the Coca-Cola or Pepsico companies. Despite all these difficulties, data

---

[16] For a rather complete survey of the field, see F. M. Scherer, *Industrial Market Structure and Economic Performance*, 2d ed. (Chicago: Rand McNally, 1980). Chapters 1 and 2 lay out the general methodology of industrial organization theory.

Table 19.1   *Representative Data on U.S. Industrial Structure, 1977*

Industry	Number of Firms	Total Output	Total Value Added ($\times$ 1,000,000)	Percentage of Output Produced by 4 Largest	8 Largest	20 Largest	50 Largest
Motor vehicles	254	$76,518	$18,724	93%	99%	99 + %	99 + %
Steel mills	395	41,998	15,332	45	65	84	95
Pharmaceuticals	655	11,459	8,214	24	43	73	91
Aircraft	151	14,834	8,134	59	81	99	99 +
Petroleum refining	192	91,689	14,424	30	53	81	94
Photographic equipment	702	9,945	6,732	72	86	90	94
Electronic computers	808	12,924	7,624	44	51	71	85
Commercial printing	10,964	9,360	5,338	6	10	17	26
Tires	121	8,971	4,347	70	88	97	99 +
Sawmills	6,966	10,867	4,453	17	23	36	49
Toilet preparations	644	6,557	4,527	40	56	79	90
Cigarettes	8	6,377	3,803	90	100	100	100
Organic fibers	37	6,380	2,804	78	90	99	100
Bottled and canned soft drinks	1,758	10,007	4,085	15	22	36	50

Source: *Statistical Abstract of the United States, 1981* (Washington, D.C.: U.S. Government Printing Office, 1981), table 1427.

similar to those provided in Table 19.1 are about all the quantitative information that is available on real-world industrial structure, and such data are widely used.

Several other aspects of market structure have been systematically examined by industrial organization economists. Particular attention has been focused on barriers to entry because this concept plays a key role both in the model of perfectly competitive pricing in the long run and in the theory of contestable markets. Two types of entry barriers have been intensively studied: (1) cost barriers derived from economies of scale and (2) barriers created by firms' strategic decisions. Barriers of the latter type include those derived from firms' pricing decisions and from product differentiation. There is a vast amount of empirical information on all of these topics.[17]

A final structural concern has been the study of mergers. "Horizontal" mergers (that is, two firms producing the same types of goods) raise no particularly novel economic issues—they will clearly increase the concentration in an in-

[17]The classic treatment is J. S. Bain, *Barriers to New Competition* (Cambridge, Mass.: Harvard University Press, 1956).

dustry and therefore may pose the threats of creating the kinds of allocational inefficiencies outlined previously in this chapter. More difficult to evaluate are "vertical" mergers, in which one firm integrates a given production process rather than relying on a network of sellers of intermediate products. In this case the results on the market price of the end product may be indeterminate. Vertical integration may produce cost efficiencies that tend to reduce prices, but it may also produce some degree of monopolistic control over prices of inputs. No theoretically unambiguous conclusion is possible.[18] Finally, in recent years "conglomerate" mergers have become commonplace among firms in very different industries. Huge firms such as ITT or Textron operate in literally hundreds of markets, and this raises the question of whether those firms' subsidiaries behave in ways similar to independent firms in such markets. As for vertical mergers a variety of analyses have been proposed, ranging from the notion that conglomerate firms provide "synergistic" cost savings and diversification for their subsidiaries to the hypothesis that conglomerates may aid in monopolization by engaging in cross-subsidization among subsidiaries. Both the theory and empirical evidence on such behavior are relatively underdeveloped.

Firm Conduct

This aspect of industrial organization theory concerns the attempt to provide some institution details with which to supplement the various pricing models discussed earlier in this chapter. Because it has proved to be quite difficult to obtain detailed information about firms' strategic motives and assumptions (say, through interviews with managers), the focus of much of this research instead has been on the narrower question of whether oligopolistic coordination in pricing decisions is possible or likely. Economists have examined the roles of explicit agreements, tacit understandings, price leadership, commonly used rules of thumb and the use of industrywide price lists as mechanisms for effecting such coordination. All of these at times have proved to be successful. But increasing legal scrutiny of such devices, combined with the instability in cartels that incentives to chisel on price create, has placed severe limits on the possibility of success. Many other aspects of market organization tend to deter oligopolistic coordination. In particular, dynamic changes in either demand or cost conditions over time may make it very difficult for a would-be cartel to decide precisely how to maximize joint profits. And the expected gains from such coordination therefore may appear to be quite small. That judgment may be altered, however, if the cartel can devise some sort of coordinating innovation or if it can enlist government aid in the pursuit of its goals.[19]

Industry Performance

A final aspect of industrial organization analysis concerns appraising industry performance. Traditionally, the primary focus has been on examining the allocational efficiency of alternative industry structures. Two different types of

---

[18] For a summary of some of the debate, see J. S. McGee and L. R. Bassett, "Vertical Integration Revisited," *Journal of Law and Economics* (April 1976): 17–38.

[19] For a survey of many of the issues surrounding oligopolistic coordination, see Scherer, *Industrial Market Structure and Economic Performance*, chaps. 6 and 7.

criteria are employed. The first concerns the "static efficiency" of the industry, which is usually taken to mean how closely behavior in that industry approaches the perfectly competitive ideal. Industries with fairly large numbers of firms, low entry barriers, and pricing close to marginal cost can be regarded as "effectively" competitive. On the other hand, important departures from these ideals will reverse that assessment, and there may be static losses in social welfare as a result of such failures. A general conclusion of this type of research is that a large portion of the U.S. economy appears to be effectively competitive and that the degree of competition may have increased in recent years. For example, W. G. Shepherd finds that in 1980, 77 percent of U.S. National Income was produced in industries that he classifies as effectively competitive, with 2 percent being produced under monopoly, 3 percent in industries with dominant firms, and 18 percent in "tight" oligopolies. He also reports that the share of oligopolies was roughly halved since the 1950s, resulting in a sharply rising incidence of competitive behavior. Shepherd attributes important roles to antitrust enforcement, increasing international trade, and government deregulation efforts in bringing about these results.[20]

A second set of allocational criteria concern "dynamic" efficiency. That is, they focus on industry progress over time. In this case there is no well-defined ideal model to serve as a standard of judgment. Rather, the criteria used involve a number of performance measures such as industry growth, productivity improvements, favorable relative price trends, and new product innovation. Much of this research stems from the initial work of Joseph Schumpeter (see Chapter 18) on the importance of entrepreneurial profit-seeking activity to the growth process. Developing and testing specific hypotheses about the effect of market structure on various performance measures has proved rather difficult, however.

In addition to allocational criteria, a number of noneconomic performance measures have also been examined by industrial organization theorists. Equity questions about the distribution of economic profits among industry participants or the impact of industry structure on relative wage rates sometimes have been raised as factors offsetting the allocational benefits of some competitive market organizations. Similarly, some authors have stressed the ability of various market organizations to generate employment for workers independent of whether such industries do so efficiently. Finally, the political influence of firms has been examined, with the goal of obtaining market structures (possibly competitive) that minimize that influence. As this partial list of other criteria makes clear, the field of industrial organization consequently may overlap many other social science disciplines.

---

[20] W. G. Shepherd, "Causes of Increased Competition in the U.S. Economy, 1939–1980," *Review of Economics and Statistics* (November 1982): 613–626.

SUMMARY

Many real-world markets resemble neither of the polar cases of perfect competition or monopoly. Rather, such markets are characterized by some degree of concentration (hence individual firms have some effect on market price—they are not price takers), but no single firm exercises complete market control. In these circumstances there is no generally accepted model of market behavior. Aspects of both competitive and monopoly theory, together with particular institutional details of the market in question, must be used in order to develop a realistic picture of behavior. Several specific issues that we have addressed in developing such models are

- The degree of market concentration and the importance of feedback effects in output and price decisions;
- The importance of nonprice methods of competition such as product differentiation and advertising;
- Entry conditions in the market and the constraints that potential entry places on attaining monopoly profits, especially in contestable markets;
- The uncertainty faced by individual firms and the strategies they may adopt to cope with it;
- The potential benefits from monopolization of a market and the costs associated with maintaining such a cartel.

Application

THE IBM CASE

On the final day of the Johnson administration (in 1969), an antitrust case was filed by the U.S. Justice Department against International Business Machines Corporation. During the ensuing 19 years, the case developed all the elements of a television soap opera. Successive Justice Department officials had considerable difficulty in designing a coherent case; legal careers were made and destroyed at the prestigious firm of Cravath, Swaine and Moore (IBM's attorneys); many economists made tidy consultants' fees on the case; and IBM even sought to have the judge in the case disqualified for being biased. In all, the case generated 66 million pages of documentation, and probably cost taxpayers and IBM hundreds of millions of dollars. Despite these vast expenditures of physical and human

resources, the IBM case was ultimately dropped by the federal government on January 8, 1982, on the argument that it was "flimsy" and "without merit." This long-running saga clearly illustrates some of the ambiguities in modern antitrust litigation and how economic considerations affect such proceedings.

Consider first the structural question of what market IBM was alleged to have monopolized. In its original complaint the Justice Department accused IBM of monopolizing the general-purpose computer market, in which, it was asserted, IBM had about a 70 percent share. But in its defense, IBM continually sought to expand the market definition (to include all information-processing and retrieval systems, for example) and to show it was really a rather small fish in a big pond. At the time the case was dropped, after 19 years of debate, the litigants had still not reached agreement on the very basic question of what market IBM was alleged to have monopolized. Although the definition of "product group" employed in this chapter helped to clarify some general questions in developing this market definition, the empirical difficulties in implementing the definition precisely proved to be great.

Similar ambiguities surrounded the legal arguments about IBM's conduct and whether IBM had attempted to monopolize the computer market. Three of the government's specific charges against IBM's conduct should illustrate the dispute. First, it was alleged that IBM introduced "fighting machines" (particularly the 360-70), whose timing was targeted specifically to undermine competitors' efforts to develop new products. Second, it was argued that IBM's practice of selling its maintenance and programming services in a "bundle" together with its machines made it difficult for competitors to gain a foothold in the market. Finally, IBM's use of discounts for educational institutions was deemed anticompetitive because it resulted in a cohort of students trained only on IBM equipment.

IBM, in its defense, attacked each of these conduct charges by asserting they simply reflected aggressive competition and good corporate citizenship. Introduction of new machines, according to IBM, was just normal business practice in the fast-moving computer industry.

Similarly, IBM argued that it "bundled" its services and equipment together simply to serve customers better. Other companies, after all, were free to adopt the same practice. Finally, educational discounts, according to IBM, were the natural response of a company seeking to promote general social well-being. To impugn their motives would be inordinately cynical.

Most uninvolved observers of the IBM case saw some truths in both the government and IBM briefs. The decision to drop the case probably reflected the sensible judgment that the case had reached a stage where the costs of further litigation outweighed any potential gains from a government victory. In the 19 years since the case was filed, the computer industry had changed greatly, with hundreds of new firms being founded and IBM's share of the market falling rather sharply. Hence there seemed to be the sense that whatever had happened in the past, the computer industry was performing rather well in the 1980s and the social gains in tampering with its current structure might be negligible.[21]

---

[21] For a detailed commentary on the economic analysis involved in this case, see F. M. Fisher, J. J. McGowan, and J. E. Greenwood, *Folded, Spindled, and Mutilated: Economic Analysis and U.S. v. IBM* (Cambridge, Mass.: MIT Press, 1983).

SUGGESTED READINGS

Bain, J. S. *Barriers to New Competition.* Cambridge, Mass.: Harvard University Press, 1956.

Classic treatment of the theory of entry barriers together with some empirical detail.

Baumol, W. J. "Contestable Markets: An Uprising in the Theory of Industry Structure." *American Economic Review* (March 1982): 1–19.

AEA presidential address summarizing Baumol's and others' research on the theory of multiproduct firms and contestable markets.

Baumol, W. J.; Panzar, J. C.; and Willig, R. D. *Contestable Markets and the Theory of Industry Structure.* San Diego, Calif.: Harcourt Brace Jovanovich, 1982.

Detailed theoretical treatment of recent theories of contestable markets.

Chamberlin, E. H. *The Theory of Monopolistic Competition.* Cambridge, Mass.: Harvard University Press, 1950.

Development of the theory of monopolistic competition. Some empirical and institutional analysis.

Fisher, F.; Griliches, Z.; and Kaysen, C. "The Cost of Automobile Model Changes Since 1949." *Journal of Political Economy* 70 (October 1962): 433–451.

Interesting attempt to quantify the costs of product differentiation in automobile production through annual model changes.

Kaplan, A. D. H.; Dirlam, J. B.; and Lanzillotti, R. G. *Pricing in Big Business: A Case Approach.* Washington, D.C.: The Brookings Institution, 1958.

Empirical case studies of pricing behavior in large industrial corporations.

Rothschild, M. "Models of Market Organization with Imperfect Information: A Survey." *Journal of Political Economy* (November–December 1973): 1283–1908.

Nice survey of the theory of the relationship between imperfect competition in markets and the absence of full market information.

Scherer, F. M. *Industrial Market Structure and Economic Performance.* 2d ed. Chicago: Rand McNally, 1980.

Principal industrial organization text. Encyclopedic coverage.

Schmalensee, R. *The Economics of Advertising.* Amsterdam: North Holland Publishing Co., 1972. Chap. 1.

Good summary of theories of advertising together with some empirical investigations (especially of cigarette advertising).

Spence, M. "Contestable Markets and the Theory of Industrial Structure." *Journal of Economic Literature* (September 1983): 981–990.

Brief, readable review of contestable markets theory.

Sweezy, P. M. "Demand under Conditions of Oligopoly." *Journal of Political Economy* 47 (August 1939): 568–573.

Development of the "kinked" demand curve model of oligopolistic pricing behavior.

PROBLEMS

19.1

Assume for simplicity that a monopolist has no costs of production and faces a demand curve given by

$$Q = 150 - P.$$

a. Calculate the profit-maximizing price-quantity combination for this monopolist. Also calculate the monopolist's profits.

b. Suppose a second firm enters the market. Let q_1 be the output of the first firm and q_2 the output of the second. Market demand is now given by:

$$q_1 + q_2 = 150 - P.$$

Assuming that this second firm also has no costs of production, use the Cournot model of duopoly (presented in Chapter 19) to determine the profit-maximizing level of production for each firm as well as the market price. Also calculate each firm's profits.

c. How do the results from parts a and b compare to what price and quantity would prevail in a perfectly competitive market? Graph the demand and marginal revenue curves and indicate the three different price-quantity combinations on the demand curve.

19.2

A monopolist can produce at constant average (and marginal) costs of $AC = MC = 5$. The firm faces a market demand curve given by

$$Q = 53 - P.$$

a.   Calculate the profit-maximizing price-quantity combination for this monopolist. Also calculate the monopolist's profits.

b.   Suppose that a second firm enters the market. Let q_1 be the output of firm 1 and q_2 the output of firm 2. Market demand now is given by

$$q_1 + q_2 = 53 - P.$$

On the assumption that firm 2 has the same costs as firm 1, calculate the profits of firms 1 and 2 as functions of q_1 and q_2.

c.   Suppose (after Cournot) that each of these two firms chooses its level of output so as to maximize profits on the assumption that the other's output is fixed. Calculate each firm's "reaction function," which expresses desired output of one firm as a function of the other's output.

d.   On the assumption in part (c), what is the only level for q_1 and q_2 with which both firms will be satisfied (what q_1, q_2 combination satisfies both reaction curves)?

e.   With q_1 and q_2 at the equilibrium level specified in part (d), what will be the market price, the profits for each firm, and the total profits earned?

f.   Suppose now that there are n identical firms in the industry. If each firm adopts the Cournot strategy toward all its rivals, what will be the profit-maximizing output level for each firm? What will be the market price? What will be the total profits earned in the industry? (All these will depend on n.)

g.   Show that when n approaches infinity, the output levels, market price, and profits approach those that would "prevail" in perfect competition.

19.3

Use the analysis developed in this chapter and elsewhere in this part to explain the following price behavior:

a.   Doctors charge poor patients less for identical services than they charge rich patients.

b.   Banks announce a widely publicized prime rate and change it only occasionally.

c.   Blacks pay more than whites for identical houses.

d.   Insurance companies continue to solicit automobile insurance business in spite of their plea that "we lose money on every policy we write."

e.   A certain brand of beer used to be sold in cans and returnable bottles (with a deposit required). It was less expensive to buy beer in bottles and throw them away than to buy beer in cans.

19.4

Some critics contend that U.S. automobile companies pursue a strategy of planned obsolescence: that is, they produce cars that are intended to become obsolete in a few years. Would that strategy make sense in a monopoly market? How might the production of obsolescence depend on the characteristics of market demand? How would oligopolistic competition affect the profitability of the strategy?

19.5

One of the major legal complaints against Standard Oil Company in the 1911 antitrust case concerned the practice of predatory pricing. That is, it was claimed that in some markets Standard Oil would price its product below average cost in an attempt to make competitors more willing to sell out their businesses. Would such a strategy be more effective than simply offering to buy out competitors directly? Develop a general theory of when predatory behavior might work (for a detailed analysis, see J. S. McGee, "Predatory Price Cutting: The Standard Oil (N.J.) Case," *Journal of Law and Economics*, October 1958: 137–169).

19.6

In the Clorox case, Procter & Gamble was alleged to be a potential entrant into the liquid bleach market. Can you devise a way to use firms' cost curves and the demand curves facing the firms to differentiate among actual entrants? Potential entrants? Non-entrants? Use your analysis to suggest what the court should have looked for in this antitrust case.

19.7

Suppose that the demand for crude oil is given by

$$Q = 2,000P + 70,000$$

where Q is the quantity of oil in thousands of barrels per year and P is the dollar price per barrel. Suppose also that there are 1,000 identical small producers of crude oil, each with marginal costs given by

$$MC = q + 5$$

where q is the output of the typical firm.

  a. Assuming that each small oil producer acts as a price taker, calculate the market supply curve and the market equilibrium price and quantity.

  b. Suppose a practically infinite supply of crude oil is discovered in New Jersey by a would-be price leader and that this oil can be produced at a constant average and marginal cost of $15 per barrel. Assuming that the supply behavior of the competitive fringe described in part (a) is not changed by this discovery, how much should the price leader produce in order to maximize profits? What price and quantity will now prevail in the market?

  c. Graph your results. Does consumer surplus increase as a result of the New Jersey oil discovery? How does consumer surplus after the discovery compare to what would exist if the New Jersey oil were supplied competitively?

19.8

Suppose a firm is considering investing in research that would lead to a cost-saving innovation. Assuming the firm can retain this innovation solely for its own use, will the additional profits from the lower (marginal) costs be greater if the firm is a competitive price taker or if the firm is a monopolist? Develop a careful graphical argument. More generally, develop a verbal analysis to suggest whether competitive or monopoly firms are more likely to adopt cost-saving innovations. (For an early analysis of this issue see W. Fellner, "The Influence of Market Structure on Technological Progress," *Quarterly Journal of Economics*, November 1951: 560–567.)

EXTENSIONS

MONOPO- LISTIC COMPETITION

In Chapter 19 we mentioned Chamberlin's model of monopolistic competition as an example of a model of a market structure with many firms in which each firm sells a slightly differentiated product. Here we will explore this model with a specific numerical example. Suppose there are n firms in a market and that each firm has the same total cost schedule of the form:

$$c_i = 9 + 4q_i.$$

Each firm also faces a demand curve for its product of the form:

$$q_i = -0.01(n - 1)p_i + 0.01 \sum_{j \neq i} p_i + \frac{303}{n},$$

where p_i are the prices charged by other firms and n is the number of firms in the industry. Notice that the demand curve for each firm is a downward sloping function of its own price and depends positively on the prices charged by its competitors. In equilibrium for this industry all prices must be equal ($p_i = p_j$ for all i and j).

E19.1
What is the equilibrium output for each firm and the total output? (Your answer will depend on *n*.) What are the profits of the *i*th firm as a function of p_i, p_j, and *n*?

E19.2
If the firm maximizes its profits on the assumption that p_j and *n* are constant, how will the optimal p_i depend on p_j and *n*?

E19.3
Since in equilibrium $p_i = p_j$ for all *j*, show how these equilibrium values depend on *n*.

E19.4
In the long run (assume that long-run and short-run costs are the same), the number of firms will adjust so that every firm will earn 0 economic profits. What is this equilibrium number of firms? With this long-run equilibrium number of firms, what will p_i and q_i be?

E19.5
For the long-run equilibrium in this monopolistically competitive market, graph
  a.   The demand curve facing a firm;
  b.   The associated marginal revenue curve;
  c.   The average cost curve for this firm;
  d.   The marginal cost curve for this firm.

REFERENCES

Chamberlin, E. H. *The Theory of Monopolistic Competition* (Cambridge, Mass.: Harvard University Press, 1950).

Friedman, J. W. "Oligopoly Theory" in K. J. Arrow and M. D. Intriligator (Eds.) *Handbook of Mathematical Economics*, Vol. 2 (Amsterdam: North Holland, 1982), pp. 491–534.

CHAPTER 20

Strategy and Game Theory

In Chapter 19 we examined some of the problems that arise in modeling markets in which there are only a few firms. Perhaps the most difficult of these problems concerned questions of strategy—that is, with few firms each firm must, to some extent, be concerned with what its rivals will do. As we saw, making profit-maximizing decisions requires that each firm make some conjectures about its competitors' behavior. Under perfect competition such strategic thinking was unnecessary because the prevailing market price conveyed all the external information that was relevant to the firm. With relatively few firms the situation is much more complicated.

One of the primary tools that economists use to study strategic choices is formal *game theory*. This subject was originally developed during the 1920s and grew rapidly during World War II in response to the need to develop formal ways of thinking about military strategy.[1] Today the theory has applicability to problems as diverse as the development of optimal strategies for five-card stud poker to the analysis of antimissile defenses. In this chapter we will provide a brief introduction to game theory with a primary focus on its use in explaining behavior in oligopolistic markets. A few other applications will also be mentioned.

BASIC CONCEPTS

Fundamentally, game theory modeling seeks to portray complex strategic situations in a highly simplified and stylized setting. Much like the previous models in this book, game theory models abstract from most of the personal and institutional details of a problem in order to arrive at a representation of the situation that is mathematically tractable. This ability to get to the "heart" of the problem is the greatest strength of this type of modeling.

Game theory views any situation in which individuals must make strategic choices and in which the outcome will depend on what everyone does as a

---

[1] Much of the pioneering work in game theory was done by the mathematician John von Neumann. The main reference is J. von Neumann and O. Morgenstern, *The Theory of Games and Economic Behavior* (Princeton, N.J.: Princeton University Press, 1944).

game. All games have three basic elements: (1) players; (2) strategies; and (3) payoffs. Some games may also have a fourth element—an equilibrium outcome. Here we will describe each of these basic concepts.

Players

Each decision-maker in a game is called a "player." These players may be individuals (as in poker games), firms (as in oligopoly markets), or entire nations (as in military conflicts). All players are characterized as having the ability to choose from among a set of possible actions they might take.[2] Usually, the number of players is fixed throughout the "play" of a game, and games are often characterized by the number of players (that is, 2-player, 3-player, or *n*-player games). In this chapter we will primarily study 2-player games and will denote these players (usually firms) by *A* and *B*. One of the important assumptions usually made in game theory is that the specific identity of players is irrelevant. There are no "good guys" or "bad guys" in a game, and players are not assumed to have any special abilities or shortcomings. Each player is simply assumed to choose that course of action that yields the most favorable outcome.

Strategies

Each course of action open to a player in a game is called a "strategy." Depending on the game being examined, a strategy may be a very simple action (take another card in blackjack) or a very complex one (build a laser-based anti-missile defense), but each strategy is assumed to be a well-defined, specific course of action.[3] In our 2-player examples we will denote *A*'s strategies by a_1, $a_2 \ldots a_K$ and *B*'s strategies by b_1, $b_2 \ldots b_K$. Usually, the number of strategies available to each player will be finite; many aspects of game theory can be illustrated for situations in which each player has only two strategies available.

Payoffs

The final returns to the players of a game at its conclusion are called "payoffs." The payoffs are measured in levels of utility obtained by the players although frequently monetary payoffs are used instead. In general, it is assumed that players can rank the payoffs of a game ordinally from most preferred to least preferred and will seek the highest ranked payoff attainable. Payoffs incorporate all aspects associated with outcomes of a game; these include both explicit monetary payoffs and implicit feelings by the players about the outcomes such as whether they are embarrassed or gain self-esteem.

---

[2] Sometimes one of the players in a game is taken to be "nature." For this player, actions are not "chosen" but rather occur with certain probabilities. For example, the weather may affect the outcome of a game, but it is not "chosen" by nature. Rather, particular weather outcomes are assumed to occur with various probabilities. Games against nature are discussed briefly later in this chapter.

[3] In games involving a sequence of actions (for example, most board games such as chess), a specification of strategies may involve several decision points (each move in chess). Assuming perfect knowledge of how the game is played, such complex patterns can often be expressed as choices among a large but finite set of pure strategies, each of which specifies a complete course of action until the game is completed. For a discussion, see R. D. Luce and H. Raiffa, *Games and Decisions* (New York: John Wiley & Sons, 1957), chap. 3.

Table 20.1   *Payoff Matrices for 2-Player Games*

		A's Payoff Matrix B's Strategies					B's Payoff Matrix B's Strategies		
		b_1	b_2	$b_3 \ldots b_n$			b_1	b_2	$b_3 \ldots b_n$
	a_1	A_{11}	A_{12}	$A_{13} \ldots A_{1n}$		a_1	B_{11}	B_{12}	$B_{13} \ldots B_{1n}$
	a_2	A_{21}	A_{22}	$A_{23} \ldots A_{2n}$		a_2	B_{21}	B_{22}	$B_{23} \ldots B_{2n}$
A's Strategies	a_3	A_{31}	A_{32}	$A_{33} \ldots A_{3n}$	*A's Strategies*	a_3	B_{31}	B_{32}	$B_{33} \ldots B_{3n}$
	.					.			
	.					.			
	.					.			
	a_n	A_{n1}	A_{n2}	$A_{n3} \ldots A_{nn}$		a_n	B_{n1}	B_{n2}	$B_{n3} \ldots B_{nn}$

In our 2-player examples we will use A_{ij} to represent the payoff to player A of a game in which A plays strategy i and B plays strategy j. Similarly, B_{ij} records the payoff to B when these strategies are used. Table 20.1 shows these payoffs and strategies in matrix form for each player. Sometimes in simple cases we will combine A's and B's payoffs into a single payoff-matrix for ease of presentation.

*Strategic
Equilibrium*

In the theory of markets we developed the concept of equilibrium in which both suppliers and demanders were content with the market outcome. Given the equilibrium price and quantity, no market participant has an incentive to change his or her behavior. The question therefore arises whether there are similar equilibrium concepts in game theory models. Are there strategic choices that, once made, provide no incentives for the players to alter this behavior further?

Although there are several ways to formalize this equilibrium notion, the most frequently used approach was originally proposed by Cournot (see Chapter 19) in the nineteenth century and generalized in the early 1950s by J. Nash.[4] Under Nash's procedure a pair of strategies, say, (a^*, b^*), is defined to be an equilibrium if a^* represents player A's best move when B plays b^* and b^* represents B's best move when A plays a^*. Even if one of the players makes a fixed commitment never to deviate from an equilibrium strategy, the other player cannot benefit from knowing this. For nonequilibrium strategies, as we shall see, this is not the case. If one player knows what the other's strategy will be, he or she can often benefit from that knowledge and, in the process, take actions that reduce the payoff received by the player who has chosen a fixed strategy.

---

[4]John Nash, "Equilibrium Points in *n*-person Games," *Proceedings of the National Academy of Sciences* 36 (1950): 48–49.

Table 20.2   *Payoff Matrix for Equilibrium Zero-Sum Game*

		B's Strategies	
		b_1 (low budget)	b_2 (high budget)
A's Strategies	a_1 (low budget)	A: $+5$ B: -5	A: -5 B: $+5$
	a_2 (high budget)	A: $\;\;0$ B: $\;\;0$	A: $\;\;0$ B: $\;\;0$

Not every game has an equilibrium set of strategies. And, in some cases, a game may have many different equilibria, some of which are far more desirable than others—perhaps even for every player in the game. This observation suggests there is a rather complex relationship between game theory equilibria and Pareto optimality—a topic we will discuss briefly at the end of the chapter. First, however, we have a working definition with which to start our study of game theory:

Definition:

Equilibrium Strategies
A pair of strategies (a^*, b^*) represents an equilibrium solution to a 2-player game if a^* is an optimal strategy for A against b^* and b^* is an optimal strategy for B against a^*.[5]

ZERO-SUM GAMES

In *zero-sum games* the players are directly competitive—what A wins, B loses and vice versa. In formal terms, the payoffs to zero-sum games are of the form

$$A_{ij} = -B_{ij}. \tag{20.1}$$

An example of such a game in oligopoly theory might arise if the total quantity demanded of a good were absolutely fixed with the division of sales (and profits) between the firms being determined by which advertising policies are adopted (this has sometimes been asserted to be true for cigarette advertising, for example). This game is zero-sum because whatever one firm gains in sales and profits, the other loses. A simple payoff matrix reflecting this possibility is shown in Table 20.2. There each firm has two advertising strategies—adoption of a "high" or "low" budget. The entries in the table record the outcomes (in terms of dollars of profits) that accrue to A and B when the particular strategy

---

[5]Although this definition is stated only for 2-player games, the generalization to *n*-persons is straightforward, though notationally cumbersome.

choices are made. For example, the upper left-hand corner of the matrix records the fact that when A "plays" a_1 and B "plays" b_1, A receives profits of 5 and B receives profits of -5. Similarly, when both firms have high advertising budgets, profits for each are 0. The other entries in the table are to be interpreted in the same way. Notice that total profits for the industry are always 0, thus indicating that the game is truly "zero-sum."

Assuming that both A and B fully understand the outcomes of the game, it is possible to examine how they might decide on which strategy to pursue. First, notice that for firm B, strategy b_2 *dominates* b_1: No matter what A does, B can do best by playing b_2. Against a_1, that strategy promises a gain of 5, and against a_2 it promises 0 profits.

Maximin Decisions

In this game A has no dominant strategy; against b_1, strategy a_1 is preferred whereas against b_2, strategy a_2 is preferred. There are numerous ways in which A might choose a strategy in this situation. One method would be for A to adopt the pessimistic assumption that "no matter what I do, B will choose the strategy that harms me the most." Under this assumption, A should choose that strategy for which the worst possible outcome is as good as possible. Formally, A is then choosing a strategy based on a *maximin decision rule*. The firm is choosing the best outcome from a set of worst-case scenarios. Here A's maximin strategy is a_2. By choosing a_2, A can assure itself 0 profits no matter what B does. On the other hand, choosing a_1 runs some risk of getting a profit of -5. Consequently, A chooses a_2, B chooses b_2, and both end up earning 0 profits. The choice (a_2, b_2) is, in this situation, an *equilibrium* pair of strategies. If either A or B knew ahead of time what its competitor was going to do, its decision would not be affected: Knowing B will choose b_2 does not alter A's determination to choose a_2 and vice versa.

Nonequilibrium Zero-Sum Games

Not all zero-sum games, however, have equilibrium strategy pairs. For example, consider the payoffs shown in Table 20.3 (notice again that all the payoffs sum to 0). By following the maximin decision rule, A would choose strategy a_2 since under this choice the firm can at most suffer a profit loss of

Table 20.3   *Payoff Matrix for Nonequilibrium Zero-Sum Game*

		B's Strategies	
		b_1 (low budget)	b_2 (high budget)
A's Strategies	a_1 (low budget)	A: 0 B: 0	A: -10 B: $+10$
	a_2 (high budget)	A: -5 B: $+5$	A: $+5$ B: -5

-5. If B chooses b_1, it would be assured at least 0 profits. The choice a_2, b_1 is not, however, an equilibrium. For example, A might reason "I know B will choose b_1, so why should I suffer a loss of -5; instead, I'll choose a_1 and end up even." However, B can anticipate this trickery and opt for b_2 thus gaining profits of 10 and imposing a loss of -10 on A. Of course, A will see this and will choose a_2 to avoid the loss. The cycle can continue indefinitely since there is no equilibrium for the game. Each player will keep switching strategies in an effort to keep one step ahead of its competitor.

Mixed Strategies   Although the list of pure strategies in a game is intended to specify all possible discrete courses of action that the players might take, nothing in the rules requires the players to tell their opponents how they will choose. One way of preventing an opponent from correctly guessing which strategy will be used is to employ some sort of random device (flipping a coin) to choose among strategies. Even though an opponent has full knowledge of the game, it will therefore not be able to predict exactly which strategy will be chosen. Adoption of such probabilistic mixed strategies also offers some advantages to a risk-averse player.

Suppose, for example, player A in the game in Table 20.3 gives up trying to outguess B and decides instead to flip a coin to choose a strategy—a_1 will be chosen if the coin comes up heads, a_2 will be chosen if it comes up tails. The expected value (see Chapter 9) of A's loss against B's strategies in this case are

$$\text{expected loss against } b_1 = \tfrac{1}{2}(0) + \tfrac{1}{2}(-5) = -2\tfrac{1}{2}$$
$$\text{expected loss against } b_2 = \tfrac{1}{2}(-10) + \tfrac{1}{2}(+5) = -2\tfrac{1}{2}. \tag{20.2}$$

The mixed strategy, therefore, provides an expected loss of $-2\tfrac{1}{2}$ to A whereas the maximin choice of the pure strategy a_2 offers some possibility of having a loss of -5. If we focus only on minimum expectations, the mixed strategy seems clearly better.[6]

Even if B knows that A is flipping a coin to choose strategies, there is no way to benefit from this information in this zero-sum game. Since B's expected gain is $2\tfrac{1}{2}$ no matter which strategy it chooses, B should seemingly be indifferent about how it plays the game. But this is where the nonequilibrium property of this game again becomes important. If B has some reason for, say, favoring b_1 and A knows this, A would drop the mixed strategy and play a_1. B might also opt to flip a coin between b_1 and b_2, but even knowledge of this fact would be useful to A who would, in this case, find it profitable to play only a_2.[7]

---

[6] Actually, the notion of "preference" in game theory involves several complications, the most important of which concerns the question of risk aversion and how it should be modeled. We will not pursue this subject here, however, and will instead use fairly heuristic notions of preference.

[7] With this choice A raises the expected return from $-2\tfrac{1}{2}$ against B's mixed strategy to $0 = \tfrac{1}{2}(-5) + \tfrac{1}{2}(5)$.

There is, however, a mixed strategy for B that does not offer this type of opportunity for A. If B plays strategy b_1 with probability ¾ and strategy b_2 with probability ¼, expected payoffs will be

$$\text{expected payoff against } a_1 = \tfrac{3}{4}(0) + \tfrac{1}{4}(10) = 2\tfrac{1}{2}$$
$$\text{expected payoff against } a_2 = \tfrac{3}{4}(5) + \tfrac{1}{4}(-5) = 2\tfrac{1}{2}, \qquad (20.3)$$

and there is no incentive for A to depart from the mixed strategy originally chosen. Consequently, even though the game illustrated in Table 20.3 does not have an equilibrium pair of pure strategies, it does have such a pair when all possible mixed strategies are examined. Notice that with these equilibrium mixed strategies the expected payoffs are the same for A ($-2\tfrac{1}{2}$) and B ($+2\tfrac{1}{2}$). This reflects the zero-sum nature of the game being played—the basic nature of the situation is favorable to B.

Fundamental Theorem of Zero-Sum Games

The existence of an equilibrium pair of mixed strategies for the advertising game in Table 20.3 is not accidental. A fundamental mathematical result of game theory states that all 2-player zero-sum games have such equilibrium points if mixed strategies are allowed.[8] In most cases it is a fairly easy matter to compute the probabilities required for these equilibrium mixed strategies. Thus the subject of 2-person zero-sum games is a finished, rather neat package.

The numbers and precision of this result suggest that something must be incomplete about it—real-world strategy and bargaining situations, even if only between two players, are just too varied and complex to believe that they can always be characterized with a determinate equilibrium solution. The problem with applying the fundamental theorem to the study of actual strategic relationships among firms is that few, if any, such situations are truly zero-sum. Even in dueling (perhaps the prototype 2-player game), both players prefer a solution in which they both live to one in which they both die—the sum of the payoffs in the former case is greater than the sum in the latter case. In actual market situations, zero-sum games are even less likely since some strategy pairs will usually yield payoffs that are Pareto-superior (that is, everyone is better off) to others. The results for zero-sum games might therefore best be viewed as mathematically instructive rather than empirically valid.

NON-ZERO-SUM GAMES

To begin our examination of non-zero-sum games, consider the advertising example illustrated in Table 20.4.[9] The table should be interpreted in exactly the same way that the previous two were, except that the outcomes no longer

[8] This theorem is sometimes called the "minimax theorem" since the equilibrium mixed strategies would be chosen by a player who wished to maximize his or her minimum payoff against all possible strategies by an opponent. For a discussion and proof, see Luce and Raiffa, *Games and Decisions*, appendices 2–5.

[9] Actually, the games to be examined here should be properly termed "non-constant-sum" since the sum of the payoffs differs for different strategy pairs. Since any constant-sum game can be converted to a zero-sum game through a suitable choice of the origin for measuring payoffs, the previous discussion applies to such games as well. The important feature introduced here is dropping the constant-sum assumption.

Table 20.4 *Non-Zero-Sum Game*

		B's Strategies	
		b_1 (low budget)	b_2 (high budget)
A's Strategies	a_1 (low budget)	A: +7 B: +7	A: +3 B: +10
	a_2 (high budget)	A: +10 B: +3	A: +5 B: +5

sum to a constant value. In this game, strategy a_2 dominates a_1 for firm A: No matter what B does, A is better off with a_2. Similarly, b_2 dominates b_1 for firm B. Consequently, each firm will choose to have a high advertising budget and will receive a profit of +5. Notice, however, that an ironclad agreement by the firms to pursue low advertising budgets would result in a profit level of +7 for each. The difficulty with this twin low-budget strategy choice is that it is unstable. If A knows that B will choose b_1, it is to A's advantage to choose a_2 and increase its profits from +7 to +10. Similarly, if B knows A will choose a_1, B too has an incentive to cheat. Consequently, both firms by pursuing their own self-interest will choose high-budget strategies even though, in a broader sense, Pareto optimality would suggest the twin low-budget strategy.

The Prisoner's Dilemma

The game shown in Table 20.4 is one example of what has come to be known as the *Prisoner's Dilemma*. This game was first discussed by A. W. Tucker in the 1940s. The origin of the title stems from the following game situation. Two people are arrested for a crime. The district attorney has little evidence in the case and is anxious to extract a confession. She separates the suspects and tells each, "If you confess and your companion doesn't, I can promise you a reduced (6-month) sentence, whereas on the basis of your confession, your companion will get 10 years. If you both confess, you will each get a 3-year sentence." Each suspect also knows that if neither of them confesses, the lack of evidence will cause them to be tried for a lesser crime for which they will receive 2-year sentences. The payoff matrix for this situation is illustrated in Table 20.5. Notice how closely this game resembles that shown in Table 20.4. The "confess" strategy dominates for both A and B. However, an agreement by both not to confess would reduce their terms from 3 to 2 years. This "rational" solution is not stable, and there is an incentive for either prisoner to squeal on his or her colleague. This then is the dilemma—outcomes that appear to be optimal are not stable.

Prisoner's Dilemma–type problems may arise in many real-world market situations. The example of advertising budgets may actually occur. As we dis-

Table 20.5   *The Prisoner's Dilemma*

		B	
		Confess	Not Confess
A	*Confess*	A: 3 years B: 3 years	A: 6 months B: 10 years
	Not Confess	A: 10 years B: 6 months	A: 2 years B: 2 years

cussed in Chapter 19, much advertising may be merely "defensive" in the sense that a mutual agreement to reduce expenditures would be profitable to both parties. Such an agreement might be unstable, however, if one firm could increase its profits even further by cheating on the agreement. Similar situations arise in the tendency for airlines to give "bonus mileage" (there would be larger profits if all firms stopped offering free trips, but such a solution is unstable); or in the instability of farmers' agreements to restrict output (it is just too tempting for an individual farmer to try to sell more milk). As these examples show, the difficulty of enforcing agreements may be very detrimental to the profits of an industry. Whether a particular occurrence of the Prisoner's Dilemma represents an efficient assertion of competition (as in the farm case) or an inefficient outcome arising from strategic considerations (as possibly in the advertising case) is an important issue that must be addressed on a case-by-case basis.

Numerical Example: The Stackelberg Equilibrium

In Chapter 19 we developed a numerical example of a duopoly market in which the outcomes depended on the strategic assumptions made by the competitors. Under the Stackelberg version of that model, each firm had two possible strategies—to be a "leader" (produce $q = 60$) or a "follower" (produce $q = 30$). Results from employing these strategies can be viewed as a 2×2 game, the payoff matrix for which is shown in Table 20.6. As we discussed in the previous chapter, adoption of the leader-leader strategy is disastrous for the two firms, resulting in zero profits for each. A follower-follower strategy (the Cournot solution) is much more profitable for both firms, but this is unstable because it provides each firm with an incentive to cheat and grab the leader position. This particular strategy pair is not an equilibrium in the sense that we defined earlier. The game is not a Prisoner's Dilemma game either, however, since the leader-leader solution is not an equilibrium—if firm 1 knows that firm 2 will be a leader, it might as well be a follower and vice versa. Each of the leader-follower strategy pairs is an equilibrium, but, as before, the formal problem offers no guidance on which pair will be chosen. Presumably,

Table 20.6   *Payoff Matrix for the Stackelberg Model*

| | | Firm 2's Strategies | |
		Leader ($q_2 = 60$)	Follower ($q_2 = 30$)
Firm 1's Strategies	*Leader* *($q_1 = 60$)*	1: 0 2: 0	1: $1,800 2: $ 900
	Follower *($q_1 = 30$)*	1: $ 900 2: $1,800	1: $1,600 2: $1,600

Table 20.7   *Payoff Matrix for a Threat Game*

| | | B's Strategies | |
		b_1 (low budget)	b_2 (high budget)
A's Strategies	*a₁* *(low budget)*	A: +20 B: +5	A: +15 B: +10
	a₂ *(high budget)*	A: +10 B: −50	A: +5 B: −25

it will depend on such outside factors as the history of the industry or the personalities of the firms' managers.[10]

Cooperation and Repetition

Communication between participants can be an important part of a game. In the Prisoner's Dilemma, for example, the inability to reach an unbreakable agreement leads to a second-best outcome. If the parties could cooperate, they might do better. Similarly, in the Stackelberg game, an agreement to operate as a cartel would raise profits above any of those listed in Table 20.6.

As another example of how pregame communication can affect the outcome of a game, consider the payoff matrix shown in Table 20.7. In this version of the advertising game, the adoption of strategy a_2 by firm A has disastrous

---

[10] This observation shows both that non-constant-sum games may have multiple equilibria and that the equilibria may not have any particular optimality properties. For a discussion, see M. Shubik, *Game Theory in the Social Sciences* (Cambridge, Mass.: MIT Press, 1982), chap. 9.

consequences for firm B, causing a loss of -50 when B plays b_1 and -25 when b_2 is chosen. Without any communication, A would choose a_1 (this dominates a_2) and B would choose b_2 (which dominates b_1). Firm A would therefore end up with $+15$ and B with $+10$. However, by recognizing the potency of strategy a_2, A may be able to improve its situation. It can threaten to play a_2 unless B plays b_1.

If games are to be played many times, communication may be enhanced and cooperative behavior fostered. In the Prisoner's Dilemma game, for example, it seems doubtful that the district attorney's play would work if it were used repeatedly. In this case prisoners might hear about the method and act accordingly in their interrogations.[11] In other contexts, firms that are continually exasperated by their inability to obtain favorable market outcomes may come to perceive the kind of cooperative behavior that is necessary. In antitrust theory, for example, some markets are believed to be characterized by "implicit collusion" among the participants. Firms act as a cartel even though they never meet in hotel rooms to plot a common strategy. Finally, repetition of the threat game (Table 20.7) offers player A the opportunity to take reprisals on B for failing to choose b_1. Imposing severe losses on B for "improper" behavior may be far more persuasive than simply making abstract threats.

These observations suggest that cooperative and repeated games may result in very complex scenarios about how the game will be "played." Ultimately, it may not be possible to model such complexities with any degree of accuracy. Indeed, the participants themselves may find it difficult and costly to think through all of the strategic options open to them. In some cases it may be possible to simplify these decision problems by converting a game theory situation into a simpler problem involving uncertainty. In the next section we illustrate that approach.

GAMES AGAINST NATURE AND BAYESIAN DECISION MAKING

If the strategic considerations in a game are complex, it may sometimes be appropriate for one of the players to simplify the problem by treating it as a *game against nature*. Under this approach, the opponent ("nature") is assumed to be neither benevolent nor malevolent—nature does not engage in strategic thinking. Rather, nature chooses strategies on a random basis with no particular thought being given to the consequences of the "choice." Under this approach then, an opponent's choice of strategy is treated much like the weather in a firm's decisions: The strategy nature chooses will affect the payoffs received (weather certainly affects farmers' crops), but the opponent is not considered to be an active player in the game.

To illustrate this approach, consider the advertising game payoffs shown in Table 20.8. In this game neither player has a dominant strategy, so each will choose what to do based on whatever information and intuition it has available. One approach would be for, say, firm A to treat this as a game against nature—in this case A would pay no attention to B's decision problem. Instead

---

[11] The repeated Prisoner's Dilemma game is discussed in Luce and Raiffa, *Games and Decisions*, section 5.5.

Table 20.8 *Playoff Matrix for Advertising Game*

		B's Strategies	
		b_1 (low budget)	b_2 (high budget)
A's Strategies	a_1 (low budget)	A: 0 B: 3	A: 3 B: 5
	a_2 (high budget)	A: 4 B: 2	A: 1 B: 1

A would focus only on its own payoff matrix and treat the occurrence of a particular strategy for B as a state of nature, subject to some random process.[12]

Bayesian Decision Rules

Faced with this situation, there are a variety of ways in which firm A might select a strategy. Application of the maximin logic, for example, would suggest choosing strategy a_2 since the minimum payoff there (1) exceeds that for a_1 (0). This would not be a very appealing choice, however, if B were known to have a proclivity for high advertising budgets.

An approach to this problem that is consistent with usual economic models of choice in uncertain situations would be for firm A to assign (subjective) probabilities that reflect the likelihood of strategies b_1 and b_2 occurring. Using these probabilities, A would then choose the strategy that offered the highest expected value (see Chapter 9). If, for example, A believed b_1 and b_2 were equally likely, the expected payoff would be

$$\text{expected payoff of } a_1 = \tfrac{1}{2}(0) + \tfrac{1}{2}(3) = 1\tfrac{1}{2}$$
$$\text{expected payoff of } a_2 = \tfrac{1}{2}(4) + \tfrac{1}{2}(1) = 2\tfrac{1}{2},$$

(20.4)

and a_2 would be the preferred strategy. On the other hand, if A believed B really did tend to prefer b_2, it might assign a probability of $\tfrac{3}{4}$ to that strategy (and $\tfrac{1}{4}$ to b_1) in which case expected payoffs would be

$$\text{expected payoff of } a_1 = \tfrac{1}{4}(0) + \tfrac{3}{4}(3) = 2\tfrac{1}{4}$$
$$\text{expected payoff of } a_2 = \tfrac{1}{4}(4) + \tfrac{3}{4}(1) = 1\tfrac{3}{4},$$

(20.5)

and now a_1 would be preferred. At a subjective probability of $\tfrac{1}{3}$ for b_1, $\tfrac{2}{3}$ for b_2, firm A would be indifferent about which advertising strategy to choose.

---

[12] This approach is similar to the one we used to describe choices in uncertain situations in Chapter 9. Much of the theory developed there (about risk aversion, for example) is relevant here as well.

This approach to decision making is sometimes termed "Bayesian decision theory" after the eighteenth-century English statistician Thomas Bayes who first developed the mathematics associated with the calculation of subjective probabilities.[13] In Bayes's view, the probability of any event occurring is not an objective fact, but rather a subjective parameter derived from the information available to the decision-maker. The probability that a coin will come up heads is not, in the view of Bayesians, precisely ½, but rather an ever-changing estimate based on individuals' recent experiences. As new information arrives (that, for example, a coin was heads on its last 100 tosses), a rational decision-maker would alter his or her subjective probability estimate.

Bayes's approach to probability theory, therefore, leads to the following definition:

Definition:

Bayesian Decision Rule

A player in a game against nature will be following a *Bayesian decision rule* if he or she derives subjective probability estimates for various states of the world (nature's strategies) and chooses a strategy that yields the highest expected payoff based on those probability estimates.

Probably, the most desirable property of this decision rule is that it is the only decision procedure that agrees in spirit with the von Neumann–Morgenstern axioms of rational choice in uncertain situations. If a player in a game is an expected utility maximizer, it can be shown (by adding a few seemingly innocuous axioms to the von Neumann–Morgenstern set) that he or she will make decisions in a Bayesian manner when "objective" probabilities are unknown.[14] The Bayesian approach to strategic decisions is therefore widely used in economics and other disciplines.

Bayesian Decisions and Information Theory

Adoption of Bayesian decision theory does involve one major complication over our prior game theory models—the introduction of subjective probabilities. How do individuals develop their *a priori* views of the probabilities of various events and how do they gather information with which to revise these

---

[13] Formally, Bayes's theorem states that the *a priori* probability of any event, E [which we denote by $P(E)$] is modified by the arrival of new information (I) according to the equation

$$P(E|I) = P(E) \cdot \left[\frac{P(I|E)}{P(I)} \right],$$

where $P(I|E)$ is the probability of obtaining information I conditional on the occurrence of E. Intuitively, Bayes's theorem states that *a priori* probabilities should be adjusted in response to new information if that new information reflects anything about the likelihood of E. Notice that if I and E are independent, $P(I|E) = P(I)$ and Bayes's theorem indicates no change in $P(E)$. For additional details, see H. Kohler, *Statistics for Business and Economics*, 2d ed. (Glenview, Il.: Scott Foresman and Company, 1988), pp. 172–175.

[14] See Luce and Raiffa, *Games and Decisions*, chap. 13.

probability estimates? In assessing the risks connected with using a consumer product such as a lawn mower, for example, how do buyers decide the relevant risks to attach to various models? Or, in the oligopoly context, how does firm A decide how likely firm B is to adopt a high-cost advertising budget?

As these questions suggest, it is in the study of the formulation of subjective probabilities that Bayesian decision theory and formal information theory merge. In Chapter 9 we discussed some conceptual questions about how utility-maximizing individuals engage in information acquisition, and Bayesian analysis requires an adaptation of these concepts to the question of estimating subjective probabilities. Some experimental research on this topic shows that individuals are able to formulate rather rough probability estimates to use in their decisions, but a number of paradoxical results (such as a prevalent tendency to underestimate small probabilities) have been found.[15] The Bayesian decision model has not, therefore, been widely used in the study of actual oligopoly markets.

n-PLAYER GAME THEORY

All of the game theory examples we have developed so far in this chapter involve only two players. Although this limitation is useful for illustrating some of the strategic issues that arise in the play of a game (or the operation of a duopoly market), it also tends to obscure some important questions. In this final section, therefore, we briefly examine more general n-player games.

Coalitions

The most important element added to game theory when one moves beyond two players is the possibility for the formation of subsets of players who agree on coordinated strategies. Although the possibility for forming such *coalitions* exists in 2-player games (the two firms in a duopoly could form a cartel), the number of possible coalitions expands rapidly as games with larger numbers of players are considered. In some games simply listing the number of potential coalitions and the payoffs they might receive can be a major analytical task.

As in the formation of cartels in oligopolistic markets, the likelihood of forming successful coalitions in n-player games is importantly influenced by organizational costs. These costs involve both information costs associated with determining coalition strategies and enforcement costs associated with ensuring that a coalition's chosen strategy is actually followed by its members. If there are incentives for members to cheat on established coalition strategies, then monitoring and enforcement costs may be high. In some cases, such costs may be so high as to make the establishment of coalitions prohibitively costly. For these games, then, all n-players operate independently.

Game Theory, General Equilibrium, and the Core

In its most abstract theoretical development, n-player game theory has many similarities to the type of general economic equilibrium theory described in Chapters 15 and 16. An economy of n individuals can be viewed as an n-player game, and the coalitions formed may be thought of as firms, local govern-

---

[15] For a survey of some of these paradoxical results, see M. J. Machina, "Choice under Uncertainty: Problems Solved and Unsolved," *Journal of Economic Perspectives* (Summer 1987): 121–154.

ments, or any other type of economic organization. Of course, this way of modeling the economy is quite abstract, and the results are therefore probably not appropriate for any kind of detailed empirical study. Nonetheless, *n*-player game theory has been widely used as a conceptual tool for understanding the nature of some types of economic activity.

Central to these abstract uses of *n*-player game theory is the concept of the *core* of a game. This represents an attempt to generalize the notion of Pareto optimality to situations where subsets of individuals may form coalitions to improve the welfare of subset members. We have already illustrated some theoretical results related to the core in Chapter 8 when we discussed the Edgeworth model of exchange. Here we briefly illustrate how that concept has been adapted to game theory. We begin with a definition:[16]

Definition:

Core of an *n*-Player Game

The *core of an* n-*player game* consists of that set of payoffs in which no subset of players would find it advantageous to seek improvements through further coalition activity.

This core concept, therefore, includes the Pareto definition of optimality as a special case (since every individual in a game can form his or her own one-person coalition) and also allows for the balancing of power among multiplayer coalitions. Many games do not have a core under this definition—as in some of the duopoly models of the previous chapter, the play of such games represents an endless jockeying of the players (and coalitions) for favorable outcomes. But, for games that have a core, a wide variety of results relevant to economics have been obtained.

Perhaps the most interesting of these results concerns the relationship between the core and market-type institutions. Several authors have demonstrated that core solutions in *n*-player games can often be given a price system interpretation.[17] Other questions that have been examined include the modeling of public goods and externalities in game theoretic contexts and ways of introducing money and financial institutions into economic games.[18] Such applications serve to illustrate in a conceptual way how particular laws and institutions may arise to solve problems that are common to practically all economies. The general theory of games has therefore proven to be an important tool in the study of economic anthropology.

---

[16] This definition must necessarily be rather informal. For a complete development, see Shubik, *Game Theory in the Social Sciences*, chap. 6.

[17] For an example, see R. M. Anderson, "An Elementary Core Equivalence Theorem," *Econometrica* (November 1978): 1483–1487.

[18] For some references, see Shubik, *Game Theory in the Social Sciences*, chap. 12.

SUMMARY

In this chapter we have briefly examined some of the concepts associated with the modern theory of games. Although much of the discussion was presented in the context of oligopoly theory, the tools of game theory have relevance to many kinds of choices of strategy in uncertain situations. Our introduction to the game theoretic approach made several basic points:

- Concepts such as players, strategies, and payoffs are common to all types of games. The specification of games abstracts from personal and institutional peculiarities of the players and seeks to illustrate fundamental strategic issues in a simplified setting.

- A game has an equilibrium set of strategies if no player, upon learning the strategies chosen by rival players, has an incentive to alter his or her strategic choices.

- Zero-sum games represent particularly simple situations in which the net outcome across all players in the game is zero (or some other constant) no matter which strategies are chosen. Although not all zero-sum games have equilibrium points if only pure strategies are allowed, they do have such equilibria if mixed, probabilistic strategies are permitted.

- Non-constant-sum games provide a more accurate portrayal of oligopolistic situations in which all firms find some outcomes preferable to others. A particularly important illustration of such a game is the Prisoner's Dilemma in which the preferable outcome is unstable because each player has an incentive to cheat on it.

- *n*-player game theory provides the opportunity for meaningful coalitions (perhaps of firms) among the players. The theory associated with such games has many similarities to modern general equilibrium theory and can be used to explain a variety of economic institutions.

Application

THE GAME OF CHICKEN

Although the Prisoner's Dilemma is perhaps the most widely used 2-person non-cooperative game, it is not the only one that reflects commonly occurring strategic situations. Another example is provided by the game of "Chicken" for which a typical payoff matrix is shown in Table 20.9. In this game each player has two strategies: (1) to "cooperate" or (2) "not to cooperate." Payoffs to the players are recorded in the table with 0 being the least favorable outcome and 3 being the most favorable for

each player. This game has two Nash equilibria points—both off-diagonal solutions are stable in the sense described in Chapter 20. Both of these solutions are, as we shall see, vulnerable to threats, however. It is the possibility of these threats that gives this game its name and makes the game empirically interesting.

Basic Scenario of the Game
Use of the title "Chicken" to describe this game derives from a 1950s "game" played by hot-rod gangs (for the true flavor of the game see

Table 20.9 *The Game of Chicken*

		B's Strategies	
		Cooperate	Do Not Cooperate
A's Strategies	*Cooperate*	2, 2	1, 3
	Do Not Cooperate	3, 1	0, 0

the great James Dean movie, *Rebel Without a Cause*). The game's players start at opposite ends of a deserted road with their left wheels on the center line of the road. They then race toward each other with the one veering off first being branded the "chicken." In this game then "cooperation" consists of veering off the center line whereas "non-cooperation" refers to a determined strategy of staying on that line. If both drivers chicken-out, they both live, but gain no special prestige from peers. Hence, the twin cooperative strategy is unstable with each driver having an incentive to cheat on it (that is, stick to the center line). If one driver succeeds in cheating in this way, he or she receives considerable prestige (a "3") whereas the chicken loses face (a "1"). A twin strategy of non-cooperation is a disaster, however, since the cars crash and both drivers die (a "0"). Unlike the Prisoner's Dilemma, this non-cooperative solution is unstable—all the entries in the table are Pareto-superior to the crash solution. But each driver has an incentive to threaten to take a non-cooperative strategy in the hope that the opponent will be cajoled into taking a cooperative strategy. It is in each player's interest to appear to be committed to a non-cooperative strategy even if he or she intends to "chicken-out" at some point along the way. This type of strategic interaction is often found in both oligopolistic and international political situations.

Applications to Oligopoly

Most applications of the game of Chicken to explaining oligopoly behavior focus on the seeming stability of situations in which one firm could gain a clear advantage by altering its behavior. That is, they focus on explaining why "cooperative" solutions appear to be stable despite the fact that they do not meet the Nash criteria for stability. Consider, for example, the decision of U.S. auto makers to refrain from building small cars in the 1950s and early 1960s. Such restraint appeared to many observers to be unstable—a company that built small cars could have made a significant profit by doing so. But the threat that its competitors would quickly enter the market also (thereby seriously eroding profits on both small and large cars) kept any one company from proceeding. Of course, this cooperative solution ultimately failed because the rapid growth of imported small cars forced the U.S. companies to respond. The paralysis induced by the strategic situation of the 1950s placed U.S. makers at a considerable disadvantage because they had not developed the production expertise that they needed in later years.

A related situation concerns the pricing of gasoline on major highways. Although there are relatively many sellers, all seem to charge about the same price and they change prices together, usually on the same day. Presumably any one seller faces a fairly elastic demand for its gasoline and could gain significant sales by dropping its price a few cents a gallon. But its competitors would probably retaliate, and, since the total demand for gasoline along the highway is relatively inelastic, all firms would be worse off. Gas "wars" arise because of the periodic breakdown of the cooperative solution and prices drop dramatically (your author once purchased gasoline for $.12 per gallon in the 1960s). But these price breaks are usually quite short-lived (the $.12 price lasted only about four hours) and discipline quickly returns to the market.

Chicken, Nuclear Strategy, and the "Star Wars" Program

Some authors claim that the game of Chicken provides the best representation of the current strategic nuclear deterrence practiced by the United States and the Soviet Union.[19] In this game-theoretic interpretation, both superpowers refrain from the use of nuclear weapons because of the threat that the other side will use them too (similar arguments are also made about chemical and biological weapon use in World War II). Although this cooperative solution is unstable in that one party could gain by being the first to use such weapons, the threat that the other will follow suit maintains this unstable solution. Some authors have criticized this in-

terpretation because, in their view, the threat of "Mutually Assured Destruction" is fundamentally "irrational"—only a Dr. Strangelove would threaten to destroy the world if attacked. This has led to considerable analysis of the nature of threats in the Chicken game including issues of which threats are "credible" and whether threats can be probabilistic in nature. No simple, acceptable model of the nuclear stalemate has yet been developed, however.

Because we do not have a complete model of nuclear deterrence, it is difficult to predict how technical innovations will affect the strategic balance. This is especially important in appraising the Strategic Defense Initiative (or "Star Wars") proposed in the early 1980s. Antimissile defenses have both desirable and undesirable effects on the stability of strategic deterrence. The principal positive effect is that such defenses reduce the probability that accidents or third parties could initiate a major superpower confrontation. They offer the chance to destroy a few missiles that are launched in error. But such defensive systems also introduce some uncertainty into the deterrence calculation because they make retaliation more difficult. From the perspective of the Chicken game, they reduce the credibility of threats and thereby may make the cooperative solution less stable. Hence, even discounting the cost and technical difficulties that SDI poses, the overall desirability of the system cannot be appraised fully until better theoretical representations of the strategic balance become available.

---

[19] See, for example, S. J. Brams *Superpower Games: Applying Game Theory to the Superpower Conflict*, New Haven, Yale University Press, 1985.

SUGGESTED READINGS

Brams, S. J. *Superpower Games.* New Haven: Yale University Press, 1985.

Application of game theory to the study of nuclear strategy and arms control. Brams has several other books on game theory (including one on game theory and the Bible) that also make interesting reading.

Friedman, J. W. *Oligopoly and the Theory of*

Games. Amsterdam: North Holland Publishing Co., 1977.

Extensive theoretical analysis of game theoretic interpretations of oligopoly models. Excellent treatment of repeated games.

Luce, R. D., and Raiffa, H. *Games and Decisions.* New York: John Wiley & Sons, 1957.

Classic text on game theory. Very readable and complete—but only through the mid-1950s.

Raiffa, H. *Decision Analysis: Introductory Lectures on Choices under Uncertainty.* Reading, Ma.: Addison-Wesley, 1968.

Extended, easy-to-follow analysis of a single problem in decision theory. For more formal treatment, see Raiffa and Schlaiffer, Applied Statistical Decision Theory.

Schelling, T. C. *Micromotives and Macrobehavior.* New York: Norton, 1978.

Informal analysis of many situations with game theoretic interpretations. Very readable.

Schotter, A., and Schwodiauer, G. "Economics and Game Theory: A Survey." *Journal of Economic Literature* (June 1980): 479–527.

Useful survey of the basic concepts of n-person game theory. Good reference for some of the uses of game theory in explaining institutional relationships.

Shubik, M. *Game Theory in the Social Sciences.* Cambridge, Ma.: MIT Press, 1982.

Complete survey of many aspects of game theory. Many instructive examples make the book fairly informal and readable.

———. "Game Theory Models and Methods in Political Economy." In K. J. Arrow and M. D. Intriligator, eds., *Handbook of Mathematical Economics,* vol. 1. Amsterdam: North Holland Publishing Co., 1981. Pp. 285–330.

Good theoretical survey with useful geometric illustrations of solution concepts.

von Neumann, J., and Morgenstern, O. *Theory of Games and Economic Behavior.* Princeton, N.J.: Princeton University Press, 1944.

Classic work with rather heavy mathematics. Although many of the proofs are now available in simpler form, much of the conceptual background material is still useful reading.

PROBLEMS

20.1

The game of "Rock, Scissors, Paper" is played by each of two players choosing one of these items secretly and then displaying them simultaneously. Ties do not count, rock defeats scissors, scissors defeat paper, and paper defeats rock. Illustrate the payoff matrix for this game and show that it does not have an equilibrium strategy pair.

20.2

Smith and Jones are playing a number matching game. Each chooses either 1, 2, or 3. If the numbers match, Jones pays Smith $3. If they differ, Smith pays Jones $1.

  a.   Describe the payoff matrix for this game and show that it does not possess an equilibrium strategy pair.

  b.   Show that with mixed strategies this game does have an equilibrium if each player plays each number with probability ⅓. What is the value of this game?

20.3

An individual is thinking about going on a picnic but is worried about the weather. Utilities from the picnic are

	Rain	No Rain
Picnic	0	20
No Picnic	5	10

  a.   If this individual follows a maximin decision rule, will he or she choose the picnic or no picnic strategy?

  b.   If this individual believes that the probability of rain is .10 and follows a Bayesian decision rule, which strategy will be chosen? Explain why this choice differs from that in part a.

20.4

An alternative to the maximin criterion for selecting strategies in risky games is the "minimax regret" criterion. This criterion begins by computing the "maximum regret" matrix, which shows for each state of the world the *difference* between the utility obtainable for a given strategy in that state of the world and the highest utility possible with that state of the world. Hence, the matrix shows the individual's "regret" at having chosen a particular strategy when a specific state of the world occurs. A final choice is then made by choosing that strategy for which the maximum regret is as small as possible.

a. For the picnic example of Problem 20.3, show that the maximum regret matrix is given by

| | States of the World | |
	Rain	No Rain
Picnic	5	0
No Picnic	0	10

and that the minimax regret criterion results in a different choice (picnic) than does the maximin criterion. Contrast these two criteria.

b. Reformulate the Prisoner's Dilemma game in terms of a regret matrix. Does use of the minimax regret criterion change the nature of the solution?

20.5

In the ice cream cone stand example of Chapter 19, assume each stand has five possible locational strategies—locating 0, 25, 50, 75, or 100 yards from the left end of the beach. Describe the payoff matrix for this game and describe whether it has an equilibrium strategy pair.

20.6

The entire world's supply of kryptonite is controlled by 20 people with each having 10,000 grams of this potent mineral. The world demand for kryptonite is given by

$$Q = 10,000 - 1,000P$$

where P is the price per gram.

a. If all owners could conspire to rig the price of kryptonite, what price would they set and how much of their supply would they sell?

b. Why is the price computed in part a an unstable equilibrium?

c. Does there exist a price for kryptonite that would be a stable equilibrium in the sense that no firm could gain by altering its output from that required to maintain this market price?

20.7

Smith and Jones are stranded on a desert island with fixed initial endowments of clams and bread. Instead of seeking mutually beneficial trades directly, they opt for a bidding strategy in which they use their initial clam endowments to bid for bread. That is, the bread is deposited in a safe place and each person states how many clams he or she will offer for the bread. Upon revealing the bids the available bread is then split in proportion to each bid. If, for example, Smith bids one clam and Jones bids two clams, Smith gets ⅓ of the bread and Jones gets ⅔.

a. Sketch an Edgeworth Box diagram that shows the initial endowments of Smith and Jones.

b. On your Edgeworth Box, show how a final allocation is determined given a particular set of bids by Smith and Jones.

      c.   Use your construction from part b to show Smith's optimal reply to a particular bid by Jones. Develop a similar construction for Jones.

      d.   Is there an equilibrium pair of strategies for the situation described in part c? That is, is there a bid for Smith that is optimal given Jones's bid and vice versa?

      e.   Is the equilibrium described in part d necessarily on the contract curve for this exchange economy?

(*Note*: This is an example of a "strategic market game." For a further discussion, see M. Shubik, *Game Theory in the Social Sciences* [Cambridge, Mass., MIT Press, 1982], pp. 316–322.)

PART
VII

Pricing in the Factor Market

Factors of production also have prices. Labor services are purchased for a wage rate per labor-hour, machines have rental rates, and something must be paid for the use of land. In this part we shall investigate how those prices are determined. As a starting point, it might be assumed that those prices are established by the forces of supply and demand (as is the case for the prices of goods). Individuals supply labor services demanded by firms. Similarly, owners of capital and land are willing to rent these resources to a firm for a price. In some way, then, prices are determined by the operation of the market.

In Chapter 21 we discuss the general principles that might be used to develop models of this process of determining factor prices. We begin by showing how the demand for any factor of production is derived from the demand for the products it produces. Profit-maximizing firms play the role of intermediary in bringing together individuals' demands for economic goods with factor suppliers' abilities to produce those goods—if no one wants a good, firms will not hire anyone to produce it.

As in our examination of markets for goods, we use this notion of derived demand to study

factor pricing in two different cases. First we treat the firm as a price taker in input markets—that is, we assume that firms cannot affect factor prices through their actions. This assumption permits us to develop quite a general theory of factor pricing under competitive conditions.

The second part of Chapter 21 concerns factor pricing in imperfectly competitive markets. In these sections we relax the price-taker assumption in several different ways and illustrate the implications of those relaxations for factor pricing. As we show, the results of this analysis closely mirror those we obtained in our study of monopoly in Chapter 18.

The development of Chapter 21 is quite general in that it applies to any factor of production. In Chapters 22 and 23 we take up several issues specifically related to pricing in the labor and capital markets. Chapter 22 discusses three particular aspects of the supply and demand for labor services. First, we analyze the simple labor supply decision for a single individual and develop a market supply of labor curve in much the same way we developed a market demand curve in Part II. Next, we briefly discuss occupational choice and the concept of *compensating wage differentials*. Finally, we take note of the fact that important portions of the labor market are characterized by the presence of unions, and we show how these organizations can be incorporated into the general theory of factor pricing.

In Chapter 23 the market for capital is analyzed. The central purpose of the chapter is to emphasize the interconnection between capital and the study of the allocation of resources over time. An economy's stock of capital represents some output that was produced in the past but was not consumed, and we shall analyze the choices that were made in this process. Some care is also taken to integrate the theory of capital into the models of firms' behavior that we developed in Part III. Appendix A to Chapter 23 presents some useful mathematical results about interest rates and provides an alternative derivation of the basic conclusion of the chapter. Appendix B to Chapter 23 discusses some basic principles of optimal economic behavior over time.

In *The Principles of Political Economy and Taxation*, Ricardo wrote

> The produce of the earth . . . is divided among three classes of the community, namely, the proprietor of the land, the owner of the stock of capital necessary for its cultivation, and the laborers by whose industry it is cultivated. To determine the laws which regulate this distribution is the principal problem in Political Economy.[1]

The purpose of Part VII is to analyze how the prices of those factors of production are determined. An understanding of this pricing mechanism not only provides insights into how the market distributes income among the various factors of production but also suggests how this distribution might change over time.

[1]D. Ricardo, *The Principles of Political Economy and Taxation* (1817; reprinted, London: J. M. Dent and Son, 1965), p. 1.

CHAPTER 21

Firms' Demands for Factors of Production

In this chapter we will examine several general models of the pricing of factors of production. For the most part we will study how differences in the nature of firms' demands for factors can affect their prices and will devote relatively little attention to the supply side of the market. Chapters 22 and 23 are concerned with issues related to the supply of labor and capital, respectively, so we will postpone any very explicit treatment of factor supply until then.

PROFIT MAXI-MIZATION AND DERIVED DEMAND

In Chapter 12 we showed that a firm's hiring of inputs is directly related to its desire to maximize profits. No firm hires workers or rents equipment simply to provide its managers with companionship. Rather, hiring of inputs is a primary component of the profit-maximization process. Specifically, as we showed in Chapter 12, any firm's profits (π) can be expressed as the difference between total revenues (TR) and total costs (TC), each of which can be regarded as functions of the inputs used (say, capital, K, and labor, L):

$$\pi = TR(K, L) - TC(K, L). \tag{21.1}$$

The first-order conditions for a profit maximum are

$$\frac{\partial \pi}{\partial K} = \frac{\partial TR}{\partial K} - \frac{\partial TC}{\partial K} = 0$$

$$\frac{\partial \pi}{\partial L} = \frac{\partial TR}{\partial L} - \frac{\partial TC}{\partial L} = 0 \tag{21.2}$$

or

$$\frac{\partial TR}{\partial K} = \frac{\partial TC}{\partial K}$$

and

$$\frac{\partial TR}{\partial L} = \frac{\partial TC}{\partial L}. \tag{21.3}$$

In words, Equations 21.3 report the rather obvious result that any profit-maximizing firm should hire additional units of each factor of production up to the point at which the extra revenue yielded by hiring one more unit is equal to the extra cost of hiring that unit. The firm's demand for any input, therefore, depends both on how productive a particular input is in producing goods, and thereby yielding revenue to the firm, and on how hiring of inputs affects costs. This result follows directly from the profit-maximization hypothesis and applies to any factor market.

Marginal Revenue Product

All of the derivatives in Equations 21.3 are given special names in the theory of factor demand. Expressions for the change in revenue with respect to a change in an input (that is, the terms on the left in Equations 21.3) are termed the *marginal revenue product* (MRP) for that input. By recognizing that the hiring of an extra unit of an input results in extra revenue only through the output (q) it yields, we can gain some further insights into the nature of this concept. For the case of labor input, for example, we have

$$MRP_L = \frac{\partial TR(q)}{\partial L} = \frac{\partial TR(q)}{\partial q} \cdot \frac{\partial q}{\partial L} = MR \cdot MP_L, \qquad (21.4)$$

where MR is the marginal revenue for the firm's output and MP_L is the marginal physical product of labor. Suppose that, at current production levels, hiring an extra apple picker for one hour would yield three extra bushels of apples and that the marginal revenue yielded from selling a bushel of apples is $4. Then the extra revenue yielded to an orchard owner from hiring an extra hour of an apple picker's time would be $12—that is, the marginal revenue product of labor is $12. An identical argument would follow for the hiring of any other input. We have, therefore, developed the following:

Definition:

Marginal Revenue Product
The *marginal revenue product* (MRP) from hiring an extra unit of any input is the extra revenue yielded by selling what that extra input produces. It can be found by multiplying the input's marginal physical productivity times the marginal revenue obtainable from the firm's output in the market for goods:

$$MRP = MR \cdot MP. \qquad (21.5)$$

Marginal Expense

Equations 21.3 show that any additional units of input should be hired up to the point at which the inputs' *MRP* is equal to the cost of hiring those inputs. If the supply curves facing the firm for the inputs it hires are infinitely elastic at prevailing prices (that is, if the firm can hire all it wants without affecting input prices), this extra cost is simply the inputs' price. If our orchard owner can hire any number of pickers at a market wage of $10 per hour, then the *marginal expense* of hiring labor is given by this market wage. In this case, it would indeed make sense to hire the worker since his or her MRP_L ($12) exceeds this market wage. Sometimes, however, a firm's hiring decisions may have some effect on input costs if the supply of such inputs is not infinitely elastic. In this case, as we will show later in this chapter, the marginal expense of hiring another unit of input will exceed its market price because the firm's hiring will drive up input prices. For the moment, however, we will not examine this possibility and will instead assume the firm is a price taker for the inputs it buys. That is,

$$\frac{\partial TC}{\partial K} = v$$

$$\frac{\partial TC}{\partial L} = w,$$

(21.6)

where v and w are the prevailing per-unit hiring costs of capital and labor. The first-order conditions for profit maximization (Equations 21.3) therefore become

$$MRP_K = v$$

$$MRP_L = w.$$

(21.7)

An Alternative Derivation

Before turning to examine the implications of Equations 21.7 for the firm's demand for inputs, we present an alternative derivation of these profit-maximizing conditions that offers additional insights into the relationship between the firm's input and output choices. In Chapter 11 we examined a model in which the firm was assumed to minimize the costs of producing any level of its output (say, q_0). The Lagrangian expression associated with this minimization problem is:

$$\mathcal{L} = vK + wL + \lambda[q_0 - f(K, L)],$$

(21.8)

where $f(K, L)$ is the firm's production function. Assuming again that the firm's input choices do not affect the input prices, v and w, the first-order conditions for a minimum are

$$\frac{\partial \mathcal{L}}{\partial K} = v - \lambda \frac{\partial f}{\partial K} = 0$$

$$\frac{\partial \mathcal{L}}{\partial L} = w - \lambda \frac{\partial f}{\partial L} = 0$$

(21.9)

$$\frac{\partial \mathcal{L}}{\partial \lambda} = q_0 - f(K, L) = 0.$$

The first two of these equations can be written as

$$\lambda \frac{\partial f}{\partial K} = \lambda MP_K = v$$

$$\lambda \frac{\partial f}{\partial L} = \lambda MP_L = w.$$

(21.10)

But, as we pointed out in Chapter 11, the Lagrangian multiplier, λ, can be interpreted as marginal cost (MC) in this problem because it reflects the change in the objective (total costs) for a one-unit change in the constraint (output − q_0). Using this interpretation, we have

$$MC \cdot MP_K = v$$
$$MC \cdot MP_L = w. \tag{21.11}$$

Output choices can now be incorporated into this theory of input choice by introducing the old reliable $MR = MC$ rule for profit maximization:

$$MR \cdot MP_K = v$$
$$MR \cdot MP_L = w, \tag{21.12}$$

which is precisely the result we developed earlier. This approach makes especially clear that the firm's demand for any input stems not only from its desire to minimize costs but also from the firm's desire to make profit-maximizing output choices. As we shall see, examining how firms react to changes in input prices requires that we take account of both of these motivations.

Price-Taking in the Output Market

A final observation that might be made about profit-maximizing input choices concerns the possibility that the firm may exhibit price-taking behavior in the market for its output. In this case, marginal revenue is identical to market price, and Equations 21.12 become

$$P \cdot MP_K = v$$
$$P \cdot MP_L = w. \tag{21.13}$$

The terms on the left of these equations represent a special case of the marginal revenue product notion in which the physical quantity of output produced by one extra unit of an input is valued at its market price. Although for price takers there is no distinction between this concept and the MRP, for firms that are not price takers $MR < P$ so it does make a difference whether one values an input's physical productivity at the firm's marginal revenue or at market price for the output being produced. Sometimes the term *marginal value product* is used to refer to this valuation by market price, but we will not use that term here. Instead, we will only use the marginal revenue product concept in referring to the factors that influence a firm's demand for inputs. For the most part, however, we will also assume price-taking behavior in the goods market so there is no necessity to make the distinction.

COMPARATIVE STATICS OF INPUT DEMAND

In this section we use the profit-maximizing conditions discussed previously to study the comparative statics of input demand. Specifically, we shall look at the demand for labor (the analysis for capital would be symmetric) and ask about the direction and size of $\partial L / \partial w$. As we have indicated previously, it is likely this derivative will be negative (a decrease in w will cause more labor to be hired), but now we are in a position to give a detailed treatment of the issue.

Single-Input Case   One reason for expecting $\partial L / \partial w$ to be negative is based on the presumption that the marginal physical product of labor declines as the quantity of labor employed increases. A decrease in w means that more labor must be hired to bring about the equality $w = P \cdot MP_L$: A fall in w must be met by a fall in MP_L (since P is fixed), and this can be brought about by increasing L. That this argument is strictly correct for the case of one input can be shown as follows. Write the total differential of the profit-maximizing Equation 21.13 as

$$dw = P \cdot \frac{\partial MP_L}{\partial L} \cdot \frac{\partial L}{\partial w} \cdot dw$$

or

$$1 = P \cdot \frac{\partial MP_L}{\partial L} \cdot \frac{\partial L}{\partial w} \tag{21.14}$$

or

$$\frac{\partial L}{\partial w} = \frac{1}{P \cdot \partial MP_L / \partial L}.$$

If we assume that $\partial MP_L / \partial L < 0$ (that is, that MP_L decreases as L increases), we have

$$\frac{\partial L}{\partial w} < 0. \tag{21.15}$$

A *ceteris paribus* fall in w will cause more labor to be hired (and, parenthetically, this also will cause more output to be produced).

Two-Input Case   For the case of two (or more) inputs the story is considerably more complex. The assumption of a diminishing marginal physical product of labor can be misleading here. If w falls, there will not only be a change in L but also a change in K as a new cost-minimizing combination of inputs is chosen. When K changes, the entire MP_L function changes (labor now has a different amount of capital to work with), and an argument such as we used above cannot be made. In the remainder of this section we will use a graphic approach to suggest why, even in the two-factor case, $\partial L / \partial w$ must be negative. A more precise, mathematical analysis is presented in the next section.

Substitution Effect   In some ways, analyzing the two-factor case is similar to the analysis of the individual's response to a change in the price of a good that was presented in Chapter 5. When w falls, we can decompose the total effect on the quantity of L hired into two components. The first of these might be called the *substitution effect*. If q is held constant at q_1, there will be a tendency to substitute L for K in the productive process. This effect is illustrated in Figure 21.1a. Since the condition for minimizing the cost of producing q_1 requires that $RTS = w/v$, a fall in w will necessitate a movement from input combination A to combination B. Because the isoquants have been assumed to exhibit a diminishing RTS, it is clear from the diagram that this substitution effect must be

Figure 21.1   *The Substitution and Output Effects
of a Decrease in the Price of a Factor*

When the price of labor falls, two analytically different effects come into play. One of these, the substitution effect, would cause more labor to be purchased if output were held constant. This is shown as a movement from point *A* to point *B* in (a). At point *B* the cost-minimizing condition ($RTS = w/v$) is satisfied for the new, lower w. This change in w/v will also shift the firm's expansion path and its marginal cost curve. A normal situation might be for the *MC* curve to shift downward in response to a decrease in w as shown in (b). With this new curve (*MC'*) a higher level of output (q_2) will be chosen. Consequently, the hiring of labor will increase (to L_2), also from this output effect.

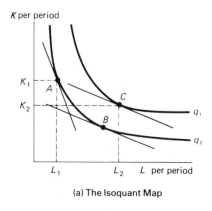

(a) The Isoquant Map

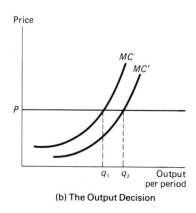

(b) The Output Decision

negative: A decrease in w will cause an increase in labor hired if output is held constant.

Output Effect

It is not correct, however, to hold output constant. It is in considering a change in q (the *output effect*) that the analogy to the individual's utility-maximization problem breaks down. The reason for this breakdown is that consumers have budget constraints, whereas firms do not. Firms produce as much as the available demand allows. In order to investigate what happens to the quantity of output produced, it is necessary to investigate the firm's profit-maximizing output decision. A change in w, because it changes relative factor costs, will shift the firm's expansion path. Consequently, all the firm's cost curves will be shifted, and probably some output level other than q_1 will be chosen. In Figure 21.1b what might be considered the "normal" case has been drawn. It has been assumed that with this new expansion path, the marginal cost curve for the firm has shifted downward to *MC'*. Consequently, the profit-maximizing level of output rises from q_1 to q_2. The profit-maximizing condition ($P = MC$) is now satisfied at a higher level of output. Returning to Figure 21.1a, this increase in output will cause even more L to be demanded, providing L is not an inferior input (see below). The result of both the substitution and output effects will be to move the input choice to point C on the firm's isoquant map. Both effects work to increase the quantity of labor hired in response to a decrease in the real wage.

The analysis provided in Figure 21.1 assumed that the market price (or marginal revenue if this does not equal price) of the good being produced remained constant. This would be an appropriate assumption if only one firm in an industry experienced a fall in unit labor costs. However, if (as seems more likely) the decline were industry-wide, a slightly different analysis would be required. In that case *all* firms' marginal cost curves would shift outward and hence the industry supply curve would shift also. Assuming that demand is downward sloping, this will lead to a decline in product price. Output for both the industry and for the typical firm will still increase and, as before, more labor will be hired. Since this latter, industry-wide output effect arising from shifts in the market supply curve is more commonly used, it is the one we will use in our subsequent mathematical development.

Cross-Price Effects

We have shown that at least in simple cases, $\partial L/\partial w$ is unambiguously negative: Both substitution and output effects cause more labor to be hired when the wage rate falls. From Figure 21.1 it should be clear that no definite statement can be made about how capital usage responds to the wage change. That is, the sign of $\partial K/\partial w$ is indeterminate. In the simple two-input case, a fall in the wage will cause a substitution away from capital; that is, less capital will be used to produce a given output level. But the output effect will cause more capital to be demanded as part of the firm's increased production plan. So, substitution and output effects in this case work in opposite directions, and no definite conclusion about the sign of $\partial K/\partial w$ is possible.

A Summary of Substitution and Output Effects

The results of this discussion can be summarized by the following principle:

Optimization Principle:

Substitution and Output Effects in Input Demand
When the price of an input falls, two effects cause the quantity demanded of that input to rise:

1. The *substitution effect* causes any given output level to be produced using more of the input; and
2. The fall in costs causes more of the good to be sold, thereby creating an additional *output effect* that increases demand for the input.

For a rise in input price, both substitution and output effects cause the quantity of an input demanded to decline.

We will now provide a more precise development of these concepts using a mathematical approach to the analysis.

**MATHE-
MATICAL
DERIVATION**

As we showed in Chapter 12, general input demand functions generated by considering the firm's profit-maximizing decision can be stated for the two-input case as

$$L = L(P, w, v)$$

$$K = K(P, w, v)$$

(21.16)

where P is the product price. The presence of this term in the demand function again illustrates the close connection between product demand and the derived demand for inputs. Here we will examine how changes in input prices affect these demands.[1] For simplicity, we will focus only on labor demand, since the argument for capital (or for any other variable input) would be identical. As in our graphic analysis, we start by dividing $\partial L/\partial w$ into two components: (1) the change in L induced by the change in w, holding output constant; and (2) the change in L induced by changes in output. Hence

$$\frac{\partial L}{\partial w} = \frac{\partial L}{\partial w} \ (q \text{ constant}) \ + \frac{\partial L}{\partial w} \ (\text{from changes in } q).$$

(21.17)

We now examine each of these terms separately.

*Constant Output
Demand
Functions and
Shephard's
Lemma*

We have already discussed the first term on the right of Equation 21.17 in connection with an analysis of cost minimization. In Chapter 11 we demonstrated "Shephard's lemma," which uses the envelope theorem to show that the constant output demand function for L can be found simply by partially differentiating total costs with respect to w (see footnote 11.9). That is,

$$\frac{\partial TC}{\partial w} = L'(q, w, v),$$

(21.18)

where the function L' permits output to be held constant in studying labor demand. Two arguments suggest why $\partial L'/\partial w$ will be negative. In the two-input case, the assumption that the rate of technical substitution diminishes for southeasterly movements along an isoquant, combined with the assumption of cost minimization, requires that w and L move in opposite directions when output is held constant. That result has already been demonstrated graphically in Figure 21.1. Second, even in the many-input case it can be shown that $\partial L'/\partial w = \partial^2 TC/\partial w^2$ must be negative if costs are truly minimized.[2] Hence the substitution effect in Equation 21.17 is unambiguously negative.

---

[1] In general $\partial L/\partial P$ and $\partial K/\partial P$ will be positive, since, assuming a positively sloped marginal cost curve, an increase in product price will increase output and the derived demand for both inputs. In the inferior input case, however, this analysis will not hold, since an increase in output will actually cause less of the inferior input to be purchased.

[2] For a proof see E. Silberberg, *The Structure of Economics: A Mathematical Analysis* (New York: McGraw-Hill Book Company, 1978), chap. 8. Silberberg also uses Shephard's lemma to show that cross-price effects in input demand functions are equal. That is, for the two-input case, $\partial L'/\partial v = \partial^2 TC/\partial w \partial v = \partial^2 TC/\partial v \partial w = \partial K'/\partial w$ (where K' is the constant output demand function for capital). An analogous proof holds for the many-input case.

Output Effects

Derivation of the output effect in Equation 21.17 is considerably more tedious, and we will provide only a heuristic proof here.[3] To do so we make use of a "chain rule" type of argument to examine the causal links that determine how changes in w affect the demand for L through induced output changes. Specifically, we can write

$$\frac{\partial L}{\partial w} \text{ (from changes in } q) \quad = \frac{\partial L}{\partial q} \cdot \frac{\partial q}{\partial P} \cdot \frac{\partial P}{\partial MC} \cdot \frac{\partial MC}{\partial w} \qquad (21.19)$$

to record the way in which w affects L through its effect on marginal costs, product prices, and market demand. Evaluation of the middle two terms on the right side of Equation 21.19 is straightforward. Since $P = MC$ for profit maximization under perfect competition, $\partial P/\partial MC = 1$. The derivative $\partial q/\partial P$ shows how market demand (or, more precisely, the firm's share of that demand) responds to price changes. In the usual case, $\partial q/\partial P < 0$. This term indicates how behavior in the goods market affects input demand. As we will see in the next section, the price elasticity of demand for goods therefore plays an important role in determining the price elasticity of demand for inputs.

Evaluation of the terms $\partial L/\partial q$ and $\partial MC/\partial w$ in Equation 21.19 is tedious. But we have already shown (in footnote 10 of Chapter 11) that both these terms must have the same sign. Hence their product must be positive. Overall then, the right-hand side of Equation 21.19 must be negative because of the negatively sloped market demand curve for the good being produced.

As in our graphic analysis, the mathematical conclusion is that $\partial L/\partial w$ must be negative because both substitution and output effects operate in the same direction. The ambiguity that arises from the Slutsky equation in the theory of demand for goods does not arise in the theory of demand for inputs. Because input demands are themselves derived from the demand for the goods being produced, the types of responses to price changes that might occur are somewhat constrained.

Numerical Example

In Chapter 12 we examined the input demand and short-run supply decisions for a hamburger emporium with a seating capacity of 16 square meters. We showed (in Equation 12.39) that the short-run supply function for this firm is

$$q = \frac{40(10P)}{(vw)^{.5}} \qquad (21.20)$$

and that the demand for labor is

$$L = \frac{(10P)^2}{v^{.5} w^{1.5}}. \qquad (21.21)$$

As we showed, if $w = v = \$4$ and $P = \$1$, this firm will supply 100 hamburgers per hour and will hire 6.25 workers each hour. If w rises to $\$9$ with P and v unchanged, the firm will produce 66.6 hamburgers per hour using only 1.9 workers.

---

[3] For a detailed proof, see C. E. Ferguson, *The Neoclassical Theory of Production and Distribution* (Cambridge: Cambridge University Press, 1969), pp. 136–153.

To examine the substitution and output effects present in this problem, suppose that the firm had continued to produce 100 hamburgers per hour even though the wage rose to $9. As we showed in Chapter 12, cost minimization requires that

$$\frac{K}{L} = \frac{w}{v} = \frac{9}{4}. \tag{21.22}$$

Using the original production function

$$q = 100 = 10K^{.25}L^{.25}F^{.5} \tag{21.23}$$

together with the cost-minimization requirement (and $F = 16$) implies

$$10 = 4(9/4L)^{.25}L^{.25}, \tag{21.24}$$

which yields a value for L of approximately 4.17. Even if output were held constant at 100 hamburgers, employment would therefore decline from 6.25 to 4.17 as the firm substitutes capital (grills) for labor. This is the substitution effect. The additional reduction in hiring from 4.17 workers to 1.9 reflects the decline in hourly hamburger output from 100 to 66.6.

To analyze this situation a bit more formally, we can compute the constant output demand for labor function using Shephard's lemma. Total costs for the hamburger firm are

$$TC = vK + wL + R, \tag{21.25}$$

where R is the fixed rental rate for space. Substituting the input demand functions for K and L calculated in Chapter 12 (Equations 12.37 and 12.38) into this expression yields

$$TC = v\left[\frac{(10P)^2}{v^{1.5}w^{.5}}\right] + w\left[\frac{(10P)^2}{v^{.5}w^{1.5}}\right] + R$$

$$= \frac{2(10P)^2}{v^{.5}w^{.5}} + R. \tag{21.26}$$

But, we can use the output supply function (Equation 21.20) to conclude

$$(10P)^2 = \frac{q^2vw}{1600} \tag{21.27}$$

so,

$$TC = \frac{q^2v^{.5}w^{.5}}{800} + R. \tag{21.28}$$

Applying Shephard's lemma yields

$$L' = \frac{\partial TC}{\partial w} = \frac{q^2}{1600}v^{.5}w^{-.5}. \tag{21.29}$$

For $q = 100$ we have

$$L' = 6.25v^{.5}w^{-.5}, \tag{21.30}$$

which for $v = \$4$, $w = \$4$ yields $L' = 6.25$; and for $v = \$4$, $w = \$9$ yields $L' = 4.17$ as we derived earlier. Notice how the constant output demand function (Equation 21.29) allows us to hold output (q) constant in our analysis whereas the total demand function for L (Equation 21.21) implicitly allows output to change and thereby provides a larger impact from the wage change.[4]

RESPONSIVENESS OF INPUT DEMAND TO CHANGES IN INPUT PRICES

The previous analysis provides a basis for explaining the degree to which input demand will respond to changes in input prices; that is, it helps to explain the price elasticity of demand for inputs. Suppose, for example, that the wage rate rose. We already know that less labor will be demanded. Now we wish to investigate whether this decrease in quantity demanded will be large or small. First, consider the substitution effect. The decrease in hiring of labor will depend on how easy it is for firms to substitute other factors of production for labor. In the terminology of Chapters 10 and 11, the size of the effect will depend on the elasticity of substitution that characterizes a firm's production function. Some firms may find it relatively simple to substitute machines for workers, and for these firms the quantity of labor demanded will decrease substantially. Other firms may produce with a fixed-proportions technology, and for them substitution will be impossible.

In addition to depending on technical properties of the production function, the size of the substitution effect will depend on the length of time that is allowed for adjustment. In the short run, firms may have a stock of machinery that requires a relatively set complement of workers. Consequently, the short-run substitution possibilities are slight. Over the long run, however, the firm may be able to adapt its machinery so as to use less labor per machine; the possibilities of substitution may therefore be substantial. For example, a rise in the wages of coal miners will have little short-run substitution effect, since existing coal-mining equipment requires a fixed complement of workers. In the long run, however, there is clear evidence that mining can be made more capital intensive by designing more complex machinery. In the long run, capital can be substituted for labor.

An increase in the wage rate will also raise firms' costs. As we have seen, this will cause the price of the good being produced to rise, and individuals will reduce their purchases of that good. This reduction in purchases is called the output effect: Because less output is being produced, less labor will be demanded. The output effect will in this way reinforce the substitution effect. In order to investigate the likely size of the output effect, we must know (1) how large the increase in costs brought about by the wage rate increase is and (2) how much quantity demanded will be reduced by a rising price. The size of the first of these components will depend on how "important" labor is in total production costs, whereas the size of the second will depend on how price

[4]The wage elasticity of demand in Equation 21.29 is $-.5$ whereas it is -1.5 in Equation 21.21. This total demand elasticity overstates the situation in a market context, however, since as we show in the next section, a rise in wages would shift the output supply curve and affect output prices.

elastic demand for the product is. In industries for which labor costs are a major portion of total costs and for which demand is very elastic, output effects will be large. For example, an increase in wages for restaurant workers is likely to induce a large output effect in the demand for such workers, since labor costs are a significant portion of restaurant operating costs and the demand for meals eaten out is relatively price elastic. An increase in wages will cause a big price rise, and this will cause individuals to reduce sharply the meals they eat out. On the other hand, output effects in the demand for pharmaceutical workers are probably small, since direct labor costs are a small fraction of drug production costs and the demand for drugs is price inelastic. Wage increases will have only a small effect on costs, and any increases in price that do result will not cause demand for drugs to be reduced significantly.

Our general conclusion then is that the price elasticity of demand for any input will be greater (in absolute value),

1. The larger is the elasticity of substitution of that input for other inputs;
2. The larger is the share of total cost represented by expenditures on that input; and
3. The larger is the price elasticity of demand for the good being produced.

Similar conclusions hold for the cross-price elasticity of demand for an input with respect to changes in some other input price.[5] As will be shown in the application at the end of this chapter, these insights into the determinants of elasticity can be quite useful in examining the operations of the low-wage labor market and for other applications.

MARGINAL PRODUCTIVITY ANALYSIS AND THE DETERMINANTS OF FACTOR SHARES

As the quotation from Ricardo in the introduction to Part VII indicated, the analysis of the determinants of the share of total output accruing to each factor of production has been of central concern in the development of economic theory. An early policy question that provided the impetus for much of this analysis was the debate in England over the repeal of the Corn Laws. These laws placing tariffs on the importation of grain into England were instituted during the Napoleonic wars. The debate over repeal centered attention on the fact that under these laws, protected landowners in England received a larger share of the nation's income than they would if the laws were repealed. In order

---

[5] All of these conclusions can be conveniently summarized for the multiple-input case. If there are n inputs $X_1 \ldots X_n$ with prices $v_1 \ldots v_n$, then

$$e_{X_i, v_j} = \frac{\partial X_i}{\partial v_j} \cdot \frac{v_j}{X_i} = K_j(\sigma_{ij} + e_{Q,P}),$$

where e_{X_i, v_j} is the elasticity of demand of the ith input with respect to the jth price, K_j is the share of total cost attributable to the jth input, σ_{ij} is the partial elasticity of substitution between X_i and X_j (see Chapter 11 for a definition of this concept), and $e_{Q,P}$ is the price elasticity of demand for the good being produced. For a proof, see R. G. D. Allen, *Mathematical Analysis for Economists* (New York: St. Martin's Press, 1938), pp. 505–508. See also the Extensions to this chapter for additional details on the elasticity of demand for inputs.

to discuss adequately the possible effects of repeal on the factor distribution of income, it was necessary to develop a theory of factor shares. The examination of this problem relied on Ricardo's earlier analysis of land rent.

As the Industrial Revolution proceeded, however, more attention came to be devoted to the determinants of the distribution of income between capital and labor.[6] In part, this emphasis was a response to the Marxian assertion that an increasing amount of capital in the economy would lead toward the impoverishment of the working class (labor). Because capital, unlike land, is not in fixed supply, Ricardian rent analysis was inappropriate for discussing these questions of factor shares. A new analytical tool was needed. The marginal productivity theory of factor demand provided this tool.

Although the marginal productivity theory of factor demand can be used to analyze the distribution of income among any arbitrary number of factors, it will be convenient here, as before, to assume that there are only two: labor and capital. We shall also assume that there is only one firm (perhaps "the economy") producing a homogeneous output using labor and capital. The production function for the firm is given by $Q = f(K, L)$, and this output sells at price P in the market. The total income received by labor from the productive process during one period is wL, whereas the total income accruing to capital is vK (where v is now used as the rental rate on capital). Since the total value of output is given by $P \times Q$, *labor's share* of output is given by the ratio wL/PQ and *capital's share* is given by vK/PQ. Sometimes it is also convenient to talk about the *relative shares* of labor and capital: wL/vK.

If the firm in question is a profit maximizer and if it operates as if it were in a perfectly competitive market, it will choose capital and labor so that the marginal revenue product of each factor is equal to its price. Hence

$$\text{labor's share} = \frac{wL}{PQ} = \frac{P \cdot MP_L \cdot L}{PQ} = \frac{MP_L \cdot L}{Q}$$

and   (21.31)

$$\text{capital's share} = \frac{vK}{PQ} = \frac{P \cdot MP_K \cdot K}{PQ} = \frac{MP_K \cdot K}{Q}.$$

The shares of capital and labor therefore are determined by purely technical properties of the production function relating the quantities of those inputs used and their respective marginal physical products. If we knew the exact

[6] In recent years discussion of the division of income between capital and labor has become less important than it once was. There are two reasons for this. First, some of the most important inequalities in income distribution that exist today are inequalities in the distribution of what is ostensibly labor income. A discussion of the incomes of "capitalists" and "laborers" may obscure these inequalities. A second, related reason for the irrelevance of this distinction is an increasing lack of precision in defining what is "labor" income and what is "capital" income. This occurs because of the large increments to "human capital" that have been made in recent years. For example, are the wages of doctors to be regarded as examples of differential labor incomes or as a return on the capital invested in medical education?

The Adding-Up Controversy

form of the production function, we could predict the behavior of the factor shares.[7]

Before proceeding to discuss changing factor shares, however, it is important to clear up one theoretical point. Although we have been speaking rather loosely of the "shares" of income, it is not clear that this usage is internally consistent. A basic fact of bookkeeping is that the total value of output must equal the total costs of factor inputs. But it is not obvious that the relationships embodied in Equation 21.31 will ensure this.

Mathematically, it is required that

$$w \cdot L + v \cdot K = P \cdot Q$$

or

$$\frac{w \cdot L}{P \cdot Q} + \frac{v \cdot K}{P \cdot Q} = 1 \tag{21.32}$$

or

labor's share + capital's share = 1.

Total product must be exhausted between those factor payments assigned by the marginal productivity theory to labor and those factor payments assigned to capital. An important question, then, is whether the marginal productivity theory of factor demand will ensure this.

In the late 1930s considerable theoretical controversy surrounded this question. If there were no reason why the shares should "add up" properly, it was argued, then perhaps the whole marginal productivity apparatus should be abandoned. One way that was proposed for answering this problem was purely formal. It can be shown that the marginal productivity theory is consistent (in the sense of Equation 21.32) if (and only if) the production function, $f(K, L)$, exhibits constant returns to scale. If this is the case, competitively determined factor payments will exactly suffice to exhaust total output.[8] In what follows

---

[7]The competitively determined factor share can also be given an interpretation as the elasticity of output with respect to the input in question. For example, in the case of labor,

$$e_{Q,L} = \frac{\partial f}{\partial L} \cdot \frac{L}{Q} = \frac{MP_L \cdot L}{Q} = \text{labor's share.}$$

This fact is often used in empirical studies of technical change (see Chapter 10).

[8]*Proof*: If $f(K, L)$ exhibits constant returns to scale, we know that

$$f(tK, tL) = t \cdot f(K, L) \qquad \text{for any } t > 0.$$

Differentiating this with respect to t gives

$$f_1 K + f_2 L = f(K, L)$$

or

$$MP_K \cdot K + MP_L \cdot L = f(K, L) = Q.$$

Multiplication of this equation by P and using the demand relations in Equations 21.13 yields Equation 21.32. For a more detailed summary of the "adding-up controversy," see E. Chamberlin, *The Theory of Monopolistic Competition*, 8th ed. (Cambridge, Mass.: Harvard University Press, 1962), appendix B.

we shall assume constant returns to scale and therefore that the factor shares will add up properly.

Factor Shares and the Elasticity of Substitution

A fact of modern industrialization is that capital-labor ratios tend to rise over time. This seems to be true for all industries, although capitalization may proceed at different rates in different industries. One important question that might be asked is how this increasing use of capital will affect the distribution of income between capital and labor: Will vK/wL rise or fall over time? If v/w falls more rapidly than K/L is rising, capital's relative share will decrease; whereas if v/w does not change greatly in response to major changes in K/L, capital's share will increase. In a sense the question is: Which changes more rapidly, relative prices or relative quantities? It might be possible to analyze the theory of factor pricing to gain some insights into the rates of change in these magnitudes.

If we are willing to assume that factor markets are perfectly competitive (or perhaps a reasonable approximation thereof), the concept of the elasticity of substitution (see Chapter 10) can be quite useful in analyzing the behavior of factor shares. Recall that the elasticity of substitution was defined as

$$\sigma = \frac{\text{percent } \Delta(K/L)}{\text{percent } \Delta RTS}. \tag{21.33}$$

Because the firm (or the economy) in question obeys the conditions of the marginal productivity theory of factor demand, the RTS (of L for K) will be equal to the ratio w/v. Relative factor rewards will be determined by relative marginal productivities (and therefore by the RTS).

Equation 21.33 then can be rewritten as

$$\sigma = \frac{\text{percent } \Delta(K/L)}{\text{percent } \Delta(w/v)}, \tag{21.34}$$

and we can use this parameter to study changes in relative factor shares. If $\sigma = 1$, Equation 21.34 says that w/v will change in exactly the same proportion that K/L does. In this case, therefore, the relative shares of capital and labor (vK/wL) will stay constant. Any increase in the capital-labor ratio over time will be exactly counterbalanced by an increase in MP_L/MP_K ($= RTS$), and this will be manifested by an identical increase in w/v.

For $\sigma > 1$ the percentage increase in K/L will exceed the percentage increase in w/v, and hence the share of capital in total income will rise as the capital-labor ratio increases. The opposite result occurs when $\sigma < 1$ (when substitution is relatively "difficult"). Capital's share will tend to decline in this case because the relative price of labor is rising rapidly in response to an increasing amount of capital per worker.

The elasticity of substitution is therefore a useful conceptual tool for understanding the effect of changing input proportions on factor shares. If factor substitution is relatively easy, the more rapidly expanding input will increase its share of total income. But this need not be the case. If substitution is difficult, the changing relative factor rewards that result from changed input proportions can reverse this result. Empirically, it seems to be the case that the shares of labor and capital income in total income have been relatively constant over time. This is one reason why the Cobb-Douglas production function is of considerable interest. Since this is the production function for which $\sigma = 1$, it is in general accord with the observed constancy of income shares.[9]

MONOPSONY IN THE INPUT MARKET

In many situations firms are not price takers for the inputs they buy. That is, the supply curve for, say, labor faced by the firm is not a horizontal line at the prevailing wage rate. It frequently may be necessary for the firm to offer a wage above that currently prevailing if it is to attract more employees. In order to study such situations it is most convenient to examine the polar case of *monopsony* (a single buyer) in the labor market. If there is only one buyer in the labor market, this firm faces the entire market supply curve. In order to increase its hiring of labor by one more unit, it must move to a higher point on this supply curve. This will involve paying not only a higher wage to the "marginal worker" but also additional wages to those workers already employed. The marginal expense associated with hiring the extra unit of labor (ME_L) therefore exceeds its wage rate. We can show this result mathematically as follows. The total cost of labor to the firm is wL. Hence the change in those costs brought about by hiring an additional worker is

$$ME_L = \frac{\partial wL}{\partial L} = w + L \frac{\partial w}{\partial L}. \tag{21.35}$$

In the competitive case, $\partial w / \partial L = 0$ and the marginal expense of hiring one more worker is simply the market wage, w. However, if the firm faces a positively sloped labor supply curve, $\partial w / \partial L > 0$ and the marginal expense exceeds the wage. These ideas are summarized by

---

Definition:

Marginal Input Expense

The *marginal expense* associated with any input (ME) is the increase in total costs of the input that results from hiring one more unit. If the firm faces an upward-sloping supply curve for the input, the marginal expense will exceed the market price of the input.

---

[9]Constancy of factor shares can be shown directly with the Cobb-Douglas production function:

$$Q = AK^\alpha L^\beta,$$

where $\alpha + \beta = 1$. Since

$$MP_L = \frac{\partial Q}{\partial L} = \beta AK^\alpha L^{\beta-1},$$

$$\text{labor's share} = \frac{P \cdot MP_L \cdot L}{PQ} = \frac{(\beta AK^\alpha L^{\beta-1}) \cdot L}{AK^\alpha L^\beta} = \beta.$$

A similar proof shows that capital's share $= \alpha$, and hence the shares are constants independent of the total supplies of labor and capital.

A profit-maximizing firm will hire any input up to the point at which its marginal revenue product is just equal to its marginal expense. This is simply a generalization of our previous discussion of marginalist choices to cover the case of monopsony power in the labor market. As before, any departure from such choices will result in lower profits for the firm. If, for example, $MRP_L > ME_L$, the firm should hire more workers, since such an action would increase revenues more than costs. Alternatively, if $MRP_L < ME_L$, employment should be reduced, since that would lower costs more rapidly than revenues.

Graphic Analysis   The monopsonist's choice of labor input is illustrated in Figure 21.2. The firm's demand curve for labor (D) is drawn negatively sloped, as we have shown it must be.[10] Here also the ME_L curve associated with the labor supply curve (S) is constructed in much the same way that the marginal revenue curve associated with a demand curve can be constructed. Because S is positively sloped, the ME_L curve lies everywhere above S. The profit-maximizing level of labor input for the monopsonist is given by L_1, for at this level of input the profit-maximizing requirement of Equation 21.3 holds. At L_1 the wage rate in the market is given by w_1. Notice that the quantity of labor demanded falls short of that which would be hired in a perfectly competitive labor market (L^*). The firm has restricted input demand by virtue of its monopsonistic position in the market. The formal similarities between this analysis and that of monopoly presented in Chapter 18 should be clear. In particular, the "demand curve" for a monopsonist consists of a single point given by L_1, w_1. The monopsonist has chosen this point as the most desirable of all those points on the supply curve, S. A different point will not be chosen unless some external change (such as a shift in the demand for the firm's output or a change in technology) affects labor's marginal revenue product.[11]

[10] Figure 21.2 is intended only as a pedagogic device and cannot be rigorously defended. In particular, the curve labeled D, although it is supposed to represent the "demand" (or marginal revenue product) curve for labor, has no precise meaning for the monopsonist buyer of labor, since we cannot construct this curve by confronting the firm with a fixed wage rate. Instead, the firm views the entire supply curve, S, and uses the auxiliary curve ME_L to choose the most favorable point on S. There is in a strict sense no such thing as the monopsonist's demand curve. This is analogous to the case of a monopoly, for which we could not speak of a monopolist's "supply curve."

When firms have some effect on the prices of the inputs they buy, another complication arises. The rule for the choice of minimum cost input combinations must be revised to take these price effects into account. It should be easy for the reader to show that inputs (K and L) should be chosen so that the RTS (of L for K) is equal to ME_L/ME_K and that this ratio is no longer equal to the ratio of the inputs' prices (w/v). However, we shall not analyze this explicitly here.

[11] For a detailed discussion of the comparative statics analysis of factor demand in the monopoly and monopsony cases, see W. E. Diewert, "Duality Approaches to Microeconomic Theory" in K. J. Arrow and M. D. Intriligator, eds., *Handbook of Mathematical Economics*, vol. 2 (Amsterdam: North Holland Publishing Co., 1982), pp. 584–590.

Figure 21.2   *Pricing in a Monopsonistic Labor Market*

If a firm faces a positively sloped supply curve for labor (S), it will base its decisions on the marginal expense of additional hiring (ME_L). Because S is positively sloped, (ME_L) lies above S. The curve S can be thought of as an "average cost of labor curve," and the (ME_L) curve is marginal to S. At L_1, the equilibrium condition $ME_L = MRP_L$ holds, and this quantity will be hired at a market wage rate w_1. Notice that the monopsonist buys less labor than would be bought if the labor market were perfectly competitive (L^*).

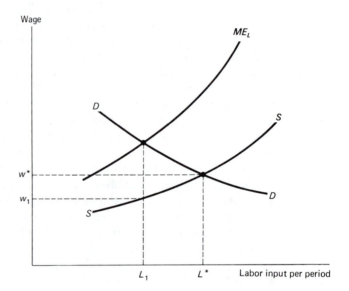

Numerical
Example

To illustrate these concepts in a very simple context, suppose a coal mine's workers can always dig two tons of coal per hour and that coal sells for $10 per ton. The marginal revenue product of a coal miner is therefore $20 per hour. If the coal mine is the only hirer of miners in a local area and faces a labor supply curve of the form

$$L = 50w, \tag{21.36}$$

this firm must recognize that its hiring decisions affect wages. Expressing the total wage bill as a function of L,

$$wL = \frac{L^2}{50} \tag{21.37}$$

permits the mine operator (perhaps only implicitly) to calculate the marginal expense associated with hiring miners:

$$ME_L = \frac{\partial wL}{\partial L} = \frac{L}{25}. \tag{21.38}$$

Equating this to miners' marginal revenue product of $20 implies that the mine operator should hire 500 workers per hour. At this level of employment the wage will be $10 per hour—only half the value of workers' marginal revenue product. If the mine operator had been forced by market competition to pay $20 per hour, regardless of the number of miners hired, market equilibrium would have been established with $L = 1000$ rather than the 500 hired under monopsonistic conditions.

Actual Examples of Monopsony

There are several real-world labor markets for which the monopsonistic model may be considered appropriate. For example, consider professional baseball, football, and hockey. The major leagues in each of these sports are the only hirers of highly skilled athletes. Drafting methods and various contract clauses in these leagues effectively prohibit interteam competitive bidding for players, so that the monopsonistic model is appropriate. One buyer (the league) is free to choose that point on the players' supply curve that is most advantageous. In any detailed analysis one would want to go considerably further than the simple monopsonistic model. Particularly important in this regard would be consideration of the differences in players' abilities, which cannot be captured in the previous models that assume homogeneous labor.

Other instances of monopsonistic behavior in the labor market are due to geographical considerations. In many mill towns the local firm is the only source of employment. Since moving costs are high for the local residents, the monopsonistic model is appropriate. Some monopsonistic positions may arise because only one firm hires a particular type of labor that has a unique technical knowledge. In this regard the government is in many situations a monopsonistic buyer. For example, consider the market for park rangers or for astronauts. In such situations the limited availability of even remotely comparable jobs creates the monopsonistic position.

Wage Discrimination in Hiring

If a monopsony can segregate the supply of a factor into two or more distinct markets, it may be able to increase profits. For example, a monopsony may be able to discriminate in hiring between men and women. Because the firm can readily identify which market a prospective employee belongs to, it will find it profitable to pay different wages in the two markets. Such a situation is shown in Figure 21.3. The assumptions that men and women are equally productive and that the firm has a constant marginal revenue product of labor no matter how much labor is hired are shown by the horizontal MRP_L curve. The supply curves for men and women are shown in the figure as sharing the same vertical axis. Given these supply curves the firm will choose that quantity of labor in each market for which the marginal expense (ME_L) is equal to labor's marginal revenue product. Consequently, the firm will hire L_m from the men's market and L_w from the women's. The wage rates in the two markets will be w_m and w_w, respectively. The way we have drawn Figure 21.3, men's wages will

Figure 21.3 *Discrimination in Hiring by a Monopsonist*

By segregating the labor market, say, between men and women, a monopsonist will minimize labor costs by choosing those quantities of labor such that the marginal revenue product of labor is equal to the marginal expense in each market. In this diagram the wages of women (w_w) will be below the wages of men (w_m), even though the marginal revenue product for both types of labor is identical.

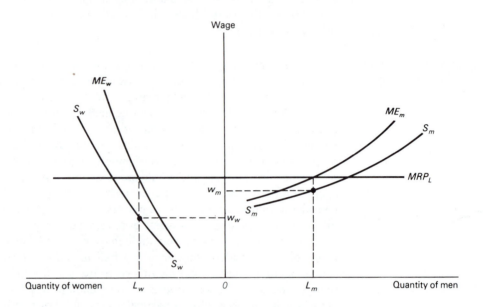

exceed women's, and this happens because women's labor supply is relatively inelastic.[12]

A similar analysis can be developed for any situation in which a monopsony can segregate the market for its inputs into two separate parts. In order to do so, it must be able to identify workers as belonging to particular markets so that its segmentation strategy will work: It must know how much of each kind of worker it is hiring. For this reason, segregation along easily identifiable lines (sex, race, or age) might be the type most often encountered. Whether existing wage differences along such lines can be explained by such a model is doubtful, however, since most labor markets seem to be more subject to the forces of competition than that depicted in Figure 21.3.

MONOPOLY IN THE SUPPLY OF INPUTS

Another way in which imperfect competition may occur in input markets is that the suppliers of the input may be able to form a monopoly. Examples of such monopolies include labor unions in "closed shop" industries, production

---

[12] Women may, for example, have a more inelastic supply curve because they have relatively few employment alternatives. The possibility of such employment alternatives, of course, would require a more complex model than the simple monopsony model presented here.

Figure 21.4   *Bilateral Monopoly*

A monopoly supplier of an input would prefer equilibrium E_1, whereas a monopsony demander of the input would prefer equilibrium E_2. Here the market outcome is indeterminate and must be settled through bargaining.

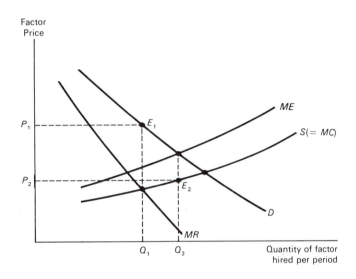

cartels for certain types of capital equipment, and firms (or countries) that control unique supplies of natural resources. Analysis of such situations proceeds in a way similar to that used for any monopoly: The monopoly supplier may choose any point on the input demand curve it faces. For example, a monopolistic input supplier could maximize its revenues from selling inputs by choosing to produce that output level for which marginal revenue is zero. Or it could choose any other level of factor supply that yields a desirable outcome.[13] To the extent that this choice results in input prices in excess of opportunity costs, monopoly rents will be earned. Those rents will persist as long as entry into the input market can be restricted.

Bilateral Monopoly

If both the supply and demand sides of an input market are monopolized, the market outcome will be indeterminate. Each participant can set bounds on the range of outcomes that may result, but the actual outcome will depend on the bargaining skills of the parties. Figure 21.4 illustrates a market in which a monopolistic supplier of some input (say, a rare metal used to produce an alloy) faces a monopsonistic buyer of the input (the only producer of the alloy). The monopolist's preferred point occurs where its marginal production cost (MC) equals the marginal revenue (MR) associated with the demand for the

---

[13] Several alternative goals of a monopolistic union are described in Chapter 22.

rare metal. At that point Q_1 would be produced at a price of P_1. The monopolist's preferred equilibrium is denoted by E_1. The monopsony, on the other hand, would prefer to trade amount Q_2 at a price of P_2, since that equilibrium (E_2) maximizes its profits. As in Figure 21.2, the monopsony wishes to hire that level of input for which the marginal revenue product (as reflected by the D curve) is equal to the marginal expense.

Thus in the bilateral monopoly situation illustrated in Figure 21.4, the desires of buyer and seller are in conflict. Neither point E_1 nor point E_2 is the equilibrium outcome, and the parties must bargain with each other to reach a solution. Although the analysis provided in the figure can place bounds on the likely outcome of such bargaining, arriving at a specific solution would require the development of a formal model of the bargaining process. Often such models draw on some of the tools of game theory that were introduced in Chapter 20.

SUMMARY

In this chapter we used the model of a profit-maximizing firm to examine that firm's demand for the inputs it uses. We illustrated several applications of our general result (first derived in Chapter 12) that the firm will hire any input up to the point at which the marginal revenue product (MRP) of the last unit hired is equal to the marginal expense (ME) of hiring that unit:

- The marginal revenue productivity from hiring extra units of an input is the product of the marginal physical productivity of the input times the firm's marginal revenue in its output market.
- If the firm is a price taker for the inputs it buys, it is possible to analyze the comparative statics of its demand fairly completely. A rise in the price of an input will cause fewer units to be hired because of both substitution and output effects. The size of these effects will depend on the firm's technology and on the price responsiveness of the demand for its output.
- The marginal productivity theory of input demand can also be used to study the determinants of relative income shares accruing to various factors of production. The elasticity of substitution indicates how these shares change in response to changing factor supplies.
- If a firm has a monopsonistic position in an input market, it will recognize how its hiring affects input prices. The marginal expense associated with hiring additional units of an input will exceed that input's price, and the firm will reduce hiring below competitive levels to maximize profits. If the firm holds a monopsonistic position in several markets, it may be able to practice input price discrimination among them.
- If input suppliers form a monopoly against a monopsonistic demander, the result is indeterminate. In such a situation of bilateral monopoly, the market equilibrium chosen will depend on the bargaining of the two parties.

Application

THE MINIMUM WAGE

The Fair Labor Standards Act of 1938 established a national minimum wage of $0.25 per hour, with provisions for increasing this figure to $0.40 per hour. Since that time the minimum wage has been raised several times in response to general inflation and changing social values. The scope of minimum wage legislation has also been expanded over time, and most employees are now covered. Economists have been far from enthusiastic over this seemingly beneficial development in social legislation. They have argued that although minimum wages may benefit some workers, others suffer substantial unemployment. The theory of input demand provides the framework from which economists draw this implication, and the study of the effects of a minimum wage provides an important application of the tools developed in this chapter.

A Graphic Analysis

Figure 21.5 illustrates the possible effects of a minimum wage. Figure 21.5a shows the supply and demand curves for labor. Given these curves, an equilibrium wage rate, w_1, is established in the market. At this wage a typical firm hires l_1, and this choice of input is shown on the firm's isoquant map in Figure 21.5b. Suppose

Figure 21.5   *Effects of a Minimum Wage in a Perfectly Competitive Labor Market*

Initially, a wage rate of w_1 is set by the forces of supply and demand. At this wage rate a typical firm chooses to use l_1 units of labor. The imposition of a minimum wage (w_2) causes the firm to reduce labor usage to l_2 because it will both substitute capital (and other inputs) for labor and cut back output. All firms' demands will be reduced to L_2 at the new wage rate. Individuals wish to supply L_3, however, and there will be unemployment of $L_3 - L_2$.

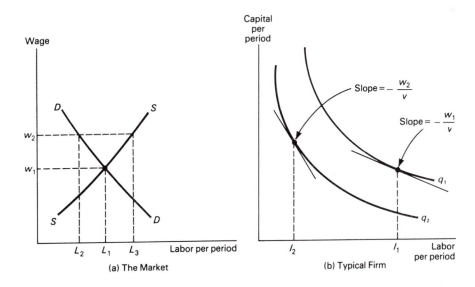

(a) The Market

(b) Typical Firm

now that a minimum wage of w_2 ($> w_1$) is imposed by law. This new wage will cause the firm to reduce its demand for labor from l_1 to l_2. The reduction comes from two effects. First, the increase in the price of labor causes the firm to substitute capital for labor along the q_1 isoquant. In addition to this substitution effect, there is a negative output effect, since the increase in costs has caused the firm's output to be reduced from q_1 to q_2. Consequently, the typical firm will reduce its demand for labor from l_1 to l_2. Similar actions by many firms will be reflected in a movement along the market demand for labor curve from L_1 to L_2. At the same time more labor (L_3) will be supplied at w_2 than was supplied at the lower wage rate. The imposition of the minimum wage therefore will result in an excess of the quantity of labor supplied over the quantity of labor demanded of $L_3 - L_2$. This excess supply is what we mean by "unemployment." At the new prevailing wage more individuals want to work than are able to find jobs. The extent of this unemployment will depend on the size of the substitution and output effects that come into play as firms are affected by the new wage. For those workers who do find jobs, wages are increased from w_1 to w_2. Whether the total wage bill ($w \cdot L$) increases or decreases will depend on the elasticity of demand for labor. If demand is inelastic, total receipts will rise; if it is elastic, the total bill will fall.

Minimum Wages and Teenage Unemployment
There is some empirical evidence that changes in the minimum wage law have had serious effects in increasing teenage unemployment. Teenagers are the labor market participants most likely to be affected by minimum wage laws, since they usually represent the lower end of the spectrum of skills. An increase in minimum wages may cause employers to substitute capital and skilled labor for what has become more expensive, unskilled teenage labor; it may also cause large negative output effects, since the products produced by teenage employees (services, for example) usually have a fairly high

price elasticity. In recent years teenage unemployment has increased rapidly. Particularly hard hit have been teenage minority group members, for whom unemployment rates often exceed 30 percent. Although there are several factors that may account for such statistics (unstable employment opportunities, discrimination in employment, long periods of searching for jobs), many economists assign an important role to statutory changes in the minimum wage. For example, one study found that each 1 percent increase in the minimum wage resulted in a reduction of .3 percent in teenagers' share of total employment.[14] A particularly important example of this reduction is in the changing employment patterns of fast-food chains in response to rising minimum wages. These businesses are highly labor-intensive and sell a product (eating out), the demand for which is relatively price-responsive. Hence the firms may find their sales falling off substantially in response to price rises stemming from minimum wage increases. In addition, the firms may attempt to substitute capital equipment (automatic cooking equipment) for teenage workers, thereby further reducing their demand for workers. In response to the major 1977 minimum wage increase, for example, the McDonald's Corporation (reputedly the largest employer of teenage workers in the United States) adopted a new program of research on labor-saving technology and initiated several changes in its teenage hiring practices.

Effects of Expanding Minimum Wage Coverage
Although periodic increases in the minimum wage undoubtedly have had a negative effect on teenage employment, those increases have not exceeded increases in wages in general. The minimum wage has remained relatively constant at about 45 percent of the average wage in manufacturing over the past 40 years. The per-

---

[14] F. Welch, "Minimum Wage Legislation in the United States," *Economic Inquiry* 12 (September 1974): 285–318.

centage of the labor force covered by minimum wage legislation, however, has been greatly expanded in recent years. Some analysts believe that this expansion has had even more significant effects than has the rise in the minimum wage itself. These effects show up both in reduced employment in industries newly covered by the minimum wage law, through the process illustrated in Figure 21.5, and in lower wages for individuals who work in uncovered industries (because of the increased supply of workers seeking such jobs). Since much of the employment in uncovered industries is not officially recorded, however, it is difficult to estimate the magnitude of the second effect.

Minimum Wages in Monopsony Markets
The predicted negative impact of minimum wage increases on employment arises from a competitive model and reflects a simple application of the theory of input demand. The substantial empirical evidence showing such negative employment effects provides considerable support for the applicability of such a model to most labor markets.[15] When labor markets are

imperfectly competitive, however, the predictions are not so clearcut.

Adoption of a minimum wage changes the labor supply curve (no one can work at below the minimum even if he or she wants to) and therefore shifts the associated marginal expense curve. In some cases, this shift may actually cause the firm to increase its profit-maximizing choice of labor input. An appropriately chosen minimum wage may therefore mitigate monopsonistic distortions to the labor market in some circumstances.

The empirical relevance of this theoretical observation is unclear. In the early years of minimum wage legislation, these requirements may have had some effect on isolated local monopsonists, and even in recent years they may have affected hiring cartels for agricultural workers. Because minimum wages tend to be set at a low fraction of average wages (usually well below one-half), however, they probably have no effect on monopsonistic hiring of relatively skilled workers. In these cases (such as professional sports) unionization and the concomitant bilateral bargaining are a far more effective control on monopsonistic behavior by employers.

[15] For a survey of some of the literature, see D. Hamermesh "Minimum Wages and the Demand for Labor," *Economic Inquiry* (July 1982): 365–380.

SUGGESTED READINGS

Allen, R. G. D. *Mathematical Analysis for Economists.* New York: St. Martin's Press, 1938. Pp. 369–374 and 505–509.

Fairly complete development of input demand relationships. Notation difficult in spots.

Becker, G. *The Economics of Discrimination.* 2d ed. Chicago: University of Chicago Press, 1971.

First theoretical analysis of economic discrimination. Shows that under competitive conditions discrimination may harm the discriminator as well.

Bordcherding, T. E. "A Neglected Social Cost of a Voluntary Military." *American Economic Review* 61 (March 1971): 195–196.

An analysis of the monopsonistic position occupied by the military in hiring soldiers.

Diewert, W. E. "Duality Approaches to Microeconomic Theory." In K. J. Arrow and M. D. Intriligator, eds., *Handbook of Mathematical Economics*, vol. 2. Amsterdam: North Holland Publishing Co., 1982. Pp. 537–584.

Advanced use of duality to study input demand.

Douglas, P. H. *The Theory of Wages.* New York: Crowell-Collier and Macmillan, 1934.

First use of the Cobb-Douglas production function to analyze input shares in the United States.

Ferguson, C. E. " 'Inferior Factors' and the Theories of Production and Input Demand." *Economica* n.s. 35 (1968): 140–150.

Detailed treatment of inferior inputs and why they pose no special problems for input demand theory.

Fuss, M., and McFadden, D., eds. *Production Economics: A Dual Approach to Theory and Application.* Amsterdam: North Holland Publishing Co., 1980.

Sophisticated development of the relationship between production functions and input demand functions.

Hamermesh, D. "The Demand for Labor in the Long Run." In O. C. Ashenfelter and R. Lagard, eds., *Handbook of Labor Economics,* vol. 1. Amsterdam: North Holland Publishing Co., 1986. Pp. 429–472.

Comprehensive review of both theoretical and empirical issues in the demand for labor. Espe-cially strong in analyzing the demand for different types of labor.

Robinson, J. "Euler's Theorem and the Problem of Distribution." *Economic Journal* 44 (1934): 398–421.

Discussion of the "adding-up" problem and some criticisms of using Euler's theorem to solve it.

Rottenberg, S. "The Baseball Players' Labor Market." *Journal of Political Economy* 64 (June 1956): 242–258.

Early work on the theory of monopsony in base-ball. Much literature has followed.

Silberberg, E. *The Structure of Economics: A Mathematical Analysis.* New York: McGraw-Hill Book Company, 1978. Chaps. 8 and 10.

Extensive use of duality and Shephard's lemma to derive input demand results.

PROBLEMS

21.1

Suppose that the demand for labor is given by

$$L = -50w + 450$$

and the supply is given by

$$L = 100w,$$

where L represents the number of people employed and w is the real wage rate per hour.

    a.   What will be the equilibrium levels for w and L in this market?

    b.   Suppose that the government wishes to raise the equilibrium wage to $4 per hour by offering a subsidy to employers for each person hired. How much will this subsidy have to be? What will the new equilibrium level of employment be? How much total subsidy will be paid?

    c.   Suppose instead that the government declared a minimum wage of $4 per hour. How much labor would be demanded at this price? How much unemployment would there be?

    d.   Graph your results.

21.2

Assume that the market for rental cars (used for business purposes) is perfectly competitive with the demand for this capital input given by

$$K = 1,500 - 25v$$

and the supply given by

$$K = 75v - 500$$

where K represents the number of cars rented by firms and v is the rental rate per day.

a. What will be the equilibrium levels for v and K in this market?

b. Suppose that following an oil embargo gas prices rise dramatically so that now business firms must take account of gas prices in their car rental decisions. Their demand for rental cars is now given by

$$K = 1{,}700 - 25v - 300g$$

where g is the per gallon price of gasoline. What will be the equilibrium levels for v and K if $g = \$2$? If $g = \$3$?

c. Graph your results.

d. Since the oil embargo brought about decreased demand for rental cars, what might be the implication for other capital input markets as a result? For example, employees may still need transportation, so how might the demand for mass transit be affected? Since businesspeople also rent cars to attend meetings, what might happen in the market for phone equipment as employees drive less and use the phone more? Can you think of any other factor input markets that might be affected?

21.3

A landowner has three farms (A, B, and C) of differing fertility. The levels of output for the three farms with one, two, and three laborers employed are as given:

Number of Laborers	Level of Output Farm A	Farm B	Farm C
1	10	8	5
2	17	11	7
3	21	13	8

For example, if three laborers were hired, one for each firm, the total output would be $10 + 8 + 5 = 23$. This would represent a poor allocation of labor, since if the Farm C laborer were assigned to help on Farm A the total output would be $17 + 8 = 25$.

a. If market conditions caused the landowner to hire five laborers, what would be the most productive allocation of that labor? How much would be produced? What is the marginal product of the last worker?

b. If that farm output is sold in a perfectly competitive market with one unit of output priced at $1, and labor market equilibrium occurs when five workers are hired, what wage is paid? How much profit does the landowner receive?

21.4

The mowing of lawns requires only labor (gardeners) and capital (lawn mowers). These factors must be used in the fixed proportions of one worker to one lawn mower, and production exhibits constant returns to scale. Suppose that the wage rate of gardeners is $2 per hour and that lawn mowers rent for $5 per hour and that the price elasticity of demand for mowed lawns is -2.

a. What is the wage elasticity of demand for gardeners (that is, what is $\partial L/\partial w \cdot w/L$)?

b. What is the elasticity of demand for lawn mowers with respect to their rental rate (that is, $\partial K/\partial v \cdot v/K$)?

c. What is the cross elasticity of demand for lawn mowers with respect to the wage rate (that is, $\partial K/\partial w \cdot w/K$)?

21.5

Assume that the quantity of envelopes licked per hour by Sticky Gums, Inc. is $Q = 10,000\sqrt{L}$ where L is the number of laborers hired per hour by the firm. Assume further that the envelope-licking business is perfectly competitive with a market price of $.01 per envelope.

    a.   How much labor would be hired at a competitive wage of $10? $5? $2? Use your results to sketch a demand curve for labor.

    b.   Assume that Sticky Gums hires its labor at an hourly wage of $10. What quantity of envelopes will be licked when the price of a licked envelope is $.10, $.05, $.02? Use your results to sketch a supply curve for licked envelopes.

21.6

Suppose there are a fixed number of 1,000 identical firms in the perfectly competitive concrete pipe industry. Each firm produces the same fraction of total market output and each firm's production function for pipe is given by

$$q = \sqrt{KL}.$$

Suppose also that the market demand for concrete pipe is given by

$$Q = 400,000 - 100,000P$$

where Q is total concrete pipe.

    a.   If $w = v = \$1$, in what ratio will the typical firm use K and L? What will be the long-run average and marginal cost of pipe?

    b.   In long-run equilibrium what will be the market equilibrium price and quantity for concrete pipe? How much will each firm produce? How much labor will be hired by each firm and in the market as a whole?

    c.   Suppose the market wage, w, rose to $2 while v remained constant at $1. How will this change the capital-labor ratio for the typical firm, and how will it affect its marginal costs?

    d.   Under the conditions of part (c) what will the long-run market equilibrium be? How much labor will now be hired by the concrete pipe industry?

    e.   How much of the change in total labor demand from part (b) to part (d) represented the substitution effect resulting from the change in wage and how much represented the output effect?

21.7

In the early 1960s President John Kennedy's Council of Economic Advisers recommended the institution of "Wage-Price Guideposts." The basic idea of the guideposts was to require wages in all industries to increase at the rate at which the national level of output per worker increases (about 3.2 percent per year). Some industries would have had rates of productivity increase of less than 3.2 percent. These industries were to be permitted to increase prices to the extent that their productivity increase fell short of the national average. On the other hand, firms that had productivity increases in excess of the national average were expected to reduce their prices to the extent of this excess.

    Adherence to these rules was intended to keep prices constant on a nationwide basis. There were numerous exceptions to these general principles, but assume for the purposes of this problem that these were not important. If the Wage-Price Guideposts were legislated as an unbreakable law, answer the following questions:

    a.   What would happen to the relative factor shares in each industry over time?

    b. What does this implicitly assume about the elasticity of substitution in all industries?

    c. What effect would this legislation have on the investment of new capital if industries did not obey the assumption discussed in (b)?

    d. In regard to your answer to (c), what effects do you think the guideposts would have on economic growth?

21.8

Carl the clothier owns a large garment factory on an isolated island. Carl's factory is the only source of employment for most of the islanders and thus Carl acts as a monopsonist. The supply curve for garment workers is given by

$$L = 80w$$

where L is the number of workers hired and w is their hourly wage. Assume also that Carl's labor demand (marginal revenue product) curve is given by

$$L = 400 - 40MRP_L$$

    a. How many workers will Carl hire in order to maximize his profits and what wage will he pay?

    b. Assume now that the government implements a minimum wage law covering all garment workers. How many workers will Carl now hire and how much unemployment will there be if the minimum wage is set at $4.00 per hour?

    c. Graph your results.

    d. How does the imposition of a minimum wage under monopsony differ in results as compared with a minimum wage imposed under perfect competition (assuming the minimum wage is above the market determined wage)?

21.9

The Ajax Coal Company is the only hirer of labor in its area. It can hire any number of female workers or male workers it wishes. The supply curve for women is given by

$$L_f = 100w_f$$

and for men by

$$L_m = 9w_m^2,$$

where w_f and w_m are, respectively, the hourly wage rate paid to female and male workers. Assume that Ajax sells its coal in a perfectly competitive market at $5 per ton and that each worker hired (both men and women) can mine 2 tons per hour. If the firm wishes to maximize profits, how many female and male workers should be hired, and what will the wage rates for these two groups be? How much will Ajax earn in profits per hour on its mine machinery? How will that result compare to one in which Ajax was constrained (say, by market forces) to pay all workers the same wage based on the value of their marginal products?

21.10

The town of Podunk has decided to provide security services to its residents by hiring workers (L) and guard dogs (D). Security services (S) are produced according to the production function

$$S = \sqrt{LD},$$

and residents of the town wish to consume 10 units of such services per period.

a. Suppose that L and D both rent for \$1 per period. How much of each input should the town hire to produce the desired services at minimal cost? What will that cost be?

b. Suppose now that Podunk is the only hirer of people who work with guard dogs and that the supply curve for such workers is given by

$$L = 10w,$$

where w is the per-period wage of guard dog handlers. If dogs continue to rent for \$1 per period, how much of each input should the town hire to produce the desired services at minimal cost? What will those costs be? What will the wage rate of dog handlers be?

21.11

Assume employers have no "taste for discrimination" against blacks but that the white employees do. A white employee considers his "psychic wage" to be a combination of the money wage and the percentage of blacks in the firm. That is, a white worker demands higher wages in order to work with blacks. Both blacks and whites offer their services in a perfectly competitive market and are equally productive. The wages for whites and blacks are given by

$$w_1 = MRP \quad (1 + \text{percent of blacks in firm})$$

and

$$w_2 = MRP$$

respectively. How might you expect a cost-minimizing firm to adjust the racial mix of its employees?

EXTENSIONS

THE ELASTICITY OF DEMAND FOR LABOR

In Chapter 21 we showed how the elasticity of demand for labor is an important concept for judging a variety of questions about how labor markets operate. Here we show explicitly how this elasticity is related to a firm's underlying production and cost functions. Following customary convention we will denote the (constant output) wage elasticity of demand for labor as

$$\eta_{LL} = \frac{\partial L}{\partial w} \cdot \frac{w}{L} \quad (q \; constant)$$

and the cross elasticity of labor demand for changes in the capital rental rate as

$$\eta_{LK} = \frac{\partial L}{\partial v} \cdot \frac{v}{L} \quad (q \; constant)$$

For the most part our discussion will focus on cases where production depends only on two inputs (K and L), but in the final Extension Problem we show how the results can be generalized.

E21.1

Suppose the total cost function can be written as

$$TC(w, v, q) = qC(w, v)$$

where $C(w, v)$ is a unit cost function that is homogeneous of degree one in w and v (this is true for all the cost functions we introduced in the Extensions to Chapter 11, for example). Use Shephard's lemma to show that

$$L = qC_w$$

and

$$K = qC_v.$$

E21.2
Use the results from E21.1 together with

$$wC_{ww} + vC_{wv} = 0$$

(which follows from Euler's Theorem for homogeneous functions) and the definition

$$\sigma = \frac{CC_{wv}}{C_w C_v}$$

(see the Extensions to Chapter 11) to prove that in the two factor case

$$\eta_{LL} = -(1 - s_L)\sigma$$

$$\eta_{LK} = (1 - s_L)\sigma$$

where s_L $(= wL/qC)$ is labor's share of total costs.

E21.3
Explain the results of E21.2 intuitively. Specifically, why does capital's share of total costs $(1 - s_L)$ enter into both expressions for the elasticity of demand for labor?

E21.4
For the three cost functions introduced in the Extensions to Chapter 11, show that the wage elasticity of demand for labor is

Total Cost Function	η_{LL}
Cobb Douglas	$-(1 - s_L)$
CES	$-(1 - s_L)\sigma$
Translog	$(2\beta_2 + s_L^2 - s_L)/s_L$
	$= (1 - s_L)\left\{\dfrac{2\beta_2 + s_L(s_L - 1)}{s_L(1 - s_L)}\right\}$
	$= (1 - s_L)\sigma$

where the notation here follows that used in the Extensions to Chapter 11.

E21.5
Use the procedure followed in Problem E21.2 to show that the total wage elasticity of demand for labor (including output effects) is given by

$$e_{L,w} = -(1 - s_L) - s_L e_{Q,P}$$

where $e_{Q,P}$ is the price elasticity of demand for the firm's output. To complete this proof assume the industry in question is in long-run competitive equilibrium so that $P = MC = AC$ (which is C, given the notation used in E21.2). Explain this equation for total elasticity intuitively. Under what circumstances would you use this total elasticity? When would the constant output elasticity be appropriate?

E21.6
For the many input case, it can be shown that

$$\eta_{ij} = \frac{\partial X_i}{\partial w_j} \cdot \frac{w_j}{X_i} = s_j \sigma_{ij}$$

(see Hamermesh, pp. 440–441).

Explain how this general equation applies directly to the cross elasticity of demand for labor (η_{LK}) in the two input case but that the own wage elasticity (η_{LL}) requires some modification.

E21.7
Since (constant output) factor demand equations are homogeneous of degree zero in all input prices, show that

$$\sum_{j=1}^{\eta} \eta_{ij} = 0$$

Because $\eta_{ii} < 0$, what do you conclude about the signs of η_{ij} for $i \neq j$?

REFERENCES

Fuss, M., and D. McFadden, eds., *Production Economics: A Dual Approach to Theory and Applications* (Amsterdam: North Holland Publishing Co., 1978).

Hamermesh, D. S., "The Demand for Labor in the Long Run" in O. C. Ashenfelter and R. Layard, eds., *Handbook of Labor Economics*, vol. 1 (Amsterdam: North Holland Publishing Co., 1986), pp. 429–471.

CHAPTER 22

Labor Supply

In this chapter we shall examine some aspects of factor pricing that are related particularly to the labor market. Because we have already discussed questions about the demand for labor (or any other factor) in some detail, we shall be concerned primarily with analyzing the supply of labor. There are several reasons why a chapter with this focus is presented here. First, the theory of labor supply provides another useful application of the model of individual choice that we developed in Parts II and III. A second reason for examining the economics of labor supply is to provide some insight into the job choices that individuals make. The concept of compensating differentials that we shall develop for this purpose also has uses that extend far beyond traditional questions of occupational choice. Finally, analyzing labor supply can provide an opportunity to examine the operation of labor unions. Because unions are important, powerful participants in the labor markets of most Western countries, any treatment of labor supply would be incomplete without such an examination.

ALLOCATION OF TIME

In Part II we analyzed the way in which an individual will choose to allocate a fixed amount of income among a variety of available goods. Individuals must make similar choices in deciding how they will spend their time. The number of hours in a day (or in a year) is absolutely fixed, and time must be used as it "passes by." It is not possible, in a strict sense, to leave some time unutilized today so that it can be used tomorrow. Given this fixed amount of time, any individual must decide how many hours to work; how many hours to spend consuming a wide variety of goods, ranging from cars and television sets to operas; how many hours to devote to self-maintenance; and how many hours to sleep. By studying how individuals choose to divide their time among these activities, economists are able to understand the decision to work. By viewing work as only one of a number of choices open to individuals in the way they allocate their time, it is possible to understand why work decisions may be changed in response to changing opportunities. In the next few sections we shall analyze this possibility.

Simple Two-Good Model

For simplicity we shall start by assuming that there are only two uses to which an individual may devote his or her time—either engaging in market work at a real wage rate of w per hour or not working. We shall refer to nonwork time as "leisure," but this word is not meant to carry any connotation of idleness. Time that is not spent in market work can be devoted to work in the home, to self-improvement, or to consumption (it takes time to use a television set or a bowling ball).[1] All of those activities contribute to an individual's well-being, and time will be allocated to them in what might be assumed to be a utility-maximizing way.

More specifically, assume that an individual's utility during a typical day depends on consumption during that period (C) and on hours of leisure enjoyed (H):

$$\text{utility} = U(C, H). \tag{22.1}$$

Notice that in writing this utility function, we have used two "composite" goods, consumption and leisure. The reader should recognize that utility is in fact derived by devoting real income and time to the consumption of a wide variety of goods and services.[2] In seeking to maximize utility, the individual is bound by two constraints. The first of these concerns available time. If we let L represent hours of work, then

$$L + H = 24. \tag{22.2}$$

That is, the day's time must be allocated either to work or to nonwork. A second constraint records the fact that the individual can purchase consumption items only by working (later in this chapter we will allow for the availability of nonlabor income). If the real hourly market wage rate that the individual can earn is given by w, the income constraint is given by

$$C = wL. \tag{22.3}$$

Combining the two constraints, we have

$$C = w(24 - H) \tag{22.4}$$

or

$$C + wH = 24w. \tag{22.5}$$

This combined constraint has an important interpretation. Any individual has a "full income" given by $24w$. That is, an individual who worked all the time would have this much command over real consumption goods each day. Individuals may spend their full income either by working (for real income and

---

[1] Perhaps the first formal theoretical treatment of the allocation of time was given by G. S. Becker, "A Theory of the Allocation of Time," *Economic Journal* 75 (September 1965): 493–517.

[2] This observation leads to the consideration of how such activities are produced in the home. For a survey see R. Gronau, "Home Production: A Survey" in O. C. Ashenfelter and R. Layard, eds., *Handbook of Economics*, vol. 1 (Amsterdam: North Holland Publishing Co., 1986), pp. 273–304.

consumption) or by not working and thereby enjoying leisure. Equation 22.5 shows that the opportunity cost of consuming leisure is w per hour: It is equal to earnings forgone by not working.

Utility
Maximization

The individual's problem then is to maximize utility, subject to the full income constraint. Setting up the Lagrangian expression

$$\mathcal{L} = U(C, H) + \lambda(24w - C - wH), \tag{22.6}$$

the first-order conditions for a maximum are

$$\frac{\partial \mathcal{L}}{\partial C} = \frac{\partial U}{\partial C} - \lambda = 0$$

$$\frac{\partial \mathcal{L}}{\partial H} = \frac{\partial U}{\partial H} - w\lambda = 0. \tag{22.7}$$

Dividing the two lines in Equation 22.7, we get

$$\frac{\partial U/\partial H}{\partial U/\partial C} = w = MRS \quad (H \text{ for } C). \tag{22.8}$$

Hence we have derived the following:

Optimization Principle:

Utility-Maximizing Labor Supply Decision
In order to maximize utility, given the real wage, w, the individual should choose to work that number of hours for which the marginal rate of substitution of leisure for consumption is equal to w.

Of course, the result derived in Equation 22.8 is only a necessary condition for a maximum. As in Chapter 5, this tangency will be a true maximum provided that the *MRS* of leisure for consumption is diminishing.

Income and
Substitution
Effects of a
Change in w

A change in the real wage rate (w) can be analyzed in a manner identical to that used in Chapter 5. When w rises, the "price" of leisure becomes higher—the individual must give up more in lost wages for each hour of leisure consumed. The substitution effect of an increase in w on the hours of leisure therefore will be negative. As leisure becomes more expensive, there is reason to consume less of it. However, the income effect will be positive—since leisure is a normal good, the higher income resulting from a higher w will increase the demand for leisure. Thus the income and substitution effects work in opposite directions. It is impossible to predict on *a priori* grounds whether an increase in w will increase or decrease the demand for leisure time. Since leisure and work are mutually exclusive ways to spend one's time, it is also impossible to predict what will happen to the number of hours worked. The substitution effect tends to increase hours worked when w increases whereas the income effect, because it increases the demand for leisure time, tends to

Figure 22.1   *Income and Substitution Effects*
of a Change in the Real Wage Rate w

Since the individual is a supplier of labor, the income and substitution effects of an increase in the real wage rate (w) work in opposite directions in their effects on the hours of leisure demanded (or on hours of work). In (a) the substitution effect (movement to point S) outweighs the income effect, and a higher wage causes hours of leisure to decline to H_1. Hours of work therefore increase. In (b) the income effect is stronger than the substitution effect, and H increases to H_1. In this case hours of work decline.

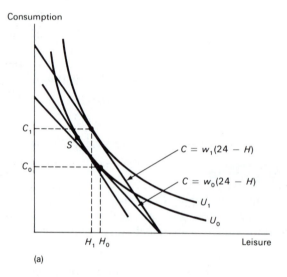

(a)

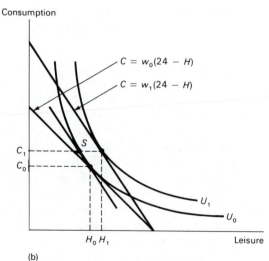

(b)

decrease the number of hours worked. Which of these two effects is the stronger is an important empirical question.[3]

The two possible reactions to a change in w are illustrated in Figure 22.1. In both graphs the initial wage is w_0, and the initial optimal choices of C and H are given by the point C_0, H_0. When the wage rate increases to w_1, the optimal combination moves to point C_1, H_1. This movement can be considered as the result of two effects. The substitution effect can be represented by the movement of the optimal point from C_0, H_0 to S and the income effect by the movement from S to C_1, H_1. In Figures 22.1a and 22.1b these two effects combine to produce different results. In Figure 22.1a the substitution effect of a change in w outweighs the income effect, and the individual demands less leisure ($H_1 < H_0$). Another way of saying this is that the individual will work longer hours when w rises.

In Figure 22.1b the situation is reversed. The income effect of a change in w more than offsets the substitution effect and the demand for leisure increases ($H_1 > H_0$). The individual works shorter hours when w rises. In the cases examined in Chapter 5 this would have been considered an unusual result— when the "price" of leisure rises, the individual demands more of it. For the case of normal consumption goods, the income and substitution effects work in the same direction. Only for "inferior" goods do they differ in sign. In the case of leisure and labor, however, the income and substitution effects always work in opposite directions. An increase in w makes an individual better off because he or she is a *supplier* of labor. In the case of a consumption good, individuals are made worse off when a price rises because they are *consumers* of that good. We can summarize this analysis by

Optimization Principle:

Income and Substitution Effects of a Change in the Real Wage
When the real wage rate increases, a utility-maximizing individual may increase or decrease hours worked. The substitution effect will tend to increase hours worked as the individual substitutes earnings for leisure, which is now relatively more costly. On the other hand, the income effect will tend to reduce hours worked as the individual uses his or her increased purchasing power to buy more leisure hours.

We now turn to examine a mathematical development of these responses that provides additional insights into the labor supply decision.

A MATHE-MATICAL ANALYSIS OF LABOR SUPPLY

In order to derive a mathematical statement of labor supply decisions, it is helpful first to amend the individual's budget constraint slightly to allow for the presence of nonlabor income. To do so, we rewrite Equation 22.3 as

$$C = wL + N, \tag{22.9}$$

[3] If the family is taken to be the relevant decision unit, even more complex questions arise about the income and substitution effects that changes in the wages of one family member, say, the husband, will have on the labor force behavior of other family members, for example, the wife.

where N is real nonlabor income and may include such items as dividend and interest income, receipt of government transfer benefits, or simply gifts from other persons. Indeed, N could stand for lump-sum taxes paid by the individual, in which case its value would be negative.

Maximization of utility subject to this new budget constraint would yield results virtually identical to those already derived. That is, the necessary condition for a maximum described in Equation 22.8 would continue to hold as long as the value of N is unaffected by the labor-leisure choices being made; that is, so long as N is a "lump-sum" receipt or loss of income,[4] the only effect of introducing nonlabor income into the analysis is to shift the budget constraints in Figure 22.1 outward in a parallel manner without affecting the trade-off rate between earnings and leisure.

This discussion suggests that we can write the individual's labor supply function as $L(w, N)$ to indicate that the number of hours worked will depend both on the real wage rate and on the amount of real nonlabor income received. On the assumption that leisure is a normal good, $\partial L/\partial N$ will be negative; that is, an increase in N will raise the demand for leisure and (since there are only 24 hours in the day) reduce L. To study wage effects on labor supply ($\partial L/\partial w$), we will find it helpful first to consider the dual problem to the individual's primary utility-maximization problem.

Dual Statement of the Problem

As we showed in Chapter 5, related to the individual's primary problem of utility maximization given a budget constraint is the dual problem of minimizing the expenditures necessary to attain a given utility level. In the present context, this problem can be phrased as choosing values for consumption (C) and leisure time ($H = 24 - L$) so that the amount of extra expenditures,

$$E = C - wL, \tag{22.10}$$

required to attain a given utility level [say, $U_0 = U(C, H)$] is as small as possible. As in Chapter 5, solving this minimization problem will yield exactly the same solution as solving the utility-maximization problem.

Now we can apply the envelope theorem to the minimum value for these extra expenditures calculated in the dual problem. Specifically, a small change in the real wage will change the minimum expenditures required by

$$\frac{\partial E}{\partial w} = -L. \tag{22.11}$$

Intuitively, each \$1 increase in w reduces the required value of E by \$$L$, since that is the extent to which labor earnings are increased by the wage change.

---

[4]In many situations, however, N itself may depend on labor supply decisions. For example, the value of welfare or unemployment benefits a person can receive depends on his or her earnings, as does the amount of income taxes paid. In such cases the slope of the individual's budget constraint will no longer be reflected by the real wage but must instead reflect the *net* return to additional work after taking increased taxes and reductions in transfer payments into account. For some examples, see the problems at the end of this chapter.

This result is very similar to Shephard's lemma in the theory of production (see Chapters 11 and 21): Here the result shows that a labor supply function can be calculated from the expenditure function by partial differentiation. Since utility is held constant in the dual expenditure minimization approach, this function should be interpreted as a "compensated" (constant utility) labor supply function, which we will denote by $L'(w, U)$ to differentiate it from the uncompensated labor supply function $L(w, N)$ introduced earlier.

Slutsky Equation of Labor Supply

Now we can use these concepts to derive a Slutsky-type equation that reflects the substitution and income effects that result from changes in the real wage. We begin by recognizing that the expenditures being minimized in the dual problem of Equation 22.11 play the role of nonlabor income in the primal utility-maximization problem. Hence, by definition, at the optimal point we have

$$L'(w, U) = L[w, E(w, U)] \equiv L(w, N). \tag{22.12}$$

Partial differentiation of both sides of Equation 22.12 with respect to w yields

$$\frac{\partial L'}{\partial w} = \frac{\partial L}{\partial w} + \frac{\partial L}{\partial E} \cdot \frac{\partial E}{\partial w}, \tag{22.13}$$

and using the envelope relation from Equation 22.11, we have

$$\frac{\partial L'}{\partial w} = \frac{\partial L}{\partial w} - L \frac{\partial L}{\partial E} = \frac{\partial L}{\partial w} - L \frac{\partial L}{\partial N}. \tag{22.14}$$

Introducing a slightly different notation for the compensated labor supply function

$$\frac{\partial L'}{\partial w} = \frac{\partial L}{\partial w} \bigg|_{U = U_0}, \tag{22.15}$$

and rearranging terms gives the final Slutsky equation for labor supply:

$$\frac{\partial L}{\partial w} = \frac{\partial L}{\partial w} \bigg|_{U = U_0} + L \frac{\partial L}{\partial N}. \tag{22.16}$$

In words (as we have previously shown), the change in labor supplied in response to a change in the real wage can be disaggregated into the sum of a substitution effect in which utility is held constant and an income effect that is analytically equivalent to an appropriate change in nonlabor income. Since the substitution effect is positive (a higher wage increases the amount of work chosen when utility is held constant) and the term $\partial L / \partial N$ is negative, this derivation shows that the substitution and income effects work in opposite directions. The mathematical development supports the earlier conclusions from our graphical analysis. The mathematical development also suggests that the importance of negative income effects may be greater the greater is labor supply, L, a possibility we will examine in the next section.

Numerical Example

The Cobb-Douglas utility function provides an instructive example of these offsetting substitution and income effects in labor supply decisions. Suppose therefore that hourly utility is a function of consumption and leisure of the form

$$U = \sqrt{CH}. \tag{22.17}$$

The individual is constrained by a budget constraint

$$C = wL + N \tag{22.18}$$

and by a time constraint

$$H = 1 - L, \tag{22.19}$$

where, for simplicity, we have set maximum work time equal to 1 (hour, day, year, or lifetime). Combining Equations 22.17–22.19, we can express utility as a function of labor supply choice only:

$$U^2 = CH = (wL + N)(1 - L)$$
$$= wL - wL^2 + N - NL. \tag{22.20}$$

Differentiation of U^2 with respect to L yields the first-order condition for a utility maximum

$$\frac{\partial U^2}{\partial L} = w - 2wL - N = 0 \tag{22.21}$$

or

$$L = \frac{1}{2} - \frac{N}{2w}. \tag{22.22}$$

This, then, is the individual's labor supply function. If $N = 0$ this individual will work $\frac{1}{2}$ of each period no matter what the wage is—that is, if $N = 0$, the substitution and income effects of a change in w precisely offset each other and leave L unaffected. A more complete analysis of why this is so requires that we examine the effects separately. Calculation of the income effect in the Slutsky Equation 22.16 is straightforward using the optimal choice in Equation 22.22

$$L \cdot \frac{\partial L}{\partial N} = \left[\frac{1}{2} - \frac{N}{2w} \right]\left[-\frac{1}{2w} \right] = -\frac{1}{4w} + \frac{N}{4w}. \tag{22.23}$$

If $N = 0$, this income effect will be simply

$$L \cdot \frac{\partial L}{\partial N} = -\frac{1}{4w},$$

where the negative sign indicates that the income effect of an increase in w will reduce L since leisure is a normal good.

Calculation of the substitution effect in the Slutsky equation is a rather messy process. First one must derive an expression for indirect utility as a function of w and N (the two exogenous elements in the individual's budget constraint) and then use this to eliminate N from the optimal labor supply choice given by Equation 22.22. Luckily, your author has made this calculation for you:[5]

$$L'(w, U) = 1 - \frac{U}{\sqrt{w}}. \tag{22.24}$$

This constant utility labor supply function shows that if only substitution effects are allowed, $\partial L'/\partial w$ is definitely positive:

$$\frac{\partial L'}{\partial w} = \frac{U}{2w^{3/2}}. \tag{22.25}$$

Replacing U with its indirect representation in terms of w and N in Equation 22.25 (see footnote 5) now yields

$$\frac{\partial L'}{\partial w} = \frac{1}{4w} + \frac{N}{4w^2}. \tag{22.26}$$

Hence, if $N = 0$,

$$\frac{\partial L'}{\partial w} = \frac{1}{4w}, \tag{22.27}$$

and the Slutsky equation

$$\frac{\partial L}{\partial w} = \frac{\partial L'}{\partial w} + L \frac{\partial L}{\partial N} = \frac{1}{4w} - \frac{1}{4w} = 0 \tag{22.28}$$

shows that the substitution and income effects are precisely offsetting.

Of course, if $N \neq 0$ (the individual has some nonlabor income), this precise offsetting would not occur. The explanation for this is that this individual will always choose to spend half of his or her nonlabor income on leisure. But leisure "costs" w per hour and a rise in w will mean that less leisure can be "bought" with a fixed number of N dollars. If, for example, $N = \$2$ per hour and w is $\$10$ per hour, Equation 22.22 shows that the individual will work

$$L = \tfrac{1}{2} - \tfrac{2}{20} = \tfrac{4}{10}. \tag{22.29}$$

This person spends $\$1$ of his or her nonlabor income on leisure each hour. At a wage of $\$10$, this $\$1$ will buy $\tfrac{1}{10}$ of an hour of leisure. If, on the other hand, $w = \$5$, the $\$1$ would buy $\tfrac{2}{10}$ of an hour and

$$L = \tfrac{1}{2} - \tfrac{2}{10} = \tfrac{3}{10}. \tag{22.30}$$

With nonlabor income, therefore, the income and substitution effects are not offsetting—the substitution effect dominates and a fall in wages reduces hours of work.

[5] The indirect utility function is

$$U = \frac{\sqrt{w}}{2} + \frac{N}{2\sqrt{w}}.$$

Figure 22.2   *Two Shapes for an Individual's Supply Curve for Labor*

In (a) a higher real wage induces the individual to supply more labor. The substitution effect of the higher wage outweighs the income effect. In (b), on the other hand, the supply curve of labor is backward bending. For relatively high wage rates, the income effect of a higher wage outweighs the substitution effect and causes the individual to demand more leisure.

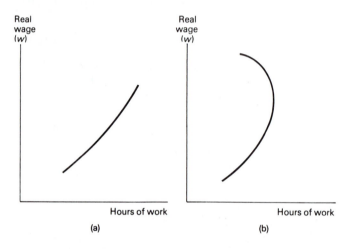

INDIVIDUAL SUPPLY CURVE FOR LABOR

Using the analysis of the previous sections, we now can discuss individual labor supply in detail. In Figure 22.2 we have drawn an individual's supply of labor curve by calculating the number of hours he or she is willing to work at every possible real wage rate. Such a curve might resemble that shown in Figure 22.2a. There the individual's labor supply curve is drawn with a positive slope: At higher real wage rates the individual chooses to work longer hours. The substitution effect of a higher wage outweighs the income effect. This need not always be the case, however, as Figure 22.2b demonstrates. There the supply curve is "backward bending"—once real wages exceed a certain level, even higher wage rates induce the individual to work fewer hours. Such a curve is entirely consistent with the theory of the allocation of time we have developed. At relatively high wage rates and hours of work, a further increase in the wage may cause individuals to choose to work fewer hours, since the income effect may come to outweigh the substitution effect. The individual uses the higher real wage rate to "buy" more leisure.

An important empirical question is which of these curves best reflects individual labor supply decisions. Although there is substantial evidence that short-run labor supply curves have a positive slope (consider, for example, the positive effect of offering higher overtime wages on hours of work), it appears that in the long run individual supply curves at times may have been backward bending. In 1890 the average work week in the United States in the manufacturing industry was about 60 hours. Real wages in 1890 were about $2.50 per

---

Figure 22.3   *Construction of the Market Supply Curve for Labor*

As the real wage rises, there are two reasons why the supply of labor may increase. First, higher real wages may cause each individual in the market to work more hours. Second, higher wages may induce more individuals (for example, individual 2) to enter the labor market.

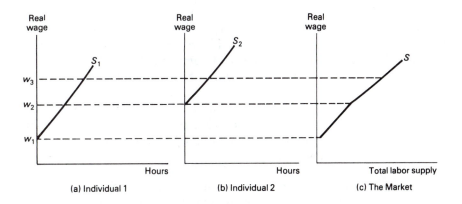

| (a) Individual 1 | (b) Individual 2 | (c) The Market |

hour (in terms of 1983 consumption prices). By 1929 the work week in manufacturing had dropped to 40 hours, in spite of the fact that real wages had risen to about $4.50 per hour. American workers chose to take some of their increasing incomes in the form of leisure, and this is consistent with the notion of a backward-bending supply curve. Since 1929, real wages in manufacturing have continued to rise (to about $8.80 per hour in 1983), but the work week has not fallen much below 40 hours per week. It appears that in recent years the substitution effect of higher wages has almost exactly balanced the income effect, at least for manufacturing workers.

MARKET SUPPLY CURVE FOR LABOR

We can construct a market supply of labor curve from individual supply curves by horizontal summation. At each possible wage rate we would add together the quantity of labor offered by each individual in order to arrive at a market total. One particularly interesting aspect of this procedure is that as the wage rate rises, more individuals may be induced to enter the labor force. Figure 22.3 illustrates this possibility for the simple case of two individuals. For a real wage below w_1 neither individual chooses to work. Consequently, the market supply curve of labor (Figure 22.3c) shows that no labor is supplied at real wages below w_1. A wage in excess of w_1 causes individual 1 to enter the labor market. However, as long as wages fall short of w_2, individual 2 will not work. Only at a wage rate above w_2 will both individuals participate in the labor market. In general the possibility of the entry of new workers makes the market supply of labor somewhat more responsive to wage rate increases than would be the case if the number of workers was assumed to be fixed.

The most important example of higher real wage rates inducing increased labor force participation is the labor force behavior of married women in the

United States in the post–World War II period. Since about 1950 the percentage of working married women has increased from 32 percent to over 60 percent; economists attribute this, at least in part, to the increasing wages that women are able to earn. In recent years a substantial portion of the annual increase in the size of the labor force has been provided by the increasing tendency for married women to work. Both recent attitudinal changes and the upward rise in real wage rates suggest that this trend will continue.

OTHER USES OF THE TIME ALLOCATION MODEL

Although we have applied the time allocation model only to the case of choices between labor and leisure time, the model itself is quite general. Choices that individuals must make among competing uses of time can usually be analyzed within a utility-maximization framework, and it is often possible to gain considerable insights by proceeding in this way. Here we shall discuss briefly three such additional applications: job search theory, the economics of childbearing, and transportation choices. Each of those applications builds on the observation that the opportunity cost of time not working is given by the market wage rate.

Job Search Theory

In seeking new jobs individuals are often faced with considerable uncertainty about available openings. Consequently, they must invest some time (and possibly other resources such as phone calls or placing of advertisements) in finding a suitable job match. To the extent that individuals must reduce potential work time to accommodate their job search plans, the hourly cost of searching can be approximated by the market wage. The higher an individual's market wage, the more likely he or she would be to adopt search techniques that economize on time (such as using an employment agency). If, on the other hand, search time is subsidized (say, by receipt of unemployment insurance benefits), it is possible that search time may be prolonged in the hope of finding a better job.[6]

The Economics of Childbearing

Individuals' decisions to have children are affected by a number of social, religious, and economic factors. Economists have tended to focus primarily on the costs associated with having children and how those costs vary among individuals. One of the most important of those costs is the forgone wages of parents who choose to care for their children rather than to pursue market employment. Indeed, by some estimates, this cost is far in excess of all other costs of childbearing combined. That type of calculation has led some authors to speculate that the increase in real wages for women in the United States since World War II is a principal reason for the decline in the birth rate during that period. Since children have become relatively more expensive, people have chosen to "consume" fewer of them. Similarly, the fact that birth rates in North America and Western Europe are lower than in the less-developed parts of the world

---

[6] For a theoretical treatment of some of these issues, see J. J. McCall, "Economics of Information and Job Search," *Quarterly Journal of Economics* 84 (1970): 113–126.

might be attributed to wage rate differences (and hence cost of children differences) between these regions.[7]

Transportation Choices

In choosing among alternative transportation modes, individuals will take both time and dollar costs into account. Transportation planners are particularly interested in how individuals respond to differences in such costs so that they can predict the effect on demand of improvements in highways or in public transit systems. Most studies have found that individuals are quite sensitive to time costs, especially those associated with walking or waiting.[8] From examinations of individuals' trade-offs between time and dollar costs, those studies generally conclude that individuals value transit time at between 50 percent and 100 percent of their market wage. These findings then offer further support for the time allocation model.

OCCUPATIONAL CHOICE AND COMPENSATING WAGE DIFFERENTIALS

Wage rates differ greatly among individuals and among jobs. There are three economic reasons why these differentials arise. First, workers have different levels of skills. These differences in skills may cause some workers to be more productive than others; in a competitive market for labor, those with greater skills will earn higher wages. Second, some workers may receive wages that are essentially a monopoly rent. If workers can successfully limit access to certain jobs, they may succeed in improving their own wages. Finally, wage rates may differ among jobs because some jobs are more pleasant than others. More enjoyable jobs will attract a large supply of applicants, and this may cause the wage rates to be lower than in less desirable ones. In this section we shall restrict our attention to this third reason for wage differentials. Even though we shall implicitly assume that all workers are equally skilled and that there are no monopolistic elements in the wage-setting process, wage differentials can (and do) arise, and we wish to examine this possibility.

The notion that differing characteristics of jobs may lead to differential wages has long been noted by economists. In *The Wealth of Nations*, for example, Adam Smith noted that

> the whole of the advantages and disadvantages of the different employments of labour . . . must, in the same neighbourhood, be either equal or continually tending to equality. If in the same neighbourhood there is any employment either more or less advantageous than the rest, so many people would crowd into it in the one case, and so many would desert it in the other, that its advantages would soon return to the level of other employments. . . .
>
> [But] pecuniary wages . . . are everywhere in Europe extremely different according to the different employments of labour . . . this difference arises

---

[7] For a seminal contribution to the economics of fertility, see G. Becker, "An Economic Analysis of Fertility" in *Demographic and Economic Change in Developed Countries* (Princeton, N.J.: Princeton University Press, 1960).

[8] See, for example, T. A. Domencich and D. McFadden, *Urban Travel Demand* (Amsterdam: North Holland Publishing Co., 1975).

Figure 22.4   *Compensating Wage Differentials*

The demand curve for labor is assumed to be the same for both a "pleasant" job and an "unpleasant" one. However, the supply curves (S_p and S_u, respectively) differ for the two types of jobs. This causes wages to differ between the jobs. The higher wage rate for the unpleasant job (w_u) is said to "compensate" for the nature of the job.

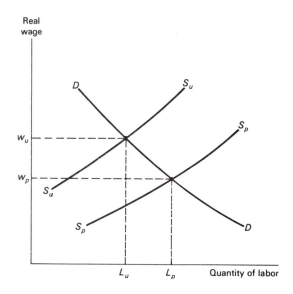

partly from certain circumstances in the employments themselves, which, either really, or at least in the imaginations of men, make up for a small pecuniary gain in some and counter-balance a great one in others. . . .[9]

Smith then stressed the difference between the "whole advantages and disadvantages" of a particular job and the wages paid for the job. Even with perfect freedom of access to jobs and no skill differentials, wage rate differences can persist because of differences in the attractiveness of certain jobs. The market operates to equate the total attractiveness of jobs, not the pecuniary rewards of these jobs. Economists refer to those wage rate differences that relate to the amenities of various jobs as *compensating differentials* because higher wages are presumed to compensate for unpleasant working conditions.

Figure 22.4 illustrates a simple example of the way in which compensating differentials might arise. It assumes that there are two jobs: one "pleasant" and the other "unpleasant." The demand curve of firms for workers to fill those jobs is assumed to be the same for both jobs. There are no differences in the skills of workers that might lead to differing demand conditions. The demand

[9]A. Smith, *The Wealth of Nations* (New York: Random House, Modern Library ed., 1937), chap. 10, p. 1.

curve for both jobs is represented by the curve DD. Because the jobs differ in their attractiveness, the supply of labor to them will differ. The curve S_u represents the supply curve to the unpleasant job, and the equilibrium wage is given by w_u. At this wage, firms in the unpleasant industry will demand L_u labor-hours of labor input, and this is what individuals are willing to supply. Similarly, the curve S_p represents the supply curve of workers to the pleasant job. This curve lies to the right of the S_u curve because of the differences in the jobs: At any given wage individuals are willing to supply more labor to the pleasant job. By the interaction of supply and demand, an equilibrium wage rate of w_p will be established for the pleasant job. This wage will be below w_u, and the difference between w_u and w_p is a wage differential that compensates for the unpleasantness of the first job. The equilibrium shown in Figure 22.4 is stable: There is no incentive for a worker to transfer from one job to the other. The net advantages of the two jobs have been equalized.

Examples

It is not hard to find examples of compensating wage differentials in the real world. Probably the most important instances arise between jobs that require identical skills but differ in their riskiness. In the construction industry, for example, iron workers who work on high-rise buildings are paid more than iron workers who stay at ground level. Similarly, laborers engaged in the digging of tunnels are paid more than laborers who dig cut-and-cover trenches. Finally, there is some evidence that on the average, doctors and lawyers in independent professional practice earn more than those working for large firms. In this case the higher mean wage compensates for the greater risk inherent in independent practice.

Other examples of wage differentials that compensate for the disadvantages of a job are commonly encountered. Wages tend to be lower in suburban jobs than in central city jobs, and these differentials serve to compensate for the costs of the trip to work. Salaries of college professors (regrettably) tend to be below those for other occupations requiring similar skills, probably because the academic "lifestyle" is regarded as being an attractive one. One particularly interesting wage differential that has been observed concerns the relationship between wage rates and unemployment rates among cities, particularly in less-developed countries. It has been found that cities with high unemployment rates also tend to have relatively high average wage rates. These higher wages, in a sense, compensate for the higher probability of becoming unemployed at some time.

LABOR UNIONS

Workers may at times find it advantageous to join together in a labor union in order to pursue goals that can more effectively be accomplished by a group. If association with a union were wholly voluntary, it could be assumed that every union member derives a positive benefit from belonging. Compulsory membership (the "closed shop"), however, is frequently enforced in order to maintain the viability of the union organization. If all workers were left on their own to decide on membership, their rational decision might be not to join the union, and hence avoid dues and other restrictions. However, they would benefit from the higher wages and better working conditions that have been won by the union. What appears to be rational from each individual worker's point of view may prove to be irrational from a group's point of view, since the union is undermined by "free riders." Compulsory membership therefore may be a necessary means of maintaining an effective union coalition.[10]

Unions' Goals

As in our discussion of the theory of the firm, we shall start our analysis of union behavior by defining the goals toward which a union strives. A first assumption we might make is that the goals of a union are in some sense an adequate representation of the goals of its members. This assumption avoids the problem of union leadership and disregards the personal aspirations of those leaders, which may be in conflict with rank-and-file goals. Union leaders therefore are assumed to be conduits for expressing the desires of the membership.[11] In the United States union goals have tended to be oriented toward "bread-and-butter" issues. The programs of major unions have not emphasized the promotion of radical social change, except briefly in the early 1900s. Rather, unions have attempted to exert an effect solely in the labor market, and in this they have had some success.

In some respects, strong unions can be analyzed in the same way as a monopoly firm. The union faces a demand curve for labor; because it is the sole source of supply, it can choose at which point on this curve it will operate. The point that is actually chosen by the union will obviously depend on what particular goals it has decided to pursue. Three possible choices are illustrated in Figure 22.5. For example, the union may choose to offer that quantity of labor that maximizes the total wage bill ($w \cdot L$). If this is the case, it will offer that quantity for which the "marginal revenue" from labor demand is equal to 0. This quantity is given by L_1 in Figure 22.5, and the wage rate associated with this quantity is w_1. The point E_1 is therefore the preferred wage-quantity combination. Notice that at wage rate w_1 there may be an excess supply of labor, and the union must somehow allocate those jobs that are available to those workers who want them. Since it may be difficult to initiate transfers between workers with jobs and those without jobs, this equilibrium may be unstable within the union itself.

Another possible goal that the union may pursue would be to choose the quantity of labor that would maximize the total economic rent (that is, wages less opportunity costs) obtained by those members who are employed. This would necessitate choosing that quantity of labor for which the additional total wages obtained by having one more employed union member (the marginal revenue) are equal to the extra cost of luring that member into the market. The

---

[10] For a more complete discussion of the issues raised in this and later sections, see J. Dunlop, *Wage Determination under Trade Unions* (New York: Crowell-Collier and Macmillan, 1944). For a more recent analysis, see H. S. Farber, "The Analysis of Union Behavior" in O. C. Ashenfelter and R. Layard, eds., *Handbook of Labor Economics*, vol. 2 (Amsterdam: North Holland Publishing Co., 1986), pp. 1039–1089.

[11] Much recent analysis, however, revolves around whether "potential" union members have some voice in setting union goals and how union goals may affect the desires of workers with differing amounts of seniority on the job.

Figure 22.5   *Three Possible Points on the Labor Demand Curve That a Monopolistic Union Might Choose*

A union has a monopoly in the supply of labor. It therefore may choose that point on the demand curve for labor that it most prefers. Three such points are shown in the figure. At point E_1 total labor payments ($w \cdot L$) are maximized; at E_2 the economic rent that workers receive is maximized; and at E_3 the total amount of labor services supplied is maximized.

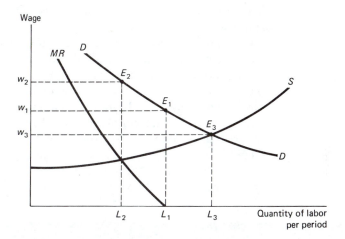

union therefore should choose that quantity, L_2, at which the marginal revenue curve crosses the supply curve.[12] The wage rate associated with this quantity is w_2, and the desired wage-quantity combination is labeled E_2 in the diagram. With the wage w_2, many individuals who desire to work at the prevailing wage are left unemployed. Perhaps the union may "tax" the large economic rent earned by those who do work in order to transfer income to those who don't.

A third possibility would be for the union to aim for maximum employment of its members. This would involve choosing the point w_3, L_3, which is precisely the point that would result if the market were organized in a perfectly competitive way. No employment greater than L_3 could be achieved, since the quantity of labor that union members supply would be reduced for wages less than w_3.

Other Goals: Job Security and Fringe Benefits

Although the union goals illustrated in Figure 22.5 are those that are easiest to diagram, the list is by no means exhaustive. Two other important goals that unions may seek, for example, are job security and a variety of nonwage "fringe" benefits. The issue of job security is a particularly important one in

---

[12] Mathematically, the union's goal is to choose L so as to maximize wL − (area under S), where S is the compensated supply curve for labor and reflects workers' opportunity costs in terms of forgone leisure.

industries such as durable goods manufacturing or construction, in which there are major cyclical influences on product demand and hence on the demand for labor. Unions may seek to reduce the risks of such fluctuations for their members by establishing contractual "rights" to jobs. In that way the variability in workers' wage incomes will be reduced, and (as we showed in Chapter 9) this reduction raises workers' utility. Fringe benefits such as pensions, vacations, insurance coverage, and generally better working conditions are also of considerable value to workers. Because such benefits are frequently of low visibility in negotiating sessions and are often nontaxable to workers, they have come to constitute an increasingly important part of firms' total labor costs.

There are two ways in which recognition of such alternative union (or for that matter, any worker's) goals should be used to modify the analysis presented previously in this chapter. First, the price of labor should be generalized to include indirect forms of compensation in addition to the usual hourly wage rate. Without this generalization it is hard to interpret many market equilibria. Related to this is a second observation: Unions may be willing to forgo wage rate goals to obtain other types of benefits. Hence one might wish to postulate a multidimensional utility function for unions rather than the simple ones we introduced previously. With such an approach a considerably larger number of types of market equilibria might be observed.

SUMMARY

This chapter was primarily concerned with the question of labor supply by individuals. By treating work as one of a number of possible ways that an individual might allocate his or her time, the analysis of labor supply was shown to be a further application of the general theory of utility maximization. Some of the results stemming from this approach were:

- A utility-maximizing individual will choose to work that number of hours for which the marginal rate of substitution of leisure for consumption is equal to his or her real wage rate.
- An increase in the real wage creates income and substitution effects that operate in different directions in their effect on labor supply. This result can be shown using a Slutsky-type equation similar to that developed in Chapter 5.
- The theory of time allocation is relevant to a number of other economic decisions in addition to the labor supply decision. Since most activities require time to complete them, the notion that they have both market prices and time prices has far-reaching consequences for economic theory.
- Jobs may differ in their relative attractiveness and this may give rise to compensating wage differentials. Such differentials represent equilibrium market outcomes and can persist until supply or demand conditions in the various job markets change.

- Unions can be treated analytically as monopoly suppliers of labor. Labor market equilibrium in the presence of unions will depend on what goals the union chooses to pursue in this supply decision.

Application

THE MILITARY DRAFT AND THE VOLUNTEER FORCE

Thus far our discussion of labor supply has been concerned primarily with the question of the total supply of labor to all potential employers. In such a case it might be expected that the supply curve would be relatively inelastic because most individuals have only limited alternative uses for their time. The supply of labor to a particular occupation, however, is likely to be considerably more elastic. Rising wages in the market for one type of labor service will not only prompt an additional supply of labor through the mechanisms analyzed previously (longer hours and increased labor force participation) but also, and more importantly, can attract workers from other employments. Small changes in (relative) wages may attract a substantially increased supply to an occupation.

The question of the elasticity of the supply of labor played an important role in the mid-1960s debate over the costs of establishing an all-volunteer army in the United States. If the supply of labor to the military were elastic, volunteers could be attracted with relatively small increments to existing pay schedules. An inelastic supply, on the other hand, would create sharp increases in defense costs as a result of the elimination of military conscription. To examine this issue, W. Y. Oi (in a 1967 study) calculated a supply curve for military personnel.[13] His basic results are presented in Table 22.1. There is clear evidence that increases in military pay encourage enlistments. For example, Oi showed that an increase in the first-term pay of enlistees from the then present level of $2,500 to a level more nearly approximating civilian wages (about $3,600 for unskilled 18-year-olds in 1965) would have increased enlistments by 40 percent. Notice, however, that the supply

[13] W. Y. Oi, "The Economic Cost of the Draft," *American Economic Review* 57 (May 1967): 39–62.

Table 22.1   *Supply Curve of Voluntary Enlistments in the Armed Forces in 1965*

Annual First-Term Pay	Enlistments
$2,500	260,000
3,600	365,000
4,700	415,000
5,900	470,000

Source: W. Y. Oi, "The Economic Cost of the Draft," *American Economic Review* 57 (May 1967): 39–62.

curve tended to become more inelastic as potential wages were raised still further. Raising wages from $4,700 to $5,900 would attract only 13 percent more enlistments. This may indicate that individuals' feelings about serving in the military vary widely across the population and that those with preferences against serving can be attracted only at very high wages.

In addition to estimating the cost of a volunteer army, one of the goals of Oi's study was to calculate the economic burden of the military draft that was then in effect. Costs of the draft fell on two types of individuals: those who were actually drafted and those who were "reluctant volunteers" in that they volunteered for service only because of fear of the draft. In 1965 Oi estimated that out of a total of 470,000 enlistments, 260,000 were "true" volunteers, 155,000 were reluctant volunteers, and 55,000 were draftees. Assuming that draftees would require a greater pay inducement to enter the armed forces voluntarily than would the reluctant volunteers, Oi conjectured that the typical individual in the latter group would have volunteered (in the absence of a draft) at a wage about halfway between $2,500 (at which level none would have volunteered) and $4,700 (at which level all 155,000 would volunteer). Hence the annual cost of the draft of reluctant volunteers was about $170 million ($3,600 required pay, less $2,500 actual pay, times 155,000).

Oi hypothesized that the wage necessary to attract actual draftees into the army was considerably above that for reluctant volunteers. Taking the rather arbitrary estimate of $5,900 as the minimum wage necessary to attract the typical draftee, he calculated a total annual cost to draftees of $187 million ($5,900 required pay, less $2,500 actual pay, times 55,000). Adding that cost to the cost that the draft imposed on reluctant volunteers, Oi concluded that the annual cost to enlistees was about $357 million. Since enlistees usually serve about two and one-half years, the total cost of the draft to one year's group of enlistees was put at $893 mil-

lion or over $3,800 per draft-related enlistee.[14] Even these high costs ignored other costs that the draft imposed on nonenlistees. Such costs included taking less preferred but draft-exempt jobs, staying in school longer to escape the draft, seeking medical exemptions or conscientious objector status, or illegal draft evasion. Political opposition to the draft in the late 1960s suggested that these costs were substantial.

Following cessation of hostilities in Vietnam in the early 1970s, the U.S. military moved rapidly toward the establishment of an all-volunteer force. Experiences since that time have been quite consistent with what had been predicted by Oi and others; that is, enlistments proved to be rather responsive to military pay. One recent study of the years 1967 to 1979, for example, finds that the supply elasticities for enlistments in the army and navy exceed unity and are especially high for later years in which the threat of a draft had largely disappeared.[15] Interestingly, these authors also found that supply elasticities to the marines and air force were much lower than for the other armed services. For the case of the Marine Corps, they attributed this finding to the special nature of that branch of the armed forces: It appears that a segment of the population wants to join almost regardless of wages. The air force is also a special case because of the specialized training it provides. The allure of high-wage civilian jobs following service in the air force appears to outweigh the effects of current wages on enlistments.

Of course, military planners also have been forced to recognize that the supply elasticity of

---

[14] For pedagogic purposes Oi's calculations have been simplified in this example, and they do not correspond exactly to those in the original article. Also it should be pointed out that the cost figures do not include forgone rents that would be earned by "true" volunteers in moving to a volunteer army (because they would be paid more under the new pay scales than was necessary to attract them into the army).

[15] See C. Ash, B. Udis, and R. F. McNown, "Enlistments in the All-Volunteer Force: A Military Personnel Supply Model and Its Forecasts," *American Economic Review* (March 1983): 145–215.

enlistments is a two-way street. If military wages lag behind comparable civilian wage rates, enlistments (especially in the army and navy) may fall precipitously. Because military pay costs have already come to represent almost 25 per-

cent of the total U.S. defense budget, there is considerable resistance to raising wages faster. But the alternative of returning to a draft, especially in peacetime, seems even less palatable.

SUGGESTED READINGS

Ashenfelter, O. C., and Layard, R. *Handbook of Labor Economics* (2 volumes). Amsterdam: North Holland Publishing Co., 1986.

Collection of survey articles on many of the topics touched on in this chapter. Particularly thorough articles on men's and women's labor supply and on the economics of unions.

Becker, G. S. "An Economic Analysis of Fertility." In *Demographic and Economic Change in Developed Countries*, National Bureau Conference Series No. 11. Princeton, N.J.: Princeton University Press, 1960.

First economic approach to the theory of childbearing.

————. "A Theory of the Allocation of Time." *Economic Journal* 75 (September 1965): 493–517.

Fundamental work on time allocation including both labor supply and consumption decisions.

Cain, G. G. *Married Women in the Labor Force: An Economic Analysis*. Chicago: University of Chicago Press, 1966.

Good theoretical and empirical analysis of women's labor supply decisions.

Mincer, J. "Labor Force Participation of Married Women." In H. G. Lewis, ed., *Aspects of Labor Economics*, National Bureau Conference Series No. 14. Princeton, N.J.: Princeton University Press, 1962.

Discusses several paradoxes in the empirical evidence on women's labor supply.

Moffitt, R. A., and Kehrer, K. C. "The Effect of Tax and Transfer Programs on Labor Supply: The Evidence from the Income Maintenance Experiments." In R. G. Ehrenberg, ed., *Research in Labor Economics*, vol. 4. Greenwich, Conn.: JAI Press, 1981. Pp. 103–150.

Complete survey of the experimental evidence in labor supply, especially in relationship to the effects of transfer programs.

Parsley, C. J. "Labor Unions and Wages: A Survey." *Journal of Economic Literature* (March 1980): 1–31.

A survey of the empirical literature with an extensive bibliography.

Rees, A. "The Effects of Unions on Resource Allocation." *Journal of Law and Economics* 6 (October 1963): 69–78.

Classic paper on the allocational effects of unions.

PROBLEMS

22.1

Suppose there are 8,000 hours in a year (actually there are 8,760) and that an individual has a potential market wage of $5 per hour.

a.   What is the individual's full income? If he or she chooses to devote 75 percent of this income to leisure, how many hours will be worked?

b.   Suppose a rich uncle dies and leaves the individual an annual income of $4,000 per year. If he or she continues to devote 75 percent of full income to leisure, how many hours will be worked?

c.   How would your answer to Part (b) change if the market wage were $10 per hour instead of $5 per hour?

d.   Graph the individual's supply of labor curve implied by parts (b) and (c).

22.2
Mr. Peabody has a utility function $U = \sqrt{C \cdot H}$ and is maximizing his utility at $U = 20$ when he works 14 hours a day. Would he be willing to give up an hour of his leisure to drive Mrs. Atterboy to the wrestling match if she offered him $5?

22.3
Use the concept of the opportunity cost of time to discuss:

    a.   who you might expect to pay the higher fares to fly the faster Concorde to Europe;

    b.   who you expect would be more likely to stand in long lines and even camp out overnight to purchase tickets to a sporting event;

    c.   for whom greens fees are a larger fraction of the total cost of a golf game—a prospering physician or a peanut vendor?

    d.   How would the degree of traffic congestion affect who drives to work and who takes mass transit?

22.4
An individual receives utility from daily income (Y), given by

$$U(Y) = 100\,Y - \frac{1}{2}\,Y^2.$$

The only source of income is earnings. Hence $Y = wL$, where w is the hourly wage and L is hours worked per day. The individual knows of a job that pays $5 per hour for a certain 8-hour day. What wage must be offered for a construction job where hours of work are random with a mean of 8 hours and a standard deviation of 6 hours to get the individual to accept this more "risky" job?

Hint: This problem makes use of the statistical identity

$$E(X^2) = \text{Var } X + E(X)^2,$$

where E means "expected value."

22.5
A family with two adult members seeks to maximize a utility function of the form

$$U(C, H_1, H_2),$$

where C is family consumption and H_1 and H_2 are hours of leisure of each family member. Choices are constrained by

$$C = w_1(24 - H_1) + w_2(24 - H_2) + N,$$

where w_1 and w_2 are the wages of each family member and N is nonlabor income.

    a.   Without attempting a mathematical presentation, use the notions of substitution and income effects to discuss the likely signs of the cross-substitution effects $\partial H_1/\partial w_2$ and $\partial H_2/\partial w_1$.

    b.   Suppose that one family member (say individual 1) can work in the home, thereby converting leisure hours into consumption according to the function

$$C_1 = f(H_1),$$

    where $f' > 0$, $f'' < 0$. How might this additional option affect the optimal division of work among family members?

22.6
A welfare program for low income people offers a family a basic grant of $6,000 per year. This grant is reduced by $.75 for each $1 of other income the family has.

a. How much in welfare benefits does the family receive if it has no other income? If the head of the family earns $2,000 per year? How about $4,000 per year?

b. At what level of earnings does the welfare grant become zero?

c. Assume that the head of this family can earn $4 per hour and that the family has no other income. What is the annual budget constraint for this family if it does not participate in the welfare program? That is, how are consumption (C) and hours of leisure (H) related?

d. What is the budget constraint if the family opts to participate in the welfare program? (Remember, the welfare grant can only be positive.)

e. Graph your results from parts (c) and (d).

f. Suppose the government changes the rules of the welfare program to permit families to keep 50 percent of what they earn. How would this change your answer to parts (d) and (e) above?

g. Using your results from part (f), can you predict whether the head of this family will work more or less under the new rules described in part (f)?

22.7

Suppose that a union has a fixed supply of labor to sell. If the union desires to maximize the total wage bill, what wage rate will it demand? How would your answer change if unemployed workers were paid unemployment insurance at the rate u per worker and the union now desired to maximize the sum of the wage bill and the total amount of unemployment compensation?

22.8

Universal Fur is located in Clyde, Baffin Island, and sells high quality fur bow ties throughout the world at a price of $4 each. The production function for fur bow ties (Q) is given by

$$Q = 50X - 2X^2$$

where X is the quantity of pelts used each week. Pelts are supplied only by Dan's Trading Post, which obtains them by hiring Eskimo trappers at a rate of $16 per day. Dan's weekly production function for pelts is given by

$$X = \sqrt{L}$$

where L represents the number of days of Eskimo time used each week.

a. For a quasi-competitive case in which both Universal Fur and Dan's Trading Post act as price takers for pelts, what will be the equilibrium price (P_X) and how many pelts will be traded?

b. Suppose Dan acts as a monopolist, while Universal Fur continues to be a price taker. What equilibrium will emerge in the pelt market?

c. Suppose Universal Fur acts as a monopsonist but that Dan acts as a price taker. What will the equilibrium be?

d. Graph your results and discuss the type of equilibrium that is likely to emerge in the bilateral monopoly bargaining between Universal Fur and Dan. (*Note*: In this problem it is possible to trade X in fractional units.)

CHAPTER 23

Capital

The study of the theory of capital as a factor of production is central to many areas of economics. Economists traditionally have assigned an important role to capital as a factor of production in the growth process. One of the major reasons for increases in per capita output over time is the increasing amount of productive equipment that workers have at their disposal. To understand where this equipment comes from and the incentives that lead to its accumulation, we must develop a theory of capital accumulation. Similarly, Keynesian economic theory assigns an important role to investment as one component of aggregate demand. Since net investment comes about because firms desire to change the stock of capital they have available, it is again important to have an understanding of the factors that go into determining the desired amount of capital. For this reason, capital theory is central to modern macroeconomics.

The study of capital theory is also controversial. Primarily, this controversy centers on the question of whether the owner of productive equipment (that is, capital) has any "right" to obtain a rent for its use. In the final analysis the answer to this question must be regarded as one aspect of the broader question of the nature and desirability of private property as a social institution. Various sections of Part VIII present a brief economic discussion of this issue. In this chapter, however, we shall avoid most normative questions in order to provide an understanding of the nature of capital and why its allocation is an important issue.

Here we shall investigate three questions: What is "capital?" What is "the" rate of return on capital and how is it determined? How can the answers to the first two questions be used to develop a theory of capital accumulation (investment) by integrating the theory of capital and the theory of the firm's choice of inputs? Two additional subjects related to the theory of capital accumulation are discussed in appendixes to this chapter. In Appendix A we present a brief summary of the mathematics of compound interest. Since the theory of capital is integrally connected to the question of allocating resources over time, compound interest rate concepts are basic to understanding the subject. Appendix B provides a more theoretical treatment of the allocation of resources over

Figure 23.1   *Two Views of Capital Accumulation*

In (a), society withdraws some current consumption (*s*) in order to gorge itself (with *x* extra consumption) in the next period. The one-period rate of return would be measured by $x/s - 1$. The society in (b) takes a more long-term view and uses *s* to increase its consumption perpetually by *y*. The perpetual rate of return would be given by y/s.

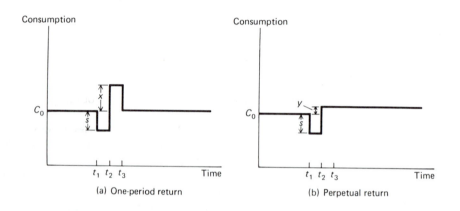

(a) One-period return   (b) Perpetual return

time. A principal purpose of that appendix is to introduce the mathematics associated with optimal decision making in a dynamic context.

CAPITAL AND THE RATE OF RETURN

When we speak of the capital stock of an economy, we mean the sum total of machines, buildings, and other manufactured, nonlabor resources that are in existence at some point in time. These assets represent some part of an economy's output in the past that was not consumed, having been set aside to be used for production in the future. All societies, from the most primitive to the most complex, engage in capital accumulation. A bushman's taking time off from hunting to make arrows, individuals in a modern society using part of their incomes to buy houses, or governments taxing citizens in order to purchase dams and post office buildings are all engaging in essentially the same sort of activity: Some portion of current output is being set aside for use in producing output in future periods. Present "sacrifice" for future gain is the essential aspect of capital accumulation.

Rate of Return

The process of capital accumulation is pictured schematically in Figure 23.1. In both panels of the figure, society is initially consuming level C_0 and has been doing so for some time. At time t_1 a decision is made to withhold some output (amount *s*) from current consumption for one period. Starting in period t_2 this withheld consumption is in some way put to use producing future consumption. An important concept connected with this process is the *rate of return*, which is earned on that consumption that is put aside. In Figure 23.1a, for example, all of the withheld consumption is used to produce additional output only in period t_2. Consumption is increased by amount x in period t_2 and then returns to the long-run level C_0. Society has saved in one year in order to have an orgy in the next year. A definition of the (one-period) rate of return from this activity would be

---

Definition:

Single Period Rate of Return
The *single period rate of return* (r_1) on an investment is the extra consumption provided in period 2 as a fraction of the consumption forgone in period 1. That is,

$$r_1 = \frac{x - s}{s} = \frac{x}{s} - 1. \tag{23.1}$$

If $x > s$ (if more consumption comes out of this process than went into it), we would say that the one-period rate of return to capital accumulation is positive. For example, if withholding 100 units from current consumption permitted society to consume an extra 110 units next year, the one period rate of return would be

$$\frac{110}{100} - 1 = 0.10$$

or 10 percent.

In Figure 23.1b society is assumed to take a more long-term view in its capital accumulation. Again an amount s is set aside at time t_1. Now, however, this set-aside consumption is used to raise the consumption level for all periods in the future. If the permanent level of consumption is raised to $C_0 + y$, we define the perpetual rate of return to be

---

Definition:

Perpetual Rate of Return
The *perpetual rate of return* (r_∞) is the permanent increment to future consumption expressed as a fraction of the initial consumption forgone. That is,

$$r_\infty = \frac{y}{s}. \tag{23.2}$$

If capital accumulation succeeds in raising C_0 permanently, r_∞ will be positive. For example, suppose that society set aside 100 units of output in period t_1 to be devoted to capital accumulation. If this capital would permit output to be raised by 10 units for every period in the future (starting at time period t_2), the perpetual rate of return would be 10 percent.

When economists speak of the rate of return to capital accumulation, then, they have in mind something between these two extremes. Somewhat loosely we shall speak of the rate of return as being a measure of the terms at which consumption today may be turned into consumption tomorrow (this will be made more explicit soon). A natural question to ask is how the economy's rate of return is determined. Again, the answer must somehow revolve around the supply and demand for present and future goods. In the next section we shall present a simple model in which this supply-demand interaction is demonstrated.

DETERMINATION OF THE RATE OF RETURN

In this section we will describe how operation of supply and demand in the market for "future" goods establishes an equilibrium rate of return. We begin by analyzing the connection between the rate of return and the "price" of future goods. Then we show how individuals and firms are likely to react to this price. Finally, these actions are brought together (as we have done for the analysis of other markets) to demonstrate the determination of an equilibrium price of future goods and to examine some of the characteristics of that solution.

Rate of Return and Price of Future Goods

For most of our analysis in this chapter, we will assume that there are only two periods to be considered—the current period (to be denoted by the subscript 0) and the next period (denoted by the subscript 1). We will use r to denote the (one-period) rate of return between these two periods. Hence, as defined in the previous section then,

$$r = \frac{\Delta C_1}{\Delta C_0} - 1, \qquad (23.3)$$

where we use the Δ notation to refer to the change in consumption in the two periods. Rewriting Equation 23.3 yields

$$\frac{\Delta C_1}{\Delta C_0} = 1 + r \qquad (23.4)$$

or

$$\frac{\Delta C_0}{\Delta C_1} = \frac{1}{1 + r}. \qquad (23.5)$$

But the term on the left of Equation 23.5 simply records how much C_0 must be forgone if C_1 is to be increased by one unit; that is, the expression represents the relative "price" of one unit of C_1. So we have defined:

Definition:

Price of Future Goods
The relative *price of future goods* (P_1) is defined to be the quantity of present goods that must be forgone to increase future consumption by one unit. That is,

$$P_1 = \frac{\Delta C_0}{\Delta C_1} = \frac{1}{1 + r}. \qquad (23.6)$$

We now proceed to develop a demand-supply analysis of the determination of P. By so doing we also will have developed a theory of the determination of r, the rate of return in this simple model.

Demand for
Future Goods

The theory of the demand for future goods is simply one further application of the utility-maximization model developed in Part II of this book. Here the individual's utility depends on present and future consumption [that is, utility $= U(C_0, C_1)$], and he or she must decide how much of current income (I) to allocate to these two goods.[1] Income not spent on current consumption can be invested at the rate of return r in order to obtain consumption next period. As before P_1 reflects the present cost of future consumption, and the individual's budget constraint is given by

$$I = C_0 + P_1 C_1. \tag{23.7}$$

This constraint is illustrated in Figure 23.2. If the individual chooses to spend all of his or her income on C_0, total current consumption will be I with no consumption occurring in period 2. Alternatively, if $C_0 = 0$, C_1 will be given by $I/P_1 = I(1 + r)$. That is, if all income is invested at the rate of return r, current income will grow to $I(1 + r)$ in period two.[2]

Imposition of the individual's indifference curve map for C_0 and C_1 onto the budget constraint in Figure 23.2 illustrates utility maximization. Here utility is maximized at the point C_0^*, C_1^*. The individual consumes C_0^* currently and chooses to save $I - C_0^*$ to consume next period. This future consumption can be found from the budget constraint as

$$P_1 C_1^* = I - C_0^* \tag{23.8}$$

or

$$C_1^* = \frac{(I - C_0^*)}{P_1} \tag{23.9}$$

$$= (I - C_0^*)(1 + r). \tag{23.10}$$

In other words, current savings ($I - C_0^*$) are invested at the rate of return, r, and grow to yield C_1^* in the next period.

[1] For an analysis of the case where the individual has income in both periods, see problem 23.1.

[2] This observation yields an alternative interpretation of the budget constraint given by Equation 23.7. That can be written in terms of the rate of return as

$$I = C_0 + \frac{C_1}{1 + r}$$

and records the fact that it is the "present value" of C_1 that enters into the individual's current budget constraint. The concept of present value is discussed in more detail later in this chapter.

Figure 23.2   *Individual's Intertemporal Utility Maximization*

When faced with the intertemporal budget constraint $I = C_0 + P_1 C_1$, the individual will maximize utility by choosing to consume C_0^* currently and C_1^* in the next period. A fall in P_1 (an increase in the rate of return, r) will cause C_1 to rise, but the effect on C_0 is indeterminate since substitution and income effects operate in opposite directions (assuming that both C_0 and C_1 are normal goods).

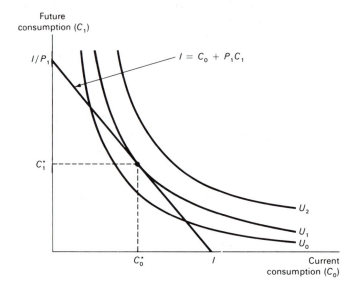

A comparative statics analysis of the equilibrium illustrated in Figure 23.2 is straightforward. If P_1 falls (that is, if r rises), both income and substitution effects will cause more C_1 to be demanded, except in the unlikely event that C_1 is an inferior good. Hence the demand curve for C_1 will be downward sloping. An increase in r effectively lowers the price of C_1 and consumption of that good thereby increases. This demand curve is labeled D in Figure 23.3.

Before leaving our discussion of individuals' intertemporal decisions, we should point out that our analysis does not permit an unambiguous statement to be made about the sign of $\partial C_0 / \partial P_1$. In Figure 23.2 substitution and income effects work in opposite directions, and no definite prediction is possible. A fall in P_1 will cause the individual to substitute C_1 for C_0 in his or her consumption plans. But the fall in P_1 raises real income, and the income effect causes both C_0 and C_1 to increase. Phrased somewhat differently, the model illustrated in Figure 23.2 does not permit a definite prediction about how changes in the rate of return affect current period savings. A higher r produces substitution effects that favor more saving and income effects that favor less. Ultimately therefore, the direction of the effect must be an empirical question.

Figure 23.3   *Determination of the Equilibrium Price of Future Goods*

The point P_1^*, C_1^* represents an equilibrium in the market for future goods. The equilibrium price of future goods determines the rate of return via Equation 23.11.

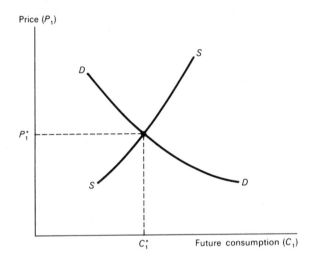

Supply of Future Goods

In one sense the analysis of the supply of future goods is quite simple. We can argue that an increase in the relative price of future goods (P_1) will induce firms to produce more of them, since the yield from doing so is now greater. This reaction is reflected in the positively sloped supply curve S in Figure 23.3. It might be expected that, as in our previous perfectly competitive analysis, this supply curve reflects the increasing marginal costs (or diminishing returns) that firms experience when attempting to turn present goods into future ones through capital accumulation.

Unfortunately, delving deeper into the nature of capital accumulation runs into complications that have occupied economists for hundreds of years.[3] Basically, all of these derive from problems in developing a tractable model of the capital accumulation process. For our model of individual behavior this problem did not arise, since we could assume that the "market" quoted a rate of return to individuals so that they could adapt their behavior to it. We shall also follow this route when describing firms' investment decisions later in this chapter. But to develop an adequate model of capital accumulation by firms, we must describe precisely how C_0 is "turned into" C_1 and to do so would take us too far afield into the intricacies of capital theory. Instead we will be content to draw the supply curve in Figure 23.3 with a positive slope on the presump-

[3] For a discussion of some of this debate, see M. Blaug, *Economic Theory in Retrospect*, rev. ed. (Homewood, Ill.: Richard D. Irwin, 1978), chap. 12.

tion that such a shape is intuitively reasonable. Much of the subsequent analysis in this chapter may serve to convince the reader that this is indeed the case.

Equilibrium Price of Future Goods

Equilibrium in the market shown in Figure 23.3 is at P_1^*, C_1^*. At that point individuals' supply and demand for future goods are in balance, and the required amount of current goods will be put into capital accumulation in order to produce C_1^* in the future.[4]

There are a number of reasons to expect that P_1 will be less than 1; that is, it will cost less than the sacrifice of one current good to "buy" one good in the future. On the demand side it might be argued that individuals require some reward for waiting. Everyday adages ("a bird in the hand is worth two in the bush," "live for today") and more substantial realities (the uncertainty of the future and the finiteness of life) suggest that individuals are generally impatient in their consumption decisions. Hence capital accumulation such as that shown in Figure 23.3 will take place only if the current sacrifice is in some way worthwhile.

There are also supply reasons for believing P_1 will be less than 1. All of these involve the idea that capital accumulation is "productive": Sacrificing one good currently will yield more than one good in the future. Some simple examples of the productivity of capital investment are provided by such pastoral activities as the growing of trees or the aging of wine and cheese. Tree nursery owners and vineyard and dairy operators "abstain" from selling their wares in the belief that time will make them more valuable in the future. Although it is obvious that capital accumulation in a modern industrial society is far more complex than growing trees (consider building a steel mill or an electric power system), economists believe the two processes have certain similarities. In both cases investing current goods makes the production process longer and more complex and therefore improves the overall productive power of other resources used in production.

The Equilibrium Rate of Return

We can now define the relationship of the rate of return (r) to what we have called the price of future goods by the formula

$$P_1^* = \frac{1}{1 + r}. \tag{23.11}$$

Since we believe that P_1^* will be less than 1, the rate of return (r) will be positive. For example, if $P_1^* = .9$, r will equal approximately .11, and we would say that the rate of return to capital accumulation is "11 percent." By withholding one unit of current consumption, the consumption of future goods can be increased by 1.11. The rate of return and P_1 are equivalent ways of measuring the terms on which present goods can be turned into future goods.

---

[4]This is a much simplified form of an analysis originally presented by I. Fisher, *The Rate of Interest* (New York: Macmillan Co., 1907).

Rate of Return,
Interest Rates,
and Nominal
Interest Rates

The concept of the rate of return that we have been analyzing so far in this chapter is sometimes used synonymously with the related concept of the "real" interest rate. In this context both are taken to refer to the real return that is available from capital accumulation. The term "interest rate" is used much more widely in economics, and it is important to point out the difference between these other uses and the one employed here. Most importantly, interest rates observed in the real world will usually be nominal rates that reflect not only real returns to capital accumulation but also expected inflation rates as well. When the general price level is changing, borrowers and lenders will want to be compensated for such changes in purchasing power. Specifically, if overall prices are expected to increase by $\dot{P}_e$ between two periods (that is, a $\dot{P}_e$ of .10 would be a 10 percent inflation rate), we would expect the nominal interest rate (R) to be given by the equation

$$1 + R = (1 + r)(1 + \dot{P}_e), \tag{23.12}$$

since a would-be lender would expect to be compensated for both the opportunity cost of not investing in real capital (r) and for the general rise in prices ($\dot{P}_e$). Expansion of Equation 23.12 yields

$$1 + R = 1 + r + \dot{P}_e + r\dot{P}_e, \tag{23.13}$$

and assuming $r \cdot \dot{P}_e$ is small, we have the simpler approximation

$$R = r + \dot{P}_e. \tag{23.14}$$

If the real rate of return is 4 percent (.04) and the expected rate of inflation is 10 percent (.10), the nominal interest rate would be approximately 14 percent (.14). The difference, therefore, between observed nominal interest rates and real interest rates may be substantial. We will mention here only three of the problems that arise in attempting to infer the real rate of return from nominal interest rates: (1) price expectations, $\dot{P}_e$, are not observable, so some estimates (such as recent inflation rates) must be used; (2) even after adjusting for price expectations, some real interest rates may reflect riskless returns (on government bonds, for example) whereas actual investment in physical capital may be risky and thereby require a higher r; and (3) observed interest rates often reflect taxable earnings and therefore may be affected by tax laws whereas the rate of return to capital accumulation is defined without reference to taxes. We will not pursue these issues here, however.

For our purposes we shall assume in the remainder of this chapter that an equilibrium rate of return (denoted simply by r) has been established by a process such as that shown in Figure 23.3. This rate of return provides a common "price" for all potential investors, telling them what they can expect to earn on a capital investment. Similarly, the rate of return provides information to savers by recording how consumption in one period may be traded for consumption in another period. The rate of return therefore plays the same role in a "two-period" model that relative prices do in a model of allocation within a single period.

THE FIRM'S DEMAND FOR CAPITAL

Thus far in this chapter we have not talked explicitly about the firm's demand for capital equipment. It is time to do so using the concepts we have already developed. Presumably, a firm will rent machines in accordance with the same principles of profit maximization that we derived in Chapter 21. Specifically, in a perfectly competitive market the firm will choose to hire that number of machines for which the marginal revenue product is precisely equal to their market rental rate. In this section we shall first investigate the determinants of this market rental rate, and we shall assume that all machines are rented. Later in the section, because most firms buy machines and hold them until they deteriorate rather than rent them, we shall examine the particular problems raised by that situation.

Determinants of Market Rental Rates

Consider a firm in the business of renting machines to other firms. Suppose that firm owns a machine (say, a car or a backhoe) that has a current market price of P. How much will the firm charge its clients for the use of the machine? The owner of the machine faces two kinds of costs: depreciation on the machine and the *opportunity cost* of having its funds tied up in a machine rather than in an investment earning the current available rate of return. If it is assumed that depreciation costs per period are a constant percentage (d) of the machine's market price and that the real interest rate is given by r, then the total costs to the machine owner for one period are given by

$$Pd + Pr = P(r + d). \tag{23.15}$$

If we assume that the machine rental market is perfectly competitive, no long-run profits can be earned by renting machines. The workings of the market will ensure that the rental rate per period for the machine (v) is exactly equal to the costs of the machine owner. Hence we have the basic result that

$$v = P(r + d). \tag{23.16}$$

The competitive rental rate is the sum of forgone interest and depreciation costs that the machine's owner must pay. For example, suppose that the real interest rate is 5 percent (that is, 0.05) and that the physical depreciation rate is 4 percent (0.04). Suppose also that the current market price of the machine is $10,000. Then, in this simple model, the machine would have an annual rental rate of $900 [= $10,000 × (0.05 + 0.04)] per year. $500 of this would represent the opportunity cost of the funds invested in the machine, and the remaining $400 would reflect the physical costs of deterioration.

In the case of a machine that does not depreciate ($d = 0$), Equation 23.16 can be written as

$$\frac{v}{P} = r. \tag{23.17}$$

This simply says that in equilibrium an infinitely long-lived (nondepreciating) machine is equivalent to a perpetual bond (see Appendix A) and, hence, must "yield" the market rate of return. The rental rate as a percentage of the machine's price must be equal to r. If $v/P > r$, everyone would rush out to buy machines, since they yield more than the rates of return elsewhere. Similarly, if $v/P < r$, no one would be in the business of renting out machines, since more could be made on alternative investments. The reader also may notice that v/P is analogous to the concept of a perpetual rate of return, which we discussed in the first section of this chapter. An amount P is given up in order to receive a return of v for every period in the future. In our previous example, if the physical depreciation rate were 0, the annual rental rate for the machine would be $500 (= 0.05 \times \$10,000)$. The owner of a machine, by renting out the machine to someone else, will earn 5 percent on the investment. This is exactly what the machine owner could earn on any other investment.

Ownership of Equipment

Our analysis so far has assumed that firms rent all of the machines they use. Although such rental does take place in the real world (for example, many firms are in the business of leasing cars, trucks, freight cars, and computers to other firms), more commonly firms own the machines they use. A firm will buy a machine and will use the services of the machine in combination with the labor it hires to produce output. The ownership of machines makes the analysis of the demand for capital somewhat more complex than that of the demand for labor. However, by recognizing the important distinction between a *stock* and a *flow*, we can show that these two demands are quite similar.

A firm uses *capital services* to produce output. These services are a *flow* magnitude. It is the number of machine-hours that is relevant to the productive process (just as it is labor-hours), not the number of machines *per se*. Frequently, however, the assumption is made that the flow of capital services is proportional to the *stock* of machines (100 machines, if fully employed for 1 hour, can deliver 100 machine-hours of service); therefore these two different concepts are used synonymously. If during a period a firm desires a certain number of machine-hours, this is usually taken to mean that the firm desires a certain number of machines.[5] The firm's demand for capital services is also a demand for capital.

A profit-maximizing firm in perfect competition will choose its level of inputs so that the marginal revenue product from an extra unit of any input is equal to its cost. This result also holds for the demand for machine hours. The cost of capital services is given by the rental rate (v) in Equation 23.16. This cost is borne by the firm whether it rents the machine in the open market or owns the machine itself. In the former case it is an explicit cost, whereas in the latter case it is an implicit cost, since the firm could rent its machine to someone else if it chose to do so. In either case the opportunity cost of machine usage is given by the market rental rate, v. The fact of ownership, to a first approximation, is irrelevant to the determination of cost. Hence we can apply our prior analysis of input demand:

---

[5]This assumption ignores the fact that the rate of capital stock utilization (that is, the flow of services from a given stock) is also an economic variable under a firm's control. A complete theory of capital should also address the question of profit-maximizing choices of utilization rates.

Optimization Principle:

Demand for Capital

A profit-maximizing firm facing a perfectly competitive rental market for capital will hire additional capital input up to the point at which its marginal revenue product (MRP_K) is equal to the market rental rate, v. Under perfect competition the rental rate will reflect both depreciation costs and opportunity costs of alternative investments. Thus we have

$$MRP_K = v = P(r + d). \qquad (23.18)$$

Theory of Investment

If a firm obeys the profit-maximizing rule of Equation 23.18 and finds that it desires more capital services than can be provided by its currently existing stock of machinery, it has two choices. First, it may hire the additional machines that are needed in the rental market. This would be formally identical to its decision to hire additional labor. Second, the firm can buy new machinery to meet its needs. This second alternative is the one most often chosen; we call the purchase of new equipment by the firm *investment*. It is an obvious, but often forgotten, fact that investment and the demand for capital services are not the same concept. Net investment (that is, investment over and above that necessary to replace what is being worn out) occurs only if the firm's demand for capital services exceeds that level of services that can be provided by its existing stock of machinery.

Investment demand is an important component of "aggregate demand" in macroeconomic theory. Frequently, it is assumed that this demand for plant and equipment (that is, machines) is inversely related to the rate of interest, or what we have called the "rate of return." Using the analysis we developed in this part of the text, we can demonstrate the links in this argument. A fall in the interest rate (r) will, *ceteris paribus*, decrease the rental rate on capital (Equation 23.16). Because forgone interest represents an implicit cost for the owner of a machine, a fall in r in effect reduces the price (that is, the rental rate) of capital inputs. This fall in v implies that capital has become a relatively less expensive input, and as we showed in Chapter 21, this will prompt firms to increase their capital usage. Firms then may either rent additional machines from others or buy new equipment for their own use.[6] It is this latter effect (the buying of new equipment) that is termed "investment." The relationship between changes in r and investment is, then, one aspect of the theory of the firms' demand for productive inputs. Because the interest rate is an important determinant of the rental rate on capital, a fall in r has an effect on investment by causing firms' demands for capital services to increase. If firms' current stock of machinery cannot deliver the desired number of machine hours, investment in new machinery will take place.

---

[6] There may be substantial lags between the perceived demand for additional capital and actual expenditures on new machines. These lags arise both because decision making takes time and because there may be costs associated with making these decisions. In empirical work the estimation of these lags is quite important.

**PRESENT
DISCOUNTED
VALUE
CRITERION**

The theory of firms' demand for capital is usually presented in a form rather different from what we have developed thus far. This alternative form is termed the *present discounted value* theory of investment demand. Rather than treating the renting of machines as analogous to the hiring of labor and centering attention on the rental rate, this approach analyzes the decision to purchase a machine. The theory is therefore a "stock" theory of the demand for machines rather than a "flow" theory of the demand for the services of a machine. The distinction between the two theories is, however, really one of semantics, not substance. Besides discussing the present discounted value criterion, a principal purpose of this section is to show that this criterion dictates the same behavior as does the rental rate approach we have outlined.

Present Value

In order to analyze the present discounted value criterion for investment, we must first discuss the procedure that should be used to add up sums of money that are to be paid in different periods, since the purchaser of a machine will collect the net income (or, more properly, the marginal value product) from the machine over several periods into the future. Although the formal mathematical aspects of this subject are presented in Appendix A of this chapter, it is possible here to provide an intuitive explanation of the logic that economists employ. A starting point is the observation that $1 today is worth more than $1 that is not to be received until some later date. If a dollar is available today it can be invested and earn interest at the prevailing rate, r. Conversely, if $1 is not received until next year, some interest must be forgone. More specifically, $1 today will grow to $(1 + r)$ dollars next year. Alternatively, we can develop the following:

Definition:

Present Discounted Value
The *present discounted value* (*PDV*) of $1 payable next year is that amount which if invested at the rate of return, r, would grow to be exactly $1 at the end of one year. That is,

$$PDV(\$1) = \frac{\$1}{1 + r}. \qquad (23.19)$$

Using this definition, future dollars can be converted into present dollars. The promise of $1 next year is identical to the promise of $1/(1 + r)$ today, since in one year an individual will have $1 in either case. It is easy to generalize the idea of present value to any number of periods. If $1 is invested for two years, for example, it will grow to $\$1 \times (1 + r) \times (1 + r) = \$1 \times (1 + r)^2$. Similarly, the present value of $1 payable in two years would be $\$1/(1 + r^2)$. This is the amount that would have to be invested today in order to obtain $1 in two years. These results can be summarized by

$$\text{present value of \$1 payable in 1 year} = \frac{\$1}{(1 + r)}$$

Table 23.1   *Present Value of $1 Payable at Future Dates*

Interest Rate (r)	1 Year	2 Years	3 Years	10 Years	20 Years
0.03	$0.970	$0.943	$0.915	$0.744	$0.554
0.04	0.962	0.925	0.889	0.676	0.456
0.05	0.952	0.907	0.864	0.614	0.377
0.06	0.943	0.890	0.840	0.558	0.312
0.07	0.935	0.873	0.816	0.508	0.258

$$\text{present value of \$1 payable in 2 years} = \frac{\$1}{(1 + r)^2}$$

$$\text{present value of \$1 payable in 3 years} = \frac{\$1}{(1 + r)^3}$$

(23.20)

$$\text{present value of \$1 payable in } n \text{ years} = \frac{\$1}{(1 + r)^n}.$$

In order to reinforce the implications of the present value concept, Table 23.1 shows the present value of $1 payable 1, 2, 3, 10, or 20 years in the future for five possible interest rates. For example, the table records the fact that if r is 4 percent, the present value of $1 payable in one year is $.962. If about $.96 is invested today at 4 percent, it will grow to $1 by the end of one year. Similarly, the table shows that if the interest rate is 7 percent, an investment of about only $.26 will grow to $1 in 20 years. In general the present value of $1 available at some date in the future declines as the interest rate increases; for a fixed interest rate, dollars payable in the distant future are worth less than those payable in the near term.

These ideas are reflected in a generalization of our previous definition:

Definition:

Present Discounted Value
The *present discounted value* (or sometimes just *present value*) of $1 payable n years in the future is

$$PDV(\$1) = \frac{\$1}{(1 + r)^n}$$

(23.21)

If \$N is to be paid n years in the future, the present value is

$$PDV(\$N) = \frac{\$N}{(1 + r)^n}. \tag{23.22}$$

Present
Discounted Value
Approach to
Investment
Decisions

When a firm buys a machine, it is in effect buying a stream of net revenues in future periods. In order to decide whether to purchase the machine, the firm must compute the current value of this stream. Since the revenues will accrue to the firm in many future periods, the logic of the preceding argument suggests that the firm should compute the present value of this stream. Only by doing so will the firm have taken adequate account of the effects of forgone interest. This is the alternative approach we shall now take to explain the investment decision.

Consider a firm in the process of deciding whether to buy a particular machine. The machine is expected to last n years and will give its owner a stream of monetary returns (that is, marginal revenue products) in each of the n years. Let the return in year i be represented by R_i. If r is the present interest rate, and if this rate is expected to prevail for the next n years, the present discounted value (PDV) of the machine to its owner is given by

$$PDV = \frac{R_1}{1 + r} + \frac{R_2}{(1 + r)^2} + \cdots + \frac{R_n}{(1 + r)^n}. \tag{23.23}$$

This present discounted value represents the total value of the stream of payments that is provided by the machine, once adequate account is taken of the fact that these payments occur in different years. If the PDV of this stream of payments exceeds the price (P) of the machine, the firm should make the purchase. Even when the effects of the interest payments that the firm could have earned on its funds had it not purchased the machine are taken into account, the machine promises to return more than its prevailing price. Consequently, firms would rush out to buy machines. On the other hand, if $P > PDV$, the firm would be better off to invest its funds in some alternative that promises a rate of return of r. When account is taken of forgone interest, the machine does not pay for itself. No profit-maximizing firm would buy a machine for which $P > PDV$. In a competitive market the only equilibrium that can prevail is the price of a machine being equal to the present discounted value of the net revenues from the machine. Only in this situation will there be neither an excess demand for machines nor an excess supply of machines. Hence market equilibrium requires that

$$P = PDV = \frac{R_1}{1 + r} + \frac{R_2}{(1 + r)^2} + \cdots + \frac{R_n}{(1 + r)^n}. \tag{23.24}$$

We shall now use this condition to show two situations in which the present discounted value criterion of investment reduces to the equilibrium conditions outlined in Equation 23.16 or 23.17.

Simple Case

Assume first that machines are infinitely long-lived and that the marginal reve-nue product (that is, R_i) is the same in every year. This uniform return also will equal the rental rate for machines (v), since that is what another firm would pay for the machine's use during the period. With these simplifying assumptions we may write the present discounted value from machine owner-ship as

$$PDV = \frac{v}{(1 + r)} + \frac{v}{(1 + r)^2} + \cdots + \frac{v}{(1 + r)^n} + \cdots$$

$$= v \cdot \left(\frac{1}{(1 + r)} + \frac{1}{(1 + r)^2} + \cdots + \frac{1}{(1 + r)^n} + \cdots\right)$$

$$= v \cdot \left(\frac{1}{1 - 1/(1 + r)} - 1\right) \tag{23.25}$$

$$= v \cdot \left(\frac{1 + r}{r} - 1\right)$$

$$= v \cdot \frac{1}{r}.$$

But since in equilibrium $P = PDV$, this says

$$P = v \cdot \frac{1}{r} \tag{23.26}$$

or

$$\frac{v}{P} = r, \tag{23.27}$$

as was shown in Equation 23.17. For this case the present discounted value criterion gives results identical to those outlined in the previous section. We again have demonstrated the algebraic relationship among a machine's price, the rental rate on the machine, and the market rate of interest. In particular, a *ceteris paribus* increase in r will decrease the machine's PDV, and firms will be less willing to buy machines for the same reasons discussed in the previous section.

General Case

Equation 23.16 can be derived for the more general case in which the rental rate on machines is not constant over time and in which there is some depre-ciation. This analysis is most easily carried out by using continuous time.[7] Sup-pose that the rental rate for a *new* machine at any time s is given by $v(s)$.

---

[7] The mathematics of continuous compound interest rates is discussed in Appendix A of this chapter.

Assume also that the machine depreciates exponentially at the rate d.[8] The net rental rate (and the marginal revenue product) of a machine therefore declines over time as the machine gets older. In year s the net rental rate on an *old* machine bought in a previous year (t) would be

$$v(s)e^{-d(s-t)}, \tag{23.28}$$

since $s - t$ is the number of years over which the machine has been decaying. For example, suppose that a machine were bought in 1984. Its net rental rate in 1989 then would be the rental rate that is earned by new machines in 1989 [$v(1989)$] discounted by the factor e^{-5d} to account for the amount of depreciation that has taken place over the five years of the machine's life.

If the firm is considering buying the machine when it is new in year t, it should discount all of these net rental amounts back to that date. The present value of the net rental in year s discounted back to year t is therefore (if r is the interest rate)

$$e^{-r(s-t)}v(s)e^{-d(s-t)} = e^{(r+d)t}v(s)e^{-(r+d)s}, \tag{23.29}$$

since, again, ($s - t$) years elapse from when the machine is bought until when the net rental is received. The present discounted value of a machine bought in year t is therefore the sum (integral) of these present values. This sum should be taken from year t (when the machine is bought) over all years into the future:

$$PDV(t) = \int_t^\infty e^{(r+d)t}v(s)e^{-(r+d)s}ds. \tag{23.30}$$

Since in equilibrium the price of the machine at year $t[P(t)]$ will be equal to this present value, we have the following fundamental equation:

$$P(t) = \int_t^\infty e^{(r+d)t}v(s)e^{-(r+d)s}ds. \tag{23.31}$$

This rather formidable equation is simply a more complex version of Equation 23.24 and can be used to derive Equation 23.16. First rewrite the equation as

$$P(t) = e^{(r+d)t}\int_t^\infty v(s)e^{-(r+d)s}ds. \tag{23.32}$$

---

[8] In this view of depreciation, machines are assumed to "evaporate" at a fixed rate per unit of time. This model of decay is in many ways identical to the assumptions of radioactive decay made in physics. There are other possible forms that physical depreciation might take; this is only the most mathematically tractable.

It is important to keep the concept of physical depreciation (depreciation that affects a machine's productivity) distinct from accounting depreciation. The latter concept is important only in that the method of accounting depreciation chosen may affect the rate of taxation on the profits from a machine. From an economic point of view, however, the cost of a machine is a sunk cost: Any choice on how to "write off" this cost is to some extent arbitrary.

Now differentiate with respect to t, using the rule for taking the derivative of a product:

$$\frac{dP(t)}{dt} = (r + d)e^{(r+d)t}\int_t^\infty v(s)e^{-(r+d)s}ds - e^{(r+d)t}v(t)e^{-(r+d)t}$$

$$= (r + d)P(t) - v(t).$$

(22.33)

Hence

$$v(t) = (r + d)P(t) - \frac{dP(t)}{dt}.$$

(23.34)

This is precisely the result shown earlier in Equation 23.16, except that the term $-dP(t)/dt$ has been added. The economic explanation for the presence of this term is that it represents the capital gains that accrue to the owner of the machine. If the machine's price can be expected to rise, for example, the owner may accept somewhat less than $(r + d)P$ for its rental.[9] On the other hand, if the price of the machine is expected to fall $[dP(t)/dt < 0]$, the owner will require more in rent than is specified in Equation 23.16. If the price of the machine is expected to remain constant over time, $dP(t)/dt = 0$ and the equations are identical. The result of this analysis is to show that there is a definite relationship among the price of a machine at any time, the stream of future profits that the machine promises, and the current rental rate for the machine.

AN EXAMPLE: WHEN TO HARVEST A TREE

As an example of the present discounted value criterion for investments, consider the case of a landowner who must decide when to cut down a tree and sell it to a sawmill. Our analysis of firms' investment decisions suggests that if the landowner allows the tree to continue growing, he or she will forgo potential interest that could be earned by investing the tree's market value in some other use. On the other hand, harvesting the tree will mean that the tree's future growth must be forgone. The profit-maximizing decision therefore would seem to be to harvest the tree at a time at which these two costs balance each other out. The *PDV* criterion permits us to show this result precisely.

Suppose that the value of the tree at any time, t, is given by $f(t)$ and that L dollars are invested initially as payments to workers who plant the tree. Assume also that the (continuous) market interest rate is given by r. Given these assumptions, the landowner will choose a harvesting date so as to maximize the *PDV* of potential profits. At any time, t, the present discounted value of the treeowner's profits is given by

$$PDV(t) = e^{-rt}f(t) - L,$$

(23.35)

which is simply the difference between (the present value of) revenues and present costs. The firm's decision, then, consists of choosing t to maximize this value. As always, this value may be found by differentiation:

[9] For example, rental houses in suburbs with rapidly appreciating house prices will usually rent for less than the landlord's actual costs because the landlord also gains from price appreciation.

$$\frac{dPDV(t)}{dt} = e^{-rt}f'(t) - re^{-rt}f(t) = 0, \tag{23.36}$$

or after dividing both sides by e^{-rt}:

$$f'(t) - rf(t) = 0; \tag{23.37}$$

therefore,

$$r = \frac{f'(t)}{f(t)}. \tag{23.38}$$

Hence t should be chosen so that Equation 23.38 holds. Two features of this optimal condition are worth noting. First, observe that the cost of the initial labor input drops out upon differentiation. This cost is (even in a literal sense) a "sunk" cost that is basically irrelevant to the profit-maximizing decision. Second, Equation 23.38 can be interpreted as saying that the tree should be harvested when the rate of interest is equal to the proportional rate of growth of the tree. This is true because $f'(t)/f(t)$ is in fact the percentage increase in $f(t)$ at time t. This result makes intuitive sense. If the tree is growing more rapidly than the prevailing interest rate, its owner should leave his or her funds invested in the tree, since the tree provides the best return available. The volume of timber in this case might be increasing at 8 percent per year, while the interest rate available in the market is only 5 percent. On the other hand, if the tree is growing less rapidly than the prevailing interest rate, the tree should be cut, and the funds obtained from its sale should be invested elsewhere at the rate r.

Equation 23.38 is only a necessary condition for a maximum. By differentiating Equation 23.37, again it is easy to see that it is also required that at the chosen value of t,

$$f''(t) - rf'(t) < 0, \tag{23.39}$$

if Equation 23.38 is to represent a true maximum. If we assume that $f'(t) > 0$ (that the tree is always growing), then the assumption that $f''(t) < 0$ will ensure that this condition holds. The necessary conditions will ensure a maximum if we assume that the tree is always growing but that this growth slows over time.

Numerical Example

As an illustration, suppose that a forester has determined that the trees in his or her woodlot are growing according to the equation

$$f(t) = e^{.4\sqrt{t}}. \tag{23.40}$$

This equation always exhibits a positive growth rate ($f'(t) > 0$) and, since

$$\frac{f'(t)}{f(t)} = \frac{.2}{\sqrt{t}}, \tag{23.41}$$

this rate diminishes over time. If the real interest rate is, say, .04, we can solve for the optimal harvesting age as

$$r = .04 = \frac{f'(t)}{f(t)} = \frac{.2}{\sqrt{t}} \tag{23.42}$$

or

$$\sqrt{t} = \frac{.2}{.04} = 5 \tag{23.43}$$

so

$$t^* = 25.$$

Up to 25 years of age, the volume of wood in the tree is increasing at a rate in excess of 4 percent per year so the optimal decision is to permit the tree to stand. But, for $t > 25$ the annual growth rate falls below 4 percent and the forester can find better investments—perhaps planting new trees.

Comparative Statics Analysis

To see how the optimal choice of t changes in response to a change in the interest rate, it is necessary to differentiate Equation 23.37 totally:

$$f''(t) \frac{\partial t}{\partial r} - rf'(t) \frac{\partial t}{\partial r} - f(t) = 0 \tag{23.44}$$

or

$$\frac{\partial t}{\partial r} = \frac{f(t)}{f''(t) - rf'(t)}.$$

This expression will be negative in view of the second-order conditions given above. We have shown, therefore, that an increase in r will cause t to decrease (the tree will be cut sooner if the interest rate rises), and vice versa. This is then another demonstration of the negative relationship between v and the level of investment (which here consists of the quantity of wood in a growing tree).

Numerical Example Revisited

If the real interest rate in our prior example rose to five percent, Equation 23.42 would become

$$r = .05 = \frac{.2}{\sqrt{t}} \tag{23.45}$$

and the optimal harvest age would be

$$t^* = \left(\frac{.2}{.05} \right) = 16. \tag{23.46}$$

The higher real interest rate thereby discourages investment in trees by prompting the forester to choose an earlier harvest date.

HUMAN CAPITAL

One important application of the theory of capital concerns a kind of investment that is very different from what we have been discussing thus far—the investment that a person can make in himself or herself. Individuals can invest in themselves in a variety of ways. They can acquire a formal education; they may accept apprenticeships and learn skills on the job; they can spend considerable efforts in looking for better jobs; or they can purchase various kinds of medical services that maintain them in good health. All of those activities can be looked upon as "investments," in that both time and money are sacrificed currently in the hope that this somehow will pay off in the future. By acquiring skills or buying "good health," individuals are adding to their stock of *human capital* in much the same way that the purchase of machines by firms adds to the firms' stock of physical capital. There is substantial empirical evidence that most such additions to human capital are quite productive in the sense that they serve to increase individuals' earnings in future periods. In fact, it has been found that many investments that individuals make in themselves that yield returns substantially in excess of those prevailing on investments in physical capital.[10]

Although the analogy between human and physical capital provides many insights into the nature of individuals' decisions about education, health care consumption, and employment experiences, the analogy should not be pushed too far. Human capital has a number of special properties that make it unique among the assets an individual can buy. Contrary to other assets, human capital cannot (in the absence of slavery) be sold. The owner of human capital is inextricably tied to his or her investment. Although the individual may rent out this investment to employers, he or she may not sell it in the way in which a firm might sell a machine it no longer needed. Human capital also depreciates in a rather unusual way. It is totally lost upon the death of its owner, and this makes the investment rather risky. Finally, the acquisition of human capital may take substantial time. Whereas a firm seeking to buy a drill press may only have to spend five minutes in the buying process, individuals seeking to improve their skills must usually invest considerable time in doing so. During that time earnings must be forgone, and they should be considered as part of the cost of acquisition. For all these reasons, we must recognize the limitations of the human capital approach as well as its great analytical strength in illuminating the human investment process.

SUMMARY

In this chapter we have examined several aspects of the theory of capital with particular emphasis on integrating that theory with the theory of the firm's demand for capital inputs. Some of the results we illustrated were

- Capital accumulation represents the sacrifice of present for future consumption. The rate of return measures the terms at which this trade can be accomplished.

---

[10] For a thorough analysis of the education aspects of human capital formation, see G. S. Becker, *Human Capital*, National Bureau of Economic Research (New York: Columbia University Press, 1964).

- The rate of return is established through mechanisms much like those that establish any equilibrium price. The equilibrium rate of return will be positive reflecting both individuals' relative preferences for present over future goods and the positive physical productivity of capital accumulation.
- The rate of return is an important element in the overall costs associated with capital ownership. It is an important determinant of the market rental rate on capital, v.
- Future returns on capital investments must be discounted at the prevailing real interest rate. Use of such present value notions provides an alternative way to approach the firm's investment decisions.
- Human capital has some similarities to physical capital as an investment. It also has some unique features that complicate the theory of individuals' and firms' human capital investment decisions.

Application

EFFECTS OF TAX POLICIES ON INVESTMENT

Federal tax policies have been widely used to influence the overall level of U.S. investment over the past 30 years. Although the general thrust of these policies has been to increase investment by lowering taxes, changes in the general tax rate have not been the primary way this has been accomplished. Rather, complex changes have been made in accounting procedures and special credits have been allowed for investment. Although it would be inappropriate to attempt to describe these changes in detail, a brief sketch of the three most important such policies may serve to indicate the ways in which investment incentives have been provided.

1. *Accelerated Depreciation*: In 1954, federal tax policy was changed to allow firms to "write off" the costs of their investments in plant and equipment more rapidly than was previously the case. That policy had the effect of allowing firms to postpone the taxes owed on the income generated by newly purchased machinery. In essence, firms received from the government an interest-free loan of their tax

liability. By one estimate this relatively subtle change in accounting principles had the effect of reducing the rental rate on capital by as much as 20 percent.[11]

2. *Useful Lifetime Guidelines*: Another provision for accelerated depreciation was instituted in 1962. Under this provision, what the tax law defined to be the "useful lifetimes" of various types of equipment were shortened. For example, the minimum useful life of a car was reduced from four to three years. This made it possible for firms to gain further benefits from accelerated depreciation, and effective rental rates on capital were reduced another 2 or 3 percent. Useful lifetimes have been redefined many times since 1962.

3. *Investment Tax Credit*: An additional tax change in 1962 was the institution of an "investment tax credit" for machinery and equipment purchases. Under that policy, 7 percent of the amount that firms in-

[11] R. E. Hall and D. W. Jorgenson, "Tax Policy and Investment Behavior," *American Economic Review* 57 (June 1967): 391–414.

Table 23.2   *Change in Gross Investment in Equipment as a Result of Federal Tax Policy in 1963 (Billions of 1954 Dollars)*

	Manufacturing Equipment	Nonmanufacturing Equipment
Total gross investment	$8.461	$17.982
Change due to		
Accelerated depreciation	0.549	1.141
Useful lifetime guidelines	0.315	0.656
Investment tax credit	0.867	1.808
Total effect of federal tax policy	1.731	3.605
Tax effect as a percent of total gross investment	20.5%	20.0%

vested could be taken as a credit against taxes due. That policy reduced effective rental rates by 7 percent: Essentially, the federal government paid 7 percent of all machinery and equipment purchases.

Quantitative Effects of the Tax Policies on Investment in the Early 1960s

Table 23.2 shows the estimated effect of each of these tax policies on firms' total gross investment in equipment in 1963. As our theoretical discussion suggested, the reduction in rental rates had a substantial effect on the demand for capital equipment, increasing total purchases by about 20 percent over what they would have been under older, less generous tax laws. Clearly, tax policy provides a powerful lever by means of which the federal government can affect investment and, through investment, the overall pace of economic activity. The relatively high levels of employment experienced during the mid-1960s in the United States may have been in part the result of such policies.

Tax Policies of the Reagan Administration

In the first year of the Reagan administration, a similar set of investment-oriented tax policies was enacted as part of the Economic Recovery

Tax Act of 1981 (ERTA). Changes introduced under this act included a new form of accelerated depreciation (Accelerated Cost Recovery System—ACRS) and an increased investment tax credit. Adoption of the ACRS was a particularly important innovation. It eliminated the prior concept of "useful lifetime guidelines" for determining depreciation allowances and substituted a simplified scheme in which any asset falls into one of four classes with a tax life of 3, 5, 10, or 15 years. For most capital assets these lives were considerably shorter than had been the case previously. Most notably, the depreciation period for all equipment used to conduct research and development activities was reduced to a short three years whereas the previous guidelines had required much longer periods. Adoption of the ACRS also brought much greater uniformity into the tax treatment of various industries' investments. For example, under prior laws depreciation periods for producers' equipment ranged from over 14 years for ships and boats and over 12 years for turbines to 5 years for trucks and tractors. Similarly, depreciation periods for buildings ranged from 23 to more than 40 years. Under the ACRS, depreciation periods were set at a uniform 5 years for most equipment and 10 or 15 years for buildings. It was hoped that such changes would result in a more uniform tax treatment of investment decisions across industries, thereby mitigating some of the anomalies that had developed under the prior system.

The overall effect of the ERTA changes was to reduce substantially taxes (and hence effective rental rates) on firms' capital investments. Indeed, some analysts even suggested that the tax rates under ERTA on many types of equipment were negative; that is, the government was effectively subsidizing this type of investment.[12]

Possibilities for this subsidy having a major effect on firms' investment behavior were rather limited, however, because the tax law was again changed in 1982 (under the pompously titled Tax Equity and Fiscal Responsibility Act), and there the subsidy was largely eliminated. Indeed this later law raised the tax rates on some types of investment to above their pre-1981 levels. In 1986 depreciation and other rules were further tightened as part of a major tax "reform" package. Hence, the overall effect of policies on investment during the Reagan administration is difficult to assess.

[12] See D. Fullerton and Y. K. Henderson, "Long-Run Effects of the Accelerated Recovery System," National Bureau of Economic Research Working Paper No. 828 (Revised, February, 1983).

SUGGESTED READINGS

Auerbach, A. J., and Hines, J. R. "Investment Tax Incentives and Frequent Tax Norms." *American Economic Review Papers and Proceedings* (May 1988): pp. 211–216.

Brief discussion and references on effects of taxation on investment.

Becker, G. S. *Human Capital: A Theoretical and Empirical Analysis with Special Reference to Education*, National Bureau of Economic Research, General Series No. 80. New York: Columbia University Press, 1964.

Basic treatment of the human capital concept and how human capital investments might be modeled.

Blaug, M. *Economic Theory in Retrospect*. Rev. ed. Homewood, Ill.: Richard D. Irwin, 1978. Chap. 12.

Good review of Austrian capital theory and of attempts to conceptualize the capital accumulation process.

Harcourt, G. C. "Some Cambridge Controversies in the Theory of Capital." *Journal of Economic Literature* 7 (June 1969): 369–405.

Summarizes the "Cambridge Controversy" about the nature and measurability of capital.

Hirshleifer, J. *Investment, Interest and Capital*. Englewood Cliffs, N.J.: Prentice-Hall, Inc., 1970.

Extended treatment of the neoclassical theory of investment.

Jorgenson, D. W. "Econometric Studies of Investment Behavior: A Survey." *Journal of Economic Literature* 9 (December 1971): 1111–1147.

Interesting survey of the 1960s empirical literature on investment behavior.

Samuelson, P. A. "Parable and Realism in Capital Theory: The Surrogate Production Function." *Review of Economic Studies* 39 (June 1962): 193–206.

A discussion of how capital might be added up for use in an aggregate production function.

Shoven, J. B., and Taubman, P. "Saving, Capital Income, and Taxation." In H. J. Aaron and M. J. Boskin, eds., *The Economics of Taxation*. Washington, D.C.: The Brookings Institution, 1980.

Use of a general equilibrium model to study the allocational effects of capital taxation.

Solow, R. M. *Capital Theory and the Rate of Return*. Amsterdam: North Holland Publishing Co., 1964.

Lectures on the nature of capital. Very readable.

PROBLEMS

23.1
An individual has a fixed amount of money (W) to allocate between consumption in two periods (C_1 and C_2). The individual's utility function is given by

$$U(C_1, C_2),$$

and the budget constraint is

$$W = C_1 + \frac{C_2}{1 + r},$$

where r is the one-period interest rate.

    a.   Show that in order to maximize utility, given this budget constraint, the individual should choose C_1 and C_2 so that the MRS (of C_1 for C_2) is equal to $1 + r$.

    b.   Show that $\partial C_2/\partial r \geq 0$ but that the sign of $\partial C_1/\partial r$ is ambiguous. If $\partial C_1/\partial r$ is negative, what can you conclude about the price elasticity of demand for C_2?

    c.   How might your analysis of this problem be amended if the individual received income in each period (Y_1 and Y_2) so that the budget constraint is given by

$$Y_1 - C_1 + \frac{Y_2 - C_2}{1 + r} = 0$$

23.2.
Assume that an individual expects to work for 40 years and then retire with a life expectancy of an additional 20 years. Suppose also that the individual's earnings rise at a rate of 3 percent per year and that the interest rate is also 3 percent (the overall price level is constant in this problem). What (constant) fraction of income must the individual save in each working year to be able to finance a level of retirement income equal to 60 percent of earnings in the year just prior to retirement?

23.3
As scotch whiskey ages, its value increases. One dollar of scotch at year 0 is worth $V(t) = e^{2\sqrt{t} - 0.15t}$ dollars at time t. If the interest rate is 5 percent, after how many years should a person sell scotch in order to maximize the PDV of this sale?

23.4
The president of the Acme Landfill Company has estimated that the purchase of 10 more deluxe dump trucks can bring in added revenues of $100,000 a year for the life of the trucks. The trucks have a life span of seven years and cost $50,000 each. If the company can earn a 10 percent rate of return on investments in alternative ventures, should it go ahead and purchase the trucks? What if the company found that it could only earn a 9 percent return on its alternative investments? Should it go ahead with the purchase?

23.5
As in the example in Chapter 23, suppose that trees are produced by applying one unit of labor at time 0. The value of the wood contained in a tree is given at any time (t) by $f(t)$. If the market wage rate is w and the instantaneous rate is r, what is the PDV of this production process and how should t be chosen to maximize this PDV?

    a.   If the optimal value of t is denoted by t^*, show that the no-pure-profit condition of perfect competition will necessitate that

$$w = e^{-rt} f(t^*).$$

Can you interpret what this expression means?

b.   A tree sold before t^* will not be cut down immediately. Rather, it still will make sense for the new owner to let the tree continue to mature until t^*. Show that the price of a u-year-old tree will be we^{ru} and that this price will exceed the value of the wood in the tree $[f(u)]$ for every value of u except $u = t^*$ when these two values are equal.

c.   Suppose that a landowner has a "balanced" wood lot with one tree of "each" age from 0 to t^*. What is the value of this wood lot? (*Hint:* It is the sum of the values of all trees in the lot.)

d.   If the value of the wood lot is V, show that the instantaneous interest on V (that is, $r \cdot V$) is equal to the "profits" earned at each instant by the landowner, where by profits we mean the difference between the revenue obtained from selling a fully matured tree $[f(t^*)]$ and the cost of planting a new one (w). This result shows that there is no pure profit in borrowing to buy a wood lot, since one would have to pay in interest at each instant exactly what would be earned from cutting a fully matured tree.

23.6 Corporate profits are currently taxed at a 46 percent rate in the United States. This problem focuses on the interaction of that tax with firms' investment decisions.

a.   Suppose (contrary to fact) that profits were defined for tax purposes as what we have called pure economic profits. How would a tax on such profits affect investment decisions?

b.   In fact, profits are defined for tax purposes as

$$\pi' = PQ - WL - \text{depreciation},$$

where depreciation is determined by governmental and industry guidelines that seek to allocate a machine's costs over its "useful" lifetime. If depreciation were equal to actual physical deterioration and if a firm were in long-run competitive equilibrium, how would a tax on π' affect the firm's choice of capitalized inputs?

c.   Under the conditions of part (b), how would capital usage be affected by adoption of "accelerated depreciation" policies that specify depreciation rates in excess of physical deterioration early in a machine's life, but much lower depreciation rates as the machine ages?

d.   Under the conditions of part (c), how might a decrease in the corporate profits tax affect capital usage?

23.7

Some foresters suggest that timber plots be managed so as to achieve "maximum sustainable yield." How might an economist evaluate this proposition?

23.8

A high-pressure life insurance salesman was heard to make the following argument: "At your age a $100,000 whole life policy is a much better buy than a similar term policy. Under a whole life policy you'll have to pay $2,000 per year for the first four years, but nothing more for the rest of your life. A term policy will cost you $400 per year, essentially forever. If you live 35 years you'll pay only $8,000 for the whole life policy, but $14,000 for the term policy. Surely the whole life is a better deal."

Assuming the salesman's life expectancy assumption is correct, how would you evaluate this argument? Specifically, calculate the present discounted value of the premium costs of the two policies assuming that the interest rate is 10 percent.

23.9

A high-pressure car-loan saleswoman (perhaps the sister of the salesman in Problem 23.8) was heard to make the following argument to a new car buyer: "Suppose you buy this $10,000 car with cash. Since you could be earning 10 percent on that money in a bank you'll lose at least $3,000 in interest over the next 3 years. On the other hand, if you take one of our low-cost auto loans for $10,000, you'll only have to pay $350 per month for 36 months. Overall then you'll pay back $12,600—$10,000 for the car and only $2,600 in interest. Hence, you actually save money by financing the car!"

How would you evaluate this argument? Is the auto loan really lost cost?

23.10

The No-flite Golfball Company manufactures cut-proof golfballs and is thinking of investing in a new name. Their media personnel have come up with two suggestions: "Astro-flite" and "Jack Nickless." It's cheaper to switch to "Astro-flite" since the second name will involve legal fees for dealing with a well-known golfer who is likely to get upset by the whole thing. The second name, however, is expected to bring in more business than the first. If the costs and payoffs are as given below, and the firm expects to go out of business in five years, is it worth it to make a name switch, and if so, to which name?

	Cost	Yearly Return	Interest Rate
Astro-flite	3,800	1,000	10%
Jack Nickless	5,000	1,400	10%

Would your answer change if the interest rate were 15%?

23.11

Suppose an individual has I dollars to allocate between consumption this period (C_0) and consumption next period (C_1) and that the interest rate is given by r.

a. Graph the individual's initial equilibrium and indicate the total value of current period savings ($I - C_0$).

b. Suppose that after the individual makes his or her savings decision (by purchasing one period bonds), the interest rate falls to r'. How will this alter the individual's budget constraint? Show the new utility-maximizing position. Discuss how the individual's improved position can be interpreted as resulting from a "capital gain" on his or her initial bond purchases.

c. Suppose the tax authorities wish to impose an "income" tax based on the value of capital gains. If all such gains are valued in terms of C_0 as they are "accrued," show how those gains should be measured. Call this value G_1.

d. Suppose instead that capital gains are measured as they are "realized"—that is, capital gains are defined to include only that portion of bonds that is cashed in to buy additional C_0. Show how these realized gains can be measured. Call this amount G_2.

e. Develop a measure of the true increase in utility that results from the fall in r, measured in terms of C_0. Call this "true" capital gain G_3. Show that $G_3 < G_2 < G_1$. What do you conclude about the current policy that taxes only realized gains?

(*Note:* This problem is adapted from J. Whalley, "Capital Gains Taxation and Interest Rate Changes," *National Tax Journal* (March 1979): 87–91.)

Appendix A to Chapter 23

The Mathematics of Compound Interest

The purpose of this appendix is to gather together some simple results concerning the mathematics of compound interest. These results have applications in a wide variety of economic problems, ranging from macroeconomic policy to the optimal way to raise Christmas trees.

We assume that there is a current prevailing market interest rate of i per period, say, one year. This interest rate is assumed to be both certain and constant over all future periods.[1] If \$1 is invested at this rate, i, and the interest is then compounded (that is, future interest is paid on past interest earned),

at the end of 1 period \$1 will be . . . $\$1 \times (1 + i)$,
at the end of 2 periods \$1 will be . . .

$$\$1 \times (1 + i) \times (1 + i) = \$1 \times (1 + i)^2,$$

and

at the end of n periods \$1 will be . . . $\$1 \times (1 + i)^n$.

Similarly, \$N grows like

$$\$N \times (1 + i)$$
$$\$N \times (1 + i)^2$$
$$.$$
$$.$$
$$.$$
$$\$N \times (1 + i)^n.$$

PRESENT DISCOUNTED VALUE

The *present value* of \$1 payable 1 period from now is

$$\frac{\$1}{(1 + i)}.$$

This is simply the amount that an individual would be willing to pay now for the promise of \$1 at the end of 1 period. Similarly, the present value of \$1

---

[1] The assumption of a constant i is obviously unrealistic. Since the problems introduced by considering an interest rate that varies from period to period greatly complicate the notation without adding a commensurate degree of conceptual knowledge, such an analysis is not undertaken here. In many cases the generalization to a varying interest rate is merely a trivial application of the notion that any multiperiod interest rate can be regarded as resulting from compounding several single-period rates. If we let r_{ij} be the interest rate prevailing between periods i and j (where $i < j$), then,

$$1 + r_{ij} = (1 + r_{i,i+1})(1 + r_{i+1,i+2}) \cdots (1 + r_{j-1,j}).$$

payable n periods from now is

$$\frac{\$1}{(1 + i)^n},$$

and the present value of $\$N$ payable n periods from now is

$$\frac{\$N}{(1 + i)^n}.$$

The *present discounted value* of a stream of payments $N_0, N_1, N_2, \ldots, N_n$ (where the subscripts indicate the period in which the payment is to be made) is

$$PDV = N_0 + \frac{N_1}{(1 + i)} + \frac{N_2}{(1 + i)^2} + \cdots + \frac{N_n}{(1 + i)^n}. \qquad \text{(23A.1)}$$

PDV is the amount that an individual would be willing to pay in return for a promise to receive the stream $N_0, N_1, N_2, \ldots, N_n$. It represents the amount that would have to be invested now if one wished to duplicate the payment stream.

Annuities and Perpetuities

An *annuity* is a promise to pay $\$N$ in each period for n periods, starting next period. The PDV of such a contract is

$$PDV = \frac{N}{(1 + i)} + \frac{N}{(1 + i)^2} + \cdots + \frac{N}{(1 + i)^n}. \qquad \text{(23A.2)}$$

Let $D = 1/(1 + i)$; then,

$$PDV = N(D + D^2 + \cdots + D^n)$$

$$= ND(1 + D + D^2 + \cdots + D^{n-1}) \qquad \text{(23A.3)}$$

$$= ND\left(\frac{1 - D^n}{1 - D}\right).$$

Notice that

$$\lim_{n \to \infty} D^n = 0.$$

Therefore, for an annuity of infinite duration,

$$PDV \text{ of infinite annuity} = \lim_{n \to \infty} PDV = ND\left(\frac{1}{1 - D}\right), \qquad \text{(23A.4)}$$

which, by the definition of D,

$$= N\left(\frac{1}{1 + i}\right)\left(\frac{1}{1 - 1/(1 + i)}\right)$$

$$= N\left(\frac{1}{1 + i}\right)\left(\frac{1 + i}{i}\right) = \frac{N}{i}. \qquad \text{(23A.5)}$$

This case of an infinite period annuity is sometimes called a *perpetuity* or a *consol*. Such annuities are rare (indeed technically illegal) in the United States but are common in Canada and in the United Kingdom. The formula simply says that the amount that must be invested if one is to obtain \$N per period forever is simply \$N/i, since this amount of money would earn \$N in interest each period ($i \cdot \$N/i = \$N$).

The Special Case of a Bond

An *n*-period *bond* is a promise to pay \$N each period, starting next period, for *n* periods. It also promises to return the principal (face) value of the bond at the end of *n* periods. If the principal value of the bond is \$P (usually \$1000 in the U.S. bond market), then the present discounted value of such a promise is

$$PDV = \frac{N}{(1 + i)} + \frac{N}{(1 + i)} + \cdots + \frac{N}{(1 + i)} + \frac{P}{(1 + i)}. \qquad (23A.6)$$

Again let $D = 1/(1 + i)$; then,

$$PDV = ND + ND^2 + \cdots + (N + P)D^n. \qquad (23A.7)$$

Equation 23A.7 can be looked at in another way. Suppose that we knew the price at which the bond is currently trading, say, B. Then we could ask what value of i gives the bond a PDV equal to B. To find this i we set

$$B = PDV = ND + ND^2 + \cdots + (N + P)D^n. \qquad (23A.8)$$

Since B, N, and P are known, we can solve this equation for D and hence for i.[2] The i that solves the equation is called the *yield* on the bond and is the best measure of the return actually available from the bond. The yield of a bond represents the return available both from direct interest payments and from any price differential between the initial price (B) and the maturity price (P).

Notice that as i increases, PDV decreases. This is a precise way of formulating the well-known concept that bond prices (PDV's) and interest rates (yields) are inversely correlated.

CONTINUOUS TIME

Thus far this appendix has dealt with discrete time—the analysis has been divided into periods. Often it is more convenient to deal with continuous time. In such a case the interest on an investment is compounded "instantaneously" and growth over time is "smooth." This facilitates the analysis of maximization problems because certain functions are more easily differentiated. Many financial intermediaries (for example, savings banks) have adopted continuous interest formulas in recent years.

---

[2] Since this equation is really an *n*th-degree polynomial, there are in reality *n* solutions (roots). Only one of these solutions is the relevant one reported in bond tables or on calculators. The other solutions are either imaginary or unreasonable. In the present example there is only one real solution.

Suppose that i is given as the (nominal) interest rate per year but that half this nominal rate is compounded every 6 months. Then, at the end of 1 year, the investment of $1 would have grown to

$$\$1 \times \left(1 + \frac{i}{2}\right)^2. \tag{23A.9}$$

Notice that this is superior to investing for 1 year at the simple rate, i, because interest has been paid on interest; that is,

$$\left(1 + \frac{i}{2}\right)^2 > (1 + i). \tag{23A.10}$$

Consider the limit of this process—for the nominal rate of i per period, consider the amount that would be realized if i were in fact "compounded n times during the period"; let $n \to \infty$:

$$\lim_{n \to \infty} \left(1 + \frac{i}{n}\right)^n. \tag{23A.11}$$

This limit exists and is simply e^i, where e is the base of natural logarithms (the value of e is approximately 2.72). It is important to note that $e^i > (1 + i)$—it is much better to have continuous compounding over the period than to have simple interest.

We can ask what continuous rate, r, yields the same amount at the end of one period as the simple rate i. We are looking for the value of r that solves the equation

$$e^r = (1 + i). \tag{23A.12}$$

Hence

$$r = \ln(1 + i). \tag{23A.12'}$$

Using this formula it is a simple matter to translate from discrete interest rates into continuous ones. If i is measured as a decimal yearly rate, then r is a yearly continuous rate. Table 23A.1 shows the effective annual interest rate (i) associated with selected interest rates (r) that are continuously compounded.[3] Tables similar to 23A.1 often appear in the windows of savings banks advertising the "true" yields on their accounts.

Continuous Growth

One dollar invested at a continuous interest rate of r will become

$$V = \$1 \cdot e^{rT} \tag{23A.13}$$

after T years. This growth formula is a very convenient one to work with. For example, it is easy to show that the instantaneous relative rate of change in V

---

[3] To compute the figures in Table 23A.1, interest rates are used in decimal rather than percent form (that is, a 5 percent interest rate is recorded as 0.05 for use in Equation 23A.12).

Table 23A.1   *Effective Annual Interest Rates for Selected Continuously Compounded Rates*

Continuously Compounded Rate	Effective Annual Rate
3.0%	3.04%
4.0	4.08
5.0	5.13
5.5	5.65
6.0	6.18
6.5	6.72
7.0	7.25
8.0	8.33
9.0	9.42
10.0	10.52

is, as would be expected, simply given by r:

$$\text{rate of change} = \frac{dV/dt}{V} = \frac{re^{rt}}{e^{rt}} = r. \tag{23A.14}$$

Continuous interest rates also are convenient for calculating present discounted values. Suppose that we wished to calculate the *PDV* of \$1 to be paid T years from now. This would be given by:[4]

$$\frac{\$1}{e^{rT}} = \$1 \cdot e^{-rT}. \tag{23A.15}$$

The logic of this calculation is exactly the same as that used in the discrete time analysis of this appendix: Future dollars are worth less than present ones.

One interesting application of continuous discounting occurs in calculating the *PDV* of \$1 per period paid in small installments at each instant of time from today (time 0) until period T. Since there would be an infinite number of payments, the mathematical tool of integration must be used to compute this result:

$$PDV = \int_0^T e^{-rt} dt. \tag{23A.16}$$

All this statement says is that we are adding all the discounted dollars over the time period 0 to T.

---

[4]In physics this formula occurs as an example of "radioactive decay." If one unit of a substance decays continuously at the rate δ, then after T periods, $e^{-\delta T}$ will remain. This amount never exactly reaches zero no matter how large T is.

The value of this definite integral is given by

$$PDV = \frac{-e^{-rt}}{r} \bigg|_0^T$$

$$= \frac{-e^{-rT}}{r} + \frac{1}{r}. \tag{23A.17}$$

If we let T go to infinity, this value becomes

$$PDV = \frac{1}{r}, \tag{23A.18}$$

as was the case for the infinitely long annuity considered in the discrete case.

Continuous discounting is particularly convenient for calculating the PDV of an arbitrary stream of payments over time. Suppose that $f(t)$ records the number of dollars to be paid during period t. Then the PDV of the payment at time T is

$$e^{-rT}f(T), \tag{23A.19}$$

and the PDV of the entire stream from the present time (year 0) until year T is given by

$$\int_0^T f(t)e^{-rt}dt. \tag{23A.20}$$

Frequently, economic agents may seek to maximize an expression such as that given in Equation 23A.20. Use of continuous time makes the analysis of such choices straightforward because standard differential calculus methods of maximization can be used.

Appendix B to Chapter 23

Control Theory and Optimal Resource Allocation over Time

The theory of capital developed in Chapter 23 was concerned primarily with the allocation of resources over time. We demonstrated how firms and individuals are led to set aside some portion of current production as capital accumulation in order to produce more in future periods. Many economic problems are of this general type: Economic agents must make decisions about additions to or reductions in the level of some stock, and those decisions will affect both current and future well-being. In this appendix we shall examine how such decisions might be made in an optimal (that is, utility-maximizing) way. We first present a general mathematical model of the accumulation process and show the conditions that must hold for an optimal solution. This model of optimal allocation is then applied to two simple examples: capital accumulation and the use of nonrenewable natural resources. Each of these examples shows the important role that prices and interest rates play in intertemporal resource allocation.

THE MATHE-MATICAL MODEL

Two variables are of primary interest for the problem of allocating resources over time: the stock being allocated (K) and a "control" variable (C) being used to effect increases or decreases in K. For our present discussion it is helpful to think of K as the capital stock, with C representing either the savings rate or total net investment, but many other interpretations arise in economics. Since these variables obviously will take on different values in different periods, they should be denoted as functions of time [($K(t)$ and $C(t)$]. For most of our development, however, it will be convenient not to record this functional dependence on time explicitly.

Choices of K and C will yield benefits over time to the economic agents involved. Those benefits at any point of time will be denoted by $U(K, C, t)$. The agents' goal is to maximize

$$\int_0^T U(K, C, t)dt, \tag{23B.1}$$

where T denotes the time period over which decisions are to be made.

There are two types of constraints in this problem. The first shows the rules by which K changes over time:

$$\frac{dK}{dt} = f(K, C, t). \tag{23B.2}$$

Here the notation indicates that changes in K will depend on the level of that variable itself, on the control decisions made (C), and (possibly) on the particular point in time being observed. In order to avoid cumbersome notation, we shall adopt the convention of denoting the time derivative of any variable, X, by $\dot{X}$. Hence the constraint given in Equation 23B.2 will be written as

$$\frac{dK}{dt} = \dot{K} = f(K, C, t). \tag{23B.3}$$

A second type of constraint in this maximization problem concerns initial and terminal conditions specified for the stock K. At the start of the problem, K will exist as a piece of historical data that cannot be altered, and at the conclusion of the planning period, some other type of requirement may be placed on K (for example, that K be zero). We shall write these end point constraints as

$$K(0) = K_0$$
$$K(T) = K_T, \tag{23B.4}$$

where the particular value of the constants K_0 and K_T will depend on the nature of the problem being analyzed.

Equations 23B.1, 23B.3, and 23B.4 therefore constitute the principal maximization problem to be examined in this appendix. We now proceed to show how this problem might be solved.

Maximum Principle: An Intuitive Approach

The dynamic optimization problem we have described requires that we find an optimum time path for the variables K and C. That is a considerably more difficult problem than other maximization problems discussed in this book, for which we required discovery of only a single optimal point rather than an entire time path of points. Our strategy for finding a solution is to convert the dynamic problem into a "single-period" problem and then show how the solution to that simplified problem for any arbitrary point in time solves the dynamic problem as well.

To convert the dynamic problem to a single-period problem, we start by recognizing that any current decision about how the stock of K should be changed will affect both current and future well-being. An optimal choice that uses C to effect current changes in K should balance the current costs of changing K against the future benefits of changing K and vice versa. To aid in this balancing process, we introduce a Lagrangian-type multiplier, $\lambda(t)$, which can be interpreted as the marginal change in future benefits brought about by a one-unit change in K. Therefore $\lambda(t)$ is a measure of the (marginal) value of the stock K at the current time t. That variable (as in our other maximization problems) permits a solution that balances benefits and costs of current decisions.

Having in this way converted the dynamic problem to a single-period one, it remains to reformulate the solution in a dynamic context. That reformulation consists of showing how $\lambda(t)$ must change over time so as to (1) keep changes in K occurring in an optimal way and (2) assure that the end point conditions on K (Equation 23B.4) are satisfied. Such a final solution will then provide a time path of values for C and K that maximizes the integral given in Equation 23B.1. As an additional feature, the optimal solution will also provide a time path for the multiplier λ that will show how the marginal evaluation of K (that is, its price) changes over time.

To proceed formally in the manner sketched in the previous section, we introduce the multiplier $\lambda(t)$ as a measure of the marginal value of the stock K at any instant. Hence the total value of the stock is given by $\lambda(t)K$ and the rate of change in this value (that is, the value of gains or losses being experienced in the capital stock) is given by

$$\frac{d\lambda(t)K}{dt} = \lambda \frac{dK}{dt} + K \frac{d\lambda}{dt} = \lambda \dot{K} + K \dot{\lambda}. \tag{23B.5}$$

Hence the total net value of utility at any time (including any effect that current changes in $\dot{K}$ may have—this is what permits this single-period problem to reflect many periods) is given by

$$H = U(K, C, t) + \lambda \dot{K} + K \dot{\lambda}, \tag{23B.6}$$

where we have labeled this expression "H" to indicate its similarity to the "Hamiltonian" function encountered in formal dynamic optimization theory.[1] The function H is in some ways similar to the Lagrangian expression we have used repeatedly to solve maximization problems elsewhere in this book.

The first-order condition for choosing C to maximize H is

$$\frac{\partial H}{\partial C} = \frac{\partial U(K, C, t)}{dC} + \lambda \frac{\partial \dot{K}}{\partial C} = 0, \tag{23B.7}$$

since λ and K (as opposed to $\dot{K}$) are not dependent on C. Rewriting this first optimal condition yields

$$\frac{\partial U}{\partial C} = -\lambda \frac{\partial \dot{K}}{\partial C}. \tag{23B.8}$$

In words, for C to be optimally chosen it must be the case that the marginal change in U from increasing C is exactly balanced by any effect that such an increase has on changes in the stock of K (where such changes are evaluated at the margin by λ).

Having chosen C to maximize our comprehensive single-period measure of utility, it is now necessary to focus on how the marginal valuation of K (that is, λ) should change over time. We can do that by asking what level of K would maximize H. Of course, in actuality K is not a choice variable at any instant—its value is determined by past history. But by "pretending" that K is at its optimal value, we can infer what the behavior of λ must be. Differentiation of H with respect to K yields

$$\frac{\partial H}{\partial K} = \frac{\partial U}{\partial K} + \lambda \frac{\partial \dot{K}}{\partial K} + \dot{\lambda} = 0 \tag{23B.9}$$

as a first-order condition for a maximum. Rearranging terms gives

---

[1]The usual Hamiltonian omits the final term in Equation 23B.6. See L. S. Pontryagin et al., *The Mathematical Theory of Optimal Processes* (New York: Interscience Publishers, 1972).

$$-\dot{\lambda} = \frac{\partial U}{\partial K} + \lambda \frac{\partial \dot{K}}{\partial K}. \tag{23B.10}$$

This expression can be interpreted as saying that any change in the marginal valuation of K must counterbalance the net productivity of K in either changing U or in changing $\dot{K}$. The value of K should be changing in a way opposite to that in which K itself imparts present and future benefits.

Bringing together the two optimal conditions, we have

$$\frac{\partial H}{\partial C} = \frac{\partial U}{\partial C} + \lambda \frac{\partial \dot{K}}{\partial C} = 0$$

$$\frac{\partial H}{\partial K} = \frac{\partial U}{\partial K} + \lambda \frac{\partial \dot{K}}{\partial K} + \dot{\lambda} = 0. \tag{23B.11}$$

These show how C and λ should evolve over time so as to keep K on its optimal path.[2] Once the system of equations is started in motion, the entire time path of the relevant variables is determined. To provide a complete solution, it is also necessary to make sure that the path of K is "feasible" in that it obeys the end point conditions of Equation 23B.4. This can usually be accomplished by adjusting the initial values for C and λ to some appropriate levels. These adjustments are quite important in applied dynamic optimization problems, but we shall not discuss them in detail here.

CAPITAL ACCUMULATION

The problem of capital accumulation over time provides one of the most straightforward applications of the optimal control problem we have described. Here we shall examine that problem in a very simple form.[3] Suppose that the population of a particular society is fixed and that the society receives utility from consumption, $C(t)$, in each period. If the society's rate of time preference is given by r, then an appropriate goal is to choose a path of capital accumulation that maximizes

$$\int_0^T e^{-rt} C(t)\, dt. \tag{23B.12}$$

To establish the constraints in this problem, first note that total output in each period (Q) depends on the quantity of capital (K) available for production:

$$Q = Q(K). \tag{23B.13}$$

Since the quantity of labor is fixed, it is reasonable to assume that capital exhibits a diminishing marginal productivity; that is, $\partial^2 Q / \partial K^2$ is negative.

Total output may be devoted to either consumption or gross investment. If it is assumed that capital depreciates at a proportional rate d, then the change in the capital stock at any point of time is given by

---

[2] These are only first-order conditions for a maximum. We shall not discuss second-order conditions here.

[3] For an early attempt to solve a problem of this type, see F. P. Ramsey, "A Mathematical Theory of Saving," *Economic Journal* 38 (December 1928): 542–559.

$$\dot{K} = Q - C - dK. \tag{23B.14}$$

Equation 23B.14 provides the "laws of motion" for the economy we have described; it is analogous to the general constraint introduced previously in Equation 23B.3. As we pointed out earlier, most optimal control problems also specify end point constraints, and we shall return to discuss those constraints briefly at the conclusion of our analysis of this problem.

We can now set up the Hamiltonian expression:

$$
\begin{aligned}
H &= e^{-rt}C + \lambda \dot{K} + \dot{\lambda} K \\
  &= e^{-rt}C + \lambda(Q - C - dK) + \dot{\lambda} K.
\end{aligned}
\tag{23B.15}
$$

From Equation 23B.11, the first-order conditions for an optimal time path are

$$\frac{\partial H}{\partial C} = e^{-rt} - \lambda = 0 \tag{23B.16}$$

$$\frac{\partial H}{\partial K} = \lambda \left(\frac{\partial Q}{\partial K} - d \right) + \dot{\lambda} = 0. \tag{23B.17}$$

The first of these equations shows that the marginal value (or "shadow price") of capital, λ, should equal the marginal value of consumption. Since consumption is continuously discounted by the factor e^{-rt}, the shadow price of capital should follow a similar path. This will ensure that the marginal contribution to utility of a unit of output devoted to current consumption is equal to the marginal utility contribution that unit of output would make to capital accumulation (and hence to future consumption).

Equation 23B.17 may be rewritten as

$$\frac{\partial Q}{\partial K} = -\frac{\dot{\lambda}}{\lambda} + d \tag{23B.18}$$

or, using Equation 23B.16 to solve for λ,

$$\frac{\partial Q}{\partial K} = r + d. \tag{23B.19}$$

In other words, the shadow price of capital should change over time so as to equate the marginal productivity of capital to $r + d$. The net output gain from having one more unit of capital should equal the sum of two costs: those related to the opportunity cost of forgone consumption, r, and those related to the physical deterioration of capital, d. This result closely resembles the equilibrium condition for perfectly competitive capital markets discussed in Chapter 23 (see especially Equation 23.34).[4]

The conditions 23B.16 and 23B.17 (together with the constraint 23B.14) therefore describe the optimal evolution of our simple economy through time.

---

[4] Equation 23.34 reduces to Equation 23B.19 for the present case, since in the present problem K and C are components of homogeneous total output (Q), and hence the relative price of a unit of K is 1.

Figure 23.B1   *Optimal Capital Accumulation Paths for Simple Economy*

The optimal path for this simple economy occurs at K^*, C^*. If the initial capital stock departs from K^*, then C should be chosen so that K^* is reached as quickly as possible.

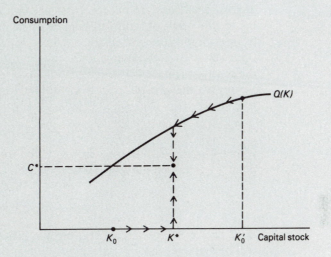

Figure 23B.1 illustrates this evolution in the K–C plane. The value of K for which Equation 23B.19 holds is K^*. That is, the "optimal" capital stock and any optimal growth path must operate to hold K constant at K^*. But if $\dot{K} = 0$, this implies (by Equation 23B.14) that

$$0 = Q(K^*) - C - dK^* \qquad (23B.20)$$

or

$$C^* = Q(K^*) - dK^*.$$

In other words, C must be chosen to be C^* so as to keep the capital stock constant. The optimal path of this economy therefore is the single point K^*, C^*.

The effect of end point constraints can be illustrated in Figure 23B.1. Suppose that the initial capital stock, K_0, is smaller than K^*. Then it is optimal initially to set $C = 0$ and have K grow as rapidly as possible. Once K reaches K^*, consumption should be increased to C^*. Similarly, if the initial capital stock, K_0', exceeds K^*, it is optimal to consume all output [by setting $C = Q(K)$ at each instant of time] until the capital stock is reduced to K^* through depreciation. Once K^* is reached, consumption should be reduced to its optimal level C^* so as to avoid "overshooting" the appropriate level of capital. Once at K^*, C^*, the economy may continue to operate there indefinitely. End period constraints on capital can be handled in ways identical to those used for the initial period constraints.[5]

USE OF EX-HAUSTIBLE RESOURCES

Concern with rising energy prices during the 1970s caused economists to re-examine theories of the optimal use of natural resource stocks. Of particular concern was the question of whether markets in which decisions (presumably) are based only on current supply-demand considerations are capable of providing for the needs of future consumers. Since that question necessarily involves examination of the optimal time pattern for the depletion of a fixed stock of some resource (for example, oil, coal, or iron ore), it can be examined using the control theory tools we have developed.[6]

Suppose that the (inverse) demand function for the resource in question is given by

$$P = P(C), \tag{23B.21}$$

where P is the market price and C is the total quantity consumed during a period. For any output level C the total utility from consumption is given by[7]

$$U(C) = \int_0^C P(c)dc. \tag{23B.22}$$

If the rate of time preference is given by r, the optimal pattern of resource usage will be that one which maximizes

$$\int_0^T e^{-rt}U(C)dt. \tag{23B.23}$$

The constraints in this problem are again of two types. First, since the stock of the resource is fixed, that stock is reduced each period by the level of consumption:

$$\dot{K} = -C. \tag{23B.24}$$

In addition to this rule for changes in K, the stock of resources must also obey the end point constraints:

$$K(0) = K_0$$

and   (23B.25)

$$K(T) = K_T.$$

---

[5] The "all-or-nothing"-type rules for consumption decisions result from the oversimplified nature of this problem. In more complex cases optimal paths will approach K^*, C^* in a continuous manner.

[6] The model developed here can be readily generalized to the case of renewable resources such as timber or fish.

[7] We have assumed here that there are no extraction costs associated with consumption. It would be a straightforward matter to develop a theory for the case when such costs are significant. The notion of total utility being the area under the compensated demand curve (Equation 23B.22) was first discussed in connection with consumers' surplus in Chapter 5.

Usually the initial stock, K_0, will represent the quantity of current "known reserves" of the resource, whereas the terminal stock, K_T, will be zero (assuming that resources left in the ground have no value).

Setting up the Hamiltonian,

$$H = e^{-rt}(U) + \lambda \dot{K} + \dot{\lambda} K \qquad (23B.26)$$
$$= e^{-rt}(U) - \lambda C + \dot{\lambda} K,$$

yields the following first-order conditions for a maximum:

$$\frac{\partial H}{\partial C} = e^{-rt}\frac{\partial U}{\partial C} - \lambda = 0 \qquad (23B.27)$$

$$\frac{\partial H}{\partial K} = \dot{\lambda} = 0. \qquad (23B.28)$$

The second equation illustrates the important result that in this problem, the shadow price of the resource should stay constant over time. Because we are allocating a fixed stock, any path in which the resource had a higher shadow price in one period than in another could be improved upon (in terms of providing more utility) by reducing consumption in the period in which the shadow price is high and increasing consumption in the period in which it is low.[8]

To interpret the first condition, Equation 23B.22 can be used to show that

$$\frac{\partial U}{\partial C} = P(C), \qquad (23B.29)$$

and hence, substituting into Equation 23B.27,

$$e^{-rt}P(C) = \lambda. \qquad (23B.30)$$

Since we know from our previous discussion that λ must be constant, this equation requires that the path for C be chosen so that market price rises at the rate r per period. That is precisely the sort of solution that would emerge in a competitive market. For any resource to provide an investment that is in equilibrium with other alternatives, its price must rise at the rate of interest. Any slower rate of price increase would prompt investors to put their funds into some alternative form of capital, whereas any faster rate would draw all available funds into investments in the resource. This result therefore suggests that at least in this simple case, competitive markets will allocate natural resources efficiently over time.

End period constraints in the natural resource case are usually handled by examining those that relate to terminal period stocks. If the resource stock is to be fully depleted, then it is required that the final period price, $P(T)$, be such

[8] One of the first authors to recognize this fundamental point was H. Hotelling, in his path-breaking article, "The Economics of Exhaustible Resources," *Journal of Political Economy* 39 (April 1931): 137–175.

that demand becomes zero at that price. In most applications such a price can be found by setting it high enough so that substitutes for the resource in question totally dominate the market. For example, if it were known that solar power would totally replace petroleum energy sources in the year 2010 if oil in that year sold for more than $50 per barrel, then $50 would be the terminal price. Using that price together with Equation 23B.30, the entire time path of prices can be computed [including the initial price $P(0)$].

One final aspect of this resource-pricing problem should be noted. Throughout we have assumed that extraction costs are zero, but that should not be taken to imply that use of the resource itself is "costless." Current consumption of the resource implies lower future consumption, and this cost is no less real than actual production costs would be. Some authors refer to costs of this nature (those related to the fixed nature of the resource stock) as "user costs" or "scarcity costs." The costs are best measured by the shadow price of the resource stock, λ.

SUGGESTED READINGS

Dorfman, R. "An Economic Interpretation of Optimal Control Theory." *American Economic Review* 59 (December 1969): 817–831.

Uses the approach of this appendix to examine optimal capital accumulation. Excellent, intuitive introduction.

Hotelling, H. "The Economics of Exhaustible Resources." *Journal of Political Economy* 39 (April 1931): 137–175.

Fundamental work on allocation of natural resources. Analyzes both competitive and monopoly cases.

Kendrick, D. "Control Theory with Applications to Economics." In K. J. Arrow and M. D. Intriligator, eds., *Handbook of Mathematical Economics*, vol. 1. Amsterdam, North Holland Publishing Co., 1981. Pp. 111–158.

Mathematically sophisticated treatment of control theory. Good set of references to the applied literature.

Ramsey, F. P. "A Mathematical Theory of Saving." *Economic Journal* 38 (December 1928): 542–559.

One of the first uses of the calculus of variations to solve economic problems.

Scott, A. D. "Notes on User Cost." *Economic Journal* 63 (June 1953): 368–384.

Basic methodological note concerning scarcity costs.

Solow, R. M. "The Economics of Resources or the Resources of Economics." *American Economic Review Papers and Proceedings* 64 (May 1974): 1–14.

AEA presidential address. Very readable, even entertaining.

PART

VIII

Limits of the Market

Prior sections of this book have focused at length on the ways in which markets allocate resources. Although the equilibria described were not always efficient, they were arrived at through some type of interaction of the forces of supply and demand. Only on a few occasions (for example, in our discussion of the regulation of natural monopolies) have we analyzed how nonmarket actors (for example, government regulators) might affect observed outcomes. In this final part, we will move away somewhat from our examination of market forces and explore some situations where nonmarket influences may be quite important. We will show that, for

some allocational questions, markets will perform relatively poorly and other economic institutions (most importantly, the government) may play decisive, though not necessarily better, allocational roles.

Chapter 24 addresses problems raised by goods that have externality or spillover effects. For these goods simple market transactions may not accurately reflect all of the economic consequences of consumption and production—some misallocations of resources may occur. In Chapter 24 we examine two common situations of such occurrences. First, we look at externalities between two specific economic actors such as a manufacturing firm that harms nearby residents because it pollutes the air. We show how this situation can be viewed as a failure to define property rights fully and how full specification of such rights may improve the resulting allocation of resources.

Our second example of externalities concerns goods that benefit a large number of individuals who cannot be prevented from receiving such benefits. Such goods are called "public goods." Besides examining in detail the attributes of such goods, we also investigate some of the problems involved in achieving an efficient level of output for them.

Chapter 25, the final chapter in this text, focuses on social choice theory. In its most general statement, this theory is concerned with how choices are made in a nonmarket context—especially through voting. More specifically, social choice theory is primarily concerned with modeling the operation of voting for governmental decisions when many other allocational decisions are made using market mechanisms. We show that the Pareto optimality of voting procedures is open to question in many important cases.

CHAPTER 24

Externalities and Public Goods

In Chapter 17 we showed that a number of problems may interfere with the allocational efficiency of perfectly competitive markets. Here we will examine two of those problems, externalities and public goods, in more detail. This examination has two purposes. First, we wish to show clearly why the existence of externalities and public goods may distort the allocation of resources. In so doing it will be possible to illustrate some additional features of the type of information that is provided by competitive prices and some of the circumstances that may diminish the usefulness of that information. Our second reason for looking more closely at externalities and public goods is to suggest ways in which the allocational problems they pose might be mitigated. We will see that, at least in some cases, the efficiency of competitive market outcomes may be more robust than might at first have been anticipated.

DEFINING EXTERNALITIES

Externalities occur because economic agents have effects on each other's activities that are not reflected in market transactions. Chemical makers spewing toxic fumes on their neighbors, jet planes waking up people, or motorists littering the highway are, from an economic point of view, all engaging in the same sort of activity—they are having a direct effect on the well-being of others that is outside traditional market channels. Such activities might be contrasted to effects that take place directly through markets. When I choose to purchase a steak, for example, I (perhaps imperceptibly) raise the price of steak generally and that may affect the well-being of other steak buyers. But such effects, because they are captured in market prices, are not true externalities and do not affect the market's ability to allocate resources efficiently.[1] Rather, the rise in the price of steak that results from my increased purchase is an accurate reflection of societal preferences, and the price rise helps to assure that the right mix

---

[1] Sometimes effects of one economic agent on another that take place through the market system are termed "pecuniary" externalities to differentiate such effects from the "technological" externalities we are discussing. Here the use of the term "externalities" will refer only to the latter type, since these are the only type with consequences for the efficiency of resource allocation.

of products is produced. However, that is not the case for untaxed toxic chemical discharges, jet noise, or litter. In these cases, market prices (of chemicals, air travel, or disposable containers) may not accurately reflect society's preferences for these activities because they may take no account of the damage being done to third parties. Information being conveyed by the prices is fundamentally inaccurate, leading to a misallocation of resources.

As a summary, therefore, we have developed the following:

Definition:

Externality

An *externality* occurs whenever the activities of one economic agent affect the activities of another agent in ways that are not taken into account by the operation of the market.

Before analyzing in detail why failing to take externalities into account can lead to a misallocation of resources, we will examine a few examples that may clarify the nature of the problem.

Interfirm Externalities

To illustrate the externality issue in its simplest form, consider two firms—one producing good X and the other producing good Y—where each firm uses only a single input, labor. The production of good Y is said to have an external effect on the production of X if the output of X depends not only on the amount of labor chosen by the X-entrepreneur but also on the level at which the production of Y is carried on. Notationally, the production function for good X can be written as

$$X = f(L_X; Y), \tag{24.1}$$

where L_X denotes the amount of labor devoted to good X, and Y appears to the right of the semicolon in the equation to show that it is an effect on production over which the X-entrepreneur has no control.[2] As an example, suppose that the two firms are located on a river, with firm X being downstream from Y. Suppose that firm Y pollutes the river in its productive process. Then the output of firm X may depend not only on the level of inputs it uses itself but also on the amount of pollutants flowing past its factory. The level of pollutants, in turn, is determined by the output of firm Y. In the production function shown by Equation 24.1, the output of firm Y would have a negative marginal physical productivity $\partial X/\partial Y < 0$. Increases in Y output would cause less X to be produced. In the next section we shall return to analyze this case more fully as it is representative of most simple types of externalities.

Beneficial Externalities

The relationship between two firms may be beneficial. Most examples of such positive externalities are rather bucolic in nature. Perhaps the most famous, proposed by J. Meade, involves two firms, one producing honey (raising bees)

[2] We shall find it necessary to redefine the assumption of "no control" considerably as the analysis of this chapter proceeds.

and the other producing apples.[3] Because the bees feed on apple blossoms, an increase in apple production will improve productivity in the honey industry. The beneficial effects of having well-fed bees is a positive externality to the beekeeper. In the notation of Equation 24.1, $\partial X/\partial Y$ would now be positive. The usual perfectly competitive case is simply the middle ground between such positive externalities and the negative externalities in the previous example. In such a middle ground case, the productive activities of one firm have no direct effect on those of other firms: $\partial X/\partial Y = 0$.

Externalities in Utility

Externalities also can occur if the activities of an economic agent directly affect an individual's utility. Most common examples of environmental externalities are of this type. From an economic perspective it makes little difference whether such effects are created by firms (in the form, say, of toxic chemicals or jet noise) or by other individuals (litter or, perhaps, the noise from a loud radio). In all such cases the amount of such activities would enter directly into the individual's utility function in much the same way as firm Y's output entered into firm X's production function in Equation 24.1. As in the firm case, such externalities may sometimes be beneficial (you may actually like the song being played on your neighbor's radio). So, again, a situation of no externalities can be regarded as simply the middle ground in which other agents' activities have no direct effect on individuals' utilities.

One special type of utility externality that is relevant to our analysis of social choices in Chapter 25 arises when one individual's utility depends directly on the utility of someone else. If, for example, Smith cares about Jones's welfare, we could write his or her utility function (U_S) as

$$\text{utility} = U_S(X_1, \ldots, X_n; U_J), \tag{24.2}$$

where $X_1, \ldots, X_n$ are the goods that Smith consumes and U_J is Jones's utility. If Smith is altruistic and wants Jones to be well off (as might happen if Jones were a close relative), $\partial U_S/\partial U_J$ would be positive. If, on the other hand, Smith were envious of Jones, it might be the case that $\partial U_S/\partial U_J$ would be negative; that is, improvements in Jones's utility make Smith worse off. The middle ground between altruism and envy would occur if Smith were indifferent to Jones's welfare ($\partial U_S/\partial U_J = 0$), and that is what we have usually assumed throughout this book.

Public Goods Externalities

Goods that are "public" or "collective" in nature provide a specific illustration of a type of externality that will be the focus for our analysis in the second half of this chapter. The defining characteristic of these goods is nonexclusion; that is, once the goods are produced (either by the government or by some private entity), they provide benefits to an entire group, perhaps to everyone. It is technically impossible to restrict these benefits to specific individuals who pay

[3] J. Meade, "External Economies and Diseconomies in a Competitive Situation," *Economic Journal* 62 (March 1952): 54–67. We shall return to examine Meade's example later in this chapter.

for them, so the benefits are available to all. As we mentioned in Chapter 17, national defense provides the traditional example. Once a defense system is established, all individuals in society are protected by it whether they wish to be or not and whether they pay for it or not. Later in this chapter we will explore the public goods concept in considerably greater detail.

EXTERNALITIES AND ALLOCATIVE EFFICIENCY

Traditionally, it has been argued that the presence of externalities such as those just described can cause a market to operate inefficiently. The reasons for this were discussed initially in Chapter 17 but will be repeated here by using our earlier example of the two firms located on a river. Suppose that the production function of the pollution-producing firm is given by

$$Y = g(L_Y), \tag{24.3}$$

where L_Y is the quantity of labor devoted to Y production. The production function for good X (which exhibits an externality) was given by Equation 24.1. The Pareto conditions for an optimal allocation of labor require that the social marginal revenue product of labor ($SMRP_L$) be equal for both firms. If P_X and P_Y are the prices of good X and Y, respectively, the $SMRP$ of labor in the production of good X is given by

$$SMRP_L^X = P_X \frac{\partial f}{\partial L_X}. \tag{24.4}$$

Because of the productive externality, the statement of the $SMRP$ of labor in the production of Y is somewhat more complex. An additional unit of labor employed by firm Y will produce some extra Y. But it will also produce some extra pollution, and this will reduce the production of X. Consequently,

$$SMRP_L^Y = P_Y \cdot \frac{\partial g}{\partial L_Y} + P_X \cdot \frac{\partial f}{\partial Y} \cdot \frac{\partial Y}{\partial L_Y}, \tag{24.5}$$

where the second term represents the effect that hiring additional workers in plant Y has on the value of production in plant X. This effect will be negative if $\partial f / \partial Y < 0$. Efficiency then requires that

$$SMRP_L^X = SMRP_L^Y. \tag{24.6}$$

The decentralized calculations of the two firm managers will not bring this condition about if "normal" market reactions are allowed. Firm X will hire labor up to the point at which its private marginal revenue product (MRP_L) is equal to the prevailing wage rate:

$$w = MRP_L^X = P_x \frac{\partial f}{\partial L_X}. \tag{24.7}$$

Firm Y will follow a similar course of action:

$$w = MRP_L^Y = P_Y \frac{\partial g}{\partial L_Y}. \tag{24.8}$$

The market therefore will cause

$$MRP_L^X = MRP_L^Y. \tag{24.9}$$

Now it is readily seen that this market equilibrium will ensure Pareto efficiency only if $\partial f / \partial Y = 0$ in Equation 24.5. In other words, as long as the externality exists, the managers' decisions will not bring about an optimal allocation. In our example we assumed that $\partial f / \partial Y < 0$, which implies that labor will be overallocated to the production of good Y. Labor's social marginal revenue product in the production of Y will fall short of its value in the production of X. The value of output could be increased by shifting labor from the production of Y into the production of X. If, on the other hand, we had assumed that $\partial f / \partial Y > 0$ (Meade's bees example), labor would have been underallocated to Y production.

TRADITIONAL WAYS OF COPING WITH EXTERNALITIES

The model we have been using to analyze externalities assumes that productive technologies and society's preferences regarding external costs are unchanging. Within the confines of this simple model,[4] there are still a number of potential solutions to the allocational problems posed. In this section we will examine two "traditional" solutions: taxation and internalization of costs. Then, in the next section, we will show that in some circumstances, externalities can be accommodated by the normal workings of the market and the traditional solutions may be unnecessary.

Taxation

The government could impose a suitable excise tax on the firm generating the external diseconomy. Presumably, this tax would cause the output of Y to be cut back and would cause labor to be shifted out of the production of Y. This classic remedy to the externality problem was first put forward lucidly in the 1920s by A. C. Pigou;[5] although it has been somewhat modified, it remains the "standard" answer to the externality problem given by economists. The central issue for regulators becomes one of obtaining sufficient empirical information so that the correct tax can be imposed directly on the polluting firm.

The taxation solution is illustrated conceptually in Figure 24.1. Suppose that firm Y's marginal cost curve is given by MC and that the market demand curve for Y is given by DD (ignore the curve D' for the moment). Assume also that Y's marginal social cost curve is represented by MC'. This curve differs from MC by the amount of extra costs that the production of Y imposes on others (here only firm X) in the economy. From a social point of view the optimal output of Y would be Y_2. At this output level the marginal benefit of Y's production (what people are willing to pay for the good) is exactly equal to the marginal social cost. However, the market will cause output level Y_1 to be

---

[4] For a more general treatment that allows for changing technologies to cope with externalities and for the possibility that individuals' valuation of external costs may change over time, see P. Burrows, *The Economic Theory of Pollution Control* (Cambridge, Mass.: MIT Press, 1980).

[5] A. C. Pigou, *The Economics of Welfare*, 4th ed. (London: Macmillan & Co., 1946). Pigou also stresses the desirability of providing subsidies to firms that produce beneficial externalities.

Figure 24.1   *Graphic Demonstration of the Costs of an Externality*

The demand for Y is given by the curve DD and the private marginal cost curve for Y by MC. The curve MC' records the social marginal cost of Y production. From society's point of view, therefore, Y_2 is the optimal output. However, the normal workings of the market will cause output level Y_1 to be produced. One way to force the market to allocate goods correctly would be to adopt an excise tax of amount t on the production of Y. The effect of the tax is to reduce the demand curve facing the firm from DD to D'D', and this will shift the profit-maximizing level of output from Y_1 to Y_2.

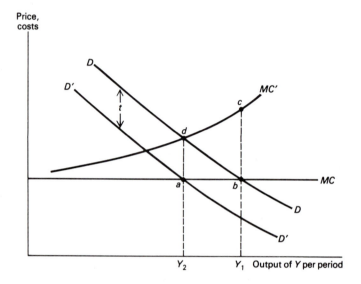

produced since, at this output, market price is equal to private marginal cost. Consequently, Y will be overproduced as we indicated previously.[6]

   A specific tax of amount t (see Chapter 14) would cause the effective demand curve for Y to shift to D'. With this new demand curve, the private profit-maximizing output will be Y_2, and this indeed will be the level of output that is socially optimal. At Y_2 the marginal external damage done by producing Y is given by the distance ad, which is precisely the amount (t) paid by the consumers of Y in the form of excise taxes. By taxing good Y the effective demand for the product has been reduced; individuals who use Y are now forced to pay for the damage that its production creates. This reduces demand and causes Y

[6] It will be convenient in our discussion to assume that firm Y acts as a perfectly *price-discriminating monopolist* in the market by selling each unit separately at the highest price it will bring. The assumption of a perfect price discriminator eliminates the need for introducing the notion of consumer surplus into this analysis, since there is in fact no such surplus (see Chapter 18). The results would not be changed materially if there were many firms such as Y in a perfectly competitive industry. In that case, however, the concept of consumers' surplus would have to be introduced explicitly. In our analysis of the next section, for example, it would be necessary to show how firm X might bribe the consumers of good Y to accept the efficient output restriction.

output to contract. Resources are shifted out of Y production, and an efficient allocation is established.

Merger and Internalization

A second traditional cure for the allocational distortions caused by the external relationship between X and Y would be for the two firms to merge. If a single firm were operating both plants X and Y, it would recognize the detrimental effect that Y production has on the production function for good X. In effect the firm (X + Y) would now pay the full social marginal costs of Y production because it also produces X. In other words, the firm's manager would now take the marginal cost curve for Y production to be MC' and would produce at the point where

$$P_Y = MC', \tag{24.10}$$

which is exactly what is required for efficiency. Economists would say that the externality in Y production has been internalized as a result of the merger.

Attempts to internalize externalities in production are quite common. Often an organization will expand in size with the purpose of encompassing all the spillover effects of its activities. Firms, for example, may merge in an attempt to capture external benefits. Recreational site developers (ski areas, golf courses, resort hotels) often operate the service industries (motels, gas stations, shops) near their projects. In this way they are able to internalize the positive benefits that such developments provide to the service industries. Another important example of attempting to internalize external effects is the recent move toward the creation of regional metropolitan governments. It has been argued that geographically limited city governments cannot handle many current urban problems because these problems spill over into neighboring communities. New York City's air pollution problems, for example, are not confined to the city itself but affect communities in New Jersey and Connecticut as well. New York City also provides benefits to neighboring communities by acting as a commercial and cultural center. Since many of the individuals who benefit from having such activities available do not live or work in New York City, there is no feasible way to get them to support the central city through taxes. By adopting a regional government, all such spillover effects would be internalized and policies that were optimal from a regional point of view could be pursued.

PROPERTY RIGHTS, ALLOCATION, AND THE COASE THEOREM

One important question we might still ask about this analysis is if firm Y's actions impose a cost on firm X, why doesn't firm X bribe firm Y to cut back on its output? Presumably, the gain of such a cutback to firm X (area *abcd* in Figure 24.1) would exceed the loss of profits to firm Y (area *abd*—remember the assumption in footnote 6 that firm Y is a perfect price discriminator), and some bargaining arrangement might be worked out that would monetarily benefit both parties. Both firms would be irrational not to recognize such a possibility, and it would seem that the benefits of internalization could be obtained without the necessity of a merger.

Property Rights

We can gain additional insights into these possibilities for bargaining by introducing the concept of property rights:

Definition:

Property Rights
Property rights establish the legal owner of a resource and specify the ways in which the resource may be used.

Two major types of property rights' specifications are "common" property and "private" property. Common property is, by definition, owned by "society at large": No individual may appropriate such a resource solely for his or her own use. Private property, on the other hand, is directly owned by individuals who have, within prevailing legal strictures, some say over how it is used. Private property may either be *exchangeable* or *nonexchangeable*, depending on whether the good in question may or may not be traded. In this book we have been concerned primarily with exchangeable private property, and these are the types of property rights that we shall consider here.[7]

The Coase Theorem and Allocation

For the purposes of the two-firm externality example, it is interesting to consider the nature of the property right that might be attached to the river shared by the firms. Suppose that property rights were defined so as to give "ownership" of the river to one of the firms but that the firms were free to bargain over how the river might be used. It might be thought that if the ownership of the river were given to firm Y, pollution would result, whereas if the right were given to firm X, the river would remain pure. This might not be the case, however, because such a conclusion disregards the bargains that might be reached by the two parties. Indeed, several authors have argued that if bargaining is costless, the two parties left on their own will arrive at the efficient output (Y_2), and this result will be independent of who "owns" the river. We now demonstrate this result, which is sometimes termed the Coase theorem, after the economist who first proposed it.[8]

If, for example, firm Y owns the river, it must then impute some cost of this ownership into its cost function. What are the costs associated with river ownership? Again the opportunity cost doctrine provides the answer: The costs are what the river would bring in its next best alternative use. In the problem, only firm X has some alternative use for the river (to keep it clean); the amount that this firm would be willing to pay for a clean river is equal to the external damage done by the pollution. Consequently, if firm Y calculates its costs correctly, its marginal cost curve (including the cost of river ownership) becomes

---

[7] Two important examples of privately owned goods that are not exchangeable are an individual's human capital (this could be sold only in a society that permitted slavery) and an individual's vote (a private good that is provided by the state). Some property may be only "partly" sold. For example, some land plots are sold, but the original owner retains "mineral rights" on those plots. Similarly, governments may buy "development rights" from farmers to ensure that their land remains in agricultural production. These examples clearly point out that the nature of the property right attached to a good is determined within the legal framework of society.

[8] See R. Coase, "The Problem of Social Cost," *Journal of Law and Economics* 3 (October 1960): 1–44.

MC' in Figure 24.1. Firm Y therefore will produce Y_2 and sell the remaining rights of river use to firm X for a fee of some amount between *abd* (Y's lost profits from producing Y_2 rather than Y_1) and *abcd* (the maximum amount X would pay to avoid having Y increased from Y_2 to Y_1).

A similar allocation would result if firm X owned the rights to the river. In this case, firm Y would be willing to pay any amount up to the total profits it earns from production for the right to pollute the river. Firm X will accept these payments as long as they exceed the costs imposed on it by the river pollution. The ultimate result of bargaining will be for firm Y to offer a payment to firm X for the use of the river in dumping pollution associated with output level Y_2. Firm X will not sell the rights to dump any further pollution because what firm Y would be willing to pay falls short of the cost of additional pollution to firm X. Again the efficient point can be reached by relying on free bargaining between the two firms. Notice that in both situations, some production of Y takes place, and there will be some pollution. Having no Y output (and no pollution) would be inefficient in the same sense that producing Y_1 is: Scarce resources would not be efficiently allocated. The example shows (by relying on the opportunity cost doctrine) that there is some "optimal" level of pollution and that this level may be achieved through bargains between the individuals involved.

The effect of this demonstration is startling. Traditional arguments, at least within this simple model, have been shown to be wrong in their assertions that markets cannot accommodate externalities. When a broad enough view of the possibility for mutually beneficial exchange is taken, the allocation difficulties raised by the externality are readily handled by bargaining between the individuals involved. Even more interesting is the fact that the market allocation of the use of the river is independent of the actual ownership of the river. The description of the allocation process is completely symmetrical, and the results are identical to those that would prevail if an "ideal" merger were to take place.

Distributional Effects

There are distributional effects that do depend on who is assigned ownership of the river. If both firms appear in court demanding property rights to the river, the court's decision on how these rights should be assigned will have important distributional effects. If firm Y is given ownership of the river, its owners will be better off than they would be if firm X were the owner. Because, in our example, allocation will be unaffected by the way in which property rights are assigned,[9] any assessment of the desirability of certain assignments must be made on equity grounds. For example, if the owners of firm Y were very wealthy and those of firm X poor, we might argue that ownership should be given to firm X on the basis of distributional equity. The price system, in

---

[9] This conclusion requires that the changing distribution of wealth implied by different assignments of property rights has no effect on the allocation of goods. Loosely speaking, it is assumed that the demand and cost curves of Figure 24.1 will not shift in response to the changing distribution of wealth. It is assumed that "income effects" are unimportant.

principle, may be capable of solving certain simple externality problems of allocation, but, as always, the price system cannot deal with problems of equity.[10]

It should be pointed out, however, that the issue of equity in the assignment of property rights arises in every allocational decision, not only in the study of externalities. The issue of which firm should be assigned ownership of the river is not essentially different from the question of which individual has the right of ownership to a particular house. In either case a government could decide that the prevailing system of property rights is undesirable and therefore might redefine those rights. The issue of income distribution is no more intertwined with the problem of externalities than it is with any other question about existing property ownership.

Relevance of the Coase Theorem

It should be repeated that the results of this section depend crucially on the assumption that bargaining is costless. If there were costs associated with striking bargains, we would have to compare those costs to the potential allocational gains from Coase bargaining. Only in situations where those gains exceed necessary bargaining costs will Coase-type results hold. When bargaining costs are high, externalities will continue to distort the allocation of resources, and the assignment of property rights can have a major effect on that allocation. If major industries are given the right to spew noxious fumes into the atmosphere, for example, an efficient allocation is unlikely to emerge, since the costs of bringing together into an effective bargaining unit all the individuals harmed by such fumes are probably quite high. Nevertheless, development of the Coase theorem and the later research based on it has had a major impact on the way economists think about the relationship among externalities, property rights, and the efficient allocation of resources. Some empirical illustrations of this relationship are provided in the application at the end of this chapter.

ATTRIBUTES OF PUBLIC GOODS

We now turn our attention to an additional set of problems about the relationship between competitive markets and the allocation of resources—those raised by the existence of public goods. We begin by providing a precise definition of this concept and then examine why such goods pose allocational problems. We then briefly discuss potential ways in which such problems might be mitigated. In the final chapter in this book, we offer a few warnings about the normative value of some of these prescriptions and stress the need for a positive, behavioral theory of government before attempting to draw policy conclusions about public goods production.

---

[10] Matters of equity cannot be established here on *a priori* grounds but, rather, require a detailed examination of the welfare level of each agent. It would be inappropriate to argue, for example, that firm Y has an inalienable right to the use of the river or, conversely, that firm X has a basic right to clean water. Since firm Y's actions affect only firm X, no such *a priori* conclusions are possible. The desires of the two firms are strictly competitive, and any arguments about the intrinsic rights of one party can be applied symmetrically to the other. For some fascinating examples of this symmetry in legal cases, see Coase, "Problem of Social Cost," 1–44.

The most common definitions of public goods stress two attributes of such goods: nonexclusivity and nonrivalness. We now turn to describe these attributes in detail.

Nonexclusivity

The first property that distinguishes public goods concerns whether individuals may be excluded from the benefits of consuming the good. For most private goods such exclusion is indeed possible: I easily can be excluded from consuming a hamburger if I don't pay for it. In some cases, however, such exclusion is either very costly or impossible. National defense is the standard example. Once a defense system is established, everyone in a country benefits from it whether they pay for it or not. Similar comments apply, on a more local level, to goods such as mosquito control or inoculation against disease programs. In these cases, once the programs are implemented, no one in the community can be excluded from those benefits whether he or she pays for them or not. Again, public goods might be contrasted to excludable private consumption goods (such as food, automobiles, and motion pictures), for which exclusion is a simple matter. Those who do not pay for such goods do not receive the services they promise. Hence we can divide goods into two categories according to the following definition.

Definition:

Exclusive Goods

A good is *exclusive* if it is relatively easy to exclude individuals from benefiting from the good once it is produced. A good is nonexclusive if it is impossible, or very costly, to exclude individuals from benefiting from the good.

Nonrivalry

A second property that characterizes some public goods is nonrivalry. A nonrival good is one for which additional units can be consumed at zero marginal social cost. For most goods, of course, consumption of additional amounts involves some marginal costs of production. Consumption of one more hot dog by someone, for example, requires that various resources be devoted to its production. For certain goods, however, this is not the case. Consider, for example, having one more automobile cross a highway bridge during an off-peak period. Since the bridge is already in place, having one more vehicle cross requires no additional resource use and does not reduce consumption elsewhere. Similarly, having one more viewer tune in to a television channel involves no additional cost, even though this action would result in additional consumption taking place. Therefore we have developed the following:

Definition:

Nonrival Goods

A good is *nonrival* if consumption of additional units of the good involves zero marginal social costs of production.

Table 24.1   *Examples Showing Typology of Public and Private Goods*

		Exclusive	
		Yes	**No**
Rival	*Yes*	Hot dogs, automobiles, houses	Fishing grounds, public grazing land, clean air
	No	Bridges, swimming pools, satellite television transmission (scrambled)	National defense, mosquito control, justice

Typology of Public Goods

The concepts of nonexclusion and nonrivalry are in some ways related. Many goods that are nonexclusive are also nonrival. National defense and mosquito control are two examples of goods for which exclusion is not possible and additional consumption takes place at zero marginal cost. Many other instances might be suggested. The concepts, however, are not identical: Some goods may possess one property, but not the other. It is, for example, impossible (or at least very costly) to exclude some fishing boats from ocean fisheries, yet arrival of another boat clearly imposes social costs in the form of a reduced catch for all concerned. Similarly, use of a bridge during off-peak hours may be nonrival, but it is possible to exclude potential users by erecting toll booths. Table 24.1 presents a cross-classification of goods by their possibilities for exclusion and their rivalry. Several examples of goods that fit into each of the categories are provided. Many of the examples other than those in the upper left corner of the table (exclusive, rival private goods) are often produced by the government. However, most economists focus on nonexclusion as the defining characteristic of "public goods" since, as will be described below, those goods pose the most significant problems for resource allocation in a market economy. Nonrival goods often are privately produced (there are, after all, private bridges, swimming pools, and highways that consumers must pay to use) as long as nonpayers can be excluded from consuming them.[11] Hence we will use the following narrow definition:

[11] Nonrival goods that permit imposition of an exclusion mechanism are sometimes referred to as *club goods* since provision of such goods might be organized along the lines of private clubs. Such clubs might then charge a "membership" fee and permit unlimited use by members. The optimal size of a club is determined by the economies of scale present in the production process for the club good. For an analysis, see R. Cornes and T. Sandler, *The Theory of Externalities, Public Goods, and Club Goods* (Cambridge: Cambridge University Press, 1986).

Definition:

Public Good

A good is a (pure) *public good* if, once produced, no one can be excluded from benefiting from its availability. Public goods usually also will be nonrival, but that need not always be the case.

EFFICIENT PROVISION OF PUBLIC GOODS

Our definition of "public goods" offers a clear illustration of why private markets may not produce such goods in adequate amounts. Purchasers of exclusive private goods can appropriate the benefits of those goods entirely for themselves. Smith's pork chop, for example, yields no benefits to Jones. The resources that were used to produce the pork chop can be seen as contributing only to Smith's utility, and he or she is willing to pay whatever this is worth. The resource cost of a private good, then, can be "attributed" to a single individual. For a public good, this will not be the case. In buying a public good, an individual would not be able to appropriate all the benefits of the good. Since others cannot be excluded from benefiting from the good, society's utility obtained from the resources devoted to the public good will exceed the utility that accrues to the single individual who pays for the good. The resource cost cannot be attributed solely to the one purchaser. However, potential purchasers will not take the benefits that their purchases have for others into account in their expenditure decisions. Consequently, private markets will tend to underallocate resources to public goods.

The distinction between "pure" public goods and "pure" private goods can be made in a simple way by considering the conditions for efficiency that must hold in the two cases. We know that for the case of any two private goods, marginal rates of substitution must be identical for all individuals and that this common *MRS* must equal the rate at which the goods can be technically transformed in production (see Chapter 16). There is no ambiguity when we say that the social *MRS* must equal the social rate of product transformation. For the case of a (nonexclusive) public good, it is still possible to speak of the rate of product transformation of this good for some private good. Exactly the same kind of resource reallocation takes place between private and public producers as takes place between two private producers when the composition of output changes. In producing more national defense, some automobiles, say, will have to be given up, just as they would if society decided to produce more trucks. It is in defining the social marginal rate of substitution between a public good and some private good that important differences arise.

An Intuitive Analysis

Because public goods are provided on a nonexclusive basis to everyone, the social marginal utility of an additional unit of a public good is the sum of the marginal utilities of all persons benefiting from the public good. For example, suppose that a flood control plan were under consideration and assume that 100,000 individuals would benefit from the plan. Assume also that each individual would be willing to trade away the benefits that the flood control program promises in exchange for one car. Clearly, then, the social marginal rate of substitution of the flood control plan for automobiles is 1 to 100,000. In the aggregate, individuals would be willing to give up 100,000 automobiles in exchange for the benefits of flood prevention.

If left to the private market, however, the flood control program would not come into being. Suppose, for example, that the opportunity cost of producing the dams and dikes necessary for flood control is 50,000 automobiles; that is, a cutback in automobile production by 50,000 would free enough resources to produce the flood control system. Under these circumstances, it is clear that no private individuals would pay for the flood control program themselves. They would only be willing to trade 1 car for the benefits of the program, whereas production conditions would require that they be willing to trade 50,000 cars. Each individual would therefore opt for a privately owned automobile.

Such a decision is clearly inefficient from a social point of view. The social *MRS* of flood control for cars is 1 to 100,000, whereas the technical rate of product transformation is only 1 to 50,000. Looked at in a social context, flood control is a much better "buy" than automobiles; resources should be transferred into flood control up to the point at which the social *MRS* is brought into line with the technological *RPT* implied by the economy's productive abilities.

Mathematical Approach

More formally, if SMU_P denotes the social marginal utility of the public good and MU_P^i (for $i = 1, \ldots, n$) represents the marginal utility of the public good to each of the n individuals in society, then (assuming that we can somehow compare utilities)

$$SMU_P = MU_P^1 + MU_P^2 + \cdots + MU_P^n. \qquad (24.11)$$

On the other hand, all the additional benefits of the production of one more private good accrue to the individual receiving the good, say, individual i. The social marginal rate of substitution ($SMR\overset{\circ}{S}$) of the public good (P) for the private good (G) therefore is defined as

$$SMRS \quad (P \text{ for } G) = \frac{SMU_P}{MU_G^i} = \frac{MU_P^1}{MU_G^i} + \frac{MU_P^2}{MU_G^i} + \cdots + \frac{MU_P^n}{MU_G^i}, \qquad (24.12)$$

and the condition for an efficient allocation of resources requires that

$$RPT \quad (P \text{ for } G) = SMRS \quad (P \text{ for } G), \qquad (24.13)$$

where RPT (P for G) is the rate of product transformation of the public good for the private good.[12]

The efficiency condition of Equation 24.13 cannot be achieved by the work-

[12] These conditions were first demonstrated in P. A. Samuelson, "The Pure Theory of Public Expenditure," *Review of Economics and Statistics* 36 (November 1954): 387–389; and in several later articles in the same journal. An equivalent definition of the *SMRS* defines it to be the sum of the *MRS* over all individuals who benefit from the public good. Implicitly this definition asks what total quantity of private goods would individuals give up if one more public good were produced whereas the text definition measures the trade-off for one additional unit of the private good.

Figure 24.2   *Derivation of the Demand for a Public Good*

Since a public good is nonexclusive, the price that individuals are willing to pay for one more unit (their "marginal valuations") is equal to the sum of what each individual would pay. Hence, for public goods, market demand curves are derived by a vertical summation rather than the horizontal summation used in the case of private goods.

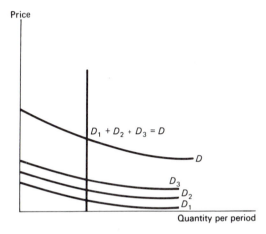

ings of the price system. Free operation of even an "ideal" perfectly competitive market will only ensure that

$$RPT \quad (P \text{ for } G) \quad = \quad MRS \quad (P \text{ for } G)$$

$$= \frac{MU_P^i}{MU_G^i} < SMRS \quad (P \text{ for } G), \tag{24.14}$$

where the final inequality sign holds as long as the public good provides some positive benefits to other individuals in addition to those provided to individual i. For this reason, the free market will tend to underallocate resources to the production of public goods.

A Graphic Analysis

Problems raised by the nonexclusive nature of public goods also can be demonstrated with partial equilibrium analysis by examining the demand curve associated with such goods. In the case of a private good the market demand curve (see Chapter 7) was found by summing individuals' demands horizontally. At any price the quantities demanded by each individual are summed to calculate the total quantity demanded in the market. The market demand curve shows the marginal evaluation that individuals place on an additional unit of output. For a public good (which is provided in fixed quantity to everyone), individual demand curves must be added vertically. To find out how society values some level of public good provision, we must ask how each individual values this level of output and then sum these valuations. This is illustrated conceptually in Figure 24.2. Here the total demand curve for the public good (DD) is the vertical sum of each individual's demand curve. Each point on the DD curve represents the social marginal evaluation of the particular level of public goods' expenditure. Producing one more unit of the public good would benefit everyone. To evaluate this benefit it is necessary to sum each individual's personal evaluation of the good. Because markets, by their nature, sum demand curves horizontally rather than vertically, Figure 24.2 again indicates why competitive markets may fail to provide public goods in adequate amounts.

LINDAHL PRICING OF PUBLIC GOODS

Since pure public goods cannot be traded efficiently in competitive markets, a number of economists have examined how such goods might be provided by the government and financed through taxation. One approach has been to investigate whether an efficient allocation of resources to public goods might come about voluntarily; that is, individuals would agree to be taxed in exchange for the benefits that the public good provides. Perhaps the clearest statement of how such an equilibrium might arise was provided by the German economist Erik Lindahl in 1919.[13] In this section we will briefly examine Lindahl's solution, showing why it is at best a conceptual answer to the public goods question.

A Graphic Approach

Lindahl's argument can be illustrated graphically for a society with only two individuals (again the ever-popular Smith and Jones). In Figure 24.3 the curve labeled *SS* shows Smith's demand for a particular public good. Rather than using the price of the public good on the vertical axis, we instead have assumed that the share of the public good's cost that Smith must pay varies from 0 percent to 100 percent. The negative slope of *SS* simply indicates that at a higher tax price for the public good, Smith will demand a smaller quantity of it.

Jones's demand for the public good is derived in much the same way. Now, however, we record the proportion paid by Jones on the right-hand vertical axis of Figure 24.3 and reverse the scale so that moving up the axis results in a lower tax price paid. Given this convention Jones's demand for the public good (*JJ*) has a positive slope.

The two demand curves in Figure 24.3 intersect at *C*, with an output level of *OE* for the public good. At this output level Smith is willing to pay, say, 60 percent of the good's cost whereas Jones pays 40 percent. That point *C* is an equilibrium is suggested by the following argument. For output levels less than *OE*, the two individuals combined are willing to pay more than 100 percent of the public good's cost. Hence they will vote to increase its level of production (but see the caveats to this statement at the end of this section). For output levels greater than *OE*, the individuals are not willing to pay the total cost of the public good being produced and therefore may vote for reductions in the amount being provided. Only for output level *OE* is there an equilibrium where the tax shares pay precisely for the level of the public good's produc-

---

[13] Most of Lindahl's writings are in German. Excerpts from them are reprinted in translation in R. A. Musgrave and A. T. Peacock, eds., *Classics in the Theory of Public Finance* (London: Macmillan, 1958).

Figure 24.3 *Lindahl Equilibrium in the Demand for Public Goods*

The curve *SS* shows that Smith's demand for a public good increases as the tax share that Smith must pay falls. Jones' demand curve for the public good (*JJ*) is constructed in a similar way. The point *C* represents a Lindahl equilibrium at which *OE* of the public good is supplied with Smith paying 60 percent of the cost. Any other quantity of the public good is not an equilibrium since either too much or too little funding would be available.

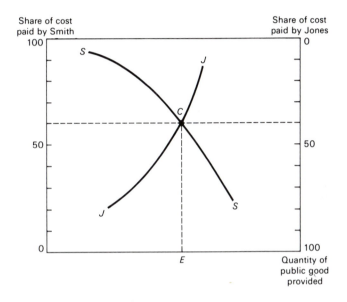

tion undertaken by the government. That this Lindahl equilibrium also will be an efficient allocation of resources can be most conveniently demonstrated mathematically.

Efficiency of the Lindahl Equilibrium

Assume, as before, that there are only two individuals (Smith and Jones) and two goods in society: pure public goods (*P*) and pure private goods (*G*). Denote the market prices of these goods by P_P and P_G, respectively. Let Smith's share of the public good's price be denoted by α. Then the tax price to Smith for each unit of public good provided is αP_P. Smith therefore will maximize utility by choosing those quantities of the two goods for which

$$\frac{\alpha P_P}{P_G} = MRS_{\text{Smith}} \quad (P \text{ for } G) \quad = \frac{MU_{\text{Smith}}(P)}{MU_{\text{Smith}}(G)}. \tag{24.15}$$

Similarly, Jones will pay a tax share of $(1 - \alpha)$ and will maximize utility by choosing *P* and *G* so that

$$\frac{(1 - \alpha)P_P}{P_G} = MRS_{\text{Jones}} \quad (P \text{ for } G) \quad = \frac{MU_{\text{Jones}}(P)}{MU_{\text{Jones}}(G)}. \tag{24.16}$$

Producers now will produce private and public goods so as to maximize their profits, requiring that

$$\frac{P_P}{P_G} = RPT \quad (P \text{ for } G). \tag{24.17}$$

Summing the utility-maximizing Equations 24.15 and 24.16 yields

$$MRS_{\text{Smith}} + MRS_{\text{Jones}} = \frac{MU_{\text{Smith}}(P)}{MU_{\text{Smith}}(G)} + \frac{MU_{\text{Jones}}(P)}{MU_{\text{Jones}}(G)}$$

$$= \frac{\alpha P_P}{P_G} + \frac{(1-\alpha)P_P}{P_G} = \frac{P_P}{P_G} = RPT \quad (P \text{ for } G), \tag{24.18}$$

where the final equality follows from the profit-maximizing condition 24.17. But these conditions are precisely those required for an efficient allocation of resources to public goods—compare Equation 24.12 to Equation 24.18. Consequently, we have shown that the Lindahl equilibrium represents an efficient allocation of resources. The tax shares introduced in that equilibrium play the role of "pseudo" prices that mimic the functioning of a competitive price system in achieving efficiency. Unfortunately, for reasons we shall now examine, this solution is at best only a conceptual one.

REVEALING THE DEMAND FOR PUBLIC GOODS: THE FREE RIDER PROBLEM

Deriving a Lindahl equilibrium requires knowledge of the optimal tax share (what we have called α) for each individual. A major problem arises in attempting to envision how such data might be collected. Although, through their voting patterns, individuals may provide some information about their preferences for public goods (a topic we take up in the next chapter), that information is usually too sketchy to permit tax shares to be computed because most voting methods do not record the intensity of individuals' preferences. As an alternative a government might choose to ask individuals how much they are willing to pay for particular packages of public goods, but the results of this poll might be extremely inaccurate. In responding to such a question, individuals may feel that they should understate their true preferences for fear they will ultimately have to pay what the good is worth to them in the form of taxes. From the individual's point of view, the proper strategy is to understate true preferences in the hope that others will bear the burden of paying for the good. Since, for a traditional public good, no one can be excluded from enjoying its benefits, the best position to occupy is that of a "free rider." Each individual, by acting in his or her own self-interest, may ensure that society underestimates the demand for public goods and hence underallocates resources to their production. As in the Prisoner's Dilemma (Chapter 20) what is individually rational proves to be collectively irrational.

The free rider problem arises in all organizations that provide collective goods to their members. For example, labor unions generally are able to obtain better wages and working conditions in unionized plants. Workers in such plants have an incentive to enjoy the benefits of unionization while at the same time refusing to join the union. They thereby avoid the payment of dues. In order to combat such free rider problems, unions quite often insist on a "closed," or "union," shop. Similar problems arise in the United States in attempting to collect blood on a voluntary basis. Since people know that they will get all the blood they need if they have to be hospitalized, the tendency is to be a free rider and refrain from donating. As these examples illustrate, the free rider problem can be solved only by some sort of compulsion. This compulsion may arise out of a sense of group solidarity or civic pride (individuals do give blood in America—far more do in England), or it may require legal or quasi-legal force (as in the union case). For governments the necessity to tax individuals to force them to pay for public services is inescapable, and some voting schemes have been proposed that gather the sort of information required for a Lindahl equilibrium.[14] None of these offers a particularly effective solution to the free rider problem, however.

Local Public Goods

Some economists have suggested that the public goods problem may be more tractable on a local than on a national level.[15] Because individuals are relatively mobile, they may indicate their preferences for local public goods by choosing to live in communities that offer them utility-maximizing public goods taxation packages. "Voting with one's feet" thereby provides a mechanism for revealing public goods demand in much the same way that "dollar voting" reveals private goods demand. Individuals who want high-quality schools or a high level of police protection can "pay" for them by choosing to live in highly taxed communities. Those who prefer not to receive such benefits can choose to live elsewhere. Similar arguments apply to other types of organizations (such as clubs) that offer packages of public goods for their members—individuals can choose which package of goods they prefer. Whether such actions can completely cope with the problem of revealing the demand for public goods (even on a local level) remains an unsettled question, however.

SUMMARY

In this chapter we have examined some technical problems with certain types of goods that raise questions about the ability of competitive markets to allocate them efficiently. All of these difficulties arise from externality (or spillover) effects involved in the consumption or production of such goods. In some cases it may be possible to design mechanisms to cope with these externalities in a market setting, but there are important limits involved in such solutions. Some specific issues we examined were:

- Externalities between two economic agents may cause a misallocation of resources because of a divergence between private and social marginal

[14] For one such method and a summary of others, see T. N. Tideman and G. Tullock, "A New and Superior Process for Making Social Choices," *Journal of Political Economy* 84 (December 1976): 1145–1159.

[15] See C. M. Tiebout, "A Pure Theory of Local Expenditures," *Journal of Political Economy* 64 (October 1956): 416–424.

cost. Traditional solutions to this divergence include mergers among the affected parties and adoption of suitable (Pigovian) taxes or subsidies.

- If transactions costs are small, private bargaining among the parties affected by an externality may bring social and private costs into line. The proof that resources will be efficiently allocated under such circumstances is sometimes called the *Coase theorem*.

- Public goods provide benefits to individuals on a nonexclusive basis—no one can be prevented from consuming such goods. Such goods may often also be nonrival in that the social marginal cost of serving another user is zero.

- Private markets will tend to underallocate resources to public goods because no single buyer can appropriate all of the benefits that such a good provides.

- A Lindahl optimal tax-sharing scheme can result in an efficient allocation of resources to the production of public goods. Computation of these tax shares requires substantial information that individuals have incentives to hide, however. Reliance on voluntary assent to tax-sharing schemes may therefore fall victim to the tendency of individuals to adopt the free rider position.

Application

PROPERTY RIGHTS

Legal assignments of property rights change over time. Some goods that were at one time commonly owned (most land, for example) have in more recent times become primarily private property. Similarly, some goods that were at one time private (roads, bridges, lighthouses, and fire companies) increasingly have come to be publicly owned. Traditionally, such changes have been regarded as primarily legal or political in origin. Although economic analysis could illustrate the implications of various property rights assignments, it was believed to have little to say about how assignments were in fact made. More recently, however, several economists have argued that the definitions societies adopt for property rights are strongly motivated by economic considerations. In particular, it has been suggested that private property rights come into existence when it becomes economical for those affected by externalities to inter-

nalize them through transactions in private property; that is, when the benefits of coping with the externalities exceed the costs of enforcing private property rights.[16] In broad terms, then, the hypothesis is that legal institutions (notably property rights) evolve over time toward economically efficient outcomes. Although it would be inappropriate here to investigate the wide variety of implications for the analysis of law that stem from this hypothesis, we shall examine four specific examples of the development of private property rights as a way of internalizing externalities.

Native Americans' Land
Prior to the arrival of large numbers of Europeans on the East Coast of North America, land

---

[16] See H. Demsetz, "Toward a Theory of Property Rights," *American Economic Review, Papers and Proceedings* 57 (May 1967): 347–359.

was commonly owned. Hunting and trapping activities by one Native American had little effect on those of another; hence there were few incentives to adopt mechanisms for coping with externalities. Opening of trade with Europe changed that situation considerably. Because of strong European demand for fur, trapping expanded greatly both in intensity and in geographic extent. Interaction effects among tribes and among individuals within tribes came to have major importance as some animals were overhunted and productivity fell. In response to the increasing importance of these externalities, private ownership of land became more common among Native Americans. By 1790 most land on the East Coast was privately owned. In that way the problem of overhunting was mitigated, as each landowner had an incentive to manage resources on a "sustained yield" basis.

Radio

A more recent example of the establishment of private property in what previously had been a common resource is the case of the radio spectrum.[17] Prior to a series of technical innovations in the early twentieth century, the radio spectrum had little economic value (other than for small-scale scientific experiments). Development of reliable long-distance radio transmitters altered that situation. Progressive "invasions" of the radio spectrum (through both a greater variety of wavelengths and the technical ability to discern between closer wavelengths) led to significant problems of interference among users. To cope with these externalities governments began to allocate portions of the spectrum for the unique use of specific individuals or firms. Those property rights came to be quite highly priced because they provided owners with substantial monopoly profits.

Bees and Apples

Earlier in this chapter we mentioned Meade's example of the beneficial externalities between beekeepers and apple growers. Since the costs of bargaining between these two producers are probably low, our analysis suggests that there may be incentives to internalize the externalities through private property contracts. In fact Cheung's investigation of beekeeping in Washington State shows that such contracts are well developed.[18] Terms of the contracts typically take into account both the benefits that various crops provide to beekeepers (in the form of honey) and the benefits that farmers get from having bees pollinate their crops. For crops such as clover and alfalfa, which have high honey yields, beekeepers usually pay rent to farmers for the right to have their bees use the farmers' land. On the other hand, apple and cherry growers must "rent" bees to provide pollination because the honey yield from those crops is low. Thus, although Meade's example has a bucolic appeal, its importance as an example of market failure has been limited by bargaining among the parties involved.

Oysters and Lobsters

Because shellfish are found along the continental shelf in relatively isolated beds, enforcement of property rights for such resources is less costly than for ocean fisheries, where common property is the prevalent institution. Property rights in shellfishing grounds may be enforced by the state like any other legal right, or they may be enforced informally by custom and heredity. Whatever the source of the property rights, our analysis suggests that shellfish producers who operate on private property will recognize any divergence between private and social marginal costs that the fishing activities have. By so doing, they will in the long run be

---

[17]This section draws on H. G. J. Aitken, *Syntony and Spark: The Origins of Radio* (New York: John Wiley & Sons, 1976).

[18]S. N. S. Cheung, "The Fable of the Bees: An Economic Investigation," *Journal of Law and Economics* 16 (April 1973): 11–33.

more productive than those who fish on common property. Some direct evidence on this possibility was provided in a 1975 study of oyster production by R. J. Agnello and L. P. Donnelley.[19] In this study the authors noted that states differ widely in the proportion of their oyster grounds that are privately owned. In Virginia, for example, about 74 percent of oysters are produced from privately owned grounds whereas in neighboring Maryland the figure is less than 17 percent. The authors found that there was clear evidence that oyster fishermen were more productive in states with a high level of private property. In Virginia, for example, the average physical productivity of oyster fishermen was nearly 60 percent higher than in Maryland. More generally, the authors found that a 10 percent increase in the proportion of oyster grounds that were privately owned led to an increase of 338 pounds in the annual oyster

catch of each fisherman. They attribute this result to the greater efficiency with which private oyster beds can be managed.

A similar result was obtained by F. W. Bell in a study of lobstering.[20] In this case, however, the author found that property rights were only weakly enforced (by custom rather than by law) and that the common property nature of most production decisions led to overfishing. In 1966, for example, the author calculated that there may have been twice as many lobster traps in use as would be dictated by efficiency considerations. A reduction in the number of traps to the optimal level would have increased the catch by nearly 10 pounds per trap. The author suggested that such a reduction might be brought about through state regulation, but our analysis indicates that it might also be achieved through a more careful definition of property rights in the industry.

[19] R. J. Agnello and L. P. Donnelley, "Property Rights and Efficiency in the Oyster Industry," *Journal of Law and Economics* 18 (October 1975): 521–533.

[20] F. W. Bell, "Technological Externalities and Common Property Resources: An Empirical Study of the U.S. Northern Lobster Industry," *Journal of Political Economy* 80 (January–February 1972): 148–158.

SUGGESTED READINGS

Alchian, A., and Demsetz, H. "Production, Information Costs, and Economic Organization." *American Economic Review* 62 (December 1972): 777–795.

Uses externality arguments to develop a theory of economic organizations.

Arrow, K. J. *The Limits of Organization.* New York: W. W. Norton & Company, 1974.

Analyzes information problems within organizations.

Cheung, S. N. S. "The Fable of the Bees: An Economic Investigation." *Journal of Law and Economics* 16 (April 1973): 11–33.

Empirical study of how the famous bee-orchard owner externality is handled by private markets in the state of Washington.

———. "Private Property Rights and Sharecropping." *Journal of Political Economy* 76 (December 1968): 1107–1122.

An analysis of the efficiency properties of various land tenancy arrangements.

Coase, R. H. "The Market for Goods and the Market for Ideas." *American Economic Review* 64 (May 1974): 384–391.

Speculative article about notions of externalities and regulation in the "marketplace of ideas."

———. "The Problem of Social Cost." *Journal of Law and Economics* 3 (October 1960): 1–44.

Classic article on externalities. Many fascinating historical-legal cases.

Cornes, R., and Sandler, T. *The Theory of Externalities, Public Goods, and Club Goods.* Cambridge: Cambridge University Press, 1986.

Good theoretical analysis of many of the issues raised in this chapter. Good discussions of the connections between returns to scale, excludability, and club goods.

Demsetz, H. "Toward a Theory of Property Rights." *American Economic Review, Papers and Proceedings* 57 (May 1967): 347–373.

Brief development of a plausible theory of how societies come to define property rights.

Friedman, M. *Capitalism and Freedom.* Chicago: University of Chicago Press, 1962.

Basic statement of the purported political benefits of private property.

Furubotn, E., and Pejovich, S. "Property Rights and Economic Theory: A Survey of the Recent Literature." *Journal of Economic Literature* 10 (December 1972): 1137–1162.

Survey of the property rights literature. Especially interesting on the economics of collective enterprises.

Samuelson, P. A. "The Pure Theory of Public Expenditures." *Review of Economics and Statistics* 36 (November 1954): 387–389.

Classic statement of the efficiency conditions for public goods production.

———. "Diagrammatic Exposition of a Theory of Public Expenditures." *Review of Economics and Statistics* 37 (November 1955): 350–356.

Diagrammatic treatment of the famous 1954 article.

Tiebout, C. M. "A Pure Theory of Local Expenditures." *Journal of Political Economy* 64 (October 1956): 416–424.

Primary reference on the local public goods concept and how such goods might be produced efficiently.

Worcester, D. A. "Pecuniary and Technological Externality, Factor Rents, and Social Costs." *American Economic Review* 59 (December 1969): 873–885.

Theoretical and historical survey of the externality concept. Good graphic treatment and a complete set of historical references.

PROBLEMS

24.1

A firm in a perfectly competitive industry has patented a new process for making widgets. The new process lowers the firm's average cost curve, meaning this firm alone (although still a price taker) can earn real economic profits in the long run.

    a. If the market price is $20 per widget and the firm's marginal cost curve is given by $MC = .4q$, where q is the daily widget production for the firm, how many widgets will the firm produce?

    b. Suppose a government study has found that the firm's new process is polluting the air and estimates the social marginal cost of widget production by this firm to be $SMC = .5q$. If the market price is still $20, what is the socially optimal level of production for the firm? What should the amount of a government imposed excise tax be in order to bring about this optimal level of production?

    c. Graph your results.

24.2.

On the island of Pago-Pago there are 2 lakes and 20 fishermen. Each fisherman can fish on either lake and keep the average catch on his particular lake. On Lake X the total number of fish caught is given by

$$F^X = 10L_X - 1/2L_x^2,$$

where L_X is the number of men fishing on the Lake.

For Lake Y the relationship is

$$F^Y = 5L_Y.$$

a. Under this organization of society, what will the total number of fish caught be?

b. The chief of Pago-Pago, having once read an economics book, believes that he can raise the total number of fish caught by restricting the number of men allowed to fish on Lake X. What is the correct number of men allowed to fish on Lake X in order to maximize the total catch of fish? What is the number of fish caught in this situation?

c. Being basically opposed to coercion, the chief decides to require a fishing license for Lake X. If the licensing procedure is to bring about the optimal allocation of labor, what should the cost of a license be (in terms of fish)?

d. Does this example prove that a "competitive" allocation of resources may not be optimal?

24.3

Suppose that the oil industry in Utopia is perfectly competitive and that all firms draw oil from a single (and practically inexhaustible) pool. Assume that each competitor believes that he or she can sell all the oil he or she can produce at a stable world price of $10 per barrel and that the cost of operating a well for one year is $1,000.

Total output per year (Q) of the oil field is a function of the number of wells (N) operating in the field. In particular,

$$Q = 500N - N^2,$$

and the amount of oil produced by each well (q) is given by

$$q = \frac{Q}{N} = 500 - N.$$

a. Describe the equilibrium output and the equilibrium number of wells in this perfectly competitive case. Is there a divergence between private and social marginal cost in the industry?

b. Suppose now that the government nationalizes the oil field. How many oil wells should it operate? What will total output be? What will the output per well be?

c. As an alternative to nationalization the Utopian government is considering an annual license fee per well to discourage over-drilling. How large should this license fee be if it is to prompt the industry to drill the optimal number of wells?

24.4

There is currently considerable controversy concerning product safety. Two extreme positions might be termed *caveat emptor* (let the buyer beware) and *caveat vendor* (let the seller beware). Under the former scheme producers would have no responsibility for the safety of their products: Buyers would absorb all losses. Under the latter scheme this liability assignment would be reversed; firms would be completely responsible under law for losses incurred from unsafe products. Using simple supply and demand analysis, discuss how the assignment of such liability might affect the allocation of resources. Would safer products be produced if firms were strictly liable under law?

24.5

Three types of contracts are used to specify the way in which tenants on a plot of agricultural land may pay rent to the landlord. Rent may be paid (1) in money (or a fixed amount of agricultural produce) or (2) as a fixed proportionate share of the crop or (3) in "labor dues" by agreeing to work on other plots owned by the landlord. How might these alternative contract specifications affect tenants' production decisions? What sorts of transactions costs might occur in the enforcement of each type of contract? What economic factors might affect the type of contract specified in different places or during different historical periods?

24.6
Suppose a monopoly produces a harmful externality. Use the concept of consumer surplus to analyze whether an optimal tax on the polluter would necessarily be a welfare improvement.

24.7
Suppose there are only two individuals in society. The demand curve for person A for mosquito control is given by

$$q_a = 100 - P.$$

For person B the demand curve for mosquito control is given by

$$q_b = 200 - P.$$

a. Suppose mosquito control is a pure public good: that is, once it is produced everyone benefits from it. What would be the optimal level of this activity if it could be produced at a constant marginal cost of $50 per unit?

b. If mosquito control were left to the private market, how much might be produced? Does your answer depend on what each person assumes about what the other will do?

c. If the government were to produce the optimal amount of mosquito control, how much will this cost? How should the tax bill for this amount be allocated between the individuals if they are to share it in proportion to benefits received from mosquito control?

24.8
Suppose there are three individuals in society who vote on whether the government should undertake specific projects. Let the net benefits of a particular project be $150, $140, and $50 for persons A, B, and C, respectively.

a. If the project costs $300 and these costs are to be shared equally, would a majority vote to undertake the project? What would be the net benefit to each person under such a scheme? Would total net benefits be positive?

b. Suppose that the project costs $375 and again that costs were to be shared equally. Now would a majority vote for the project, and would total net benefits be positive?

c. Suppose (presumably contrary to fact) votes can be bought and sold in a free market. Describe what kinds of results you might expect in parts (a) and (b).

24.9
Suppose that the production possibility frontier for an economy that produces one public good (P) and one private good (G) is given by

$$G^2 + 100P^2 = 5,000.$$

This economy is populated by 100 identical individuals, each with a utility function of the form

$$\text{utility} = \sqrt{G_i P}$$

where G_i is the individual's share of private good production ($= G/100$). Notice that the public good is nonexclusive and that everyone benefits equally from its level of production.

    a.   If the market for G and P were perfectly competitive, what levels of those goods would be produced? What would the typical individual's utility be in this situation?

    b.   What are the optimal production levels for G and P? What would the typical individual's utility level be? How should consumption of good G be taxed to achieve this result? (*Hint:* The numbers in this problem do not come out evenly, and some approximations should suffice.)

24.10

Suppose that there are N individuals in an economy with three goods. Two of the goods are pure (nonexclusive) public goods, whereas the third is an ordinary private good.

    a.   What conditions must hold for resources to be allocated efficiently between either of the public goods and the private good?

    b.   What conditions must hold for resources to be allocated efficiently between the two public goods?

24.11

In an economy characterized by a hierarchy of governmental units (for example, federal, state, and local governments), what criteria might be used to determine which public goods are produced by which level of government? How would economies or diseconomies of scale in production affect your answer?

CHAPTER 25

Social Choice Theory

Much of our analysis in this book has been primarily concerned with exploring the relationship between economic efficiency and a perfectly competitive price system. We showed that there is a clear connection between these concepts but that problems may arise that interfere with a competitive price system's ability to convey accurate information. Existence of such problems therefore may force societies to choose among second-best alternatives. In addition, as we mentioned briefly in Chapter 16, nothing within the competitive model ensures that even efficient outcomes will be regarded as fair or equitable. In choosing among efficient allocations of resources, it is inevitable that some individuals will prefer one specific allocation whereas others will prefer some alternative (where, presumably, they are better off). The competitive model provides no method for making such choices. In this chapter we will attempt to tie up these loose ends by examining the theory of social choice. That is, we will briefly describe the way economists have tried to conceptualize the problem of how societies make choices (usually through their governments) among various feasible allocations of resources. Unfortunately, the theory we will be describing is very much incomplete. Perhaps more disturbing, the theory is also replete with negative findings about whether potential social choice mechanisms (for example, voting) yield desirable results. Still, social choice theory represents a fascinating series of attempts to apply economic tools to the investigation of basic political and philosophical questions. Consequently, the subject represents a natural focus for the final chapter of this book.

Our analysis of social choice theory is divided into three major parts. First, we return to the simple model of an exchange economy and examine possible welfare criteria for choosing among efficient allocations. Next, we examine some very general results about the nature of social decision rules and introduce the principal negative "theorem" (due to K. J. Arrow), which states that no such decision rule can be completely satisfactory. The final sections of the chapter are then devoted to the question of voting and representative government. Consistent with our focus throughout this book, our primary concern will be to illustrate the connection (if any) between voting methods and efficient resource allocation.

SOCIAL WELFARE CRITERIA

We will begin our study of social choice theory by examining some of the problems associated with devising welfare criteria for choosing among efficient allocations of resources. This subject is the most normative branch of microeconomics, since it necessarily involves making hard choices about the utility levels of different individuals. In choosing between two efficient allocations, A and B, the problem arises that some individuals prefer A whereas others prefer B. In some way comparisons among people must be made in order to judge which allocation is preferable. As might be expected, there is no universally accepted criterion for making such choices. Very basic philosophical questions continue to perplex welfare economists. Our main purpose here is to illustrate these perplexities.

One initial assumption we make in defining welfare criteria is that individual tastes are to "count." The measure of social welfare is how well off the individuals in society feel. Some authors refer to this as the individualistic assumption.[1] Using this definition of social welfare, it should be clear that a Pareto optimal allocation of resources (one in which no one can be made better off without making someone else worse off) is a necessary condition for a social optimum. If resources were allocated in a way such that someone could be made better off without necessarily lowering the utility level of anyone else, this allocation could not have been socially optimal. On the other hand, there may be many Pareto optimal allocations; one purpose of social welfare economics is to establish criteria for choosing among these.

Social Welfare Criteria in an Exchange Model

The model of efficiency in exchange that we developed in Chapter 8 is useful for demonstrating the problems involved in establishing social welfare criteria, and we shall focus primarily on that in this chapter.[2] Consider the Edgeworth box diagram in Figure 25.1. Only those points on the contract curve are eligible to be considered as possible candidates for a social optimum. Points off the contract curve are dominated by points on the curve in the sense that both individuals can be made better off, and in so doing social welfare could be improved. Along the contract curve the utilities of the two individuals (Smith

---

[1] This assumption is by no means universally accepted. Many authors have stressed that individuals' preferences are in fact shaped by their economic and social environment and therefore should not be taken as fixed. This observation raises many important and difficult issues that cannot be adequately treated here.

[2] Production can be integrated into the discussion of social welfare economics. See, for example, F. M. Bator, "The Simple Analytics of Welfare Maximization," *American Economic Review* 47 (March 1957): 22–59. Although no new conceptual problems would be created by such an addition, several graphic difficulties do arise. Because goods can be produced (rather than being in fixed supply as they are in the exchange model), any contemplated change in the utility levels of individuals in society will also necessitate a change in the whole production plan (society's production possibility frontier would change). We shall not investigate these analytic complications here.

Figure 25.1   *Edgeworth Box Diagram of Exchange*

This diagram is simply a redrawing of Figure 8.3. The curve O_S, O_J is the locus of efficient allocations of X and Y between Smith and Jones. Allocations off this locus are dominated by those on it in that both individuals can be made better off by moving to the contract curve.

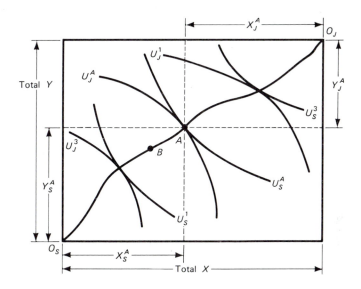

and Jones) vary, and these utilities are directly competitive. Smith's utility can be increased only by decreasing Jones's. Given this set of efficient allocations, we now wish to discuss possible criteria for choosing among them. For this purpose we shall assume for the moment that utilities are measurable and that they may be compared on a common scale. Obviously, this assumption is in direct contradiction to the warnings expressed in Chapter 3 about the measurability of utility. However, making such an assumption will permit us to conceptualize certain problems.

Using the assumption of measurability, we can use the possible utility combinations along the contract curve in Figure 25.1 to construct the utility possibility frontier shown in Figure 25.2.[3] The curve O_S, O_J records those utility levels for Smith and Jones that are obtainable from the fixed quantities of those goods that are available. Any utility combination (such as point C) that lies inside the curve O_S, O_J is inefficient in the sense that utilities could be unambiguously improved (for example, by moving to any point on the arc $C'C'$). This is simply a reflection of the way in which the contract curve is constructed.

---

[3] This construction is identical to that we used in Chapter 15 to derive the production possibility frontier.

Figure 25.2   *Utility Possibility Frontier*

Assuming measurability of utility, the utility possibility frontier can be derived from Figure 25.1. This curve (O_S, O_J) shows those combinations of utility that society can achieve. Two criteria for choosing among points on O_S, O_J might be: Choose "equal" utilities for Smith and Jones (point *A*); or choose the utilities so that their sum is the greatest (point *B*). Under the Rawl's maximin criterion, the efficient allocation *B* would be regarded as inferior to equal allocations between *D* and *A*.

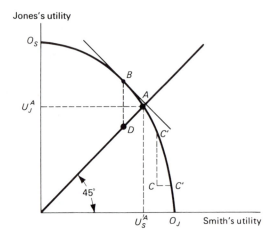

Using the utility possibility frontier, we can now rephrase the "problem" of welfare economics as being the development of criteria for selecting a point on this frontier.

Equality Criterion   A few simple criteria for choosing a point on O_S, O_J can be shown on Figure 25.2. One possible principle would require complete equality: Smith and Jones should enjoy the same level of welfare (again remember the dubious nature of the assumption of utility measurability here). This social welfare criterion would necessitate choosing point *A* on the utility possibility frontier. Since point *A* corresponds to a unique point on the contract curve, the socially op-timal allocation of goods has been determined by this choice. In Figure 25.1 this allocation is seen to require that Smith gets X_S^A and Y_S^A, whereas Jones gets X_J^A and Y_J^A. Notice that the goods *X* and *Y* are not necessarily distributed equally. It is equality of utilities that is required by the criterion, not equality of goods. If individuals have rather different tastes for the two goods, these goods could be very unequally distributed at point *A*. It might even be the case that one of the individuals would get more of both goods at the socially optimal point. This would be true, for example, if Smith were ascetic by nature, whereas Jones were materialistic. To equalize utilities, therefore, Jones should be given more goods with which to satisfy her cravings.

Utilitarian Criterion

A similar (though not necessarily identical) criterion would be to choose that point on the utility possibility frontier for which the sum of Smith's and Jones's utilities is the greatest. This would require that the optimal point (B) be chosen to maximize ($U_J + U_S$) subject to the constraint implied by the utility possibility frontier. As before, point B would imply a certain allocation of X and Y between Smith and Jones, and this allocation could be derived from Figure 25.1.

Maximin Criterion

A final criterion we can examine was first posed by the philosopher John Rawls.[4] Rawls begins by envisioning society as being in an "initial position" in which no one knows what his or her final position (and ultimate utility) will be. He then asks what kind of welfare criterion would be adopted by people who find themselves in such a position. Posed in this way, selection of a welfare criterion is a problem in behavior under uncertainty, since no one knows exactly how the criterion chosen will affect his or her personal well-being. From his initial premise Rawls concludes that individuals would be very risk averse (see Chapter 9) in their selection of a criterion. Specifically, he asserts that members of society would choose to depart from perfect equality only on the condition that the worst-off person under an unequal distribution of utilities would actually be better off than under equality. In terms of Figure 25.2 unequal distributions such as B would be permitted only when the attainable equal distributions (which lie along the 45° line) were below point D. Equal distributions that lie between D and A are, according to Rawls, superior to B because the worse-off individual (Smith) is better off there than under allocation B. The Rawls criterion (which is also termed the "maximin" criterion because of its similarity to the criterion used in game theory) therefore suggests that many efficient allocations may not be socially desirable and that societies may choose equality even at considerable efficiency costs. Such a conclusion is not universally shared by economists, many of whom argue that the criteria proposed are unnecessarily risk averse. Individuals in the initial position may instead prefer to gamble that they will be the winners under an unequal final distribution, and such motives may dominate if the likelihood of being the worse-off individual is small.[5] Still, Rawls's conception of using the "initial position" methodology to conceptualize how individuals might make social decisions is an intriguing one that has been widely used in other investigations.

SOCIAL WELFARE FUNCTIONS

A more general approach to social welfare (which as special cases includes the three criteria we discussed above) can be obtained by examining the concept of a social welfare function.[6] If we assume that individual tastes are to count, this function might depend only on Smith's and Jones's utility levels:

[4] J. Rawls, *A Theory of Justice* (Cambridge, Mass.: Harvard University Press, 1971).

[5] See, for example, K. J. Arrow, "Some Ordinalist-Utilitarian Notes on Rawls's Theory of Justice," *Journal of Philosophy* (May 1973): 245–263.

[6] This concept was first developed by A. Bergson in "A Reformulation of Certain Aspects of Welfare Economics," *Quarterly Journal of Economics* 52 (February 1938): 310–334.

Figure 25.3   *Using a Social Welfare Function to Find the Social Optimum*

If we can postulate the existence of a social welfare function having the indifference curves W_1, W_2, and W_3, it is possible to conceptualize the problem of social choice. It is clear that efficiency (being on O_S, O_J) is necessary for a welfare optimum, but this is not sufficient, as may be seen by comparing points D and F.

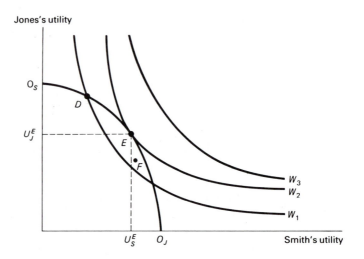

$$\text{social welfare} = W(U_S, U_J). \tag{25.1}$$

The social choice problem, then, is to allocate X and Y between Smith and Jones so as to maximize W. This procedure is pictured in Figure 25.3. The curves labeled W_1, W_2, and W_3 represent social indifference curves, in that society is indifferent about which utility combination on a particular curve is chosen.[7] These indifference curves for the function W are drawn convex on the normative assumption that "society" exhibits a diminishing rate of substitution of Smith's utility for Jones's. This assumption would seem to be reasonable if society is basically egalitarian and is progressively less willing to make Smith better off at the expense of making Jones worse off.

Point E is the optimal point of social welfare, in that this is the highest level of W achievable with the given utility possibility frontier. As before, it is necessary to go from point E to the Edgeworth box diagram in order to determine the socially optimal allocation of goods. Any of the methods we have already mentioned might be used to obtain this allocation.

---

[7]Under the "equality" criterion the social welfare function would have L-shaped indifference curves, whereas under the "maximum sum of utilities" criterion the indifference curves would be parallel straight lines with a slope of -1.

Conflicts between Efficiency and Equity

Figure 25.3 demonstrates a conceptual way of choosing a distribution of utilities that maximizes social welfare. The figure again illustrates the important distinction to be made between the goals of equity and efficiency. All of the points on O_S, O_J are efficient by the Pareto criterion. However, some of the efficient points represent far more socially desirable distributions than do others. As with the Rawls maximin criterion, there are in fact many inefficient points (such as F) that are socially preferred to efficient points (such as D). It sometimes may be in society's interest to choose seemingly inefficient allocations of resources if the truly optimal allocation (point E) is unattainable. In order to satisfy societal concepts of equity, it may make sense to accept some inefficiency.

As a practical example of this sort of inconsistency between efficiency and equity, consider the debate in the United States over the desirability of adopting a guaranteed annual income for all citizens. Opponents of this proposal assert that its acceptance would lead to great inefficiencies because, once the necessity to work was mitigated, individuals would withdraw from the labor force. Even without examining the actual size of this purported effect, on *a priori* grounds this is not necessarily a conclusive argument. For example, suppose that without income transfers only points such as D could be achieved. Perhaps initial endowments are so skewed that even perfectly efficient trading would ensure a relatively unequal outcome. On the other hand, perhaps income transfers would cause the "inefficient" point F to be achieved.[8] What has been sacrificed in efficiency therefore has more than been compensated for (in terms of social welfare) by increased equity.

NORMATIVE POLITICAL THEORY AND THE ARROW IMPOSSIBILITY THEOREM

The social welfare function, then, provides a useful tool for demonstrating particular aspects of the problem of social choice. We must recognize, however, that this tool is only a conceptual one offering little guidance for the development of practical policy. The social indifference curves of Figure 25.3 are in reality nothing more than a few casually drawn lines. We have so far begged the question of how such a function is established or what the properties of the function are likely to be. Both of these questions are at the heart of political philosophy. Although a treatment of this subject is obviously far outside the scope of this book, we shall, in this section, provide brief glimpses of some of the issues raised by political theorists in attempting to define "social welfare." We also examine in more detail the economic approach to such questions taken by K. J. Arrow and others.

Normative Political Theory

A major goal of political theorists has been to propose possible definitions of "the common good." This term is usually taken to refer to a set of moral precepts about social welfare that can act as guidelines for governmental poli-

---

[8] For example, the withdrawal of persons from the labor force may cause the total quantities of X and Y available to contract (not as much can be produced when income transfers are introduced). Graphically, the size of the Edgeworth box would be contracted, and perhaps F is the "best point" that can be obtained within this new, smaller box.

cies. Some theorists, such as J. Rawls, assume that there exist basic moral principles of fairness and justice with which most people would agree. These "social contract" philosophers therefore would argue that the role of welfare economics is to discover these universal principles and to attempt to implement them. A wide variety of ethical postulates has been proposed. These range from rather vague precepts ("provide the greatest good to the greatest number") to specific policy recommendations about the way in which social welfare could be "improved." None of these postulates has won widespread assent: The problem of finding an equitable, commonly agreed upon method for choosing among potential resource allocations remains unresolved.

A number of political theorists feel that the search for universal, pragmatic moral principles is fruitless. In any large and complex society, a wide variety of beliefs will be held; it is argued that these ultimately will prove to be irreconcilable. Economists have been most interested in those aspects of political theory that examine how these differences are accommodated by the political process. This interest derives naturally from economists' studies of the ways in which markets coordinate differences in individuals' preferences and firms' technological capabilities. The major contribution that economists have made to political theory is to demonstrate how basic economic models can be applied to political contexts as well. On a philosophical level, economists (most notably Kenneth Arrow)[9] have asked if a consistent notion of social preferences can be derived in principle from a group of differing individual preferences. Is it possible to construct a social welfare function that adequately reflects individuals' views of what social choices should be? The simple answer to this question seems to be no. Complex problems of inconsistency arise in attempting to "add up" different individuals' views, and it does not seem possible to define a set of rules that represent social preferences. Whatever social welfare function is decided upon, it must either be based on the preferences of a single individual (perhaps Plato's philosopher-king) or it must express preferences that are not completely consistent.

Arrow's Impossibility Theorem

As an illustration of the problems in deriving a social welfare function, we shall examine Arrow's basic result. Arrow views the general social problem as choosing among several feasible "social states." It is assumed that each individual in society can rank these states according to their desirability. The question Arrow raises is: Does there exist a ranking of these states on a society-wide scale that fairly records these individual preferences? Symbolically, assume there are three social states (A, B, and C) and two individuals in society (Smith and Jones). Suppose that Smith prefers A to B (we will denote this by $A\ P_S\ B$, where P_S represents the words "is preferred by Smith to") and B to C. These preferences can be written as $A\ P_S\ B$ and $B\ P_S\ C$. If the individual is to be "rational," it should then be the case that $A\ P_S\ C$: The individual's preferences should be transitive. Suppose also that among the three states, Jones

---

[9]See K. J. Arrow, *Social Choice and Individual Values* (New Haven, Conn.: Yale University Press, 1951).

has preferences $C\ P_J\ A$, $A\ P_J\ B$, and $C\ P_J\ B$. Arrow's impossibility theorem consists of showing that a reasonable social ranking of these three states (call this ranking P) cannot exist.

The crux of this theorem is to define what is meant by a "reasonable social ranking." Arrow assumes that any social ranking (P) should obey the following six seemingly unobjectionable axioms (here P is to be read "is socially preferred to"):

1. It must rank all social states: Either $A\ P\ B$, $B\ P\ A$, or A and B are equally desirable ($A\ I\ B$) for any two states A and B.
2. The ranking must be transitive: If $A\ P\ B$ and $B\ P\ C$ (or $B\ I\ C$), then $A\ P\ C$.
3. The ranking must be positively related to individual preferences: If A is unanimously preferred to B by Smith and Jones, then $A\ P\ B$.
4. If new social states become feasible, this fact should not affect the social ranking of the original states. If, between A and B, $A\ P\ B$, then this will remain true if some new state (D) becomes feasible.[10]
5. The social preference relation should not be imposed, say, by custom. It should not be the case that $A\ P\ B$ regardless of the tastes of individuals in society.
6. The relationship should be nondictatorial. One person's preferences should not determine society's preferences.

Arrow was able to show that these six conditions (all of which seem ethically reasonable on the surface) are not compatible with one another: No general social relationship obeying Conditions 1 to 6 exists. Using the preferences of Smith and Jones among A, B, and C, it is possible to see the kind of inconsistencies that can arise in social choice. Since $B\ P_S\ C$ and $C\ P_J\ B$, it must be the case that society is indifferent between B and C ($B\ I\ C$). Otherwise society's preferences would be in accord with only one individual (and against the other), and this would violate Axiom 6 requiring nondictatorship.

Since both Smith and Jones prefer A to B, Conditions 3 and 5 require that $A\ P\ B$. Hence, by transitivity Axiom 2, $A\ P\ C$. But, again, this is a violation of

---

[10] Condition 4 is sometimes called the axiom of the *independence of irrelevant alternatives*. More controversy has arisen over this axiom (and similar ones in the von Neumann–Morgenstern list) than any other. To see the sort of functions that are ruled out by the axiom, consider individuals voting for candidates in an election. Suppose that each individual can rank these candidates in order of their desirability. An election somehow combines these individual lists into a society-wide list. According to Axiom 4, the social list must have the property that if candidate X is preferred to candidate Y, this should remain true even if other candidates enter or leave the race. The most common election procedure in which each person votes only for his or her most preferred candidate may not obey the axiom because of the presence of "spoilers" in the race. For example, it is conceivable that the presence of George Wallace in the 1968 presidential election caused Hubert Humphrey to lose (Richard Nixon was shown to be "socially preferred"). With the "irrelevant alternative" Wallace out of the race, Humphrey might have won. The presidential election system therefore would not obey Arrow's Axiom 4. Many authors have examined the consequences of relaxing the axiom.

the nondictatorship assumption since $A\ P_S\ C$ but $C\ P_J\ A$. Thus, in this simple case an inconsistency arises in the attempt to construct a social preference relationship. Admittedly, this example is a bit contrived, but it does illustrate clearly the problems of trying to aggregate divergent patterns of individual preferences into some reasonable social pattern. The importance of Arrow's work is to show that any social decision rule that is chosen must violate at least one of the postulates embodied in Axioms 1 through 6.

Significance of the Arrow Theorem

Much research in social choice theory has been focused on Arrow's fundamental result and on whether it continues to hold under potential revisions in the set of basic postulates.[11] In general, the impossibility result appears to be rather robust to modest changes in these postulates. Systems with fewer basic axioms and systems under which some of Arrow's axioms are relaxed continue to demonstrate a variety of inconsistencies. It appears that to expect methods of social choice to be at the same time rational, definitive, and egalitarian may be to expect too much. Instead compromises are inevitable. Of course, where to make such compromises is a very difficult normative question.

Despite the negative nature of Arrow's conclusion, it should be remembered that all societies do in fact make choices. The U.S. Congress manages to pass a budget (often at the last minute); the Soviets and the Chinese adopt five-year plans; and Alaskan Eskimos decide how to improve upon their communal fishing methods for the next year. Rather than examining the normative question of how such choices might be made in a socially optimal way, it may be more productive to examine how these choices are actually made so that positive predictions can be made about what outcomes are likely in various situations. In the final sections of this chapter, we take such an approach in a brief review of economic analyses of voting and representative government.

DIRECT VOTING AND RESOURCE ALLOCATION

Voting is used as a social decision process in many institutions. In some instances individuals vote directly on policy questions. That is the case in some New England town meetings, many state-wide referenda (for example, California's Proposition "13" in 1977), and for many of the national policies adopted in Switzerland. Direct voting also characterizes the social decision procedure used for many smaller groups and clubs such as farmers' cooperatives, university faculties, or the local Rotary club. In other cases, however, societies have found it more convenient to utilize a representative form of government in which individuals vote directly only for political representatives, who are then charged with making decisions on policy questions. For our study of positive social choice theory, we will begin with an analysis of direct voting. This is an important subject not only because such a procedure applies to many cases, but also because elected representatives often engage in direct voting (in the U.S. Congress, for example), and the theory we will illustrate

[11] For a survey see D. H. Blair and R. A. Pollak, "Rational Collective Choice," *Scientific American* (August 1983): 88–95.

applies to those instances as well. Later in the chapter we will take up special problems raised in studying representative government.

Majority Rule

Because so many elections are conducted on a majority rule basis, we often tend to regard that procedure as a natural and, perhaps, optimal one for making social choices. But only a cursory examination should suggest that there is nothing particularly sacred about a rule requiring that a policy obtain 50 percent of the vote to be adopted. In the U.S. Constitution, for example, two-thirds of the states must adopt an amendment before it becomes law. And 60 percent of the U.S. Congress must vote to limit debate on controversial issues. Indeed in some institutions (Quaker meetings, for example), unanimity may be required for social decisions. Our discussion of the Lindahl equilibrium concept in the previous chapter suggests that there does exist a distribution of tax shares that would obtain unanimous support in voting for public goods. But arriving at such unanimous agreements may be very time-consuming and may be subject to strategic ploys by the voters involved. To examine in detail the forces that lead societies to move away from unanimity and to choose some other determining fraction would take us too far afield here. We instead will assume throughout our discussion of voting that decisions will be made by majority rule; that is, we will assume that policies will be adopted if they are favored by the next whole integer above $n/2$ voters (where n is the total number of voters). Readers may wish to ponder for themselves what kinds of situations might call for a decisive proportion of other than 50 percent.

The Paradox of Voting

In the 1780s the French social theorist M. de Condorcet observed an important peculiarity of majority rule voting systems—they may not arrive at an equilibrium but instead may cycle among alternative options. Condorcet's paradox is illustrated for a simple case in Table 25.1. Suppose there are three voters (Smith, Jones, and Fudd) choosing among three policy options. For our subsequent analysis we will assume that the policy options represent three levels of spending on a particular public good [(A) low, (B) medium, or (C) high], but Condorcet's paradox would arise even if the options being considered do not

Table 25.1   *Preferences That Produce the Paradox of Voting*

	Policy			
	A Low Spending	**B** Medium Spending	**C** High Spending	**A** Low Spending
Voter				
Smith	>	>	<	
Jones	<	>	>	
Fudd	>	<	>	

have this type of ordering associated with them.[12] Preferences of Smith, Jones, and Fudd among the three policy options are indicated by inequality signs. That is, the signs indicate that Smith prefers option A to option B, that Jones prefers option B to option A, and so forth. The preferences described in Table 25.1 give rise to Condorcet's paradox.

Consider a vote between options A and B. Here option A would win, since it is favored by Smith and Fudd and opposed only by Jones. In a vote between options A and C, option C would win, again by 2 votes to 1. But in a vote of C versus B, B would win and we would be back where we started. Social choices would endlessly cycle among the three alternatives. In subsequent votes, any choice that was initially decided upon could be defeated by an alternative, and no equilibrium would ever be reached. In this situation the option finally chosen will depend on such seemingly nongermane issues as when the balloting stops or how items are ordered on an agenda rather than being derived in some rational way from the preferences of voters.

Single-Peaked Preferences and the Median Voter Theorem

Condorcet's voting paradox arises because of the presence of a degree of irreconcilability in the preferences of voters. One therefore might ask whether restrictions on the types of preferences allowed might yield situations where equilibrium voting outcomes are more likely. A fundamental result about this probability was discovered by D. Black in 1948.[13] Black showed that equilibrium voting outcomes always occur in cases where the issue being voted upon is one-dimensional (such as how much to spend on a public good) and where voters' preferences are "single-peaked." To understand what the notion of single-peaked means, consider again Condorcet's paradox. In Figure 25.4 we illustrate the preferences that gave rise to the paradox by assigning hypothetical utility levels to options A, B, and C that are consistent with the preferences recorded in Table 25.1. For Smith and Jones, preferences are single-peaked—as levels of public goods' expenditures rise, there is only one local utility-maximizing choice (A for Smith, B for Jones). Fudd's preferences, on the other hand, have two local maxima (A and C). It is these preferences that produced the cyclical voting pattern. If instead Fudd had the preferences represented by the dashed line in Figure 25.4 (where now C is the only local utility maximum), there would be no paradox. In that case, option B would be chosen since that option would defeat both A and C by votes of 2 to 1. Here B is the preferred choice of the "median" voter (Jones) whose preferences are "between" the preferences of Smith and the revised preferences of Fudd.

Black's result is quite general and applies to any number of voters. If choices are unidimensional and preferences are single-peaked, majority rule will result in the selection of the project that is most favored by the median voter. Therefore that voter's preferences will determine what social choices are made. These

---

[12] The "public good" being voted on might represent "equality" brought about through income transfers, so that this analysis is relevant to voting on equity matters as well.

[13] D. Black, "On the Rationale of Group Decision Making," *Journal of Political Economy* (February 1948): 23–34.

Figure 25.4   *Single-Peaked Preferences and the Median Voter Theorem*

This figure illustrates the preferences in Table 25.1. Smith's and Jones's preferences are single-peaked, but Fudd's have two local peaks, and these yield the voting paradox. If Fudd's instead had been single-peaked (the dashed lines), option B would be chosen as the preferred choice of the median voter (Jones).

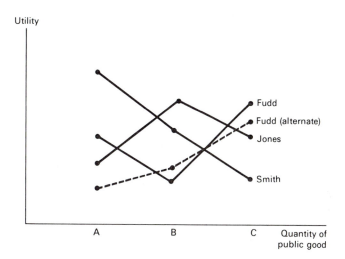

choices may not necessarily be efficient, however. The tax-spending package favored by the median voter might be quite different from a Lindahl equilibrium depending on the extent to which other voters favor the tax-spending combinations assigned to them under the plan.

Unfortunately, Black's median voter result may be of only limited importance since many issues of public choice are not one-dimensional. Consider, for example, choosing among alternative general environmental policies that involve varying levels of spending, locations of activities, and types of pollution permitted. In such a case, individuals' preferences are likely to be both varied and quite complex. In these situations the single-peaked notion loses much of its intuitive appeal, and there are no simple median voter theorems. Whether equilibrium voting choices exist in such instances and what the characteristics of such choices will be have proved to be very difficult questions to address in any general way. Still, the "median voter theorem" has intuitive appeal and has been used in many empirical applications such as those described at the end of this chapter.

Intensity of Preferences and Logrolling

Thus far we have discussed only simple voting schemes in which voters can articulate which of two options they prefer but have no opportunity to express the intensity of their feelings. In these situations majority rule can result in the adoption of policies that are only mildly favored by the majority but are despised by a minority. To prevent that, minority voters may adopt logrolling (or vote-trading) techniques.

Table 25.2   *Intensity of Preferences and Logrolling*
(Figure shows utility gain or loss from each project.)

		Project	
Voter	A	B	C
1	−5	2	2
2	−5	6	6
3	3	2	10
4	3	−5	−5
5	3	−7	−7

Table 25.2 provides an example of logrolling. In it the preferences about three projects (in terms of utility gains or losses) for five individuals are recorded. If all the projects are voted on individually, all will pass—always by a vote of 3 to 2. That this may not be a desirable outcome can be seen simply by summing the utility levels (assuming that can be done) for each project; by this criterion, only project C is "worthwhile." Both A and B yield a net negative utility level to society as a whole.

Projects A and B might be blocked through logrolling. Suppose individuals 1 and 5 agree to "trade" votes; that is, individual 1 agrees to oppose project B, providing individual 5 will oppose project A. Such a trade makes both individuals better off than they would be should both projects be adopted. With the vote trading, both projects fail by 3−2 votes.[14]

Simple vote trading does not guarantee that all projects that are, on the average, beneficial will be accepted and that those that are harmful will be turned down, however. Consider now a two-way choice between projects A and C. In that case individuals 1 and 5 can still profitably trade votes ensuring that both project A (undesirable) and project C (desirable) are defeated. As this example suggests, there is no very close connection between the concept of free trading in votes and choosing efficient resource allocations. No general efficiency theorems similar to those in Chapter 17 are possible. Nevertheless, the prevalence of "back scratching" and "pork barrel" politics in legislative bodies is a prevalent and fascinating phenomenon that deserves study.[15]

---

[14] Notice that this trade imposes a negative externality on voters 2 and 3 (who are worse off without both projects than with both) and a positive externality on voter 4.

[15] For an extended discussion of logrolling, together with the hypothesis that it may lead to the overproduction of public goods, see J. M. Buchanan and G. Tullock, *The Calculus of Consent* (Ann Arbor: University of Michigan Press, 1962).

ANALYSIS OF REPRESENTATIVE GOVERNMENT

In a representative government, voters vote for candidates, not policies. Successful candidates then represent their constituencies in making policy choices. Here we will examine a few of the issues that have been raised about this kind of indirect representation of individual preferences.

As in our discussion of the theory of the firm, we shall start our analysis by examining the motives of government leaders. It might, for instance, be proposed that government leaders act so as to maximize the "social good." At least two realities argue against assuming such benevolent motivations. First, the notion of "social good" is extremely ill-defined. Not everyone in society has the same view of the way things should be. Second, the assumption of a benevolent leadership would be in marked contrast to the self-interest assumption that underlies both the theory of the individual and the theory of the firm that we developed earlier in this book. There seems to be no very persuasive reason why people should change their basic motivations upon elevation to political office. Consequently, to be consistent with the other positive theories of this book, a less socially virtuous theory may be appropriate.

Majority Principle and Pluralism

One interesting theory of leadership motivation has been put forward by Anthony Downs. In *An Economic Theory of Democracy*, he hypothesizes that "parties in democratic politics are analogous to entrepreneurs in a profit-seeking economy. So as to attain their private ends, they formulate whatever policies they believe will gain the most votes, just as entrepreneurs produce whatever products will gain the most profits. . . ."[16] In other words, parties act so as to maximize political support. In order to pursue this goal, parties must contend with uncertainty in many respects. A party is uncertain how any particular policy choice will affect political support. This is true not only because it may be hard to ascertain who benefits from government action but also because policies must be adopted before the policies of the party (or parties) out of power are known. This strategic advantage of those out of power is significantly modified, however, by the control that the party in power has over the public's access to information.

It would be impossible to summarize the numerous insights and testable hypotheses that follow from Downs's basic assumption. Perhaps the most interesting general conclusion he draws is that the party in power generally will adopt a majority principle in its policy decisions. It will pursue only those policies for which more votes are gained than are lost, and it will pursue such policies up to the point at which the marginal gain in votes from those benefiting from the policy equals the marginal loss in votes from those being hurt by the policy. The analogy between party motivation and profit maximization is quite close. By examining corollaries to the majority principle, Downs is able to arrive at many of his most interesting results.

It is worthwhile to contrast Downs's view of the nature of the political process with another, more commonly held view. This alternative conception ex-

[16] A. Downs, *An Economic Theory of Democracy* (New York: Harper & Row, 1957), p. 295.

amines the pluralistic nature of democratic government. Social decisions are assumed to be made by the interaction of many powerful special-interest groups. Presumably, these groups wield some influence over political leaders by virtue of campaign contributions, friendship, superior knowledge of special issues, or perhaps by direct measures of corruption. Whatever the avenues of control, it is assumed that pressure groups are the primary molders of the legal system.

Two assessments of pluralism have been put forward. The first optimistically predicts that the interaction of numerous pressure groups, in some sense, will produce a socially desirable outcome. Laws that are ultimately passed represent an equilibrium among numerous groups. Because no one group has significant power (at least not on all issues), the resultant equilibrium generally will be representative of the society as a whole.

Special-Interest and Public-Interest Pressure Groups

This beneficial assessment of pluralism has been questioned by many authors. One of the most compelling objections was put forward by Olson.[17] He pointed out that there is a systematic bias in a pluralistic society that causes only certain kinds of pressure groups to exercise political power. In particular, Olson argues, only pressure groups that represent narrow special interests will arise; pressure groups representing the "public interest" will be weak or nonexistent. The reason for this tendency, Olson explains, lies in the nature of the collective good provided by a pressure group to its members. In a close-knit group, each member can recognize the benefits of group action, and there may be strong sanctions against being a free rider. Consequently, groups such as the "oil lobby" would be expected to have considerable success because each member of the group will find it in his or her interest to engage in pressure group activity.[18] On the other hand, diffuse public-interest groups will have minimal success because individual members of such groups cannot hope to obtain for themselves any major part of the benefits of their activity. The collective goods provided by public-interest groups, say, consumer legislation, have significant nonexclusion properties (everyone will benefit whether they join Common Cause or Citizens for Limited Taxation or not), so that the natural tendency is for such groups to be weak. Olson's assessment of pluralism therefore is not particularly positive. He foresees a serious absence of effective pressure groups to represent broad constituencies of public interest.

Reelection Constraint

By combining Downs's and Olson's theories of government action, we can construct an interesting third alternative. It is undoubtedly true that pressure groups exercise considerable influence over legislation, and Olson is probably right when he theorizes that the public interest will be underrepresented. How-

---

[17] See M. Olson, *The Logic of Collective Action* (Cambridge, Mass.: Harvard University Press, 1965), especially chaps. 5 and 6.

[18] Other important examples of special-interest groups are found within the government. For example, the Pentagon lobby and the "welfare" lobby may be quite powerful in distorting government expenditure decisions away from those that are socially optimal. For this reason certain kinds of public goods may be overproduced.

ever, Olson's model does not take sufficient account of the motives of political leaders. Lobby groups probably provide "utility" to political leaders in many ways, and these leaders therefore may follow the dictates of the lobbyists. But the legislator does not have an unconstrained utility-maximization problem. Rather, he or she must operate subject to the constraint of reelection. The legislator therefore must pay some attention to what Downs calls the majority principle, although this attention will by no means be absolute. Better informed voters may make a legislator's reelection constraint more binding and may mitigate the void of power on public issues noted by Olson.

Bureaucracies

Although governmental policies in a representative democracy are enacted by elected officials, they are usually implemented by and operated through bureaucratic agencies. Because those agencies typically possess monopoly power in the production of the services with which they are charged, it is possible that they exercise an independent influence on the direction of policy. For example, Niskanen hypothesizes that bureaus seek to maximize their budgets (perhaps because high budgets yield utility to bureaucrats).[19] A major implication of that hypothesis is that in the bilateral monopoly bargaining between elected officials and bureaucracies, decisions will be reached that tend to overallocate resources to the public sector (relative to what would be preferred by the median voter). Several authors have attempted to estimate such allocational effects empirically.[20] They generally conclude that the data are consistent with the budget-maximization hypothesis. However, this empirical work is, of necessity, quite preliminary.

Representative Government and the Allocation of Resources

All of these observations suggest that decision making in representative government is quite complex and subject to a variety of pressures. The notion that the government will readily improve the efficiency with which resources are allocated in a competitive market system is at least open to serious question. One cannot take the good intentions of government officials for granted. Rather, it is necessary to develop empirically valid models of government behavior and then to study the efficiency properties of these models. Within such models it is indeed possible that governments may adopt policies that foster efficiency by regulating monopolies, taxing externalities, and providing public goods. But it is also possible that governments, because they lack information or because they respond to narrow private interests or to the motives of bureaucrats, may adopt inefficient policies. Some authors refer to this latter possibility as "nonmarket failure" in contrast to private market failures brought about by externalities and public goods.[21] Instances of nonmarket failures

---

[19] W. A. Niskanen, *Bureaucracy and Representative Government* (Chicago: Aldine Publishing Company, 1971).

[20] See, for example, T. E. Borcherding, *Budgets and Bureaucrats: The Sources of Government Growth* (Durham, N.C.: Duke University Press, 1975).

[21] See, for example, C. Wolf, Jr., "A Theory of Nonmarket Failure," *The Public Interest* (Spring 1979): 114–133.

might include unwarranted interferences with free exchanges among individuals (for example, minimum wage or rent control laws), inefficient interferences with international trade (tariffs or various nonquantitative restrictions), or overproduction of public goods (for example, defense or wilderness areas) in response to interest group pressures.

SUMMARY

In this chapter we surveyed some of the concepts from the economic theory of social choice. We showed that social choice mechanisms are intrinsically more difficult to evaluate than market mechanisms. Even in relatively simple situations, Pareto inferior results may occur. For complex situations (such as voting in the U.S. Congress), developing explicit models of behavior may be impossible and evaluation must be by less formal means. In examining these issues we showed that

- Choosing equitable allocations of resources is an ambiguous process because many potential welfare criteria might be used. In some cases achieving equity (appropriately defined) may require some efficiency sacrifices.
- Arrow's impossibility theorem shows that, given fairly general assumptions, no completely satisfactory social choice mechanism exists. The problem of social choice theory is therefore to assess the relative performance of somewhat imperfect mechanisms.
- Direct voting and majority rule may not always yield an equilibrium. If preferences are single-peaked, however, majority rule voting on one-dimensional public questions will result in choosing policies most favored by the median voter. Such policies are not necessarily efficient, however.
- In representative democracy, elected representatives make choices based on their own preferences and on the need to maintain voters' support. They may not necessarily choose only those policies favored by the median voter nor only those policies that are Pareto efficient, however.

Application

THE TAX REVOLT AND SOCIAL CHOICE THEORY

In recent years a number of states have passed tax limitation statutes and a constitutional amendment has been proposed to serve the same purpose at the federal level. In this example we summarize some of the empirical re-search that has tried to explain the nature of this "tax revolt." The tax limitation idea largely originated in California with the passage of "Proposition 13" in 1977. That ballot initiative required that property in California be taxed at a maximum rate of 1 percent of the 1975 fair market value and imposed sharp limits on tax increases in future years. It resulted in a decline in local property tax revenues of nearly 60 percent between fiscal 1978 and fiscal 1979.

Two hypotheses have been proposed to explain why voters demanded such a drastic change in policy. The first views Proposition 13 as a demand for changing the sources of local tax revenues without reducing local expenditures significantly. Under this view citizens were largely content with the existing levels of local services but wanted state tax sources (primarily income and sales taxes) to take over a larger share of the burden. A second hypothesis views Proposition 13 as a statement by voters that local government had grown too large and that voters wished to see a cutback in both taxes and expenditures.

Results from Proposition 13
In a 1979 paper Attiyeh and Engle examined voting patterns on Proposition 13 in an attempt to differentiate between these hypotheses.[22] They found that such patterns tended to contradict the notion that voters simply wished to change the sources of local government financing. For example, communities in which property tax levies had been rising most dramatically did not appear to favor Proposition 13 disproportionately. On the other hand, the authors found clear evidence that voters wished a reduction in both tax rates and expenditures, although their results suggested that a somewhat less dramatic reduction might have received even more voter support. In all then, Attiyeh and Engle's results imply that local government in California had expanded beyond the bounds that voters believed to be optimal. The success of Proposition 13 clearly showed, however, that there were limits to that expansion.

Tax Limitation in Massachusetts and Michigan
Evidence from studies of other tax limitation initiatives tends to be somewhat contradictory as to voters' motivation. For example, Ladd and Wilson used personal survey data to examine voter patterns in Massachusetts in connection with the 1980 passage of "Proposition 2½"—a proposal very similar to Proposition 13.[23] Consistent with the California study they also found evidence to contradict the notion that voters simply wanted to shift the source of local revenues (say, from the property tax to the income tax). But voters feared the loss of "vital" services and did not seem to want large cutbacks. Instead they preferred "greater efficiency" in government but seemed to be quite vague as to what actual policies that might require. Gramlich, Rubinfeld, and Swift reached similar conclusions by studying voters' opinions in connection with a 1978 vote in Michigan on the "Headler amendment" to limit state taxes. Again voters clearly wanted a reduction in taxes, but the evidence on what public services they might willingly forgo was quite mixed.

The lessons for social choice theory to be drawn from recent experiences with the tax revolt therefore are ambiguous. On the one hand, some voters clearly feel that resources are currently being overallocated to public goods and express that feeling by voting for cuts in taxes and expenditures. Larger numbers of voters, however, seem to be relatively content with existing service levels but want a cut in taxes anyway. Whether this represents simply a rather confused quest for a nonexistent "free lunch" or whether voters have in mind some more systematic alteration in existing tax expenditure patterns is difficult to determine given the data currently available.

[22] R. Attiyeh and R. F. Engle, "Testing Some Propositions about Proposition 13," *National Tax Journal* 32 (June 1979): 131–146.

[23] H. Ladd and J. B. Wilson, "Why Voters Support Tax Limitations—Proposition 2½," *National Tax Journal* (June 1982): 127–148.

SUGGESTED READINGS

Arrow, K. J. *Social Choice and Individual Values.* 2d ed. New Haven, Conn.: Yale University Press, 1963.

Classic statement of the impossibility theorem. Extensive discussion of its general meaning.

————. "Some Ordinalist-Utilitarian Notes on Rawls's Theory of Justice." *Journal of Philosophy* 70 (May 1973): 245–263.

Arrow's criticism of Rawls's welfare criterion, essentially because of excessive risk aversion.

Bator, F. M. "The Simple Analytics of Welfare Maximization." *American Economic Review* 47 (March 1957): 22–59.

Good graphical presentation of most of the basic results of welfare economics.

Black, D. "On the Rationale of Group Decision Making." *Journal of Political Economy* (February 1948): 23–34. Reprinted in K. J. Arrow and T. Scitovsky, eds., *Readings in Welfare Economics.* Homewood, Ill.: Richard D. Irwin, 1969.

Early development of the "median voter" theorem.

Buchanan, J. M. "An Economic Theory of Clubs." *Economica* (February 1965): 1–14.

Develops an economic theory of the size, function, and internal operations of "clubs."

Buchanan, J. M., and Tullock, G. *The Calculus of Consent.* Ann Arbor: Michigan University Press, 1962.

Fairly complete analysis of the properties of various voting schemes.

Inman, R. P. "Markets, Governments and the 'New' Political Economy." In A. J. Auerbach and M. Feldstein, eds., *Handbook of Public Econom-*

ics, vol. 2. Amsterdam: North Holland Publishing Co., 1987. Pp. 647–777.

Extensive review of recent literature on the topics covered in this chapter. Interesting use of game theory to illustrate some concepts. Good discussion of theoretical role for tax limitation provisions.

Mishan, E. J. *Welfare Economics: Five Introductory Essays.* New York: Random House, 1964.

Interesting essays on various possible welfare criteria and the difficulties with each.

Mueller, D. C. "Public Choice: A Survey." *Journal of Economic Literature* (June 1976): 395–433.

Very readable survey of public choice theory.

Olson, M. *The Logic of Collective Action.* Cambridge, Mass.: Harvard University Press, 1965.

Analyzes the effects of individual incentives on the willingness to undertake collective action. Many fascinating examples.

Rawls, J. *A Theory of Justice.* Cambridge, Mass.: Harvard University Press, 1971.

Basic philosophical text. Makes wide use of economic concepts, especially Pareto efficiency notions and the contract curve.

————. "Some Reasons for the Maximin Criterion." *American Economic Review* 64 (May 1974): 141–146.

Rejoinder to critics of his proposed welfare criterion.

Sen, A. K. *Collective Choice and Social Welfare.* San Francisco: Holden-Day, 1970.

Complete, formal analysis of collective choice issues. Has many literary sections among the more mathematical analyses.

PROBLEMS

25.1

There are 200 pounds of food that must be allocated between two marooned sailors on an island. The utility function of the first sailor is given by

$$\text{utility} = \sqrt{F_1},$$

where F_1 is the quantity of food consumed by the first sailor. For the second sailor, utility (as a function of his food consumption) is given by

$$\text{utility} = 1/2\sqrt{F_2}.$$

a.   If the food is allocated equally between the sailors, how much utility will each receive?

b.   How should food be allocated between the sailors to assure equality of utility?

c.   How should food be allocated so as to maximize the sum of the sailors' utilities?

d.   Suppose that sailor 2 requires a utility level of at least 5 to remain alive. How should food be allocated so as to maximize the sum of utilities subject to the constraint that sailor 2 receive that minimum level of utility?

e.   Suppose that both sailors agree on a social welfare function of the form

$$W = U_1^{1/2} U_2^{1/2}.$$

How should food be allocated between the sailors so as to maximize social welfare?

25.2
In the 1930s several authors suggested a "bribe criterion" for judging the desirability of social situations. This welfare criterion states that a movement from social state A to state B is an improvement in social welfare if those who gain by this move are able to compensate those who lose sufficiently so that they will accept the change. Compensation does not actually have to be made; it is only necessary that it could be paid. If the compensation is actually made, this criterion reduces to the Pareto definition (some individuals are made better off without making anyone worse off). Hence the criterion is novel only in that compensation is not paid by the gainers to the losers. In such a situation, does the bribe criterion seem a "value-free" one, or does the criterion seem somehow to favor those who are initially rich? Can you give some simple examples?

25.3
Suppose that an economy is characterized by a linear production possibility function for its two goods (X and Y) of the form

$$X + 2Y = 180.$$

There are two individuals in this economy, each with an identical utility function for X and Y of the form

$$U(X, Y) = \sqrt{XY}.$$

a.   Suppose that Y production is set at 10. What would the utility possibility frontier for this economy be?

b.   Suppose that Y production is set at 30. What would the utility possibility frontier be?

c.   How should Y production be chosen so as to ensure the "best" utility possibility frontier?

d.   Under what conditions (contrary to those of this problem) might your answer to part (c) depend on the point on the utility possibility frontier being considered?

25.4
Suppose that seven individuals constitute a society in which individuals cast votes for their most preferred social arrangement and that the arrangement with the greatest number of votes is always chosen. Devise an example of individual rankings of the three states A, B, and C such that state A is chosen when all three states are available but that state B is chosen if the "irrelevant" alternative C is not avail-

able. (This amounts to showing that the constitution of this society does not obey Axiom 4 in Arrow's list). How reasonable is your example? What does it indicate about the nature of Arrow's axiom?

25.5

Suppose that there are two individuals in an economy. Utilities of those individuals under five possible social states are shown in the following table:

State	Utility 1	Utility 2
A	50	50
B	70	40
C	45	54
D	53	50.5
E	30	84

Individuals do not know which number (1 or 2) they will be assigned when the economy begins operating. Hence they are uncertain about the actual utility they will receive under the alternative social states. Which social state will be preferred if an individual adopts the following strategies in his or her voting behavior to deal with this uncertainty?

a.   Choose that state which assures the highest utility to the least well-off person (that is, choose a maximin strategy—see Chapter 20).

b.   Assume that there is a 50-50 chance of being either individual and choose that state with the highest expected utility.

c.   Assume that no matter what, the odds are always unfavorable such that there is a 60 percent chance of having the lower utility and a 40 percent chance of higher utility in any social state. Choose the state with the highest expected utility given these probabilities.

d.   Assume that there is a 50-50 chance of being assigned either number and that each individual dislikes inequality. Each will choose that state for which

$$\text{expected utility} - |U_1 - U_2|$$

is as large as possible (where the $|\ldots|$ notation denotes absolute value).

e.   What do you conclude from this problem about social choices under a "veil of ignorance" as to an individual's specific identity in society?

25.6

Suppose there are 3 individuals in society trying to rank three social states (A, B, and C). For each of the methods of social choice indicated develop an example to show how (at least) one of the Arrow axioms will be violated.

a.   Majority rule without vote trading.

b.   Majority rule with vote trading.

c.   Point voting where each voter can give 1, 2, or 3 points to each alternative and that alternative with the highest point total is selected.

Solutions to Odd-Numbered Problems

Only very brief solutions to most of the odd-numbered problems in the text are given here. Complete solutions to all of the problems are contained in the *Solutions Manual*, which is available to instructors upon request.

CHAPTER 2

2.1
a. 0   b. $15x$ c. $x^{-2/3}$ d. $-2x^{-3}$ e. $3x^{-1}$ f. e^x g. $15e^{3x}$ h. $3x^2 - 10x + 6$
i. $8x^7$ j. $x^2 e^x$

2.3
a. $x = 1, f(1) = -8; x = -1, f(-1) = 8$ b. $x = 2$, a maximum
c. Inflection at $x = 0$

2.5
a. $t = 5/4$ sec. $H = 25$ ft.   b. $t = 7.3$ sec. $H = 145$ ft.
c. $\partial H/\partial g = -1/2(t^*)^2$ depends on g because t^* depends on g.

2.7
$x = y = z = 0$, a minimum

2.9
$x = 1/2$ $y = 2/3$ $z = 4/3$, a maximum

2.11
$x = 3/7$ $y = 6/7$ $z = 9/7$

2.13
$x = 1/\sqrt{2}$ or $-1/\sqrt{2}$ $y = 3$ or -3

CHAPTER 3

3.1
b. $MRS = \dfrac{\partial U/\partial C}{\partial U/\partial W} = 3/2$

3.3
a. Fixed proportion, perfect complements
b. $U = 10M$ $M =$ Spending on hotdogs
c. $U = 7.5M$ Given M provides less utility

3.5
a. No   b. Yes   c. No   d. No   e. Yes   f. Yes

3.7
Shape of marginal utility function not necessarily an indicator of convexity of indifference curves.

3.9
Follows since $MRS = MU_X/MU_Y$. MU_X doesn't depend on Y and vice versa. **3.2** (i) is counterexample.

CHAPTER 4

4.1
a. $T = 5$ $S = 2$ b. $T = 5/2$ $S = 4$ costs \$2 so needs extra \$1.

4.3
a. $C = 10$ $B = 3$ $U = 127$ b. $C = 4$ $B = 1$ $U = 79$

4.5
Lagrangian leads to negative consumption of X_3. If $X_3 \geq 0$, optimum is $X_1 = 5,000$
$X_2 = 2,000$ $X_3 = 0$.

4.7
b. $G = I/(P_G + P_V/2)$ $V = I/(2P_G + P_V)$ c. Utility $= M = V = I/(2P_G + P_V)$
d. $E = M(2P_G + P_V)$

4.9
a. $C = 7.2$ $S = 6$ $L = 10.8$
b. Full income budget constraint $10C + 4S = 96$
c. Cobb-Douglas: $C = 3/4(96/P_C)$ $S = 1/4(96/P_S)$
   P_C, P_S include both time and dollar prices.
d. $E = \dfrac{27}{4} \, UP_{\bar{S}}^{1/4} P_{\bar{C}}^{3/4}$

CHAPTER 5

5.1
b. A—inferior B—luxury C—necessity

5.5
a. $X = 5$ $Y = 10$ b. $X = I/2P_X$ $Y = I/2P_Y$
c. $\partial X/\partial P_Y = 0$ no cross price effect.

5.7
a. $\partial X/\partial I = 0$ so there is no income effect.
b. $MRS = \dfrac{\partial U/\partial X}{\partial U/\partial Y} = \dfrac{1}{X}$ depends only on X.

5.9
a. Use MU_i/P_i is the same for all goods.   b. Follows from (a).

CHAPTER 6

6.1
b. Substitution elasticity and income elasticity are both 1.

6.3
a. $P_{BT} = 2P_B + P_T$
b. Since P_C and I are constant, $C = I/2P_C$ is also constant.
c. Yes—changes in P_B or P_T affect only P_{BT}.

6.5
b. Relative price $= (P_2 + t)/(P_3 + t)$
   Approaches $P_2/P_3 < 1$ as $t \to 0$
   Approaches 1 as $t \to \infty$
   So increase in t raises relative price of X_2.

c. Does not strictly apply since changes in t change relative prices.
d. May reduce spending on X_2—effect on X_3 uncertain.

6.7

Show $X_i \cdot \dfrac{\partial X_j}{\partial I} = X_j \cdot \dfrac{\partial X_i}{\partial I}$ and use symmetry of net substitution effects.

CHAPTER 7

7.1
a. $X = 100$ $e_{X,P_X} = -1$ $e_{X,P_Y} = 1/2$ $e_{X,I}$ cannot be computed without knowing distribution of changes.   b. 5.75, 10.91, 10.04, 16.26   c. $X = 10$
d. $X = 56.5$. If $P_Z = 2$, $X = 31.5$

7.3
a. $Q = 9,000 - 300P$ $P = 30$
b. $Q = 12,000 - 300P$ $P = 40$
c. $Q = 6,000 - 300P$ $P = 20$

7.5
a. $X = 15 - 3P_X + .01I_1 + .02I_2 + 2P_Y$ c. $X = 51 - 3P_X$ d. $X = 50 - 3P_X$
e. $X = 53 - 3P_X$

7.7
Apply various definitions.

7.9
Treat ham and cheese sandwiches as a composite good. Expenditures on that good completely exhaust income, so the income elasticity is 1.0.

CHAPTER 8

8.1
Use trade example—say, 3 firewood for 2 corn.

8.3
Two goods are perfect substitutes. Indifference curves have same slope for both people.

8.5
a. Contract curve is a straight line. Only equilibrium price ratio is $P_H/P_C = 2$
b. Initial equilibrium on contract curve.
c. Not on contract curve—equilibrium between $40H, 80C$ and $48H, 96C$ (for Smith).
d. Smith takes everything, Jones starves.

8.7
a. Efficient, on contract curve   b. Off contract curve
c. On contract curve, A gets all gains from trade.

CHAPTER 9

9.1
Mean wait is same, but variance lower with single feed line.

9.3
a. 1 trip
   Expected value = $.5 \cdot 0 + .5 \cdot 12 = 6$
   2 trip
   Expected value = $.25 \cdot 0 + .5 \cdot 6 + .25 \cdot 12 = 6$
b. 2 trip strategy preferred because of smaller variance.
c. Adding trips reduces variance, but at a diminishing rate. So desirability depends on trip's cost.

9.5
a. $E(U) = .75 \ln(10,000) + .25 \ln(9,000) = 9.1840$
b. $E(U) = \ln 9,750 = 9.1850$—insurance is preferable.
c. $260. d. Premium = $300 $E(U) = \ln(9,700) = 9.1799$

9.7
$P = .525$

9.9
b. rr increases for quadratic. $rr = 1$ for logarithmic.
c. $U(W) = W^k$ $0 < k < 1$

CHAPTER 10

10.1
b. $AP_L = 100/\sqrt{L}$ c. $MP_L = \partial Q/\partial L = 50/\sqrt{L}$ so $MP_L < AP_L$

10.3
a. $K = 10$ $L = 5$ b. $K = 8$ $L = 8$ c. $K = 9$ $L = 6.5$
d. Isoquant is linear between solutions (a) and (b).

10.5
Yes, the concepts are based on different assumptions about how input levels are varied.

10.7
a. $\beta_0 = 0$ b. $MP_K = \beta_2 + \frac{1}{2}\beta_1 \sqrt{L/K}$ $MP_L = \beta_3 + \frac{1}{2}\beta_1 \sqrt{K/L}$
c. σ not constant.

10.9
Apply theorem to f_K which is homogeneous of degree 0.

CHAPTER 11

11.1
Draftsman right since minimum of $SATC$ curves occurs where slope is zero. In constant returns to scale case, both are correct.

11.3
a, b. $Q = 150$ $J = 25$ $MC = 4$
$Q = 300$ $J = 100$ $MC = 8$
$Q = 450$ $J = 225$ $MC = 12$

11.5
d. $TC = K(Qw^\beta v^\alpha)^{1/\alpha+\beta}$

11.7
a. $STC = 100 + Q^2/100$
b. $SMC = Q/50$

$Q = 25$	$STC = 106.25$	$SAC = 4.25$	$SMC = .50$
$Q = 50$	$STC = 125$	$SAC = 2.50$	$SMC = 1$
$Q = 100$	$STC = 200$	$SAC = 2$	$SMC = 2$
$Q = 200$	$STC = 500$	$SAC = 2.50$	$SMC = 4$

d. $SMC = SAC$ at $Q = 100$. Lowest SAC.

11.9
a. $Q_2 = 4Q_1$ b. 1.60, 2.00, 3.20
c. Because of constant returns to scale, doesn't matter. $LTC = 2Q$.
d. If production functions are identical, $Q_1 = Q_2$.

11.11
a. $L = Q(1 + \sqrt{v/w})$ $K = Q(1 + \sqrt{w/v})$
b. $Q = (K^{-1} + L^{-1})^{-1}$
c. $\sigma = 0.5$ $(\rho = -1)$ $\varepsilon = 1$ $\delta = \gamma = .5$ generate this function.

CHAPTER 12

12.1
a. $q = 50$ b. $\pi = 200$

12.3
b. $mr = 8/\sqrt{q}$ c. $q = 400$ $P = .80$

12.5
b. if $Q = a + bP$ $P = (Q - a)/b$ $MR = (2Q - a)/b$ so $P - MR = -(1/b)Q$
c. $Q = A^b$ $P = (Q/a)^{1/b}$ $MR = (1 + 1/b)P$

12.7
a. $q = 2P/w$ b. $\pi = Pq - wq^2/4$

CHAPTER 13

13.1
Hiring costs may be quasi-fixed or variable depending on time period used.

13.3
a. $L_A = 3$ b. 4/7   c. $L_A = 1$
d. Revenue = 10.5   Wage = 2

13.5
a. Marginal utility of leisure must be zero.
b. *Hint:* Which of Mr. E's indifference curves shows the levels of π necessary to encourage him or her to provide various hours of work?

13.7
a. $Q = 50$ $C = 10$ $\pi = 395$
b. $Q = C = 30$ $\pi = 275$

13.9

a. $q = 1,500$ $\pi = 12,500$ b. $q = 2,000$ $\pi = 22,500$
c. $22,500 - 12,500 = 10,000$ per week.

CHAPTER 14

14.1

a. $q = 10\sqrt{P} - 20$ b. $Q = 1,000\sqrt{P} - 2,000$
c. $P = 25$ $Q = 3,000$

14.3

a. $P = 6$ b. $q = 60,000 - 10,000P$
c. $P = 6.01$, $P = 5.99$ d. $e_{Q,F} = -.6$ $e_{qP} = -600$
a. $P = 6$ b. $Q = 359,800 - 59,950P$ c. $P = 6.002$, $P = 5.998$
d. $e_{qP} = -3,600$.

14.5

a. $P = 3$ $Q = 2,000,000$ $n = 2,000$ farms
b. $P = 6$ $\pi = 3,000$/farm   c. $P = 3$ $Q = 2,600,000$ $n = 2,600$ farms

14.7

a. $n = 50$, $Q = 1,000$, $q = 20$, $P = 10$, $w = 200$
b. $n = 72$, $Q = 1,728$, $q = 24$, $P = 14$, $w = 288$

14.9

a. $q = 10$ b. $P = 10$, $Q = 30,000$, $n = 3,000$
c. $q = 5$, $AC = 15$, $Q = 25,000$, $n = 5,000$
a. same   b. $P = 10$, $Q = 50,000$, $n = 5,000$
c. $P = 5$, $Q = 45,000$, $n = 9,000$.

CHAPTER 15

15.1

b. $C = 300$ $M = 150$ c. $P_C/P_M = 1/2$

15.3

a. Efficiency requires $k_X = 2k_Y$
c.–d. $k_Y = \dfrac{1/2}{(1 + \alpha_X)}$ $k_X = \dfrac{1}{(1 + \alpha_X)}$
    Hence $k_X > k_Y$ good X is capital-intensive.

15.5

a. Use production possibility frontier, then Edgeworth box.
b. If p doesn't change, land-labor ratio must stay same in each industry. Can happen only if production of labor-intensive commodity expands.

15.7

b. $P_1 ED_1 = -[3P_2^2 + 6P_2 P_3 - 2P_3^2 - P_1 P_2 - 2P_1 P_3]P_1$
c. $P_2/P_1 = 3$ $P_3/P_1 = 5$ $P_3/P_2 = 5/3$

15.9

a. Value of transactions $= 240 =$ Income
    Wage $= 240/20 = 12$ per hour. Since $P_X/P_Y = 3/2$ and $P_X \cdot X + P_Y \cdot Y = 240$,
    $P_X = 6$ $P_Y = 4$.

b. Wage = 18 per hour, $P_X = 9$ $P_Y = 6$
   Yes, system does exhibit classical dichotomy.

CHAPTER 16

16.1
a. $C = F = 10$ $RPT = 1$ $U = 10$
b. $C = 2F$ so $C = 15$ $F = 15/2$ $U = \sqrt{112.5}$
c. $C = 5\sqrt{10}$ $F = \dfrac{5\sqrt{10}}{2}$ $U = \sqrt{125}$

16.3
a. $F + C = 100$ b. $2F + C = 150$
c. Need to satisfy both constraints   d. Relative cost of F increases as F rises.
e. $P_F/P_C = 1$ for $F < 50$ $P_F/P_C = 2$ for $F > 50$ f. $P_F/P_C = 5/4$
g. Because production possibility frontier is kinked at $F = C = 50$
h. $.8F + .9C = 100$ lies outside previous frontier does not affect answers to (a)–(g).

16.5
Both inputs fully employed only when $W = S = 50$.

16.7
Tangencies will be unstable because individuals will have incentives to make utility-improving transactions.

CHAPTER 17

17.1
Show Walrasian and Marshallian adjustment rules differ when supply curve has negative slope.

17.3
a. $P = 10, Q = 80$
b. $P_0 = 8, P_1 = 11$ $P_2 = 9.5, P_3 = 10.25$ takes 3 periods.
c. Choose $E(P) = P^* = 10$.

17.5
a. $\overline{P} = 10,000$ $P^* = 10,000$ b. $\overline{P} = 7,500$
c. $P^* = 8,125$ $\overline{P} = 6,062$ d. No.

17.7
a. If new information arrives randomly (as it must), prices will move randomly.
b. Advisers may sell something besides stock performance.

CHAPTER 18

18.1
a. $Q = 24$ $P = 29$ $\pi = 576$ b. $MC = P = 5$ $Q = 48$
c. Consumers Surplus $= 1,152$
   Under monopoly, consumer surplus $= 288$
   Profits $= 576$ Deadweight loss $= 288$

18.3
a. $Q = 25$ $P = 35$ $\pi = 625$
b. $Q = 20$ $P = 50$ $\pi = 800$
c. $Q = 40$ $P = 30$ $\pi = 400$

18.5
a. $P = 15$ $Q = 5$ $TC = 65$ $\pi = 10$
b. $A = 3$ $P = 15$ $Q = 6.05$ $\pi = 12.25$

18.7
a. $Q_1 = 25$ $P_1 = 30$ $Q_2 = 30$ $P_2 = 20$ $\pi = 1,075$
b. $P_1 = 26.66$ $P_2 = 21.66$ $\pi = 1,058.33$
c. $P_1 = P_2 = 23\frac{1}{3}$ $\pi = 1,008\frac{1}{3}$

CHAPTER 19

19.1
a. $Q = 75$ $P = 75$ $\pi = 5,625$
b. $q_1 = q_2 = 50$ $P = 50$ $\pi_1 = \pi_2 = 2,500$
c. Under perfect competition $P = 0$ $Q = 150$.

19.3
a. Price discrimination   b. Price leadership   c. Price discrimination (by sellers)
d. Probably incorrect accounting   e. Buyers have a preference for cans—perhaps
   because they stack more easily.

19.5
McGee's conclusion is that predatory pricing is less profitable than outright
acquisition because of the losses involved on the monopolist's sales.

19.7
a. $P = 25$ $Q = 20,000$
b. $P = 20$ $Q = 30,000$ q (for leader) $= 15,000$
c.

Price	Consumer Surplus
25	100,000
20	225,000
15	400,000

CHAPTER 20

20.1
If one player knows what the other will do, he or she has an opportunity to adopt a
winning strategy.

20.3
a. Choose "no picnic."
b. $U(\text{Picnic}) = .10 \cdot 0 + .90 \cdot 20 = 18$
   $U(\text{No Picnic}) = .10 \cdot 5 + .90 \cdot 10 = 9.5$
   Choose picnic.

20.5
Equilibrium with each stand at 50.

20.7
a–c. *Hint:* A bid can be represented by a straight line through the initial endowment.
d. Yes, there is an equilibrium.
e. Not necessarily.

CHAPTER 21

21.1
a. $w = 3$ $L = 300$
b. $w = 4$ $s = 3$ $L = 400$ total subsidy $= 1,200$
c. $w = 4$ $D = 250$ $S = 400$ $u = 150$

21.3
a. Hire 5   Output $= 34$ $MP_L = 4$
b. $w = P$ $MP_L = 4$ $wL = 20$ $\pi = 14$

21.5
a. $w = 10$ $L = 25$
   $w = 5$ $L = 100$
   $w = 2$ $L = 625$
b. $P = .1$ $Q = 500,000$
   $P = .05$ $Q = 250,000$
   $P = .20$ $Q = 100,000$

21.7
a. Factor shares constant   b. Assumes $\sigma = 1$
c. If $\sigma > 1$, capital discouraged $\sigma < 1$, capital encouraged
d. If advanced firms have $\sigma > 1$, investment there is discouraged.

21.9
$L_m = 400$ $w_m = 20/3$ $L_f = 500$ $w_f = 5$ $\pi = 3,833$
If same wage, $w = 10$ $L = 1900$ $\pi = 0$

21.11
Hire only blacks or only whites.

CHAPTER 22

22.1
a. Full income $= 40,000$ $L = 2,000$ hours
b. $L = 1,400$ hours   c. $L = 1,700$ hours
d. Supply asymptotic to 2,000 hours as w rises.

22.3
a. Those with high values of time.   b. Desire to see event or low value of time.
c. Peanut vendor since physician has high opportunity cost.
d. People with high time value will take transit if congestion worsens.

22.5
a. Income effect probably dominates.
b. Person 1 may work less in the market.

22.7
$MR_L = 0$ if no unemployment benefits.
$MR_L = u$ if there is UI.

CHAPTER 23

23.1
b. Income and substitution effects work in opposite directions.
   If $\partial C_1/\partial r < 0$, C_2 is price elastic.
d. Budget constraint passes through Y_1, Y_2.

23.3
25 years

23.5
a. $w = PDV$ of harvested tree   b. Treat tree as any other asset.
c. Use integration, $t = 0 \ldots t^*$ d. $rV = f(t^*) - w$

23.7
If "maximum substantial yield" means $f'(t) = 0$, this allows trees to grow too long.

23.9
$350 payment also involves some repayment of principal. $10,000 not being borrowed for 3 years.

23.11
Hint: Use two period graph. Measure all gains in terms of C_0.

CHAPTER 24

24.1
a. $P = 20$ $q = 50$ b. $P = 20$ $q = 40$ $MC = 16$ tax $= 4$

24.3
a. $N = 400$ The externality arises because one well's drilling affects all wells'
    output.
b. $N = 200$ c. Fee $= 2,000/$well.

24.5
An essay question. Should consider: services provided by parties, risks, information costs, incentives under the various contracts, and so forth.

24.7
a. set $q_a = q_b$, optimal $q = 125$ b. Free rider problem might result in $q = 0$
c. Total cost 6,250 Area under D 4,688 for (a), 17,188 for (b). May want to share
    costs in this ratio.

24.9
a. If each person is a free rider, utility will be 0.
b. $P = 5$ $G = 50$ $G/100 = 0.5$ Utility $= \sqrt{2.5}$.

24.11
Also an essay question. Should look at: Demand revelation problem, economies of scale and spillover effects among communities.

CHAPTER 25

25.1
a. 100 each $U_1 = 10$ $U_2 = 5$ b. $F_1 = 40$ $F_2 = 160$
c. $F_1 = 160$ $F_2 = 40$ d. $F_1 = F_2 = 100$ e. $F_1 = F_2 = 100$

25.3
a. $X = 160$ $(U_1 + U_2)^2 = 1,600$ b. $(U_1 + U_2)^2 = 3,600$
c. Max XY subject to $X + 2Y = 180$ $X = 90$ $Y = 45$ $(U_1 + U_2)^2 = 4,050$

25.5
a. D b. E c. B d. A e. Choice depends on criterion used.

Glossary of Frequently Used Terms

Some of the terms that are used frequently in this book are defined below. The reader may wish to use the Index to find those sections of the text that give more complete descriptions of these concepts.

Adverse Selection—When buyers and sellers have asymmetric information about market transactions, trades actually completed may be biased to favor the actor with better information.

Agent—A person who makes economic decisions for another economic actor. A hired manager operates as an agent for a firm's owner.

Arrow Impossibility Theorem—Fundamental result of social choice theory: any social decision rule must violate at least one of the axioms of rational choice that Arrow developed.

Bayesian Decision Rule—Use of subjective probabilities to rank and choose strategies according to their expected utilities.

Ceteris Paribus Assumption—The assumption that all other relevant factors are held constant when examining the influence of one particular variable in an economic model. Reflected in mathematical terms by the use of partial differentiation.

Coase Theorem—Result attributable to R. Coase: if bargaining costs are zero, an efficient allocation of resources can be attained in the presence of externalities through reliance on bargaining among the parties involved.

Compensated Demand Curve—Curve showing relationship between the price of a good and the quantity consumed while holding real income (or utility) constant. Denoted by $h(P_X, P_Y, U)$.

Compensating Wage Differentials—Differences in real wages that arise when the characteristics of occupations cause workers in their supply decisions to prefer one job over another.

Compensation Formula—A representation of the way in which the hourly wage paid to a worker is determined.

Complements (Gross)—Two goods such that if the price of one rises, the quantity consumed of the other will fall. Goods X and Y are gross complements if $\partial X/\partial P_Y < 0$. *See also* Substitutes (Gross).

Complements (Net)—Two goods such that if the price of one rises, the quantity consumed of the other will fall, holding real income (utility) constant. Goods X and Y are net complements if

$$\left. \partial X/\partial P_Y \right|_{U = \overline{U}} < 0.$$

Such compensated cross-price effects are symmetric; that is,

$$\left. \partial X/\partial P_Y \right|_{U = \overline{U}} = \left. \partial Y/\partial P_X \right|_{U = \overline{U}}.$$

See also Substitutes (Net). Also called Hicksian substitutes and complements.

Composite Commodity—A group of goods whose prices all move together—the relative prices of goods in the group do not change. Such goods can be treated as a single commodity in many applications.

Constant Cost Industry—An industry in which expansion of output and entry by new firms have no effect on the cost curves of individual firms.

Constant Returns to Scale—*See* Returns to Scale.

Consumer Surplus—The difference between the total value consumers receive from the consumption of a particular good and the total amount they pay for the good. It is the area under the compensated demand curve and above the market price.

Contestable Market—A market in which entry and exit are absolutely free. Markets subject to such "hit-and-run" entry and exit will produce where $P = MC = AC$ even if there are not a large number of firms.

Contour Line—The set of points along which a function has a constant value. Useful for graphing three-dimensional functions in two dimensions. Individuals' indifference curve maps and firms' production isoquant maps are examples.

Contract Curve—The set of all the efficient allocations of goods among those individuals in an exchange economy. Each of these allocations has the property that no one individual can be made better off without making someone else worse off.

Convexity Assumptions—Assumptions about the shapes of individuals' utility functions and firms' production functions. Based on the presumption that the relative marginal effectiveness of a particular good or input diminishes as the quantity of that good or input increases. Important because they ensure that the application of first-order conditions will indeed yield a true maximum.

Core of an Exchange Economy—The set of allocations that is not blocked by any coalition. Every allocation in the core is Pareto optimal, but some Pareto-efficient allocations may not be in the core.

Core of an *n*-player game—The set of payoffs in an *n*-player game for which no subset of players would find it advantageous to seek additional improvements through further coalition activity.

Decreasing Cost Industry—An industry in which expansion of output generates cost-reducing externalities that cause the cost curves of those firms in the industry to shift downward.

Decreasing Returns to Scale—*See* Returns to Scale.

Demand Curve—A graph showing the *ceteris paribus* relationship between the price of a good and the quantity of that good pur-

chased. A two-dimensional representation of the demand function $X = D_X(P_X, P_Y, I)$.

Diminishing Marginal Productivity—*See* Marginal Physical Product.

Diminishing Marginal Rate of Substitution—*See* Marginal Rate of Substitution.

Discrimination, Price—Occurs whenever a buyer or seller is able to use its market power effectively to separate markets and to follow a different price policy in each market. *See also* Perfect Price Discrimination.

Duality—The relationship between any constrained maximization problem and its related "dual" constrained minimization problem.

Economic Efficiency—Exists when resources are allocated so that no activity can be increased without cutting back on some other activity. *See also* Pareto Optimality.

Edgeworth Box Diagram—A graphic device used to demonstrate economic efficiency. Most frequently used to illustrate the contract curve in an exchange economy but also useful in the theory of production.

Elasticity—A measure of the percentage change in one variable brought about by a 1 percent change in some other variable. If $y = f(x)$, then the elasticity of y with respect to $x(e_{y,x})$ is given by $dy/dx \cdot x/y$. Most often used to describe how the quantity of a good demanded responds to a change in its price. For example, if $e_{Q,P} = -2$, a 1 percent rise in price causes quantity demanded to fall by 2 percent. The price elasticity of supply is defined in an analogous way.

Entry Conditions—Characteristics of an industry that determine the ease with which a new firm may begin production. Under perfect competition, entry is assumed to be costless, whereas in a monopolistic industry there are significant barriers to entry.

Envelope Theorem—A mathematical result: the change in the maximum value of a function brought about by a change in a parameter of the function can be found by partially differentiating the function with respect to the parameter (when all other variables take on their optimal values).

Equilibrium—A situation in which supply and demand are in balance. At an equilibrium price, the quantity demanded by individuals is exactly equal to that which is supplied by all firms.

Equilibrium Strategies—A set of strategies in game theory for which each strategy is optimal for a particular player against those being used by the other players. Even if strategies were known, no player would have an incentive to switch strategies.

Euler's Theorem—A mathematical theorem: if $f(X_1, \ldots, X_n)$ is homogeneous of degree k, then

$$f_1 X_1 + f_2 X_2 + \cdots + f_n X_n$$
$$= k f(X_1, \ldots, X_n).$$

Exchange Economy—An economy in which the supply of goods is fixed (that is, no production takes place). The available goods, however, may be reallocated among individuals in the economy.

Expansion Path—The locus of those cost-minimizing input combinations that a firm will choose to produce various levels of output (when the prices of inputs are held constant).

Expected Utility—The average utility expected from a risky situation. If there are n outcomes, $X_1, \ldots, X_n$ with probabilities $P_1, \ldots, P_n$ ($\Sigma P_i = 1$), then the expected utility is given by

$$E(U) = P_1 U(X_1) + P_2 U(X_2)$$
$$+ \cdots + P_n U(X_n).$$

Expenditure Function—A function derived from the individual's dual expenditure minimization problem. Shows the minimum expenditure necessary to achieve a given utility level:

$$\text{expenditures} = E(P_X, P_Y, U).$$

Externality—An effect of one economic agent on another that is not taken into account by normal market behavior.

First-Order Conditions—Mathematical conditions that must necessarily hold if a function is to take on its maximum or minimum value. Usually show that any activity should be increased to the point at which marginal benefits equal marginal costs.

Fixed Costs—Costs that do not change as the level of output changes in the short run. Fixed costs are in many respects irrelevant to the theory of short-run price determination. *See also* Variable Costs.

General Equilibrium Model—A model of an economy that portrays the operation of many markets simultaneously.

Giffen's Paradox—A situation in which the increase in a good's price leads individuals to consume more of the good. Arises because the good in question is inferior and because the income effect induced by the price change is stronger than the substitution effect.

Homogeneous Function—A function, $f(X_1, X_2, \ldots, X_n)$, is homogeneous of degree k if

$$f(mX_1, mX_2, \ldots, mX_n) = m^k f(X_1, X_2, \ldots, X_n).$$

Homothetic Function—A function which can be represented as a monotonic transformation of a function that is homogeneous of degree one. The slopes of the contour lines for such a function depend only on the ratios of the variables that enter the function not on their absolute levels.

Income and Substitution Effects—Two analytically different effects that come into play when an individual is faced with a changed price for some good. Arise because a change in the price of a good will affect an individual's purchasing power. Even if purchasing power is held constant, however, substitution effects will cause individuals to reallocate their expenditures. Substitution effects are reflected in movements along an indifference curve, whereas income effects entail a movement to a different indifference curve. *See also* Slutsky Equation.

Increasing Cost Industry—An industry in which the expansion of output creates cost-increasing externalities, which cause the cost curves of those firms in the industry to shift upward.

Increasing Returns to Scale—*See* Returns to Scale.

Indifference Curve Map—A contour map of an individual's utility function showing those alternative bundles of goods from which the individual derives equal levels of welfare.

Indirect Utility Function—A representation of utility as a function of all prices and income.

Inferior Good—A good that is bought in smaller quantities as an individual's income rises.

Inferior Input—A factor of production that is used in smaller amounts as a firm's output expands.

Input demand function—Function showing the firm's demand for an input (say labor) which depends on input costs (w, v) and on the level of output (q)

$$L = L(w, v, q).$$

Isoquant Map—A contour map of the firm's production function. The contours show the alternative combinations of productive inputs that can be used to produce a given level of output.

Lindahl Equilibrium—A hypothetical solution to the public goods problem: the tax share that each individual pays plays the same role as an equilibrium market price in a competitive allocation.

Long Run—*See* Short Run–Long Run Distinction.

Marginal Cost (*MC*)—The additional cost incurred by producing one more unit of output: $MC = \partial TC/\partial q$.

Marginal Physical Product (*MP*)—The additional output that can be produced by one more unit of a particular input while holding all other inputs constant. It is usually assumed that an input's marginal productivity diminishes as additional units of the input are put into use while holding other inputs fixed. If $Q = f(K, L)$, $MP_L = \partial Q/\partial L$.

Marginal Rate of Substitution (*MRS*)—The rate at which an individual is willing to trade one good for another while remaining equally well off. The *MRS* is the absolute value of the slope of an indifference curve. It is usually assumed that the *MRS* (of X for Y) will diminish as X is progressively substituted for Y.

Marginal Revenue (*MR*)—The additional revenue obtained by a firm when it is able to sell one more unit of output. $MR = \partial P \cdot q/\partial q = P(1 + 1/e_{q,P})$.

Marginal Revenue Product (*MRP*)—The extra revenue that accrues to a firm when it sells the output that is produced by one more unit of some input. In the case of labor, for example, $MRP_L = MR \cdot MP_L$.

Marginal Utility (*MU*)—The extra utility that an individual receives by consuming one more unit of a particular good.

Marginal Value Product—A specific case of marginal revenue product that applies when the good being produced is sold in a perfectly competitive market. If the competitive price is given by P (= *MR* in this case), then Marginal Value Product = $P \cdot MP_L$.

Market Period—A very short period over which quantity supplied is fixed and not responsive to changes in market price.

Marshallian Quantity Adjustment—The assumption that markets are cleared through quantity adjustments in response to excess demand or supply.

Maximin Decision Rule—A rule for selecting that strategy in a game for which the minimum payoff is as large as possible against all possible opponents' strategies.

Monopoly—An industry in which there is only a single seller of the good in question.

Monopsony—An industry in which there is only a single buyer of the good in question.

Normative Analysis—Economic analysis that takes a position on how economic actors or markets should operate.

Offer Curve—A curve showing those trades an individual would willingly make away from a particular initial endowment at alternative price ratios.

Oligopoly—An industry in which there are only a few sellers of the good in question.

Opportunity Cost Doctrine—The simple, though far-reaching, observation that the true cost of any action can be measured by the value of the best alternative that must be forgone when the action is taken.

Output and Substitution Effects—Come into play when a change in the price of an input that a firm uses causes the firm to change the quantities of inputs it will demand. The substitution effect would occur even if output were held constant, and it is reflected by movements along an isoquant. Output effects, on the other hand, occur when output levels change and the firm moves to a new isoquant.

Paradox of Voting—Illustrates the possibility that majority rule voting may not yield a determinate outcome but may instead cycle among alternatives.

Pareto Optimality—An allocation of resources in which no one individual can be made better off without making someone else worse off.

Partial Equilibrium Model—A model of a single market that ignores repercussions in other markets.

Perfect Competition—The most widely used economic model: there are assumed to be a large number of buyers and sellers for any good and each agent is a price taker. *See also* Price Taker.

Perfect Price Discrimination—The ability of a seller to auction off each unit of output for the maximum revenue it will bring. Differs from usual market situations in which all units of a particular good are sold at the same price.

Positive Analysis—Economic analysis that seeks to explain and predict actual economic events.

Present Discounted Value (*PDV*)—The current value of a sum of money that is payable sometime in the future. Takes into account the effect of interest payments.

Price Taker—An economic agent that makes decisions on the assumption that these decisions will have no effect on prevailing market prices.

Prisoner's Dilemma—Originally studied in the theory of games but has widespread applicability. The crux of the dilemma is that each individual, faced with the uncertainty of how others will behave, may be led to adopt a course of action that proves to be detrimental for all those individuals making the same decision. A strong coalition might have led to a solution preferred by everyone in the group.

Production Function—A conceptual mathematical function that records the relationship between a firm's inputs and its outputs. If output is a function of capital and labor only, this would be denoted by $Q = f(K, L)$.

Production Possibility Frontier—The locus of all the alternative quantities of several outputs that can be produced with fixed amounts of productive inputs.

Profit Function—The relationship between a firm's maximum profits (π^*) and the output and input prices it faces:

$$\pi^* = \pi^*(P, v, w).$$

Profits—The difference between the total revenue a firm receives and its total economic costs of production. Economic profits equal zero under perfect competition in the long run. Monopoly profits may be positive, however.

Property Rights—Legal specification of ownership and the rights of owners.

Public Good—A good that once produced is available to all on a nonexclusive basis. Many public goods are also non-rival—additional individuals may benefit from the good at zero marginal costs.

Rate of Product Transformation (*RPT*)—The rate at which one output can be traded for another in the productive process while holding the total quantities of inputs constant. The *RPT* is the absolute value of the slope of the production possibility frontier.

Rate of Return—The rate at which present goods can be transformed into future goods. For example, a one-period rate of return of 10 percent implies that forgoing 1 unit of output this period will yield 1.10 units of output next period.

Rate of Technical Substitution (*RTS*)—The rate at which one input may be traded off against another in the productive process while holding output constant. The *RTS* is the absolute value of the slope of an isoquant.

Rent—Payments to a factor of production that are in excess of that amount necessary to keep it in its current employment.

Rental Rate—The cost of hiring one machine for one hour. Denoted by v in the text.

Returns to Scale—A way of classifying production functions that records how output responds to proportional increases in all inputs. If a proportional increase in all inputs causes output to increase by a smaller proportion, the production function is said to exhibit decreasing returns to scale. If output increases by a greater proportion than the inputs, the production function exhibits increasing returns. Constant returns to scale is the middle ground where both inputs and outputs increase by the same proportions. Mathematically, if $f(mK, mL) = m^k f(K, L)$, $k > 1$ implies increasing returns, $k = 1$ constant returns, and $k < 1$ decreasing returns.

Risk Aversion—Unwillingness to accept fair bets. Arises when an individual's utility of wealth function is concave (that is, $U'(W) > 0$, $U''(W) < 0$).

Second Best—The best allocation of resources that is obtainable when various constraints preclude attaining true economic efficiency.

Second-Order Conditions—Mathematical conditions required to ensure that points for which first-order conditions are satisfied are indeed true maximum or true minimum points. These conditions are satisfied by functions that obey certain convexity assumptions.

Shephard's Lemma—Application of the envelope theorem which shows that a consumer's compensated demand functions and a firm's (constant output) input demand functions can be derived from partial differentiation of expenditure functions or total cost functions respectively.

Shifting of a Tax—Market responses to the imposition of a tax that cause the incidence of the tax to be on some economic agent other than the one who actually pays the tax.

Short Run–Long Run Distinction—A conceptual distinction made in the theory of production that differentiates between a period of time over which some inputs are regarded as being fixed and a longer period in which all inputs can be varied by the producer.

Slutsky Equation—A mathematical representation of the substitution and income effects of a price change on utility maximizing choices:

$$\partial X / \partial P_X = \partial X / \partial P_X \bigg|_{U = \overline{U}} - X \frac{\partial X}{\partial I}.$$

Social Rates of Transformation and Substitution—When externalities are present, private rates of trade-off and social rates of trade-off will differ. To study the optimal allocation of resources, it is necessary to examine social rates.

Social Welfare Function—A hypothetical device that records societal views about equity among individuals.

Substitutes (Gross)—Two goods such that if the price of one increases, more of the other good will be demanded. That is, X and Y are gross substitutes if $\partial X / \partial P_Y > 0$. *See also* Complements; Slutsky Equation.

Substitutes (Net)—Two goods such that if the price of one increases, more of the other good will be demanded if utility is held constant. That is, X and Y are net substitutes if

$$\left. \partial X / \partial P_Y \right|_{U \,=\, \overline{U}} > 0.$$

Net substitutability is symmetric in that

$$\left. \partial X / \partial P_Y \right|_{U \,=\, \overline{U}} = \left. \partial Y / \partial P_X \right|_{U \,=\, \overline{U}}.$$

See also Complements; Slutsky Equation.

Substitution Effects—*See* Income and Substitution Effects; Output and Substitution Effects; Slutsky Equation.

Supply Function—For a profit-maximizing firm, a function that shows quantity supplied (q^*) as a function of output price (P) and input prices (v, w):

$$q^* = q^*(P, v, w).$$

Supply Response—Increases in production prompted by changing demand conditions and market prices. Usually a distinction is made between short-run and long-run supply responses.

Total Cost Curve—The relationship between (minimized) total costs and output, holding input prices constant. Derived from the total cost function

$$TC = TC(v, w, q).$$

Utility Function—A mathematical conceptualization of the way in which individuals rank alternative bundles of commodities. If there are only two goods, X and Y, utility is denoted by

$$\text{utility} = U(X, Y).$$

Variable Costs—Costs that change in response to changes in the level of output being produced by a firm. This is in contrast to fixed costs, which do not change.

von Neumann–Morgenstern Utility—A ranking of outcomes in uncertain situations such that individuals choose among these outcomes on the basis of their expected utility values.

Wage—The cost of hiring one worker for one hour. Denoted by w in the text.

Walrasian Price Adjustment—The assumption that markets are cleared through price adjustments in response to excess demand or supply.

Zero-Sum Game—A game in which winnings for one player are losses for the other player.

Author Index

Subject Index

Note: Key terms and the page on which they are defined are set in boldface type in this index.